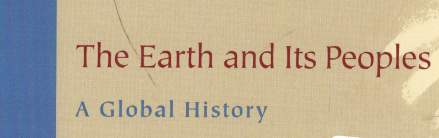

The Earth and Its Peoples

A Global History

The Earth and Its Peoples

A Global History

THIRD EDITION

Volume B: From 1200 to 1870

Richard W. Bulliet
Columbia University

Pamela Kyle Crossley
Dartmouth College

Daniel R. Headrick
Roosevelt University

Steven W. Hirsch
Tufts University

Lyman L. Johnson
University of North Carolina–Charlotte

David Northrup
Boston College

Houghton Mifflin Company   Boston   New York

Publisher: Charles Hartford
Editor-in-Chief: Jean L. Woy
Senior Sponsoring Editor: Nancy Blaine
Senior Development Editor: Jennifer Sutherland
Editorial Associate: Annette Fantasia
Senior Project Editor: Carol Newman
Editorial Assistant: Trinity Peacock-Broyles
Senior Design Coordinator: Jill Haber
Senior Designer: Henry Rachlin
Manufacturing Manager: Florence Cadran
Senior Marketing Manager: Sandra McGuire

Cover illustration: *The Flower Gatherers* by Vasanti Ragim, Kulu c. 1700. The Art Archive/Victoria and Albert Museum London/Sally Chappell.

Part opener credits

Pt. 4, p. 333: Bibliothèque nationale de France; Pt. 5, p. 445: Library of Congress; Pt. 6, p. 577: © Hulton-Deutsch/Corbis.

Chapter opener credits

Ch. 12, p. 305: Justin Kerr; Ch. 13, p. 336: Imperial Household Agency/International Society for Educational Information, Japan; Ch. 14, p. 366: Imperial Household Collection, Kyoto; Ch. 15, p. 391: Copyright Brussels, Royal Library of Belgium; Ch. 16, p. 417: G. Dagli Orti/The Art Archive; Ch. 17, p. 448: Kunsthistorisches Museum, Vienna/The Bridgeman Art Library, New York and London; Ch. 18, p. 473: Archivo General de la Nación, Buenos Aires; Ch. 19, p. 499: From William Clark, *Ten Views in the Islands of Antigua*, 1823. British Library; Ch. 20, p. 525: V&A Picture Library; Ch. 21, p. 550: Novosti; Ch. 22, p. 580: Jean-Loup Charmet/ The Bridgeman Art Library; Ch. 23, p. 608: Science & Society Picture Library; Ch. 24, p. 632: *Estación de Orizaba*, 1877. From Casimiro Castro, *Album del Ferro-Carril Mexicano: Coleccion de Vista Pintadas* (Victor Debray and Company, 1877); Ch. 25, p. 663: Eyre and Hobbs House Art Gallery; Ch. 26, p. 690: Mary Evans Picture Library.

Printed in U.S.A.

Library of Congress Catalog Card Number: 2003115591

ISBN: 0-618-42768-6

1 2 3 4 5 6 7 8 9—VH—2008 2007 2006 2005 2004

Brief Contents

12 Peoples and Civilizations of the Americas, 200–1500 305

PART FOUR
Interregional Patterns of Culture and Contact, 1200–1550   333
13 Mongol Eurasia and Its Aftermath, 1200–1500 336
14 Tropical Africa and Asia, 1200–1500 366
15 The Latin West, 1200–1500 391
16 The Maritime Revolution, to 1550 417

PART FIVE
The Globe Encompassed, 1500–1750   445
17 Transformations in Europe, 1500–1750 448
18 The Diversity of American Colonial Societies, 1530–1770 473
19 The Atlantic System and Africa, 1550–1800 499
20 Southwest Asia and the Indian Ocean, 1500–1750 525
21 Northern Eurasia, 1500–1800 550

PART SIX
Revolutions Reshape the World, 1750–1870   577
22 Revolutionary Changes in the Atlantic World, 1750–1850 580
23 The Early Industrial Revolution, 1760–1851 608
24 Nation Building and Economic Transformation in the Americas, 1800–1890 632
25 Africa, India, and the New British Empire, 1750–1870 663
26 Land Empires in the Age of Imperialism, 1800–1870 690

Contents

MAPS xii

ENVIRONMENT AND TECHNOLOGY xiii

DIVERSITY AND DOMINANCE xiii

ISSUES IN WORLD HISTORY xiii

PREFACE xv

ABOUT THE AUTHORS xx

NOTE ON SPELLING AND USAGE xxi

12 Peoples and Civilizations of the Americas, 200–1500 305

Classic-Era Culture and Society in Mesoamerica, 200–900 307
Teotihuacan 308 • The Maya 310

The Postclassic Period in Mesoamerica, 900–1500 313
The Toltecs 313 • The Aztecs 314

Northern Peoples 316
Southwestern Desert Cultures 316 • Mound Builders: The Adena, Hopewell, and Mississippian Cultures 318

Andean Civilizations, 200–1500 320
Cultural Response to Environmental Challenge 320 • Moche and Chimu 322 • Tiwanaku and Wari 323 • The Inca 327

CONCLUSION 329 / KEY TERMS 329 / SUGGESTED READING 329 / NOTES 330

■ ENVIRONMENT AND TECHNOLOGY: Inca Roads 326

■ DIVERSITY AND DOMINANCE: Burials as Historical Texts 324

ISSUES IN WORLD HISTORY: Religious Conversion 331

PART FOUR
Interregional Patterns of Culture and Contact, 1200–1550
333

13 Mongol Eurasia and Its Aftermath, 1200–1500 336

The Rise of the Mongols, 1200–1260 337
Nomadism in Central and Inner Asia 338 • The Mongol Conquests, 1215–1283 338 • Overland Trade and the Plague 344

The Mongols and Islam, 1260–1500 344
Mongol Rivalry 345 • Islam and the State 345 • Culture and Science in Islamic Eurasia 346

Regional Responses in Western Eurasia 349
Russia and Rule from Afar 349 • New States in Eastern Europe and Anatolia 350

Mongol Domination in China, 1271–1368 351
The Yuan Empire, 1279–1368 352 • Cultural and Scientific Exchange 353 • The Fall of the Yuan Empire 354

The Early Ming Empire, 1368–1500 354
Ming China on a Mongol Foundation 354 • Technology and Population 356 • The Ming Achievement 357

Centralization and Militarism in East Asia, 1200–1500 359
Korea from the Mongols to the Yi, 1231–1500 359 • Political Transformation in Japan, 1274–1500 360 • The Emergence of Vietnam, 1200–1500 363

CONCLUSION 363 / KEY TERMS 364 / SUGGESTED READING 364 / NOTES 365

■ ENVIRONMENT AND TECHNOLOGY: From Gunpowder to Guns 358

■ DIVERSITY AND DOMINANCE: Mongol Politics, Mongol Women 340

14 Tropical Africa and Asia, 1200–1500 366

Tropical Lands and Peoples 367
The Tropical Environment 367 • Human Ecosystems 369 • Water Systems and Irrigation 370 • Mineral Resources 371

New Islamic Empires 372
Mali in the Western Sudan 372 • The Delhi Sultanate in India 375

Indian Ocean Trade 380
Monsoon Mariners 380 • Africa: The Swahili and Zimbabwe 381 • Arabia: Aden and the Red Sea 384 • India: Gujarat and the Malabar Coast 384 • Southeast Asia: The Rise of Malacca 385

Social and Cultural Change 385
Architecture, Learning, and Religion 385 • Social and Gender Distinctions 387

CONCLUSION 389 / KEY TERMS 389 / SUGGESTED READING 389 / NOTES 390

■ ENVIRONMENT AND TECHNOLOGY: The Indian Ocean Dhow 382

■ DIVERSITY AND DOMINANCE: Personal Styles of Rule in India and Mali 376

15 The Latin West, 1200–1500 391

Rural Growth and Crisis 393
Peasants and Population 394 • The Black Death and Social Change 395 • Mines and Mills 397

Urban Revival 398
Trading Cities 398 • Civic Life 400 • Gothic Cathedrals 404

Learning, Literature, and the Renaissance 406
Universities and Learning 406 • Humanists and Printers 407 • Renaissance Artists 409

Political and Military Transformations 410
Monarchs, Nobles, and Clergy 410 • The Hundred Years War, 1337–1453 413 • New Monarchies in France and England 413 • Iberian Unification 414

CONCLUSION 415 / KEY TERMS 415 / SUGGESTED READING 415 / NOTES 416

■ ENVIRONMENT AND TECHNOLOGY: The Clock 405

■ DIVERSITY AND DOMINANCE: Persecution and Protection of Jews, 1272–1349 402

16 The Maritime Revolution, to 1550 417

Global Maritime Expansion Before 1450 418
The Pacific Ocean 419 • The Indian Ocean 421 • The Atlantic Ocean 423

European Expansion, 1400–1550 424
Motives for Exploration 425 • Portuguese Voyages 425 • Spanish Voyages 428

Encounters with Europe, 1450–1550 431
Western Africa 431 • Eastern Africa 433 • Indian Ocean States 433 • The Americas 435 • Patterns of Dominance 440

CONCLUSION 441 / KEY TERMS 441 / SUGGESTED READING 441 / NOTES 442

■ ENVIRONMENT AND TECHNOLOGY: Vasco da Gama's Fleet 429

■ DIVERSITY AND DOMINANCE: Kongo's Christian King 438

■ ISSUES IN WORLD HISTORY: Climate and Population, to 1500 443

PART FIVE
The Globe Encompassed, 1500–1750
445

17 Transformations in Europe, 1500–1750 448

Culture and Ideas 449
Religious Reformation 450 • Traditional Thinking and Witch-Hunts 453 • The Scientific Revolution 454 • The Early Enlightenment 456

Social and Economic Life 456
The Bourgeoisie 456 • Peasants and Laborers 460 • Women and the Family 461

Political Innovations 462
State Development 462 • Religious Policies 463 • Monarchies in England and France 466 • Warfare and Diplomacy 467 • Paying the Piper 469

CONCLUSION 471 / KEY TERMS 472 / SUGGESTED READING 472 / NOTES 472

■ ENVIRONMENT AND TECHNOLOGY: Mapping the World 458

■ DIVERSITY AND DOMINANCE: Political Craft and Craftiness 464

18 The Diversity of American Colonial Societies, 1530–1770 473

The Columbian Exchange 474
Demographic Changes 475 • Transfer of Plants and Animals 476

Spanish America and Brazil 477
State and Church 477 • Colonial Economies 480 • Society in Colonial Latin America 483

English and French Colonies in North America 488
Early English Experiments 488 • The South 488 • New England 490 • The Middle Atlantic Region 492 • French America 493

Colonial Expansion and Conflict 495
Imperial Reform in Spanish America and Brazil 495 • Reform and Reorganization in British America 497

CONCLUSION 497 / KEY TERMS 498 / SUGGESTED READING 498 / NOTES 498

■ ENVIRONMENT AND TECHNOLOGY: A Silver Refinery at Potosí, Bolivia, 1700 481

■ DIVERSITY AND DOMINANCE: Race and Ethnicity in the Spanish Colonies: Negotiating Hierarchy 484

19 The Atlantic System and Africa, 1550–1800 499

Plantations in the West Indies 501
Colonization Before 1650 501 • Sugar and Slaves 502

Plantation Life in the Eighteenth Century 503
Technology and Environment 504 • Slaves' Lives 505 •
Free Whites and Free Blacks 508

Creating the Atlantic Economy 510
Capitalism and Mercantilism 510 • The Atlantic
Circuit 511

Africa, the Atlantic, and Islam 515
The Gold Coast and the Slave Coast 515 • The Bight
of Biafra and Angola 517 • Africa's European and Islamic
Contacts 518

CONCLUSION 523 / KEY TERMS 523 /
SUGGESTED READING 524 / NOTES 524

■ ENVIRONMENT AND TECHNOLOGY: Amerindian Foods
in Africa 506

■ DIVERSITY AND DOMINANCE: Slavery in West Africa
and the Americas 520

20 Southwest Asia and the Indian Ocean, 1500–1750 525

The Ottoman Empire, to 1750 526
Expansion and Frontiers 528 • Central Institutions 530 •
Crisis of the Military State, 1585–1650 534 • Economic
Change and Growing Weakness, 1650–1750 534

The Safavid Empire, 1502–1722 536
The Rise of the Safavids 537 • Society and Religion 537 •
A Tale of Two Cities: Isfahan and Istanbul 538 • Economic
Crisis and Political Collapse 540

The Mughal Empire, 1526–1761 541
Political Foundations 541 • Hindus and Muslims 542 •
Central Decay and Regional Challenges, 1707–1761 544

Trade Empires in the Indian Ocean, 1600–1729 544
Muslims in the East Indies 545 • Muslims in East
Africa 545

CONCLUSION 548 / KEY TERMS 548 /
SUGGESTED READING 549 / NOTES 549

■ ENVIRONMENT AND TECHNOLOGY: Metal Currency
and Inflation 535

■ DIVERSITY AND DOMINANCE: Islamic Law and Ottoman
Rule 532

21 Northern Eurasia, 1500–1800 550

Japanese Reunification 551
Civil War and the Invasion of Korea, 1500–1603 551 •
The Tokugawa Shogunate, to 1800 552 • Japan
and the Europeans 553 • Elite Decline and Social
Crisis 555

The Later Ming and Early Qing Empires 556
The Ming Empire, 1500–1644 557 • Ming Collapse
and the Rise of the Qing 558 • Trading Companies
and Missionaries 558 • Emperor Kangxi
(r. 1662–1722) 559 • Chinese Influences on
Europe 563 • Tea and Diplomacy 564 • Population
and Social Stress 564

The Russian Empire 565
The Drive Across Northern Asia 566 • Russian Society
and Politics to 1725 567 • Peter the Great 569 •
Consolidation of the Empire 571

Comparative Perspectives 571
Political Comparisons 572 • Cultural, Social, and
Economic Comparisons 572

CONCLUSION 573 / KEY TERMS 574 /
SUGGESTED READING 574 / NOTES 574

■ ENVIRONMENT AND TECHNOLOGY: East Asian Porcelain 554

■ DIVERSITY AND DOMINANCE: Gendered Violence:
The Yangzhou Massacre 560

ISSUES IN WORLD HISTORY: The Little Ice Age 575

PART SIX
Revolutions Reshape the World, 1750–1870
577

22 Revolutionary Changes in the Atlantic World, 1750–1850 580

**Prelude to Revolution: The Eighteenth-Century
Crisis** 582
Colonial Wars and Fiscal Crises 582 • The Enlightenment
and the Old Order 582 • Folk Cultures and Popular
Protest 586

The American Revolution, 1775–1800 587
Frontiers and Taxes 587 • The Course of Revolution,
1775–1783 589 • The Construction of Republican
Institutions, to 1800 591

The French Revolution, 1789–1815 592
French Society and Fiscal Crisis 592 • Protest Turns
to Revolution, 1789–1792 593 • The Terror,
1793–1794 595 • Reaction and Dictatorship,
1795–1815 597

**Revolution Spreads, Conservatives Respond,
1789–1850** 601
The Haitian Revolution, 1789–1804 601 • The Congress of
Vienna and Conservative Retrenchment, 1815–1820 603 •
Nationalism, Reform, and Revolution, 1821–1850 604

CONCLUSION 605 / KEY TERMS 606 /
SUGGESTED READING 606 / NOTES 607

■ ENVIRONMENT AND TECHNOLOGY: The Pencil 584

■ DIVERSITY AND DOMINANCE: Robespierre and
Wollstonecraft Defend and Explain the Terror 598

23 The Early Industrial Revolution,
1760–1851 608

Causes of the Industrial Revolution 609
Population Growth 609 • The Agricultural
Revolution 610 • Trade and Inventiveness 610 •
Britain and Continental Europe 611

The Technological Revolution 614
Mass Production: Pottery 614 • Mechanization:
The Cotton Industry 615 • The Iron Industry 616 •
The Steam Engine 618 • Railroads 620 •
Communication over Wires 620

The Impact of the Early Industrial Revolution 622
The New Industrial Cities 622 • Rural
Environments 624 • Working Conditions 624 •
Changes in Society 626

New Economic and Political Ideas 627
Laissez Faire and Its Critics 627 • Positivists and Utopian
Socialists 628 • Protests and Reforms 628

Industrialization and the Nonindustrial World 629

CONCLUSION 630 / KEY TERMS 630 /
SUGGESTED READING 631 / NOTES 631

■ ENVIRONMENT AND TECHNOLOGY: The Origin of
Graphs 613

■ DIVERSITY AND DOMINANCE: Adam Smith and the
Division of Labor 616

24 Nation Building and Economic
Transformation in the Americas,
1800–1890 632

Independence in Latin America, 1800–1830 633
Roots of Revolution, to 1810 634 • Spanish South
America, 1810–1825 634 • Mexico, 1810–1823 637 •
Brazil, to 1831 638

The Problem of Order, 1825–1890 639
Constitutional Experiments 639 • Personalist
Leaders 642 • The Threat of Regionalism 644 • Foreign
Interventions and Regional Wars 646 • Native Peoples
and the Nation-State 647

The Challenge of Social and Economic Change 650
The Abolition of Slavery 650 • Immigration 652 •
American Cultures 654 • Women's Rights and the
Struggle for Social Justice 655 • Development and
Underdevelopment 656 • Altered Environments 659

CONCLUSION 660 / KEY TERMS 661 /
SUGGESTED READING 661 / NOTES 662

■ ENVIRONMENT AND TECHNOLOGY: Constructing the Port
of Buenos Aires, Argentina 658

■ DIVERSITY AND DOMINANCE: The Afro-Brazilian Experience,
1828 640

25 Africa, India, and the New British
Empire, 1750–1870 663

Changes and Exchanges in Africa 664
New Africa States 665 • Modernization in Egypt and
Ethiopia 668 • European Penetration 669 • Abolition
and Legitimate Trade 670 • Secondary Empires in Eastern
Africa 672

India Under British Rule 673
Company Men 673 • Raj and Rebellion, 1818–1857 674 •
Political Reform and Industrial Impact 676 • Rising
Indian Nationalism 680

Britain's Eastern Empire 681
Colonies and Commerce 681 • Imperial Policies and
Shipping 683 • Colonization of Australia and New
Zealand 684 • New Labor Migrations 686

CONCLUSION 687 / KEY TERMS 688 /
SUGGESTED READING 688 / NOTES 689

■ ENVIRONMENT AND TECHNOLOGY: Whaling 685

■ DIVERSITY AND DOMINANCE: Ceremonials of Imperial
Domination 678

26 Land Empires in the Age of Imperialism, 1800–1870 690

The Ottoman Empire 691
Egypt and the Napoleonic Example, 1798–1840 692 •
Ottoman Reform and the European Model, 1807–
1853 693 • The Crimean War and Its Aftermath,
1853–1877 699

The Russian Empire 703
Russia and Europe 703 • Russia and Asia 705 •
Cultural Trends 706

The Qing Empire 707
Economic and Social Disorder, 1800–1839 707 • The
Opium War and Its Aftermath, 1839–1850 708 • The

Taiping Rebellion, 1850–1864 710 • Decentralization at
the End of the Qing Empire, 1864–1875 712

CONCLUSION 715 / KEY TERMS 715 /
SUGGESTED READING 715

■ ENVIRONMENT AND TECHNOLOGY: The Web of War 702

■ DIVERSITY AND DOMINANCE: The French Occupation
of Egypt 694

ISSUES IN WORLD HISTORY: State Power, the Census,
and the Question of Identity 717

GLOSSARY G-1

INDEX I-1

Maps

12.1 Major Mesoamerican Civilizations, 1000 B.C.E.–1519 C.E.   308

12.2 Culture Areas of North America   319

12.3 Andean Civilizations, 200 B.C.E.–1532 C.E.   321

13.1 The Mongol Domains in Eurasia in 1300   343

13.2 Western Eurasia in the 1300s   346

13.3 The Ming Empire and Its Allies, 1368–1500   355

13.4 Korea and Japan, 1200–1500   361

14.1 Africa and the Indian Ocean Basin: Physical Characteristics   368

14.2 Africa, 1200–1500   373

14.3 South and Southeast Asia, 1200–1500   378

14.4 Arteries of Trade and Travel in the Islamic World, to 1500   381

15.1 The Black Death in Fourteenth-Century Europe   396

15.2 Trade and Manufacturing in Later Medieval Europe   399

15.3 Europe in 1453   411

16.1 Exploration and Settlement in the Indian and Pacific Oceans Before 1500   420

16.2 Middle America to 1533   424

16.3 European Exploration, 1420–1542   427

17.1 Religious Reformation in Europe   452

17.2 The European Empire of Charles V   463

17.3 Europe in 1740   470

18.1 Colonial Latin America in the Eighteenth Century   479

18.2 European Claims in North America, 1755–1763   494

19.1 The Atlantic Economy   512

19.2 The African Slave Trade, 1500–1800   514

19.3 West African States and Trade, 1500–1800   516

20.1 Muslim Empires in the Sixteenth and Seventeenth Centuries   529

20.2 European Colonization in the Indian Ocean to 1750   546

21.1 The Qing Empire, 1644–1783   559

21.2 Climate and Diversity in the Qing Empire   566

21.3 The Expansion of Russia, 1500–1800   568

22.1 The American Revolutionary War   590

22.2 Napoleon's Europe, 1810   600

22.3 The Haitian Revolution   602

23.1 The Industrial Revolution in Britain, ca. 1850   612

23.2 Industrialization in Europe, ca. 1850   621

24.1 Latin America by 1830   636

24.2 Dominion of Canada, 1873   642

24.3 Territorial Growth of the United States, 1783–1853   645

24.4 The Expansion of the United States, 1850–1920   659

25.1 Africa in the Nineteenth Century   666

25.2 India, 1707–1805   674

25.3 European Possessions in the Indian Ocean and South Pacific, 1870   682

26.1 The Ottoman and Russian Empires, 1829–1914   697

26.2 Conflicts in the Qing Empire, 1839–1870   709

Environment and Technology

Inca Roads   326
Gunpowder to Guns   358
The Indian Ocean Dhow   382
The Clock   405
Vasco da Gama's Fleet   429
Mapping the World   458
A Silver Refinery at Potosí, Bolivia, 1700   481
Amerindian Foods in Africa   506

Metal Currency and Inflation   535
East Asian Porcelain   554
The Pencil   584
The Origin of Graphs   613
Constructing the Port of Buenos Aires, Argentina   658
Whaling   685
The Web of War   702

Diversity and Dominance

Burials as Historical Texts   324
Mongol Politics, Mongol Women   340
Personal Styles of Rule in India and Mali   376
Persecution and Protection of Jews, 1272–1349   402
Kongo's Christian King   438
Political Craft and Craftiness   464
Race and Identity in the Spanish Colonies: Negotiating Hierarchy   484

Slavery in West Africa and the Americas   520
Islamic Law and Ottoman Rule   532
Gendered Violence: The Yangzhou Massacre   560
Robespierre and Wollstonecraft Defend and Explain the Terror   598
Adam Smith and the Division of Labor   616
The Afro-Brazilian Experience, 1828   640
Ceremonials of Imperial Domination   678
The French Occupation of Egypt   694

Issues in World History

Religious Conversion   331
Climate and Population, to 1500   443
The Little Ice Age   575
State Power, the Census, and the Question of Identity   717

Preface

Reaching the point of preparing the third edition of a textbook is particularly gratifying for its authors. The sustained appeal of their writing tells them that they have done something good and useful. But that in turn prompts them to ponder what they can do to make their book still better. Fortunately, feedback from teachers and students provides a regular stream of helpful suggestions. We have tried to respond to the most frequent and constructive of these suggestions in preparing the third edition.

Our overall goal remains unchanged: to produce a textbook that not only speaks for the past but speaks to today's student and today's teacher. Students and instructors alike should take away from this text a broad vision of human societies beginning as sparse and disconnected communities reacting creatively to local circumstances; experiencing ever more intensive stages of contact, interpenetration, and cultural expansion and amalgamation; and arriving at a twenty-first century world in which people increasingly visualize a single global community.

Process, not progress, is the keynote of this book: a steady process of change over time, at first differently experienced in various regions, but eventually connecting peoples and traditions from all parts of the globe. Students should come away from this book with a sense that the problems and promises of their world are rooted in a past in which people of every sort, in every part of the world, confronted problems of a similar character and coped with them as best they could. We believe that our efforts will help students see where their world has come from and learn thereby something useful for their own lives.

Central Themes

We subtitled *The Earth and Its Peoples* "A Global History" because the book explores the common challenges and experiences that unite the human past. Although the dispersal of early humans to every livable environment resulted in a myriad of different economic, social, political, and cultural systems, all societies displayed analogous patterns in meeting their needs and exploiting their environments. Our challenge was to select the particular data and episodes that would best illuminate these global patterns of human experience.

To meet this challenge, we adopted two themes to serve as the spinal cord of our history: "technology and the environment" and "diversity and dominance." The first theme represents the commonplace material bases of all human societies at all times. It grants no special favor to any cultural group even as it embraces subjects of the broadest topical, chronological, and geographical range. The second theme expresses the reality that every human society has constructed or inherited structures of domination. We examine practices and institutions of many sorts: military, economic, social, political, religious, and cultural, as well as those based on kinship, gender, and literacy. Simultaneously we recognize that alternative ways of life and visions of societal organization continually manifest themselves both within and in dialogue with every structure of domination.

With respect to the first theme, it is vital for students to understand that technology, in the broad sense of experience-based knowledge of the physical world, underlies all human activity. Writing is a technology, but so is oral transmission from generation to generation of lore about medicinal or poisonous plants. The magnetic compass is a navigational technology, but so is Polynesian mariners' hard-won knowledge of winds, currents, and tides that made possible the settlement of the Pacific islands.

All technological development has come about in interaction with environments, both physical and human, and has, in turn, affected those environments. The story of how humanity has changed the face of the globe is an integral part of our first theme. Yet technology and the environment do not explain or underlie all important episodes of human experience. The theme of "diversity and dominance" informs all our discussions of politics, culture, and society. Thus when narrating the histories of empires, we describe a range of human experiences within and beyond the imperial frontiers without assuming that imperial institutions are a more fit topic for discussion than the economic and social organization of pastoral nomads or the lives of peasant women. When religion and culture occupy our narrative, we focus not only on the dominant tradition but also on the diversity of alternative beliefs and practices.

Changes in the Third Edition

A reader comparing the second and third editions will notice changes in both structure and coverage. Most apparent among the structural changes are two new features. In each chapter a two-page primary source feature, "Diversity and Dominance," has replaced the brief "Society and Culture" excerpts of the previous edition. The new feature fills two needs. First, it gives students extended documentary selections on which to hone their analytical skills. This, we believe, will serve well the desire of many teachers to expose their students to the raw material with which historians work. Second, it provides a focus for students to consider the many forms of dominance that have developed over time and the many ways in which human diversity has continued to express itself regardless of these forms of dominance. The topics covered under "Diversity and Dominance" range from "Hierarchy and Conduct in the Analects of Confucius" (Chapter 3) and "Archbishop Adalbert of Hamburg and the Christianization of the Scandinavians and Slavs" (Chapter 10) to "The Afro-Brazilian Experience, 1828" (Chapter 24) and "Women, Family Values, and the Russian Revolution" (Chapter 30).

"Issues in World History," the second new feature, comprises original essays that appear at the end of Parts One through Seven. As we surveyed the burgeoning field of global history, we became aware of issues of such broad significance, often involving new kinds of historical evidence, that they could not easily be discussed in a chapter concentrating on a specific time and place. We therefore highlight seven of these issues in part-ending essays: "Animal Domestication," "Oral Societies and the Consequences of Literacy," "Religious Conversion," "Climate and Population, to 1500," "The Little Ice Age," "State Power, the Census, and the Question of Identity," and "Famines and Politics." We believe that teachers and students will be stimulated to see the great reach and exciting potential of the field of global history and be encouraged to pose broader questions of their own.

We sifted through a mass of helpful suggestions on how to revise and reorganize the content itself. Along with hundreds of minor revisions and clarifications, we effected a number of major changes:

- Chapters 3 and 4 have been rethought and reorganized: Chapter 3 now deals with several civilizations that emerged independently in different parts of the world in the second and first millennia B.C.E., while Chapter 4 focuses on the same time period in Western Asia and the Mediterranean, giving greater stress to continuity and interaction in that region.
- Chapter 10, on early medieval Europe, has been reorganized so that it opens with Byzantium and proceeds from there to western Europe. Two new maps have been added—one on German kingdoms, c. 530, and the other on Kievan Russia and the Byzantine Empire in the eleventh century.
- We greatly increased the coverage of Russian history, including expanded discussions in Chapters 10 and 21 and an entirely new section in Chapter 26.
- The history and impact of the Mongols are now covered in a single chapter, Chapter 13, "Mongol Eurasia and Its Aftermath, 1200–1500." Combining previously separated materials allowed us to make more evident the parallels and contrasts between the impact of the Mongols in the west and in the east.
- Chapter 17, on early modern Europe, has been reorganized and streamlined.
- Coverage of the United States in the late nineteenth century, previously in two separate chapters, has been reorganized and consolidated in Chapter 24.
- Chapter 26 now includes an extended discussion of the beginnings of European impact on Egypt.
- Discussions of the modernization of Japan in the late nineteenth century have been combined in Chapter 27. The discussion of nationalism now includes coverage of the unification of Italy as well as two new maps on the unifications of Italy and Germany.
- Chapter 33 brings the account of threats and strains to the global environment up to the present, including a new map showing stresses on the world's fresh water supplies.
- The final chapter, Chapter 34, "Globalization at the Turn of the Millennium," has been entirely rewritten to reflect current developments in global politics, the global economy, and global culture. New maps have been added showing regional trade associations and the unequal distribution of wealth around the world. The terrorist attacks of September 11 and the responses to them receive special attention.
- Suggested Reading lists were updated with important recent scholarship.

Organization

The Earth and Its Peoples uses eight broad chronological divisions to define its conceptual scheme of global historical development. In **Part One: The Emergence of Human Communities, to 500 B.C.E.,** we examine important patterns of human communal organization in both the Eastern and Western Hemispheres. Small, dispersed human communities living by foraging spread to most parts of the world over tens of thousands of years. They responded to enormously diverse environmental conditions, at different times in different ways, discovering how to cultivate plants and utilize the products of domestic animals. On the basis of these new modes of sustenance, population grew, permanent towns appeared, and political and religious authority, based on collection and control of agricultural surpluses, spread over extensive areas.

Part Two: The Formation of New Cultural Communities, 1000 B.C.E.–400 C.E., introduces the concept of a "cultural community," in the sense of a coherent pattern of activities and symbols pertaining to a specific human community. While all human communities develop distinctive cultures, including those discussed in Part One, historical development in this stage of global history prolonged and magnified the impact of some cultures more than others. In the geographically contiguous African-Eurasian land mass, the cultures that proved to have the most enduring influence traced their roots to the second and first millennia B.C.E.

Part Three: Growth and Interaction of Cultural Communities, 300 B.C.E.–1200 C.E., deals with early episodes of technological, social, and cultural exchange and interaction on a continental scale both within and beyond the framework of imperial expansion. These are so different from earlier interactions arising from more limited conquests or extensions of political boundaries that they constitute a distinct era in world history, an era that set the world on the path of increasing global interaction and interdependence that it has been following ever since.

In Part Four: Interregional Patterns of Culture and Contact, 1200–1550, we look at the world during the three and a half centuries that saw both intensified cultural and commercial contact and increasingly confident self-definition of cultural communities in Europe, Asia, and Africa. The Mongol conquest of a vast empire extending from the Pacific Ocean to eastern Europe greatly stimulated trade and interaction. In the West, strengthened European kingdoms began maritime expansion in the Atlantic, forging direct ties with sub-Saharan Africa and beginning the conquest of the civilizations of the Western Hemisphere.

Part Five: The Globe Encompassed, 1500–1750, treats a period dominated by the global effects of European expansion and continued economic growth. European ships took over, expanded, and extended the maritime trade of the Indian Ocean, coastal Africa, and the Asian rim of the Pacific Ocean. This maritime commercial enterprise had its counterpart in European colonial empires in the Americas and a new Atlantic trading system. The contrasting capacities and fortunes of traditional land empires and new maritime empires, along with the exchange of domestic plants and animals between the hemispheres, underline the technological and environmental dimensions of this first era of complete global interaction.

In Part Six: Revolutions Reshape the World, 1750–1870, the word *revolution* is used in several senses: in the political sense of governmental overthrow, as in France and the Americas; in the metaphorical sense of radical transformative change, as in the Industrial Revolution; and in the broadest sense of a perception of a profound change in circumstances and worldview. Technology and environment lie at the core of these developments. With the rapid ascendancy of the Western belief that science and technology could overcome all challenges—environmental or otherwise—technology became an instrument not only of transformation but also of domination, to the point of threatening the integrity and autonomy of cultural traditions in nonindustrial lands.

Part Seven: Global Diversity and Dominance, 1850–1945, examines the development of a world arena in which people conceived of events on a global scale. Imperialism, world war, international economic connections, and world-encompassing ideological tendencies, such as nationalism and socialism, present the picture of a globe becoming increasingly interconnected. European dominance took on a worldwide dimension, seeming at times to threaten the diversity of human cultural experience with permanent subordination to European values and philosophies, while at other times triggering strong political or cultural resistance.

For Part Eight: Perils and Promises of a Global Community, 1945 to the Present, we divided the last half of the twentieth century into three time periods: 1945–1975, 1975–1991, and 1991 to the present. The challenges of the Cold War and post-colonial nation building dominated most of the period and unleashed global economic, technological, and political forces that became increasingly important in all aspects of human life. Technology plays a central role in Part Eight, because of its integral role in the growth of a global community and because its many benefits in improving the quality of life seem clouded by real and potential negative impacts on the environment.

Formats

To accommodate different academic calendars and approaches to the course, *The Earth and Its Peoples* is available in three formats. There is a one-volume hard-cover version containing all 34 chapters, along with a two-volume paperback edition: Volume I: *To 1550* (Chapters 1–16) and Volume II: *Since 1500* (Chapters 16–34). For readers at institutions with the quarter system, we offer a three-volume paperback version: Volume A: *To 1200* (Chapters 1–12); Volume B: *From 1200 to 1870* (Chapters 12–26); and Volume C: *Since 1750* (Chapters 22–34). Volume II includes an Introduction that surveys the main developments set out in Volume I and provides a groundwork for students studying only the period since 1500.

Supplements

We have assembled an array of supplements to aid students in learning and instructors in teaching. These supplements, including our new *History Companion*, a *Study Guide*, an *Instructor's Resource Manual, Test Items, Blackboard* and *Web CT* course cartridges, and *Map Transparencies* provide a tightly integrated program of teaching and learning.

In keeping with Houghton Mifflin's goal of being your primary source for history, we are proud to announce the *History Companion,* your new primary source for history technology solutions. History instructors have enough to do without having to master new software or download the latest plug-in to gain access to primary sources, maps, and other tools of the trade. The *History Companion* provides hundreds of resources with only a few clicks of your mouse. The *History Companion* has three components:

The *Instructor Companion* is an easily searchable CD-ROM that makes hundreds of historical images and maps instantly accessible in PowerPoint format. Each image is accompanied by notes that place it in its proper historical context and tips for ways it can be presented in the classroom. This CD is free to instructors with the adoption of this or any Houghton Mifflin history textbook. In addition to visual presentation materials, the CD includes our *HM Testing* program; a computerized version of the *Test Items* to enable instructors to alter, replace, or add questions; as well as resources from the *Instructor's Resource Manual.*

The *Student Research Companion* is a free Internet-based tool with 100 interactive maps and 500 primary sources. The primary sources include headnotes that provide pertinent background information and questions that students can answer and email to their instructors.

The *Student Study Companion* is a free online study guide that contains ACE self-tests, which feature 25 to 30 multiple-choice questions per chapter with feedback, an audio pronunciation guide, web-based flashcards, chapter chronologies, and web links. In addition, *History WIRED: Web Intensive Research Exercises and Documents,* updated by John Reisbord (Ph.D. Northwestern University), offers text-specific links to visual and written sources on the World Wide Web, along with exercises to enhance learning. These study tools will help make your students succeed in the classroom.

The *Study Guide,* authored by Michele G. Scott James of MiraCosta College, contains learning objectives, chapter outlines (with space for students' notes on particular sections), key-term identifications, multiple-choice questions, short-answer and essay questions, and map exercises. Included too are distinctive "comparison charts" to help students organize the range of information about different cultures and events discussed in each chapter. The *Study Guide* is published in two volumes, to correspond to Volumes I and II of the textbook: Volume I contains Chapters 1–16; Volume II, Chapters 16–34.

The *Instructor's Resource Manual,* thoroughly revised by John Reisbord (Ph.D. Northwestern University), provides useful teaching strategies for the global history course and tips for getting the most out of the text. Each chapter contains instructional objectives, a detailed chapter outline, discussion questions, in-depth learning projects, and audio-visual resources.

Our *Test Items,* prepared by Jane Scimeca of Brookdale Community College, offers 20 to 25 key-term identifications, 5 to 10 essay questions with answer guidelines, 35 to 40 multiple-choice questions, and 2 to 3 history and geography exercises.

We have designed *Blackboard* and *WebCT* course cartridges for institutions using these platforms, so that students and instructors can access a wealth of resources including learning objectives, chapter outlines, and Internet assignments, in addition to our testing and quizzing programs.

Finally, a set of transparencies of all the maps in the textbook is available on adoption.

Acknowledgments

In preparing the third edition, we benefited from the critical readings of many colleagues. Our sincere thanks go in particular to the following instructors: Joseph Adams, Walton High School, Cobb County, Georgia; William H. Alexander, Norfolk State University; Corinne Blake, Rowan University; Olwyn M. Blouet, Virginia State University; Eric Bobo, Hinds Community College; James Boyden, Tulane University; Craige B.

Champion, Syracuse University; Eleanor A. Congdon, Youngstown State University; Philip Daileader, The College of William and Mary; Donald M. Fisher, Niagara County Community College; Nancy Fitch, California State University, Fullerton; Jay Harmon, Catholic High School, Baton Rouge, Louisiana; Carol A. Keller, San Antonio College; Susan Maneck, Jackson State University; Laurie S. Mannino, Magruder High School, North Potomac, Maryland; Margaret Malamud, New Mexico State University; Randall McGowen, University of Oregon; Diethelm Prowe, Carleton College; Michael D. Richards, Sweet Briar College; William Schell, Jr., Murray State University; Jeffrey M. Shumway, Brigham Young University; Jonathan Skaff, Shippensburg University of Pennsylvania; Tracy L. Steele, Sam Houston State University; and Peter von Sivers, University of Utah.

When textbook authors set out on a project, they are inclined to believe that 90 percent of the effort will be theirs and 10 percent that of various editors and production specialists employed by their publisher. How very naïve. This book would never have seen the light of day had it not been for the unstinting labors of the great team of professionals who turned the authors' words into beautifully presented print. Our debt to the staff of Houghton Mifflin remains undiminished in the third edition. Nancy Blaine, Senior Sponsoring Editor, has offered us firm but sympathetic guidance throughout the revision process. Jennifer Sutherland, Senior Development Editor, offered astute and sympathetic assistance as the authors worked to incorporate many new ideas and subjects into the text. Carol Newman, Senior Project Editor, moved the work through the production stages to meet what had initially seemed like an unachievable schedule. Carole Frolich did an outstanding job of art and photo research. Jill Haber, Senior Production Design Coordinator, dealt with many of the technological issues that arise in producing a text of this size. We also recognize the invaluable contributions of Senior Designer Henry Rachlin, who created the book's elegant new design, Editorial Associate Annette Fantasia, who oversaw the review process and the preparation of supplemental material, and Florence Cadran, Manufacturing Manager, who saw to it that the text was printed on schedule.

We thank also the many students whose questions and concerns, expressed directly or through their instructors, shaped much of this revision. We continue to welcome all readers' suggestions, queries, and criticisms. Please contact us at our respective institutions or at this e-mail address: history@hmco.com

About the Authors

Richard W. Bulliet Professor of Middle Eastern History at Columbia University, Richard W. Bulliet received his Ph.D. from Harvard University. He has written scholarly works on a number of topics: the social history of medieval Iran (*The Patricians of Nishapur*), the historical competition between pack camels and wheeled transport (*The Camel and the Wheel*), the process of conversion to Islam (*Conversion to Islam in the Medieval Period*), and the overall course of Islamic social history (*Islam: The View from the Edge*). He is the editor of the *Columbia History of the Twentieth Century*. He has published four novels, co-edited *The Encyclopedia of the Modern Middle East*, and hosted an educational television series on the Middle East. He was awarded a fellowship by the John Simon Guggenheim Memorial Foundation.

Pamela Kyle Crossley Pamela Kyle Crossley received her Ph.D. in Modern Chinese History from Yale University. She is Professor of History and Rosenwald Research Professor in the Arts and Sciences at Dartmouth College. Her books include *A Translucent Mirror: History and Identity in Qing Imperial Ideology; The Manchus; Orphan Warriors: Three Manchu Generations and the End of the Qing World;* and (with Lynn Hollen Lees and John W. Servos) *Global Society: The World Since 1900.* Her research, which concentrates on the cultural history of China, Inner Asia, and Central Asia, has been supported by the John Simon Guggenheim Memorial Foundation and the National Endowment for the Humanities.

Daniel R. Headrick Daniel R. Headrick received his Ph.D. in History from Princeton University. Professor of History and Social Science at Roosevelt University in Chicago, he is the author of several books on the history of technology, imperialism, and international relations, including *The Tools of Empire: Technology and European Imperialism in the Nineteenth Century; The Tentacles of Progress: Technology Transfer in the Age of Imperialism; The Invisible Weapon: Telecommunications and International Politics;* and *When Information Came of Age: Technologies of Knowledge in the Age of Reason and Revolution, 1700–1850.* His articles have appeared in the *Journal of World History* and the *Journal of Modern History,* and he has been awarded fellowships by the National Endowment for the Humanities, the John Simon Guggenheim Memorial Foundation, and the Alfred P. Sloan Foundation.

Steven W. Hirsch Steven W. Hirsch holds a Ph.D. in Classics from Stanford University and is currently Associate Professor Classics and History at Tufts University. He has received grants from the National Endowment for the Humanities and the Massachusetts Foundation for Humanities and Public Policy. His research and publications include *The Friendship of the Barbarians: Xenophon and the Persian Empire,* as well as articles and reviews in the *Classical Journal,* the *American Journal of Philology,* and the *Journal of Interdisciplinary History.* He is currently working on a comparative study of ancient Mediterranean and Chinese civilizations.

Lyman L. Johnson Professor of History at the University of North Carolina at Charlotte, Lyman L. Johnson earned his Ph.D. in Latin American History from the University of Connecticut. A two-time Senior Fulbright-Hays Lecturer, he also has received fellowships from the Tinker Foundation, the Social Science Research Council, the National Endowment for the Humanities, and the American Philosophical Society. His recent books include *Death, Dismemberment, and Memory; The Faces of Honor* (with Sonya Lipsett-Rivera); *The Problem of Order in Changing Societies; Essays on the Price History of Eighteenth-Century Latin America* (with Enrique Tandeter); and *Colonial Latin America* (with Mark A. Burkholder). He also has published in journals, including the *Hispanic American Historical Review,* the *Journal of Latin American Studies,* the *International Review of Social History, Social History,* and *Desarrollo Económico.* He recently served as president of the Conference on Latin American History.

David Northrup Professor of History at Boston College, David Northrup earned his Ph.D. in African and European History from the University of California at Los Angeles. He earlier taught in Nigeria with the Peace Corps and at Tuskegee Institute. Research supported by the Fulbright-Hays Commission, the National Endowment for the Humanities, and the Social Science Research Council led to publications concerning pre-colonial Nigeria, the Congo (1870–1940), the Atlantic slave trade, and Asian, African, and Pacific Islander indentured labor in the nineteenth century. A contributor to the *Oxford History of the British Empire* and *Blacks in the British Empire,* his latest book is *Africa's Discovery of Europe, 1450–1850.* For 2004 and 2005 he serves as president of the World History Association.

Note on Spelling and Usage

Where necessary for clarity, dates are followed by the letters C.E. or B.C.E. The abbreviation C.E. stands for "Common Era" and is equivalent to A.D. (*anno Domini*, Latin for "in the year of the Lord"). The abbreviation B.C.E stands for "before the Common Era" and means the same as B.C. ("before Christ"). In keeping with our goal of approaching world history without special concentration on one culture or another, we chose these neutral abbreviations as appropriate to our enterprise. Because many readers will be more familiar with English than with metric measurements, however, units of measure are generally given in the English system, with metric equivalents following in parentheses.

In general, Chinese has been romanized according to the *pinyin* method. Exceptions include proper names well established in English (e.g., Canton, Chiang Kaishek) and a few English words borrowed from Chinese (e.g., kowtow). Spellings of Arabic, Ottoman Turkish, Persian, Mongolian, Manchu, Japanese, and Korean names and terms avoid special diacritical marks for letters that are pronounced only slightly differently in English. An apostrophe is used to indicate when two Chinese syllables are pronounced separately (e.g., Chang'an).

For words transliterated from languages that use the Arabic script—Arabic, Ottoman Turkish, Perisan, Urdu— the apostrophe indicating separately pronounced syllables may represent either of two special consonants, the *hamza* or the *ain*. Because most English-speakers do not hear the distinction between these two, they have not been distinguished in transliteration and are not indicated when they occur at the beginning or end of a word. As with Chinese, some words and commonly used placenames from these languages are given familiar English spellings (e.g., Quran instead of Qur'an, Cairo instead of al-Qahira). Arabic romanization has normally been used for terms relating to Islam, even where the context justifies slightly different Turkish or Persian forms, again for ease of comprehension.

Before 1492 the inhabitants of the Western Hemisphere had no single name for themselves. They had neither a racial consciousness nor a racial identity. Identity was derived from kin groups, language, cultural practices, and political structures. There was no sense that physical similarities created a shared identity. America's original inhabitants had racial consciousness and racial identity imposed on them by conquest and the occupation of their lands by Europeans after 1492. All of the collective terms for these first American peoples are tainted by this history. *Indians, Native Americans, Amerindians, First Peoples, and Indigenous Peoples* are among the terms in common usage. In this book the names of individual cultures and states are used wherever possible. *Amerindian* and other terms that suggest transcultural identity and experience are used most commonly for the period after 1492.

There is an ongoing debate about how best to render Amerindian words in English. It has been common for authors writing in English to follow Mexican usage for Nahuatl and Yucatec Maya words and place-names. In this style, for example, the capital of the Aztec state is spelled Tenochtitlán, and the important late Maya city-state is spelled Chichén Itzá. Although these forms are still common even in the specialist literature, we have chosen to follow the scholarship that sees these accents as unnecessary. The exceptions are modern place-names, such as Mérida and Yucatán, which are accented. A similar problem exists for the spelling of Quechua and Aymara words from the Andean region of South America. Although there is significant disagreement among scholars, we follow the emerging consensus and use the spellings khipu (not quipu), Tiwanaku (not Tiahuanaco), and Wari (not Huari). However, we keep Inca (not Inka) and Cuzco (not Cusco), since these spellings are expected by most of our potential readers and we hope to avoid confusion.

The Earth and Its Peoples

A Global History

Peoples and Civilizations of the Americas, 200–1500

Maya Scribe   Mayan scribes used a complex writing system to record religious concepts and memorialize the actions of their kings. This picture of a scribe was painted on a ceramic plate.

CHAPTER OUTLINE

Classic-Era Culture and Society in Mesoamerica, 200–900

The Postclassic Period in Mesoamerica, 900–1500

Northern Peoples

Andean Civilizations, 200–1500

DIVERSITY AND DOMINANCE: Burials as Historical Texts

ENVIRONMENT AND TECHNOLOGY: Inca Roads

In late August 682 C.E. the Maya° princess Lady Wac-Chanil-Ahau° walked down the steep steps from her family's residence and mounted a sedan chair decorated with rich textiles and animal skins. As the procession exited from the urban center of Dos Pilas°, her military escort spread out through the fields and woods along its path to prevent ambush by enemies. Lady Wac-Chanil-Ahau's destination was the Maya city of Naranjo°, where she was to marry a powerful nobleman. Her marriage had been arranged to re-establish the royal dynasty that had been eliminated when Caracol, the region's major military power, had defeated Naranjo. Lady Wac-Chanil-Ahau's passage to Naranjo symbolized her father's desire to forge a military alliance that could resist Caracol. For us, the story of Lady Wac-Chanil-Ahau illustrates the importance of marriage and lineage in the politics of the classic-period Maya.

Smoking Squirrel, the son of Lady Wac-Chanil-Ahau, ascended the throne of Naranjo as a five-year-old in 693 C.E. During his long reign he proved to be a careful diplomat and formidable warrior. He was also a prodigious builder, leaving behind an expanded and beautified capital as part of his legacy. Mindful of the importance of his mother and her lineage from Dos Pilas, he erected numerous stelae (carved stone monuments) that celebrated her life.[1]

When population increased and competition for resources grew more violent, warfare and dynastic crisis convulsed the world of Wac-Chanil-Ahau. The defeat of the city-states of Tikal and Naranjo by Caracol undermined long-standing commercial and political relations in much of southern Mesoamerica and led to more than a century of conflict. Caracol, in turn, was challenged by the dynasty created at Dos Pilas by the heirs of Lady Wac-Chanil-Ahau. Despite a shared culture and religion, the great Maya cities remained divided by the dynastic ambitions of their rulers and by the competition for resources.

As the story of Lady Wac-Chanil-Ahau's marriage and her role in the development of a Maya dynasty suggests, the peoples of the Americas were in constant competition for resources. Members of hereditary elites organized their societies to meet these challenges, even as their ambition for greater power predictably ignited new conflicts. No single set of political institutions or technologies worked in every environment, and enormous cultural diversity existed in the ancient Americas. In Mesoamerica (Mexico and northern Central America) and in the Andean region of South America, Amerindian peoples developed an extraordinarily productive and diversified agriculture.[2] They also built great cities that rivaled the capitals of the Chinese and Roman Empires in size and beauty. The Olmecs of Mesoamerica and Chavín° of the Andes were among the earliest civilizations of the Americas (see Chapter 3). In the rest of the hemisphere, indigenous peoples adapted combinations of hunting and agriculture to maintain a wide variety of settlement patterns, political forms, and cultural traditions. All the cultures and civilizations of the Americas experienced cycles of expansion and contraction as they struggled with the challenges of environmental changes, population growth, social conflict, and war.

As you read this chapter, ask yourself the following questions:

- How did differing environments influence the development of Mesoamerican, Andean, and northern peoples?

- What technologies were developed to meet the challenges of these environments?

- How were the civilizations of Mesoamerica and the Andean region similar? How did they differ?

- How did religious belief and practice influence political life in the ancient Americas?

Maya (MY-ah)   Wac-Chanil-Ahau (wac-cha-NEEL-ah-HOW)
Dos Pilas (dohs PEE-las)   Naranjo (na-ROHN-hoe)

Chavín (cha-VEEN)

C H R O N O L O G Y

	Mesoamerica	Northern peoples	Andes
100	**100** Teotihuacan founded	**100–400** Hopewell culture in Ohio River Valley	**100–600** Nazca culture
			200–700 Moche culture
	250 Maya early clasic period begins		
400			
			500–1000 Tiwanaku and Wari control Peruvian highlands
700		**700–1200** Anasazi culture	
	ca. 750 Teotihuacan destroyed		
	800–900 Maya centers abandoned, end of classic period	**919** Pueblo Bonito founded	
	968 Toltec capital of Tula founded		
1000			
		1050–1250 Cahokia reaches peak power	
	1156 Tula destroyed	**1150** Collapse of Anasazi centers begins	**1200** Chimu begin military expansion
1300			
	1325 Aztec capital Tenochtitlan founded		
			1438 Inca expansion begins
			1465 Inca conquer Chimu
1500		**1500** Mississippian culture declines	**1500–1525** Inca conquer Ecuador
	1502 Moctezuma II crowned Aztec ruler		

CLASSIC-ERA CULTURE AND SOCIETY IN MESOAMERICA, 200–900

Between about 200 and 900 C.E. the peoples of Mesoamerica created a remarkable civilization. Despite enduring differences in language and the absence of regional political integration, Mesoamericans were unified by similarities in material culture, religious beliefs and practices, and social structures. Building on the earlier achievements of the Olmecs and others, the peoples of the area that is now Central America and south and central Mexico developed new forms of political organization, made great strides in astronomy and mathematics, and improved the productivity of their agriculture. This mix of achievements is called the classic period by archaeologists. During this period, population grew, a greater variety of products were traded over longer distances, and social hierarchies became more complex. Great cities were constructed, serving as centers of political life and as arenas of religious ritual and spiritual experience.

Classic-period civilizations built on the religious and political foundations established earlier in Olmec centers. The cities of the classic period continued to be

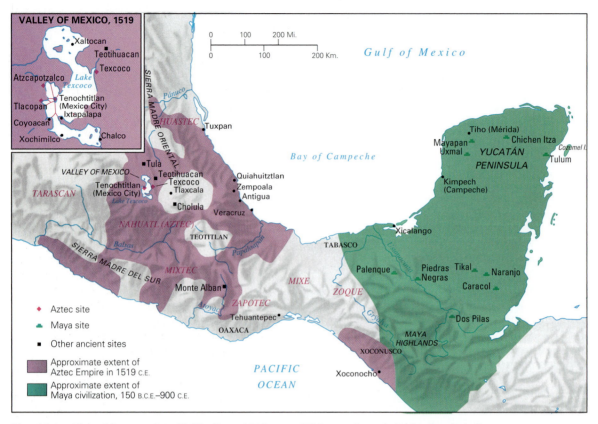

Map 12.1   Major Mesoamerican Civilizations, 1000 B.C.E.–1519 C.E. From their island capital of Tenochtitlan, the Aztecs militarily and commercially dominated a large region. Aztec achievements were built on the legacy of earlier civilizations such as the Olmecs and Maya.

dominated by platforms and pyramids devoted to religious functions, but they were more impressive and architecturally diversified. They had large full-time populations divided into classes and dominated by hereditary political and religious elites who controlled nearby towns and villages and imposed their will on the rural peasantry.

The political and cultural innovations of this period did not depend on the introduction of new technologies. The agricultural foundation of Mesoamerican civilization had been developed centuries earlier. Major innovations in agriculture such as irrigation, the draining of wetlands, and the terracing of hillsides had all been in place for more than a thousand years when great cities were developed after 200 C.E. Instead, the achievements of the classic era depended on the ability of increasingly powerful elites to organize and command growing numbers of laborers and soldiers. What had changed was the reach and power of religious and political leaders. The

scale and impressive architecture found at Teotihuacan° or at the great Maya cities illustrate both Mesoamerican aesthetic achievements and the development of powerful political institutions.

Teotihuacan

Located about 30 miles (48 kilometers) northeast of modern Mexico City, **Teotihuacan** (100 B.C.E.–750 C.E.) was one of Mesoamerica's most important classic-period civilizations (see Map 12.1). At the height of its power, from 450 to 600 C.E., it was the largest city in the Americas. With between 125,000 and 200,000 inhabitants, it was larger than all but a small number of contemporary European and Asian cities.

Religious architecture rose above a city center aligned with nearby sacred mountains and reflecting the

---

Teotihuacan (teh-o-tee-WAH-kahn)

Temple of Quetzalcoatl in Teotihuacan   This impressive temple was decorated with images of two gods, Quetzalcoatl and Tlaloc. Along both sides of the main temple steps are arrayed the serpent images associated with Quetzalcoatl, a culture god common to most of the Mesoamerican civilizations. Along the front of the temple the image of Quetzalcoatl is decorated with a feathered necklace. The image with the goggle-like decoration is Tlaloc, the rain or storm god.   (Jean Mazenod/Citadelles & Mazenod, Paris)

duty toward the gods and as essential to the well-being of human society.

The rapid growth in urban population initially resulted from a series of volcanic eruptions that disrupted agriculture. Later, as the city elite increased its power, farm families from the smaller villages in the region were forced to relocate to the urban core. As a result, more than two-thirds of the city's residents retained their dependence on agriculture, walking out from urban residences to their fields. The elite of Teotihuacan used the city's growing labor resources to bring marginal lands into production. Swamps were drained, irrigation works were constructed, terraces were built into hillsides, and the use of chinampas was expanded. **Chinampas°,** sometimes called "floating gardens," were narrow artificial islands constructed along lakeshores or in marshes. They were created by heaping lake muck and waste material on beds of reeds that were then anchored to the shore by trees. Chinampas permitted year-round agriculture—because of subsurface irrigation and resistance to frost—and thus played a crucial role in sustaining the region's growing population. The productivity of the city's agriculture made possible its accomplishments in art, architecture, and trade.

As population grew, the housing of commoners underwent dramatic change. Apartment-like stone buildings were constructed for the first time. These apartment compounds were unique to Teotihuacan. They commonly housed members of a single kinship group, but some were used to house craftsmen working in the same trade. The two largest craft groups produced pottery and obsidian tools, the most important articles of long-distance trade. It appears that more than 2 percent of the urban population was engaged in making obsidian tools and weapons. The city's pottery and obsidian have been found throughout central Mexico and even in the Maya region of Guatemala.

The city's role as a religious center and commercial power provided both divine approval of and a material basis for the elite's increased wealth and status. Members of the elite controlled the state bureaucracy, tax collection, and commerce. Their prestige and wealth were reflected in their style of dress and diet and in the separate residence compounds built for aristocratic families. The central position and great prestige of the priestly class were evident in temple and palace murals. Teotihuacan's economy and religious influence drew pilgrims from as far away as Oaxaca and Veracruz. Some of them became permanent residents.

Unlike the other classic-period civilizations, the people of Teotihuacan did not concentrate power in the

movement of the stars. Enormous pyramids dedicated to the Sun and Moon and more than twenty smaller temples devoted to other gods were arranged along a central avenue. The people recognized and worshiped many gods and lesser spirits. Among the gods were the Sun, the Moon, a storm-god, and Quetzalcoatl°, the feathered serpent. Quetzalcoatl was a culture-god believed to be the originator of agriculture and the arts. Like the earlier Olmecs, people living at Teotihuacan practiced human sacrifice. More than a hundred sacrificial victims were found during the excavation of the temple of Quetzalcoatl at Teotihuacan. Sacrifice was viewed as a sacred

---

Quetzalcoatl (kate-zahl-CO-ah-tal)

chinampas (chee-NAM-pahs)

hands of a single ruler. Although the ruins of their impressive housing compounds demonstrate the wealth and influence of the city's aristocracy, there is no clear evidence that individual rulers or a ruling dynasty gained overarching political power. In Teotihuacan the deeds of individual rulers were not featured in public art, nor were their images represented by statues or other monuments as in other Mesoamerican civilizations. In fact, some scholars suggest that Teotihuacan was ruled by alliances forged among elite families or by weak kings who were the puppets of these powerful families. Regardless of what form political decision making took, we know that this powerful classic-period civilization achieved regional preeminence without subordinating its political life to the personality of a powerful individual ruler or lineage.

Historians debate the role of the military in the development of Teotihuacan. The absence of walls or other defensive structures before 500 C.E. suggests that Teotihuacan enjoyed relative peace during its early development. Archaeological evidence, however, reveals that the city created a powerful military to protect long-distance trade and to compel peasant agriculturalists to transfer their surplus production to the city. The discovery of representations of soldiers in typical Teotihuacan dress in the Maya region of Guatemala suggests to some that Teotihuacan used its military to expand trade relations. Unlike later postclassic civilizations, however, Teotihuacan was not an imperial state controlled by a military elite.

It is unclear what forces brought about the collapse of Teotihuacan about 650 C.E. Weakness was evident as early as 500 C.E., when the urban population declined to about 40,000 and the city began to build defensive walls. These fortifications and pictorial evidence from murals suggest that the city's final decades were violent. Early scholars suggested that the city was overwhelmed militarily by a nearby rival city or by nomadic warrior peoples from the northern frontier. More recently, investigators have uncovered evidence of conflict within the ruling elite and the mismanagement of resources. This, they argue, led to class conflict and the breakdown of public order. As a result, most important temples in the city center were pulled down and religious images defaced. Elite palaces were also systematically burned and many of the residents killed. Regardless of the causes, the eclipse of Teotihuacan was felt throughout Mexico and into Central America.

The Maya

During Teotihuacan's ascendancy in the north, the **Maya** developed an impressive civilization in the region that today includes Guatemala, Honduras, Belize, and southern Mexico (see Map 12.1).

Given the difficulties imposed by a tropical climate and fragile soils, the cultural and architectural achievements of the Maya were remarkable. Although they shared a single culture, they were never unified politically. Instead, rival kingdoms led by hereditary rulers struggled with each other for regional dominance, much like the Mycenaean-era Greeks (see Chapter 4).

Today Maya farmers prepare their fields by cutting down small trees and brush and then burning the dead vegetation to fertilize the land. Swidden agriculture (also called shifting agriculture or slash and burn agriculture) can produce high yields for a few years. However, it uses up the soil's nutrients, eventually forcing people to move to more fertile land. The high population levels of the Maya classic period (250–900 C.E.) required more intensive forms of agriculture. Maya living near the major urban centers achieved high agricultural yields by draining swamps and building elevated fields. They used irrigation in areas with long dry seasons, and they terraced hillsides in the cooler highlands. Nearly every household planted a garden to provide condiments and fruits to supplement dietary staples. Maya agriculturists also managed nearby forests, favoring the growth of the trees and shrubs that were most useful to them, as well as promoting the conservation of deer and other animals hunted for food.

During the classic period, Maya city-states proliferated. The most powerful cities controlled groups of smaller dependent cities and a broad agricultural zone by building impressive religious temples and by creating rituals that linked the power of kings to the gods. Classic-period cities, unlike earlier sites, had dense central precincts that were visually dominated by monumental architecture. These political and ceremonial centers were commonly aligned with the movements of the sun and Venus. Open plazas were surrounded by high pyramids and by elaborately decorated palaces often built on high ground or on constructed mounds. The effect was to awe the masses drawn to the centers for religious and political rituals.

The Maya loved decoration. Nearly all of their public buildings were covered with bas-relief and painted in bright colors. Religious allegories, the genealogies of rulers, and important historical events were the most common motifs. Beautifully carved altars and stone monoliths were erected near major temples. This rich legacy of monumental architecture was constructed without the aid of wheels—no pulleys, wheelbarrows, or carts—or metal tools. Masses of men and women aided only by levers and stone tools cut and carried construction materials and lifted them into place.

The Maya cosmos was divided into three layers connected along a vertical axis that traced the course of the

The Great Plaza at Tikal   Still visible in the ruins of Tikal, in modern Guatemala, are the impressive architectural and artistic achievements of the classic-era Maya. Maya centers provided a dramatic setting for the rituals that dominated public life. Construction of Tikal began before 150 B.C.E.; the city was abandoned about 900 C.E. A ball court and residences for the elite were part of the Great Plaza.   (Martha Cooper/Peter Arnold, Inc.)

sun. The earthly arena of human existence held an intermediate position between the heavens, conceptualized by the Maya as a sky-monster, and a dark underworld. A sacred tree rose through the three layers; its roots were in the underworld, and its branches reached into the heavens. The temple precincts of Maya cities physically represented essential elements of this religious cosmology. The pyramids were sacred mountains reaching to the heavens. The doorways of the pyramids were portals to the underworld.

Rulers and other members of the elite served both priestly and political functions. They decorated their bodies with paint and tattoos and wore elaborate costumes of textiles, animal skins, and feathers to project both secular power and divine sanction. Kings communicated directly with the supernatural residents of the other worlds and with deified royal ancestors through bloodletting rituals and hallucinogenic trances. Scenes of rulers drawing blood from lips, ears, and penises are common in surviving frescoes and on painted pottery.

Warfare in particular was infused with religious meaning and attached to elaborate rituals. Battle scenes and the depiction of the torture and sacrifice of captives were frequent decorative themes. Typically, Maya military forces fought to secure captives rather than territory. Days of fasting, sacred ritual, and rites of purification preceded battle. The king, his kinsmen, and other ranking nobles actively participated in war. Elite captives were nearly always sacrificed; captured commoners were more likely to be forced to labor for their captors.

Only two women are known to have ruled Maya kingdoms. Maya women of the ruling lineages did play

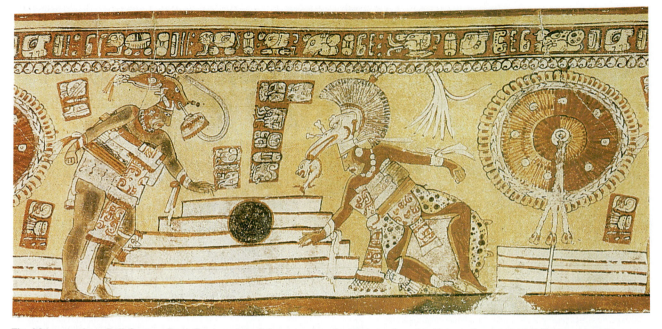

The Mesoamerican Ball Game   From Guatemala to Arizona, archaeologists have found evidence of an ancient ball game played with a solid rubber ball on slope-sided courts shaped like a capital T. Among the Maya the game was associated with a creation myth and thus had deep religious meaning. There is evidence that some players were sacrificed. In this scene from a ceramic jar, players wearing elaborate ritual clothing—which includes heavy, protective pads around the chest and waist—play with a ball much larger than the ball actually used in such games. Some representations show balls drawn to suggest a human head. (Chrysler Museum of Art/Justin Kerr)

important political and religious roles, however. The consorts of male rulers participated in bloodletting rituals and in other important public ceremonies, and their noble blood helped legitimate the rule of their husbands. Although Maya society was patrilineal (tracing descent in the male line), there is evidence that some male rulers traced their lineages bilaterally (in both the male and the female lines). Like Lady Wac-Chanil-Ahau's son Smoking Squirrel, some rulers emphasized the female line if it held higher status. Much less is known about the lives of the women of the lower classes, but scholars believe that women played a central role in the religious rituals of the home. They were also healers and shamans. Women were essential to the household economy, maintaining essential garden plots and weaving, and in the management of family life.

Building on what the Olmecs had done, the Maya made important contributions to the development of the Mesoamerican calendar and to mathematics and writing. Their interest in time and in the cosmos was reflected in the complexity of their calendric system. Each day was identified by three separate dating systems. Like other peoples throughout Mesoamerica, the Maya had a calendar that tracked the ritual cycle (260 days divided into thirteen months of 20 days) as well as a solar calendar (365 days divided into eighteen months of 20 days, plus 5 unfavorable days at the end of the year). The concurrence of these two calendars every fifty-two years was believed to be especially ominous. Alone among Mesoamerican peoples, the Maya also maintained a continuous "long count" calendar, which began at a fixed date in the past that scholars have identified as 3114 B.C.E., a date that the Maya probably associated with creation.

Both the calendars and the astronomical observations on which they were based depended on Maya mathematics and writing. Their system of mathematics incorporated the concept of the zero and place value but had limited notational signs. Maya writing was a form of hieroglyphic inscription that signified whole words or concepts as well as phonetic cues or syllables. Aspects of public life, religious belief, and the biographies of rulers and their ancestors were recorded in deerskin and bark-paper books, on pottery, and on the stone columns and monumental buildings of the urban centers. In this sense every Maya city was a sacred text.

Between 800 and 900 C.E. many of the major urban centers of the Maya were abandoned or destroyed, although a small number of classic-period centers survived for centuries. This collapse was preceded in some areas by decades of urban population decline and increased warfare. Some scholars have proposed that epidemic disease and pestilence played a role in this catastrophe, although there is little evidence to support this argument. Other experts have contended that the earlier destruction of Teotihuacan around 650 C.E. disrupted trade, thus undermining the legitimacy of Maya rulers who had used the goods in rituals. There is growing consensus that the growing population led to environmental degradation and declining agricultural productivity. This environmental crisis, in turn, led to social conflict and increased levels of warfare as desperate elites sought to acquire additional agricultural land through conquest.

THE POSTCLASSIC PERIOD IN MESOAMERICA, 900–1500

The division between the classic and postclassic periods is somewhat arbitrary. Not only is there no single explanation for the collapse of Teotihuacan and many of the major Maya centers, but these events occurred over more than a century and a half. In fact, some important classic-period civilizations survived unscathed. Moreover, the essential cultural characteristics of the classic period were carried over to the postclassic. The two periods are linked by similarities in religious belief and practice, architecture, urban planning, and social organization.

There were, however, some important differences between the periods. There is evidence that the population of Mesoamerica expanded during the postclassic period. Resulting pressures led to an intensification of agricultural practices and to increased warfare. The governing elites of the major postclassic states—the Toltecs and the Aztecs—responded to these harsh realities by increasing the size of their armies and by developing political institutions that facilitated their control of large and culturally diverse territories acquired through conquest.

The Toltecs

Little is known about the **Toltecs**° prior to their arrival in central Mexico. Some scholars speculate that they were originally a satellite population that Teotihuacan had placed on the northern frontier to protect against the incursions of nomads. After their migration south, the Toltecs borrowed from the cultural legacy of Teotihuacan and created an important postclassic civilization. Memories of their military achievements and the violent imagery of their political and religious rituals dominated the Mesoamerican imagination in the late postclassic period. In the fourteenth century, the Aztecs and their contemporaries erroneously believed that the Toltecs were the source of nearly all the great cultural achievements of the Mesoamerican world. As one Aztec source later recalled:

> In truth [the Toltecs] invented all the precious and marvelous things. . . . All that now exists was their discovery. . . . And these Toltecs were very wise; they were thinkers, for they originated the year count, the day count. All their discoveries formed the book for interpreting dreams. . . . And so wise were they [that] they understood the stars which were in the heavens.[3]

In fact, all these contributions to Mesoamerican culture were in place long before the Toltecs gained control of central Mexico. The most important Toltec innovations were instead political and military.

The Toltecs created the first conquest state based largely on military power, and they extended their political influence from the area north of modern Mexico City to Central America. Established about 968 C.E., the Toltec capital of Tula° was constructed in a grand style (see Map 12.1). Its public architecture featured colonnaded patios and numerous temples. Although the population of Tula never reached the levels of classic-period Teotihuacan, the Toltec capital dominated central Mexico. Toltec decoration had a more warlike and violent character than did the decoration of earlier Mesoamerican cultures. Nearly all Toltec public buildings and temples were decorated with representations of warriors or with scenes suggesting human sacrifice.

Two chieftains or kings apparently ruled the Toltec state together. Evidence suggests that this division of responsibility eventually weakened Toltec power and led to the destruction of Tula. Sometime after 1000 C.E. a struggle between elite groups identified with rival religious cults undermined the Toltec state. According to legends that survived among the Aztecs, Topiltzin°—one of the two rulers and a priest of the cult of Quetzalcoatl—and his followers bitterly accepted exile in the east, "the land of the rising sun." These legendary events coincided with growing Toltec influence among the Maya of the Yucatán Peninsula. One of the ancient texts relates these events in the following manner:

Toltec (TOLL-tek)

Tula (TOO-la) **Topilitzin** (tow-PEELT-zeen)

Thereupon he [Topiltzin] looked toward Tula, and then wept. . . . And when he had done these things . . . he went to reach the seacoast. Then he fashioned a raft of serpents. When he had arranged the raft, he placed himself as if it were his boat. Then he set off across the sea.[4]

After the exile of Topiltzin, the Toltec state began to decline, and around 1156 C.E. northern invaders overcame Tula itself. After its destruction, a centuries-long process of cultural and political assimilation produced a new Mesoamerican political order based on the urbanized culture and statecraft of the Toltecs. Like Semitic peoples of the third millennium B.C.E. interacting with Sumerian culture (see Chapter 2), the new Mesoamerican elites were drawn in part from the invading cultures. The Aztecs of the Valley of Mexico became the most important of these late postclassic peoples.

The Aztecs

The Mexica°, more commonly known as the **Aztecs,** were among the northern peoples who pushed into central Mexico in the wake of the collapse of Tula. At the time of their arrival they had a clan-based social organization. In their new environment they began to adopt the political and social practices that they found among the urbanized agriculturalists of the valley. At first, the Aztecs served their more powerful neighbors as serfs and mercenaries. As their strength grew, they relocated to small islands near the shore of Lake Texcoco, and around 1325 C.E. they began the construction of their twin capitals, **Tenochtitlan°** and Tlatelolco (together the foundation for modern Mexico City).

Military successes allowed the Aztecs to seize control of additional agricultural land along the lakeshore. With the increased economic independence and greater political security that resulted from this expansion, the Aztecs transformed their political organization by introducing a monarchical system similar to that found in more powerful neighboring states. The kinship-based organizations that had organized political life earlier survived to the era of Spanish conquest, but lost influence relative to monarchs and hereditary aristocrats. Aztec rulers did not have absolute power, and royal succession was not based on primogeniture. A council of powerful aristocrats selected new rulers from among male members of the ruling lineage. Once selected, the ruler was forced to renegotiate the submission of tribute dependencies and then demonstrate his divine mandate by undertaking a new round of military conquests. War was infused with religious meaning, providing the ruler with legitimacy and increasing the prestige of successful warriors.

With the growing power of the ruler and aristocracy, social divisions were accentuated. These alterations in social organization and political life were made possible by Aztec military expansion. Territorial conquest allowed the warrior elite of Aztec society to seize land and peasant labor as spoils of war (see Map 12.1). In time, the royal family and highest-ranking members of the aristocracy possessed extensive estates that were cultivated by slaves and landless commoners. The Aztec lower classes received some material rewards from imperial expansion but lost most of their ability to influence or control decisions. Some commoners were able to achieve some social mobility through success on the battlefield or by entering the priesthood, but the highest social ranks were always reserved for hereditary nobles.

The urban plan of Tenochtitlan and Tlatelolco continued to be organized around the clans, whose members maintained a common ritual life and accepted civic responsibilities such as caring for the sick and elderly. Clan members also fought together as military units. Nevertheless, the clans' historical control over common agricultural land and other scarce resources, such as fishing and hunting rights, declined. By 1500 C.E. great inequalities in wealth and privilege characterized Aztec society.

Aztec kings and aristocrats legitimated their ascendancy by creating elaborate rituals and ceremonies to distinguish themselves from commoners. One of the Spaniards who participated in the conquest of the Aztec Empire remembered his first meeting with the Aztec ruler Moctezuma° II (r. 1502–1520): "many great lords walked before the great Montezuma [Moctezuma II], sweeping the ground on which he was to tread and laying down cloaks so that his feet should not touch the earth. Not one of these chieftains dared look him in the face."[5] Commoners lived in small dwellings and ate a limited diet of staples, but members of the nobility lived in large, well-constructed two-story houses and consumed a diet rich in animal protein and flavored by condiments and expensive imports like chocolate from the Maya region to the south. Rich dress and jewelry also set apart the elite. Even in marriage customs the two groups were different. Commoners were monogamous, great nobles polygamous.

The Aztec state met the challenge of feeding an urban population of approximately 150,000 by efficiently

---

Mexica (meh-SHE-ca)   **Tenochtitlan** (teh-noch-TIT-lan)   **Moctezuma** (mock-teh-ZU-ma)

Costumes of Aztec Warriors In Mesoamerican warfare individual warriors sought to gain prestige and improve their status by taking captives. This illustration from the sixteenth-century Codex Mendoza was drawn by an Amerindian artist. It shows the Aztecs' use of distinctive costumes to acknowledge the prowess of warriors. These costumes indicate the taking of two (top left) to six captives (bottom center). The individual on the bottom right shown without a weapon was a military leader. As was common in Mesoamerican illustrations of military conflict, the captives, held by their hair, are shown kneeling before the victors. (The Bodleian Library, University of Oxford, Selder. A.I. fol. 64r)

organizing the labor of the clans and additional laborers sent by defeated peoples to expand agricultural land. The construction of a dike more than 5½ miles (9 kilometers) long by 23 feet (7 meters) wide to separate the freshwater and saltwater parts of Lake Texcoco was the Aztecs' most impressive land reclamation project. The dike allowed a significant extension of irrigated fields and the construction of additional chinampas. One expert has estimated that the project consumed 4 million person-days to complete. Aztec chinampas contributed maize, fruits, and vegetables to the markets of Tenochtitlan. The imposition of a **tribute system** on conquered peoples also helped relieve some of the pressure of Tenochtitlan's growing population. Unlike the tribute system of Tang China, where tribute had a more symbolic character (see Chapter 11), one-quarter of the Aztec capital's food requirements was satisfied by tribute payments of maize, beans, and other foods sent by nearby political dependencies. The Aztecs also demanded cotton cloth, military equipment, luxury goods like jade and feathers, and sacrificial victims as tribute. Trade supplemented these supplies.

A specialized class of merchants controlled long-distance trade. Given the absence of draft animals and wheeled vehicles, this commerce was dominated by lightweight and valuable products like gold, jewels, feathered garments, cacao, and animal skins. Merchants also provided essential political and military intelligence for the Aztec elite. Operating outside the protection of Aztec military power, merchant expeditions were armed and often had to defend themselves. Although merchants became wealthy and powerful as the Aztecs expanded their empire, they were denied the privileges of the high nobility, which was jealous of its power. As a result, the merchants feared to publicly display their affluence.

Like commerce throughout the Mesoamerican world, Aztec commerce was carried on without money and credit. Barter was facilitated by the use of cacao, quills filled with gold, and cotton cloth as standard units of value to compensate for differences in the value of bartered goods. Aztec expansion facilitated the integration of producers and consumers in the central Mexican economy. As a result, the markets of Tenochtitlan and

Tlatelolco offered a rich array of goods from as far away as Central America and what is now the southwestern border of the United States. Hernán Cortés (1485–1547), the Spanish adventurer who eventually conquered the Aztecs, expressed his admiration for the abundance of the Aztec marketplace:

> One square in particular is twice as big as that of Salamanca and completely surrounded by arcades where there are daily more than sixty thousand folk buying and selling. Every kind of merchandise such as may be met with in every land is for sale. . . . There is nothing to be found in all the land which is not sold in these markets, for over and above what I have mentioned there are so many and such various things that on account of their very number . . . I cannot detail them.[6]

The Aztecs succeeded in developing a remarkable urban landscape. The combined population of Tenochtitlan and Tlatelolco and the cities and hamlets of the surrounding lakeshore was approximately 500,000 by 1500 C.E. The island capital was designed so that canals and streets intersected at right angles. Three causeways connected the city to the lakeshore.

Religious rituals dominated public life in Tenochtitlan. Like the other cultures of the Mesoamerican world, the Aztecs worshiped a large number of gods. Most of these gods had a dual nature—both male and female. The major contribution of the Aztecs to the religious life of Mesoamerica was the cult of Huitzilopochtli°, the southern hummingbird. As the Aztec state grew in power and wealth, the importance of this cult grew as well. Huitzilopochtli was originally associated with war, but eventually the Aztecs identified this god with the Sun, worshiped as a divinity throughout Mesoamerica. Huitzilopochtli, they believed, required a diet of human hearts to sustain him in his daily struggle to bring the Sun's warmth to the world. Tenochtitlan was architecturally dominated by a great twin temple devoted to Huitzilopochtli and Tlaloc, the rain god, symbolizing the two bases of the Aztec economy: war and agriculture.

War captives were the preferred sacrificial victims, but large numbers of criminals, slaves, and people provided as tribute by dependent regions were also sacrificed. Although human sacrifice had been practiced since early times in Mesoamerica, the Aztecs and other societies of the late postclassic period transformed this religious ritual by dramatically increasing its scale. There are no reliable estimates for the total number of sacrifices, but the numbers clearly reached into the thousands each year. This form of violent public ritual had political consequences and was not simply the celebration of religious belief. Some scholars have emphasized the political nature of the rising tide of sacrifice, noting that sacrifices were carried out in front of large crowds that included leaders from enemy and subject states as well as the masses of Aztec society. The political subtext must have been clear: rebellion, deviancy, and opposition were extremely dangerous.

NORTHERN PEOPLES

By the end of the classic period in Mesoamerica, around 900 C.E., important cultural centers had appeared in the southwestern desert region and along the Ohio and Mississippi river valleys of what is now the United States. In both regions improved agricultural productivity and population growth led to increased urbanization and complex social and political structures. In the Ohio Valley Amerindian peoples who depended on locally domesticated seed crops as well as traditional hunting and gathering developed large villages with monumental earthworks. The introduction of maize, beans, and squash into this region from Mesoamerica after 1000 B.C.E. played an important role in the development of complex societies. Once established, these useful food crops were adopted throughout North America.

As growing populations came to depend on maize as a dietary staple, large-scale irrigation projects were undertaken in both the southwestern desert and the eastern river valleys. This development is a sign of increasingly centralized political power and growing social stratification. The two regions, however, evolved different political traditions. The Anasazi° and their neighbors in the southwest maintained a relatively egalitarian social structure and retained collective forms of political organization based on kinship and age. The mound builders of the eastern river valleys evolved more hierarchical political institutions: groups of small towns were subordinate to a political center ruled by a hereditary chief who wielded both secular and religious authority.

Southwestern Desert Cultures

Immigrants from Mexico introduced agriculture based on irrigation to present-day Arizona around 300 B.C.E. Because irrigation allowed the planting of two crops per year, the population grew and settled village life soon appeared.

Huitzilopochtli (wheat-zeel-oh-POSHT-lee)

Anasazi (ah-nah-SAH-zee)

Mesa Verde Cliff Dwelling   Located in southern Colorado, the Anasazi cliff dwellings of the Mesa Verde region hosted a population of about 7,000 in 1250 C.E. The construction of housing complexes and religious buildings in the area's large caves was probably prompted by increased warfare in the region.   (David Muench Photography)

Of all the southwestern cultures, the Hohokam of the Salt and Gila river valleys show the strongest Mexican influence. Hohokam sites have platform mounds and ball courts similar to those of Mesoamerica. Hohokam pottery, clay figurines, cast copper bells, and turquoise mosaics also reflect Mexican influence. By 1000 C.E. the Hohokam had constructed an elaborate irrigation system that included one canal more than 18 miles (30 kilometers) in length. Hohokam agricultural and ceramic technology spread over the centuries to neighboring peoples, but it was the Anasazi to the north who left the most vivid legacy of these desert cultures.

Archaeologists use **Anasazi,** a Navajo word meaning "ancient ones," to identify a number of dispersed, though similar, desert cultures located in what is now

the Four Corners region of Arizona, New Mexico, Colorado, and Utah (see Map 12.2). Between 450 and 750 C.E. the Anasazi developed an economy based on maize, beans, and squash. Their successful adaptation of these crops permitted the formation of larger villages and led to an enriched cultural life centered in underground buildings called kivas. Evidence suggests that the Anasazi may have used kivas for weaving and pottery making, as well as religious rituals. They produced pottery decorated with geometric patterns, learned to weave cotton cloth, and, after 900 C.E., began to construct large multistory residential and ritual centers.

One of the largest Anasazi communities was located in Chaco Canyon in what is now northwestern Mexico. Eight large towns were built in the canyon and four more on surrounding mesas, suggesting a regional population of approximately 15,000. Many smaller villages were located nearby. Each town contained hundreds of rooms arranged in tiers around a central plaza. At Pueblo Bonito, the largest town, more than 650 rooms were arranged in a four-story block of residences and storage rooms. Pueblo Bonito had thirty-eight kivas, including a great kiva more than 65 feet (19 meters) in diameter. Social life and craft activities were concentrated in small open plazas or common rooms. Hunting, trade, and the need to maintain irrigation works often drew men away from the village. Women shared in agricultural tasks and were specialists in many crafts. They also were responsible for food preparation and childcare. If the practice of the modern Pueblos, cultural descendants of the Anasazi, is a guide, houses and furnishings may have belonged to the women, who formed extended families with their mothers and sisters.

At Chaco Canyon high-quality construction, the size and number of kivas, and the system of roads linking the canyon to outlying towns all suggest that Pueblo Bonito and its nearest neighbors exerted some kind of political or religious dominance over a large region. Some archaeologists have suggested that the Chaco Canyon culture originated as a colonial appendage of Mesoamerica, but the archaeological record provides little evidence for this theory. Merchants from Chaco provided Toltec-period peoples of northern Mexico with turquoise in exchange for shell jewelry, copper bells, macaws, and trumpets. But these exchanges occurred late in Chaco's development, and more important signs of Mesoamerican influence such as pyramid-shaped mounds and ball courts are not found at Chaco. Nor is there evidence from the excavation of burials and residences of clear class distinctions, a common feature of Mesoamerican culture. Instead, it appears that the Chaco Canyon culture developed from earlier societies in the region.

The abandonment of the major sites in Chaco Canyon in the twelfth century most likely resulted from a long drought that undermined the culture's fragile agricultural economy. Nevertheless, the Anasazi continued in the Four Corners region for more than a century after the abandonment of Chaco Canyon. There were major centers at Mesa Verde in present-day Colorado and at Canyon de Chelly and Kiet Siel in Arizona. Anasazi settlements on the Colorado Plateau and in Arizona were constructed in large natural caves high above valley floors. This hard-to-reach location suggests increased levels of warfare, probably provoked by population pressure on limited arable land. Elements of this cultural tradition survive today among the Pueblo peoples of the Rio Grande Valley and Arizona who still live in multistory villages and worship in kivas.

Mound Builders: The Adena, Hopewell, and Mississippian Cultures

The Adena people of the Ohio River Valley constructed large villages with monumental earthworks from about 500 B.C.E. This early mound-building culture was based on traditional hunting and gathering supplemented by limited cultivation of locally domesticated seed crops. Nearly all of the Adena mounds contained burials. Items found in these graves indicate a hierarchical society with an elite distinguished by its access to rare and valuable goods such as mica from North Carolina and copper from the Great Lakes region.

Around 100 C.E. the Adena culture blended into a successor culture now called Hopewell, also centered in the Ohio River Valley. The largest Hopewell centers appeared in present-day Ohio; but Hopewell influence, in the form of either colonies or trade dependencies, spread west to Illinois, Michigan, and Wisconsin, east to New York and Ontario, and south to Alabama, Louisiana, Mississippi, and even Florida (see Map 12.2). For the necessities of daily life Hopewell people were dependent on hunting and gathering and a limited agriculture inherited from the Adena.

Hopewell is an early example of a North American **chiefdom**—territory that had a population as large as 10,000 and was ruled by a chief, a hereditary leader with both religious and secular responsibilities. Chiefs organized periodic rituals of feasting and gift giving that established bonds among diverse kinship groups and guaranteed access to specialized crops and craft goods. They also managed long-distance trade, which provided luxury goods and additional food supplies.

The largest Hopewell towns in the Ohio River Valley served as ceremonial and political centers and had several thousand inhabitants. Villages had populations of a few hundred. Large mounds built to house elite burials and as platforms for temples and the residences of chiefs dominated major Hopewell centers. Chiefs and other members of the elite were buried in vaults surrounded by valuable goods such as river pearls, copper jewelry, and, in some cases, women and retainers who seem to have been sacrificed to accompany a dead chief into the afterlife. As was true of the earlier Olmec culture of Mexico, the abandonment of major Hopewell sites around 400 C.E. has no clear environmental or political explanation.

Map 12.2 Culture Areas of North America In each of the large ecological regions of North America, native peoples evolved distinctive cultures and technologies. Here the Anasazi of the arid southwest and the mound-building cultures of the Ohio and Mississippi river valleys are highlighted.

ARCTIC

SUBARCTIC

NORTHWEST

PLATEAU

PLAINS

NORTHEAST

CALIFORNIA

GREAT
BASIN

Mesa
Verde

Kiet Siel

Canyon
de Chelly

Chaco
Canyon

Cahokia

SOUTHEAST

SOUTHWEST

0   300   600 Km.

0   300   600 Mi.

☐ Approximate extent of Anasazi culture

☐ Approximate extent of mound-building cultures

Hopewell technology and mound building continued in smaller centers that have been linked to the development of Mississippian culture (700–1500 C.E.). As in the case of the Anasazi, some experts have suggested that contacts with Mesoamerica influenced Mississippian culture, but there is no convincing evidence to support this theory. It is true that maize, beans, and squash, all first domesticated in Mesoamerica, were closely associated with the development of the urbanized Mississippian culture. But these plants and related technologies were probably passed along through numerous intervening cultures.

The development of urbanized Mississippian chiefdoms resulted instead from the accumulated effects of small increases in agricultural productivity, the adoption of the bow and arrow, and the expansion of trade networks. An improved economy led to population growth, the building of cities, and social stratification. The largest towns shared a common urban plan based on a central plaza surrounded by large platform mounds. Major towns were trade centers where people bartered essential commodities, such as the flint used for weapons and tools.

The Mississippian culture reached its highest stage of evolution at the great urban center of Cahokia, located near the modern city of East St. Louis, Illinois (see Map 12.2). At the center of this site was the largest mound constructed in North America, a terraced structure 100 feet (30 meters) high and 1,037 by 790 feet (316 by 241 meters) at the base. Areas where commoners lived ringed the center area of elite housing and temples. At its height in about 1200 C.E., Cahokia had a population of about 20,000—about the same as some of the largest postclassic Maya cities.

Cahokia controlled surrounding agricultural lands and a number of secondary towns ruled by subchiefs. The urban center's political and economic influence depended on its location on the Missouri, Mississippi and Illinois Rivers. This location permitted canoe-based commercial exchanges as far away as the coasts of the Atlantic and the Gulf of Mexico. Sea shells, copper, mica, and flint were drawn to the city by trade and tribute from distant sources and converted into ritual goods and tools. Burial evidence suggests that the rulers of Cahokia enjoyed most of the benefits of this exalted position. In one burial more than fifty young women and retainers were apparently sacrificed to accompany a ruler on his travels after death.

As at Hopewell sites, no evidence links the decline and eventual abandonment of Cahokia, which occurred after 1250 C.E., with military defeat or civil war. Climate changes and population pressures undermined the center's vitality. Environmental degradation caused by deforestation, as more land was cleared to feed the growing population, and more intensive farming practices played roles as well. After the decline of Cahokia, smaller Mississippian centers continued to flourish in the southeast of the present-day United States until the arrival of Europeans.

ANDEAN CIVILIZATIONS, 200–1500

The Andean region of South America was an unlikely environment for the development of rich and powerful civilizations (see Map 12.3). Much of the region's mountainous zone is at altitudes that seem too high for agriculture and human habitation. Along the Pacific coast an arid climate posed a difficult challenge to the development of agriculture. To the east of the Andes Mountains, the hot and humid tropical environment of the Amazon headwaters also offered formidable obstacles to the organization of complex societies. Yet the Amerindian peoples of the Andean area produced some of the most socially complex and politically advanced societies of the Western Hemisphere. The very harshness of the environment compelled the development of productive and reliable agricultural technologies and attached them to a complex fabric of administrative structures and social relationships that became the central features of Andean civilization.

Cultural Response to Environmental Challenge

From the time of Chavín (see Chapter 3) all of the great Andean civilizations succeeded in connecting the distinctive resources of the coastal region with its abundant fisheries and irrigated maize fields to the mountainous interior with its herds of llamas and rich mix of grains and tubers. Both regions faced significant environmental challenges. The coastal region's fields were periodically overwhelmed by droughts or shifting sands that clogged irrigation works. The mountainous interior presented some of the greatest environmental challenges, averaging between 250 and 300 frosts per year.

The development of compensating technologies required an accurate calendar to time planting and harvests and the domestication of frost-resistant varieties of potatoes and grains. Native peoples learned to practice dispersed farming at different altitudes to reduce risks

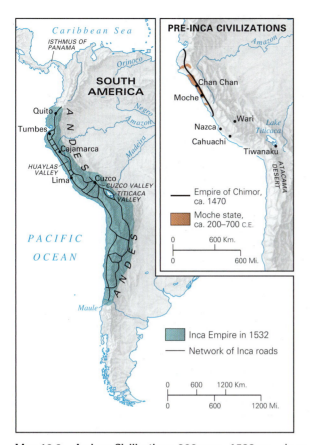

Map 12.3   Andean Civilizations, 200 B.C.E.–1532 C.E.   In response to environmental challenges posed by an arid coastal plain and high interior mountain ranges, Andean peoples made complex social and technological adaptations. Irrigation systems, the domestication of the llama, metallurgy, and shared labor obligations helped provide a firm economic foundation for powerful, centralized states. In 1532 the Inca Empire's vast territory stretched from modern Chile in the south to Colombia in the north.

environments. The remarkable collective achievements of Andean peoples were accomplished with a record-keeping system more limited than the one found in Mesoamerica. A system of knotted colored cords, **khipus°**, was used to aid administration and record population counts and tribute obligations. Large-scale drainage and irrigation works and the terracing of hillsides to control erosion and provide additional farmland led to an increase in agricultural production. Andean people also collectively undertook road building, urban construction, and even textile production.

The sharing of responsibilities began at the household level. But it was the clan, or **ayllu°**, that provided the foundation for Andean achievement. Members of an ayllu held land communally. Although they claimed descent from a common ancestor, they were not necessarily related. Ayllu members thought of each other as brothers and sisters and were obligated to aid each other in tasks that required more labor than a single household could provide. These reciprocal obligations provided the model for the organization of labor and the distribution of goods at every level of Andean society. Just as individuals and families were expected to provide labor to kinsmen, members of an ayllu were expected to provide labor and goods to their hereditary chief.

With the development of territorial states ruled by hereditary aristocracies and kings after 1000 B.C.E., these obligations were organized on a larger scale. The **mit'a°** was a rotational labor draft that organized members of ayllus to work the fields and care for the llama and alpaca herds owned by religious establishments, the royal court, and the aristocracy. Each ayllu contributed a set number of workers for specific tasks each year. Mit'a laborers built and maintained roads, bridges, temples, palaces, and large irrigation and drainage projects. They produced textiles and goods essential to ritual life, such as beer made from maize and coca (dried leaves chewed as a stimulant and now also the source of cocaine). The mit'a system was an essential part of the Andean world for more than a thousand years.

Work was divided along gender lines, but the work of men and women was interdependent. Hunting, military service, and government were largely reserved for men. Women had numerous responsibilities in textile production, agriculture, and the home. One early Spanish commentator described the responsibilities of Andean women in terms that sound very modern:

> [T]hey did not just perform domestic tasks, but also [labored] in the fields, in the cultivation of their lands,

from frosts, and they terraced hillsides to create micro environments within a single area. They also discovered how to use the cold, dry climate to produce freeze-dried vegetable and meat products that prevented famine when crops failed. The domestication of the llama and alpaca also proved crucial, providing meat, wool, and long-distance transportation that linked coastal and mountain economies. Even though the Andean environment was harsher than that of Mesoamerica, the region's agriculture proved more dependable, and Andean peoples faced fewer famines.

The effective organization of human labor allowed the peoples of both the high mountain valleys and dry coastal plain to overcome the challenges posed by their

khipus (KEY-pooz)   **ayllu** (aye-YOU)   **mit'a** (MEET-ah)

in building houses, and carrying burdens. . . . [A]nd more than once I heard that while women were carrying these burdens, they would feel labor pains, and giving birth, they would go to a place where there was water and wash the baby and themselves. Putting the baby on top of the load they were carrying, they would then continue walking as before they gave birth. In sum, there was nothing their husbands did where their wives did not help.[7]

The ayllu was intimately tied to a uniquely Andean system of production and exchange. Because the region's mountain ranges created a multitude of small ecological areas with specialized resources, each community sought to control a variety of environments so as to guarantee access to essential goods. Coastal regions produced maize, fish, and cotton. Mountain valleys contributed quinoa (the local grain) as well as potatoes and other tubers. Higher elevations contributed the wool and meat of llamas and alpacas, and the Amazonian region provided coca and fruits. Ayllus sent out colonists to exploit the resources of these ecological niches. Colonists remained linked to their original region and kin group by marriage and ritual. Historians commonly refer to this system of controlled exchange across ecological boundaries as vertical integration, or verticality.

The historical periodization of Andean history is similar to that of Mesoamerica. Both regions developed highly integrated political and economic systems long before 1500. The pace of agricultural development, urbanization, and state formation in the Andes also approximated that in Mesoamerica. Due to the unique environmental challenges in the Andean region, however, distinctive highland and coastal cultures appeared. In the Andes, more than in Mesoamerica, geography influenced regional cultural integration and state formation.

Moche and Chimu

Around 200 C.E., some four centuries after the collapse of Chavín (see Chapter 3), the **Moche°** developed cultural and political tools that allowed them to dominate the north coastal region of Peru. Moche identity was cultural in character. They did not establish a formal empire or create unified political structures. The most powerful of the Moche urban centers, such as Cerro Blanco located near the modern Peruvian city of Trujillo (see Map 12.3), did establish hegemony over smaller towns and villages. There is also evidence that the Moche extended political and economic control over their neighbors militarily.

***

Moche (MO-che)

Moche Portrait Vase   The Moche of ancient Peru were among the most accomplished ceramic artists of the Americas. Moche potters produced representations of gods and spirits, scenes of daily life, and portrait vases of important people. This man wears a headdress adorned by two birds and seashells. The stains next to the eyes of the birds represent tears.   (Museo de Arqueologica y Antropologia, Lima/Lee Bolton Picture Library)

Archaeological evidence indicates that the Moche cultivated maize, quinoa, beans, manioc, and sweet potatoes with the aid of massive irrigation works. At higher elevations they also produced coca, which they used ritually. Archaeological excavations reveal the existence of complex networks of canals and aqueducts that connected fields with water sources as far away as 75 miles (121 kilometers). These hydraulic works were maintained by mit'a labor imposed on Moche commoners or on subject peoples. The Moche maintained large herds of alpacas and llamas to transport goods across the region's difficult terrain. Their wool, along with cotton provided by farmers, provided the raw material for the thriving Moche textile production. Their meat provided an important part of the diet.

Evidence from surviving murals and decorated ceramics suggests that Moche society was highly stratified and theocratic. The need to organize large numbers of laborers to construct and maintain the irrigation system helped promote class divisions. Wealth and power among the Moche was concentrated, along with political control, in the hands of priests and military leaders. Hierarchy was further reinforced by the military conquest of neighboring regions. The residences of the elite were constructed atop large platforms at Moche ceremonial centers. The elite literally lived above the commoners. Their power was also apparent in their rich clothing and jewelry, which confirmed their divine status and set them farther apart from commoners. Moche rulers and other members of the elite wore tall headdresses. They used gold and gold alloy jewelry to mark their social position: gold plates suspended from their noses concealed the lower portion of their faces, and large gold plugs decorated their ears.

These deep social distinctions also were reflected in Moche burial practices. A recent excavation in the Lambeyeque Valley discovered the tomb of a warrior-priest who was buried with a rich treasure of gold, silver, and copper jewelry, textiles, feather ornaments, and shells (see Diversity and Dominance: Burials as Historical Texts). Retainers and servants were also buried with this powerful man to serve him in the afterlife.

Most commoners, on the other hand, devoted their time to subsistence farming and to the payment of labor dues owed to their ayllu and to the elite. Both men and women were involved in agriculture, care of llama herds, and the household economy. They lived with their families in one-room buildings clustered in the outlying areas of cities and in surrounding agricultural zones.

The high quality of Moche textiles, ceramics, and metallurgy indicates the presence of numerous skilled artisans. As had been true centuries earlier in Chavín, women had a special role in the production of textiles; even elite women devoted time to weaving. Moche culture developed a brilliant representational art. Moche craftsmen produced highly individualized portrait vases that today adorn museum collections in nearly every city of the world. Ceramics were also decorated with line drawings representing myths and rituals. The most original Moche ceramic vessels were decorated with explicit sexual acts. The Moche were also accomplished metalsmiths, producing beautiful gold and silver religious and decorative objects and items for elite adornment. Metallurgy served more practical ends as well: artisans produced a range of tools made of heavy copper and copper alloy for agricultural and military purposes.

Since we have no written sources, a detailed history of the Moche can never be written. The archaeological record makes clear that the rapid decline of the major centers coincided with a succession of natural disasters in the sixth century and with the rise of a new military power in the Andean highlands. When an earthquake altered the course of the Moche River, major flooding seriously damaged urban centers. The Moche region also was threatened by long-term climate changes. A thirty-year drought expanded the area of coastal sand dunes during the sixth century, and powerful winds pushed sand onto fragile agricultural lands, overwhelming the irrigation system. As the land dried, periodic heavy rains caused erosion that damaged fields and weakened the economy that had sustained ceremonial and residential centers. This succession of disasters undermined the authority of the religious and political leaders, whose privileges were based on their ability to control natural forces through rituals. Despite massive efforts to keep the irrigation canals open and despite the construction of new urban centers in less vulnerable valleys to the north, Moche civilization never recovered. In the eighth century, the rise of a new military power, the **Wari°,** also contributed to the disappearance of the Moche by putting pressure on trade routes that linked the coastal region with the highlands.

At the end of the Moche period the **Chimu°** developed a new and more powerful coastal civilization. Chan Chan, capital of the Empire of Chimor, was constructed around 800 C.E. near the earlier Moche cultural center. After 1200 C.E. Chimu began a period of aggressive military expansion. At the apex of its power, The Empire of Chimor controlled 625 miles (1,000 kilometers) of the Peruvian coast.

Within Chan Chan was a series of walled compounds, each one containing a burial pyramid. Scholars believe that each ruler built his own compound and was buried in it on death. Sacrifices and rich grave goods accompanied each royal burial. As did the Moche, Chimor's rulers separated themselves from the masses of society by their consumption of rare and beautiful textiles, ceramics, and precious metals as a way of suggesting the approval of the gods. Some scholars suggest that the Chimu dynasty practiced split inheritance: goods and lands of the deceased ruler went to secondary heirs or for religious sacrifices. The royal heir who inherited the throne was forced to construct his own residence compound and then undertake new conquests to fund his household. After the Inca conquered the northern coast in 1465, they borrowed from the rich rituals and court customs of the Chimu.

Tiwanaku and Wari

After 500 C.E. two powerful civilizations developed in the Andean highlands. At nearly 13,000 feet (3,962 meters) on the high treeless plain near Lake Titicaca in modern Bolivia stand the ruins of **Tiwanaku°** (see Map 12.3). Initial

---

Wari (WAH-ree) **Chimu** (chee-MOO)
Tiwanaku (tee-wah-NA-coo)

DIVERSITY AND DOMINANCE

BURIALS AS HISTORICAL TEXTS

Efforts to reveal the history of the Americas before the arrival of Europeans depend on the work of archaeologists. The burials of rulers and other members of elites can be viewed as historical texts that describe how textiles, precious metals, beautifully decorated ceramics, and other commodities were used to reinforce the political and cultural power of ruling lineages. In public, members of the elite were always surrounded by the most desirable and rarest products as well as by elaborate rituals and ceremonies. The effect was to create an aura of godlike power. The material elements of political and cultural power were integrated into the experience of death and burial as members of the elite were sent into the afterlife.

The first photograph is of an excavated Moche tomb in Sipán, Peru. The Moche (100 C.E.–ca. 700 C.E.) were one of the most important of the pre-Inca civilizations of the Andean region. They were masters of metallurgy, ceramics, and textiles. The excavations at Sipán revealed a "warrior/priest" buried with an amazing array of gold ornaments, jewels, textiles, and ceramics. He was also buried with two women, perhaps wives or concubines, two male servants, and a warrior. The warrior, one woman, and one man are missing feet, as if this deformation would guarantee their continued faithfulness to the deceased ruler.

The second photograph shows the excavation of a Classic-Era (250 C.E.–ca. 800 C.E.) Maya burial at Río Azul in Guatemala. Here a member of the elite was laid out on a carved wooden platform and cotton mattress; his body painted with decorations. He was covered in beautifully woven textiles and surrounded by valuable goods. Among the discoveries were a necklace of individual stones carved in the shape of heads, perhaps a symbol of his prowess in battle, high-quality ceramics, some filled with foods consumed by the elite like cacao. The careful preparation of the burial chamber had required the work of numerous artisans and laborers, as was the case in the burial of the Moche warrior/priest. In death, as in life, these early American civilizations acknowledged the high status, political power, and religious authority of their elites.

QUESTIONS FOR ANALYSIS

1. If these burials are texts, what are stories?
2. Are there any visible differences in the two burials?
3. What questions might historians ask of these burials that cannot be answered?
4. Are modern burials texts in similar ways to these ancient practices?

---

occupation may have occurred as early as 400 B.C.E., but significant urbanization began only after 200 C.E. Tiwanaku's expansion depended on the adoption of technologies that increased agricultural productivity. Modern excavations provide the outline of vast drainage projects that reclaimed nearly 200,000 acres (8,000 hectares) of rich lakeside marshes for agriculture. This system of raised fields and ditches permitted intensive cultivation similar to that achieved by use of chinampas in Mesoamerica. Fish from the nearby lake and llamas added protein to a diet largely dependent on potatoes and grains. Llamas were also crucial for the maintenance of long-distance trade relationships that brought in corn, coca, tropical fruits, and medicinal plants.

The urban center of Tiwanaku was distinguished by the scale of its construction and by the high quality of its stone masonry. Large stones and quarried blocks were moved many miles to construct a large terraced pyramid, walled enclosures, and a reservoir—projects that probably required the mobilization of thousands of laborers over a period of years. Despite a limited metallurgy that produced only tools of copper alloy, Tiwanaku's artisans built large structures of finely cut stone that required little mortar to fit the blocks. They also produced gigantic human statuary. The largest example, a stern figure with a military bearing, is cut from a single block of stone that measures 24 feet (7 meters) high.

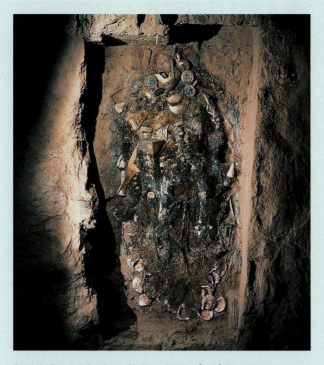

Burials Reveal Ancient Civilizations (Left) Buried around 300 C.E., this Moche warrior-priest was buried amid rich tribute at Sipán in Peru. Also, buried were the bodies of retainers or kinsmen probably sacrificed to accompany this powerful man. The body lies with the head on the right and the feet on the left. (Right) Similarly, the burial of a member of the Maya elite at Río Azul in northern Guatemala indicates the care taken to surround the powerful with fine ceramics, jewelry and other valuable goods. (*left:* Heinze Plenge/NGS Image Collection; *right:* George Mobley/NGS Image Collection)

Little is known of the social structure or daily life of this civilization. Neither surviving murals nor other decorative arts offer the suggestive guidance found in the burial goods of the Moche. Nevertheless, it is clear that Tiwanaku was a highly stratified society ruled by a hereditary elite. Most women and men devoted their time to agriculture and the care of llama herds. However, the presence of specialized artisans is evident in the high-quality construction in public buildings and in locally produced ceramics. The distribution of these ceramics to distant places suggests the presence of a specialized merchant class as well.

Many scholars portray Tiwanaku as the capital of a vast empire, a precursor to the later Inca state. It is clear that the elite controlled a large, disciplined labor force in the surrounding region. Military conquests and the establishment of colonial populations provided the highland capital with dependable supplies of products from ecologically distinct zones. Tiwanaku cultural influence extended eastward to the jungles and southward to the coastal regions and oases of the Atacama Desert in Chile. But archaeological evidence suggests that Tiwanaku, in comparison with contemporary Teotihuacan in central Mexico, had a relatively small full-time population of around 30,000. It was not a metropolis like the largest Mesoamerican cities; it was a ceremonial and political center for a large regional population.

Inca Roads

From the time of Chavin (900–250 B.C.E.), Andean peoples built roads to facilitate trade across ecological boundaries and to project political power over conquered peoples. In the fifteenth and sixteenth centuries, the Inca extended and improved the networks of roads constructed in earlier eras. Roads were crucially important to Inca efforts to collect and redistribute tribute paid in food, textiles, and chicha (corn liquor).

Two roads connected Cuzco, the Inca capital in southern Peru, to Quito, Ecudaor, in the north and to Chile farther south. One ran along the flat and arid coastal plain, the other through the mountainous interior. Shorter east-west roads connected important coastal and interior cities. Evidence suggests that administrative centers were sited along these routes to expedite rapid communication with the capital. Rest stops at convenient distances provided shelter and food to traveling officials and runners who carried messages between Cuzco and the empire's cities and towns. Warehouses were constructed along the roads to provide food and military supplies for passing Inca armies or to supply local laborers working on construction projects or cultivating the ruler's fields.

Because communication with regional administrative centers and the movement of troops were the central objectives of the Inca leadership, routes were selected to avoid natural obstacles and to reduce travel time. Mit'a laborers recruited from nearby towns and villages built and maintained the roads. Roads were commonly paved with stone or packed earth and often were bordered by stone or adobe walls to keep soldiers or pack trains of llamas from straying into farmers' fields. Whenever possible, roadbeds were made level. In mountainous terrain some roads were little more than improved paths, but in flat country three or four people could walk abreast. Care was always taken to repair damage caused by rain runoff or other drainage problems.

The achievement of Inca road builders is clearest in the mountainous terrain of the interior. They built suspension bridges across high gorges and cut roadbeds into the face of cliffs. A Spanish priest living in Peru in the seventeenth century commented that the Inca roads "were magnificent constructions, which could be compared favorably with the most superb roads of the Romans."

Source: Quotation from Father Bernabe Cobo, *History of the Inca Empire. An account of the Indians' customs and origin together with a treatise on Inca legends, history, and social institutions* (Austin: University of Texas Press, 1983), 223.

Inca Road   The Inca built roads to connect distant parts of the empire to Cuzco, the Inca capital. These roads are still used in Peru.   (Loren McIntyre/Woodfin Camp & Associates)

The contemporary site of Wari was located about 450 miles (751 kilometers) to the northwest of Tiwanaku, near the modern Peruvian city of Ayacucho. Wari clearly shared elements of the culture and technology of Tiwanaku, but the exact nature of this relationship remains unclear. Some scholars argue that Wari began as a dependency of Tiwanaku, while others suggest that they were joint capitals of a single empire. Recent archaeological discoveries indicate that Wari was also closely tied to Nazca, a powerful state located to the south. As was common throughout the history of the Andes, Wari benefited from its contacts and commercial exchanges with other powerful societies in the region.

Wari was larger than Tiwanaku, measuring nearly 4 square miles (10 square kilometers). The city center was surrounded by a massive wall and included a large temple. The center had numerous multifamily housing blocks. Less-concentrated housing for commoners was located in a sprawling suburban zone. Wari's development, unlike that of most other major urban centers in the Andes, appears to have occurred without central planning.

The small scale of its monumental architecture and the near absence of cut stone masonry in public and private buildings distinguish Wari from Tiwanaku. It is not clear that these characteristics resulted from the relative weakness of the elite or the absence of specialized construction crafts. There is a distinctive Wari ceramic style that has allowed experts to trace Wari's expanding power to the coastal area earlier controlled by the Moche and to the northern highlands. Wari's military expansion occurred at a time of increasing warfare throughout the Andes. As a result, roads were built to maintain communication with remote fortified dependencies. Perhaps as a consequence of military conflict, both Tiwanaku and Wari declined to insignificance by about 1000 C.E. The Inca inherited their political legacy.

The Inca

In little more than a hundred years, the **Inca** developed a vast imperial state, which they called "Land of Four Corners." By 1525 the empire had a population of more than 6 million and stretched from the Maule River in Chile to northern Ecuador and from the Pacific coast across the Andes to the upper Amazon and, in the south, into Argentina (see Map 12.3). In the early fifteenth century the Inca were one of many competing military powers in the southern highlands, an area of limited political significance after the collapse of Wari. Centered in the valley of Cuzco, the Inca were initially organized as a chiefdom based on reciprocal gift giving and the redistribution of food and textiles. Strong and resourceful leaders consolidated political authority in the 1430s and undertook an ambitious campaign of military expansion.

The Inca state, like earlier highland powers, was built on traditional Andean social customs and economic practices. Tiwanaku had relied in part on the use of colonists to provide supplies of resources from distant, ecologically distinct zones. The Inca built on this legacy by conquering additional distant territories and increasing the scale of forced exchanges. Crucial to this process was the development of a large, professional military. Unlike the peoples of Mesoamerica, who distributed specialized goods by developing markets and tribute relationships, Andean peoples used state power to broaden and expand the vertical exchange system that had permitted ayllus to exploit a range of ecological niches.

Like earlier highland civilizations, the Inca were pastoralists. Inca prosperity and military strength depended on vast herds of llamas and alpacas, which provided food and clothing as well as transport for goods. Both men and women were involved in the care of these herds. Women were primarily responsible for weaving; men were drivers in long-distance trade. This pastoral tradition provided the Inca with powerful metaphors that helped shape their political and religious beliefs. They believed that the gods and their ruler shared the obligations of the shepherd to his flock—an idea akin to references to "The Lord is my Shepherd."

Collective efforts by mit'a laborers made the Inca Empire possible. Cuzco, the imperial capital, and the provincial cities, the royal court, the imperial armies, and the state's religious cults all rested on this foundation. The mit'a system also created the material surplus that provided the bare necessities for the old, weak, and ill of Inca society. Each ayllu contributed approximately one-seventh of its adult male population to meet these collective obligations. These draft laborers served as soldiers, construction workers, craftsmen, and runners to carry messages along post roads. They also drained swamps, terraced mountainsides, filled in valley floors, built and maintained irrigation works, and built storage facilities and roads. Inca laborers constructed 13,000 miles (20,930 kilometers) of road, facilitating military troop movements, administration, and trade (see Environment and Technology: Inca Roads).

Imperial administration was similarly superimposed on existing political structures and established elite groups. The hereditary chiefs of ayllus carried out administrative and judicial functions. As the Inca expanded, they generally left local rulers in place. By leaving the rulers of defeated societies in place, the Inca risked rebellion, but they controlled these risks by means of a thinly veiled system of hostage taking and the

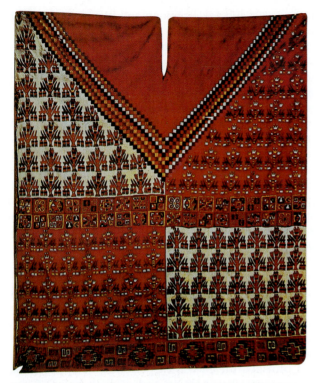

Inca Tunic Andean weavers produced beautiful textiles from cotton and from the wool of llamas and alpacas. The Inca inherited this rich craft tradition and produced some of the world's most remarkable textiles. The quality and design of each garment indicated the weaver's rank and power in this society. This tunic was an outer garment for a powerful male. (From *Textile Art of Peru*. Collection created and directed by Jose Antonio de Lavalle and Jose Alejandro Gonzalez Garcia [L. L. Editores, 1989])

use of military garrisons. The rulers of defeated regions were required to send their heirs to live at the Inca royal court in Cuzco. Inca leaders even required that representations of important local gods be brought to Cuzco and made part of the imperial pantheon. These measures promoted imperial integration while at the same time providing hostages to ensure the good behavior of subject peoples.

Conquests magnified the authority of the Inca ruler and led to the creation of an imperial bureaucracy drawn from among his kinsmen. The royal family claimed descent from the Sun, the primary Inca god. Members of the royal family lived in palaces maintained by armies of servants. The lives of the ruler and members of the royal family were dominated by political and religious rituals that helped legitimize their authority. Among the many obligations associated with kingship was the require-

ment to extend imperial boundaries by warfare. Thus each new ruler began his reign with conquest.

Tenochtitlan, the Aztec capital, had a population of about 150,000 in 1520. At the height of Inca power in 1530, Cuzco had a population of less than 30,000. Nevertheless, Cuzco was a remarkable place. The Inca were highly skilled stone craftsmen: their most impressive buildings were constructed of carefully cut stones fitted together without mortar. The city was laid out in the shape of a giant puma (a mountain lion). At the center were the palaces that each ruler built when he ascended to the throne, as well as the major temples. The richest was the Temple of the Sun. Its interior was lined with sheets of gold, and its patio was decorated with golden representations of llamas and corn. The ruler made every effort to awe and intimidate visitors and residents alike with a nearly continuous series of rituals, feasts, and sacrifices. Sacrifices of textiles, animals, and other goods sent as tribute dominated the city's calendar. The destruction of these valuable commodities, and a small number of human sacrifices, helped give the impression of splendor and sumptuous abundance that appeared to demonstrate the ruler's claimed descent from the Sun.

Inca cultural achievement rested on the strong foundation of earlier Andean civilizations. We know that astronomical observation was a central concern of the priestly class, as in Mesoamerica; the Inca calendar, however, is lost to us. All communication other than oral was transmitted by the khipus borrowed from earlier Andean civilizations. In weaving and metallurgy, Inca technology, building on earlier regional developments, was more advanced than in Mesoamerica. Inca craftsmen produced utilitarian tools and weapons of copper and bronze as well as decorative objects of gold and silver. Inca women produced textiles of extraordinary beauty from cotton and the wool of llamas and alpacas.

Although the Inca did not introduce new technologies, they increased economic output and added to the region's prosperity. The conquest of large populations in environmentally distinct regions allowed the Inca to multiply the yields produced by the traditional exchanges between distinct ecological niches. But the expansion of imperial economic and political power was purchased at the cost of reduced equality and diminished local autonomy. The imperial elite, living in richly decorated palaces in Cuzco and other urban centers, was increasingly cut off from the masses of Inca society. The royal court held members of the provincial nobility at arm's length, and commoners were subject to execution if they dared to look directly at the ruler's face.

After only a century of regional dominance, the Inca Empire faced a crisis in 1525. The death of the Inca ruler

Huayna Capac at the conclusion of the conquest of Ecuador initiated a bloody struggle for the throne. Powerful factions coalesced around two sons whose rivalry compelled both the professional military and the hereditary Inca elite to choose sides. Civil war was the result. The Inca state controlled a vast territory spread over more than 3,000 miles (4,830 kilometers) of mountainous terrain. Regionalism and ethnic diversity had always posed a threat to the empire. Civil war weakened imperial institutions and ignited the resentments of conquered peoples. On the eve of the arrival of Europeans, the destructive consequences of this violent conflict undermined the institutions and economy of Andean civilizations.

CONCLUSION

The indigenous societies of the Western Hemisphere developed unique technologies and cultural forms in mountainous regions, tropical rain forests, deserts, woodlands, and arctic regions. In Mesoamerica, North America, and the Andean region, the natural environment powerfully influenced cultural development. The Maya of southern Mexico, for example, developed agricultural technologies that compensated for the tropical cycle of heavy rains followed by long dry periods. On the coast of Peru the Moche used systems of trade and mutual labor obligation to meet the challenge of an arid climate and mountainous terrain, while the mound builders of North America expanded agricultural production by utilizing the rich floodplains of the Ohio and Mississippi Rivers. Across the Americas, hunting and gathering peoples and urbanized agricultural societies produced rich religious and aesthetic traditions as well as useful technologies and effective social institutions in response to local conditions. Once established, these cultural traditions proved very durable.

The Aztec and Inca Empires represented the culmination of a long developmental process that had begun before 1000 B.C.E. Each imperial state controlled extensive and diverse territories with populations that numbered in the millions. The capital cities of Tenochtitlan and Cuzco were great cultural and political centers that displayed some of the finest achievements of Amerindian technology, art, and architecture. Both states were based on conquests and were ruled by powerful hereditary elites who depended on the tribute of subject peoples. In both traditions religion met spiritual needs while also organizing collective life and legitimizing political authority.

The Aztec and Inca Empires were created militarily, their survival depending as much on the power of their armies as on the productivity of their economies or the wisdom of their rulers. Both empires were ethnically and environmentally diverse, but there were important differences. Elementary markets had been developed in Mesoamerica to distribute specialized regional production, although the forced payment of goods as tribute remained important. In the Andes reciprocal labor obligations and managed exchange relationships were used to allocate goods. The Aztecs used their military to force defeated peoples to provide food, textiles, and even sacrificial captives as tribute, but they left local hereditary elites in place. The Incas, in contrast, created a more centralized administrative structure managed by a trained bureaucracy.

As the Western Hemisphere's long isolation drew to a close in the late fifteenth century, both empires were challenged by powerful neighbors or by internal revolts. In earlier periods similar challenges had contributed to the decline of great civilizations in both Mesoamerica and the Andean region. In those cases, a long period of adjustment and the creation of new indigenous institutions followed the collapse of dominant powers such as the Toltecs in Mesoamerica and Tiwanaku in the Andes. With the arrival of Europeans, this cycle of crisis and adjustment would be transformed, and the future of Amerindian peoples would become linked to the cultures of the Old World.

■ Key Terms

Teotihuacan	khipu
chinampas	ayllu
Maya	mit'a
Toltecs	Moche
Aztecs	Wari
Tenochtitlan	Chimu
tribute system	Tiwanaku
Anasazi	Inca
chiefdom	

■ Suggested Reading

In *Prehistory of the Americas* (1987) Stuart Fiedel provides an excellent summary of the early history of the Western Hemisphere. Alvin M. Josephy, Jr., in *The Indian Heritage of America* (1968), also provides a thorough introduction to the topic. *Canada's First Nations* (1992) by Olive Patricia Dickason is a well-written survey that traces the history of Canada's Amerindian peoples to the modern era. *Early Man in the New World,* ed. Richard Shutler, Jr. (1983), provides a helpful addition to these works. *Atlas of Ancient America* (1986) by Michael Coe, Elizabeth P. Benson, and Dean R. Snow is a useful compendium of maps and information. George Kubler, *The Art and Architecture of Ancient America* (1962), is a valuable resource, though now dated.

Eric Wolf provides an enduring synthesis of Mesoamerican history in *Sons of the Shaking Earth* (1959). A good summary of recent research on Teotihuacan is found in Esther Pasztori, *Teotihuacan* (1997). Linda Schele and David Freidel summarize the most recent research on the classic-period Maya in their excellent *A Forest of Kings* (1990). See also David Drew, *The Lost Chronicles of the Maya Kings* (1999). The best summary of Aztec history is Nigel Davies, *The Aztec Empire: The Toltec Resurgence* (1987). Jacques Soustelle, *Daily Life of the Aztecs*, trans. Patrick O'Brian (1961), is a good introduction. Though controversial in some of its analysis, Inga Clendinnen's *Aztecs* (1991) is also an important contribution.

Chaco and Hohokam (1991), ed. Patricia L. Crown and W. James Judge, is a good summary of research issues. Robert Silverberg, *Mound Builders of Ancient America* (1968), supplies a good introduction to this topic. See also *Understanding Complexity in the Prehistoric Southwest*, ed. George J. Gumerman and Murray Gell-Mann (1994).

A helpful introduction to the scholarship on early Andean societies is provided by Karen Olsen Bruhns, *Ancient South America* (1994). For the Moche see Garth Bawden, *The Moche* (1996). *The History of the Incas* (1970) by Alfred Metraux is dated but offers a useful summary. The best recent modern synthesis is María Rostworowski de Diez Canseco, *History of the Inca Realm*, trans. by Harry B. Iceland (1999). John Murra, *The Economic Organization of the Inca State* (1980), and Irene Silverblatt, *Moon, Sun, and Witches: Gender Ideologies and Class in Inca and Colonial Peru* (1987), are challenging, important works on Peru before the arrival of Columbus in the Western Hemisphere. Frederich Katz, *The Ancient Civilizations of the Americas* (1972), offers a useful comparative perspective on ancient American developments.

◼ Notes

1. This summary closely follows the historical narrative and translation of names offered by Linda Schele and David Freidel in *A Forest of Kings: The Untold Story of the Ancient Maya* (New York: Morrow, 1990), 182–186.
2. From the Florentine Codex, quoted in Inga Clendinnen, *Aztecs* (New York: Cambridge University Press, 1991), 213.
3. Quoted in Nigel Davies, *The Toltec Heritage: From the Fall of Tula to the Rise of Tenochtitlán* (Norman: University of Oklahoma Press, 1980), 3.
4. Bernal Díaz del Castillo, *The Conquest of New Spain*, trans. J. M. Cohen (London: Penguin Books, 1963), 217.
5. Hernando Cortés, *Five Letters, 1519–1526*, trans. J. Bayard Morris (New York: Norton, 1991), 87.
6. Quoted in Irene Silverblatt, *Moon, Sun, and Witches: Gender Ideologies and Class in Inca and Colonial Peru* (Princeton, NJ: Princeton University Press, 1987), 10.
7. Quoted in Irene Silverblatt, *Moon, Sun, and Witches: Gender Ideologies and Class in Inca and Colonial Peru* (Princeton, N.J.: Princeton University Press, 1987), 10.

Religious Conversion

Religious conversion has two meanings that often get confused. The term can refer to the inner transformation an individual may feel on joining a new religious community or becoming revitalized in his or her religious belief. Conversions of this sort are often sudden and deeply emotional. In historical terms, they may be important when they transform the lives of prominent individuals.

In its other meaning, *religious conversion* refers to a change in the religious identity of an entire population, or a large portion of a population. This generally occurs slowly and is hard to trace in historical documents. As a result, historians have sometimes used superficial indicators to trace the spread of a religion. Doing so can result in misleading conclusions, such as considering the spread of the Islamic faith to be the result of forced conversion by Arab conquerors, or taking the routes traveled by Christian or Buddhist missionaries as evidence that the people they encountered adopted their spiritual message, or assuming that a king or chieftain's adherence to a new religion immediately resulted in a religious change among subjects or followers.

In addition to being difficult to document, religious conversion in the broad societal sense has followed different patterns according to changing circumstances of time and place. Historians have devised several models to explain the different conversion patterns. According to one model, religious labels in a society change quickly, through mass baptism, for example, but devotional practices remain largely the same. Evidence for this can be found in the continuation of old religious customs among people who identify themselves as belonging to a new religion. Another model sees religious change as primarily a function of economic benefit or escape from persecution. Taking this approach makes it difficult to explain the endurance of certain religious communities in the face of hardship and discrimination. Nevertheless, most historians pay attention to economic advantage in their assessments of mass conversion. A third model associates a society's religious conversion with its desire to adopt a more sophisticated way of life, by shifting, for example, from a religion that does not use written texts to one that does.

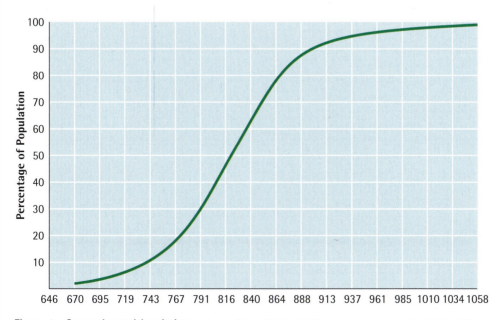

Figure 1   Conversion to Islam in Iran   *Source:* Richard W. Bulliet, *Conversion to Islam in the Medieval Period,* Cambridge, MA: Harvard University Press, 1979, 23. Copyright ©1979 by the President and Fellows of Harvard College.

One final conceptual approach to explaining the process of mass religious change draws on the quantitative models of innovation diffusion that were originally developed to analyze the spread of new technologies in the twentieth century. According to this approach, new ideas, whether in the material or religious realm, depend on the spread of information. A few early adopters—missionaries, pilgrims, or conquerors, perhaps—spread word of the new faith to the people they come in contact with, some of whom follow their example and convert. Those converts in turn spread the word to others, and a chain reaction picks up speed in what might be called a bandwagon effect. The period of bandwagon conversion tapers off when the number of people who have not yet been offered an opportunity to convert diminishes. The entire process can be graphed as a *logistic* or S-shaped curve. Figure 1, the graph of conversion to Islam in Iran based on changes from Persian (non-Islamic) to Arabic (Islamic) names in family genealogies, shows such a curve over a period of almost four centuries.

In societies that were largely illiterate, like those in which Buddhism, Christianity, and Islam slowly achieved spiritual dominance, information spread primarily by word of mouth. The proponents of the new religious views did not always speak the same language as the people they hoped to bring into the faith. Under these circumstances, significant conversion, that is, conversion that involved some understanding of the new religion, as opposed to forced baptism or imposed mouthing of a profession of faith, must surely have started with fairly small numbers.

Language was crucial. Chinese pilgrims undertook lengthy travels to visit early Buddhist sites in India. There they acquired Sanskrit texts, which they translated into Chinese. These translations became the core texts of Chinese Buddhism. In early Christendom, the presence of bilingual (Greek-Aramaic) Jewish communities in the eastern parts of the Roman Empire facilitated the early spread of the religion beyond its Aramaic-speaking homeland. By contrast, Arabic, the language of Islam, was spoken only in the Arabian peninsula and the desert borderlands that extended northwards from Arabia between Syria, Jordan, and Iraq. This initial impediment to the spread of knowledge about Islam dissolved only when intermarriage with non-Muslim, non-Arab women, many of them taken captive and distributed as booty during the conquests, produced bilingual offspring. Bilingual preachers of the Christian faith were similarly needed in the Celtic, Germanic, and Slavic language areas of western and eastern Europe.

This slow process of information diffusion, which varied from region to region, made changing demands on religious leaders and institutions. When a faith was professed primarily by a ruler, his army, and his dependents, religious leaders gave the highest priority to servicing the needs of the ruling minority and perhaps discrediting, denigrating, or exterminating the practices of the majority. Once a few centuries had passed and the new faith had become the religion of the great majority of the population, religious leaders turned to establishing popular institutions and reaching out to the common people. Historical interpretation can benefit from knowing where a society is in a long-term process of conversion.

These various models reinforce the importance of distinguishing between emotional individual conversion experiences and broad changes in a society's religious identity. New converts are commonly thought of as especially zealous in their faith, and that description is often apt in instances of individual conversion experiences. It is less appropriate, however, to broader episodes of conversion. In a conversion wave that starts slowly, builds momentum in the bandwagon phase, and then tapers off, the first individuals to convert are likely to be more spiritually motivated than those who join the movement toward its end. Religious growth depends as much on making the faith attractive to late converts as to ecstatic early converts.

PART FOUR

Interregional Patterns of Culture and Contact, 1200–1550

CHAPTER 13
Mongol Eurasia and Its
Aftermath, 1200–1500

CHAPTER 14
Tropical Africa and Asia,
1200–1500

CHAPTER 15
The Latin West, 1200–1500

CHAPTER 16
The Maritime Revolution,
to 1550

In Eurasia, overland trade along the Silk Road, which had begun before the Roman and Han empires, reached its peak during the era of the Mongol empires. Beginning in 1206 with the rise of Genghis Khan, the Mongols tied Europe, the Middle East, Russia, and East Asia together with threads of conquest and trade centered on Central and Inner Asia. For over a century and a half, some communities thrived on the continental connections that the Mongols fostered, while others groaned under the tax burdens and physical devastation of Mongol rule. But whether for good or ill, Mongol power was based on the skills, strategies, and technologies of the overland trade and life on the steppes.

The impact of the Mongols was also felt by societies that escaped conquest. In Eastern Europe, the Mediterranean coastal areas of the Middle East, Southeast Asia, and Japan, fear of Mongol attack stimulated societies to organize more intensively in their own defense, accelerating processes of urbanization, technological development, and political centralization that in many cases were already underway.

By 1500, Mongol dominance was past, and new powers had emerged. A new Chinese empire, the Ming, was expanding its influence in Southeast

Asia. The Ottomans had captured Constantinople and overthrown the Byzantine Empire. And the Christian monarchs who had defeated the Muslims in Spain and Portugal were laying the foundations of new overseas empires. With the fall of the Mongol Empire, Central and Inner Asia were no longer at the center of Eurasian trade.

As the overland trade of Eurasia faded, merchants, soldiers, and explorers took to the seas. The most spectacular of the early state-sponsored long-distance ocean voyages were undertaken by the Chinese admiral Zheng He. The 1300s and 1400s also saw African exploration of the Atlantic and Polynesian colonization of the central and eastern Pacific. By 1500 the navigator Christopher Columbus, sailing for Spain, had reached the Americas; within twenty-five years a Portuguese ship would sail all the way around the world. New sailing technologies and a sounder knowledge of the size of the globe and the contours of its shorelines made sub-Saharan Africa, the Indian Ocean, Asia, Europe, and finally the Americas more accessible to each other than ever before.

The great overland routes of Eurasia had generated massive wealth in East Asia and a growing hunger for commerce in Europe. These factors animated the development of the sea trade, too. Exposure to the achievements, wealth, and resources of societies in the Americas, sub-Saharan Africa, and Asia enticed the emerging European monarchies to pursue further exploration and control of the seas.

	1200	1250	1300	1350
Americas	• 1200 Population of Cahokia reaches 30,000		• 1325 Aztecs found Tenochtitlan	
	1200–1300 Collapse of Anasazi centers			
Europe	• 1215 Magna Carta	• 1286 Champagne fairs begin to promote regional trade	• 1347 Black Death	
	• 1240 Mongol conquest of Russia	• 1300 First clocks	1337–1453 Hundred Years War	
	• 1241 Mongol invasion of Europe			
Africa	Kingdom of Benin founded ca. 1250 •	• 1270 Solomonic dynasty founded in Ethiopia	• 1324–1325 Mansa Musa's pilgrimage to Mecca brings Islamic learning to Mali	
	1240–1500 Mali Empire			
Middle East	• 1221 Mongols attack Iran	• 1260 Mamluks defeat Mongols at Ain Jalut	• 1300 Emergence of Ottomans in Anatolia	1370–1405 Reign of Timur
			1295–1304 Rule of Muslim Il-khan Ghazan	
		• 1258 Mongols take Baghdad, end Abbasid Caliphate		
Asia and Oceania	• 1200 Polynesians settle New Zealand	• 1274, 1281 Mongol attacks on Japan	• 1336 Ashikaga Shogunate founded	
	1206–1227 Reign of Genghis Khan	Polynesians settle Hawaii 1300 •	Yuan Empire in China 1279–1368	
	• 1206 Delhi Sultanate founded in India	1265–1294 Reign of Khubilai Khan	Ming Empire founded in China 1368 •	

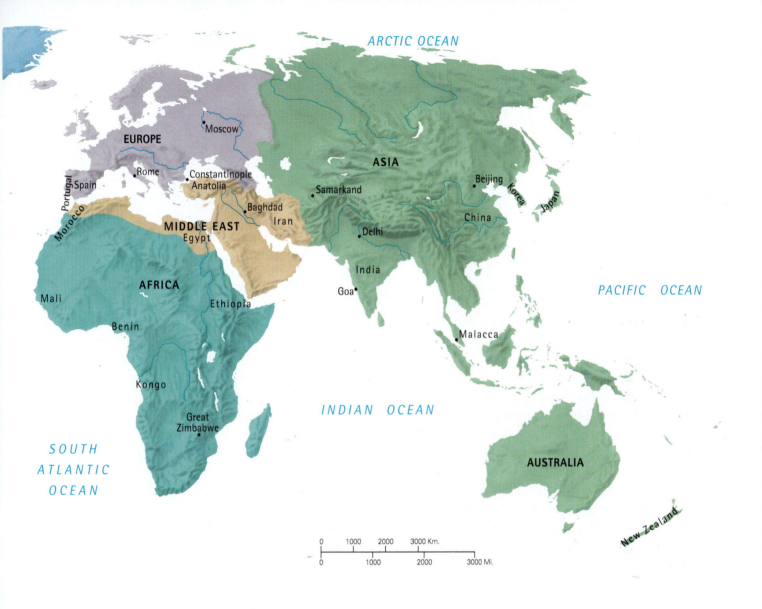

ARCTIC OCEAN

EUROPE

• Moscow

ASIA

• Rome

Constantinople
Anatolia

Beijing •

Portugal
Spain

• Samarkand

Korea

Japan

Morocco

Baghdad

China

MIDDLE EAST
Egypt

Iran

• Delhi

PACIFIC OCEAN

AFRICA

Ethiopia

India

Mali

Goa •

Benin

Malacca •

Kongo

INDIAN OCEAN

Great
Zimbabwe •

SOUTH
ATLANTIC
OCEAN

AUSTRALIA

New Zealand

| 0 | 1000 | 2000 | 3000 Km. |
| 0 | 1000 | 2000 | 3000 Mi. |

1400   1450   1500   1550

1438–1533 Inca Empire   • **1533** Pizarro conquers Inca Empire

• **1520** Cortés conquers Aztec Empire

• **1492** Columbus reaches Caribbean

Voyages of Henry the Navigator **1418–1460**   **1462–1505** Ivan III unites Russia   Portugal establishes trading empire
in Indian Ocean **1499–1572**

• **1454** Gutenberg Bible printed

1400–1550 Italian Renaissance   • **1492** Christian reconquest of Spain

1400–1450 Great Zimbabwe at its peak   • **1471** Portuguese establish Elmina   • **1526** Christian king of Kongo urges end of slave trade

• **1486** Benin and Portugal initiate trade

Vasco da Gama rounds Africa **1499** •

• **1539** Portuguese aid Ethiopia

• **1415** Portuguese seize Morocco

• **1453** Ottomans take Constantinople

• **1517** Ottomans conquer Egypt

1405–1433 Voyages of Zheng He   Annam conquers Champa **1500** •   • **1510, 1511** Portuguese seize Goa, Malacca

• **1482** Japanese invasion of Korea

• **1392** Yi kingdom founded in Korea   • **ca. 1449** Ulugh Beg builds observatory in Samarkand

13

Mongol Eurasia and Its Aftermath, 1200–1500

Defending Japan   Japanese warriors board Mongol warships with swords to prevent the landing of the invasion force in 1281.

CHAPTER OUTLINE

The Rise of the Mongols, 1200–1260
The Mongols and Islam, 1260–1500
Regional Responses in Western Eurasia
Mongol Domination in China, 1271–1368
The Early Ming Empire, 1368–1500
Centralization and Militarism in East Asia, 1200–1500
DIVERSITY AND DOMINANCE: Mongol Politics, Mongol Women
ENVIRONMENT AND TECHNOLOGY: From Gunpowder to Guns

When the Mongol leader Temüjin° was a boy, a rival group murdered his father. Temüjin's mother tried to shelter him (and protect him from dogs, which he feared), but she could not find a safe haven. At fifteen Temüjin sought refuge with the leader of the Keraits°, one of Mongolia's many warring confederations. The Keraits spoke Turkic and respected both Christianity and Buddhism. Gifted with strength, courage, and intelligence, Temüjin learned the importance of religious tolerance, the necessity of dealing harshly with enemies, and the variety of Central Asia's cultural and economic traditions.

In 1206 the **Mongols** and their allies acknowledged Temüjin as **Genghis Khan°,** or supreme leader. His advisers included speakers of many languages and adherents of all the major religions of the Middle East and East Asia. His deathbed speech, which cannot be literally true even though a contemporary recorded it, captures the strategy behind Mongol success: "If you want to retain your possessions and conquer your enemies, you must make your subjects submit willingly and unite your diverse energies to a single end."[1] By implementing this strategy, Genghis Khan became the most famous conqueror in history, initiating an expansion of Mongol dominion that by 1250 stretched from Poland to northern China.

Scholars today stress the immense impact Temüjin and his successors had on the later medieval world, and the positive developments that transpired under Mongol rule. European and Asian sources of the time, however, vilify the Mongols as agents of death, suffering, and conflagration, a still-common viewpoint based on reliable accounts of horrible massacres.

The tremendous extent of the Mongol Empire promoted the movement of people and ideas from one end of Eurasia to the other. Specialized skills developed in different parts of the world spread rapidly throughout the Mongol domains. Trade routes improved, markets expanded, and the demand for products grew. Trade on the Silk Road, which had declined with the fall of the Tang Empire (see Chapter 11), revived.

During their period of domination, lasting from 1218 to about 1350 in western Eurasia and to 1368 in China, the Mongols focused on specific economic and strategic interests and usually permitted local cultures to survive and continue to develop. In some regions, local reactions to Mongol domination and unification sowed seeds of regional and ethnic identity that grew extensively in the period of Mongol decline. Societies in regions as widely separated as Russia, Iran, China, Korea, and Japan benefited from the Mongol stimulation of economic and cultural exchange and also found in their opposition to the Mongols new bases for political consolidation and affirmation of cultural difference.

As you read this chapter, ask yourself the following questions:

- What accounts for the magnitude and speed of the Mongol conquests?
- What benefits resulted from the integration of Eurasia in the Mongol Empire?
- How did the effect of Mongol rule on Russia and the lands of Islam differ from its effect on East Asia?
- In what ways did the Ming Empire continue or discontinue Mongol practices?

THE RISE OF THE MONGOLS, 1200–1260

The environment, economic life, cultural institutions, and political traditions of the steppes (prairies) and deserts of Central and Inner Asia contributed to the expansion and contraction of empires. The Mongol Empire owes much of its success to these long-term conditions. Yet the interplay of environment and technology, on the one hand, and specific human actions, on the other, cannot easily be determined. The way of life known as **nomadism** gives rise to imperial expansion only occasionally, and historians disagree about what triggers these episodes. In the case of the Mongols, a precise assessment of the personal contributions of Genghis Khan and his followers remains uncertain.

Temüjin (TEM-uh-jin)   **Keraits** (keh-rates)
Genghis Khan (GENG-iz KAHN)

Nomadism in Central and Inner Asia

Descriptions of steppe nomads from as early as the Greek writer Herodotus in the sixth century B.C.E. portray them as superb riders, herdsmen, and hunters. Traditional accounts maintain that the Mongols put their infants on goats to accustom them to riding. Moving regularly and efficiently with flocks and herds required firm decision making, and the independence of individual Mongols and their families made this decision making public, with many voices being heard. A council with representatives from powerful families ratified the decisions of the leader, the *khan*. Yet people who disagreed with a decision could strike off on their own. Even during military campaigns, warriors moved with their families and possessions.

Menial work in camps fell to slaves—people who were either captured during warfare or who sought refuge in slavery to escape starvation. Weak groups secured land rights and protection from strong groups by providing them with slaves, livestock, weapons, silk, or cash. More powerful groups, such as Genghis Khan's extended family and descendants, lived almost entirely off tribute, so they spent less time and fewer resources on herding and more on warfare designed to secure greater tribute.

Leading families combined resources and solidified intergroup alliances through arranged marriages and other acts, a process that helped generate political federations. Marriages were arranged in childhood—in Temüjin's case, at the age of eight—and children thus became pawns of diplomacy. Women from prestigious families could wield power in negotiation and management, though they ran the risk of assassination or execution just like men (see Diversity and Dominance: Mongol Politics, Mongol Women).

Families often included believers in two or more religions, most commonly Buddhism, Christianity, or Islam. Virtually all Mongols observed the practices of traditional shamanism, rituals in which special individuals visited and influenced the supernatural world. Whatever their faith, the Mongols believed in world rulership by a khan who, with the aid of his shamans, could speak to and for an ultimate god, represented as Sky or Heaven. This universal ruler transcended particular cultures and dominated them all.

The Mongols were not unfamiliar with agriculture or unwilling to use products grown by farmers, but their ideal was self-sufficiency. Since their wanderings with their herds normally took them far from any farming region, self-sufficiency dictated foods they could provide for themselves—primarily meat and milk—and clothing made from felt, leather, and furs. Women oversaw the breeding and birthing of livestock and the preparation of furs.

Mongol dependency on settled regions related primarily to iron for bridles, stirrups, cart fittings, and weapons. They acquired iron implements in trade and reworked them to suit their purposes. As early as the 600s the Turks, a related pastoral people, had large iron-working stations south of the Altai Mountains in western Mongolia. Neighboring agricultural states tried to limit the export of iron but never succeeded. Indeed, Central Asians developed improved techniques of iron forging, which the agricultural regions then adopted. The Mongols revered iron and the secrets of ironworking. Temüjin means "blacksmith," and several of his prominent followers were the sons of blacksmiths.

Steppe nomads situated near settled areas traded wool, leather, and horses for wood, cotton and cottonseed, silk, vegetables, grain, and tea. An appreciation of the value of permanent settlements for growing grain and cotton, as well as for working iron, led some nomadic groups to establish villages at strategic points, often with the help of migrants from the agricultural regions. The frontier regions east of the Caspian Sea and in northern China thus became economically and culturally diverse. Despite their interdependence, nomads and farmers often came into conflict. On rare occasion such conflicts escalated into full-scale invasions in which the martial prowess of the nomads usually resulted in at least temporary victory.

The Mongol Conquests, 1215–1283

Shortly after his acclamation in 1206 Genghis set out to convince the kingdoms of Eurasia to pay him tribute. Two decades of Mongol aggression followed. By 1209 he had forced the Tanggut rulers of northwest China to submit, and in 1215 he captured the Jin capital of Yanjing, today known as Beijing. He began to attack the west in 1219 with a full-scale invasion of a Central Asian state centered on Khwarezm, an oasis area east of the Caspian Sea. By 1221 he had overwhelmed most of Iran. By this time his conquests had gained such momentum that Genghis did not personally participate in all campaigns, and subordinate generals sometimes led the Mongol armies, which increasingly contained non-Mongol nomads as well.

Genghis Khan died in 1227. His son and successor, the Great Khan Ögödei° (see Figure 13.1), continued to

Ögödei (ERG-uh-day)

C H R O N O L O G Y

	Mongolia and China	Central Asia and Middle East	Russia	Korea, Japan, and Southeast Asia
1200	**1206** Temüjin chosen Genghis Khan of the Mongols			
	1227 Death of Genghis Khan	**1221–1223** First Mongol attacks in Iran	**1221–1223** First Mongol attacks on Russia	
	1227–1241 Reign of Great Khan Ögödei			
	1234 Mongols conquer northern China		**1240** Mongols sack Kiev	
		1250 Mamluk regime controls Egypt and Syria	**1242** Alexander Nevskii defeats Teutonic Knights	
		1258 Mongols sack Baghdad and kill the caliph		**1258** Mongols conquer Koryo rulers in Korea
	1271 Founding of Yuan Empire	**1260** Mamluks defeat Il-khans at Ain Jalut	**1260** War between Il-khans and Golden Horde	**1274, 1281** Mongols attack Japan
	1279 Mongol conquest of Southern Song			**1283** Yuan invades Annam
1300		**1295** Il-khan Ghazan converts to Islam		**1293** Yuan attacks Java
		1349 End of Il-khan rule	**1346** Plague outbreak at Kaffa	**1333–1338** End of Kamakura Shogunate in Japan, beginning of Ashikaga
	1368 Ming Empire founded	**ca. 1350** Egypt infected by plague		
		1370–1405 Reign of Timur		**1392** Founding of Yi kingdom in Korea
1400	**1403–1424** Reign of Yongle	**1402** Timur defeats Ottoman sultan		
	1405–1433 Voyages of Zheng He			
	1449 Mongol attack on Beijing	**1453** Ottomans capture Constantinople	**1462–1505** Ivan III establishes authority as tsar. Moscow emerges as major political center.	**1471–1500** Annam conquers Champa

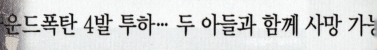

DIVERSITY AND DOMINANCE

MONGOL POLITICS, MONGOL WOMEN

Women in nomadic societies often enjoy more freedom and wield greater influence than women in villages and towns. The wives or mothers of Mongol rulers traditionally managed state affairs during the interregnum between a ruler's death and the selection of a successor. Princes and heads of ministries treated such regents with great deference and obeyed their commands without question. Since a female regent could not herself succeed to the position of khan, her political machinations usually focused on gaining the succession for a son or other male relative.

The History of the World-Conqueror *by the Iranian historian 'Ata-Malik Juvaini, elegantly written in Persian during the 1250s, combines a glorification of the Mongol rulers with an unflinching picture of the cruelties and devastation inflicted by their conquests. As a Muslim, he explains these events as God's punishment for Muslim sins. But this religious viewpoint does not detract from his frank depiction of the instruments of Mongol domination and the fate of those who tried to resist.*

When [Qa'an, i.e., Ögödei, Genghis Khan's son and successor] was on his hunting ground someone brought him two or three water-melons. None of his attendants had any [money] or garments available, but Möge Khatun [his wife], who was present, had two pearls in her ears like the two bright stars of the Lesser Bear when rendered auspicious by conjunction with the radiant moon. Qa'an ordered these pearls to be given to the man. But as they were very precious she said: "This man does not know their worth and value: it is like giving saffron to a donkey. If he is commanded to come to the *ordu* [residence] tomorrow, he will there receive [money] and clothing." "He is a poor man," said Qa'an, "and cannot bear to wait until tomorrow. And whither should these pearls go? They too will return to us in the end. . . ."

At Qa'an's command she gave the pearls to the poor man, and he went away rejoicing and sold them for a small sum, round about two thousand dinars [Note: this is actually a very large sum]. The buyer was very pleased and thought to himself: "I have acquired two fine jewels fit for a present to the Emperor. He is rarely brought such gifts as these." He ac-

cordingly took the pearls to the Emperor, and at that time Möge Khatun was with him. Qa'an took the pearls and said: "Did we not say they would come back to us?" . . . And he distinguished the bearer with all kinds of favours. . . .

When the decree of God Almighty had been executed and the Monarch of the World . . . . Qa'an had passed away, Güyük, his eldest son, had not returned from the campaign against the Qifchaq, and therefore in accordance with precedent the dispatch of orders and the assembling of the people took place at the door of the *ordu*, or palace of his wife, Möge Khatun, who, in accordance with the Mongol custom, had come to him from his father, Chinggiz-Khan. But since Töregene Khatun was the mother of his eldest sons and was moreover shrewder and more sagacious than Möge Khatun, she sent messages to the princes, i.e. the brothers and nephews of the Qa'an, and told them of what had happened and of the death of Qa'an, and said that until a Khan was appointed by agreement someone would have to be ruler and leader in order that the business of state might not be neglected nor the affairs of the commonweal thrown into confusion; in order, too, that the army and the court might be kept under control and the interests of the people protected.

Chaghatai [another of Genghis's sons] and the other princes sent representatives to say that Töregene Khatun was the mother of the princes who had a right to the Khanate; therefore, until a *quriltai* [family council] was held, it was she that should direct the affairs of the state, and the old ministers should remain in the service of the Court, so that the old and new *yasas* [imperial decrees] might not be changed from what was the law.

Now Töregene Khatun was a very shrewd and capable woman, and her position was greatly strengthened by this unity and concord. And when Möge Khatun shortly followed in the wake of Qa'an [i.e., died], by means of finesse and cunning she obtained control of all the affairs of state and won over the hearts of her relatives by all kind of favours and kindnesses and by the sending of gifts and presents. And for the most part strangers and kindred, family and army inclined towards her, and submitted themselves obediently and gladly to her commands and prohibitions, and came under her sway. . . .

And when Güyük came to his mother, he took no part in affairs of state, and Töregene Khatun still executed the decrees of the Empire although the Khanate was settled upon her son. But when two or three months had passed and the son was somewhat estranged from his mother on account of Fatima [see below], the decree of God the Almighty and Glorious was fulfilled and Töregene passed away. . . .

And at that time there was a woman called Fatima, who had acquired great influence in the service of Töregene Khatun and to whose counsel and capability were entrusted all affairs of state. . . .

At the time of the capture of the place [Mashhad, Iran] in which there lies the Holy Shrine of 'Ali ar-Riza [the eighth Shi'ite Imam], she was carried off into captivity. It so chanced she came to Qara-Qorum [Karakorum], where she was a procuress in the market; and in the arts of shrewdness and cunning the wily Delilah could have been her pupil. During the reign of Qa'an she had constant access to the *ordu* of Töregene Khatun; and when times changed and Chinqai [a high official] withdrew from the scene, she enjoyed even greater favour, and her influence became paramount; so that she became the sharer of intimate confidences and the depository of hidden secrets, and the ministers were debarred from executing business, and she was free to issue commands and prohibitions. And from every side the grandees sought her protection, especially the grandees of Khorasan [where Mashhad is located]. And there also came to her certain of the *sayyids* [i.e., descendants of Muhammad] of the Holy Shrine [the tomb of 'Ali ar-Riza], for she claimed to be of the race of the great *sayyids*.

When Güyük succeeded to the Khanate, a certain native of Samarqand, who was said to be an 'Alid [i.e., descendant of Muhammad], one Shira . . . hinted that Fatima had bewitched Köten [another of Töregene Khatun's sons], which was why he was so indisposed. When Köten returned, the malady from which he was suffering grew worse, and he sent a messenger to his brother Güyük to say that he had been attacked by that illness because of Fatima's magic and that if anything happened to him Güyük should seek retribution from her. Following on this message there came tidings of Köten's death. Chinqai, who was now a person of authority, reminded Güyük of the message, and he sent an envoy to his mother to fetch Fatima. His mother refused to let her go saying that she would bring her herself. He sent again several times, and each time she refused him in a different way. As a result his relations with his mother became very bad, and he sent the man from Samarqand with instructions to bring Fatima by force if his mother should still delay in sending her or find some reason for refusing. It being no longer possible to excuse herself, she agreed to send Fatima; and shortly afterwards she passed away. Fatima was brought face to face with Güyük, and was kept naked, and in bonds, and hungry and thirsty for many days and nights; she was plied with all manner of violence, severity, harshness and intimidation; and at last she confessed to the calumny of the slanderous talebearer and avowed her falseness . . . She was rolled up in a sheet of felt and thrown into the river.

And everyone who was connected with her perished also. And messengers were sent to fetch certain persons who had come from the Shrine and claimed to be related to her; and they suffered many annoyances.

This was the year in which Güyük Khan went to join his father, and it was then that 'Ali Khoja of Emil accused Shira of the same crime, namely of bewitching Khoja. He was cast into bonds and chains and remained imprisoned for nearly two years, during which time by reason of all manner of questioning and punishment he despaired of the pleasure of life. And when he recognized and knew of a certainty that this was [his] punishment he resigned himself to death and surrendering his body to the will of Fate and Destiny confessed to a crime which he had not committed. He too was cast into the river, and his wives and children were put to the sword. . . .

[I]n that same year, in a happy and auspicious hour, the Khanate had been settled upon Mengü Qa'an. . . . And when Khoja was brought to the Qa'an, a messenger was sent to 'Ali Khoja, who was one of his courtiers. Some other person brought the same accusation against him, and Mengü-Qa'an ordered him to be beaten from the left and the right until all his limbs were crushed; and so he died. And his wives and children were cast into the baseness of slavery and disgraced and humiliated.

And it is not hidden from the wise and intelligent man, who looks at these matters in the light of understanding and reflects and ponders on them, that the end of treachery and the conclusion of deceit, which spring from evil ways and wicked pretensions, is shameful and the termination thereof unlucky. . . . God preserve us from the like positions and from trespassing into the region of deliberate offenses!

QUESTIONS FOR ANALYSIS

1. How do the stories of Töregene Khatun and Fatima differ in their presentation of female roles?

2. What does the passage indicate concerning the respect of the Mongols for women?

3. What does Güyük's refusal to take over the affairs of state while his mother is still alive imply?

Source: Reprinted by permission of the publisher from 'Ala-ad-Din 'Ata-Malik Juvaini, *The History of the World-Conqueror*, vol. 1, trans. John Andrew Boyle (Cambridge, MA: Harvard University Press, 1958), 211–212, 239–248. Copyright © 1958 by Manchester University Press.

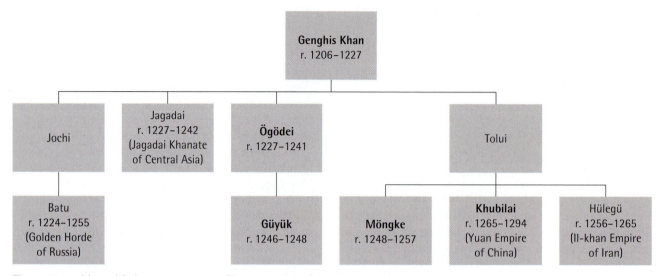

Figure 13.1 Mongol Rulers, 1206–1260 The names of the Great Khans are shown in bold type. Those who founded the regional khanates are listed with their dates of rule.

assault China. He destroyed the Tanggut and then the Jin and put their territories under Mongol governors. In 1236 Genghis's grandson Batu° (d. 1255) attacked Russian territories, took control of all the towns along the Volga° River, and within five years conquered Kievan Russia, Moscow, Poland, and Hungary. Europe would have suffered grave damage in 1241 had not the death of Ögödei compelled the Mongol forces to suspend their campaign. With Genghis's grandson Güyük° installed as the new Great Khan, the conquests resumed. By 1234 the Mongols controlled most of northern China and were threatening the Southern Song. In the Middle East they sacked Baghdad in 1258 and executed the last Abbasid caliph (see Chapter 9).

Although the Mongols' original objective may have been tribute, the scale and success of the conquests created a new historical situation. Ögödei unquestionably sought territorial rule. Between 1240 and 1260 his imperial capital at Karakorum° attracted merchants, ambassadors, missionaries, and adventurers from all over Eurasia. A European who visited in 1246 found the city isolated but well populated and cosmopolitan.

The Mongol Empire remained united until about 1265, as the Great Khan in Mongolia exercised authority over the khans of the Golden Horde in Russia, the khans of the Jagadai domains in Central Asia, and the Il-khans

in Iran (see Map 13.1). After Ögödei's death in 1241 family unity began to unravel. When Khubilai° declared himself Great Khan in 1265, the descendants of Jagadai and other branches of the family refused to accept him. The destruction of Karakorum in the ensuing fighting contributed to Khubilai's transferring his court to the old Jin capital that is now Beijing. In 1271 he declared himself founder of the **Yuan Empire.**

Jagadai's descendants, who continued to dominate Central Asia, had much closer relations with Turkic-speaking nomads than did their kinsmen farther east. This, plus a continuing hatred of Khubilai and the Yuan, contributed to the strengthening of Central Asia as an independent Mongol center and to the adoption of Islam in the western territories.

After the Yuan destroyed the Southern Song (see Chapter 11) in 1279, Mongol troops crossed south of the Red River and attacked Annam—now northern Vietnam. They occupied Hanoi three times and then withdrew after arranging for the payment of tribute. In 1283 Khubilai's forces invaded Champa in what is now southern Vietnam and made it a tribute nation as well. A plan to invade Java by sea failed, as did two invasions of Japan in 1274 and 1281.

In tactical terms, the Mongols did not usually outnumber their enemies, but like all steppe nomads for many centuries, they displayed extraordinary abilities

Batu (BAH-too) **Volga** (VOHL-gah) **Güyük** (gi-yik)
Karakorum (kah-rah-KOR-um)

Khubilai (KOO-bih-lie)

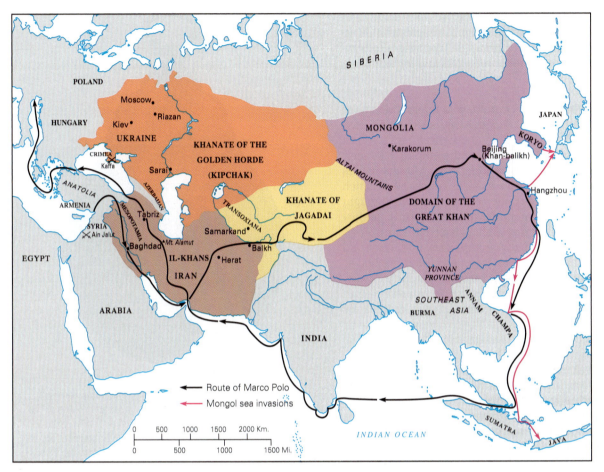

Map 13.1   The Mongol Domains in Eurasia in 1300   After the death of Genghis Khan in 1227, his empire was divided among his sons and grandsons. Son Ögödei succeeded Genghis as Great Khan. Grandson Khubilai expanded the domain of the Great Khan into southern China by 1279. Grandson Hülegü was the first Il-khan in the Middle East. Grandson Batu founded the Khanate of the Golden Horde in southern Russia. Son Jagadai ruled the Jagadai Khanate in Central Asia.

on horseback and utilized superior bows. The Central Asian bow, made strong by laminated layers of wood, leather, and bone, could shoot one-third farther (and was significantly more difficult to pull) than the bows used by their enemies in the settled lands.

Mounted Mongol archers rarely expended all of the five dozen or more arrows they carried in their quivers. As the battle opened, they shot arrows from a distance to decimate enemy marksmen. Then they galloped against the enemy's infantry to fight with sword, lance, javelin, and mace. The Mongol cavalry met its match only at the Battle of Ain Jalut°, where it confronted Mamluk forces whose war techniques shared some of the same traditions (see Chapter 9).

To penetrate fortifications, the Mongols fired flaming arrows and hurled enormous projectiles—sometimes flaming—from catapults. The first Mongol catapults, built on Chinese models, transported easily but had short range and poor accuracy. During western campaigns in Central Asia, the Mongols encountered a catapult design that was half again as powerful as the Chinese model. They used this improved weapon against the cities of Iran and Iraq.

Cities that resisted Mongol attack faced mass slaughter or starvation under siege. Timely surrender brought food, shelter, and protection. The bloodletting the Mongols inflicted on cities such as Balkh° (in present-day northern Afghanistan) spread terror and made it easier

Ain Jalut (ine jah-LOOT)

Balkh (bahlk)

for the Mongols to persuade cities to surrender. Each conquered area helped swell the "Mongol" armies. In campaigns in the Middle East a small Mongol elite oversaw armies of recently recruited Turks and Iranians.

Overland Trade and the Plague

Commercial integration under Mongol rule strongly affected both the eastern and western wings of the empire. Like their aristocratic predecessors in Inner Asia, Mongol nobles had the exclusive right to wear silk, almost all of which came from China. Trade under Mongol dominion brought new styles and huge quantities of silk westward, not just for clothing but also for wall hangings and furnishings. Abundant silk fed the luxury trade in the Middle East and Europe. Artistic motifs from Japan and Tibet reached as far as England and Morocco. Porcelain was another eastern luxury product that became important in trade and strongly influenced later cultural tastes in the Islamic world.

Traders from all over Eurasia enjoyed the benefits of Mongol control. Merchants encountered ambassadors, scholars, and missionaries over the long routes to the Mongol courts. Some of the resulting travel literature, like the account of the Venetian Marco Polo° (1254–1324), freely mixed the fantastic with the factual. Stories of fantastic wealth stimulated a European ambition to find easier routes to Asia.

Exchange also held great dangers. In southwestern China **bubonic plague** had festered in Yunnan province since the early Tang period. In the mid-thirteenth century Mongol troops established a garrison in Yunnan whose military and supply traffic provided the means for flea-infested rats to carry the plague into central China, northwestern China, and Central Asia. Marmots and other desert rodents along the routes became infected and passed the disease to dogs and people. The caravan traffic infected the oasis towns. The plague incapacitated the Mongol army during their assault on the city of Kaffa° in Crimea° in 1346. They withdrew, but the plague remained. From Kaffa rats infected by fleas reached Europe and Egypt by ship (see Chapter 15).

Typhus, influenza, and smallpox traveled with the plague. The combination of these and other diseases created what is often called the "great pandemic" of 1347–1352 and spread devastation far in excess of what the Mongols inflicted in war. Peace and trade, not conquest, gave rise to the great pandemic.

Marco Polo (mar-koe POE-loe) **Kaffa** (KAH-fah)
Crimea (cry-MEE-ah)

Passport The Mongol Empire facilitated the movement of products, merchants, and diplomats over long distances. Travelers frequently encountered new languages, laws, and customs. The *paisa* (from a Chinese word for "card" or "sign"), with its inscription in Mongolian, proclaimed that the traveler had the ruler's permission to travel through the region. Europeans later adopted the practice, thus making the *paisa* the ancestor of modern passports. (The Metropolitan Museum of Art, purchase bequest of Dorothy Graham Bennett, 1993 [1993.256]. Photograph 1997 The Metropolitan Museum of Art)

THE MONGOLS AND ISLAM, 1260–1500

From the perspective of Mongol imperial history, the issue of which branches of the family espoused Islam and which did not mostly concerns their political rivalries and their respective quests for allies. From the standpoint of the history of Islam, however, recovery from the political, religious, and physical devastation that culminated in the destruction of the Abbasid caliphate in Baghdad in 1258 attests to the vitality of the faith and the ability of Muslims to overcome adversity. Within fifty years of its darkest hour, Islam had reemerged as a potent ideological and political force.

Mongol Rivalry

By 1260 the **Il-khan°** state, established by Genghis's grandson Hülegü, controlled parts of Armenia and all of Azerbaijan, Mesopotamia, and Iran. The Mongols who had conquered southern Russia settled north of the Caspian Sea and established the capital of their Khanate of the **Golden Horde** (also called the Kipchak° Khanate) at Sarai° on the Volga River. There they established dominance over the indigenous Muslim Turkic population, both settled and pastoral.

Some members of the Mongol imperial family had professed Islam before the Mongol assault on the Middle East, and Turkic Muslims had served the family in various capacities. Indeed, Hülegü himself, though a Buddhist, had a trusted Shi'ite adviser and granted privileges to the Shi'ites. As a whole, however, the Mongols under Hülegü's command came only slowly to Islam.

The passage of time did little to reconcile Islamic doctrines with Mongol ways. Muslims abhorred the Mongols' worship of idols, a fundamental part of shamanism. Furthermore, Mongol law specified slaughtering animals without spilling blood, which involved opening the chest and stopping the heart. This horrified Muslims, who were forbidden to consume blood and slaughtered animals by slitting their throats and draining the blood.

Islam became a point of inter-Mongol tension when Batu's successor as leader of the Golden Horde declared himself a Muslim, swore to avenge the murder of the Abbasid caliph, and laid claim to the Caucasus—the region between the Black and Caspian Seas—which the Il-khans also claimed (see Map 13.2).

Some European leaders believed that if they helped the non-Muslim Il-khans repel the Golden Horde from the Caucasus, the Il-khans would help them relieve Muslim pressure on the crusader states in Syria, Lebanon, and Palestine (see Chapter 9). This resulted in a brief correspondence between the Il-khan court and Pope Nicholas IV (r. 1288–1292) and a diplomatic mission that sent two Christian Turks to western Europe as Il-khan ambassadors in the late 1200s. Many Christian crusaders enlisted in the Il-khan effort, but the pope later excommunicated some for doing so.

The Golden Horde responded by seeking an alliance with the Muslim Mamluks in Egypt (see Chapter 9) against both the crusaders and the Il-khans. These complicated efforts effectively extended the life of the crusader states; the Mamluks did not finish ejecting the crusaders until the fifteenth century.

Before the Europeans' diplomatic efforts could produce a formal alliance, however, a new Il-khan ruler, Ghazan° (1271–1304), declared himself a Muslim in 1295. Conflicting indications of Sunni and Shi'ite affiliation on such things as coins indicate that the Il-khans did not pay too much attention to theological matters. Nor is it clear whether the many Muslim Turkic nomads who served alongside the Mongols in the army were Shi'ite or Sunni.

Islam and the State

Like the Turks before them (see Chapter 9), the Il-khans gradually came to appreciate the traditional urban culture of the Muslim territories they ruled. Though nomads continued to serve in their armies, the Il-khans used tax farming, a fiscal method developed earlier in the Middle East, to extract maximum wealth from their domain. The government sold tax-collecting contracts to small partnerships, mostly consisting of merchants who might also work together to finance caravans, small industries, or military expeditions. The corporations that offered to collect the most revenue for the government won the contracts. They could use whatever methods they chose and could keep anything over the contracted amount.

Initially, the cost of collecting taxes fell, but over the long term, the exorbitant rates the tax farmers charged drove many landowners into debt and servitude. Agricultural productivity declined. The government had difficulty procuring supplies for the soldiers and resorted to taking land to grow its own grain. Like land held by religious trusts, this land paid no taxes. Thus the tax base shrank even as the demands of the army and the Mongol nobility continued to grow.

Ghazan faced many economic problems. Citing the humane values of Islam, he promised to reduce taxes, but the need for revenues kept the decrease from being permanent. He also witnessed the failure of a predecessor's experiment with the Chinese practice of using paper money. Having no previous exposure to paper money, the Il-khan's subjects responded negatively. The economy quickly sank into a depression that lasted beyond the end of the Il-khan state in 1349. High taxes caused widespread popular unrest and resentment. Mongol nobles competed fiercely among themselves for the decreasing revenues, and fighting among Mongol factions destabilized the government.

In the mid-fourteenth century Mongols from the Golden Horde moved through the Caucasus into the

---

Il-khan (IL-con)   **Kipchak** (KIP-chahk)   **Sarai** (sah-RYE)

Ghazan (haz-ZAHN)

Map 13.2   Western Eurasia in the 1300s   Ghazan's conversion to Islam in 1295 upset the delicate balance of power in Mongol domains. European leaders abandoned their hope of finding an Il-khan ally against the Muslim defenders in Palestine, while an alliance between the Mamluks and the Golden Horde kept the Il-khans from advancing west. This helped the Europeans retain their lands in Palestine and Syria.

western regions of the Il-khan Empire and then into the Il-khan's central territory, Azerbaijan, briefly occupying its major cities. At the same time a new power was emerging to the east, in the Central Asian Khanate of Jagadai (see Map 13.1). The leader **Timur°**, known to Europeans as Tamerlane, skillfully maneuvered himself into command of the Jagadai forces and launched campaigns into western Eurasia, apparently seeing himself as a new Genghis Khan. By ethnic background he was a Turk with only an in-law relationship to the family of the Mongol conqueror. This prevented him from assuming the title *khan*, but not from sacking the Muslim sultanate of Delhi in northern India in 1398 or defeating

the sultan of the rising Ottoman Empire in Anatolia in 1402. By that time he had subdued much of the Middle East, and he was reportedly preparing to march on China when he died in 1405. The Timurids (descendants of Timur) could not hold the empire together, but they laid the groundwork for the establishment in India of a Muslim Mongol-Turkic regime, the Mughals, in the sixteenth century.

Culture and Science in Islamic Eurasia

The Il-khans of Iran and Timurids of Central Asia presided over a brilliant cultural flowering in Iran, Afghanistan, and Central Asia based on the shar-

---

Timur (tem-EER)

Tomb of Timur in Samarqand   The turquoise tiles that cover the dome are typical of Timurid architectural decoration. Timur's family ornamented his capital with an enormous mosque, three large religious colleges facing one another on three sides of an open plaza, and a lane of brilliantly tiled Timurid family tombs in the midst of a cemetery. Timur brought craftsmen to Samarqand from the lands he conquered to build these magnificent structures.   (Sassoon/Robert Harding Picture Library)

ing of artistic trends, administrative practices, and political ideas between Iran and China, the dominant urban civilizations at opposite ends of the Silk Road. The dominant cultural tendencies of the Il-khan and Timurid periods are Muslim, however. Although Timur died before he could reunite Iran and China, his forcible concentration of Middle Eastern scholars, artists, and craftsmen in his capital, Samarkand, fostered advancement in some specific activities under his descendants.

The historian Juvaini° (d. 1283), the literary figure who noted Genghis Khan's deathbed speech, came from the city of Balkh, which the Mongols had devastated in 1221. His family switched their allegiance to the Mongols, and both Juvaini and his older brother assumed high government posts. The Il-khan Hülegü, seeking to immortalize and justify the Mongol conquest of the Middle East, enthusiastically supported Juvaini's writing. This resulted in the first comprehensive narrative of the rise of the Mongols under Genghis Khan.

Juvaini combined a florid style with historical objectivity—he often criticized the Mongols—and served as an inspiration to **Rashid al-Din°,** Ghazan's prime minister, when he attempted the first history of the world. Rashid al-Din's work included the earliest known general history of Europe, derived from conversations with European monks, and a detailed description of China based on information from an important Chinese Muslim official stationed in Iran. The miniature paintings that accompanied some copies of Rashid al-Din's work included depictions of European and Chinese people and events and reflected the artistic traditions of both cultures. The Chinese techniques of composition helped inaugurate the greatest period of Islamic miniature painting under the Timurids.

Rashid al-Din traveled widely and collaborated with administrators from other parts of the far-flung Mongol dominions. His idea that government should be in accord with the moral principles of the majority of the population buttressed Ghazan's adherence to Islam. Administratively, however, Ghazan did not restrict himself to Muslim precedents but employed financial and monetary techniques that roughly resembled those in use in Russia and China.

Under the Timurids, the tradition of the Il-khan historians continued. After conquering Damascus, Timur himself met there with the greatest historian of the age, Ibn Khaldun° (1332–1406), a Tunisian. In a scene reminiscent of Ghazan's answering Rashid al-Din's questions on the history of the Mongols, Timur and Ibn Khaldun exchanged historical, philosophical, and geographical viewpoints. Like Genghis, Timur saw himself as a world conqueror. At their capitals of Samarkand and Herat (in western Afghanistan), later Timurid rulers sponsored historical writing in both Persian and Turkish.

A Shi'ite scholar named **Nasir al-Din Tusi°** represents the beginning of Mongol interest in the scientific traditions of the Muslim lands. Nasir al-Din may have

Juvaini (joo-VINE-nee)   Rashid al-Din (ra-SHEED ad-DEEN)
Ibn Khaldun (ee-bin hal-DOON)
Nasir al-Din Tusi (nah-SEER ad-DEEN TOO-si)

Astronomy and Engineering   Observational astronomy went hand in hand not only with mathematics and calendrical science but also with engineering as the construction of platforms, instruments for celestial measurement, and armillary spheres became more sophisticated. This manual in Persian, completed in the 1500s but illustrating activities of the Il-khan period, illustrates the use of a plumb line with an enormous armillary sphere.   (Istanbul University Library)

he laid new foundations for algebra and trigonometry. Some followers working at an observatory built for Nasir al-Din at Maragheh°, near the Il-khan capital of Tabriz, used the new mathematical techniques to solve a fundamental problem in classical cosmology.

Islamic scholars had preserved and elaborated on the insights of the Greeks in astronomy and mathematics and adopted the cosmological model of Ptolemy°, which assumed a universe with the earth at its center surrounded by the sun, moon, and planets traveling in concentric circular orbits. However, the motions of these orbiting bodies did not coincide with predictions based on circular orbits. Astronomers and mathematicians had long sought a mathematical explanation for the movements that they observed.

Nasir al-Din proposed a model based on the idea of small circles rotating within a large circle. One of his students reconciled this model with the ancient Greek idea of epicycles (small circles rotating around a point on a larger circle) to explain the movement of the moon around the earth. The mathematical tables and geometric models devised by this student somehow became known to Nicholas Copernicus (1473–1543), a Polish monk and astronomer. Copernicus adopted the lunar model as his own, virtually without revision. He then proposed the model of lunar movement developed under the Il-khans as the proper model for planetary movement as well—but with the planets circling the sun.

Sponsorship of observational astronomy and the making of calendars had engaged the interest of earlier Central Asian rulers, particularly the Uighurs° and the Seljuks. Under the Il-khans, the astronomers of Maragheh excelled in predicting lunar and solar eclipses. Astrolabes, armillary spheres, three-dimensional quadrants, and other instruments acquired new precision.

The remarkably accurate eclipse predictions and tables prepared by Il-khan and Timurid astronomers reached the hostile Mamluk lands in Arabic translation. Byzantine monks took them to Constantinople and translated them into Greek, while Christian scholars working in Muslim Spain translated them into Latin. In India the sultan of Delhi ordered them translated into Sanskrit. The Great Khan Khubilai (see below) summoned a team of Iranians to Beijing to build an observatory for him. Timur's grandson Ulugh Beg° (1394–1449), who mixed science and rule, constructed a great observatory in Samarkand and actively participated in compiling observational tables that were later translated into Latin and used by European astronomers.

joined the entourage of Hülegü during a campaign in 1256 against the Assassins, a Shi'ite religious sect derived from the Fatimid dynasty in Egypt and at odds with his more mainstream Shi'ite views (see Chapter 9). Nasir al-Din wrote on history, poetry, ethics, and religion, but made his most outstanding contributions in mathematics and cosmology. Following Omar Khayyam° (1038?–1131), a poet and mathematician of the Seljuk° period,

Omar Khayyam (oh-mar kie-YAM)   Seljuk (SEL-jook)

Maragheh (mah-RAH-gah)   Ptolemy (TOHL-uh-mee)
Uigur (WEE-ger)   Ulugh Beg (oo-loog bek)

A further advance made under Ulugh Beg came from the mathematician Ghiyas al-Din Jamshid al-Kashi°, who noted that Chinese astronomers had long used one ten-thousandth of a day as a unit in calculating the occurrence of a new moon. This seems to have inspired him to employ decimal fractions, by which quantities less than one could be represented by a marker to show place. Al-Kashi's proposed value for *pi* (π) was far more precise than any previously calculated. This innovation arrived in Europe by way of Constantinople, where a Greek translation of al-Kashi's work appeared in the fifteenth century.

REGIONAL RESPONSES IN WESTERN EURASIA

Safe, reliable overland trade throughout Eurasia benefited Mongol ruling centers and commercial cities along the length of the Silk Road. But the countryside, ravaged by conquest, sporadically continuing violence, and heavy taxes, suffered terribly. As Mongol control weakened, regional forces in Russia, eastern Europe, and Anatolia reasserted themselves. All were influenced by Mongol predecessors, and all had to respond to the social and economic changes of the Mongol era. Sometimes this meant collaborating with the Mongols. At other times it meant using local ethnic or religious traditions to resist or roll back Mongol influence.

Russia and Rule from Afar

The Golden Horde established by Genghis's grandson Batu after his defeat of a combined Russian and Kipchak (a Turkic people) army in 1223 started as a unified state but gradually lost its unity as some districts crystallized into smaller khanates. The White Horde, for instance, came to rule much of southeastern Russia in the fifteenth century, and the Crimean khanate on the northern shore of the Black Sea succumbed to Russian invasion only in 1783.

Trade routes east and west across the steppe and north and south along the rivers of Russia and Ukraine conferred importance on certain trading entrepôts, as they had under Kievan Russia (see Chapter 10). The Mongols of the Golden Horde settled at (Old) Sarai, just north of where the Volga flows into the Caspian Sea (see Map 13.1). They ruled their Russian domains to the north and east from afar. To facilitate their control, they granted privileges to the Orthodox Church, which then helped reconcile the Russian people to their distant masters.

The politics of language played a role in subsequent history. Old Church Slavonic, an ecclesiastical language, revived; but Russian steadily acquired greater importance and eventually became the dominant written language. Russian scholars shunned Byzantine Greek, previously the main written tongue, even after the Golden Horde permitted renewed contacts with Constantinople. The Golden Horde enlisted Russian princes to act as their agents, primarily as tax collectors and census takers. Some had to visit the court of the Great Khans at Karakorum to secure the documents upon which their authority was based.

The flow of silver and gold into Mongol hands starved the local economy of precious metal. Like the Il-khans, the khans of the Golden Horde attempted to introduce paper money as a response to the currency shortage. This had little effect in a largely nonmonetary economy, but the experiment left such a vivid memory that the Russian word for money (*denga*°) comes from the Mongolian word for the stamp (*tamga*°) used to create paper currency. But commerce depended more on direct exchange of goods than on currency transactions.

Alexander Nevskii° (ca. 1220–1263), the prince of Novgorod, persuaded some fellow princes to submit to the Mongols. In return, the Mongols favored both Novgorod and the emerging town of Moscow, ruled by Alexander's son Daniel. These towns eclipsed devastated Kiev as political, cultural, and economic centers. This, in turn, drew people northward to open new agricultural land far from the Mongol steppe lands to the southwest. Decentralization continued in the 1300s, with Moscow only very gradually becoming Russia's dominant political center (see Map 13.2).

Russia was deeply affected by the Mongol presence. Bubonic plague became endemic among rodents in the Crimea. Ukraine°, a fertile and well-populated region in the late Kievan period (1000–1230), suffered severe population loss as Mongol armies passed through on campaigns against eastern Europe and raided villages to collect taxes.

Historians debate the Mongol impact on Russia. Some see the destructiveness of the Mongol conquests and the subsequent domination of the khans as isolating

---

Ghiyas al-Din Jamshid al-Kashi   (gee-YASS ad-DIN jam-SHEED al-KAH-shee)

denga (DENG-ah)   *tamga* (TAHM-gah)   **Nevskii** (nih-EFF-skee)
Ukraine (you-CRANE)

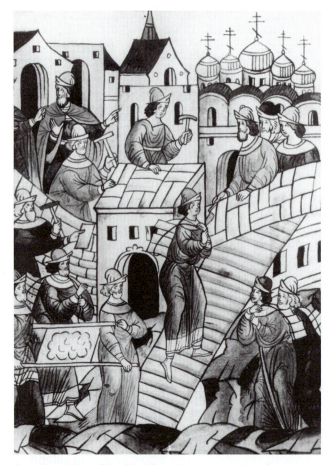

Transformation of the Kremlin   Like other northern Europeans, the Russians preferred to build in wood, which was easy to handle and comfortable to live in. But they fortified important political centers with stone ramparts. In the 1300s, the city of Moscow emerged as a new capital, and its old wooden palace, the Kremlin, was gradually transformed into a stone structure.   (Novosti)

Russia and parts of eastern Europe from developments to the west. These historians refer to the "Mongol yoke" and hypothesize a sluggish economy and dormant culture under the Mongols.

Others point out that Kiev declined economically well before the Mongols struck and that the Kievan princes had already ceased to mint coins. Moreover, the Russian territories regularly paid their heavy taxes in silver. These payments indicate both economic surpluses and an ability to convert goods into cash. The burdensome taxes stemmed less from the Mongols than from their tax collectors, Russian princes who often exempted their own lands and shifted the load to the peasants.

As for Russia's cultural isolation, skeptics observe that before the Mongol invasion, the powerful and constructive role played by the Orthodox Church oriented Russia primarily toward Byzantium (see Chapter 10). This situation discouraged but did not eliminate contacts with western Europe, which probably would have become stronger after the fall of Constantinople to the Ottomans in 1453 regardless of Mongol influence.

The traditional structure of local government survived Mongol rule, as did the Russian princely families, who continued to battle among themselves for dominance. The Mongols merely added a new player to those struggles.

Ivan° III, the prince of Moscow (r. 1462–1505), established himself as an autocratic ruler in the late 1400s. Before Ivan, the title **tsar** (from "caesar"), of Byzantine origin, applied only to foreign rulers, whether the emperors of Byzantium or the Turkic khans of the steppe. Ivan's use of the title, which began early in his reign, probably represents an effort to establish a basis for legitimate rule with the decline of the Golden Horde and disappearance of the Byzantine Empire.

New States in Eastern Europe and Anatolia

The interplay between religion, political maneuvering, and new expressions of local identity affected Anatolia and parts of Europe confronted with the Mongol challenge as well. Raised in Sicily, the Holy Roman Emperor Frederick II (r. 1212–1250) appreciated Muslim culture and did not recoil from negotiating with Muslim rulers. When the pope threatened to excommunicate him unless he went on a crusade, Frederick nominally regained Jerusalem through a flimsy treaty with the Mamluk sultan in Egypt. This did not satisfy the pope, and the preoccupation of both pope and emperor with their quarrel left Hungary, Poland, and other parts of eastern Europe to deal with the Mongol onslaught on their own. Many princes capitulated and went to (Old) Sarai to offer their submission of Batu.

The Teutonic° Knights, however, resisted. Like the Knights Templar in the Middle East (see Chapter 9), the German-speaking Teutonic Knights had a crusading goal: to Christianize the Slavic and Kipchak populations of northern Europe, whose territories they colonized with thousands of German-speaking settlers. Having an interest in protecting Slav territory from German expansion, Alexander Nevskii cooperated in the Mongol campaigns against the Teutonic Knights and their Finnish allies. The latter suffered a catastrophic setback in 1242,

Ivan (ee-VAHN)   **Teutonic** (two-TOHN-ik)

when many broke through ice on Lake Chud (see Map 13.2) and drowned. This destroyed the power of the Knights, and the northern Crusades virtually ceased.

The "Mongol" armies encountered by the Europeans were barely Mongol other than in most command positions. Mongol recruitment and conscription created an international force of Mongols, Turks, Chinese, Iranians, a few Europeans, and at least one Englishman, who had gone to the Middle East as a crusader but joined the Mongols and served in Hungary.

Initial wild theories describing the Mongols as coming from Hell or from the caves where Alexander the Great confined the monsters of antiquity gave way to more sophisticated understanding as European embassies to the Golden Horde, the Il-khan, and the Great Khan in Mongolia reported on Mongol trade routes and the internal structure of Mongol rule. In some quarters terror gave way to awe and even idealization of Mongol wealth and power. Europeans learned about diplomatic passports, coal mining, movable type, high-temperature metallurgy, higher mathematics, gunpowder, and, in the fourteenth century, the casting and use of bronze cannon. Yet with the outbreak of bubonic plague in the late 1340s (see Chapter 15), the memory of Mongol terror helped ignite religious speculation that God might be punishing the Christians of eastern and central Europe with a series of tribulations.

In the fourteenth century several regions, most notably Lithuania° (see Map 13.2), escaped the Mongol grip. When Russia fell to the Mongols and eastern Europe was first invaded, Lithuania had experienced an unprecedented centralization and military strengthening. Like Alexander Nevskii, the Lithuanian leaders maintained their independence by cooperating with the Mongols. In the late 1300s Lithuania capitalized on its privileged position to dominate its neighbors—particularly Poland—and ended the Teutonic Knights' hope of regaining power.

In the Balkans independent and well-organized kingdoms separated themselves from the chaos of the Byzantine Empire and thrived amidst the political uncertainties of the Mongol period. The Serbian king Stephen Dushan (ca. 1308–1355) proved to be the most effective leader. Seizing power from his father in 1331, he took advantage of Byzantine weakness to raise the archbishop of Serbia to the rank of an independent patriarch. In 1346 the patriarch crowned him "tsar and autocrat of the Serbs, Greeks, Bulgarians, and Albanians," a title that fairly represents the wide extent of his rule. As in the case of Timur, however, his kingdom declined after his death

Lithuania (lith-oo-WAY-nee-ah)

in 1355 and disappeared entirely after a defeat by the Ottomans at the battle of Kosovo in 1389.

The Turkic nomads from whom the rulers of the **Ottoman Empire** descended had come to Anatolia in the same wave of Turkic migrations as the Seljuks (see Chapter 9). Though centered in Iran and preoccupied with quarrels with the Golden Horde, the Il-khans exerted great influence in eastern Anatolia. However, a number of small Turkic principalities emerged farther to the west. The Ottoman principality was situated in the northwest, close to the Sea of Marmara. This not only put them in a position to cross into Europe and take part in the internal dynastic struggles of the declining Byzantine state, but it also attracted Muslim religious warriors who wished to extend the frontiers of Islam in battle with the Christians. Though the Ottoman sultan suffered defeat at the hands of Timur in 1402, this was only a temporary setback. In 1453 Sultan Mehmet II captured Constantinople and brought the Byzantine Empire to an end.

The Ottoman sultans, like the rulers of Russia, Lithuania, and Serbia, seized the political opportunity that arose with the decay of Mongol power. The new and powerful states they created put strong emphasis on religious and linguistic identity, factors that the Mongols themselves did not stress. As we shall see, Mongol rule stimulated similar reactions in the lands of east and southeast Asia.

MONGOL DOMINATION IN CHINA, 1271–1368

After the Mongols conquered northern China in the 1230s, Great Khan Ögödei told a newly recruited Confucian adviser that he planned to turn the heavily populated North China Plain into a pasture for livestock. The adviser reacted calmly but argued that taxing the cities and villages would bring greater wealth. The Great Khan agreed, but he imposed the oppressive tax-farming system in use in the Il-khan Empire, rather than the fixed-rate method traditional to China.

The Chinese suffered under this system during the early years, but Mongol rule under the Yuan Empire, established by Genghis Khan's grandson Khubilai in 1271, also brought benefits: secure routes of transport and communication; exchange of experts and advisers between eastern and western Eurasia; and transmission of information, ideas, and skills.

The Yuan Empire, 1279–1368

Just as the Il-khans in Iran and the Golden Horde in Russia came to accept many aspects of Muslim and Christian culture, so the Mongols in China sought to construct a fruitful synthesis of the Mongol and Chinese religious and moral traditions. **Khubilai Khan** gave his oldest son a Chinese name and had Confucianists participate in the boy's education. In public announcements and the crafting of laws, he took Confucian conventions into consideration. Buddhist and Daoist leaders visited the Great Khan and came away believing that they had all but convinced him to accept their beliefs.

The teachings of Buddhist priests from Tibet called **lamas°** became increasingly popular with some Mongol rulers in the 1200s and 1300s. Their idea of a militant universal ruler bringing the whole world under control of the Buddha and thus pushing it nearer to salvation mirrored an ancient Central Asia idea of universal rulership.

Beijing, the Yuan capital, became the center of cultural and economic life. Where Karakorum had been remote from any major settled area, Beijing served as the eastern terminus of the caravan routes that began near Tabriz, the Il-khan capital, and (Old) Sarai, the Golden Horde capital. An imperial horseback courier system utilizing hundreds of stations maintained close communications along routes that were generally policed and safe for travelers. Ambassadors and merchants arriving in Beijing found a city that was much more Chinese in character than its predecessor in Mongolia.

Called Great Capital (Dadu) or City of the Khan (*khan-balikh°*, Marco Polo's "Cambaluc"), Khubilai's capital featured massive Chinese-style walls of rammed earth, a tiny portion of which can still be seen. Khubilai's engineers widened the streets and developed linked lakes and artificial islands at the city's northwest edge to form a closed imperial complex, the Forbidden City. For his summer retreat, Khubilai maintained the palace and parks at Shangdu°, now in Inner Mongolia. This was "Xanadu°" celebrated by the English poet Samuel Taylor Coleridge, its "stately pleasure dome" the hunting preserve where Khubilai and his courtiers practiced riding and shooting.

"China" as we think of it today did not exist before the Mongols. Before they reunified it, China had been divided into three separate states (see Chapter 11). The Tanggut and Jin empires controlled the north, the Southern Song most of the area south of the Yellow River. These states had different languages, writing systems, forms of government, and elite cultures. The Great Khans destroyed all three and encouraged the restoration or preservation of many features of Chinese government and society, thereby reuniting China in what proved to be a permanent fashion.

By law, Mongols had the highest social ranking. Below them came, in order, Central Asians and Middle Easterners, then northern Chinese, and finally southern Chinese. This apparent racial ranking also reflected a hierarchy of functions, the Mongols being the empire's warriors, the Central Asians and Middle Easterners its census takers and tax collectors. The northern Chinese outranked the southern Chinese because they had come under Mongol control almost two generations earlier.

Though Khubilai included some "Confucians" (under the Yuan, a formal and hereditary status) in government, their position compared poorly with their status as elite officeholders in pre-Mongol times. The Confucians criticized the favoring of merchants, many of whom were from the Middle East or Central Asia, and physicians. They regarded doctors as mere technicians, or even heretical practitioners of Daoist mysticism. The Yuan encouraged medicine and began the long process of integrating Chinese medical and herbal knowledge with western approaches derived from Greco-Roman and Muslim sources.

Like the Il-khan rulers in the Middle East, the Yuan rulers concentrated on counting the population and collecting taxes. They brought Persian, Arab, and Uighur administrators to China to staff the offices of taxation and finance, and Muslim scholars worked at calendar making and astronomy. For census taking and administration, the Mongols organized all of China into provinces. Central appointment of provincial governors, tax collectors, and garrison commanders marked a radical change by systematizing government control in all parts of the country.

The scarcity of contemporary records and the hostility of later Chinese writers make examination of the Yuan economy difficult. Many cities seem to have prospered: in north China by being on the caravan routes; in the interior by being on the Grand Canal; and along the coast by participation in maritime grain shipments from south China. The reintegration of East Asia (though not Japan) with the overland Eurasian trade, which had lapsed with the fall of the Tang (see Chapter 11), stimulated the urban economies.

The privileges and prestige that merchants enjoyed changed urban life and the economy of China. With only

---

lama (LAH-mah)   ***khan-balikh*** (kahn-BAL-ik)
Shangdu (shahng-DOO)   **Xanadu** (ZAH-nah-doo)

a limited number of government posts open to the old Chinese elite, great families that had previously spent fortunes on educating sons for government service sought other outlets. Many gentry families chose commerce, despite its lesser prestige. Corporations—investor groups that behaved as single commercial and legal units and shared the risk of doing business—handled most economic activities, starting with financing caravans and expanding into tax farming and lending money to the Mongol aristocracy. Central Asians and Middle Easterners headed most corporations in China in the early Yuan period; but as Chinese bought shares, most corporations acquired mixed membership, or even complete Chinese ownership.

The agricultural base, damaged by war, overtaxation, and the passage of armies, could not satisfy the financial needs of the Mongol aristocracy. Following earlier precedent, the imperial government issued paper money to make up the shortfall. But the massive scale of the Yuan experiment led people to doubt the value of the notes, which were unsecured. Copper coinage partially offset the failure of the paper currency. During the Song, exports of copper to Japan, where the metal was scarce, had caused a severe shortage in China, leading to a rise in value of copper in relation to silver. By cutting off trade with Japan, the Mongols intentionally or unintentionally stabilized the value of copper coins.

Gentry families that had previously prepared their sons for the state examinations moved from their traditional homes in the countryside to engage in urban commerce, and city life began to cater to the tastes of merchants instead of scholars. Specialized shops selling clothing, grape wine, furniture, and religiously butchered meats became common. Teahouses featured sing-song girls, drum singers, operas, and other entertainments previously considered coarse. Writers published works in the style of everyday speech. And the increasing influence of the northern, Mongolian-influenced Chinese language, often called Mandarin in the West, resulted in lasting linguistic change.

Cottage industries linked to the urban economies dotted the countryside, where 90 percent of the people lived. Some villages cultivated mulberry trees and cotton using dams, water wheels, and irrigation systems patterned in part on Middle Eastern models. Treatises on planting, harvesting, threshing, and butchering were published. One technological innovator, Huang Dao Po°, brought knowledge of cotton growing, spinning, and weaving from her native Hainan Island to the fertile

Yangzi Delta. Some villagers came to revere such innovators as local gods.

Yet on the whole, the countryside did poorly during the Yuan period. After the initial conquests, the Mongol princes evicted many farmers and subjected the rest to brutal tax collection. As in Iran under the Il-khans, by the time the Yuan shifted to lighter taxes and encouragement of farming at the end of the 1200s, it was too late. Servitude or homelessness had overtaken many farmers. Neglect of dams and dikes caused disastrous flooding, particularly on the Yellow River.

According to Song records from before the Mongol conquest and the Ming census taken after their overthrow—each, of course, possibly subject to inaccuracy or exaggeration—China's population may have shrunk by 40 percent during eighty years of Mongol rule, with many localities in northern China losing up to five-sixths of their inhabitants. Scholars have suggested several causes, not all of them directly associated with Mongol rule: prolonged warfare, privations in the countryside causing people to resort to female infanticide, a southward movement of people fleeing the Mongols, and flooding on the Yellow River. The last helps explain why losses in the north exceeded those in the south and why the population along the Yangzi River markedly increased.

The bubonic plague and its attendant diseases, spread by the population movements, contributed as well. The Mongol incorporation of Yunnan°, a mountainous southwestern province where rodents commonly carried bubonic plague, into the centralized provincial system of government exposed the lowlands to plague (see Map 13.1). Cities seem to have managed outbreaks of disease better than rural areas as the epidemic moved from south to north in the 1300s.

Cultural and Scientific Exchange

Government officials in Yuan China maintained regular contact with their counterparts in Il-khan Iran and pursued similar economic and financial policies. While Chinese silks and porcelains affected elite tastes at the western end of the Silk Road, Il-khan engineering, astronomy, and mathematics reached China and Korea. Just as Chinese painters taught Iranian artists appealing new ways of drawing clouds, rocks, and trees, Muslims from the Middle East oversaw most of the weapons manufacture and engineering projects for

---

Huang Dao Po (hwahng DOW poh)

Yunnan (YOON-nahn)

Khubilai's armies. Similarly, the Il-khans imported scholars and texts that helped them understand Chinese technological advances, including stabilized sighting tubes for precisely noting the positions of astronomical objects, mechanically driven armillary spheres that showed how the sun, moon, and planets moved in relation to one another, and new techniques for measuring the movement of the moon. And Khubilai brought Iranians to Beijing to construct an observatory and an institute for astronomical studies similar to the Il-khans' facility at Maragheh. He made the state responsible for maintaining and staffing the observatory.

Muslim doctors and Persian medical texts—particularly in anatomy, pharmacology, and ophthalmology—circulated in China during the Yuan. Khubilai, who suffered from alcoholism and gout, accorded high status to doctors. New seeds and formulas from the Middle East stimulated medical practice. The traditional Chinese study of herbs, drugs, and potions came in for renewed interest and publication.

The Fall of the Yuan Empire

In the 1340s power contests broke out among the Mongol princes. Within twenty years farmer rebellions and feuds among the Mongols engulfed the land. Amidst the chaos, a charismatic Chinese leader, Zhu Yuanzhang°, mounted a campaign that destroyed the Yuan Empire and brought China under control of his new empire, the Ming, in 1368. Many Mongols—as well as the Muslims, Jews, and Christians who had come with them—remained in China, some as farmers or shepherds, some as high-ranking scholars and officials. Most of their descendants took Chinese names and became part of the diverse cultural world of China.

Many other Mongols, however, had never moved out of their home territories in Mongolia. Now they welcomed back refugees from the Yuan collapse. Though Turkic peoples were becoming predominant in the steppe region in the west of Central Asia, including territories still ruled by descendants of Genghis Khan, Mongols retained control of Inner Asia, the steppe regions bordering on Mongolia. Their reconcentration in this region fostered a renewed sense of Mongol unity. Some Mongol groups adopted Islam; others favored Tibetan Buddhism. But religious affiliation proved less important than Mongol identity.

The Ming thus fell short of dominating all the Mongols. The Mongols of Inner Asia paid tribute to the Ming only to the extent that doing so facilitated their trade.

The Mongols remained a continuing threat on the northern Ming frontier.

THE EARLY MING EMPIRE, 1368–1500

The history of the **Ming Empire** raises questions about the overall impact of the Mongol era in China. Just as historians of Russia and Iran divide over whether Mongol invasion and political domination retarded or stimulated the pace and direction of political and economic change, so historians of China have differing opinions about the Mongols. Since the Ming reestablished many practices that are seen as purely Chinese, they receive praise from people who ascribe central importance to Chinese traditions. On the other hand, historians who look upon the Mongol era as a pivotal historical moment when communication across the vast interior of Eurasia served to bring east and west together sometimes see the inward-looking Ming as less dynamic and productive than the Yuan.

Ming China on a Mongol Foundation

Zhu Yuanzhang, a former monk, soldier, and bandit, had watched his parents and other family members die of famine and disease, conditions he blamed on Mongol misrule. During the Yuan Empire's chaotic last decades, he vanquished rival rebels and assumed imperial power under the name Hongwu (r. 1368–1398). He ruled a highly centralized, militarily formidable empire.

Hongwu moved the capital to Nanjing° ("southern capital") on the Yangzi River, turning away from the Mongol's Beijing ("northern capital"; see Map 13.3). Though Zhu Yuanzhang the rebel had espoused a radical Buddhist belief in a coming age of salvation, once in power he used Confucianism to depict the emperor as the champion of civilization and virtue, justified in making war on uncivilized "barbarians."

Hongwu choked off the close relations with Central Asia and the Middle East fostered by the Mongols and imposed strict limits on imports and foreign visitors. Silver replaced paper money for tax payments and commerce. These practices, illustrative of an anti-Mongol ideology, proved as economically unhealthy as some of the Yuan economic policies and did not last. Instead, the Ming government gradually came to resemble the Yuan. Ming

---

Zhu Yuanzhang (JOO yuwen-JAHNG)

Nanjing (nahn-JING)

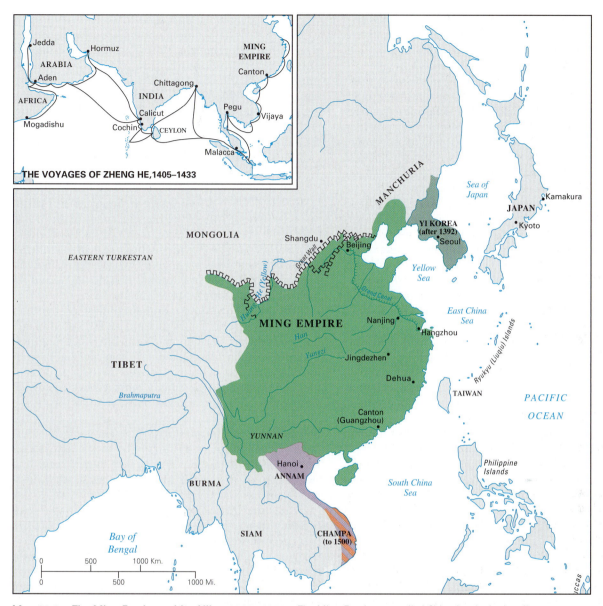

THE VOYAGES OF ZHENG HE, 1405–1433

Map 13.3   The Ming Empire and Its Allies, 1368–1500   The Ming Empire controlled China but had a hostile relationship with peoples in Mongolia and Inner Asia who had been under the rule of the Mongol Yuan emperors. Mongol attempts at conquest by seas were continued by the Ming mariner Zheng He. Between 1405 and 1433 he sailed to Southeast Asia and then beyond, to India, the Persian Gulf, and East Africa.

rulers retained the provincial structure and continued to observe the hereditary professional categories of the Yuan period. Muslims made calendars and astronomical calculations at a new observatory at Nanjing, a replica of Khubilai's at Beijing. The Mongol calendar continued in use.

Continuities with the Yuan became more evident after an imperial prince seized power through a coup d'état

to rule as the emperor **Yongle**° (r. 1403–1424). He returned the capital to Beijing, enlarging and improving Khubilai's imperial complex. The central area—the Forbidden City—acquired its present character, with moats, orange-red outer walls, golden roofs, and marble bridges.

Yongle (yoong-LAW)

Yongle intended this combination fortress, religious site, bureaucratic center, and imperial residential park to overshadow Nanjing, and it survives today as China's most imposing traditional architectural complex.

Yongle also restored commercial links with the Middle East. Because hostile Mongols still controlled much of the caravan route, Yongle explored maritime connections. In Southeast Asia, Annam became a Ming province as the early emperors continued the Mongol program of aggression. This focus on the southern frontier helped inspire the naval expeditions of the trusted imperial eunuch **Zheng He°** from 1405 to 1433.

A Muslim whose father and grandfather had made the pilgrimage to Mecca, Zheng He had a good knowledge of the Middle East; and his religion eased relations with the states of the Indian subcontinent, where he directed his first three voyages. Subsequent expeditions reached Hormuz on the Persian Gulf, sailed the southern coast of Arabia and the Horn of Africa (modern Somalia), and possibly reached as far south as the Strait of Madagascar (see Map 13.3).

On early voyages he visited long-established Chinese merchant communities in Southeast Asia in order to cement their allegiance to the Ming Empire and to collect taxes. When a community on the island of Sumatra resisted, he slaughtered the men to set an example. By pursuing commercial relations with the Middle East and possibly Africa, he also publicized Yongle's reversal of Hongwu's opposition to foreign trade.

The expeditions added some fifty new tributary states to the Ming imperial universe, but trade did not increase as dramatically. Sporadic embassies reached Beijing from rulers in India, the Middle East, Africa, and Southeast Asia. During one visit the ruler of Brunei° died and received a grand burial at the Chinese capital. Occasional expeditions continued until the 1430s, after the death of both Yongle and Zheng He, when they stopped.

Having demonstrated such abilities at long-distance navigation, why did the Chinese not develop seafaring for commercial and military gain? Contemporaries considered the voyages a personal project of Yongle, an upstart ruler who had always sought to prove his worthiness. Building the Forbidden City in Beijing and sponsoring gigantic encyclopedia projects might be taken to reflect a similar motivation. Yongle may also have been emulating Khubilai Khan, who had sent enormous fleets against Japan and Southeast Asia. This would fit with the rumor spread by Yongle's political enemies that he was actually a Mongol.

A less speculative approach to the question starts with the fact that the new commercial opportunities fell short of expectations, despite bringing foreign nations into the Ming orbit. In the meantime, Japanese coastal piracy intensified, and Mongol threats in the north and west grew. The human and financial demands of fortifying the north, redesigning and strengthening Beijing, and outfitting military expeditions against the Mongols ultimately took priority over the quest for maritime empire.

Technology and Population

Although innovation continued in all areas of the Ming economy, advances were less frequent and less significant than under the Song, particularly in agriculture. Agricultural production peaked around the mid-1400s and remained level for more than a century.

The Ming government limited mining, partly to reinforce the value of metal coins and partly to control and tax the industry. Farmers had difficulty obtaining iron and bronze for farm implements. The peace that had followed the Mongol conquest resulted in a decline in techniques for making high-quality bronze and steel, which were especially used for weapons. Central Asian and Middle Eastern technicians rather than Chinese cast the bronze instruments for Khubilai's observatory at Beijing. Japan quickly surpassed China in the production of extremely high-quality steel swords. Copper, iron, and steel became expensive in Ming China, leading to a lessened use of metal.

After the death of Emperor Yongle in 1424, shipbuilding also declined, and few advances occurred in printing, timekeeping, and agricultural technology. New weaving techniques did appear, but technological development in this field had peaked by 1500.

Reactivation of the examination system as a way of recruiting government officials (see Chapter 11) drew large numbers of educated, ambitious men into a renewed study of the Confucian classics. This reduced the vitality of commerce, where they had previously been employed, just as population increase was creating a labor surplus. Records indicating a growth from 60 million at the end of the Yuan period in 1368 to nearly 100 million by 1400 may not be entirely reliable, but rapid population growth encouraged the production of staples—wheat, millet, and barley in the north and rice in the south—at the expense of commercial crops such as cotton that had stimulated many technological innovations under the Song. Staple crops yielded lower profits, which further discouraged capital improvements. New

---

Zheng He (JEHNG HUH)   **Brunei** (broo-NIE)

Ming Porcelain Bowl High-quality Chinese blue-and-white ware commanded an international market under the Ming Empire. This piece, bearing a Portuguese inscription showing that it was made in 1541 for the Portuguese governor of Malacca, is one of the earliest examples of works made specifically for a European. (Collection, Junta de Baixo Alentago, Beja, Portugal)

foods, such as sweet potatoes, became available but were little adopted. Population growth in southern and central China caused deforestation and raised the price of wood.

The Mongols that the Ming confronted in the north fought on horseback with simple weapons. The Ming fought back with arrows, scattershot mortars, and explosive canisters. They even used a few cannon, which they knew about from contacts with the Middle East and later with Europeans (see Environment and Technology: From Gunpowder to Guns). Fearing that technological secrets would get into enemy hands, the government censored the chapters on gunpowder and guns in early Ming encyclopedias. Shipyards and ports shut down to avoid contact with Japanese pirates and to prevent Chinese from migrating to Southeast Asia.

A technology gap with Korea and Japan opened up nevertheless. When superior steel was needed, supplies came from Japan. Korea moved ahead of China in the design and production of firearms and ships, in printing techniques, and in the sciences of weather prediction and calendar making. The desire to tap the wealthy Ming market fueled some of these advances.

The Ming Achievement

In the late 1300s and the 1400s the wealth and consumerism of the early Ming stimulated high achievement in literature, the decorative arts, and painting. The Yuan period interest in plain writing had produced some of the world's earliest novels. This type of literature flourished under the Ming. *Water Margin*, which originated in the raucous drum-song performances loosely related to Chinese opera, features dashing Chinese bandits who struggle against Mongol rule, much as Robin Hood and his merry men resisted Norman rule in England. Many authors had a hand in the final print version.

Luo Guanzhong°, one of the authors of *Water Margin*, is also credited with *Romance of the Three Kingdoms*, based on a much older series of stories that in some ways resemble the Arthurian legends. It describes the attempts of an upright but doomed war leader and his followers to restore the Han Empire of ancient times and resist the power of the cynical but brilliant villain. *Romance of the Three Kingdoms* and *Water Margin* expressed much of the militant but joyous pro-China sentiment of the early Ming era and remain among the most appreciated Chinese fictional works.

Probably the best-known product of Ming technological advance was porcelain. The imperial ceramic works at Jingdezhen° experimented with new production techniques and new ways of organizing and rationalizing workers. "Ming ware," a blue-on-white style developed in the 1400s from Indian, Central Asian, and Middle Eastern motifs, became especially prized around the world. Other Ming goods in high demand included furniture, lacquered screens, and silk, all eagerly transported by Chinese and foreign merchants throughout Southeast Asia and the Pacific, India, the Middle East, and East Africa.

Luo Guanzhong (LAW GWAHB-JOONG)
Jingdezhen (JING-deh-JUHN)

From Gunpowder to Guns

Long before the invention of guns, gunpowder was used in China and Korea to excavate mines, build canals, and channel irrigation. Alchemists in China used related formulas to make noxious gas pellets to paralyze enemies and expel evil spirits. A more realistic benefit was eliminating disease-carrying insects, a critical aid to the colonization of malarial regions in China and Southeast Asia. The Mongol Empire staged fireworks displays on ceremonial occasions, delighting European visitors to Karakorum who saw them for the first time.

Anecdotal evidence in Chinese records gives credit for the introduction of gunpowder to a Sogdian Buddhist monk of the 500s. The monk described the wondrous alchemical transformation of elements produced by a combination of charcoal and saltpeter. In this connection he also mentioned sulfur. The distillation of naphtha, a light, flammable derivative of oil or coal, seems also to have been first developed in Central Asia, the earliest evidence coming from the Gandhara region (in modern Pakistan).

By the eleventh century, the Chinese had developed flamethrowers powered by burning naphtha, sulfur, or gunpowder in a long tube. These weapons intimidated and injured foot soldiers and horses and also set fire to thatched roofs in hostile villages and, occasionally, the rigging of enemy ships.

In their long struggle against the Mongols, the Song learned to enrich saltpeter to increase the amount of nitrate in gunpowder. This produced forceful explosions rather than jets of fire. Launched from catapults, gunpowder-filled canisters could rupture fortifications and inflict mass casualties. Explosives hurled from a distance could sink or burn ships.

The Song also experimented with firing projectiles from metal gun barrels. The earliest gun barrels were broad and squat and were transported on special wagons to their emplacements. The mouths of the barrels projected saltpeter mixed with scattershot minerals. The Chinese and then the Koreans adapted gunpowder to shooting masses of arrows—sometimes flaming—at enemy fortifications.

In 1280 weapons makers of the Yuan Empire produced the first device featuring a projectile that completely filled the mouth of the cannon and thus concentrated the explosive force. The Yuan used cast bronze for the barrel and iron for the cannonball. The new weapon shot farther and more accurately, and was much more destructive, than the earlier Song devices.

Knowledge of the cannon and cannonball moved westward across Eurasia. By the end of the thirteenth century cannon were being produced in the Middle East. By 1327 small, squat cannon called "bombards" were being used in Europe.

Launching Flaming Arrows   Song soldiers used gunpowder to launch flaming arrows.   (British Library)

CENTRALIZATION AND MILITARISM IN EAST ASIA, 1200–1500

Korea, Japan, and Annam, the other major states of East Asia, were all affected by confrontation with the Mongols, but with differing results. Japan and Annam escaped Mongol conquest but changed in response to the Mongol threat, becoming more effective and expansive regimes with enhanced commitments to independence.

As for Korea, just as the Ming stressed Chinese traditions and identity in the aftermath of Yuan rule, so Mongol domination contributed to revitalized interest in Korea's own language and history. The Mongols conquered Korea after a difficult war, and though Korea suffered socially and economically under Mongol rule, members of the elite associated closely with the Yuan Empire. After the fall of the Yuan, merchants continued the international connections established in the Mongol period, while Korean armies consolidated a new kingdom and fended off pirates.

Korea from the Mongols to the Yi, 1231–1500

In their effort to establish control over all of China, the Mongols searched for coastal areas from which to launch naval expeditions and choke off the sea trade of their adversaries. Korea offered such possibilities. When the Mongols attacked in 1231, the leader of a prominent Korean family assumed the role of military commander and protector of the king (not unlike the shoguns of Japan). His defensive war, which lasted over twenty years, left a ravaged countryside, exhausted armies, and burned treasures, including the renowned nine-story pagoda at Hwangnyong-sa° and the wooden printing blocks of the *Tripitaka*°, a ninth-century masterpiece of printing art. The commander's underlings killed him in 1258. Soon afterward the Koryo° king surrendered to the Mongols and became a subject monarch by linking his family to the Great Khan by marriage.

By the mid-1300s the Koryo kings were of mostly Mongol descent, and they favored Mongol dress, customs, and language. Many lived in Beijing. The kings, their families, and their entourages often traveled between China and Korea, thus exposing Korea to the philosophical and artistic styles of Yuan China: neo-Confucianism, Chan Buddhism (called *Sōn* in Korea), and celadon (light green) ceramics.

Mongol control was a stimulus after centuries of comparative isolation. Cotton began to be grown in southern Korea; gunpowder came into use; and the art of calendar making, including eclipse prediction and vector calculation, stimulated astronomical observation and mathematics. Celestial clocks built for the royal observatory at Seoul reflected Central Asian and Islamic influences more than Chinese. Avenues of advancement opened for Korean scholars willing to learn Mongolian, landowners willing to open their lands to falconry and grazing, and merchants servicing the new royal exchanges with Beijing. These developments contributed to the rise of a new landed and educated class.

When the Yuan Empire fell in 1368, the Koryo ruling family remained loyal to the Mongols and had to be forced to recognize the new Ming Empire. In 1392 the **Yi**° established a new kingdom with a capital in Seoul and sought to reestablish a local identity. Like Russia and China after the Mongols, the Yi regime publicly rejected the period of Mongol domination. Yet the Yi government continued to employ Mongol-style land surveys, taxation in kind, and military garrison techniques.

Like the Ming emperors, the Yi kings revived the study of the Confucian classics, an activity that required knowledge of Chinese and showed the dedication of the state to learning. This revival may have led to a key technological breakthrough in printing technology.

Koreans had begun using Chinese woodblock printing in the 700s. This technology worked well in China, where a large number of buyers wanted copies of a comparatively small number of texts. But in Korea, the comparatively few literate men had interests in a wide range of texts. Movable wooden or ceramic type appeared in Korea in the early thirteenth century and may have been invented there. But the texts were frequently inaccurate and difficult to read. In the 1400s Yi printers, working directly with the king, developed a reliable device to anchor the pieces of type to the printing plate: they replaced the old beeswax adhesive with solid copper frames. The legibility of the printed page improved, and high-volume, accurate production became possible. Combined with the phonetic *han'gul*° writing system, this printing technology laid the foundation for a high literacy rate in Korea.

Yi publications told readers how to produce and use fertilizer, transplant rice seedlings, and engineer reservoirs. Building on Eurasian knowledge imported by the Mongols and introduced under the Koryo, Yi scholars

---

Hwanghnyong-sa (hwahng-NEEYAHNG-sah)
Tripitaka (tri-PIH-tah-kah)   **Koryo** (KAW-ree-oh)

Yi (YEE)   *han'gul* (HAHN-goor)

Movable Type The improvement of cast bronze tiles, each showing a single character, eliminated the need to cast or carve whole pages. Individual tiles—the ones shown are Korean—could be moved from page frame to page frame and gave an even and pleasing appearance. All parts of East Asia eventually adopted this form of printing for cheap, popular books. In the mid-1400s Korea also experimented with a fully phonetic form of writing, which in combination with movable type allowed Koreans unprecedented levels of literacy and access to printed works.   (Courtesy, Yushin Yoo)

developed a meteorological science of their own. They invented or redesigned instruments to measure wind speed and rainfall and perfected a calendar based on minute comparisons of the systems of China and the Islamic world.

In agriculture, farmers expanded the cultivation of cash crops, the reverse of what was happening in Ming China. Cotton, the primary crop, enjoyed such high value that the state accepted it for tax payments. The Yi army used cotton uniforms, and cotton became the favored fabric of the Korean civil elite. With cotton gins and spinning wheels powered by water, Korea advanced more rapidly than China in mechanization and began to export considerable amounts of cotton to China and Japan.

Although both the Yuan and the Ming withheld the formula for gunpowder from the Korean government, Korean officials acquired the information by subterfuge.

By the later 1300s they had mounted cannon on ships that patrolled against pirates and used gunpowder-driven arrow launchers against enemy personnel and the rigging of enemy ships. Combined with skills in armoring ships, these techniques made the small Yi navy a formidable defense force.

Political Transformation in Japan, 1274–1500

Having secured Korea, the Mongols looked toward Japan, a target they could easily reach from Korea and a possible base for controlling China's southern coast. Their first thirty-thousand-man invasion force in 1274 included Mongol cavalry and archers and sailors from Korea and northeastern Asia. Its weaponry included light catapults and incendiary and explosive projectiles of Chinese manufacture. The Mongol forces landed successfully and decimated the Japanese cavalry, but a great storm on Hakata° Bay on the north side of Kyushu° Island (see Map 13.4) prevented the establishment of a beachhead and forced the Mongols to sail back to Korea.

The invasion deeply impressed Japan's leaders and hastened social and political changes that were already under way. Under the Kamakura° Shogunate established in 1185—another powerful family actually exercised control—the shogun, or military leader, distributed land and privileges to his followers. In return they paid him tribute and supplied him with soldiers. This stable, but decentralized, system depended on the balancing of power among regional warlords. Lords in the north and east of Japan's main island were remote from those in the south and west. Beyond devotion to the emperor and the shogun, little united them until the alien and terrifying Mongol threat materialized.

After the return of his fleet, Khubilai sent envoys to Japan demanding submission. Japanese leaders executed them and prepared for war. The shogun took steps to centralize his military government. The effect was to increase the influence of warlords from the south and west of Honshu (Japan's main island) and from the island of Kyushu, because this was where invasion seemed most likely, and they were the local commanders acting under the shogun's orders.

Military planners studied Mongol tactics and retrained and outfitted Japanese warriors for defense against advanced weaponry. Farm laborers drafted from all over the country constructed defensive fortifications at Hakata and other points along the Honshu and Kyushu coasts. This effort demanded, for the first time, a national system to move resources toward western points rather than toward the imperial or shogunal centers to the east.

The Mongols attacked in 1281. They brought 140,000 warriors, including many non-Mongols, as well as thousands of horses, in hundreds of ships. However, the wall the Japanese had built to cut off Hakata Bay from the mainland deprived the Mongol forces of a reliable landing point. Japanese swordsmen rowed out and boarded the Mongol ships lingering offshore. Their superb steel swords shocked the invaders. After a prolonged standoff, a typhoon struck and sank perhaps half of the Mongol ships. The remainder sailed away, never again to harass Japan. The Japanese gave thanks to the "wind of the Gods"—*kamikaze*°—for driving away the Mongols.

Nevertheless, the Mongol threat continued to influence Japanese development. Prior to his death in 1294,

Map 13.4 Korea and Japan, 1200–1500 The proximity of Korea and northern China to Japan gave the Mongols the opportunity to launch enormous fleets against the Kamakura Shogunate, which controlled most of the three islands (Honshu, Shikoku, and Kyushu) of central Japan.

Khubilai had in mind a third invasion. His successors did not carry through with it, but the shoguns did not know that the Mongols had given up the idea of conquering Japan. They rebuilt coastal defenses well into the fourteenth century, helping to consolidate the social position of Japan's warrior elite and stimulating the development of a national infrastructure for trade and communication. But the Kamakura Shogunate, based on regionally collected and regionally dispersed revenues, suffered financial strain in trying to pay for centralized road and defense systems.

Between 1333 and 1338 the emperor Go-Daigo broke the centuries-old tradition of imperial seclusion and aloofness from government and tried to reclaim power from the shoguns. This ignited a civil war that destroyed the Kamakura system. In 1338, with the Mongol

---

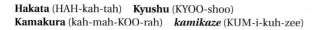

Hakata (HAH-kah-tah) **Kyushu** (KYOO-shoo)
Kamakura (kah-mah-KOO-rah) *kamikaze* (KUM-i-kuh-zee)

Painting by Sesshu   Sesshu Toyo (1420–1506) created a distinctive style of ink painting that contrasted with the Chinese styles that predominated earlier in Japan. Benefiting from growing Japanese commerce in the period of the Ashikaga Shogunate, he traveled to China as a youth and studied Chinese techniques. As he developed his style, a market for his art developed among merchant communities and other urban elites.   (Collection of the Tokyo National Museum)

threat waning, the **Ashikaga Shogunate°,** took control at the imperial center of Kyoto.

Provincial warlords enjoyed renewed independence. Around their imposing castles, they sponsored the development of market towns, religious institutions, and schools. The application of technologies imported in earlier periods, including water wheels, improved plows, and Champa rice, increased agricul-

tural productivity. Growing wealth and relative peace stimulated artistic creativity, mostly reflecting Zen Buddhist beliefs held by the warrior elite. In the simple elegance of architecture and gardens, in the contemplative landscapes of artists like Sesshu Toyo, and in the eerie, stylized performances of the No theater, the unified aesthetic code of Zen became established in the Ashikaga era.

Despite the technological advancement, artistic productivity, and rapid urbanization of this period,

---

Ashikaga (ah-shee-KAH-gah)

competition among warlords and their followers led to regional wars. By the later 1400s these conflicts resulted in the near destruction of the warlords. The great Onin War in 1477 left Kyoto devastated and the Ashikaga Shogunate a central government in name only. Ambitious but low-ranking warriors, some with links to trade with the continent, began to scramble for control of the provinces.

After the fall of the Yuan in 1368 Japan resumed trade with China and Korea. Japan exported raw materials as well as folding fans, invented in Japan during the period of isolation, and swords. Japan's primary imports from China were books and porcelain. The volatile political environment in Japan gave rise to partnerships between warlords and local merchants. All worked to strengthen their own towns and treasuries through overseas commerce or, sometimes, through piracy.

The Emergence of Vietnam, 1200–1500

Before the first Mongol attack in 1257, the states of Annam (northern Vietnam) and Champa (southern Vietnam) had clashed frequently. Annam (once called Dai Viet) looked toward China and had once been subject to the Tang. Chinese political ideas, social philosophies, dress, religion, and language heavily influenced its official culture. Champa related more closely to the trading networks of the Indian Ocean; its official culture was strongly influenced by Indian religion, language, architecture, and dress. Champa's relationship with China depended in part on how close its enemy Annam was to China at any particular time. During the Song period Annam was neither formally subject to China nor particularly threatening to Champa militarily, so Champa inaugurated a trade and tribute relationship with China that spread fast-ripening Champa rice throughout East Asia.

The Mongols exacted submission and tribute from both Annam and Champa until the fall of the Yuan Empire in 1368. Mongol political and military ambitions were mostly focused elsewhere, however, which minimized their impact on politics and culture. The two Vietnamese kingdoms soon resumed their warfare. When Annam moved its army to reinforce its southern border, Ming troops occupied the capital, Hanoi, and installed a puppet government. Almost thirty years elapsed before Annam regained independence and resumed a tributary status. By then the Ming were turning to meet Mongol challenges to their north. In a series of ruthless campaigns, Annam terminated Champa's independence, and by 1500 the ancestor of the modern state of Vietnam, still called Annam, had been born.

The new state still relied on Confucian bureaucratic government and an examination system, but some practices differed from those in China. The Vietnamese legal code, for example, preserved group landowning and decision making within the villages, as well as women's property rights. Both developments probably had roots in an early rural culture based on the growing of rice in wet paddies; by this time the Annamese considered them distinctive features of their own culture.

CONCLUSION

Despite their brutality and devastation, the Mongol conquests brought a degree of unity to the lands between China and Europe that had never before been known. Nomadic mobility and expertise in military technology contributed to communication across vast spaces and initially, at least, an often-callous disregard for the welfare of farmers, as manifested in oppressive tax policies. Trade, on the other hand, received active Mongol stimulation through the protection of routes and encouragement of industrial production. The Mongol regimes were characterized by an unprecedented openness, employing talented people irrespective of their linguistic, ethnic, or religious affiliations. As a consequence, the period of comparative Mongol unity, which lasted less than a century, saw a remarkable exchange of ideas, techniques, and products across the breadth of Eurasia. Chinese gunpowder spurred the development of Ottoman and European cannon; Muslim astronomers introduced new instruments and mathematical techniques to Chinese observatories.

However, rule over dozens of restive peoples could not endure. Where Mongol military enterprise reached its limit of expansion, it stimulated local aspirations for independence. Division and hostility among branches of Genghis Khan's family—between the Yuan in China and the Jagadai in Central Asia or between the Golden Horde in Russia and the Il-khans in Iran—provided opportunities for achieving these aspirations. The Russians gained freedom from Mongol domination in western Eurasia, and the general political disruption and uncertainty of the Mongol era assisted the emergence of the Lithuanian, Serbian, and Ottoman states. In the east, China, Korea, and Annam similarly found renewed political identity in the aftermath of Mongol rule, while Japan fought off two Mongol invasions and transformed its internal political and cultural identity in the process. In every case, the reality or threat of Mongol attack and domination encouraged centralization of government, improvement of military techniques, and renewed stress on local cultural identity. Thus, in retrospect, despite its traditional association with death and destruction, the Mongol period appears as a watershed establishing new connections between widespread parts of Eurasia and leading to the development of strong, assertive, and culturally creative regional states.

■ Key Terms

Mongols	tsar
Genghis Khan	Ottoman Empire
nomadism	Khubilai Khan
Yuan Empire	lama
bubonic plague	Beijing
Il-khan	Ming Empire
Golden Horde	Yongle
Timur	Zheng He
Rashid al-Din	Yi
Nasir al-Din Tusi	kamikaze
Alexander Nevskii	Ashikaga Shogunate

■ Suggested Reading

David Morgan's *The Mongols* (1986) affords an accessible introduction to the Mongol Empire. Morgan and Reuven Amitai-Preiss have also edited a valuable collection of essays, *The Mongol Empire and Its Legacy* (2000). Thomas T. Allsen has written more-specialized studies: *Mongol Imperialism: The Policies of the Grand Qan Möngke in China, Russia, and the Islamic Lands, 1251–1259* (1987); *Commodity and Exchange in the Mongol Empire: A Cultural History of Islamic Textiles* (2002); and *Culture and Conquest in Mongol Eurasia* (2001). Larry Moses and Stephen A. Halkovic, Jr., *Introduction to Mongolian History and Culture* (1985) links early and modern Mongol history and culture. Tim Severin, *In Search of Chinggis Khan* (1992), revisits the paths of Genghis's conquests.

William H. McNeill's *Plagues and Peoples* (1976) outlines the demographic effects of the Mongol conquests, and Joel Mokyr discusses their technological impact in *The Lever of Riches: Technological Creativity and Economic Progress* (1990). Connections between commercial development in Europe and Eurasian trade routes of the Mongol era within a broad theoretical framework inform Janet L. Abu-Lughod's *Before European Hegemony: The World System A.D. 1250–1350* (1989).

The only "primary" document relating to Genghis Khan, *Secret History of the Mongols,* has been reconstructed in Mongolian from Chinese script and has been variously produced in scholarly editions by Igor de Rachewilz and Francis Woodman Cleaves, among others. Paul Kahn produced a readable prose English paraphrase of the work in 1984. Biographies of Genghis Khan include Leo de Hartog, *Genghis Khan, Conqueror of the World* (1989); Michel Hoang, *Genghis Khan,* trans. Ingrid Canfield (1991); and Paul Ratchnevsky, *Genghis Khan: His Life and*

Legacy, trans. and ed. Thomas Nivison Haining (1992), which is most detailed on Genghis's childhood and youth.

On Central Asia after the conquests see S. A. M. Adshead, *Central Asia in World History* (1993). The most recent scholarly study of Timur is Beatrice Manz, *The Rise and Rule of Tamerlane* (1989).

David Christian, *A History of Russia, Central Asia, and Mongolia* (1998), and Charles Halperin, *Russia and the Golden Horde: The Mongol Impact on Medieval Russian History* (1987), provide one-volume accounts of the Mongols in Russia. A more detailed study is John Lister Illingworth Fennell, *The Crisis of Medieval Russia, 1200–1304* (1983). See also Donald Ostrowski, *Muscovy and the Mongols: Cross-Cultural Influences on the Steppe Frontier* (1998). Religion forms the topic of Devin DeWeese, *Islamization and Native Religion in the Golden Horde* (1994). *The Cambridge History of Iran*: Volume 5, *The Saljuq and Mongol Periods*, ed. J. A. Boyle (1968) and Volume 6, *The Timurid and Safavid Periods*, eds. Peter Jackson and Laurence Lockhart (rprt 2001) contain detailed scholarly articles covering the period in Iran and Central Asia.

Translations from the great historians of the Il-khan period include Juvaini, 'Ala al-Din 'Ata Malek, *The History of the World-Conqueror,* trans. John Andrew Boyle (1958), and Rashid al-Din, *The Successors of Genghis Khan,* trans. John Andrew Boyle (1971). The greatest traveler of the time was Ibn Battuta; see C. Defremery and B. R. Sanguinetti, eds., *The Travels of Ibn Battuta, A.D. 1325–1354,* translated with revisions and notes from the Arabic text by H. A. R. Gibb (1994), and Ross E. Dunn, *The Adventures of Ibn Battuta, a Muslim Traveler of the 14th Century* (1986).

On Europe's Mongol encounter see James Chambers, *The Devil's Horsemen: The Mongol Invasion of Europe* (1979). Christopher Dawson, ed., *Mission to Asia* (1955; reprinted 1981), assembles some of the best-known European travel accounts. See also Marco Polo, *The Travels of Marco Polo* (many editions), and the controversial skeptical appraisal of his account in Frances Wood, *Did Marco Polo Really Go to China?* (1995). Morris Rossabi's *Visitor from Xanadu* (1992) deals with the European travels of Rabban Sauma, a Christian Turk.

For China under the Mongols see Morris Rossabi's *Khubilai Khan: His Life and Times* (1988). On the Mongol impact on economy and technology in Yuan and Ming China see Mark Elvin, *The Pattern of the Chinese Past* (1973); Joseph Needham, *Science in Traditional China* (1981). Also see the important interpretation of Ming economic achievement in Andre Gunder Frank, *ReORIENT: Global Economy in the Asian Age* (1998).

The Cambridge History of China, Vol. 8, The Ming Dynasty 1368–1644, part 2, ed. Denis Twitchett and Frederick W. Mote (1998), provides scholarly essays about a little studied period. See also Albert Chan, *The Glory and Fall of the Ming Dynasty* (1982), and Edward L. Farmer, *Early Ming Government: The Evolution of Dual Capitals* (1976).

On early Ming literature see Lo Kuan-chung, *Three Kingdoms: A Historical Novel Attributed to Luo Guanzhong,* translated and annotated by Moss Roberts (1991); Pearl Buck's translation of

Water Margin, entitled *All Men Are Brothers,* 2 vols. (1933), and a later translation by J. H. Jackson, *Water Margin, Written by Shih Nai-an* (1937); and Shelley Hsüeh-lun Chang, *History and Legend: Ideas and Images in the Ming Historical Novels* (1990).

Joseph R. Levenson, ed., *European Expansion and the Counter-Example of Asia, 1300–1600* (1967), recounts the Zheng He expeditions. Philip Snow's *The Star Raft* (1988) contains more recent scholarship, while Louise Levathes, *When China Ruled the Seas* (1993) makes for lively reading.

For a general history of Korea in this period see Andrew C. Nahm, *Introduction to Korean History and Culture* (1993); Ki-Baik Lee, *A New History of Korea* (1984); and William E. Henthorn, *Korea: The Mongol Invasions* (1963). On a more specialized topic see Joseph Needham et al., *The Hall of Heavenly Records: Korean Astronomical Instruments and Clocks, 1380–1780* (1986).

For a collection of up-to-date scholarly essays on Japan, see Kozo Yamamura, ed., *The Cambridge History of Japan, Vol. 3: Medieval Japan* (1990). See also John W. Hall and Toyoda Takeshi, eds., *Japan in the Muromachi Age* (1977); H. Paul Varley, trans., *The Onin War: History of Its Origins and Background with a Selective Translation of the Chronicle of Onin* (1967); Yamada Nakaba, *Ghenko, the Mongol Invasion of Japan, with an Introduction by Lord Armstrong* (1916); and the novel *Fûtô* by Inoue Yasushi, translated by James T. Araki as *Wind and Waves* (1989).

◼ Notes

1. Quotation adapted from Desmond Martin, *Chingis Khan and His Conquest of North China* (Baltimore: The John Hopkins Press, 1950), 303.

14

Tropical Africa and Asia, 1200–1500

East African Pastoralists Herding large and small livestock has long been a way of life in drier parts of the tropics.

CHAPTER OUTLINE

Tropical Lands and Peoples

New Islamic Empires

Indian Ocean Trade

Social and Cultural Change

DIVERSITY AND DOMINANCE: Personal Styles of Rule in India and Mali

ENVIRONMENT AND TECHNOLOGY: The Indian Ocean Dhow

Sultan Abu Bakr° customarily offered his personal hospitality to every distinguished visitor to his city of Mogadishu, an Indian Ocean port in northeast Africa. In 1331 he provided food and lodging for Muhammad ibn Abdullah ibn Battuta° (1304–1369), a young Muslim scholar from Morocco who had set out to explore the Islamic world. Before beginning his tour of the trading cities of the Red Sea and East Africa, Ibn Battuta had completed a pilgrimage to Mecca and had traveled throughout the Middle East. Subsequent travels took him through Central Asia and India, China and Southeast Asia, Muslim Spain, and sub-Saharan West Africa. Logging some 75,000 miles (120,000 kilometers) in twenty-nine years, Ibn Battuta became the most widely traveled man of his times. For this reason the journals he wrote about his travels provide valuable information about these lands.

Other Muslim princes and merchants welcomed Ibn Battuta as graciously as did the ruler of Mogadishu. Hospitality was a noble virtue among Muslims, and they ignored visitors' physical and cultural differences. Although the Moroccan traveler noted that Sultan Abu Bakr had skin darker than his own and spoke a different native language (Somali), that was of little consequence. They were brothers in faith when they prayed together at Friday services in the Mogadishu mosque, where the sultan greeted his foreign guest in Arabic, the common language of the Islamic world: "You are heartily welcome, and you have honored our land and given us pleasure." When Sultan Abu Bakr and his jurists heard cases after the mosque service, they decided them on the basis of the law code familiar in all the lands of Islam.

Islam was not the only thing that united the diverse peoples of Africa and southern Asia. They also shared a tropical environment itself and a network of land and sea trade routes. The variations in tropical environments led societies to develop different specialties, which stimulated trade among them. Tropical winds governed the trading patterns of the Indian Ocean. Older than Islam, these routes were important for spreading beliefs and technologies as well as goods. Ibn Battuta made his way down the coast of East Africa in merchants' ships and joined their camel caravans across the Sahara to West Africa. His path to India followed overland trade routes, and a merchant ship carried him on to China.

As you read this chapter, ask yourself the following questions:

- How did environmental differences shape cultural differences in tropical Africa and Asia?

- How did cultural and ecological differences promote trade in specialized goods from one place to another?

- How did trade and other contacts promote state growth and the spread of Islam?

TROPICAL LANDS AND PEOPLES

To obtain food, the people who inhabited the tropical regions of Africa and Asia used methods that had proved successful during generations of experimentation, whether at the desert's edge, in grasslands, or in tropical rain forests. Much of their success lay in learning how to blend human activities with the natural order, but their ability to modify the environment to suit their needs was also evident in irrigation works and mining.

The Tropical Environment

Because of the angle of earth's axis, the sun's rays warm the **tropics** year-round. The equator marks the center of the tropical zone, and the Tropic of Cancer and Tropic of Capricorn mark its outer limits. As Map 14.1 shows, Africa lies almost entirely within the tropics, as do southern Arabia, most of India, and all of the Southeast Asian mainland and islands.

Lacking the hot and cold seasons of temperate lands, the Afro-Asian tropics have their own cycle of rainy and dry seasons caused by changes in wind patterns across the surrounding oceans. Winds from a permanent high-pressure air mass over the South Atlantic deliver heavy rainfall to the western coast of Africa during much of the year. In December and January large

---

Abu Bakr (a-BOO BAK-uhr)   **Ibn Battuta** (IB-uhn ba-TOO-tuh)

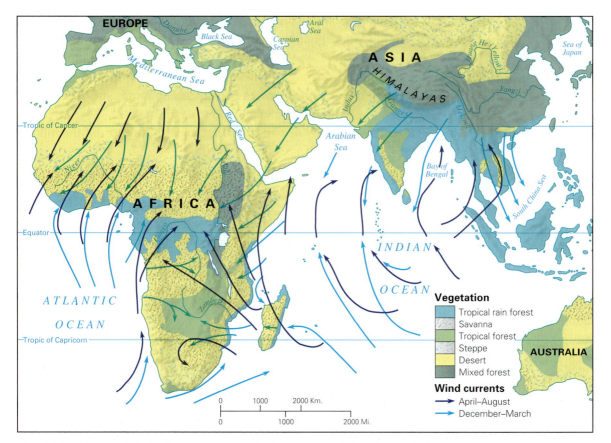

Map 14.1   Africa and the Indian Ocean Basin: Physical Characteristics   Seasonal wind patterns control rainfall in the tropics and produce the different tropical vegetation zones to which human societies have adapted over thousands of years. The wind patterns also dominated sea travel in the Indian Ocean.

high-pressure zones over northern Africa and Arabia produce a southward movement of dry air that limits the inland penetration of the moist ocean winds.

In the lands around the Indian Ocean the rainy and dry seasons reflect the influence of alternating winds known as **monsoons.** A gigantic high-pressure zone over the Himalaya° Mountains that is at its peak from December to March produces a strong southward air movement (the northeast monsoon) in the western Indian Ocean. This is southern Asia's dry season. Between April and August a low-pressure zone over India creates a northward movement of air from across the ocean (the southwest monsoon) that brings southern Asia its heaviest rains. This is the wet season.

Areas with the heaviest rainfall—coastal West Africa and west-central Africa, Southeast Asia, and much of India—have dense rain forests. Lighter rains produce other

tropical forests. The English word *jungle* comes from an Indian word for the tangled undergrowth in the tropical forests that once covered most of southern India.

Other parts of the tropics rarely see rain at all. The Sahara, the world's largest desert, stretches across northern Africa. This arid zone continues eastward across Arabia and into northwest India. Another desert zone occupies southwestern Africa. Most of the people of tropical India and Africa live between the deserts and the rain forests in lands that are favored with moderate amounts of moisture during the rainy seasons. These lands range from fairly wet woodlands to the much drier grasslands characteristic of much of East Africa.

Altitude produces other climatic changes. Thin atmospheres at high altitudes hold less heat than atmospheres at lower elevations. Snow covers some of the volcanic mountains of eastern Africa all or part of the year. The snowcapped Himalayas rise so high that they block cold air from moving south, thus giving northern

---

Himalaya (him-uh-LAY-uh)

C H R O N O L O G Y	
Tropical Africa	**Tropical Asia**
1200	
1230s Mali Empire founded	1206 Delhi Sultanate founded in India
1300	
1270 Solomonic dynasty in Ethiopia founded	1298 Delhi Sultanate annexes Gujarat
1324–1325 Mansa Musa's pilgrimage to Mecca	
1400	
1400s Great Zimbabwe at its peak	1398 Timur sacks Delhi, Delhi Sultanate declines
1433 Tuareg retake Timbuktu, Mali declines	
1500	
	1500 Port of Malacca at its peak

India a more tropical climate than its latitude would suggest. The many plateaus of inland Africa and the Deccan° Plateau of central India also make these regions somewhat cooler than the coastal plains.

The mighty rivers that rise in these mountains and plateaus redistribute water far from where it falls. Heavy rains in the highlands of Central Africa and Ethiopia supply the Nile's annual floods that make Egypt bloom in the desert. On its long route to the Atlantic, the Niger River of West Africa arcs northward to the Sahara's edge, providing waters to the trading cities along its banks. In like fashion, the Indus River provides nourishing waters from the Himalayas to arid northwest India. The Ganges° and its tributaries provide valuable moisture to northeastern India during the dry season. Mainland Southeast Asia's great rivers, such as the Mekong, are similarly valuable.

Human Ecosystems

Thinkers in temperate lands once imagined that surviving in the year-round warmth of the tropics was simply a matter of picking wild fruit off trees. In fact, mastering the tropics' many different environments was a long and difficult struggle. A careful observer touring the tropics in 1200 would have noticed that the many differences in societies derived from their particular ecosystems—that is, how people made use of the plants, animals, and other resources of their physical environments.

Domesticated plants and animals had been commonplace long before 1200, but people in some environments found it preferable to rely primarily on wild food that they obtained by hunting, fishing, and gathering. The small size of the ancient Pygmy° people in the dense forests of Central Africa permitted them to pursue their prey through dense undergrowth. Hunting also continued as a way of life in the upper altitudes of the Himalayas and in some desert environments. According to a Portuguese expedition in 1497, the people along the arid coast of southwestern Africa were well fed from a diet of "the flesh of seals, whales, and gazelles, and the roots of wild plants." Fishing was common along all the major lakes and rivers as well as in the oceans. The boating skills of ocean fishermen in East Africa, India, and Southeast Asia often led them to engage in ocean trade.

Tending herds of domesticated animals was common in areas too arid for agriculture. Unencumbered by bulky personal possessions and elaborate dwellings, they used their knowledge of local water and rain patterns to find adequate grazing for their animals in all but the severest droughts. Pastoralists consumed milk from their herds and traded hides and meat to neighboring farmers for grain and vegetables. The arid and semiarid lands of northeastern Africa and Arabia were home to the world's largest concentration of pastoralists. Like Ibn Battuta's host at Mogadishu, some Somali were urban dwellers, but most grazed their herds of goats and camels in the desert hinterland of the Horn of Africa. The western Sahara sustained

---

Deccan (de-KAN) **Ganges** (GAN-jeez)   **Pygmy** (PIG-mee)

herds of sheep and camels belonging to the Tuareg°, whose intimate knowledge of the desert also made them invaluable as guides to caravans, such as the one **Ibn Battuta** joined on the two-month journey across the desert. Along the Sahara's southern edge the cattle-herding Fulani° people gradually extended their range during this period. By 1500 they had spread throughout the western and central Sudan. Pastoralists in southern Africa sold meat to early Portuguese visitors.

By 1200 most Africans had been making their livelihood through agricultural for many centuries. Favorable soils and rainfall made farming even more dominant in South and Southeast Asia. High yields from intensive cultivation supported dense populations in Asia. In 1200 over 100 million people may have lived in South and Southeast Asia, more than four-fifths of them on the fertile Indian mainland. Though a little less than the population of China, this was triple the number of people living in all of Africa at that time and nearly double the number of people in Europe.

India's lush vegetation led one Middle Eastern writer to call it "the most agreeable abode on earth . . . its delightful plains resemble the garden of Paradise."[1] Rice cultivation dominated in the fertile Ganges plain of northeast India, in mainland Southeast Asia, and in southern China. Farmers in drier areas grew grains—such as wheat, sorghum, millet, and ensete—and legumes such as peas and beans, whose ripening cycle matched the pattern of the rainy and dry seasons. Tubers and tree crops characterized farming in rain-forest clearings.

Many useful domesticated plants and animals spread around the tropics. By 1200 Bantu-speaking farmers (see Chapter 8) had introduced grains and tubers from West Africa throughout the southern half of the continent. Bananas, brought to southern Africa centuries earlier by mariners from Southeast Asia, had become the staple food for people farming the rich soils around the Great Lakes of East Africa. Yams and cocoyams of Asian origin had spread across equatorial Africa. Asian cattle breeds grazed contentedly in pastures throughout Africa, and coffee of Ethiopian origin would shortly become a common drink in the Middle East.

Water Systems and Irrigation

In most parts of sub-Saharan Africa and many parts of Southeast Asia until quite recent times, the basic form of cultivation was extensive rather than intensive. Instead of enriching fields with manure and vegetable compost so they could be cultivated year after year, farmers abandoned fields every few years when the natural fertility of the soil was exhausted, and they cleared new fields. Ashes from the brush, grasses, and tree limbs that were cut down and burned gave the new fields a significant boost in fertility. Even though a great deal of work was needed to clear the fields initially, modern research suggests that such shifting cultivation was an efficient use of labor in areas where soils were not naturally rich in nutrients.

In other parts of the tropics, environmental necessity and population pressure led to the adoption of more intensive forms of agriculture. A rare area of intensive cultivation in sub-Saharan Africa was the inland delta of the Niger River, where large crops of rice were grown using the river's naturally fertilizing annual floods. The rice was probably sold to the trading cities along the Niger bend.

The uneven distribution of rainfall during the year was one of the great challenges faced by many Asian farmers. Unlike pastoralists who could move their herds to the water, they had to find ways of moving the water to their crops. Farmers in Vietnam, Java, Malaya, and Burma constructed special water-control systems to irrigate their terraced rice paddies. Villagers in southeast India built a series of stone and earthen dams across rivers to store water for gradual release through elaborate irrigation canals. Over many generations these canals were extended to irrigate more and more land. Although the dams and channels covered large areas, they were relatively simple structures that local people could keep working by routine maintenance. Other water-storage and irrigation systems were constructed in other parts of India in this period.

As had been true since the days of the first river-valley civilizations (see Chapter 2), the largest irrigation systems in the tropics were government public works projects. The **Delhi° Sultanate** (1206–1526) introduced extensive new water-control systems in northern India. Ibn Battuta commented appreciatively on one reservoir that supplied the city of Delhi with water. He reported that enterprising farmers planted sugar cane, cucumbers, and melons along the reservoir's rim as the water level fell during the dry season. A sultan in the fourteenth century built a network of irrigation canals in the Ganges plain that were not surpassed in size until the nineteenth century. These irrigation systems made it possible to grow crops throughout the year.

Since the tenth century the Indian Ocean island of Ceylon (modern Sri Lanka°) had been home to the greatest concentration of irrigation reservoirs and canals

---

Tuareg (TWAH-reg)   **Fulani** (foo-LAH-nee)

Delhi (DEL-ee)   **Sri Lanka** (sree LAHNG-kuh)

in the world. These facilities enabled the powerful Sinhalese° kingdom in arid northern Ceylon to support a large population. There was another impressive waterworks in Southeast Asia, where a system of reservoirs and canals served Cambodia's capital city Angkor°.

These complex systems were vulnerable to disruption. Between 1250 and 1400 the irrigation complex in Ceylon fell into ruin when invaders from South India disrupted the Sinhalese government. The population of Ceylon then suffered from the effects of malaria, a tropical disease spread by mosquitoes breeding in the irrigation canals. The great Cambodian system fell into ruin in the fifteenth century when the government that maintained it collapsed. Neither system was ever rebuilt.

The vulnerability of complex irrigation systems built by powerful governments suggests an instructive contrast. Although village-based irrigation systems could be damaged by invasion and natural calamity, they usually bounced back because they were the product of local initiative, not centralized direction, and they depended on simpler technologies.

Mineral Resources

Throughout the tropics people mined and refined metal-rich ores, which skilled metalworkers turned into tools, weapons, and decorative objects. The more valuable metals, copper and gold, became important in long-distance trade.

Iron was the most abundant and useful of the metals worked in the tropics. Farmers depended on iron hoes, axes, and knives to clear and cultivate their fields and to open up parts of the rain forests of coastal West Africa and Southeast Asia for farming. Iron-tipped spears and arrows improved hunting success. Needles facilitated making clothes and leather goods; nails held timbers together. Indian metalsmiths were renowned for making strong and beautiful swords. In Africa the ability of iron smelters and blacksmiths to transform metal fostered a belief in their magical powers.

Copper and its alloys were of special importance in Africa. In the Copperbelt of southeastern Africa, the refined metal was cast into large X-shaped ingots (metal castings). Local coppersmiths worked these copper ingots into wire and decorative objects. Ibn Battuta described a town in the western Sudan that produced two sizes of copper bars that were used as a currency in place of coins. Skilled artisans in West Africa cast copper and brass (an alloy of copper and zinc) statues and heads that are considered among the masterpieces of world

King and Queen of Ife This copper-alloy work shows the royal couple of the Yoruba kingdom of Ife, the oldest and most sacred of the Yoruba kingdoms of southwestern Nigeria. The casting dates to the period between 1100 and 1500, except for the reconstruction of the male's face, the original of which shattered in 1957 when the road builder who found it accidentally struck it with his pick.   (Andre Held, Switzerland)

art. These works were made by the "lost-wax" method, in which molten metal melts a thin layer of wax sandwiched between clay forms, replacing the "lost" wax with hard metal.

Africans exported large quantities of gold across the Sahara, the Red Sea, and the Indian Ocean. Some gold came from stream beds along the upper Niger River and farther south in modern Ghana°. In the hills south of the

---

Sinhalese (sin-huh-LEEZ)   **Angkor** (ANG-kor)

Ghana (GAH-nuh)

Zambezi° River (in modern Zimbabwe°) archaeologists have discovered thousands of mine shafts, dating from 1200, that were sunk up to 100 feet (30 meters) into the ground to get at gold ores. Although panning for gold remained important in the streams descending from the mountains of northern India, the gold and silver mines in India seem to have been exhausted by this period. For that reason, Indians imported considerable quantities of gold from Southeast Asia and Africa for jewelry and temple decoration.

Although they are rarely given credit for it, ordinary farmers, fishermen, herders, metalworkers, and others made possible the rise of powerful states and profitable commercial systems. Caravans could not have crossed the Sahara without the skilled guidance of desert pastoralists. The seafaring skills of the coastal fishermen underlay the trade of the Indian Ocean. Cities and empires rested on the food, labors, and taxes of these unsung heroes.

NEW ISLAMIC EMPIRES

The empires of Mali in West Africa and Delhi in South Asia were the largest and richest tropical states of the period between 1200 and 1500. Both utilized Islamic administrative and military systems introduced from the Islamic heartland, but in other ways these two Muslim sultanates were very different. **Mali** was founded by an indigenous African dynasty that had earlier adopted Islam through the peaceful influence of Muslim merchants and scholars. In contrast, the Delhi Sultanate was founded and ruled by invading Turkish and Afghan Muslims. Mali's wealth depended heavily on its participation in the trans-Saharan trade, but long-distance trade played only a minor role in Delhi.

Mali in the Western Sudan

The consolidation of the Middle East and North Africa under Muslim rule during the seventh and eighth centuries (see Chapter 9) greatly stimulated exchanges along the routes that crossed the Sahara. In the centuries that followed, the faith of Muhammad gradually spread to the lands south of the desert, which the Arabs called the *bilad al-sudan*°, "land of the blacks."

The role of force in spreading Islam south of the Sahara was limited. Muslim Berbers invading out of the

desert in 1076 caused the collapse of Ghana, the empire that preceded Mali in the western Sudan (see Chapter 8), but their conquest did little to spread Islam. To the east, the Muslim attacks that destroyed the Christian Nubian kingdoms on the upper Nile in the late thirteenth century opened that area to Muslim influences, but Christian Ethiopia successfully withstood Muslim advances. Instead, the usual pattern for the spread of Islam south of the Sahara was through gradual and peaceful conversion. The expansion of commercial contacts in the western Sudan and on the East African coast greatly promoted the process of conversion. African converts found the teachings of Islam meaningful, and rulers and merchants found that the administrative, legal, and economic aspects of Islamic traditions suited their interests. The first sub-Saharan African ruler to adopt the new faith was in Takrur° in the far western Sudan, about 1030.

Shortly after 1200 Takrur expanded in importance under King Sumanguru°. Then in about 1240 Sundiata°, the upstart leader of the Malinke° people, handed Sumanguru a major defeat. Even though both leaders were Muslims, the Malinke epic sagas recall their battles as the clash of two powerful magicians, suggesting how much older beliefs shaped popular thought. The sagas say that Sumanguru was able to appear and disappear at will, assume dozens of shapes, and catch arrows in midflight. Sundiata defeated Sumanguru's much larger forces through superior military maneuvers and by successfully wounding his adversary with a special arrow that robbed him of his magical powers. This victory was followed by others that created Sundiata's Mali empire (see Map 14.2).

Like Ghana before it, Mali depended on a well-developed agricultural base and control of the lucrative regional and trans-Saharan trade routes. But Mali differed from Ghana in two ways. First, it was much larger. Mali controlled not only the core trading area of the upper Niger but the gold fields of the Niger headwaters to the southwest as well. Second, from the beginning its rulers were Muslims who fostered the spread of Islam among the political and trading elite of the empire. Control of the important gold and copper trades and contacts with North African Muslim traders gave Mali and its rulers unprecedented prosperity. The pilgrimage to Mecca of the ruler **Mansa Kankan Musa**° (r. 1312–1337), in fulfillment of his personal duty as a Muslim, also gave him an opportunity to display Mali's exceptional wealth. As befitted a powerful ruler, he

---

Zambezi (zam-BEE-zee)   Zimbabwe (zim-BAHB-way)
bilad al-sudan (bih-LAD uhs–soo-DAN)

Takrur (TAHK-roor)   Sumanguru (soo-muhn-GOO-roo)
Sundiata (soon-JAH-tuh)   Malinke (muh-LING-kay)
Mansa Kankan Musa (MAHN-suh KAHN-kahn MOO-suh)

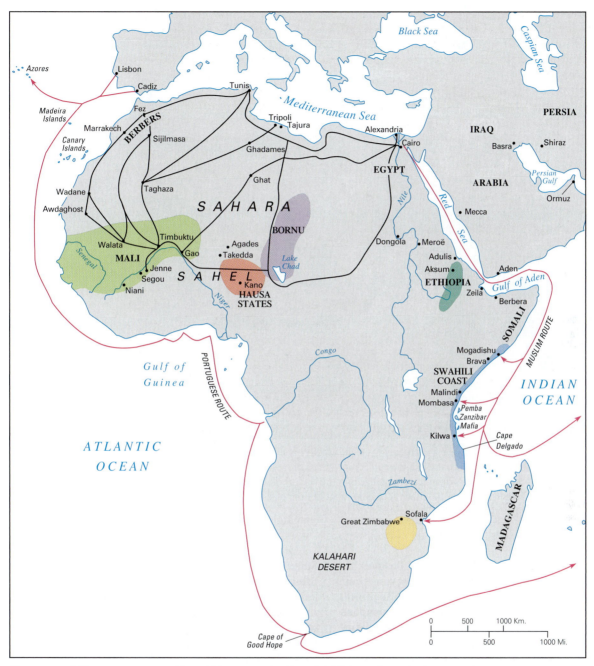

Map 14.2   Africa, 1200–1500   Many African states had beneficial links to the trade that crossed the Sahara and the Indian Ocean. Before 1500, sub-Saharan Africa's external ties were primarily with the Islamic world.

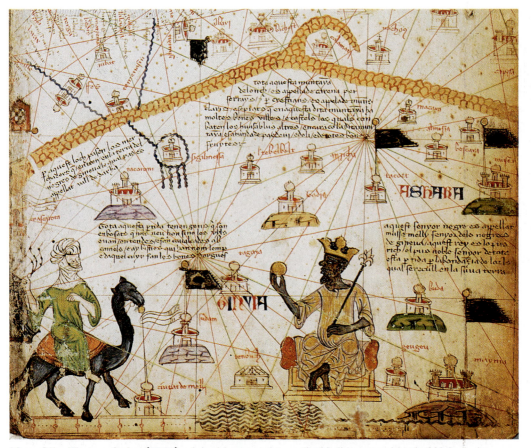

Map of the Western Sudan (1375)   A Jewish geographer on the Mediterranean island of Majorca drew this lavish map in 1375, incorporating all that was known in Europe about the rest of the world. This portion of the Catalan Atlas shows a North African trader approaching the king of Mali, who holds a gold nugget in one hand and a golden scepter in the other. A caption identifies the black ruler as Mansa Musa, "the richest and noblest king in all the land."   (Bibliothèque Nationale de France)

departed in 1324 with a large entourage. Besides his senior wife and 500 of her ladies in waiting and their slaves, according to one account, there were also 60,000 porters and a vast caravan of camels carrying supplies and provisions. For purchases and gifts he took eighty packages of gold each weighing 122 ounces (3.8 kilograms). In addition, 500 slaves each carried a golden staff. Mansa Musa was so lavish with his gifts when the entourage passed through Cairo that the value of gold there remained depressed for years.

After his return from the pilgrimage in 1325, Mansa Musa was eager to promote the religious and cultural influence of Islam in his empire. He built new mosques and opened Quranic schools in the cities along the Niger bend. When Ibn Battuta visited Mali from 1352 to 1354, during the reign of Mansa Musa's successor Mansa

Suleiman° (r. 1341–1360), he praised the Malians for their faithful recitation of Islamic prayers and for their zeal in teaching children the Quran.

Ibn Battuta also had high praise for Mali's government. He reported that "complete and general safety" prevailed in the vast territories ruled by Suleiman and that foreign travelers had no reason to fear being robbed by thieves or having their goods confiscated if they died. (For Ibn Battuta's account of the sultan's court and his subjects' respect see Diversity and Dominance: Personal Styles of Rule in India and Mali.)

Two centuries after Sundiata founded the empire, Mali began to disintegrate. When Mansa Suleiman's successors proved to be less able rulers, rebellions broke out

---

Mansa Suleiman (MAHN-suh SOO-lay-mahn)

among the diverse peoples who had been subjected to Malinke rule. Avid for Mali's wealth, other groups attacked from without. The desert Tuareg retook their city of Timbuktu° in 1433. By 1500 the rulers of Mali had dominion over little more than the Malinke heartland.

The cities of the upper Niger survived Mali's collapse, but some of the western Sudan's former trade and intellectual life moved east to other African states in the central Sudan. Shortly after 1450 the rulers of several of the Hausa city-states adopted Islam as their official religion. The Hausa states were also able to increase their importance as manufacturing and trading centers, becoming famous for their cotton textiles and leatherworking. Also expanding in the late fifteenth century was the central Sudanic state of Kanem-Bornu°. It was descended from the ancient kingdom of Kanem, whose rulers had accepted Islam in about 1085. At its peak about 1250, Kanem had absorbed the state of Bornu south and west of Lake Chad and gained control of important trade routes crossing the Sahara. As Kanem-Bornu's armies conquered new territories in the late fifteenth century, they also spread the rule of Islam.

Salt Making in the Central Sahara   For many centuries, people have extracted salt from the saline soils of places like Tegguida N'Tisent. Spring water is poured into shallow pits to dissolve the salt. The desert sun soon evaporates the water, leaving pure salt behind.   (Afrique Photo, Cliché Naud, Paris)

The Delhi Sultanate in India

The arrival of Islam in India was more violent than in West Africa. Having long before lost the defensive unity of the Gupta Empire (see Chapter 7), the divided states of northwest India were subject to raids by Afghan warlords beginning in the early eleventh century. Motivated by a wish to spread their Islamic faith and by a desire for plunder, the raiders looted Hindu and Buddhist temples of their gold and jewels, kidnapped women for their harems, and slew Indian defenders by the thousands.

In the last decades of the twelfth century a new Turkish dynasty mounted a furious assault that succeeded in capturing the important northern Indian cities of Lahore and Delhi. The Muslim warriors could fire powerful crossbows from the backs of their galloping horses thanks to the use of iron stirrups. One partisan Muslim chronicler recorded, "The city [Delhi] and its vicinity was freed from idols and idol-worship, and in the sanctuaries of the images of the [Hindu] Gods, mosques were raised by the worshippers of one God."[2] The invaders' strength was bolstered by a ready supply of Turkish adventurers from Central Asia eager to follow individual leaders and by the unifying force of their common religious faith. Although Indians fought back bravely, their small states,

often at war with one another, were unable to present an effective united front.

Between 1206 and 1236, the Muslim invaders extended their rule over the Hindu princes and chiefs in much of northern India. Sultan Iltutmish° (r. 1211–1236) consolidated the conquest of northern India in a series of military expeditions that made his empire the largest state in India (see Map 14.3). He also secured official recognition of the Delhi Sultanate as a Muslim state by the caliph of Baghdad. Although the looting and destruction of temples, enslavement, and massacres continued, especially on the frontiers of the empire, the Muslim invaders gradually underwent a transformation from brutal conquerors to more benign rulers. Muslim commanders accorded protection to the conquered, freeing them from persecution in return for payment of a special tax. Yet Hindus never forgot the intolerance and destruction of their first contacts with the invaders.

Timbuktu (tim-buk-TOO)
Kanem-Bornu (KAH-nuhm–BOR-noo)

Iltutmish (il-TOOT-mish)

DIVERSITY AND DOMINANCE

PERSONAL STYLES OF RULE IN INDIA AND MALI

Ibn Battuta wrote vivid descriptions of the powerful men who dominated the Muslim states he visited. Although his accounts are explicitly about the rulers, they also raise important issues about their relations with their subjects. The following account of Sultan Muhammad ibn Tughluq of Delhi may be read as a treatise on the rights and duties of rulers and ways in which individual personalities shaped diverse governing styles.

Muhammad is a man who, above all others, is fond of making presents and shedding blood. There may always be seen at his gate some poor person becoming rich, or some living one condemned to death. His generous and brave actions, and his cruel and violent deeds, have obtained notoriety among the people. In spite of this, he is the most humble of men, and the one who exhibits the greatest equity. The ceremonies of religion are dear to his ears, and he is very severe in respect of prayer and the punishment which follows its neglect. . . .

When drought prevailed throughout India and Sind, . . . the Sultan gave orders that provisions for six months should be supplied to all the inhabitants of Delhi from the royal granaries. . . . The officers of justice made registers of the people of the different streets, and these being sent up, each person received sufficient provisions to last him for six months.

The Sultan, notwithstanding all I have said about his humility, his justice, his kindness to the poor, and his boundless generosity, was much given to bloodshed. It rarely happened that the corpse of some one who had been killed was not seen at the gate of his palace. I have often seen men killed and their bodies left there. One day I went to his palace and my horse shied. I looked before me, and I saw a white heap on the ground, and when I asked what it was, one of my companions said it was the trunk of a man cut into three pieces. The sovereign punished little faults like great ones, and spared neither the learned, the religious, nor the noble. Every day hundreds of individuals were brought chained into his hall of audience; their hands tied to their necks and their feet bound together. Some of them were killed, and others were tortured, or well beaten . . . .

The Sultan has a brother named Masud Khan, [who] was one of the handsomest fellows I have even seen. The king suspected him of intending to rebel, so he questioned him, and, under fear of the torture, Masud confessed the charge. Indeed, every one who denies charges of this nature, which the Sultan brings against him, is put to the torture, and most people prefer death to being tortured. The Sultan had his brother's head cut off in the palace, and the corpse, according to custom, was left neglected for three days in the same place. The mother of Masud had been stoned two years before in the same place on a charge of debauchery or adultery. . . .

One of the most serious charges against this Sultan is that he forced all the inhabitants of Delhi to leave their homes. [After] the people of Delhi wrote letters full of insults and invectives against [him,] the Sultan . . . decided to ruin Delhi, so he purchased all the houses and inns from the inhabitants, paid them the price, and then ordered them to remove to Daulatabad. . . .

The greater part of the inhabitants departed, but [h]is slaves found two men in the streets: one was paralyzed, the other blind. They were brought before the sovereign, who ordered the paralytic to be shot away from a *manjanik* [catapult], and the blind man to be dragged from Delhi to Daulatabad, a journey of forty days' distance. The poor wretch fell to pieces during the journey, and only one of his legs reached Daulatabad. All of the inhabitants of Delhi left; they abandoned their baggage and their merchandize, and the city remained a perfect desert.

A person in whom I felt confidence assured me that the Sultan mounted one evening upon the roof of his palace, and, casting his eyes over the city of Delhi, in which there was neither fire, smoke, nor light, he said, "Now my heart is satisfied, and my feelings are appeased." . . . When we entered this capital, we found it in the state which has been described. It was empty, abandoned, and had but a small population.

In his description of Mansa Suleiman of Mali in 1353, Ibn Battuta places less emphasis on personality, a difference that may only be due to the fact that he had little personal contact with him. He stresses the huge social distance between the ruler and the ruled, between the master and the slave, and goes on to tell more of the ways in which Islam had altered life in Mali's cities as well as complaining about customs that the introduction of Islam had not changed.

The sultan of Mali is *Mansa* Suleiman, *mansa* meaning sultan, and Suleiman being his proper name. He is miserly, not a man from which one might hope for a rich present. It happened that I spent these two months without seeing him on account of my illness. Later on he held a banquet . . . to which the commanders, doctors, *qadi* and preacher were invited, and I went along with them. . . .

On certain days the sultan holds audiences in the palace yard, where there is a platform under a tree . . . carpeted with silk, [over which] is raised the umbrella, . . . surmounted by a bird in gold, about the size of a falcon. The sultan comes out of a door in a corner of the palace, carrying a bow in his hand and a quiver on his back. On his head he has a golden skull-cap, bound with a gold band which has narrow ends shaped like knives, more than a span in length. His usual dress is a velvety red tunic, made of the European fabrics called *mutanfas*. The sultan is preceded by his musicians, who carry gold and silver [two-stringed guitars], and behind him come three hundred armed slaves. He walks in a leisurely fashion, affecting a very slow movement, and even stops and looks round the assembly, then ascends [the platform] in the sedate manner of a preacher ascending a mosque-pulpit. As he takes his seat, the drums, trumpets, and bugles are sounded. Three slaves go at a run to summon the sovereign's deputy and the military commanders, who enter and sit down. . . .

The blacks are of all people the most submissive to their king and the most abject in their behavior before him. They swear by his name, saying *Mansa Suleiman ki* [by Mansa Suleiman's law]. If he summons any of them while he is holding an audience in his pavilion, the person summoned takes off his clothes and puts on worn garments, removes his turban and dons a dirty skullcap and enters with his garments and trousers raised knee-high. He goes forward in an attitude of humility and dejection, and knocks the ground hard with his elbows, then stands with bowed head and bent back listening to what he says. If anyone addresses the king and receives a reply from him, he uncovers his back and throws dust over his head and back, for all the world like a bather splashing himself with water. I used to wonder how it was that they did not blind themselves.

Among the admirable qualities of these people, the following are to be noted:

1. The small number of acts of injustice that one finds there; for the blacks are of all people those who most abhor injustice. The sultan pardons no one who is guilty of it.
2. The complete and general safety one enjoys throughout the land. The traveller has no more reason than the man who stays at home to fear brigands, thieves, or ravishers.
3. The blacks do not confiscate the goods of white men [i.e., North Africans and the Middle Easterners] who die in their country, not even when these consist of big treasure, They deposit them, on the contrary, with a man of confidence among the whites until those who have a right to the goods present themselves and take possession.
4. They make all their prayers punctually; they assiduously attend their meetings of the faithful, and punish their children if these should fail in this. On Fridays, anyone who is late at the mosque will find nowhere to pray, the crowd is so great. . . .
5. The blacks wear fine white garments on Fridays. If by chance a man has no more than one shirt or a soiled tunic, at least he washes it before putting it on to go to public prayer.
6. They zealously learn the Koran by heart. Those children who are neglectful in this are put in chains until they have memorized the Koran by heart. . . .

But these people have some deplorable customs, as for example:

1. Women servants, slave women, and young girls go about quite naked, not even covering their sexual parts. I saw many like this during Ramadan. . . .
2. Women go naked in the sultan's presence, too, without even a veil; his daughters also go about naked. On the twenty-seventh night of Ramadan I saw about a hundred women slaves coming out of the sultan's palace with food and they were naked. Two daughters of the sultan were with them, and these had no veil either, although they had big breasts.
3. The blacks throw dust and cinders on their heads as a sign of good manners and respect.
4. They have buffoons who appear before the sultan when his poets are reciting their praise songs.
5. And then a good number of the blacks eat the flesh of dogs and donkeys.

QUESTIONS FOR ANALYSIS

1. How would the actions of these rulers have enhanced their authority? To what extent do their actions reflect Islamic influences?
2. Although Ibn Battuta tells what the rulers did, can you imagine how one of their subjects would have described his or her perception of the same events and customs?
3. Which parts of Ibn Battuta's descriptions seem to be objective and believable? Which parts are more reflective of his personal values?

Source: The first excerpt is from Henry M. Elliot, *The History of India as Told by Its Own Historians* (London: Trübner and Co., 1869–1871) 3:611–614. The second excerpt is adapted from H. A. R. Gibb, ed., *Selections from the Travels of Ibn Battuta in Asia and Africa, 1325-1354* (London: Cambridge University Press, 1929), pp. 326–328. Copyright © 1929. Reprinted with permission of the Cambridge University Press.

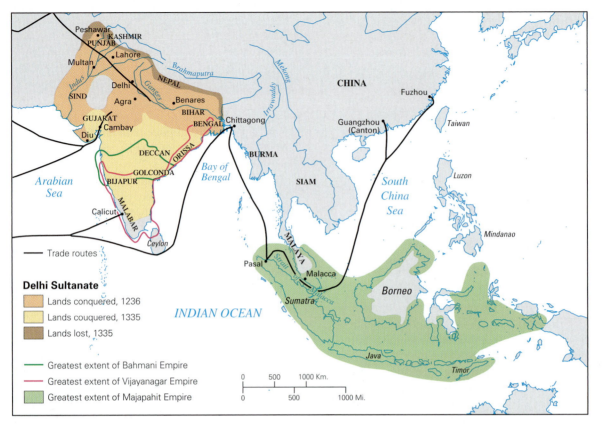

Map 14.3   South and Southeast Asia, 1200–1500   The rise of new empires and the expansion of maritime trade reshaped the lives of many tropical Asians.

To the astonishment of his ministers, Iltutmish passed over his weak and pleasure-seeking sons and designated his beloved and talented daughter Raziya° as his heir. When they questioned the unprecedented idea of a woman ruling a Muslim state, he said, "My sons are devoted to the pleasures of youth: no one of them is qualified to be king. . . . There is no one more competent to guide the State than my daughter."

In the event, her brother—whose great delight was riding his elephant through the bazaar, showering the crowds with coins—ruled ineptly for seven months before the ministers relented and put Raziya (r. 1236–1240) on the throne.

A chronicler who knew her explained why the reign of this able ruler lasted less than four years:

Sultan Raziya was a great monarch. She was wise, just, and generous, a benefactor to her kingdom, a dispenser of justice, the protector of her subjects, and the leader of her armies. She was endowed with all

the qualities befitting a king, but that she was not born of the right sex, and so in the estimation of men all these virtues were worthless. May God have mercy upon her![3]

Doing her best to prove herself a proper king, Raziya dressed like a man and rode at the head of her troops atop an elephant. Nothing, however, could overcome the prejudice against a woman ruler. In the end the Turkish chiefs imprisoned her. Soon after she escaped, she died at the hands of a robber.

After a half-century of stagnation and rebellion, the ruthless but efficient policies of Sultan Ala-ud-din Khalji° (r. 1296–1316) increased his control over the empire's outlying provinces. Successful frontier raids and high taxes kept his treasury full; wage and price controls in Delhi kept down the cost of maintaining a large army; and a network of spies stifled intrigue. When a Mongol threat from the northeast eased, Ala-ud-din's forces extended the sultanate's southern flank, seizing the rich

---

Raziya (rah-ZEE-uh)

Ala-ud-din Khalji (uh-LAH–uh-DEEN KAL-jee)

Meenakshi Temple, Madurai, India   Some 15,000 pilgrims a day visit the large Hindu temple of Meenakshi (the fish-eyed goddess) in the ancient holy city of Madurai in India's southeastern province of Tamil Nadu. The temple complex dates from at least 1000 c.e., although the elaborately painted statues of these gopuram (gate towers) have been rebuilt and restored many times. The largest gopura rises 150 feet (46 meters) above the ground.   (Jean Louis NOU/akg-images)

trading state of **Gujarat**° in 1298. Then troops drove southward, briefly seizing the southern tip of the Indian peninsula.

At the time of Ibn Battuta's visit, Delhi's ruler was Sultan Muhammad ibn Tughluq° (r. 1325–1351), who received his visitor at his palace's celebrated Hall of a Thousand Pillars. The world traveler praised the sultan's piety and generosity, but also recounted his cruelties (see Diversity and Dominance: Personal Styles of Rule in India and Mali). In keeping with these complexities, the sultan resumed a policy of aggressive expansion that enlarged the sultanate to its greatest extent. He balanced that policy with religious toleration intended to win the loyalty of Hindus and other non-Muslims. He even attended Hindu religious festivals. However, his successor Firuz Shah° (r. 1351–1388) alienated powerful Hindus by taxing the Brahmins, preferring to cultivate good relations with the Muslim elite. Muslim chroniclers praised

him for constructing forty mosques, thirty colleges, and a hundred hospitals.

A small minority in a giant land, the Turkish rulers relied on terror more than on toleration to keep their subjects submissive, on harsh military reprisals to put down rebellion, and on pillage and high taxes to sustain the ruling elite in luxury and power. Though little different from most other large states of the time (including Mali) in being more a burden than a benefit to most of its subjects, the sultanate never lost the disadvantage of foreign origins and alien religious identity. Nevertheless, over time, the sultans incorporated some Hindus into their administration. Some members of the ruling elite also married women from prominent Hindu families, though the brides had to become Muslims.

Personal and religious rivalries within the Muslim elite, as well as the discontent of the Hindus, threatened the Delhi Sultanate with disintegration whenever it showed weakness and finally hastened its end. In the mid-fourteenth century Muslim nobles challenged the sultan's dominion and successfully established the

---

Gujarat (goo-juh-RAHT)   **Tughluq** (toog-LOOK)
Firuz Shah (fuh-ROOZ shah)

Bahmani° kingdom (1347–1482), which controlled the Deccan Plateau. To defend themselves against the southward push of Bahmani armies, the Hindu states of southern India united to form the Vijayanagar° Empire (1336–1565), which at its height controlled the rich trading ports on both coasts and held Ceylon as a tributary state.

The rulers of Vijayanagar and the Bahmani turned a blind eye to religious differences when doing so favored their interests. Bahmani rulers sought to balance devotion to Muslim domination with the practical importance of incorporating the leaders of the majority Hindu population into the government, marrying Hindu wives, and appointing Brahmins to high offices. Vijayanagar rulers hired Muslim cavalry specialists and archers to strengthen their military forces, and they formed an alliance with the Muslim-ruled state of Gujarat.

By 1351, when all of South India was independent of Delhi's rule, much of north India was also in rebellion. In the east, Bengal successfully broke away from the sultanate in 1338, becoming a center of the mystical Sufi tradition of Islam (see Chapter 9). In the west, Gujarat had regained its independence by 1390. The weakening of Delhi's central authority revived Mongol interests in the area. In 1398 the Turko-Mongol leader Timur (see Chapter 13) seized the opportunity to invade and captured the city of Delhi. When his armies withdrew the next year with vast quantities of pillage and tens of thousands of captives, the largest city in southern Asia lay empty and in ruins. The Delhi Sultanate never recovered.

For all its shortcomings, the Delhi Sultanate was important in the development of centralized political authority in India. It established a bureaucracy headed by the sultan, who was aided by a prime minister and provincial governors. There were efforts to improve food production, promote trade and economic growth, and establish a common currency. Despite the many conflicts that Muslim conquest and rule provoked, Islam gradually acquired a permanent place in South Asia.

INDIAN OCEAN TRADE

The maritime network that stretched across the Indian Ocean from the Islamic heartland of Iran and Arabia to Southeast Asia connected to Europe, Africa, and China. The Indian Ocean region was the world's richest maritime trading network and an area of rapid Muslim expansion.

Bahmani (bah MAHN-ee) **Vijayanagar** (vee-juh-yah-NAH-gar)

Monsoon Mariners

The rising prosperity of Asian, European, and African states stimulated the expansion of trade in the Indian Ocean after 1200. Some of the growth was in luxuries for the wealthy—precious metals and jewels, rare spices, fine textiles, and other manufactures. The construction of larger ships also made shipments of bulk cargoes of ordinary cotton textiles, pepper, food grains (rice, wheat, barley), timber, horses, and other goods profitable. When the collapse of the Mongol Empire in the fourteenth century disrupted overland trade routes across Central Asia, the Indian Ocean routes assumed greater strategic importance in tying together the peoples of Eurasia and Africa.

Some goods were transported from one end of this trading network to the other, but few ships or crews made a complete circuit. Instead the Indian Ocean trade was divided into two legs: one from the Middle East across the Arabian Sea to India, and the other from India across the Bay of Bengal to Southeast Asia (see Map 14.4).

The characteristic cargo and passenger ship of the Arabian Sea was the **dhow°** (see Environment and Technology: The Indian Ocean Dhow). Ports on the Malabar coast of southwestern India constructed many of these vessels, which grew from an average capacity of 100 tons in 1200 to 400 tons in 1500. On a typical expedition, a dhow might sail west from India to Arabia and Africa on the northeast monsoon winds (December to March) and return on the southwest monsoons (April to August). Small dhows kept the coast in sight. Relying on the stars to guide them, skilled pilots steered large vessels by the quicker route straight across the water. A large dhow could sail from the Red Sea to mainland Southeast Asia in from two to four months, but few did so. Instead, cargoes and passengers normally sailed eastward to India in junks, which dominated travel in the Bay of Bengal and the South China Sea.

The largest, most technologically advanced, and most seaworthy vessel of this time, the junk had been developed in China. Junks were built from heavy spruce or fir planks held together with enormous nails. The space below the deck was divided into watertight compartments to minimize flooding in case of damage to the ship's hull. According to Ibn Battuta, the largest junks had twelve sails made of bamboo and carried a crew of a thousand men, of whom four hundred were soldiers. A large junk might have up to a hundred passenger cabins and could carry a cargo of over 1,000 tons. Chinese junks dominated China's foreign shipping to Southeast Asia

dhow (dow)

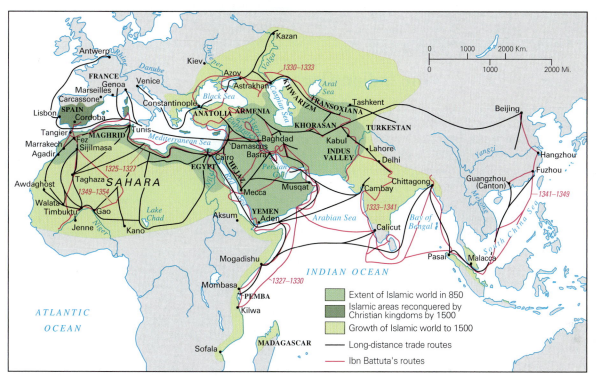

Map 14.4   Arteries of Trade and Travel in the Islamic World, to 1500   Ibn Battuta's journeys across Africa and Asia made use of land and sea routes along which Muslim traders and the Islamic faith had long traveled.

and India, but not all of the junks that plied these waters were Chinese. During the fifteenth century, vessels of this type came from shipyards in Bengal and Southeast Asia and were sailed by local crews.

The trade of the Indian Ocean was decentralized and cooperative. Commercial interests, rather than political authorities, tied several distinct regional networks together (see Map 14.4). Eastern Africa supplied gold from inland areas. Ports around the Arabian peninsula shipped horses and goods from the northern parts of the Middle East, the Mediterranean, and eastern Europe. At the center of the Indian Ocean trade, merchants in the cities of coastal India received goods from east and west, sold some locally, passed others along, and added vast quantities of Indian goods to the trade. The Strait of Malacca°, between the eastern end of the Indian Ocean and the South China Sea, was the meeting point of trade from Southeast Asia, China, and the Indian Ocean. In each region certain ports functioned as giant emporia, consolidating goods from smaller ports

and inland areas for transport across the seas. The operation of this complex trading system can best be understood by looking at some of the regions and their emporia in greater detail.

Africa: The Swahili and Zimbabwe

Trade expanded steadily along the East African coast from about 1250, giving rise to between thirty and forty separate city-states by 1500. As a result of this rising prosperity, new masonry buildings, sometimes three or four stories high, replaced many of the mud and thatch African fishing villages. Archaeology reveals the growing presence of imported glass beads, Chinese porcelain, and other exotic goods. As a result of trading contacts, many loan words from Arabic and Persian enriched the language of the coastal Africans, and the first to write in it used Arabic script. The visitors called these people "Swahili,"° from the Arabic name *sawahil*° *al-sudan*, meaning "shores of the blacks," and the name stuck.

Malacca (meh-LAK-eh)

Swahili (swah-HEE-lee)   *sawahil* (suh-WAH-hil)

The Indian Ocean Dhow

The sailing vessels that crossed the Indian Ocean shared the diversity of that trading area. The name by which we know them, *dhow*, comes from the Swahili language of the East African coast. The planks of teak from which their hulls were constructed were hewn from the tropical forests of South India and Southeast Asia. Their pilots, who navigated by stars at night, used the ancient technique that Arabs had used to find their way across the desert. Some pilots used a magnetic compass, which originated in China.

Dhows came in various sizes and designs, but all had two distinctive features in common. The first was hull construction. The hulls of dhows consisted of planks that were sewn together, not nailed. Cord made of fiber from the husk of coconuts or other materials was passed through rows of holes drilled in the planks. Because cord is weaker than nails, outsiders considered this shipbuilding technique strange. Marco Polo fancifully suggested that it indicated sailors' fear that large ocean magnets would pull any nails out of their ships. More probable explanations are that pliant sewn hulls were cheaper to build than rigid nailed hulls and were less likely to be damaged if the ships ran aground on coral reefs.

The second distinctive feature of dhows was their triangular (lateen) sails made of palm leaves or cotton. The sails were suspended from tall masts and could be turned to catch the wind.

The sewn hull and lateen sails were technologies developed centuries earlier, but there were two innovations between 1200 and 1500. First, a rudder positioned at the stern (rear end) of the ship replaced the large side oar that formerly had controlled steering. Second, shipbuilders increased the size of dhows to accommodate bulkier cargoes.

Dhow This modern model shows the vessel's main features. (National Maritime Museum, London)

Royal Enclosure, Great Zimbabwe   Inside these oval stone walls the rulers of the trading state of Great Zimbabwe lived. Forced to enter the enclosure through a narrow corridor between two high walls, visitors were meant to be awestruck.   (Courtesy of the Department of Information, Rhodesia)

At the time of Ibn Battuta's visit, the southern city of Kilwa had displaced Mogadishu as the **Swahili Coast's** most important commercial center. The traveler declared Kilwa "one of the most beautiful and well-constructed towns in the world." He noted that its dark-skinned inhabitants were devout and pious Muslims, and he took special pains to praise their ruler as a man rich in the traditional Muslim virtues of humility and generosity.

Swahili oral traditions associate the coast's commercial expansion with the arrival of Arab and Iranian merchants, but do not say what had attracted them. In Kilwa's case the answer is gold. By the late fifteenth century the city was exporting a ton of gold a year. The gold was mined by inland Africans much farther south. Much of it came from or passed through a powerful state on the plateau south of the Zambezi River, whose capital city is known as **Great Zimbabwe.** At its peak in about 1400, the city, which occupied 193 acres (78 hectares), may have had 18,000 inhabitants.

Between about 1250 and 1450, local African craftsmen built stone structures for Great Zimbabwe's rulers, priests, and wealthy citizens. The largest structure, a walled enclosure the size and shape of a large football stadium, served as the king's court. Its walls of unmortared stone were up to 17 feet (5 meters) thick and 32 feet (10 meters) high. Inside the walls were many buildings, including a large conical stone tower. The stone ruins of Great Zimbabwe are one of the most famous historical sites in sub-Saharan Africa.

Mixed farming and cattle-herding was Great Zimbabwe's economic base, but, as in Mali, the state's wealth came from long-distance trade. Trade began regionally with copper ingots from the upper Zambezi Valley, salt, and local manufactures. The gold exports into the Indian Ocean in the fourteenth and fifteenth centuries brought Zimbabwe to the peak of its political and economic power. However, historians suspect that the city's residents depleted nearby forests for firewood while their cattle overgrazed surrounding grasslands. The resulting ecological crisis hastened the empire's decline in the fifteenth century.

Arabia: Aden and the Red Sea

The city of **Aden**° had a double advantage in the Indian Ocean trade. Most of the rest of Arabia was desert, but monsoon winds brought Aden enough rainfall to supply drinking water to a large population and to grow grain for export. In addition, Aden's location (see Map 14.2) made it a convenient stopover for trade with India, the Persian Gulf, East Africa, and Egypt. Aden's merchants sorted out the goods from one place and sent them on to another: cotton cloth and beads from India, spices from Southeast Asia, horses from Arabia and Ethiopia, pearls from the Red Sea, luxurious manufactures from Cairo, slaves, gold, and ivory from Ethiopia, and grain, opium, and dyes from Aden's own hinterland.

After visiting Mecca in 1331, Ibn Battuta sailed down the Red Sea to Aden, probably wedged among bales of trade goods. His comments on the great wealth of Aden's leading merchants include a story about the slave of one merchant who paid the fabulous sum of 400 dinars for a ram in order to keep the slave of another merchant from buying it. Instead of punishing the slave for this extravagance, the master freed him as a reward for outdoing his rival. Ninety years later a Chinese Muslim visitor, Ma Huan, found "the country . . . rich, and the people numerous," living in stone residences several stories high.

Common commercial interests generally promoted good relations among the different religions and cultures of this region. For example, in the mid-thirteenth century a wealthy Jew from Aden named Yosef settled in Christian Ethiopia, where he acted as an adviser. South Arabia had been trading with neighboring parts of Africa since before the time of King Solomon of Israel. The dynasty that ruled Ethiopia after 1270 claimed descent from Solomon and from the South Arabian princess Sheba. Solomonic Ethiopia's consolidation was associated with a great increase in trade through the Red Sea port of Zeila°, including slaves, amber, and animal pelts, which went to Aden and on to other destinations.

Friction sometimes arose, however. In the fourteenth century the Sunni Muslim king of Yemen sent materials for the building of a large mosque in Zeila, but the local Somalis (who were Shi'ite Muslims) threw the stones into the sea. The result was a year-long embargo of Zeila ships in Aden. In the late fifteenth century Ethiopia's territorial expansion and efforts to increase control over the trade provoked conflicts with Muslims who ruled the coastal states of the Red Sea.

India: Gujarat and the Malabar Coast

The state of Gujarat in western India prospered as its ports shared in the expanding trade of the Arabian Sea and the rise of the Delhi Sultanate. Blessed with a rich agricultural hinterland and a long coastline, Gujarat attracted new trade after the Mongol capture of Baghdad in 1258 disrupted the northern land routes. Gujarat's forcible incorporation into the Delhi Sultanate in 1298 had mixed results. The state suffered from the violence of the initial conquest and from subsequent military crackdowns, but it also prospered from increased trade with Delhi's wealthy ruling class. Independent again after 1390, Gujarat's Muslim rulers extended their control over neighboring Hindu states and regained their preeminent position in the Indian Ocean trade.

The state derived much of its wealth from its export of cotton textiles and indigo to the Middle East and Europe, largely in return for gold and silver. Gujaratis also dominated the trade from India to the Swahili Coast, selling cotton cloth, carnelian beads, and foodstuffs in exchange for ebony, slaves, ivory, and gold. During the fifteenth century traders expanded their trade from Gujarat eastward to the Strait of Malacca. These Gujarati merchants helped spread the Islamic faith among East Indian traders, some of whom even imported specially carved gravestones from Gujarat.

Unlike Kilwa and Aden, Gujarat was important for its manufactures as well as its commerce. According to the thirteenth-century Venetian traveler Marco Polo, Gujarat's leatherworkers dressed enough skins in a year to fill several ships to Arabia and other places and also made beautiful sleeping mats for export to the Middle East "in red and blue leather, exquisitely inlaid with figures of birds and beasts, and skilfully embroidered with gold and silver wire," as well as leather cushions embroidered in gold. Later observers considered the Gujarati city of Cambay the equal of cities in Flanders and northern Italy (see Chapter 15) in the size, skill, and diversity of its textile industries.

Gujarat's cotton, linen, and silk cloth, as well as its carpets and quilts, found a large market in Europe, Africa, the Middle East, and Southeast Asia. Cambay also was famous for its polished gemstones, gold jewelry, carved ivory, stone beads, and both natural and artificial pearls. At the height of its prosperity in the fifteenth century, this substantial city's well-laid-out streets and open places boasted fine stone houses with tiled roofs. Al-

Aden (AY-den) **Zeila** (ZEYE-luh)

though most of Gujarat's overseas trade was in the hands of its Muslim residents, members of its Hindu merchant caste profited so much from related commercial activities that their wealth and luxurious lives were the envy of other Indians.

More southerly cities on the Malabar Coast duplicated Gujarat's importance in trade and manufacturing. Calicut° and other coastal cities prospered from their commerce in locally made cotton textiles and locally grown grains and spices, and as clearing-houses for the long-distance trade of the Indian Ocean. The Zamorin° (ruler) of Calicut presided over a loose federation of its Hindu rulers along the Malabar Coast. As in eastern Africa and Arabia, rulers were generally tolerant of other religious and ethnic groups that were important to commercial profits. Most trading activity was in the hands of Muslims, many originally from Iran and Arabia, who intermarried with local Indian Muslims. Jewish merchants also operated from Malabar's trading cities.

Southeast Asia: The Rise of Malacca

At the eastern end of the Indian Ocean, the principal passage into the South China Sea was through the Strait of Malacca between the Malay Peninsula and the island of Sumatra (see Map 14.3). As trade increased in the fourteenth and fifteenth centuries, this commercial choke point became the object of considerable political rivalry. The mainland kingdom of Siam gained control of most of the upper Malay Peninsula, while the Java-based kingdom of Majapahit° extended its dominion over the lower Malay Peninsula and much of Sumatra. Majapahit, however, was not strong enough to suppress a nest of Chinese pirates who had gained control of the Sumatran city of Palembang° and preyed on ships sailing through the strait. In 1407 a fleet sent by the Chinese government smashed the pirates' power and took their chief back to China for trial.

Weakened by internal struggles, Majapahit was unable to take advantage of China's intervention. The chief beneficiary of the safer commerce was the newer port of **Malacca** (or Melaka), which dominated the narrowest part of the strait. Under the leadership of a prince from Palembang, Malacca had quickly grown from an obscure fishing village into an important port by means of a series of astute alliances. Nominally subject to the king of Siam, Malacca also secured an alliance with China that was sealed by the visit of the imperial fleet in 1407. The

conversion of an early ruler from Hinduism to Islam helped promote trade with the Gujarati and other Muslim merchants who dominated so much of the Indian Ocean commerce. Merchants also appreciated Malacca's security and low taxes.

Malacca served as the meeting point for traders from India and China as well as an emporium for Southeast Asian trade: rubies and musk from Burma, tin from Malaya, gold from Sumatra, cloves and nutmeg from the Moluccas (or Spice Islands, as Europeans later dubbed them) to the east. Shortly after 1500, when Malacca was at its height, one resident counted eighty-four languages spoken among the merchants gathered there, who came from as far away as Turkey, Ethiopia, and the Swahili Coast. Four officials administered the large foreign merchant communities: one official for the very numerous Gujaratis, one for other Indians and Burmese, one for Southeast Asians, and one for the Chinese and Japanese. Malacca's wealth and its cosmopolitan residents set the standard for luxury in Malaya for centuries to come.

SOCIAL AND CULTURAL CHANGE

State growth, commercial expansion, and the spread of Islam between 1200 and 1500 led to many changes in the social and cultural life of tropical peoples. The political and commercial elites at the top of society grew more numerous, as did the slaves who served their needs. The spread of Islamic practices and beliefs affected social and cultural life—witness words of Arabic origin like *Sahara, Sudan, Swahili,* and *monsoon*—yet local traditions remained important.

Architecture, Learning, and Religion

Social and cultural changes typically affect cities more than rural areas. As Ibn Battuta observed, wealthy merchants and the ruling elite spent lavishly on new mansions, palaces, and places of worship.

Places of worship from this period exhibit fascinating blends of older traditions and new influences. African Muslims strikingly rendered Middle Eastern mosque designs in local building materials: sun-baked clay and wood in the western Sudan, coral stone on the Swahili Coast. Hindu temple architecture influenced the design of mosques, which sometimes incorporated pieces of older structures. The congregational mosque at Cambay, built in 1325, was assembled out of pillars,

---

Calicut (KAL-ih-cut)   Zamorin (ZAH-much-ruhn)
Majapahit (mah-jah-PAH-hit)   Palembang (pah-lem-BONG)

Church of Saint George, Ethiopia King Lalibela, who ruled the Christian kingdom of Ethiopia between about 1180 and 1220, had a series of churches carved out of solid volcanic rock to adorn his kingdom's new capital (also named Lalibela). The church of Saint George, excavated to a depth of 40 feet (13 meters) and hollowed out inside, has the shape of a Greek cross. (S. Sassoon/ Robert Harding Picture Library)

porches, and arches taken from sacked Hindu and Jain° temples. The culmination of a mature Hindu-Muslim architecture was the congregational mosque erected at the Gujarati capital of Ahmadabad° in 1423. It had an open courtyard typical of mosques everywhere, but the surrounding verandas incorporated many typical Gujarati details and architectural conventions.

Even more unusual than these Islamic architectural amalgams were the Christian churches of King Lalibela° of Ethiopia, constructed during the first third of the thirteenth century. As part of his new capital, Lalibela directed Ethiopian sculptors to carve eleven churches out of solid rock, each commemorating a sacred Christian site in Jerusalem. These unique structures carried on an old Ethiopian tradition of rock sculpture, though on a far grander scale.

Mosques, churches, and temples were centers of education as well as prayer. Muslims promoted literacy among their sons (and sometimes their daughters) so

that they could read the religion's classic texts. Ibn Battuta reported seeing several boys in Mali who had been placed in chains until they finished memorizing passages of the Quran. In sub-Saharan Africa the spread of Islam was associated with the spread of literacy, which had previously been confined largely to Christian Ethiopia. Initially, literacy was in Arabic, but in time Arabic characters were used to write local languages.

Islam affected literacy less in India, which had an ancient heritage of writing. Arabic served primarily for religious purposes, while Persian became the language of high culture and was used at court. Eventually, **Urdu°** arose, a Persian-influenced literary form of Hindi written in Arabic characters. Muslims also introduced papermaking in India.

Advanced Muslim scholars studied Islamic law, theology, and administration, as well as works of mathematics, medicine, and science, derived in part from ancient Greek writings. By the sixteenth century in the West African city **Timbuktu,** there were over 150 Quranic

---

Jain (jine)   **Ahmadabad** (AH-muhd-ah-bahd)
Lalibela (LAH-lee-BEL-uh)

Urdu (ER-doo)

schools, and advanced classes were held in the mosques and homes of the leading clerics. So great was the demand for books that they were the most profitable item to bring from North Africa to Timbuktu. At his death in 1536 one West African scholar, al-Hajj Ahmed of Timbuktu, possessed some seven hundred volumes, an unusually large library for that time. In Southeast Asia, Malacca became a center of Islamic learning from which scholars spread Islam throughout the region. Other important centers of learning developed in Muslim India, particularly in Delhi, the capital.

Even in conquered lands, such as India, Muslim rulers generally did not impose their religion. Example and persuasion by merchants and Sufis proved a more effective way of making converts. Many Muslims were active missionaries for their faith and worked hard to persuade others of its superiority. Islam's influence spread along regional trade routes from the Swahili Coast, in the Sudan, in coastal India, and in Southeast Asia. Commercial transactions could take place between people of different religions, but the common code of morality and law that Islam provided attracted many local merchants.

Marriage also spread Islam. Single Muslim men who journeyed along the trade routes often married local women and raised their children in the Islamic faith. Since Islam permitted a man to have up to four legal wives and many men took concubines as well, some wealthy men had dozens of children. In large elite Muslim households the many servants, both free and enslaved, were also required to be Muslims. Although such conversions were not fully voluntary, individuals could still find personal fulfillment in the Islamic faith.

In India Islamic invasions practically destroyed the last strongholds of long-declining Buddhism. In 1196 invaders overran the great Buddhist center of study at Nalanda° in Bihar° and burned its manuscripts, killing thousands of monks or driving them into exile in Nepal and Tibet. With Buddhism reduced to a minor faith in the land of its birth (see Chapter 8), Islam emerged as India's second most important religion. Hinduism was still India's dominant faith in 1500, but in most of maritime Southeast Asia Islam displaced Hinduism.

Islam also spread among the pastoral Fulani of West Africa and Somali of northeastern Africa, as well as among pastoralists in northwest India. In Bengal Muslim religious figures oversaw the conversion of jungle into farmland and thereby gained many converts among low-caste Hindus who admired the universalism of Islam.

Nalanda (nuh-LAN-duh)   **Bihar** (bee-HAHR)

The spread of Islam did not simply mean the replacement of one set of beliefs by another. Islam also adapted to the cultures of the regions it penetrated, developing African, Indian, and Indonesian varieties.

Social and Gender Distinctions

The conquests and commerce brought new wealth to some and new hardships to others. The poor may not have become poorer, but a significant growth in slavery accompanied the rising prosperity of the elite. According to Islamic sources, military campaigns in India reduced hundreds of thousands of Hindu "infidels" to slavery. Delhi overflowed with slaves. Sultan Ala-ud-din owned 50,000; Firuz Shah had 180,000, including 12,000 skilled artisans. Sultan Tughluq sent 100 male slaves and 100 female slaves as a gift to the emperor of China in return for a similar gift. His successor prohibited any more exports of slaves, perhaps because of reduced supplies in the smaller empire.

Mali and Bornu sent slaves across the Sahara to North Africa, including young maidens and eunuchs (castrated males). Ethiopian expansion generated a regular supply of captives for sale to Aden traders at Zeila. About 2.5 million enslaved Africans may have crossed the Sahara and the Red Sea between 1200 and 1500. Other slaves were shipped from the Swahili Coast to India, where Africans played conspicuous roles in the navies, armies, and administrations of some Indian states, especially in the fifteenth century. A few African slaves even found their way to China, where a Chinese source dating from about 1225 says that rich families preferred gatekeepers whose bodies were "black as lacquer."

With "free" labor abundant and cheap, most slaves were trained for special purposes. In some places, skilled trades and military service were dominated by hereditary castes of slaves, some of whom were rich and powerful. Indeed, the earliest rulers of the Delhi Sultanate rose from military slaves. A slave general in the western Sudan named Askia Muhammad seized control of the Songhai Empire (Mali's successor) in 1493. Less fortunate slaves, like the men and women who mined copper in Mali, did hard menial work.

Wealthy households in Asia and Africa employed many slaves as servants. Eunuchs guarded the harems of wealthy Muslims; female slaves were in great demand as household servants, entertainers, and concubines. Some rich men aspired to have a concubine from every part of the world. One of Firuz Shah's nobles was said to have two thousand harem slaves, including women from Turkey and China.

Indian Woman Spinning, ca. 1500 This drawing of a Muslim woman by an Indian artist shows the influence of Persian styles. The spinning of cotton fiber into thread—women's work—was made much easier by the spinning wheel, which the Muslim invaders introduced. Men then wove the threads into the cotton textiles for which India was celebrated. (British Library, Oriental and Indian Office Library, Or 3299, f. 151)

Sultan Ala-ud-din's campaigns against Gujarat at the end of the thirteenth century yielded a booty of twenty thousand maidens in addition to innumerable younger children of both sexes. The supply of captives became so great that the lowest grade of horse sold for five times as much as an ordinary female slave destined for service, although beautiful young virgins destined for the harems of powerful nobles commanded far higher prices. Some decades later, when Ibn Battuta was given ten girls captured from among the "infidels," he commented: "Female captives [in Delhi] are very cheap because they are dirty and do not know civilized ways. Even the educated ones are cheap." It would seem fairer to say that such slaves were cheap because the large numbers offered for sale had made them so.

Hindu legal digests and commentaries suggest that the position of Hindu women may have improved somewhat overall. The ancient practice of sati°—in which an upper-caste widow threw herself on her husband's funeral pyre—remained a meritorious act strongly approved by social custom. But Ibn Battuta believed that sati was strictly optional, an interpretation reinforced by the Hindu commentaries that devote considerable attention to the rights of widows.

Indian parents still gave their daughters in marriage before the age of puberty, but consummation of the marriage was supposed to take place only when the young woman was ready. Wives were expected to observe far stricter rules of fidelity and chastity than were their husbands and could be abandoned for many serious breaches. But women often were punished by lighter penalties than men for offenses against law and custom.

A female's status was largely determined by the status of her male master—father, husband, or owner. Women usually were not permitted to play the kind of active roles in commerce, administration, or religion that would have given them scope for personal achievements. Even so, women possessed considerable skills within those areas of activity that social norms allotted to them.

Besides child rearing, one of the most widespread female skills was food preparation. So far, historians have paid little attention to the development of culinary skills, but preparing meals that were healthful and tasty required much training and practice, especially given the limited range of foods available in most places. One kitchen skill that has received greater attention is brewing, perhaps because men were the principal consumers. In many parts of Africa women commonly made beer from grains or bananas. These mildly alcoholic beverages, taken in moderation, were a nutritious source of vitamins and minerals. Socially they were an important part of male rituals of hospitality and relaxation.

Throughout tropical Africa and Asia women did much of the farm work. They also toted home heavy loads of food, firewood, and water for cooking, balanced on their heads. Other common female activities included making clay pots for cooking and storage and making clothing. In India the spinning wheel, introduced by the Muslim invaders, greatly reduced the cost of making yarn for weaving. Spinning was a woman's activity done in the home; the weavers were generally men. Marketing was a common activity among women, especially in West Africa, where they commonly sold agricultural products, pottery, and other craftwork in the markets.

Some free women found their status improved by becoming part of a Muslim household, while many others were forced to become servants and concubines. Adopting Islam did not require accepting all the social customs of the Arab world. Ibn Battuta was appalled that Muslim women in Mali did not completely cover their

sati (suh-TEE)

bodies and veil their faces when appearing in public. He considered their nakedness an offense to women's (and men's) modesty. In another part of Mali he berated a Muslim merchant from Morocco for permitting his wife to sit on a couch and chat with a male friend of hers. The husband replied, "The association of women with men is agreeable to us and part of good manners, to which no suspicion attaches." Ibn Battuta's shock at this "laxity" and his refusal to ever visit the merchant again reveal the patriarchal precepts that were dear to most elite Muslims. So does the fate of Sultan Raziya of Delhi.

CONCLUSION

Tropical Africa and Asia contained nearly 40 percent of the world's population and over a quarter of its habitable land. Between 1200 and 1500 commercial, political, and cultural expansion drew the region's diverse peoples closer together. The Indian Ocean became the world's most important and richest trading area. The Delhi Sultanate brought South Asia its greatest political unity since the decline of the Guptas. In the western Sudan, Mali extended the political and trading role pioneered by Ghana. This growth of trade and empires was closely connected with the enlargement of Islam's presence in the tropical world along with the introduction of greater diversity into Islamic practice.

But if change was an important theme of this period, so too was social and cultural stability. Most tropical Africans and Asians never ventured far outside the rural communities in which their families had lived for generations. Their lives followed the familiar pattern of the seasons, the cycle of religious rituals and festivals, and the stages from childhood to elder status. Custom and necessity defined occupations. Most people engaged in food production by farming, herding, and fishing; some specialized in crafts or religious leadership. Based on the accumulated wisdom about how best to deal with their environment, such village communities were remarkably hardy. They might be ravaged by natural disaster or pillaged by advancing armies, but over time most recovered. Empires and kingdoms rose and fell in these centuries, but the villages endured.

In comparison, social, political, and environmental changes taking place in the Latin West, described in the next chapter, were in many ways more profound and disruptive. They would have great implications for tropical peoples after 1500.

Key Terms

tropics
monsoon
Ibn Battuta
Delhi Sultanate
Mali
Mansa Kankan Musa
Gujarat
dhow
Swahili Coast
Great Zimbabwe
Aden
Malacca
Urdu
Timbuktu

Suggested Reading

The trading links among the lands around the Indian Ocean have attracted the attention of recent scholars. A fine place to begin is Patricia Risso, *Merchants and Faith: Muslim Commerce and Culture in the Indian Ocean* (1995). More ambitious but perhaps more inclined to overreach the evidence is Janet Abu-Lughod, *Before European Hegemony: The World System, A.D. 1250–1350* (1989), which may usefully be read with K. N. Chaudhuri, *Asia Before Europe: Economy and Civilization of the Indian Ocean from the Rise of Islam to 1750* (1991). Students will find clear summaries of Islam's influences in tropical Asia and Africa in Ira Lapidus, *A History of Islamic Societies,* 2d ed. (2002), part II, and of commercial relations in Philip D. Curtin, *Cross-Cultural Trade in World History* (1984).

Greater detail about tropical lands is found in regional studies. For Southeast Asia see Nicholas Tarling, ed., *The Cambridge History of Southeast Asia,* vol. 1 (1992); John F. Cady, *Southeast Asia: Its Historical Development* (1964); and G. Coedes, *The Indianized States of Southeast Asia,* ed. Walter F. Vella (1968). India is covered comprehensively by R. C. Majumdar, ed., *The History and Culture of the Indian People,* vol. 4, *The Delhi Sultanate,* 2d ed. (1967); with brevity by Stanley Wolpert, *A New History of India,* 6th ed. (1999); and from an intriguing perspective by David Ludden, *A Peasant History of South India* (1985). For advanced topics see Tapan Raychaudhuri and Irfan Habib, eds., *The Cambridge Economic History of India,* vol. 1, *c. 1200–c. 1750* (1982).

A great deal of new scholarship on Africa in this period is summarized in chapters 6 and 7 of Christopher Ehret's *The Civilizations of Africa: A History to 1800* (2002). See also the latter parts of Graham Connah's *African Civilizations: Precolonial Cities and States in Tropical Africa: An Archaeological Perspective* (1987), and, for greater depth, D. T. Niane, ed., *UNESCO General History of Africa,* vol. 4, *Africa from the Twelfth to the Sixteenth Century* (1984), and Roland Oliver, ed., *The Cambridge History of Africa,* vol. 3, *c. 1050 to c. 1600* (1977).

For accounts of slavery and the slave trade see Salim Kidwai, "Sultans, Eunuchs and Domestics: New Forms of Bondage in Medieval India," in *Chains of Servitude: Bondage and Slavery in India,* ed. Utsa Patnaik and Manjari Dingwaney (1985), and the first two chapters of Paul E. Lovejoy, *Transformations in Slavery: A History of Slavery in Africa,* 2d ed. (2000).

Three volumes of Ibn Battuta's writings have been translated by H. A. R. Gibb, *The Travels of Ibn Battuta*, A.D. *1325–1354* (1958–1971). Ross E. Dunn, *The Adventures of Ibn Battuta: A Muslim of the 14th Century* (1986), provides a modern retelling of his travels with commentary. For annotated selections see Said Hamdun and Noël King, *Ibn Battuta in Black Africa* (1995).

The most accessible survey of Indian Ocean sea travel is George F. Hourani, *Arab Seafaring,* expanded ed. (1995). For a Muslim Chinese traveler's observations see Ma Huan, *Ying-yai Sheng-lan, "The Overall Survey of the Ocean's Shore"* [1433], trans. and ed. J. V. G. Mills (1970). Another valuable contemporary account of trade and navigation in the Indian Ocean is G. R. Tibbetts, *Arab Navigation in the Indian Ocean Before the Coming of the Portuguese, Being a Translation of the Kitab al-Fawa'id . . . of Ahmad b. Majidal-Najdi* (1981).

■ Notes

1. Tarikh-i-Wassaf, in Henry M. Elliot, *The History of India as Told by Its Own Historians,* ed. John Dowson (London: Trübner and Co., 1869–1871), 2:28.
2. Hasan Nizami, Taju-l Ma-asir, in Elliot, *The History of India as Told by Its Own Historians,* 2:219.
3. Minhaju-s Siraj, Tabakat-i Nasiri, in Elliot, *The History of India as Told by Its Own Historians,* 2:332–333.

The Latin West, 1200–1500

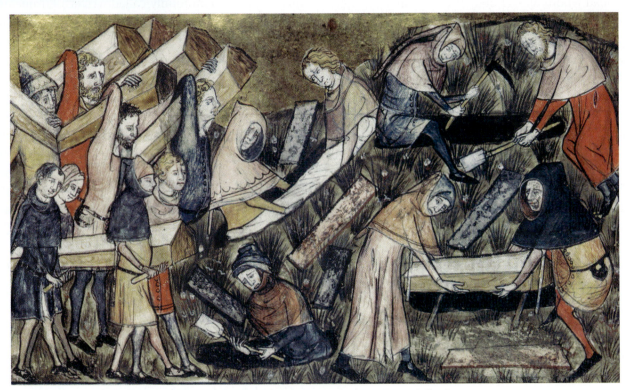

15

Burying Victims of the Black Death   This scene from Tournai, Flanders, captures the magnitude of the plague.

CHAPTER OUTLINE

Rural Growth and Crisis

Urban Revival

Learning, Literature, and the Renaissance

Political and Military Transformations

DIVERSITY AND DOMINANCE: **Persecution and Protection of Jews, 1272–1349**

ENVIRONMENT AND TECHNOLOGY: **The Clock**

In the summer of 1454, a year after the Ottoman Turks had captured the Greek Christian city of Constantinople, Aeneas Sylvius Piccolomini° was trying to stir up support for a crusade to halt the Muslim advances that were engulfing southeastern Europe and that showed no sign of stopping. The man who in four years would become pope doubted that anyone could persuade the rulers of Christian Europe to take up arms together against the Muslims: "Christendom has no head whom all will obey," he lamented, "neither the pope nor the emperor receives his due."

Aeneas Sylvius had good reason to believe that Latin Christians were more inclined to fight with each other than to join a common front against the Turks. French and English armies had been at war for more than a century. The German emperor presided over dozens of states that were virtually independent of his control. The numerous kingdoms and principalities of Mediterranean Europe had never achieved unity. With only slight exaggeration Aeneas Sylvius complained, "Every city has its own king, and there are as many princes as there are households."

He attributed this lack of unity to Europeans' being so preoccupied with personal welfare and material gain that they would never sacrifice themselves to stop the Turkish armies. During the century since a devastating plague had carried off a third of western Europe's population, people had become cynical about human nature and preoccupied with material things.

Yet despite all these divisions, disasters, and wars, historians now see the period from 1200 to 1500 (Europe's later Middle Ages) as a time of unusual progress. The avarice and greed Aeneas Sylvius lamented were the dark side of the material prosperity that was most evident in the splendid architecture, institutions of higher learning, and cultural achievements of the cities. Frequent wars caused havoc and destruction, but in the long run they promoted the development of more powerful weapons and more unified monarchies.

A European fifty years later would have known that the Turks did not overrun Europe, that a truce in the Anglo-French conflict would hold, and that explorers sent by Portugal and a newly united Spain would extend Europe's reach to other continents. In 1454 Aeneas Sylvius knew only what had been, and the conflicts and calamities of the past made him shudder.

Although their contemporary Muslim and Byzantine neighbors commonly called western Europeans "Franks," western Europeans ordinarily referred to themselves as "Latins." That term underscored their allegiance to the Latin rite of Christianity (and to its patriarch, the pope) as well as the use of the Latin language by their literate members. The **Latin West** deserves special attention because its achievements during this period had profound implications for the future of the world. The region was emerging from the economic and cultural shadow of its Islamic neighbors and, despite grave disruptions caused by plague and warfare, boldly setting out to extend its dominance. Some common elements promoted the Latin West's remarkable resurgence: competition, the pursuit of success, and the effective use of borrowed technology and learning.

As you read this chapter, ask yourself the following questions:

- How well did inhabitants of the Latin West deal with their natural environment?

- How did warfare help rulers in the Latin West acquire the skills, weapons, and determination that enabled them to challenge other parts of the world?

- How did superior technology in the Latin West promote excellence in business, learning, and architecture?

- How much did the region's achievements depend on its own people, and how much on things borrowed from Muslim and Byzantine neighbors?

Aeneas Sylvius Piccolomini (uh-NEE-uhs SIL-vee-uhs pee-kuh-lo-MEE-nee)

CHRONOLOGY

	Technology and Environment	Culture	Politics and Society
1200	**1200s** Use of crossbows and longbows becomes widespread; windmills in increased use		**1200s** Champagne fairs flourish
			1204 Fourth Crusade launched
		1210s Religious orders founded: Teutonic Knights, Franciscans, Dominicans	**1215** Magna Carta issued
		1225–1274 Thomas Aquinas, monk and philosopher	
		1265–1321 Dante Alighieri, poet	
		ca. 1267–1337 Giotto, painter	
1300	**1300** First mechanical clocks in the West	**1300–1500** Rise of universities	
		1304–1374 Francesco Petrarch, humanist writer	
	1315–1317 Great Famine	**1313–1375** Giovanni Boccaccio, humanist writer	
	1347–1351 Black Death	**ca. 1340–1400** Geoffrey Chaucer, poet	**1337** Start of Hundred Years War
	ca. 1350 Growing deforestation		**1381** Wat Tyler's Rebellion
		1389–1464 Cosimo de' Medici, banker	
		ca. 1390–1441 Jan van Eyck, painter	
1400	**1400s** Large cannon in use in warfare; hand-held firearms become prominent		**1415** Portuguese take Ceuta
		1449–1492 Lorenzo de' Medici, art patron	**1431** Joan of Arc burned as witch
	ca. 1450 First printing with movable type in the West	**1452–1519** Leonardo da Vinci, artist	**1453** End of Hundred Years War; Turks take Constantinople
	1454 Gutenberg Bible printed	**ca. 1466–1536** Erasmus of Rotterdam, humanist	**1469** Marriage of Ferdinand of Aragon and Isabella of Castile
		1472–1564 Michelangelo, artist	**1492** Fall of Muslim state of Granada
		1492 Explusion of Jews from Spain	

RURAL GROWTH AND CRISIS

Between 1200 and 1500 the Latin West brought more land under cultivation, adopted new farming techniques, and made greater use of machinery and mechanical forms of energy. Yet for most rural Europeans—more than nine out of ten people were rural—this period was a time of calamity and struggle. Most rural men and women worked hard for meager returns and suffered mightily from the effects of famine, epidemics, warfare, and social exploitation. After the devastation caused from 1347 to 1351 by the plague known as the Black Death, social changes speeded up by peasant revolts released many persons from serfdom and brought some improvements to rural life.

Rural French Peasants Many scenes of peasant life in winter are visible in this small painting by the Flemish Limbourg brothers from the 1410s. Above the snow-covered beehives one man chops firewood, while another drives a donkey loaded with firewood to a little village. At the lower right a woman, blowing on her frozen fingers, heads past the huddled sheep and hungry birds to join other women warming themselves in the cottage (whose outer wall the artists have cut away). (Musée Conde, Chantilly, France/Art Resource, NY)

Peasants and Population

Society was divided by class and gender. In 1200 most western Europeans were serfs, obliged to till the soil on large estates owned by the nobility and the church (see Chapter 10). Each noble household typically rested on the labors of from fifteen to thirty peasant families. The standard of life in the lord's stone castle or manor house stood in sharp contrast to that in the peasant's one-room thatched cottage containing little furniture and no luxuries. Despite numerous religious holidays, peasant cultivators labored long hours, but more than half of the fruits of their labor went to the landowner. Because of these meager returns, serfs were not motivated to introduce extensive improvements in farming practices.

Scenes of rural life show both men and women at work in the fields, although there is no reason to believe that equality of labor meant equality of decision making at home. In the peasant's hut, as elsewhere in medieval Europe, women were subordinate to men. The influential theologian Thomas Aquinas° (1225–1274) spoke for his age when he argued that, although both men and women were created in God's image, there was a sense in which "the image of God is found in man, and not in woman: for man is the beginning and end of woman; as God is the beginning and end of every creature."[1]

Rural poverty was not simply the product of inefficient farming methods and social inequality. It also re-

Aquinas (uh-KWY-nuhs)

sulted from the rapid growth of Europe's population. In 1200 China's population may have surpassed Europe's by two to one; by 1300 the population of each was about 80 million. China's population fell because of the Mongol conquest (see Chapter 13). Why Europe's more than doubled between 1100 and 1345 is uncertain. Some historians believe that the reviving economy may have stimulated the increase. Others argue that warmer-than-usual temperatures reduced the number of deaths from starvation and exposure, while the absence of severe epidemics lessened deaths from disease.

Whatever the causes, more people required more productive ways of farming and new agricultural settlements. One new technique gaining widespread acceptance in northern Europe increased the amount of farmland available for producing crops. Instead of following the custom of leaving half of their land fallow (uncultivated) every year to regain its fertility, some farmers tried a new **three-field system.** They grew crops on two-thirds of their land each year and planted the third field in oats. The oats stored nitrogen and rejuvenated the soil, and they could be used to feed plow horses. In much of Europe, however, farmers continued to let half of their land lie fallow and to use oxen (less efficient but cheaper than horses) to pull their plows.

Population growth also led to the foundation of new agricultural settlements. In the twelfth and thirteenth centuries large numbers of Germans migrated into the fertile lands east of the Elbe River and into the eastern Baltic states. Knights belonging to Latin Christian religious orders slaughtered or drove away native inhabitants who had not yet adopted Christianity. For example, during the thirteenth century, the Order of Teutonic Knights conquered, resettled, and administered a vast area along the eastern Baltic that later became Prussia (see Map 15.3). Other Latin Christians founded new settlements on lands conquered from the Muslims and Byzantines in southern Europe and on Celtic lands in the British Isles.

Draining swamps and clearing forests also brought new land under cultivation. But as population continued to rise, some people had to farm lands that had poor soils or were vulnerable to flooding, frost, or drought. As a result average crop yields declined after 1250, and more people were vulnerable to even slight changes in the food supply resulting from bad weather or the disruptions of war. According to one historian, "By 1300, almost every child born in western Europe faced the probability of extreme hunger at least once or twice during his expected 30 to 35 years of life."[2] One unusually cold spell led to the Great Famine of 1315–1317, which affected much of Europe.

The Black Death and Social Change

The **Black Death** cruelly resolved the problem of overpopulation by killing off a third of western Europeans. This terrible plague spread out of Asia and struck Mongol armies attacking the city of Kaffa° on the Black Sea in 1346 (see Chapter 13). A year later Genoese° traders in Kaffa carried the disease back to Italy and southern France. During the next two years the Black Death spread across Europe, sparing some places and carrying off two-thirds of the populace in others.

The plague's symptoms were ghastly to behold. Most victims developed boils the size of eggs in their groins and armpits, black blotches on their skin, foul body odors, and severe pain. In most cases, death came within a few days. To prevent the plague from spreading, town officials closed their gates to people from infected areas and burned victims' possessions. Such measures helped spare some communities but could not halt the advance of the disease across Europe (see Map 15.1). It is now believed that the Black Death was a combination of two diseases. One was anthrax, a disease that can spread to humans from cattle and sheep. The primary form of the Black Death was bubonic plague, a disease spread by contact with an infected person or from the bites of fleas that infest the fur of certain rats. But even if medieval Europeans had been aware of that route of infection, they could have done little to eliminate the rats, which thrived on urban refuse.

The plague left its mark on the survivors, bringing home how sudden and unexpected death could be. Some people became more religious, giving money to the church or flogging themselves with iron-tipped whips to atone for their sins. Others turned to reckless enjoyment, spending their money on fancy clothes, feasts, and drinking. Whatever their mood, most people soon resumed their daily routines.

Periodic returns of plague made recovery from population losses slow and uneven. By 1400 Europe's population regained the size it had had in 1200. Not until after 1500 did it rise above its preplague level.

In addition to its demographic and psychological effects, the Black Death triggered social changes in western Europe. Skilled and manual laborers who survived demanded higher pay for their services. At first authorities tried to freeze wages at the old levels. Seeing such repressive measures as a plot by the rich, peasants rose up against wealthy nobles and churchmen. During a widespread revolt in France in 1358 known as the Jacquerie,

Kaffa (KAH-fah)   **Genoese** (JEN-oh-eez)

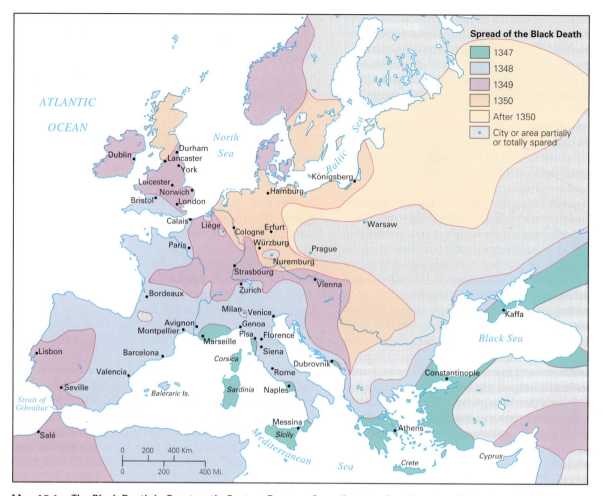

Map 15.1   The Black Death in Fourteenth–Century Europe   Spreading out of southwestern China along the routes opened by Mongol expansion, the plague reached the Black Sea port of Kaffa in 1346. This map documents its deadly progress year by year from there into the Mediterranean and north and east across the face of Europe.

peasants looted castles and killed dozens of persons. Urban unrest also took place. In a large revolt led by Wat Tyler in 1381, English peasants invaded London, calling for an end to all forms of serfdom and to most kinds of manorial dues. Angry demonstrators murdered the archbishop of Canterbury and many royal officials. Authorities put down these rebellions with even greater bloodshed and cruelty, but they could not stave off the higher wages and other social changes the rebels demanded.

Serfdom practically disappeared in western Europe as peasants bought their freedom or ran away. Free agricultural laborers used their higher wages to purchase land that they could farm for themselves. Some English

landowners who could no longer afford to hire enough fieldworkers used their land to pasture sheep for their wool. Others grew less-labor-intensive crops or made greater use of draft animals and labor-saving tools. Because the plague had not killed wild and domesticated animals, more meat was available for each survivor and more leather for shoes. Thus the welfare of the rural masses generally improved after the Black Death, though the gap between rich and poor remained wide.

In urban areas employers had to raise wages to attract enough workers to replace those killed by the plague. Guilds (see below) found it necessary to reduce the period of apprenticeship. Competition within crafts also became more common. Although the overall econ-

Watermills on the Seine River in Paris   Sacks of grain were brought to these mills under the bridge called the Grand Pont to be ground into flour. The water wheels were turned by the river flowing under them. Gears translated the vertical motion of the wheels into the horizontal motion of the millstones. (Bibliothèque Nationale de France)

omy shrank with the decline in population, per capita production actually rose.

Mines and Mills

Mining, metalworking, and the use of mechanical energy expanded so much in the centuries before 1500 that some historians have spoken of an "industrial revolution" in medieval Europe. That may be too strong a term, but the landscape fairly bristled with mechanical devices. Mills powered by water or wind were used to grind grain and flour, saw logs into lumber, crush olives, tan leather, make paper, and perform other useful tasks.

England's many rivers had some fifty-six hundred functioning watermills in 1086. After 1200 such mills spread rapidly across the western European mainland. By the early fourteenth century entrepreneurs had crammed sixty-eight watermills into a one-mile section of the Seine° River in Paris. The flow of the river below turned the simplest **water wheels.** Greater efficiency came from channeling water over the top of the wheel. Dams ensured these wheels a steady flow of water throughout the year. Some watermills in France and England even harnessed the power of ocean tides.

Windmills were common in comparatively dry lands like Spain and in northern Europe, where ice made water wheels useless in winter. Water wheels and windmills had long been common in the Islamic world, but people in the Latin West used these devices on a much larger scale than did people elsewhere.

Wealthy individuals or monasteries built many mills, but because of the expenses involved groups of investors undertook most of the construction. Since nature furnished the energy to run them for free, mills could be very profitable, a fact that often aroused the jealousy of their neighbors. In his *Canterbury Tales* the English poet Geoffrey Chaucer (ca. 1340–1400) captured millers' unsavory reputation (not necessarily deserved) by portraying a miller as "a master-hand at stealing grain" by pushing down on the balance scale with his thumb.[3]

Waterpower also made possible such a great expansion of iron making that some historians say Europe's real Iron Age came in the later Middle Ages, not in antiquity. Water powered the stamping mills that broke up the iron, the trip hammers that pounded it, and the bellows (first documented in the West in 1323) that raised temperatures to the point where the iron was liquid enough to pour into molds. Blast furnaces capable of producing high-quality iron are documented from 1380. The finished products included everything from armor and nails to horseshoes and agricultural tools.

Iron mining expanded in many parts of Europe to meet the demand. In addition, new silver, lead, and copper mines in Austria and Hungary supplied metal for coins, church bells, cannon, and statues. Techniques of deep mining that developed in Central Europe spread farther west in the latter part of the fifteenth century. To keep up with a building boom France quarried more

Seine (sen)

stone during the eleventh, twelfth, and thirteenth centuries than ancient Egypt had done during two millennia for all of its monuments.

The rapid growth of industry changed the landscape significantly. Towns grew outward and new ones were founded; dams and canals changed the flow of rivers; and the countryside was scarred by quarry pits and mines tunneled into hillsides. Pollution sometimes became a serious problem. Urban tanneries (factories that cured and processed leather) dumped acidic wastewater back into streams, where it mixed with human waste and the runoff from slaughterhouses. The first recorded antipollution law was passed by the English Parliament in 1388, although enforcing it was difficult.

One of the most dramatic environmental changes was deforestation. Trees were cut to provide timber for buildings and for ships. Tanneries stripped bark to make acid for tanning leather. Many forests were cleared to make room for farming. The glass and iron industries consumed great quantities of charcoal, made by controlled burning of oak or other hardwood. It is estimated that a single iron furnace could consume all the trees within five-eighths of a mile (1 kilometer) in just forty days. Consequently, the later Middle Ages saw the depletion of many once-dense forests in western Europe.

URBAN REVIVAL

In the tenth century not a single town in the Latin West could compare in wealth and comfort—still less in size—with the cities in the Byzantine Empire and the Islamic caliphates. Yet by the later Middle Ages wealthy commercial centers stood all along the Mediterranean, Baltic, and Atlantic, as well as on major rivers draining into these bodies of water (see Map 15.2). The greatest cities in the East were still larger, but those in the West were undergoing greater commercial, cultural, and administrative changes. Their prosperity was visible in impressive new churches, guild halls, and residences. This urban revival is a measure of the Latin West's recovery from the economic decline that had followed the collapse of the Roman Empire (see Chapter 10) as well as an illustration of how the West's rise was aided by its ties to other parts of the world.

Trading Cities

Most urban growth in the Latin West after 1200 was a result of the continuing growth of trade and manufacturing. Most of the trade was between cities and their hinterlands, but long-distance trade also stimulated urban revival. Cities in northern Italy in particular benefited from maritime trade with the bustling port cities of the eastern Mediterranean and, through them, with the great markets of the Indian Ocean and East Asia. In northern Europe commercial cities in the County of Flanders (roughly today's Belgium) and around the Baltic Sea profited from growing regional networks and from overland and sea routes to the Mediterranean.

Venice's diversion of the Fourth Crusade into an assault in 1204 against the city of Constantinople temporarily removed an impediment to Italian commercial expansion in the eastern Mediterranean. By crippling this Greek Christian stronghold, Venetians were able to seize the strategic island of Crete in the eastern Mediterranean and expand their trading colonies around the Black Sea.

Another boon to Italian trade was the westward expansion of the Mongol Empire, which opened trade routes from the Mediterranean to China (see Chapter 13). In 1271 the young Venetian merchant Marco Polo set out to reach the Mongol court by a long overland trek across Central Asia. There he spent many years serving the emperor Khubilai Khan as an ambassador and as the governor of a Chinese province. Some scholars question the truthfulness of Polo's later account of these adventures and of his treacherous return voyage through the Indian Ocean that finally brought him back to Venice in 1295, after an absence of twenty-four years. Few in Venice could believe Polo's tales of Asian wealth.

Even after the Mongol Empire's decline disrupted the trans-Asian caravan trade in the fourteenth century, Venetian merchants continued to purchase the silks and spices that reached Constantinople, Beirut, and Alexandria. Three times a year galleys (ships powered by some sixty oarsmen each) sailed in convoys of two or three from Venice, bringing back some 2,000 tons of goods. Other merchants began to explore new overland or sea routes.

Venice was not the only Latin city whose trade expanded in the thirteenth century. The sea trade of Genoa on the west coast of northern Italy probably equaled that of Venice. Genoese merchants established colonies on the shores of the eastern Mediterranean and around the Black Sea as well as in the western Mediterranean. In northern Europe an association of trading cities known as the **Hanseatic° League** traded extensively in the Baltic, including the coasts of Prussia, newly conquered by German knights. Their merchants ranged eastward to Novgorod in Russia and westward across the North Sea to London.

Hanseatic (han-see-AT-ik)

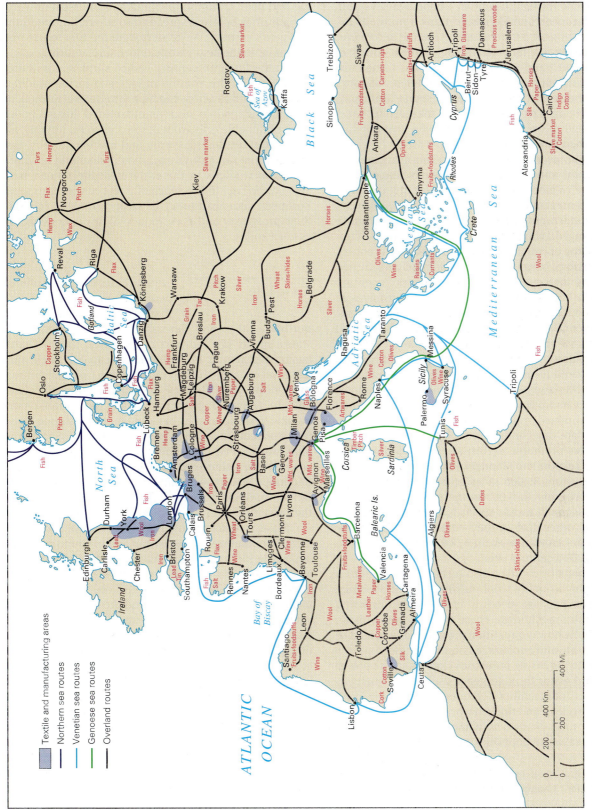

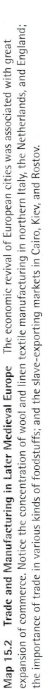

Map 15.2 Trade and Manufacturing in Later Medieval Europe The economic revival of European cities was associated with great expansion of commerce. Notice the concentration of wool and linen textile manufacturing in northern Italy, the Netherlands, and England; the importance of trade in various kinds of foodstuffs; and the slave-exporting markets in Cairo, Kiev, and Rostov.

By the late thirteenth century Genoese galleys from the Mediterranean and Hanseatic ships from the Baltic were converging on a third area, the trading and manufacturing cities in Flanders. In the Flemish towns of Bruges°, Ghent°, and Ypres° skilled artisans turned raw wool from English sheep into a fine cloth that was softer and smoother than the coarse "homespuns" from simple village looms. Dyed in vivid hues, these Flemish textiles appealed to wealthy Europeans who formerly had imported their fine textiles from Asia.

Along the overland route connecting Flanders and northern Italy, important trading fairs developed in the Champagne° region of Burgundy. The Champagne fairs began as regional markets, meeting once or twice a year, where manufactured goods, livestock, and farm produce were exchanged. When Champagne came under the control of the king of France at the end of the twelfth century, royal guarantees of safe conduct to all merchants turned the regional markets into international fairs. A century later fifteen Italian cities had permanent consulates in Champagne to represent the interests of their citizens. The fairs were also important for currency exchange and other financial transactions. During the fourteenth century the volume of trade grew so large that it became cheaper to send Flemish woolens to Italy by sea than to send them overland on pack animals. As a consequence, the fairs of Champagne lost some of their international trade but remained important regional markets.

In the late thirteenth century higher English taxes made it more profitable to turn wool into cloth in England than to export it to Flanders. Raw wool exports from England fell from 35,000 sacks at the beginning of the fourteenth century to 8,000 in the mid-fifteenth. With the aid of Flemish textile specialists and the spinning wheels and other devices they introduced, English exports of wool cloth rose from 4,000 pieces just before 1350 to 54,000 a century later.

Local banking families also turned Florence into a center for high-quality wool making. In 1338 Florence manufactured 80,000 pieces of cloth, while importing only 10,000 from Flanders. These changes in the textile industry show how competition promoted the spread of manufacturing and encouraged new specialties.

The growing textile industries channeled the power of wind and water through gears, pulleys, and belts to drive all sorts of machinery. Flanders, for example, used windmills to clean and thicken woven cloth by beating it in water, a process known as fulling. Another application of mill power was in papermaking. Although papermak-

ing had been common in China and the Muslim world for centuries before it spread to southern Europe in the thirteenth century, Westerners were the first to use machines to do the heavy work in its manufacturing.

In the fifteenth century Venice surpassed its European rivals in the volume of its trade in the Mediterranean as well as across the Alps into Central Europe. Its skilled craftspeople also manufactured luxury goods once obtainable only from eastern sources, notably silk and cotton textiles, glassware and mirrors, jewelry, and paper. At the same time, exports of Italian and northern European woolens to the eastern Mediterranean were also on the rise. In the space of a few centuries western European cities had used the eastern trade to increase their prosperity and then reduce their dependence on eastern goods.

Civic Life

Trading cities in Europe offered people more social freedom than did rural places. Most northern Italian and German cities were independent states, much like the port cities of the Indian Ocean basin (see Chapter 14). Other European cities held special royal charters that exempted them from the authority of local nobles. Because of their autonomy, they were able to adapt to changing market conditions more quickly than were cities in China and the Islamic world that were controlled by imperial authorities. Social mobility was also easier in the Latin West because anyone who lived in a chartered city for over a year might claim freedom. Thus cities became a refuge for all sorts of ambitious individuals, whose labor and talent added to their wealth.

Cities were also home to most of Europe's Jews. The largest population of Jews was in Spain, where earlier Islamic rulers had made them welcome. Many commercial cities elsewhere welcomed Jews for their manufacturing and business skills. Despite the official protection they received from Christian rulers and the church, Jews were subject to violent religious persecutions or expulsions (see Diversity and Dominance: Persecution and Protection of Jews, 1272–1349). Persecution peaked in times of crisis, such as during the Black Death. In the Spanish kingdom of Castile violent attacks on Jews were widespread in 1391 and brought the once vibrant Jewish community in Seville to an end. Terrified Jews left or converted to Christianity, but Christian fanaticism continued to rise over the next century, leading to new attacks on Jews and Jewish converts. In the Latin West only the papal city of Rome left its Jews undisturbed throughout the centuries before 1500.

Bruges (broozh)   **Ghent** (gent [hard g as in *get*])
Ypres (EE-pruh)   **Champagne** (sham-PAIN)

Flemish Weavers, Ypres   The spread of textile weaving gave employment to many people in the Netherlands. The city of Ypres in Flanders (now northern Belgium) was an important textile center in the thirteenth century. This drawing from a fourteenth-century manuscript shows a man and a woman weaving cloth on a horizontal loom, while a child makes thread on a spinning wheel.   (Stedelijke Openbare Bibliotheek, Ypres)

Opportunities for individual enterprise in European cities came with many restrictions. In most towns and cities powerful associations known as guilds dominated civic life. A **guild** was an association of craft specialists, such as silversmiths, or of merchants that regulated the business practices of its members and the prices they charged. Guilds also trained apprentices and promoted members' interests with the city government. By denying membership to outsiders and all Jews, guilds perpetuated the interests of the families that already were members. Guilds also perpetuated male dominance of most skilled jobs.

Nevertheless, in a few places women were able to join guilds either on their own or as the wives, widows, or daughters of male guild members. Large numbers of poor women also toiled in nonguild jobs in urban textile industries and in the food and beverage trades, generally receiving lower wages than men. Some women advanced socially through marriage. One of Chaucer's *Canterbury Tales* concerns a woman from Bath, a city in southern England, who became wealthy by marrying a succession of old men for their money (and then two other husbands for love), "aside from other company in youth." Chaucer says she was also a skilled weaver: "In making cloth she showed so great a bent, / She bettered those of Ypres and of Ghent."

By the fifteenth century a new class of wealthy merchant-bankers operated on a vast scale and specialized in money changing, loans, and investments. The merchant-bankers handled the financial transactions of a variety of merchants as well as of ecclesiastical and secular officials. They arranged for the transmission to the pope of funds known as Peter's pence, a collection taken up annually in every church in the Latin West. Their loans supported rulers' wars and lavish courts. Some merchant-bankers even developed their own news services, gathering information on any topic that could affect business.

Florence became a center of new banking services from checking accounts and shareholding companies

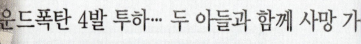

DIVERSITY AND DOMINANCE

PERSECUTION AND PROTECTION OF JEWS, 1272–1349

Because they did not belong to the dominant Latin Christian faith, Jews suffered from periodic discrimination and persecution. For the most part, religious and secular authorities tried to curb such anti-Semitism. Jews, after all, were useful citizens who worshipped the same God as their Christian neighbors. Still it was hard to know where to draw the line between justifiable and unjustifiable discrimination. The famous reviser of Catholic theology, St. Thomas Aquinas, made one such distinction in his Summa Theologica *with regard to attempts at forced conversion.*

Now, the practice of the Church never held that the children of Jews should be baptized against the will of their parents. . . . Therefore, it seems dangerous to bring forward this new view, that contrary to the previously established custom of the Church, the children of Jews should be baptized against the will of their parents.

There are two reasons for this position. One stems from danger to faith. For, if children without the use of reason were to receive baptism, then after reaching maturity they could easily be persuaded by their parents to relinquish what they had received in ignorance. This would tend to do harm to the faith.

The second reason is that it is opposed to natural justice . . . it [is] a matter of natural right that a son, before he has the use of reason, is under the care of his father. Hence, it would be against natural justice for the boy, before he has the use of reason, to be removed from the care of his parents, or for anything to be arranged for him against the will of his parents.

The "new view" Aquinas opposed was much in the air, for in 1272 Pope Gregory X issued a decree condemning forced baptism. The pope's decree reviews the history of papal protection given to the Jews, starting with a quotation from Pope Gregory I dating from 598, and decrees two new protections of Jews' legal rights.

Even as it is not allowed to the Jews in their assemblies presumptuously to undertake for themselves more than that which is permitted them by law, even so they ought not to suffer any disadvantage in those [privileges] which have been granted them.

Although they prefer to persist in their stubbornness rather than to recognize the words of their prophets and the mysteries of the Scriptures, and thus to arrive at a knowledge of Christian faith and salvation; nevertheless, inasmuch as they have made an appeal for our protection and help, we therefore admit their petition and offer them the shield of our protection through the clemency of Christian piety. In so doing we follow in the footsteps of our predecessors of happy memory, the popes of Rome—Calixtus, Eugene, Alexander, Clement, Celestine, Innocent, and Honorius.

We decree moreover that no Christian shall compel them or any one of their group to come to baptism unwillingly. But if any one of them shall take refuge of his own accord with Christians, because of conviction, then, after his intention will have been made manifest, he shall be made a Christian without any intrigue. For indeed that person who is known to come to Christian baptism not freely, but unwillingly, is not believed to possess the Christian faith.

Moreover, no Christian shall presume to seize, imprison, wound, torture, mutilate, kill, or inflict violence on them; furthermore no one shall presume, except by judicial action of the authorities of the country, to change the good customs in the land where they live for the purpose of taking their money or goods from them or from others.

In addition, no one shall disturb them in any way during the celebration of their festivals, whether by day or by night, with clubs or stones or anything else. Also no one shall exact any compulsory service of them unless it be that which they have been accustomed to render in previous times.

Inasmuch as the Jews are not able to bear witness against the Christians, we decree furthermore that the testimony of Christians against Jews shall not be valid unless there is among these Christians some Jew who is there for the purpose of offering testimony.

Since it occasionally happens that some Christians lose their Christian children, the Jews are accused by their enemies of secretly carrying off and killing these same Christian children, and of making sacrifices of the heart and blood of these very children. It happens, too, that the parents of these children, or some other Christian enemies of these Jews, secretly hide these very children in order that they may be able to injure these Jews, and in order that they may be able to extort from them a certain amount of money by redeeming them from their straits.

And most falsely do these Christians claim that the Jews have secretly and furtively carried away these children and killed them, and that the Jews offer sacrifice from the heart and the blood of these children, since their law in this matter precisely and expressly forbids Jews to sacrifice, eat, or drink the blood, or eat the flesh of animals having claws. This has been demonstrated many times at our court by Jews converted to the Christian faith: nevertheless very many Jews are often seized and detained unjustly because of this.

We decree, therefore, that Christians need not be obeyed against Jews in such a case or situation of this type, and we order that Jews seized under such a silly pretext be freed from imprisonment, and that they shall not be arrested henceforth on such a miserable pretext, unless—which we do not believe—they be caught in the commission of the crime. We decree that no Christian shall stir up anything against them, but that they should be maintained in that status and position in which they were from the time of our predecessors, from antiquity till now.

We decree, in order to stop the wickedness and avarice of bad men, that no one shall dare to devastate or to destroy a cemetery of the Jews or to dig up human bodies for the sake of getting money [by holding them for ransom]. Moreover, if anyone, after having known the content of this decree, should—which we hope will not happen—attempt audaciously to act contrary to it, then let him suffer punishment in his rank and position, or let him be punished by the penalty of excommunication, unless he makes amends for his boldness by proper recompense. Moreover, we wish that only those Jews who have not attempted to contrive anything toward the destruction of the Christian faith be fortified by the support of such protection....

*D*espite such decrees violence against Jews might burst out when fears and emotions were running high. This selection is from the official chronicles of the upper-Rhineland towns.

In the year 1349 there occurred the greatest epidemic that ever happened. Death went from one end of the earth to the other, on that side and this side of the [Mediterranean] sea, and it was greater among the Saracens [Muslims] than among the Christians. In some lands everyone died so that no one was left. Ships were also found on the sea laden with wares; the crew had all died and no one guided the ship. The Bishop of Marseilles and priests and monks and more than half of all the people there died with them. In other kingdoms and cities so many people perished that it would be horrible to describe. The pope at Avignon stopped all sessions of court, locked himself in a room, allowed no one to approach him and had a fire burning before him all the time. And from what this epidemic came, all wise teachers and physicians could only say that it was the God's will. And the plague was now here, so it was in other places, and lasted more than a whole year. This epidemic also came to Strasbourg in the summer of the above mentioned year, and it is estimated about sixteen thousand people died.

In the matter of this plague the Jews throughout the world were reviled and accused in all lands of having caused it through the poison which they are said to have put into the water and the wells—that is what they were accused of—and for this reason the Jews were burnt all the way from the Mediterranean into Germany, but not in Avignon, for the pope protected them there.

Nevertheless they tortured a number of Jews in Berne and Zofingen who admitted they had put poison into many wells, and they found the poison in the wells. Thereupon they burnt the Jews in many towns and wrote of this affair to Strasbourg, Freibourg, and Basel in order that they too should burn their Jews. . . . The deputies of the city of Strasbourg were asked what they were going to do with their Jews. They answered and said that they knew no evil of them. Then . . . there was a great indignation and clamor against the deputies from Strasbourg. So finally the Bishop and the lords and the Imperial Cities agreed to do away with the Jews. The result was that they were burnt in many cities, and wherever they were expelled they were caught by the peasants and stabbed to death or drowned. . . .

On Saturday—that was St. Valentine's Day—they burnt the Jews on a wooden platform in their cemetery. There were about two thousand people of them. Those who wanted to baptize themselves were spared. Many small children were taken out of the fire and baptized against the will of their fathers and mothers. And everything that was owed to the Jews was cancelled, and the Jews had to surrender all pledges and notes that they had taken for debts. The council, however, took the cash that the Jews possessed and divided it among the working-men proportionately. The money was indeed the thing that killed the Jews. If they had been poor and if the feudal lords had not been in debt to them, they would not have been burnt.

QUESTIONS FOR ANALYSIS

1. Why do Aquinas and Pope Gregory oppose prejudicial actions against Jews?

2. Why did prejudice increase at the time of the Black Death?

3. What factors account for the differences between the views of Christian leaders and the Christian masses?

Source: First selection reprinted with permission of Pocket Books, an imprint of Simon & Schuster Adult Publishing Group, from *The Pocket Aquinas*, edited with translations by Vernon J. Bourke. Copyright © 1960 by Washington Square Press. Copyright renewed © 1988 by Simon & Schuster Adult Publishing Group. Second selection from Jacob R. Marcus, ed., *The Jew in the Medieval World: A Source Book, 315–1791* (Cincinnati: Union of American Hebrew Congregations, 1938), 152–154, 45–47. Reprinted with permission of the Hebrew Union College Press, Cincinnati.

to improved bookkeeping. In the fifteenth century the Medici° family of Florence operated banks in Italy, Flanders, and London. Medicis also controlled the government of Florence and were important patrons of the arts. By 1500 the greatest banking family in western Europe was the Fuggers° of Augsburg, who had ten times the Medici bank's lending capital. Starting out as cloth merchants under Jacob "the Rich" (1459–1525), the family branched into many other activities, including the trade in Hungarian copper, essential for casting cannon.

Christian bankers had to devise ways to profit indirectly from loans in order to get around the Latin Church's condemnation of usury (charging interest). Some borrowers agreed to repay a loan in another currency at a rate of exchange favorable to the lender. Others added a "gift" in thanks to the lender to the borrowed sum. For example, in 1501 papal officials agreed to repay a loan of 6,000 gold ducats in five months to the Fuggers along with a "gift" of 400 ducats, amounting to an effective interest rate of 16 percent a year. In fact, the return was much smaller since the church failed to repay the loan on time. Because they were not bound by church laws, Jews were important moneylenders.

Despite the money made by some, for most residents of western European cities poverty and squalor were the norm. Even for the wealthy, European cities generally lacked civic amenities, such as public baths and water supply systems, that had existed in the cities of Western antiquity and still survived in cities of the Islamic Middle East.

Gothic Cathedrals

Master builders were in great demand in the thriving cities of late medieval Europe. Cities vied to outdo one another in the magnificence of their guild halls, town halls, and other structures (see Environment and Technology: The Clock). But the architectural wonders of their times were the new **Gothic cathedrals,** which made their appearance in about 1140 in France.

The hallmark of the new cathedrals was the pointed Gothic arch, which replaced the older round Roman arch. External (flying) buttresses stabilized the high, thin stone columns below the arches. This method of construction enabled master builders to push the Gothic cathedrals to great heights and fill the outside walls with giant windows of brilliantly colored stained glass. During the next four centuries, interior heights went ever higher,

Medici (MED-ih-chee)   Fuggers (FOOG-uhrz)

Strasbourg Cathedral   Only one of the two spires originally planned for this Gothic cathedral was completed when work ceased in 1439. But the Strasbourg Cathedral was still the tallest masonry structure of medieval Europe. This engraving is from 1630.   (Courtesy of the Trustees of the British Museum)

towers and spires pierced the heavens, and walls dazzled worshippers with religious scenes in stained glass.

The men who designed and built the cathedrals had little or no formal education and limited understanding of the mathematical principles of modern civil engineering. Master masons sometimes miscalculated, and parts of some overly ambitious cathedrals collapsed. For instance, the record-high choir vault of Beauvais Cathedral—154 feet (47 meters) in height—came tumbling down in 1284. But as builders gained experience, they devised new ways to push their steeples heavenward. The spire of the Strasbourg cathedral reached

The Clock

Clocks were a prominent feature of the Latin West in the late medieval period. The Song-era Chinese had built elaborate mechanical clocks centuries earlier (see Chapter 11), but the West was the first part of the world where clocks became a regular part of urban life. Whether mounted in a church steeple or placed on a bridge or tower, mechanical clocks proclaimed Western people's delight with mechanical objects, concern with precision, and display of civic wealth.

The word *clock* comes from a word for bell. The first mechanical clocks that appeared around 1300 in western Europe were simply bells with an automatic mechanical device to strike the correct number of hours. The most elaborate Chinese clock had been powered by falling water, but this was impractical in cold weather. The levers, pulleys, and gears of European clocks were powered by a weight hanging from a rope wound around a cylinder. An "escapement" lever regulated the slow, steady unwinding.

Enthusiasm for building expensive clocks came from various parts of the community. For some time, monks had been using devices to mark the times for prayer.

Employers welcomed chiming clocks to regulate the hours of their employees. Universities used them to mark the beginning and end of classes. Prosperous merchants readily donated money to build a splendid clock that would display their city's wealth. The city of Strasbourg, for example, built a clock in the 1350s that included statues of the Virgin, the Christ Child, and the three Magi; a mechanical rooster; the signs of the zodiac; a perpetual calendar; and an astrolabe—and it could play hymns, too!

By the 1370s and 1380s clocks were common enough for their measured hours to displace the older system that varied the length of the hour in proportion to the length of the day. Previously, for example, the London hour had varied from thirty-eight minutes in winter to eighty-two minutes in summer. By 1500 clocks had numbered faces with hour and minute hands. Small clocks for indoor use were also in vogue. Though not very accurate by today's standards, these clocks were still a great step forward. Some historians consider the clock the most important of the many technological advances of the later Middle Ages because it fostered so many changes during the following centuries.

Early Clock This weight-driven clock dates from 1454. (Bodleian Library Oxford, Ms. Laud Misc. 570, 25v.)

466 feet (142 meters) into the air—as high as a 40-story building. Such heights were unsurpassed until the twentieth century.

LEARNING, LITERATURE, AND THE RENAISSANCE

Throughout the Middle Ages people in the Latin West lived amid reminders of the achievements of the Roman Empire. They wrote and worshiped in a version of its language, traveled its roads, and obeyed some of its laws. Even the vestments and robes of medieval popes, kings, and emperors were modeled on the regalia of Roman officials. Yet early medieval Europeans lost touch with much of the learning of Greco-Roman antiquity. More vivid was the biblical world they heard about in the Hebrew and Christian scriptures.

A small revival of classical learning associated with the court of Charlemagne in the ninth century was followed by a larger renaissance (rebirth) in the twelfth century. The growing cities were home to intellectuals, artists, and universities after 1200. In the mid-fourteenth century the pace of intellectual and artistic life quickened in what is often called the **Renaissance,** which began in northern Italy and later spread to northern Europe. Some Italian authors saw the Italian Renaissance as a sharp break with an age of darkness. A more balanced view might reveal this era as the high noon of a day that had been dawning for several centuries.

Universities and Learning

Before 1100 Byzantine and Islamic scholarship generally surpassed scholarship in Latin Europe. When southern Italy was wrested from the Byzantines and Sicily and Toledo from the Muslims in the eleventh century, many manuscripts of Greek and Arabic works came into Western hands and were translated into Latin for readers eager for new ideas. These included philosophical works by Plato and Aristotle°; newly discovered Greek treatises on medicine, mathematics, and geography; and scientific and philosophical writings by medieval Muslims. Latin translations of the Iranian philosopher Ibn Sina° (980–1037), known in the West as Avicenna°, were particularly influential. Jewish scholars contributed significantly to the translation and explication of Arabic and other manuscripts.

Two new religious orders, the Dominicans and the Franciscans, contributed many talented professors to the growing number of new independent colleges after 1200. Some scholars believe that the colleges established in Paris and Oxford in the late twelfth and thirteenth centuries may have been modeled after similar places of study then spreading in the Islamic world—*madrasas,* which provided subsidized housing for poor students and paid the salaries of their teachers. The Latin West, however, was the first part of the world to establish modern **universities,** degree-granting corporations specializing in multidisciplinary research and advanced teaching.

Between 1300 and 1500 sixty new universities joined the twenty existing institutions of higher learning in the Latin West. Students banded together to found some of them; guilds of professors founded others. Teaching guilds, like the guilds overseeing manufacturing and commerce, set the standards for membership in their profession, trained apprentices and masters, and defended their professional interests.

Universities set the curriculum of study for each discipline and instituted comprehensive final examinations for degrees. Students who passed the exams at the end of their apprenticeship received a teaching diploma known as a "license." Students who completed longer training and successfully defended a scholarly treatise became "masters" or "doctors." The colleges of Paris were gradually absorbed into the city's university, but the colleges of Oxford and Cambridge remained independent, self-governing organizations.

Universally recognized degrees, well-trained professors, and exciting new texts promoted the rapid spread of universities in late medieval Europe. Because all university courses were taught in Latin, students and masters could move freely across political and linguistic lines, seeking out the university that offered the courses they wanted and that had the most interesting professors. Universities offered a variety of programs of study but generally were identified with a particular specialty. Bologna° was famous for the study of law; Montpellier and Salerno specialized in medicine; Paris and Oxford excelled in theology.

The prominence of theology partly reflected the fact that many students were destined for ecclesiastical careers, but theology was also seen as "queen of the sciences"—the central discipline that encompassed all knowledge. For this reason thirteenth-century theologians sought to synthesize the newly rediscovered philosophical works of Aristotle, as well as the commentaries of Avicenna, with the revealed truth of the Bible. Their

---

Aristotle (AR-ih-stah-tahl)   **Ibn Sina** (IB-uhn SEE-nah)
Avicenna (av-uh-SEN-uh)

Bologna (buh-LOHN-yuh)

daring efforts to synthesize reason and faith were known as **scholasticism°.**

The most notable scholastic work was the *Summa Theologica°*, issued between 1267 and 1273 by Thomas Aquinas, a brilliant Dominican priest who was a professor of theology at the University of Paris. Although Aquinas's exposition of Christian belief organized on Aristotelian principles was later accepted as a masterly demonstration of the reasonableness of Christianity, scholasticism upset many traditional thinkers. Some church authorities even tried to ban Aristotle from the curriculum. There also was much rivalry between the leading Dominican and Franciscan theological scholars over the next two centuries. However, the considerable freedom of medieval universities from both secular and religious authorities eventually enabled the new ideas of accredited scholars to prevail over the fears of church administrators.

Humanists and Printers

The intellectual achievements of the later Middle Ages were not confined to the universities. Talented writers of this era made important contributions to literature and literary scholarship. A new technology in the fifteenth century helped bring works of literature and scholarship to a larger audience.

Dante Alighieri° (1265–1321) completed a long, elegant poem, the *Divine Comedy*, shortly before his death. This supreme expression of medieval preoccupations tells the allegorical story of Dante's journey through the nine circles of hell and the seven terraces of purgatory (a place where the souls not deserving eternal punishment were purged of their sinfulness), followed by his entry into Paradise. His guide through hell and purgatory is the Roman poet Virgil. His guide through Paradise is Beatrice, a woman whom he had loved from afar since childhood and whose death inspired him to write the poem.

The *Divine Comedy* foreshadows some of the literary fashions of the later Italian Renaissance. Like Dante, later Italian writers made use of Greco-Roman classical themes and mythology and sometimes chose to write not in Latin but in the vernacular languages spoken in their regions, in order to reach broader audiences. (Dante used the vernacular spoken in Tuscany°.)

The English poet Geoffrey Chaucer was another vernacular writer of this era. Many of his works show the influence of Dante, but he is most famous for the *Canterbury Tales*, the lengthy poem written in the last dozen years of his life. These often humorous and earthy tales, told by fictional pilgrims on their way to the shrine of Thomas à Becket in Canterbury, are cited several times in this chapter because they present a marvelous cross-section of medieval people and attitudes.

Dante also influenced the literary movement of the **humanists** that began in his native Florence in the mid-fourteenth century. The term refers to their interest in the humanities, the classical disciplines of grammar, rhetoric, poetry, history, and ethics. With the brash exaggeration characteristic of new intellectual fashions, humanist writers such as the poet Francesco Petrarch° (1304–1374) and the poet and storyteller Giovanni Boccaccio° (1313–1375) claimed that their new-found admiration for the classical values revived Greco-Roman traditions that for centuries had lain buried under the rubble of the Middle Ages. This idea of a rebirth of learning long dead overlooks the fact that scholars at the monasteries and universities had been recovering and preserving all sorts of Greco-Roman learning for many centuries. Dante (whom the humanists revered) had anticipated humanist interests by a generation.

Yet it is hard to exaggerate the beneficial influences of the humanists as educators, advisers, and reformers. Their greatest influence was in reforming secondary education. Humanists introduced a curriculum centered on the languages and literature of Greco-Roman antiquity, which they felt provided intellectual discipline, moral lessons, and refined tastes. This curriculum dominated secondary education in Europe and the Americas well into the twentieth century. Despite the humanists' influence, theology, law, medicine, and branches of philosophy other than ethics remained prominent in university education during this period. After 1500 humanist influence grew in university education.

Believing the pinnacle of learning, beauty, and wisdom had been reached in antiquity, many humanists tried to duplicate the elegance of classical Latin or Greek. Others followed Dante in composing literary works in vernacular languages. Boccaccio is most famous for his vernacular writings, especially the *Decameron*, an earthy work that has much in common with Chaucer's boisterous tales. Under Petrarch's influence, however, Boccaccio turned to writing in classical Latin, including *De mulieribus claris (Famous Women)*, a chronicle of 106

---

scholasticism (skoh-LAS-tih-sizm)
Summa Theologica (SOOM-uh thee-uh-LOH-jih-kuh)
Dante Alighieri (DAHN-tay ah-lee-GYEH-ree)
Tuscany (TUS-kuh-nee)

Franceso Petrarch (fran-CHES-koh PAY-trahrk)
Giovanni Boccaccio (jo-VAH-nee boh-KAH-chee-oh)

A French Printshop, 1537   A workman operates the "press," quite literally a screw device that presses the paper to the inked type. Other employees examine the printed sheets, each of which holds four pages. When folded, the sheets make a book. (Giraudon/Art Resource, NY)

famous women from Eve to his own day. It was the first collection of women's lives in Western literature.

Once they had mastered classical Latin and Greek, a number of humanist scholars of the fifteenth century worked to restore the original texts of Greco-Roman writers and of the Bible. By comparing many different manuscripts, they eliminated errors introduced by generations of copyists. To aid in this task, Pope Nicholas V (r. 1447–1455) created the Vatican Library, buying scrolls of Greco-Roman writings and paying to have accurate copies and translations made. Working independently, the respected Dutch scholar Erasmus° of Rotterdam (ca. 1466–1536) produced a critical edition of the New Testament in Greek.

Erasmus (uh-RAZ-muhs)

Erasmus was able to correct many errors and mistranslations in the Latin text that had been in general use throughout the Middle Ages. In later years this humanist priest and theologian also wrote—in classical Latin—influential moral guides including the *Enchiridion militis christiani* (*The Manual of the Christian Knight*, 1503) and *The Education of a Christian Prince* (1515).

The influence of the humanists was enhanced after 1450 because new printing technology increased the availability of their critical editions of ancient texts, literary works, and moral guides. The Chinese were the first to use carved wood blocks for printing (see Chapter 13), and block-printed playing cards from China were circulating in Europe before 1450. Then, around 1450, three technical improvements revolutionized printing: (1) mov-

The Medici Family   This detail of a mural painting of 1459 by Benozzo Gozzoli depicts the arrival of the Magi at the birthplace of the Christ Child, but the principal figures are important members of the wealthy Medici family of Florence and their entourage in costumes of their day. The bowman on the left suggests how common African servants and slaves became in southern Europe during the Renaissance.   (Art Resource, NY)

able pieces of type consisting of individual letters, (2) new ink suitable for printing on paper, and (3) the **printing press,** a mechanical device that pressed inked type onto sheets of paper.

The man who did most to perfect printing was Johann Gutenberg° (ca. 1394–1468) of Mainz. The Gutenberg Bible of 1454, the first book in the West printed from movable type, was a beautiful and finely crafted work that bore witness to the printer's years of diligent experimentation. As printing spread to Italy and France, humanists worked closely with printers. Erasmus worked for years as an editor and proofreader for the great scholar-printer Aldo Manuzio (1449–1515), whose press in Venice published critical editions of many classical Latin and Greek texts.

By 1500 at least 10 million printed copies had issued forth from presses in 238 towns in western Europe. Though mass-produced paperbacks were still in the future, the printers and humanists had launched a revolution that was already having an effect on students, scholars, and a growing number of literate people who could gain access to ancient texts as well as to unorthodox political and religious tracts.

Renaissance Artists

The fourteenth and fifteenth centuries were as distinguished for their masterpieces of painting, sculpture, and architecture as they were for their scholarship. Although artists continued to depict biblical subjects, the spread of Greco-Roman learning led many artists, especially in Italy, to portray Greco-Roman deities and mythical tales. Another popular trend was depicting the scenes of daily life.

However, neither daily life nor classical images were entirely new subjects. Renaissance art, like Renaissance scholarship, owed a major debt to earlier generations. The Florentine painter Giotto° (ca. 1267–1337) had a formidable influence on the major Italian painters of the fifteenth century, who credited him with single-handedly reviving the "lost art of painting." In his religious scenes Giotto replaced the stiff, staring figures of the Byzantine style, which were intended to overawe viewers, with more natural and human portraits with whose emotions of grief and love viewers could identify. Rather than floating on backgrounds of gold leaf, his saints inhabit earthly landscapes.

Johann Gutenberg (yoh-HAHN GOO-ten-burg)

Giotto (JAW-toh)

Another important contribution to the early Italian Renaissance was a new painting technology from north of the Alps. The Flemish painter Jan van Eyck° (ca. 1390–1441) mixed his pigments with linseed oil instead of the diluted egg yolk of earlier centuries. Oil paints were slower drying and more versatile, and they gave pictures a superior luster. Van Eyck's use of the technique for his own masterfully realistic paintings on religious and domestic themes was quickly copied by talented painters of the Italian Renaissance.

The great Italian Leonardo da Vinci° (1452–1519), for example, used oil paints for his famous *Mona Lisa*. Renaissance artists like Leonardo were masters of many media. His other works include the fresco (painting in wet plaster) *The Last Supper*, bronze sculptures, and imaginative designs for airplanes, submarines, and tanks. Leonardo's younger contemporary Michelangelo° (1472–1564) painted frescoes of biblical scenes on the ceiling of the Sistine Chapel in the Vatican, sculpted statues of David and Moses, and designed the dome for a new Saint Peter's Basilica.

The patronage of wealthy and educated merchants and prelates did much to foster an artistic blossoming in the cities of northern Italy and Flanders. The Florentine banker Cosimo de' Medici (1389–1464), for example, spent immense sums on paintings, sculpture, and public buildings. His grandson Lorenzo (1449–1492), known as "the Magnificent," was even more lavish. The church was also an important source of artistic commissions. Seeking to restore Rome as the capital of the Latin Church, the papacy° launched a building program culminating in the construction of the new Saint Peter's Basilica and a residence for the pope.

These scholarly and artistic achievements exemplify the innovation and striving for excellence of the Late Middle Ages. The new literary themes and artistic styles of this period had lasting influence on Western culture. But the innovations in the organization of universities, in printing, and in oil painting had wider implications, for they were later adopted by cultures all over the world.

POLITICAL AND MILITARY TRANSFORMATIONS

Stronger and more unified states and armies developed in western Europe in parallel with the economic and cultural revivals. In no case were transformations smooth and steady, and the political changes unfolded somewhat differently in each state (see Map 15.3). During and after the prolonged struggle of the Hundred Years War, French and English monarchs forged closer ties with the nobility, the church, and the merchants. The consolidation of Spain and Portugal was linked to crusades against Muslim states. In Italy and Germany, however, political power remained in the hands of small states and loose alliances.

Monarchs, Nobles, and Clergy

Thirteenth-century states still shared many features of early medieval states (see Chapter 10). Hereditary monarchs occupied the peak of the political pyramid, but their powers were limited by modest treasuries and the rights possessed by others. Below them came the powerful noblemen who controlled vast estates and whose advice and consent were often required on important matters of state. The church, jealous of its traditional rights and independence, was another powerful body within each kingdom. Towns, too, had acquired many rights and privileges. Indeed, the towns in Flanders, the Hanseatic League, and Italy were nearly independent from royal interference.

In theory, nobles were vassals of the reigning monarchs and were obliged to furnish them with armored knights in time of war. In practice, vassals sought to limit the monarch's power and protect their own rights and privileges. The nobles' privileged economic and social position rested on the large estates that had been granted to their ancestors in return for supporting and training knights in armor to serve in a royal army.

In the year 1200 knights were still the backbone of western European fighting forces, but two changes in weaponry were bringing their central military role, and thus the system of estates that supported them, into question. The first involved the humble arrow. Improved crossbows could shoot metal-tipped arrows with such force that they could pierce helmets and light body armor. Professional crossbowmen, hired for wages, became increasingly common and much feared. Indeed, a church council in 1139 outlawed the crossbow as being too deadly for use against Christians. The ban was largely ignored. The second innovation in military technology that weakened the feudal system was the firearm. This Chinese invention, using gunpowder to shoot stone or metal projectiles, further transformed the medieval army.

The church also resisted royal control. In 1302 the outraged Pope Boniface VIII (r. 1294–1303) went so far as to assert that divine law made the papacy superior to

---

Jan van Eyck (yahn vahn-IKE)
Leonardo da Vinci (lay-own-AHR-doh dah-VIN-chee)
Michelangelo (my-kuhl-AN-juh-low)　**papacy** (PAY-puh-see)

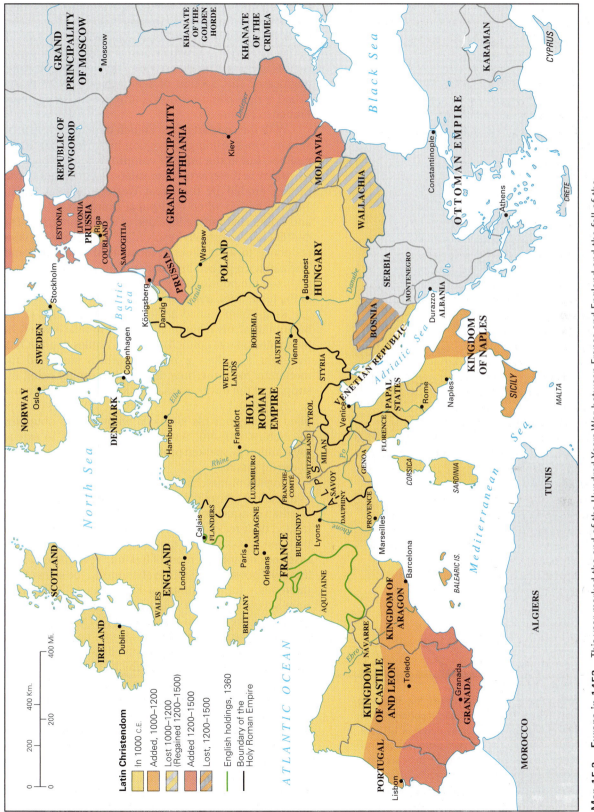

Map 15.3 Europe in 1453 This year marked the end of the Hundred Years War between France and England and the fall of the Byzantine capital city of Constantinople to the Ottoman Turks. Muslim advances into southeastern Europe were offset by the Latin Christian reconquests of Islamic holdings in southern Italy and the Iberian Peninsula and by the conversion of Lithuania.

Latin Christendom
- In 1000 C.E.
- Added, 1000–1200
- Lost 1000–1200 (Regained 1200–1500)
- Added 1200–1500
- Lost, 1200–1500
- English holdings, 1360
- Boundary of the Holy Roman Empire

The Magna Carta   One of four extant copies, this document shows the ravages of time, but the symbolic importance of the charter King John of England signed under duress in 1215 for English constitutional history has not been dimished. Originally a guarantee of the baron's feudal rights, it came to be seen as a limit on the monarch's authority over all subjects.   (The National Archives, Public Record Office and Historical Manuscripts Commission)

"every human creature," including monarchs. This theoretical claim of superiority was challenged by force. Issuing his own claim of superiority, King Philip "the Fair" of France (r. 1285–1314) sent an army to arrest the pope. After this treatment hastened Pope Boniface's death, Philip engineered the election of a French pope who established a new papal residence at Avignon° in southern France in 1309.

With the support of the French monarchy, a succession of popes residing in Avignon improved church discipline—but at the price of compromising the papacy's neutrality in the eyes of other rulers. Papal authority was further eroded by the **Great Western Schism** (1378–1415), a period when rival papal claimants at Avignon and Rome vied for the loyalties of Latin Christians. The conflict was eventually resolved by returning the papal residence to its traditional location, the city of Rome. The papacy regained its independence, but the long crisis broke the pope's ability to challenge the rising power of the larger monarchies.

King Philip gained an important advantage at the beginning of his dispute with Pope Boniface when he persuaded a large council of French nobles to grant him the right to collect a new tax, which sustained the monarchy for some time. Earlier, by adroitly using the support of the towns, the saintly King Louis IX of France (r. 1226–1270) had been able to issue ordinances that applied throughout his kingdom without first obtaining the nobles' consent. But later kings' efforts to extend royal authority sparked prolonged resistance by the most powerful vassals.

English monarchs wielded more centralized power as a result of consolidation that had taken place after the Norman conquest of 1066. Anglo-Norman kings also extended their realm by assaults on their Celtic neighbors. Between 1200 and 1400 they incorporated Wales and reasserted control over most of Ireland. Nevertheless, English royal power was far from absolute. In the span of just three years the ambitions of King John (r. 1199–1216) were severely set back. First he was compelled to acknowledge the pope as his overlord (1213). Then he lost his bid to reassert claims to Aquitaine in southern France (1214). Finally he was forced to sign the Magna Carta ("Great Charter," 1215), which affirmed that monarchs were subject to established law, confirmed the independence of the church and the city of London, and guaranteed nobles' hereditary rights.

Separate from the challenges to royal authority by the church and the nobles were the alliances and conflicts generated by the hereditary nature of monarchial

Avignon (ah-vee-NYON)

rule. Monarchs and their vassals entered into strategic marriages with a view to increasing their lands and their wealth. Such marriages showed scant regard for the emotions of the wedded parties or for "national" interests. Besides unhappiness for the parties involved, these marriages often led to conflicts over far-flung inheritances. Although these dynastic struggles and shifting boundaries make European politics seem chaotic in comparison with the empires of Asia, some important changes were emerging from them. Aided by the changing technology of war, monarchs were strengthening their authority and creating more stable (but not entirely fixed) state boundaries within which the nations of western Europe would in time develop. Nobles lost autonomy and dominance on the battlefield but retained their social position and important political roles.

The Hundred Years War, 1337–1453

The long conflict between the king of France and his vassals known as the **Hundred Years War** (1337–1453) was a key example of the transformation in politics and warfare. This long conflict set the power of the French monarchy against the ambitions of his vassals, who included the kings of England (for lands that belonged to their Norman ancestors) and the heads of Flanders, Brittany, and Burgundy. In typical fashion, the conflict grew out of a marriage alliance.

Princess Isabella of France married King Edward II of England (r. 1307–1327) to ensure that this powerful vassal remained loyal to the French monarchy. However, when none of Isabella's three brothers, who served in turn as kings of France, produced a male heir, Isabella's son, King Edward III of England (r. 1327–1377), laid claim to the French throne in 1337. Edward decided to fight for his rights after French courts awarded the throne to a more distant (and more French) cousin. Other vassals joined in a series of battles for the French throne that stretched out over a century.

New military technology shaped the conflict. Early in the war, hired Italian crossbowmen reinforced the French cavalry, but arrows from another late medieval innovation, the English longbow, nearly annihilated the French force. Adopted from the Welsh, the 6-foot (1.8-meter) longbow could shoot farther and more rapidly than the crossbow. Although arrows from longbows could not pierce armor, in concentrated volleys they often found gaps in the knights' defenses or struck their less-well-protected horses. To defend against these weapons, armor became heavier and more encompassing, making it harder for a knight to move. A knight who was pulled off his steed by a foot soldier armed with a pike (hooked pole) was usually unable to get up to defend himself.

Firearms became prominent in later stages of the Hundred Years War. Early cannon were better at spooking the horses than at hitting rapidly moving targets. As cannon grew larger, they proved quite effective in blasting holes through the heavy walls of medieval castles and towns. The first use of such artillery, against the French in the Battle of Agincourt (1415), gave the English an important victory.

A young French peasant woman, Joan of Arc, brought the English gains to a halt. Believing she was acting on God's instructions, she donned a knight's armor and rallied the French troops, which defeated the English in 1429 just as they seemed close to conquering France. Shortly after this victory, Joan had the misfortune of falling into English hands. English churchmen tried her for witchcraft and burned her at the stake in 1431.

In the final battles of the Hundred Years War, French forces used large cannon to demolish the walls of once-secure castles held by the English and their allies. The truce that ended the struggle in 1453 left the French monarchy in firm control.

New Monarchies in France and England

The war proved to be a watershed in the political history of France and England. The **new monarchies** that emerged differed from their medieval predecessors in having greater centralization of power, more fixed "national" boundaries, and stronger representative institutions. English monarchs after 1453 strove to consolidate control within the British Isles, though the Scots strongly defended their independence. French monarchs worked to tame the independence of their powerful noble vassals. Holdings headed by women were especially vulnerable. Mary of Burgundy (1457–1482) was forced to surrender much of her family's vast holdings to the king. Anne of Brittany's forced marriage to the king led to the eventual incorporation of her duchy° into France.

Changes in military technology helped undermine nobles' resistance. Smaller, more mobile cannon developed in the late fifteenth century blasted through their castle walls. More powerful hand-held firearms that could pierce even the heaviest armor hastened the demise of the armored knights. New armies depended less on knights from noble vassals and more on bowmen,

---

duchy (DUTCH-ee)

pikemen, musketeers, and artillery units paid by the royal treasury.

The new monarchies tried several strategies to pay for their standing armies. Monarchs encouraged noble vassals to make monetary payments in place of military service and levied additional taxes in time of war. For example, Charles VII of France (r. 1422–1461) won the right to impose a land tax on his vassals that enabled him to pay the costs of the last years of war with England. This new tax sustained the royal treasury for the next 350 years.

Taxes on merchants were another important revenue source. The taxes on the English wool trade, begun by King Edward III, paid most of the costs of the Hundred Years War. Some rulers taxed Jewish merchants and extorted large contributions from wealthy towns. Individual merchants sometimes curried royal favor with loans, even though such debts could be difficult or dangerous to collect. For example, the wealthy fifteenth-century French merchant Jacques Coeur° gained many social and financial benefits for himself and his family by lending money to important members of the French court, but he was ruined when his jealous debtors accused him of murder and had his fortune confiscated.

The church was a third source of revenue. The clergy often made voluntary contributions to a war effort. English and French monarchs gained further control of church funds in the fifteenth century by gaining the right to appoint important ecclesiastical officials in their realms. Although reformers complained that this subordinated the church's spiritual mission to political and economic concerns, the monarchs often used state power to enforce religious orthodoxy in their realms more vigorously than the popes had ever been able to do.

The shift in power to the monarchs and away from the nobility and the church did not deprive nobles of social privileges and special access to high administrative and military offices. Moreover, towns, nobles, and clergy found new ways to check royal power in the representative institutions that came into existence in England and France. By 1500 Parliament had become a permanent part of English government: the House of Lords contained all the great nobles and English church officials; the House of Commons represented the towns and the leading citizens of the counties. In France a similar but less effective representative body, the Estates General, represented the church, the nobles, and the towns.

Iberian Unification

The growth of Spain and Portugal into strong, centralized states was also shaped by struggles between kings and vassals, dynastic marriages and mergers, and warfare. But Spain and Portugal's **reconquest** of Iberia from Muslim rule was also a religious crusade. Religious zeal did not rule out personal gain. The Christian knights who gradually pushed the borders of their kingdoms southward expected material rewards. The spoils of victory included irrigated farmland, cities rich in Moorish architecture, and trading ports with access to the Mediterranean and the Atlantic. Serving God, growing rich, and living off the labor of others became a way of life for the Iberian nobility.

The reconquest advanced in waves over several centuries. Christian knights took Toledo in 1085. The Atlantic port of Lisbon fell in 1147 with the aid of English crusaders on their way to capture the Holy Land. It became the new capital of Portugal and the kingdom's leading city, displacing the older capital of Oporto, whose name (meaning "the port") is the root of the word *Portugal*. A Christian victory in 1212 broke the back of Muslim power in Iberia. During the next few decades Portuguese and Castilian forces captured the beautiful and prosperous cities of Cordova (1236) and Seville (1248) and in 1249 drove the Muslims from the southwestern corner of Iberia, known as Algarve° ("the west" in Arabic). Only the small kingdom of Granada hugging the Mediterranean coast remained in Muslim hands.

By incorporating Algarve in 1249, Portugal attained its modern territorial limits. After a long pause to colonize, Christianize, and consolidate this land, Portugal took the Christian crusade to North Africa. In 1415 Portuguese knights seized the port city of Ceuta° in Morocco, where they learned more about the trans-Saharan caravan trade in gold and slaves (see Chapter 14). During the next few decades, Portuguese mariners sailed down the Atlantic coast of Africa seeking access to this rich trade and alliances with rumored African Christians (see Chapter 16).

Although it took the other Iberian kingdoms much longer to complete the reconquest, the struggle served to bring them together and to keep their Christian religious zealotry at a high pitch. The marriage of Princess Isabella of Castile and Prince Ferdinand of Aragon in 1469 led to the permanent union of their kingdoms into Spain a decade later when they inherited their respective thrones. Their conquest of Granada in 1492 secured the final piece of Muslim territory in Iberia for the new kingdom.

Coeur (cur)

Algarve (ahl-GAHRV) **Ceuta** (say-OO-tuh)

The year 1492 was also memorable because of Ferdinand and Isabella's sponsorship of the voyage led by Christopher Columbus in search of the riches of the Indian Ocean (see Chapter 16). A third event that year also reflected Spain's crusading mentality. Less than three months after Granada's fall, the monarchs ordered all Jews to be expelled from their kingdoms. Efforts to force the remaining Muslims to convert or leave led to a Muslim revolt at the end of 1499 that was not put down until 1501. Portugal also began expelling Jews in 1493, including many thousands who had fled from Spain.

CONCLUSION

From an ecological perspective, the later medieval history of the Latin West is a story of triumphs and disasters. Westerners excelled in harnessing the inanimate forces of nature with their windmills, water wheels, and sails. They mined and refined the mineral wealth of the earth, although localized pollution and deforestation were among the results. But their inability to improve food production and distribution as rapidly as their population grew created a demographic crisis that became a demographic calamity when the Black Death swept through Europe in the mid-fourteenth century.

From a regional perspective, the period witnessed the coming together of the basic features of the modern West. States were of moderate size but had exceptional military capacity honed by frequent wars with one another. The ruling class, convinced that economic strength and political strength were inseparable, promoted the welfare of the urban populations that specialized in trade, manufacturing, and finance—and taxed their profits. Autonomous universities fostered intellectual excellence, and printing diffused the latest advances in knowledge. Art and architecture reached peaks of design and execution that set the standard for subsequent centuries. Perhaps most fundamentally, later medieval Europeans were fascinated by tools and techniques. In commerce, warfare, and industry, new inventions and improved versions of old ones underpinned the region's continuing dynamism.

From a global perspective, these centuries marked the Latin West's change from a region dependent on cultural and commercial flows from the East to a region poised to export its culture and impose its power on other parts of the world. It is one of history's great ironies that many of the tools that the Latin West used to challenge Eastern supremacy had originally been borrowed from the East. Medieval Europe's mills, printing, firearms, and navigational devices owed much to Eastern designs, just as its agriculture, alphabet, and numerals had in earlier times. Western European success depended as much on strong motives for expansion as on adequate means. Long before the first voyages overseas, population pressure, religious zeal, economic motives, and intellectual curiosity had expanded the territory and resources of the Latin West. From the late eleventh century onward such expansion of frontiers was notable in the English conquest of Celtic lands, in the establishment of crusader and commercial outposts in the eastern Mediterranean and Black Seas, in the massive German settlement east of the Elbe River, and in the reconquest of southern Iberia from the Muslims. The early voyages into the Atlantic were an extension of similar motives in a new direction.

■ Key Terms

Latin West	universities
three-field system	scholasticism
Black Death	humanists (Renaissance)
water wheel	printing press
Hanseatic League	Great Western Schism
guild	Hundred Years War
Gothic cathedral	new monarchies
Renaissance (European)	reconquest

■ Suggested Reading

A fine guide to the Latin West (including its ties to eastern Europe, Africa, and the Middle East) is Robert Fossier, ed., *The Cambridge Illustrated History of the Middle Ages*, vol. 3, *1250–1520* (1986). George Holmes, *Europe: Hierarchy and Revolt, 1320–1450*, 2d ed. (2000), and Denys Hay, *Europe in the Fourteenth and Fifteenth Centuries*, 2d ed. (1989), are comprehensive overviews. For the West's economic revival and growth, see Robert S. Lopez, *The Commercial Revolution of the Middle Ages, 950–1350* (1976), and Harry A. Miskimin, *The Economy of Early Renaissance Europe, 1300–1460* (1975). For greater detail see *The New Cambridge Medieval History*, vol. 6, *1300–c.1415*, ed. M. Jones (1998), and vol. 7, *1415–1500*, ed. C. Allmand (1999).

For fascinating primary sources see James Bruce Ross and Mary Martin McLaughlin, eds., *The Portable Medieval Reader* (1977) and *The Portable Renaissance Reader* (1977). *The Notebooks of Leonardo da Vinci*, ed. Pamela Taylor (1960), show this versatile genius at work.

Technological change is surveyed by Arnold Pacey, *The Maze of Ingenuity: Ideas and Idealism in the Development of Technology* (1974); Jean Gimpel, *The Medieval Machine: The Industrial Revolution of the Middle Ages* (1977); and William H. McNeill, *The Pursuit of Power: Technology, Armed Force, and Society Since A.D. 1000* (1982). For a key aspect of the environment see Roland Bechmann, *Trees and Man: The Forest in the Middle Ages* (1990).

Charles Homer Haskins, *The Rise of the Universities* (1923; reprint, 1957), is a brief, lighthearted introduction; more detailed and scholarly is Olef Pedersen, *The First Universities: Studium Generale and the Origins of University Education in Europe* (1998). Johan Huizinga, *The Waning of the Middle Ages* (1924), is the classic account of the "mind" of the fifteenth century. A multitude of works deal with the Renaissance, but few in any broad historical context. Lisa Jardine, *Worldly Goods: A New History of the Renaissance* (1996), is well illustrated and balanced; see also John R. Hale, *The Civilization of Europe in the Renaissance* (1995).

For social history see Georges Duby, *Rural Economy and Country Life in the Medieval West* (1990), for the earlier centuries. George Huppert, *After the Black Death: A Social History of Early Modern Europe* (1986), takes the analysis past 1500. Brief lives of individuals are found in Eileen Power, *Medieval People,* new ed. (1997), and Frances Gies and Joseph Gies, *Women in the Middle Ages* (1978). More systematic are the essays in Mary Erler and Maryanne Kowaleski, eds., *Women and Power in the Middle Ages* (1988). Vita Sackville-West, *Saint Joan of Arc* (1926; reprint, 1991), is a readable introduction to this extraordinary person.

Key events in the Anglo-French dynastic conflict are examined by Christopher Alland, *The Hundred Years War: England and France at War, ca. 1300–ca. 1450* (1988). Joseph F. O'Callaghan, *A History of Medieval Spain* (1975), provides the best one-volume coverage; for more detail see Jocelyn N. Hillgarth, *The Spanish Kingdoms,* 2 vols. (1976, 1978). Barbara W. Tuchman, *A Distant Mirror: The Calamitous 14th Century* (1978), is a popular ac-

count of the crises of that era. Norman F. Cantor, *In the Wake of the Plague: The Black Death and the World It Made* (2001), supplies a thorough introduction.

The Latin West's expansion is well treated by Robert Bartlett, *The Making of Europe: Conquest, Colonization, and Cultural Change* (1993); J. R. S. Phillips, *The Medieval Expansion of Europe,* 2d ed. (1998); and P. E. Russell, *Portugal, Spain and the African Atlantic, 1343–1492* (1998).

Francis C. Oakley, *The Western Church in the Later Middle Ages* (1985), is a reliable summary of modern scholarship. Kenneth R. Stow, *Alienated Minority: The Jews of Medieval Latin Europe* (1992), provides a fine survey up through the fourteenth century. For pioneering essays on the Latin West's external ties see Khalil I. Semaan, ed., *Islam and the Medieval West: Aspects of Intercultural Relations* (1980).

◼ Notes

1. Quoted in Marina Warner, *Alone of All Her Sex: The Myth and Cult of the Virgin Mary* (New York: Random House, 1983), 179.
2. Harry Miskimin, *The Economy of the Early Renaissance, 1300–1460* (Englewood Cliffs, NJ: Prentice-Hall, 1969), 26–27.
3. Quotations here and later in the chapter are from Geoffrey Chaucer, *The Canterbury Tales,* trans. Nevill Coghill (New York: Penguin Books, 1952), 25, 29, 32.

16

The Maritime Revolution, to 1550

Columbus Prepares to Cross the Atlantic, 1492   This later representation shows Columbus with the ships, soldiers, priests, and seamen that were part of Spain's enterprise.

CHAPTER OUTLINE

Global Maritime Expansion Before 1450

European Expansion, 1400–1550

Encounters with Europe, 1450–1550

ENVIRONMENT AND TECHNOLOGY: **Vasco da Gama's Fleet**

DIVERSITY AND DOMINANCE: **Kongo's Christian King**

In 1511 young Ferdinand Magellan sailed from Europe around the southern tip of Africa and eastward across the Indian Ocean as a member of the first Portuguese expedition to explore the East Indies (maritime Southeast Asia). Eight years later, this time in the service of Spain, he headed an expedition that sought to demonstrate the feasibility of reaching the East Indies by sailing westward from Europe. By the middle of 1521 Magellan's expedition had achieved its goal by sailing across the Atlantic, rounding the southern tip of South America, and crossing the Pacific Ocean—but at a high price.

One of the five ships that had set out from Spain in 1519 was wrecked on a reef, and the captain of another deserted and sailed back to Spain. The passage across the vast Pacific took much longer than anticipated, resulting in the deaths of dozens of sailors due to starvation and disease. In the Philippines, Magellan himself was killed on April 27, 1521, while aiding a local king who had promised to become a Christian. Magellan's successor met the same fate a few days later.

To consolidate their dwindling resources, the expedition's survivors burned the least seaworthy of their remaining three ships and transferred the men and supplies from that ship to the smaller *Victoria*, which continued westward across the Indian Ocean, around Africa, and back to Europe. Magellan's flagship, the *Trinidad*, tried unsuccessfully to recross the Pacific to Central America. The *Victoria*'s return to Spain on September 8, 1522, was a crowning example of Europeans' new ability and determination to make themselves masters of the oceans. A century of daring and dangerous voyages backed by the Portuguese crown had opened new routes through the South Atlantic to Africa, Brazil, and the rich trade of the Indian Ocean. Rival voyages sponsored by Spain since 1492 had opened new contacts with the American continents. Now the unexpectedly broad Pacific Ocean had been crossed as well. A maritime revolution was under way that would change the course of history.

That new maritime skill marked the end of an era in which the flow of historical influences tended to move from east to west. Before 1500 most overland and maritime expansion had come from Asia, as had the most useful technologies and the most influential systems of belief. Asia also had been home to the most powerful states and the richest trading networks. The Iberians set out on their voyages of exploration to reach Eastern markets, and their success began a new era in which the West gradually became the world's center of power, wealth, and innovation.

The maritime revolution created many new contacts, alliances, and conflicts. Some ended tragically for individuals like Magellan. Some were disastrous for entire populations: Amerindians, for instance, suffered conquest, colonization, and a rapid decline in numbers. Sometimes the results were mixed: Asians and Africans found both risks and opportunities in their new relations with the visitors from Europe.

As you read this chapter, ask yourself the following questions:

- Why did Portugal and Spain undertake voyages of exploration?

- Why do the voyages of Magellan and other Iberians mark a turning point in world history?

- What were the consequences for the different peoples of the world of the new contacts resulting from these voyages?

GLOBAL MARITIME EXPANSION BEFORE 1450

Since ancient times travel across the salt waters of the world's seas and oceans had been one of the great challenges to people's technological ingenuity. Ships had to be sturdy enough to survive heavy winds and waves, and pilots had to learn how to cross featureless expanses of water to reach their destinations. In time ships, sails, and navigational techniques perfected in the more protected seas were tried on the vast, open oceans.

However complex the solutions and dangerous the voyages, the rewards of sea travel made them worthwhile. Ships could move goods and people more quickly and cheaply than any form of overland travel then possible. Because of its challenges and rewards, sea travel attracted adventurers. To cross the unknown waters, find

CHRONOLOGY

	Pacific Ocean	Atlantic Ocean	Indian Ocean
1400	**400–1300** Polynesian settlement of Pacific islands	**770–1200** Viking voyages **1300s** Settlement of Madeira, Azores, Canaries **Early 1300s** Mali voyages **1418–1460** Voyages of Henry the Navigator **1440s** Slaves from West Africa **1482** Portuguese at Gold Coast and Kongo **1486** Portuguese at Benin **1488** Bartolomeu Dias reaches Indian Ocean **1492** Columbus reaches Caribbean **1492–1500** Spanish conquer Hispaniola **1493** Columbus returns to Caribbean (second voyage) **1498** Columbus reaches mainland of South America (third voyage)	**1405–1433** Voyages of Zheng He **1497–1498** Vasco da Gama reaches India
1500	 **1519–1522** Magellan expedition	**1500** Cabral reaches Brazil **1513** Ponce de León explores Florida **1519–1520** Cortés conquers Aztec Empire **1531–1533** Pizarro conquers Inca Empire	**1505** Portuguese bombard Swahili Coast cities **1510** Portuguese take Goa **1511** Portuguese take Malacca **1515** Portuguese take Hormuz **1535** Portuguese take Dui **1538** Portuguese defeat Ottoman fleet **1539** Portuguese aid Ethiopia

new lands, and open up new trade or settlements was an exciting prospect. For these reasons, some men on every continent had long turned their attention to the sea.

By 1450 much had been accomplished and much remained undone. Daring mariners had discovered and settled most of the islands of the Pacific, the Atlantic, and the Indian Oceans. The greatest success was the trading system that united the peoples around the Indian Ocean. But no individual had yet crossed the Pacific in either direction. Even the narrower Atlantic was a barrier that kept the peoples of the Americas, Europe, and Africa in ignorance of each other's existence. The inhabitants of Australia were likewise completely cut off from contact with the rest of humanity. All this was about to change.

The Pacific Ocean

The voyages of Polynesian peoples out of sight of land over vast distances across the Pacific Ocean are one of the most impressive feats in maritime history before 1450 (see Map 16.1). Though they left no written records, over several thousand years

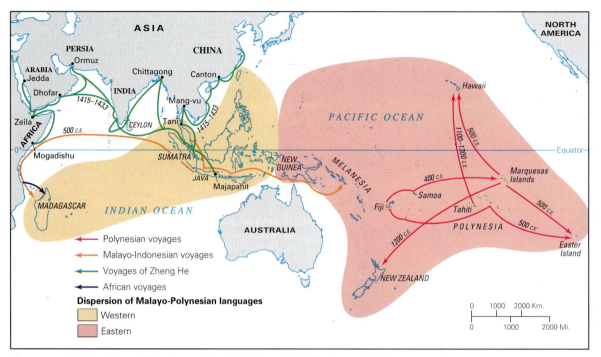

Map 16.1   Exploration and Settlement in the Indian and Pacific Oceans Before 1500   Over many centuries, mariners originating in Southeast Asia gradually colonized the islands of the Pacific and Indian Oceans. The Chinese voyages led by Zheng He in the fifteenth century were lavish official expeditions.

intrepid mariners from the Malay° Peninsula of Southeast Asia explored and settled the island chains of the East Indies and moved onto New Guinea and the smaller islands of Melanesia°. Beginning sometime before the Common Era (C.E.), a new wave of expansion from the area of Fiji brought the first humans to the islands of the central Pacific known as Polynesia. The easternmost of the Marquesas° Islands were reached about 400 C.E.; Easter Island, 2,200 miles (3,540 kilometers) off the coast of South America, was settled a century later. From the Marquesas, Polynesian sailors sailed to the Hawaiian Islands as early as 500 C.E. They settled New Zealand about 1200. Then, between 1100 and 1300, new voyages northward from Tahiti to Hawaii brought more Polynesian settlers across the more than 2,000 nautical miles (4,000 kilometers) to Hawaii.

Until recent decades some historians argued that Polynesians could have reached the eastern Pacific islands only by accident because they lacked navigational devices to plot their way. Others wondered how Polynesians could have overcome the difficulties, illustrated by

Magellan's flagship, *Trinidad*, of sailing eastward across the Pacific. In 1947 one energetic amateur historian of the sea, Thor Heyerdahl°, argued that Easter Island and Hawaii were actually settled from the Americas. He sought to prove his theory by sailing his balsa-wood raft, *Kon Tiki*, westward from Peru.

Although some Amerindian voyagers did use ocean currents to travel northward from Peru to Mexico between 300 and 900 C.E., there is now considerable evidence that the settlement of the islands of the eastern Pacific was the result of planned expansion by Polynesian mariners. The first piece of evidence is the fact that the languages of these islanders are all closely related to the languages of the western Pacific and ultimately to those of Malaya. The second is the finding that accidental voyages could not have brought sufficient numbers of men and women for founding a new colony along with all the plants and domesticated animals that were basic to other Polynesian islands.

In 1976 a Polynesian crew led by Ben Finney used traditional navigational methods to sail an ocean canoe from Hawaii south to Tahiti. The *Hokulea* was a 62-foot-

---

Malay (May-LAY)   **Melanesia** (mel-uh-NEE-zhuh)
Marquesas (mar-KAY-suhs)

Heyerdahl (HIGH-uhr-dahl)

Polynesian Canoes Pacific Ocean mariners sailing canoes such as these, shown in an eighteenth-century painting, made epic voyages of exploration and settlement. A large platform connects two canoes at the left, providing more room for the members of the expedition, and a sail supplements the paddlers. ("Tereoboo, King of Owyhee, bringing presents to Captain Cook," D. L. Ref. p. xx 2f. 35. Courtesy, The Dixon Library, State Library of New South Wales)

long (19-meter-long) double canoe patterned after old oceangoing canoes, which sometimes were as long as 120 feet (37 meters). Not only did the *Hokulea* prove seaworthy, but, powered by an inverted triangular sail and steered by paddles (not by a rudder), it was able to sail across the winds at a sharp enough angle to make the difficult voyage, just as ancient mariners must have done. Perhaps even more remarkable, the *Hokulea*'s crew was able to navigate to their destination using only their observation of the currents, stars, and evidence of land.

The Indian Ocean

While Polynesian mariners were settling Pacific islands, other Malayo-Indonesians were sailing westward across the Indian Ocean and colonizing the large island of Madagascar off the southeastern coast of Africa. These voyages continued through the fifteenth century. To this day the inhabitants of Madagascar speak Malayo-Polynesian languages. However, part of the island's population is descended from Africans who had crossed the 300 miles (500 kilometers) from the mainland to Madagascar, most likely in the centuries leading up to 1500.

Other peoples had been using the Indian Ocean for trade since ancient times. The landmasses of Southeast Asia and eastern Africa that enclose the Indian Ocean on each side, and the Indian subcontinent that juts into its middle, provided coasts that seafarers might safely follow and coves for protection. Moreover, seasonal winds known as monsoons are so predictable and steady that navigation using sailing vessels called dhows° was less difficult and dangerous in ancient times than elsewhere.

The rise of medieval Islam gave Indian Ocean trade an important boost. The great Muslim cities of the Middle East provided a demand for valuable commodities. Even more important were the networks of Muslim traders that tied the region together. Muslim traders shared a common language, ethic, and law and actively spread their religion to distant trading cities. By 1400 there were Muslim trading communities all around the Indian Ocean.

The Indian Ocean traders operated largely independently of the empires and states they served, but in East Asia imperial China's rulers were growing more and more interested in these wealthy ports of trade. In 1368

dhow (dow)

Chinese Junk This modern drawing shows how much larger one of Zheng He's ships was than one of Vasco da Gama's vessels. Watertight interior bulkheads made junks the most seaworthy large ships of the fifteenth century. Sails made of pleated bamboo matting hung from the junk's masts, and a stern rudder provided steering. European ships of exploration, though smaller, were faster and more maneuverable. (Dugald Stermer)

the Ming dynasty overthrew Mongol rule and began expansionist policies to reestablish China's predominance and prestige abroad.

Having restored Chinese dominance in East Asia, the Ming next moved to establish direct contacts with the peoples around the Indian Ocean. In choosing to send out seven imperial fleets between 1405 and 1433, the Ming may have been motivated partly by curiosity. The fact that most of the ports the fleets visited were important in the Indian Ocean trade suggests that enhancing China's commerce was also a motive. Yet because the expeditions were far larger than needed for exploration or promoting trade, their main purpose probably was to inspire awe of Ming power and achievements.

The Ming expeditions into the Indian Ocean basin were launched on a scale that reflected imperial China's resources and importance. The first consisted of sixty-two specially built "treasure ships," large Chinese junks each about 300 feet long by 150 feet wide (90 by 45 meters). There were also at least a hundred smaller vessels, most of which were larger than the flagship in which Columbus later sailed across the Atlantic. Each treasure ship had nine masts, twelve sails, many decks, and a car-rying capacity of 3,000 tons (six times the capacity of Columbus's entire fleet). One expedition carried over 27,000 individuals, including infantry and cavalry troops. The ships would have been armed with small cannon, but in most Chinese sea battles arrows from highly accurate crossbows dominated the fighting.

At the command of the expeditions was Admiral **Zheng He°** (1371–1435). A Chinese Muslim with ancestral connections to the Persian Gulf, Zheng was a fitting emissary to the increasingly Muslim-dominated Indian Ocean basin. The expeditions carried other Arabic-speaking Chinese as interpreters.

One of these interpreters kept a journal recording the customs, dress, and beliefs of the people visited, along with the trade, towns, and animals of their countries. He observed exotic animals such as the black panther of Malaya and the tapir of Sumatra; beliefs in legendary "corpse headed barbarians" whose heads left their bodies at night and caused infants to die; the division of coastal Indians into five classes, which correspond to the four Hindu varna and a separate Muslim class; and the fact

Zheng He (jung huh)

that traders in the rich Indian trading port of Calicut° could perform error-free calculations by counting on their fingers and toes rather than using the Chinese abacus. After his return, the interpreter went on tour in China, telling of these exotic places and "how far the majestic virtue of [China's] imperial dynasty extended."[1]

The Chinese "treasure ships" carried rich silks, precious metals, and other valuable goods intended as gifts for distant rulers. In return those rulers sent back gifts of equal or greater value to the Chinese emperor. Although the main purpose of these exchanges was diplomatic, they also stimulated trade between China and its southern neighbors. For that reason they were welcomed by Chinese merchants and manufacturers. Yet commercial profits could not have offset the huge cost of the fleets.

Interest in new contacts was not confined to the Chinese side. In 1415–1416 at least three trading cities on the Swahili° Coast of East Africa sent delegations to China. The delegates from one of them, Malindi, presented the emperor of China with a giraffe, creating quite a stir among the normally reserved imperial officials. Such African delegations may have encouraged more contacts, for the next three of Zheng's voyages were extended to the African coast. Unfortunately, no documents record how Africans and Chinese reacted to each other during these historic meetings between 1417 and 1433. It appears that China's lavish gifts stimulated the Swahili market for silk and porcelain. An increase in Chinese imports of pepper from southern Asian lands also resulted from these expeditions.

Had the Ming court wished to promote trade for the profit of its merchants, Chinese fleets might have continued to play a dominant role in Indian Ocean trade. But some high Chinese officials opposed increased contact with peoples whom they regarded as barbarians with no real contribution to make to China. Such opposition caused a suspension in the voyages from 1424 to 1431, and after the final expedition of 1432 to 1433, no new fleets were sent out. Later Ming emperors focused their attention on internal matters in their vast empire. China's withdrawal left a power vacuum in the Indian Ocean.

The Atlantic Ocean

The greatest mariners of the Atlantic in the early Middle Ages were the Vikings. These northern European raiders and pirates used their small, open ships to attack coastal European settlements for several centuries. They also dis-

covered and settled one island after another in the North Atlantic during these warmer than usual centuries. Like the Polynesians, the Vikings had neither maps nor navigational devices, but they managed to find their way wonderfully well using their knowledge of the heavens and the seas.

The Vikings first settled Iceland in 770. From there some moved to Greenland in 982, and by accident one group sighted North America in 986. Fifteen years later Leif Ericsson established a short-lived Viking settlement on the island of Newfoundland, which he called Vinland. When a colder climate returned after 1200, the northern settlements in Greenland went into decline, and Vinland became only a mysterious place mentioned in Norse sagas.

Some southern Europeans also used the maritime skills they had acquired in the Mediterranean and coastal Atlantic to explore the Atlantic. In 1291 two Vivaldo brothers from Genoa set out to sail through the South Atlantic and around Africa to India. They were never heard of again. Other Genoese and Portuguese expeditions into the Atlantic in the fourteenth century discovered (and settled) the islands of Madeira°, the Azores°, and the Canaries.

There is also written evidence of African voyages of exploration in the Atlantic in this period. The celebrated Syrian geographer al-Umari (1301–1349) relates that when Mansa Kankan Musa°, the ruler of the West African empire of Mali, passed through Egypt on his lavish pilgrimage to Mecca in 1324, he told of voyages to cross the Atlantic undertaken by his predecessor, Mansa Muhammad. Muhammad had sent out four hundred vessels with men and supplies, telling them, "Do not return until you have reached the other side of the ocean or if you have exhausted your food or water." After a long time one canoe returned, reporting that the others had been swept away by a "violent current in the middle of the sea." Muhammad himself then set out at the head of a second, even larger, expedition, from which no one returned.

In addition to sailing up the Pacific coast, early Amerindian voyagers from South America also colonized the West Indies. By the year 1000 Amerindians known as the **Arawak**° had moved up from the small islands of the Lesser Antilles (Barbados, Martinique, and Guadeloupe) into the Greater Antilles (Cuba, Hispaniola, Jamaica, and Puerto Rico) as well as into the Bahamas

---

Calicut (KAL-ih-kut)   Swahili (swah-HEE-lee)

Madeira (muh-DEER-uh)   Azores (A-zorz)
Mansa Kankan Musa (MAHN-suh KAHN-kahn MOO-suh)
Arawak (AR-uh-wahk)

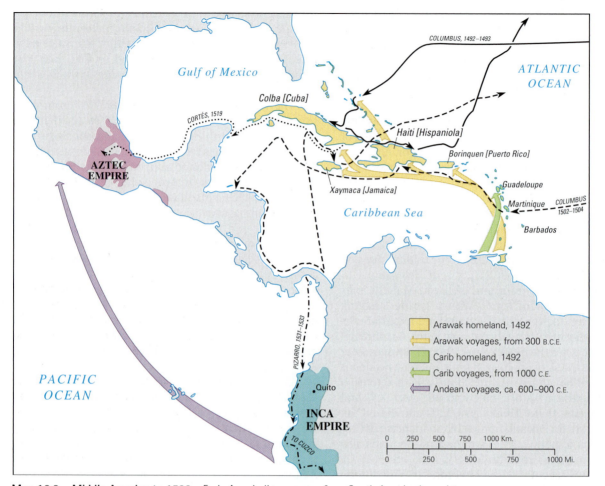

Map 16.2   Middle America to 1533   Early Amerindian voyages from South America brought new settlers to the West Indies and western Mexico. The arrival of Europeans in 1492 soon led to the conquest and depopulation of Amerindians.

(see Map 16.2). The Carib followed the same route in later centuries and by the late fifteenth century had overrun most Arawak settlements in the Lesser Antilles and were raiding parts of the Greater Antilles. From the West Indies Arawak and Carib also undertook voyages to the North American mainland.

EUROPEAN EXPANSION, 1400–1550

The preceding survey shows that maritime expansion occurred in many parts of the world before 1450. The epic sea voyages sponsored by the Iberian kingdoms of Portugal and Spain are of special interest because they began a maritime revolution that profoundly altered the course of world history. The Portuguese and Spanish expeditions ended the isolation of the Americas and increased global interaction. The influence in world affairs of the Iberians and other Europeans who followed them overseas rose steadily in the centuries after 1500.

Iberian overseas expansion was the product of two related phenomena. First, Iberian rulers had strong economic, religious, and political motives to expand their contacts and increase their dominance. Second, improvements in their maritime and military technologies gave them the means to master treacherous and unfamiliar ocean environments, seize control of existing maritime trade routes, and conquer new lands.

Motives for Exploration

Why did Iberian kingdoms decide to sponsor voyages of exploration in the fifteenth century? Part of the answer lies in the individual ambitions and adventurous personalities of these states' leaders. Another part of the answer can be found in long-term tendencies in Europe and the Mediterranean. In many ways these voyages continued four trends evident in the Latin West since about the year 1000: (1) the revival of urban life and trade, (2) a struggle with Islamic powers for dominance of the Mediterranean that mixed religious motives with the desire for trade with distant lands, (3) growing intellectual curiosity about the outside world, and (4) a peculiarly European alliance between merchants and rulers.

The city-states of northern Italy took the lead in all these developments. By 1450 they had well-established trade links to northern Europe, the Indian Ocean, and the Black Sea, and their merchant princes had also sponsored an intellectual and artistic Renaissance. But there were two reasons why Italian states did not take the lead in exploring the Atlantic, even after the expansion of the Ottoman Empire disrupted their trade to the East and led other Christian Europeans to launch new religious wars against the Ottomans in 1396 and 1444. The first was that the trading states of Venice and Genoa preferred to continue the system of alliances with the Muslims that had given their merchants privileged access to the lucrative trade from the East. The second was that the ships of the Mediterranean were ill suited to the more violent weather of the Atlantic. However, many individual Italians played leading roles in the Atlantic explorations.

In contrast, the special history and geography of the Iberian kingdoms led them in a different direction. Part of that special history was centuries of anti-Muslim warfare that dated back to the eighth century, when Muslim forces overran most of Iberia. By about 1250 the Iberian kingdoms of Portugal, Castile, and Aragon had conquered all the Muslim lands in Iberia except the southern kingdom of Granada. United by a dynastic marriage in 1469, Castile and Aragon conquered Granada in 1492. These territories were gradually amalgamated into Spain, sixteenth-century Europe's most powerful state.

Christian militancy continued to be an important motive for both Portugal and Spain in their overseas ventures. But the Iberian rulers and their adventurous subjects were also seeking material returns. With only a modest share of the Mediterranean trade, they were much more willing than the Italians to take risks to find new routes through the Atlantic to the rich trade of Africa and Asia. Moreover, both were participants in the shipbuilding changes and the gunpowder revolution that were under way in Atlantic Europe. Though not centers of Renaissance learning, both were especially open to new geographical knowledge. Finally, both states were blessed with exceptional leaders.

Portuguese Voyages

Portugal's decision to invest significant resources in new exploration rested on well-established Atlantic fishing and a history of anti-Muslim warfare. When the Muslim government of Morocco in northwestern Africa showed weakness in the fifteenth century, the Portuguese went on the attack, beginning with the city of Ceuta° in 1415. This assault combined aspects of a religious crusade, a plundering expedition, and a military tournament in which young Portuguese knights displayed their bravery. The capture of the rich North African city, whose splendid homes, they reported, made those of Portugal look like pigsties, also made the Portuguese better informed about the caravans that brought gold and slaves to Ceuta from the African states south of the Sahara. Despite the capture of several more ports along Morocco's Atlantic coast, the Portuguese were unable to push inland and gain access to the gold trade. So they sought more direct contact with the gold producers by sailing down the African coast.

The attack on Ceuta was led by young Prince Henry (1394–1460), third son of the king of Portugal. Because he devoted the rest of his life to promoting exploration of the South Atlantic, he is known as **Henry the Navigator**. His official biographer emphasized Henry's mixed motives for exploration—converting Africans to Christianity, making contact with existing Christian rulers in Africa, and launching joint crusades with them against the Ottomans. Prince Henry also wished to discover new places and hoped that such new contacts would be profitable. His initial explorations were concerned with Africa. Only later did reaching India become an explicit goal of Portuguese explorers.

Despite being called "the Navigator," Prince Henry himself never ventured much farther from home than North Africa. Instead, he founded a sort of research institute at Sagres° for studying navigation and collecting information about the lands beyond Muslim North Africa. His staff drew on the pioneering efforts of Italian merchants, especially the Genoese, who had learned some of the secrets of the trans-Saharan trade, and of fourteenth-century Jewish cartographers who used information from Arab and European sources to produce remarkably

Ceuta (say-OO-tuh)   **Sagres** (SAH-gresh)

accurate sea charts and maps of distant places. Henry also oversaw the collection of new geographical information from sailors and travelers and sent out ships to explore the Atlantic. His ships established permanent contact with the islands of Madeira in 1418 and the Azores in 1439.

Henry devoted resources to solving the technical problems faced by mariners sailing in unknown waters and open seas. His staff studied and improved navigational instruments that had come into Europe from China and the Islamic world. These instruments included the magnetic compass, first developed in China, and the astrolabe, an instrument of Arab or Greek invention that enabled mariners to determine their location at sea by measuring the position of the sun or the stars in the night sky. Even with such instruments, however, voyages still depended on the skill and experience of the navigators.

Another achievement of Portuguese mariners was the design of vessels appropriate for the voyages of exploration. The galleys in use in the Mediterranean were powered by large numbers of oarsmen and were impractical for long ocean voyages. The square sails of the three-masted European ships of the North Atlantic were propelled by friendly winds but could not sail at much of an angle against the wind. The voyages of exploration made use of a new vessel, the **caravel**°. Caravels were small, only one-fifth the size of the largest European ships of their day and of the large Chinese junks. Their size permitted them to enter shallow coastal waters and explore upriver, but they were strong enough to weather ocean storms. When equipped with lateen sails, caravels had great maneuverability and could sail deeply into the wind; when sporting square Atlantic sails, they had great speed. The addition of small cannon made them good fighting ships as well. The caravels' economy, speed, agility, and power justified a contemporary's claim that they were "the best ships that sailed the seas."[2]

To conquer the seas, pioneering captains had to overcome crew's fears that the South Atlantic waters were boiling hot and contained ocean currents that would prevent any ship entering them from ever returning home. It took Prince Henry fourteen years—from 1420 to 1434—to coax an expedition to venture beyond southern Morocco (see Map 16.3). The crew's fears proved unfounded, but the next stretch of coast, 800 miles (1,300 kilometers) of desert, offered little of interest to the explorers. Finally, in 1444 the mariners reached the Senegal River and the well-watered and well-populated lands below the Sahara beginning at what they named "Cape Verde" (Green Cape) because of its vegetation.

In the years that followed, Henry's explorers made an important addition to the maritime revolution by learning how to return speedily to Portugal. Instead of battling the prevailing northeast trade winds and currents back up the coast, they discovered that by sailing northwest into the Atlantic to the latitude of the Azores, ships could pick up prevailing westerly winds that would blow them back to Portugal. The knowledge that ocean winds tend to form large circular patterns helped explorers discover many other ocean routes.

To pay for the research, the ships, and the expeditions during the many decades before the voyages became profitable, Prince Henry drew partly on the income of the Order of Christ, a military religious order of which he was governor. The Order of Christ had inherited the properties and crusading traditions of the Order of Knights Templar, which had disbanded in 1314. The Order of Christ received the exclusive right to promote Christianity in all the lands that were discovered, and the Portuguese emblazoned their ships' sails with the crusaders' red cross.

The first financial return from the voyages came from selling into slavery Africans captured by the Portuguese in raids on the northwest coast of Africa and the Canary Islands during the 1440s. The total number of Africans captured or purchased on voyages exceeded eighty thousand by the end of the century and rose steadily thereafter. However, the gold trade quickly became more important than the slave trade as the Portuguese made contact with the trading networks that flourished in West Africa and reached across the Sahara. By 1457 enough African gold was coming back to Portugal for the kingdom to issue a new gold coin called the *cruzado* (crusade), another reminder of how deeply the Portuguese entwined religious and secular motives.

By the time of Prince Henry's death in 1460, his explorers had established a secure base of operations in the uninhabited Cape Verde Islands and had explored 600 miles (950 kilometers) of coast beyond Cape Verde, as far as what they named Sierra Leone° (Lion Mountain). From there they knew the coast of Africa curved sharply toward the east. It had taken the Portuguese four decades to cover the 1,500 miles (2,400 kilometers) from Lisbon to Sierra Leone; it took only three decades to explore the remaining 4,000 miles (6,400 kilometers) to the southern tip of the African continent.

The Portuguese crown continued to sponsor voyages of exploration, but speedier progress resulted from the growing participation of private commercial interests. In 1469 a prominent Lisbon merchant named

---

caravel (KAR-uh-vel)

Sierra Leone (see- ER-uh lee-OWN)

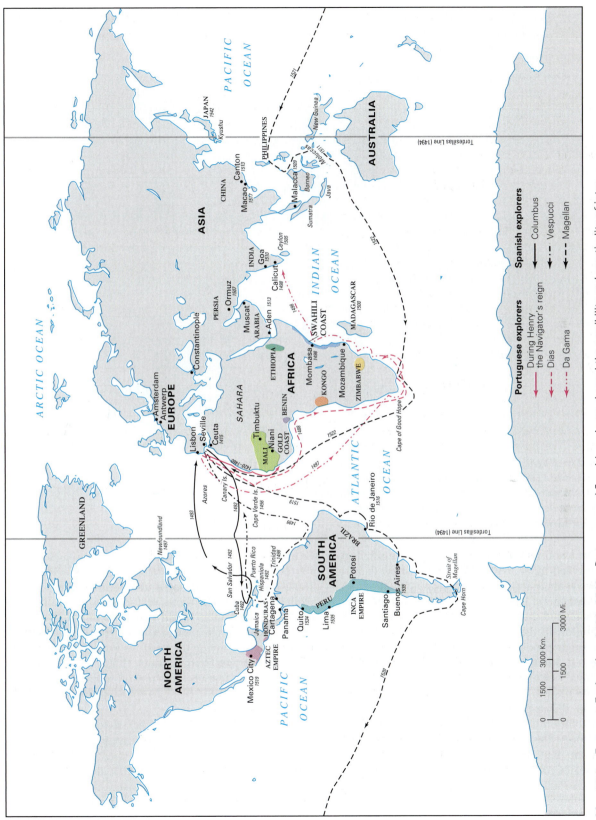

Map 16.3   European Exploration, 1420–1542   Portuguese and Spanish explorers showed the possibility and practicality of inter-continental maritime trade. Before 1540 European trade with Africa and Asia was much more important than that with the Americas, but after the Spanish conquest of the Aztec and Inca Empires transatlantic trade began to increase. Notice the Tordesillas line, which in theory separated the Spanish and Portuguese spheres of activity.

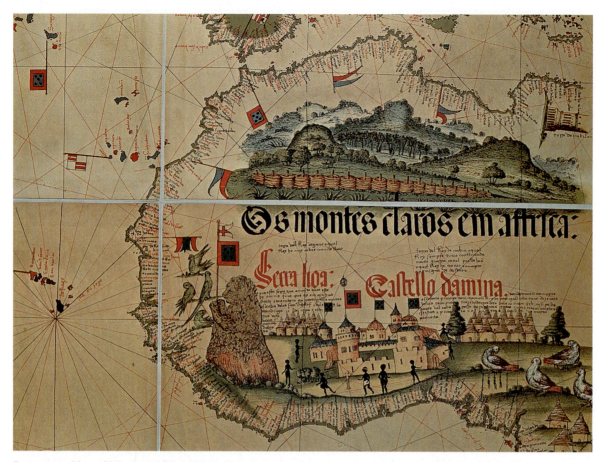

Os montes claros em affrica.

Serra lioa.   **Castello damina.**

Portuguese Map of Western Africa, 1502   This map shows in great detail a section of African coastline that Portuguese explorers charted and named in the fifteenth century. The cartographer illustrated the African interior, which was almost completely unknown to Europeans, with drawings of birds and views of coastal sights: Sierra Leone (Serra lioa), named for a mountain shaped like a lion, and the Portuguese Castle of the Mine (Castello damina) on the Gold Coast.   (akg-images)

Fernão Gomes purchased from the Crown the privilege of exploring 350 miles (550 kilometers) of new coast a year for five years in return for a monopoly on the trade he developed there. During the period of his contract, Gomes discovered the uninhabited island of São Tomé° on the equator; in the next century it became a major source of sugar produced with African slave labor. He also explored what later Europeans called the **Gold Coast**, which became the headquarters of Portugal's West African trade.

The final thrust down the African coast was spurred by the expectation of finding a passage around Africa to the rich trade of the Indian Ocean. In 1488 **Bartolomeu Dias** was the first Portuguese explorer to round the southern tip of Africa and enter the Indian Ocean. In 1497–1498 a Portuguese expedition led by **Vasco da Gama** sailed around Africa and reached India (see Environment and Technology: Vasco da Gama's Fleet). In 1500 ships in an expedition under Pedro Alvares Cabral°, while swinging wide to the west in the South Atlantic to catch the winds that would sweep them around southern Africa and on to India, came on the eastern coast of South America, laying the basis for Portugal's later claim to Brazil. The gamble that Prince Henry had begun eight decades earlier was about to pay off handsomely.

Spanish Voyages

In contrast to the persistence and planning behind Portugal's century-long exploration of the South Atlantic, haste and blind luck lay behind Spain's early discoveries. Throughout most of the fifteenth cen-

São Tomé (sow toh-MAY)

Cabral (kah-BRAHL)

Vasco da Gama's Fleet

The four small ships that sailed for India from Lisbon in June 1497 may seem a puny fleet compared to the sixty-two Chinese vessels that Zheng He had led into the Indian Ocean ninety-five years earlier. But given the fact that China had a hundred times as many people as Portugal, Vasco da Gama's fleet represented at least as great a commitment of resources. In any event, the Portuguese expedition had a far greater impact on the course of history. Having achieved its aim of inspiring awe at China's greatness, the Chinese throne sent out no more expeditions after 1432. Although da Gama's ships seemed more odd than awesome to Indian Ocean observers, that modest fleet began a revolution in global relations.

Portugal spared no expense in ensuring that the fleet would make it to India and back. Craftsmen built extra strength into the hulls to withstand the powerful storms that Dias had encountered in 1488 at the tip of Africa. Small enough to be able to navigate any shallow harbors and rivers they might encounter, the ships were crammed with specially strengthened casks and barrels of water, wine, oil, flour, meat, and vegetables far in excess of what was required even on a voyage that would take the better part of a year. Arms and ammunition were also in abundance.

Three of da Gama's ships were rigged with square sails on two masts for speed and a lateen sail on the third mast. The fourth vessel was a caravel with lateen sails. Each ship carried three sets of sails and plenty of extra rigging so as to be able to repair any damages due to storms. The crusaders' red crosses on the sails signaled one of the expedition's motives.

The captains and crew—Portugal's most talented and experienced—received extra pay and other rewards for their service. Yet there was no expectation that the unprecedented sums spent on this expedition would bring any immediate return. According to a contemporary chronicle, the only immediate return the Portuguese monarch received was

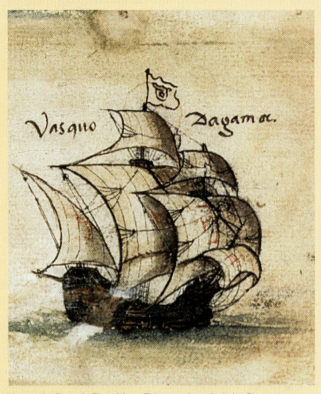

Vasco da Gama's Flagship This vessel carried the Portuguese captain on his second expedition to India in 1505. (The Pierpont Morgan Library/Art Resource, NY)

"the knowledge that some part of Ethiopia and the beginning of Lower India had been discovered." However, the scale and care of the preparations suggest that the Portuguese expected the expedition to open up profitable trade to the Indian Ocean. And so it did.

tury, the Spanish kingdoms had been preoccupied with internal affairs: completion of the reconquest of southern Iberia; amalgamation of the various dynasties; and the conversion or expulsion of religious minorities. Only in the last decade of the century were Spanish monarchs ready to turn again to overseas exploration, by which time the Portuguese had already found a new route to the Indian Ocean.

The leader of their overseas mission was **Christopher Columbus** (1451–1506), a Genoese mariner. His four voyages between 1492 and 1502 established the existence of a vast new world across the Atlantic, whose existence few in "old world" Eurasia and Africa had ever suspected. But Columbus refused to accept that he had found unknown continents and peoples, insisting that he had succeeded in his goal of finding a shorter route to the Indian Ocean than the one the Portuguese had found.

As a younger man Columbus had gained considerable experience of the South Atlantic while participating in Portuguese explorations along the African coast, but he had become convinced there was a shorter way to reach the riches of the East than the route around Africa. By his reckoning (based on a serious misreading of a ninth-century Arab authority), the Canaries were a mere 2,400 nautical miles (4,450 kilometers) from Japan. The actual distance was five times as far.

It was not easy for Columbus to find a sponsor willing to underwrite the costs of testing his theory that one could reach Asia by sailing west. Portuguese authorities twice rejected his plan, first in 1485 following a careful study and again in 1488 after Dias had established the feasibility of a route around Africa. Columbus received a more sympathetic hearing in 1486 from Castile's able ruler, Queen Isabella, but no commitment of support. After a four-year study a Castilian commission appointed by Isabella concluded that a westward sea route to the Indies rested on many questionable geographical assumptions, but Columbus's persistence finally won over the queen and her husband, King Ferdinand of Aragon. In 1492 they agreed to fund a modest expedition. Their elation at expelling the Muslims from Granada may have put them in a favorable mood.

Columbus recorded in his log that he and his mostly Spanish crew of ninety men "departed Friday the third day of August of the year 1492," toward "the regions of India." Their mission, the royal contract stated, was "to discover and acquire certain islands and mainland in the Ocean Sea." He carried letters of introduction from the Spanish sovereigns to Eastern rulers, including one to the "Grand Khan" (meaning the Chinese emperor). Also on board was a Jewish convert to Christianity whose knowledge of Arabic was expected to facilitate communication with the peoples of eastern Asia. The expedition traveled in three small ships, the *Santa María*, the *Santa Clara* (nicknamed the *Niña*), and a third vessel now known only by its nickname, the *Pinta*. The *Niña* and the *Pinta* were caravels.

The expedition began well. Other attempts to explore the Atlantic west of the Azores had been impeded by unfavorable headwinds. But on earlier voyages along the African coast, Columbus had learned that he could find west-blowing winds in the latitudes of the Canaries, which is why he chose that southern route. After reaching the Canaries, he had the *Niña's* lateen sails replaced with square sails, for he knew that from then on speed would be more important than maneuverability.

In October 1492 the expedition reached the islands of the Caribbean. Columbus insisted on calling the inhabitants "Indians" because he believed that the islands were part of the East Indies. A second voyage to the Caribbean in 1493 did nothing to change his mind. Even when, two months after Vasco da Gama reached India in 1498, Columbus first sighted the mainland of South America on a third voyage, he stubbornly insisted it was part of Asia. But by then other Europeans were convinced that he had discovered islands and continents previously unknown to the Old World. Amerigo Vespucci's explorations, first on behalf of Spain and then for Portugal, led mapmakers to name the new continents "America" after him, rather than "Columbia" after Columbus.

To prevent disputes arising from their efforts to exploit their new discoveries and to spread Christianity among the people there, Spain and Portugal agreed to split the world between them. The Treaty of Tordesillas°, negotiated by the pope in 1494, drew an imaginary line down the middle of the North Atlantic Ocean. Lands east of the line in Africa and southern Asia could be claimed by Portugal; lands to the west in the Americas were reserved for Spain. Cabral's discovery of Brazil, however, gave Portugal a valid claim to the part of South America that bulged east of the line.

But if the Tordesillas line were extended around the earth, where would Spain's and Portugal's spheres of influence divide in the East? Given Europeans' ignorance of the earth's true size in 1494, it was not clear whether the Moluccas°, whose valuable spices had been a goal of the Iberian voyages, were on Portugal's or Spain's side of the line. The missing information concerned the size of the Pacific Ocean. By chance, in 1513 a Spanish adventurer named Vasco Núñez de Balboa° crossed the

---

Tordesillas (tor-duh-SEE-yuhs) **Moluccas** (muh-LOO-kuhz)
Balboa (bal-BOH-uh)

isthmus (a narrow neck of land) of Panama from the east and sighted the Pacific Ocean on the other side. And the 1519 expedition of **Ferdinand Magellan** (ca. 1480–1521) was designed to complete Columbus's interrupted westward voyage by sailing around the Americas and across the Pacific, whose vast size no European then guessed. The Moluccas turned out to lie well within Portugal's sphere, as Spain formally acknowledged in 1529.

Magellan's voyage laid the basis for Spanish colonization of the Philippine Islands after 1564. Nor did Magellan's death prevent him from being considered the first person to encircle the globe, for a decade earlier he had sailed from Europe to the East Indies as part of an expedition sponsored by his native Portugal. His two voyages took him across the Tordesillas line, through the separate spheres claimed by Portugal and Spain—at least until other Europeans began demanding a share. Of course, in 1500 European claims were largely theoretical. Portugal and Spain had only modest settlements overseas.

Although Columbus failed to find a new route to the East, the consequences of his voyages for European expansion were momentous. Those who followed in his wake laid the basis for Spain's large colonial empires in the Americas and for the empires of other European nations. In turn, these empires promoted, among the four Atlantic continents, the growth of a major new trading network whose importance rivaled and eventually surpassed that of the Indian Ocean network. The more immediately important consequence was Portugal's entry into the Indian Ocean, which quickly led to a major European presence and profit. Both the eastward and the westward voyages of exploration marked a tremendous expansion of Europe's role in world history.

ENCOUNTERS WITH EUROPE, 1450–1550

European actions alone did not determine the consequences of the new contacts that Iberian mariners had opened. The ways in which Africans, Asians, and Amerindians perceived their new visitors and interacted with them also influenced their future relations. Some welcomed the Europeans as potential allies; others viewed them as rivals or enemies. In general, Africans and Asians had little difficulty in recognizing the benefits and dangers that European contacts might bring. However, the long isolation of the Amerindians from the rest of the world added to the strangeness of their encounter

with the Spanish and made them more vulnerable to the unfamiliar diseases that these explorers inadvertently introduced.

Western Africa

Many Africans along the West African coast were eager for trade with the Portuguese. It would give them new markets for their exports and access to imports cheaper than those that reached them through the middlemen of the overland routes to the Mediterranean. This reaction was evident along the Gold Coast of West Africa, first visited by the Portuguese in 1471. Miners in the hinterland had long sold their gold to African traders, who took it to the trading cities along the southern edge of the Sahara, where it was sold to traders who had crossed the desert from North Africa. Recognizing that they might get more favorable terms from the new sea visitors, coastal Africans were ready to negotiate with the royal representative of Portugal who arrived in 1482 seeking permission to erect a trading fort.

The Portuguese noble in charge and his officers (likely including the young Christopher Columbus, who had entered Portuguese service in 1476) were eager to make a proper impression. They dressed in their best clothes, erected and decorated a reception platform, celebrated a Catholic Mass, and signaled the start of negotiations with trumpets, tambourines, and drums. The African king, Caramansa, staged his entrance with equal ceremony, arriving with a large retinue of attendants and musicians. Through an African interpreter, the two leaders exchanged flowery speeches pledging goodwill and mutual benefit. Caramansa then gave his permission for a small trading fort to be built, assured, he said, by the appearance of these royal delegates that they were honorable persons, unlike the "few, foul, and vile" Portuguese visitors of the previous decade.

Neither side made a show of force, but the Africans' upper hand was evident in Caramansa's warning that if the Portuguese failed to be peaceful and honest traders, he and his people would simply move away, depriving their post of food and trade. Trade at the post of Saint George of the Mine (later called Elmina) enriched both sides. From there the Portuguese crown was soon purchasing gold equal to one-tenth of the world's production at the time. In return, Africans received large quantities of goods that Portuguese ships brought from Asia, Europe, and other parts of Africa.

After a century of aggressive expansion, the kingdom of Benin in the Niger Delta was near the peak of its power when it first encountered the Portuguese. Its oba (king) presided over an elaborate bureaucracy from a spacious palace in his large capital city, also known as Benin. In response to a Portuguese visit in 1486, the oba sent an ambassador to Portugal to learn more about the homeland of these strangers. Then he established a royal monopoly on trade with the Portuguese, selling pepper and ivory tusks (to be taken back to Portugal) as well as stone beads, textiles, and prisoners of war (to be resold at Elmina). In return, the Portuguese merchants provided Benin with copper and brass, fine textiles, glass beads, and a horse for the king's royal procession. In the early sixteenth century, as the demand for slaves for the Portuguese sugar plantations on the nearby island of São Tomé grew, the oba first raised the price of slaves and then imposed restrictions that limited their sale.

Early contacts generally involved a mixture of commercial, military, and religious interests. Some African rulers were quick to appreciate that the European firearms could be a useful addition to their spears and arrows in conflicts with their enemies. Because African religions did not presume to have a monopoly on religious knowledge, coastal rulers were also willing to test the value of Christian practices, which the Portuguese eagerly promoted. The rulers of Benin and Kongo, the two largest coastal kingdoms, invited Portuguese missionaries and soldiers to accompany them into battle to test the Christians' religion along with their muskets.

Portuguese efforts to persuade the king and nobles of Benin to accept the Catholic faith ultimately failed. Early kings showed some interest, but after 1538 the rulers declined to receive any more missionaries. They also closed the market in male slaves for the rest of the sixteenth century. Exactly why Benin chose to limit its contacts with the Portuguese is uncertain, but the rulers clearly had the power to control the amount of interaction.

Farther south, on the lower Congo River, relations between the kingdom of Kongo and the Portuguese began similarly but had a very different outcome. Like the oba of Benin, the manikongo° (king of Kongo) sent delegates to Portugal, established a royal monopoly on trade with the Portuguese, and expressed interest in missionary teachings. Deeply impressed with the new religion, the royal family made Catholicism the kingdom's official faith. But Kongo, lacking ivory and pepper, had less to trade than Benin. To acquire the goods brought by Portugal and to pay the costs of the missionaries, it had to sell more and more slaves.

Soon the manikongo began to lose his royal monopoly over the slave trade. In 1526 the Christian manikongo, Afonso I (r. 1506–ca. 1540), wrote to his royal

Afro–Portuguese Ivory   A skilled ivory carver from the kingdom of Benin probably made this saltcellar. Intended for a European market, it depicts a Portuguese ship on the cover and Portuguese nobles around the base. However European the subject, the craftsmanship is typical of Benin.   (Courtesy of the Trustees of the British Museum)

"brother," the king of Portugal, begging for his help in stopping the trade because unauthorized Kongolese were kidnapping and selling people, even members of good families (see Diversity and Dominance: Kongo's Christian King). Alfonso's appeals for help received no reply from Portugal, whose interests had moved to the Indian Ocean. Some subjects took advantage of the manikongo's weakness to rebel against his authority. After 1540 the major part of the slave trade from this part of Africa moved farther south.

---

manikongo (mah-NEE-KONG-goh)

Eastern Africa

Different still were the reactions of the Muslim rulers of the trading coastal states of eastern Africa. As Vasco da Gama's fleet sailed up the coast in 1498, most rulers gave the Portuguese a cool reception, suspicious of the intentions of these visitors who painted crusaders' crosses on their sails. But the ruler of one of the ports, Malindi, saw in the Portuguese an ally who could help him expand the city's trading position and provided da Gama with a pilot to guide him to India. The suspicions of most rulers were justified seven years later when a Portuguese war fleet bombarded and looted most of the coastal cities of eastern Africa in the name of Christ and commerce, though they spared Malindi.

Another eastern African state that saw potential benefit in an alliance with the Portuguese was Christian Ethiopia. In the fourteenth and early fifteenth centuries, Ethiopia faced increasing conflicts with Muslim states along the Red Sea. Emboldened by the rise of the Ottoman Turks, who had conquered Egypt in 1517 and launched a major fleet in the Indian Ocean to counter the Portuguese, the talented warlord of the Muslim state of Adal launched a furious assault on Ethiopia. Adal's decisive victory in 1529 reduced the Christian kingdom to a precarious state. At that point Ethiopia's contacts with the Portuguese became crucial.

For decades, delegations from Portugal and Ethiopia had been exploring a possible alliance between their states based on their mutual adherence to Christianity. A key figure was Queen Helena of Ethiopia, who acted as regent for her young sons after her husband's death in 1478. In 1509 Helena sent a letter to "our very dear and well-beloved brother," the king of Portugal, along with a gift of two tiny crucifixes said to be made of wood from the cross on which Christ had died in Jerusalem. In her letter she proposed an alliance of her land army and Portugal's fleet against the Turks. No such alliance was completed by the time Helena died in 1522. But as Ethiopia's situation grew increasingly desperate, renewed appeals for help were made.

Finally, a small Portuguese force commanded by Vasco da Gama's son Christopher reached Ethiopia in 1539, at a time when what was left of the empire was being held together by another woman ruler. With Portuguese help, the queen rallied the Ethiopians to renew their struggle. Christopher da Gama was captured and tortured to death, but the Muslim forces lost heart when their leader was mortally wounded in a later battle. Portuguese aid helped the Ethiopian kingdom save itself from extinction, but a permanent alliance faltered because Ethiopian rulers refused to transfer their Christian affiliation from the patriarch of Alexandria to the Latin patriarch of Rome (the pope) as the Portuguese wanted.

As these examples illustrate, African encounters with the Portuguese before 1550 varied considerably, as much because of the strategies and leadership of particular African states as because of Portuguese policies. Africans and Portuguese might become royal brothers, bitter opponents, or partners in a mutually profitable trade, but Europeans remained a minor presence in most of Africa in 1550. By then the Portuguese had become far more interested in the Indian Ocean trade.

Indian Ocean States

Vasco da Gama's arrival on the Malabar Coast of India in May 1498 did not make a great impression on the citizens of Calicut. After more than ten months at sea, many members of the crew were in ill health. Da Gama's four small ships were far less imposing than the Chinese fleets of gigantic junks that had called at Calicut sixty-five years earlier and no larger than many of the dhows that filled the harbor of this rich and important trading city. The samorin (ruler) of Calicut and his Muslim officials showed mild interest in the Portuguese as new trading partners, but the gifts da Gama had brought for the samorin evoked derisive laughter. Twelve pieces of fairly ordinary striped cloth, four scarlet hoods, six hats, and six wash basins seemed inferior goods to those accustomed to the luxuries of the Indian Ocean trade. When da Gama tried to defend his gifts as those of an explorer, not a rich merchant, the samorin cut him short, asking whether he had come to discover men or stones: "If he had come to discover men, as he said, why had he brought nothing?"

Coastal rulers soon discovered that the Portuguese had no intention of remaining poor competitors in the rich trade of the Indian Ocean. Upon da Gama's return to Portugal in 1499, the jubilant King Manuel styled himself "Lord of the Conquest, Navigation, and Commerce of Ethiopia, Arabia, Persia, and India," setting forth the ambitious scope of his plans. Previously the Indian Ocean had been an open sea, used by merchants (and pirates) of all the surrounding coasts. Now the Portuguese crown intended to make it Portugal's sea, the private property of the Portuguese alone, which others might use only on Portuguese terms.

The ability of little Portugal to assert control over the Indian Ocean stemmed from the superiority of its ships and weapons over the smaller and lightly armed merchant dhows. In 1505 the Portuguese fleet of eighty-one ships and some seven thousand men bombarded Swahili Coast cities. Next on the list were Indian ports. Goa, on the

Portuguese in India In the sixteenth century Portuguese men moved to the Indian Ocean basin to work as administrators and traders. This Indo-Portuguese drawing from about 1540 shows a Portuguese man speaking to an Indian woman, perhaps making a proposal of marriage. (Ms. 1889, c. 97, Biblioteca Casanateunse Rome. Photo: Humberto Nicoletti Serra)

west coast of India, fell to a well-armed fleet in 1510, becoming the base from which the Portuguese menaced the trading cities of Gujarat° to the north and Calicut and other Malabar Coast cities to the south. The port of Hormuz, controlling the entry to the Persian Gulf, was taken in 1515. Aden, at the entrance to the Red Sea, used its intricate natural defenses to preserve its independence. The addition of the Gujarati port of Diu in 1535 consolidated Portuguese dominance of the western Indian Ocean.

Meanwhile, Portuguese explorers had been reconnoitering the Bay of Bengal and the waters farther east. The independent city of Malacca° on the strait between the Malay Peninsula and Sumatra became the focus of their attention. During the fifteenth century Malacca had become the main entrepôt° (a place where goods are stored or deposited and from which they are distributed) for the trade from China, Japan, India, the Southeast Asian mainland, and the Moluccas. Among the city's more than 100,000 residents an early Portuguese counted

eighty-four different languages, including those of merchants from as far west as Cairo, Ethiopia, and the Swahili Coast of East Africa. Many non-Muslim residents supported letting the Portuguese join this cosmopolitan trading community, perhaps to offset the growing solidarity of Muslim traders. In 1511, however, the Portuguese seized this strategic trading center with a force of a thousand fighting men, including three hundred recruited in southern India.

Force was not always necessary. On the China coast, local officials and merchants interested in profitable new trade with the Portuguese persuaded the imperial government to allow the Portuguese to establish a trading post at Macao° in 1557. Operating from Macao, Portuguese ships nearly monopolized the trade between China and Japan.

In the Indian Ocean, the Portuguese used their control of the major port cities to enforce an even larger trading monopoly. They required all spices, as well as all goods on the major ocean routes such as between Goa

---

Gujarat (goo-juh-RAHT)   **Malacca** (muh-LAH-kuh)
entrepôt (ON-truh-poh)

Macao (muh-COW)

and Macao, to be carried in Portuguese ships. In addition, the Portuguese also tried to control and tax other Indian Ocean trade by requiring all merchant ships entering and leaving one of their ports to carry a Portuguese passport and to pay customs duties. Portuguese patrols seized vessels that attempted to avoid these monopolies, confiscated their cargoes, and either killed the captain and crew or sentenced them to forced labor.

Reactions to this power grab varied. Like the emperors of China, the Mughal° emperors of India largely ignored Portugal's maritime intrusions, seeing their interests as maintaining control over their vast land possessions. The Ottomans responded more aggressively. From 1501 to 1509 they supported Egypt's fleet of fifteen thousand men against the Christian intruders. Then, having absorbed Egypt into their empire, the Ottomans sent another large expedition against the Portuguese in 1538. Both expeditions failed because the Ottoman galleys were no match for the faster, better-armed Portuguese vessels in the open ocean. However, the Ottomans retained the advantage in the Red Sea and Persian Gulf, where they had many ports of supply.

The smaller trading states of the region were even less capable of challenging Portuguese domination head on, since their mutual rivalry impeded the formation of any common front. Some chose to cooperate with the Portuguese to maintain their prosperity and security. Others engaged in evasion and resistance. Two examples illustrate the range of responses among Indian Ocean peoples.

The merchants of Calicut put up some of the most sustained local resistance. In retaliation, the Portuguese embargoed all trade with Aden, Calicut's principal trading partner, and centered their trade on the port of Cochin, which had once been a dependency of Calicut. Some Calicut merchants became adept at evading the patrol, but the price of resistance was the shrinking of Calicut's importance as Cochin gradually became the major pepper-exporting port on the Malabar Coast.

The traders and rulers of the state of Gujarat farther north had less success in keeping the Portuguese at bay. At first they resisted Portuguese attempts at monopoly and in 1509 joined Egypt's failed effort to sweep the Portuguese from the Arabian Sea. But in 1535, finding his state at a military disadvantage due to Mughal attacks, the ruler of Gujarat made the fateful decision to allow the Portuguese to build a fort at Diu in return for their support. Once established, the Portuguese gradually extended their control, so that by midcentury they were licensing and taxing all Gujarati ships. Even after the Mughals (who were Muslims) took control of Gujarat in

Mughal (MOO-gahl)

1572, the Mughal emperor Akbar permitted the Portuguese to continue their maritime monopoly in return for allowing one ship a year to carry pilgrims to Mecca without paying the Portuguese any fee.

The Portuguese never gained complete control of the Indian Ocean trade, but their domination of key ports and the main trade routes during the sixteenth century brought them considerable profit, which they sent back to Europe in the form of spices and other luxury goods. The effects were dramatic. The Portuguese sold the large quantities of pepper that they exported for less than the price charged by Venice and Genoa for pepper obtained through Egyptian middlemen, thus breaking the Italian cities' monopoly.

In Asia the consequences were equally startling. Asian and East African traders were at the mercy of Portuguese warships, but their individual responses affected their fates. Some were devastated. Others prospered by meeting Portuguese demands or evading their patrols. Because the Portuguese were ocean-based, they had little impact on the Asian and African mainlands, in sharp contrast to what was occurring in the Americas.

The Americas

In the Americas the Spanish established a vast territorial empire, in contrast to the trading empires the Portuguese created in Africa and Asia. This outcome had little to do with differences between the two Iberian kingdoms, except for the fact that the Spanish kingdoms had somewhat greater resources to draw on. The Spanish and Portuguese monarchies had similar motives for expansion and used identical ships and weapons. Rather, the isolation of the Amerindian peoples made their responses to outside contacts different from the responses of peoples in Africa and the Indian Ocean cities. In dealing with the small communities in the Caribbean, the first European settlers resorted to conquest and plunder rather than trade. This practice was later extended to the more powerful Amerindian kingdoms on the American mainland. The spread of deadly new diseases among the Amerindians after 1518 weakened their ability to resist.

The first Amerindians to encounter Columbus were the Arawak of Hispaniola (modern Haiti and the Dominican Republic) in the Greater Antilles and the Bahamas to the north (see Map 16.2). They cultivated maize (corn), cassava (a tuber), sweet potatoes, and hot peppers, as well as cotton and tobacco, and they met their other material needs from the sea and wild plants. Although they were skilled at mining and working gold, the Arawak did not trade gold over long distances as

Africans did, and they had no iron. The Arawak at first extended a cautious welcome to the Spanish but were unprepared to sell them large quantities of gold. Instead, they told Columbus exaggerated stories about gold in other places to persuade him to move on.

When Columbus made his second trip to Hispaniola in 1493, he brought several hundred settlers from southern Iberia who hoped to make their fortune and missionaries who were eager to persuade the Indians to accept Christianity. The settlers stole gold ornaments, confiscated food, and raped women, provoking the Hispaniola Arawak to war in 1495. In this and later conflicts, horses and body armor gave the Spaniards a great advantage. Tens of thousands of Arawak were slaughtered. Those who survived were forced to pay a heavy tax in gold, spun cotton, and food. Any who failed to meet the quotas were condemned to forced labor. Meanwhile, the cattle, pigs, and goats introduced by the settlers devoured the Arawak's food crops, causing deaths from famine and disease. A governor appointed by the Spanish crown in 1502 forced the Arawak remaining on Hispaniola to be laborers under the control of Spanish settlers.

The actions of the Spanish in the Antilles were reflections of Spanish actions and motives during the wars against the Muslims in Spain in the previous centuries: seeking to serve God by defeating nonbelievers and placing them under Christian control—and becoming rich in the process. Individual **conquistadors**° (conquerors) extended that pattern around the Caribbean. Some attacked the Bahamas to get gold and labor as both became scarce on Hispaniola. Many Arawak from the Bahamas were taken to Hispaniola as slaves. Juan Ponce de León (1460–1521), who had participated in the conquest of Muslim Spain and the seizure of Hispaniola, conquered the island of Borinquen (Puerto Rico) in 1508 and explored southeastern Florida in 1513.

An ambitious and ruthless nobleman, **Hernán Cortés**° (1485–1547), led the most audacious expedition to the mainland. Cortés left Cuba in 1519 with six hundred fighting men and most of the island's stock of weapons to assault the Mexican mainland in search of slaves and to establish trade. When the expedition learned of the rich Aztec Empire in central Mexico, Cortés brought to the American mainland, on a massive scale, the exploitation and conquest begun in the reconquest of Muslim Iberia and continued in the Greater Antilles.

The Aztecs themselves had conquered their vast empire only during the previous century, and many of the Amerindians they had subjugated were far from loyal subjects. Many resented the tribute they had to pay the

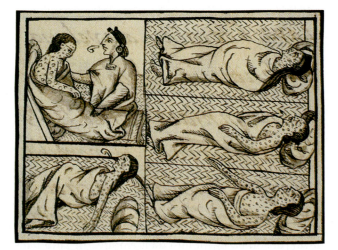

Death from Smallpox   This Aztec drawing shows a healer attending smallpox victims. The little puffs coming from their mouths represent speech.   (Biblioteca Medicea Laurenziana. Photo: MicroFoto, Florence)

Aztecs, the forced labor, and the large-scale human sacrifices to the Aztec gods. Many subject people saw the Spaniards as powerful human allies against the Aztecs and gave them their support. Like the Caribbean people, the Amerindians of Mexico had no precedent by which to judge these strange visitors.

Aztec accounts suggest that some believed Cortés to be the legendary ruler Quetzalcoatl°, whose return to earth had been prophesied, and treated him with great deference. Another consequence of millennia of isolation was far more significant: the lack of acquired immunity to the diseases of the Old World. Smallpox was the most deadly of the early epidemics that accompanied the Spanish conquistadors. It appeared for the first time on the island of Hispaniola late in 1518. An infected member of the Cortés expedition then transmitted smallpox to Mexico in 1519, where it spread with deadly efficiency.

From his glorious capital city Tenochtitlan°, the Aztec emperor **Moctezuma**° II (r. 1502–1520) sent messengers to greet Cortés and determine whether he was god or man, friend or foe. Cortés advanced steadily toward Tenochtitlan, overcoming Aztec opposition with cavalry charges and steel swords and gaining the support of thousands of Amerindian allies from among the unhappy subjects of the Aztecs. When the Spaniards

---

conquistador (kon-KEY-stuh-dor)   **Cortés** (kor-TEZ)

Quetzalcoatl (ket-zahl-COH-ah-tal)
Tenochtitlan (teh-noch-TIT-lan)
Moctezuma (mock-teh-ZOO-ma)

Coronation of Emperor Moctezuma This painting by an unnamed Aztec artist depicts the Aztec ruler's coronation. Moctezuma, his nose pierced by a bone, receives the crown from a prince in the palace at Tenochtitlan.   (Oronoz)

were near, the emperor went out in a great procession, dressed in all his finery, to welcome Cortés with gifts and flower garlands.

Despite Cortés's initial promise that he came in friendship, Moctezuma quickly found himself a prisoner in his own palace. The Spanish looted his treasury and melted down its golden objects. Soon a battle was raging in and about the capital between the Spaniards (helped by their new Amerindian allies) and the Aztecs and their supporters. Briefly the Aztecs gained the upper hand. They destroyed half of the Spanish force and four thousand of the Spaniards' Amerindian allies, and they sacrificed to their gods fifty-three Spanish prisoners and four horses, displaying their severed heads in rows on pikes. In the battle Moctezuma was killed.

The Spanish survivors retreated from the city and rebuilt their strength. Their successful capture of Tenochtitlan in 1521 was greatly facilitated by the spread of smallpox, which weakened and killed more of the city's defenders than died in the fighting. One source remembered that the disease "spread over the people as a great destruction." The bodies of the afflicted were covered with oozing sores, and large numbers soon died. It is likely that many Amerindians as well as Europeans blamed the devastating spread of this disease on supernatural forces.

After the capital fell, the conquistadors took over other parts of Mexico. Then some Spaniards began eyeing the vast Inca Empire, stretching nearly 3,000 miles (5,000 kilometers) south from the equator and containing half of the population in South America. The Inca had conquered the inhabitants of the Andes Mountains and the Pacific coast of South America during the previous century, and their rule was not fully accepted by all of the peoples they had defeated.

With the vast Pacific Ocean on one side of their realm and the sparsely inhabited Amazon forests on the other, it is not surprising that Inca rulers believed they controlled most of the world worth controlling. Theirs was a great empire with highly productive agriculture, exquisite stone cities (such as the capital, Cuzco), and rich gold and silver mines. The power of the Inca emperor was sustained by beliefs that he was descended from the Sun God and by an efficient system of roads and messengers that kept him informed about major events in the empire. Yet all was not well.

At the end of the 1520s, before even a whisper of news about the Spanish reached the Inca rulers, small-

DIVERSITY AND DOMINANCE

KONGO'S CHRISTIAN KING

The new overseas voyages brought conquest to some and opportunities for fruitful borrowings and exchanges to others. The decision of the ruler of the kingdom of Kongo to adopt Christianity in 1491 added cultural diversity to Kongolese society and in some ways strengthened the hand of the king. From then on Kongolese rulers sought to introduce Christian beliefs and rituals while at the same time Africanizing Christianity to make it more intelligible to their subjects. In addition, the kings of Kongo sought a variety of more secular aid from Portugal, including schools and medicine. Trade with the Portuguese introduced new social and political tensions, especially in the case of the export trade in slaves for the Portuguese sugar plantations on the island of São Tomé to the north.

Two letters sent to King João (zhwao) III of Portugal in 1526 illustrate how King Afonso of Kongo saw his kingdom's new relationship with Portugal and the problems that resulted from it. (Afonso adopted that name when he was baptized as a young prince.) After the death of his father in 1506, Afonso successfully claimed the throne and ruled until 1542. His son Henrique became the first Catholic bishop of the Kongo in 1521.

These letters were written in Portuguese and penned by the king's secretary João Teixera (tay-SHER-uh), a Kongo Christian, who, like Afonso, had been educated by Portuguese missionaries.

6 July 1526

To the very powerful and excellent prince Dom João, our brother:

On the 20th of June just past, we received word that a trading ship from your highness had just come to our port of Sonyo. We were greatly pleased by that arrival for it had been many days since a ship had come to our kingdom, for by it we would get news of your highness, which many times we had desired to know, . . . and likewise as there was a great and dire need for wine and flour for the holy sacrament; and of this we had had no great hope for we have the same need frequently. And

that, sir, arises from the great negligence of your highness's officials toward us and toward shipping us those things. . . .

Sir, your highness should know how our kingdom is being lost in so many ways that we will need to provide the needed cure, since this is caused by the excessive license given by your agents and officials to the men and merchants who come to this kingdom to set up shops with goods and many things which have been prohibited by us, and which they spread throughout our kingdoms and domains in such abundance that many of our vassals, whose submission we could once rely on, now act independently so as to get the things in greater abundance than we ourselves; whom we had formerly held content and submissive and under our vassalage and jurisdiction, so it is doing a great harm not only to the service of God, but also to the security and peace of our kingdoms and state.

And we cannot reckon how great the damage is, since every day the mentioned merchants are taking our people, sons of the land and the sons of our noblemen and vassals and our relatives, because the thieves and men of bad conscience grab them so as to have the things and wares of this kingdom that they crave; they grab them and bring them to be sold. In such a manner, sir, has been the corruption and deprivation that our land is becoming completely depopulated, and your highness should not deem this good nor in your service. And to avoid this we need from these kingdoms [of yours] no more than priests and a few people to teach in schools, and no other goods except wine and flour for the holy sacrament, which is why we beg of your highness to help and assist us in this matter. Order your agents to send here neither merchants nor wares, because it is our will that in these kingdoms there should not be any dealing in slaves nor outlet for them, for the reasons stated above. Again we beg your highness's agreement, since otherwise we cannot cure such manifest harm. May Our Lord in His mercy have your highness always under His protection and may you always do the things of His holy service. I kiss your hands many times.

From our city of Kongo. . . .

The King, Dom Afonso

18 October 1526

Very high and very powerful prince King of Portugal, our brother,

Sir, your highness has been so good as to promise us that anything we need we should ask for in our letters, and that everything will be provided. And so that there may be peace and health of our kingdoms, by God's will, in our lifetime. And as there are among us old folks and people who have lived for many days, many and different diseases happen so often that we are pushed to the ultimate extremes. And the same happens to our children, relatives, and people, because this country lacks physicians and surgeons who might know the proper cures for such diseases, as well as pharmacies and drugs to make them better. And for this reason many of those who had been already confirmed and instructed in the things of the holy faith of Our Lord Jesus Christ perish and die. And the rest of the people for the most part cure themselves with herbs and sticks and other ancient methods, so that they live putting all their faith in the these herbs and ceremonies, and die believing that they are saved; and this serves God poorly.

And to avoid such a great error, I think, and inconvenience, since it is from God and from your highness that all the good and the drugs and medicines have come to us for our salvation, we ask your merciful highness to send us two physicians and two pharmacists and one surgeon, so that they may come with their pharmacies and necessary things to be in our kingdoms, for we have extreme need of each and everyone of them. We will be very good and merciful to them, since sent by your highness, their work and coming should be for good. We ask your highness as a great favor to do this for us, because besides being good in itself it is in the service of God as we have said above.

Moreover, sir, in our kingdoms there is another great inconvenience which is of little service to God, and this is that many of our people, out of great desire for the wares and things of your kingdoms, which are brought here by your people, and in order to satisfy their disordered appetite, seize many of our people, freed and exempt men. And many times noblemen and the sons of noblemen, and our relatives are stolen, and they take them to be sold to the white men who are in our kingdoms and take them hidden or by night, so that they are not recognized. And as soon as they are taken by the white men, they are immediately ironed and branded with fire. And when they are carried off to be embarked, if they are caught by our guards, the whites allege that they have bought them and cannot say from whom, so that it is our duty to do justice and to restore to the free their freedom. And so they went away offended.

And to avoid such a great evil we passed a law so that every white man living in our kingdoms and wanting to purchase slaves by whatever means should first inform three of our noblemen and officials of our court on whom we rely in this matter, namely Dom Pedro Manipunzo and Dom Manuel Manissaba, our head bailiff, and Gonçalo Pires, our chief supplier, who should investigate if the said slaves are captives or free men, and, if cleared with them, there will be no further doubt nor embargo and they can be taken and embarked. And if they reach the opposite conclusion, they will lose the aforementioned slaves. Whatever favor and license we give them [the white men] for the sake of your highness in this case is because we know that it is in your service too that these slaves are taken from our kingdom; otherwise we should not consent to this for the reasons stated above that we make known completely to your highness so that no one could say the contrary, as they said in many other cases to your highness, so that the care and remembrance that we and this kingdom have should not be withdrawn. . . .

We kiss your hands of your highness many times.

From our city of Kongo, the 18th day of October,

The King, Dom Afonso

QUESTIONS FOR ANALYSIS

1. What sorts of things does King Afonso desire from the Portuguese?
2. What is he willing and unwilling to do in return?
3. What problem with his own people has the slave trade created and what has King Afonso done about it?
4. Does King Afonso see himself as an equal to King João or his subordinate? Do you agree with that analysis?

Source: From António Brásio, ed., *Monumenta Missionaria Africana: Africa Ocidental (1471–1531)* (Lisbon: Agência Geral do Ultramar, 1952), I:468, 470–471, 488–491. Translated by David Northrup.

pox claimed countless Amerindian lives, perhaps including the Inca emperor in 1530. Even more devastating was the threat awaiting the empire from **Francisco Pizarro°** (ca. 1478– 1541) and his motley band of 180 men, 37 horses, and two cannon.

With limited education and some military experience, Pizarro had come to the Americas in 1502 at the age of twenty-five to seek his fortune. He had participated in the conquest of Hispaniola and in Balboa's expedition across the Isthmus of Panama. By 1520 Pizarro was a wealthy landowner and official in Panama, yet he gambled his fortune on more adventures, exploring the Pacific coast to a point south of the equator, where he learned of the riches of the Inca. With a license from the king of Spain, he set out from Panama in 1531 to conquer them.

In November 1532 Pizarro arranged to meet the new Inca emperor, **Atahualpa°** (r. 1531–1533), near the Andean city of Cajamarca°. With supreme boldness and brutality, Pizarro's small band of armed men seized Atahualpa off a rich litter borne by eighty nobles as it passed through an enclosed courtyard. Though surrounded by an Inca army of at least forty thousand, the Spaniards were able to use their cannon to create confusion while their swords sliced thousands of the emperor's lightly armed retainers and servants to pieces. The strategy to replicate the earlier Spanish conquest of Mexico was working.

Noting the glee with which the Spaniards seized gold, silver, and emeralds, the captive Atahualpa offered them what he thought would satisfy even the greediest among them in exchange for his freedom: a roomful of gold and silver. But when the ransom of 13,400 pounds (6,000 kilograms) of gold and 26,000 pounds (12,000 kilograms) of silver was paid, the Spaniards gave Atahualpa a choice: he could be burned at the stake as a heathen or baptized as a Christian and then strangled. He chose the latter. His death and the Spanish occupation broke the unity of the Inca Empire.

In 1533 the Spaniards took Cuzco and from there set out to conquer and loot the rest of the empire. The defeat of a final rebellion in 1536 spelled the end of Inca rule. Five years later Pizarro himself met a violent death at the hands of Spanish rivals, but the conquest of the mainland continued. Incited by the fabulous wealth of the Aztecs and Inca, conquistadors extended Spanish conquest and exploration in South and North America, dreaming of new treasuries to loot.

Pizarro (pih-ZAHR-oh)   **Atahualpa** (ah-tuh-WAHL-puh)
Cajamarca (kah-hah-MAHR-kah)

Patterns of Dominance

Within fifty years of Columbus's first landing in 1492, the Spanish had located and occupied all of the major population centers of the Americas, and the penetration of the more thinly populated areas was well under way. In no other part of the world was European dominance so complete. Why did the peoples of the Americas suffer a fate so different from that of peoples in Africa and Asia? Why were the Spanish able to erect a vast land empire in the Americas so quickly? Three factors seem crucial.

First, long isolation from the rest of humanity made the inhabitants of the Americas vulnerable to new diseases. The unfamiliar illnesses first devastated the native inhabitants of the Caribbean islands and then spread to the mainland. Contemporaries estimated that between 25 and 50 percent of those infected with smallpox died. Repeated epidemics inhibited Amerindians' ability to regain control. Because evidence is very limited, estimates of the size of the population before Columbus's arrival vary widely, but there is no disputing the fact that the Amerindian population fell sharply during the sixteenth century. The Americas became a "widowed land," open to resettlement from across the Atlantic.

A second major factor was Spain's military superiority. Steel swords, protective armor, and horses gave the Spaniards an advantage over their Amerindian opponents in many battles. Though few in number, muskets and cannon also gave the Spaniards a significant psychological edge. However, it should not be forgotten that the Spanish conquests depended heavily on large numbers of Amerindian allies armed with the same weapons as the people they defeated. Perhaps the Spaniards' most decisive military advantage came from the no-holds-barred fighting techniques they had developed during a long history of warfare at home.

The patterns of domination previously established in reconquest of Iberia were a third factor in Spain's ability to govern its New World empire. The forced labor, forced conversion, and system for administering conquered lands all had their origins in the Iberian reconquest.

The same three factors help explain the quite different outcomes elsewhere. Because of centuries of contacts before 1500, Europeans, Africans, and Asians shared the same Old World diseases. Only small numbers of very isolated peoples in Africa and Asia suffered the demographic calamity that undercut Amerindians' ability to retain control of their lands. The Iberians enjoyed a military advantage at sea, as the conquest of the Indian Ocean trade routes showed, but on land they had no decisive advantage against more numerous indigenous people who were not weakened by disease. Everywhere, Iberian religious zeal to conquer non-Christians went hand in hand with a desire for riches. In Iberia and America conquest brought wealth. But in Africa and Asia, where existing trading networks were already well established, Iberian desire for wealth from trade restrained or negated the impulse to conquer.

CONCLUSION

Historians agree that the century between 1450 and 1550 was a major turning point in world history. It was the beginning of an age to which they have given various names: the "Vasco da Gama epoch," the "Columbian era," the "age of Magellan," or simply the "modern period." During those years European explorers opened new long-distance trade routes across the world's three major oceans, for the first time establishing regular contact among all the continents. By 1550 those who followed them had broadened trading contacts with sub-Saharan Africa, gained mastery of the rich trade routes of the Indian Ocean, and conquered a vast land empire in the Americas.

As dramatic and momentous as these events were, they were not completely unprecedented. The riches of the Indian Ocean trade that brought a gleam to the eye of many Europeans had been developed over many centuries by the trading peoples who inhabited the surrounding lands. European conquests of the Americas were no more rapid or brutal than the earlier Mongol conquests of Eurasia. Even the crossing of the Pacific had been done before, though in stages.

What gave this maritime revolution unprecedented importance had more to do with what happened after 1550 than with what happened earlier. Europeans' overseas empires would endure longer than the Mongols' and would continue to expand for three-and-a-half centuries after 1550. Unlike the Chinese, the Europeans did not turn their backs on the world after an initial burst of exploration. Not content with dominance in the Indian Ocean trade, Europeans opened an Atlantic maritime network that grew to rival the Indian Ocean network in the wealth of its trade. They also pioneered regular trade across the Pacific. The maritime expansion begun in the period from 1450 to 1550 marked the beginning of a new age of growing global interaction.

■ Key Terms

Zheng He	Christopher Columbus
Arawak	Ferdinand Magellan
Henry the Navigator	conquistadors
caravel	Hernán Cortés
Gold Coast	Moctezuma
Bartolomeu Dias	Francisco Pizarro
Vasco da Gama	Atahualpa

■ Suggested Reading

There is no single survey of the different expansions covered by this chapter, but the selections edited by Joseph R. Levenson, *European Expansion and the Counter Example of Asia, 1300–1600* (1967), remain a good introduction to Chinese expansion and Western impressions of China. Janet Abu-Lughod, *Before European Hegemony: The World System, A.D. 1250–1350* (1989), provides a stimulating speculative reassessment of the importance of the Mongols and the Indian Ocean trade in the creation of the modern world system; she summarizes her thesis in the American Historical Association booklet *The World System in the Thirteenth Century: Dead-End or Precursor?* (1993).

The Chinese account of Zheng He's voyages is Ma Huan, *Ying-yai Sheng-lan: "The Overall Survey of the Ocean's Shores"* [1433], ed. and trans. J. V. G. Mills (1970). A reliable guide to Polynesian expansion is Jesse D. Jennings, ed., *The Prehistory of Polynesia* (1979), especially the excellent chapter "Voyaging" by Ben R. Finney, which encapsulates his *Voyage of Rediscovery: A Cultural Odyssey Through Polynesia* (1994). The medieval background to European intercontinental voyages is summarized by Felipe Fernandez-Armesto, *Before Columbus: Exploration and Colonization from the Mediterranean to the Atlantic, 1229–1492* (1987). Tim Severin, *The Brendan Voyage* (2000) vividly recounts a modern retracing of even earlier Irish voyages.

A simple introduction to the technologies of European expansion is Carlo M. Cipolla, *Guns, Sails, and Empires: Technological Innovation and the Early Phases of European Expansion, 1400–1700* (1965; reprint, 1985). More advanced is Roger C. Smith, *Vanguard of Empire: Ships of Exploration in the Age of Columbus* (1993).

The European exploration is well documented and the subject of intense historical investigation. Clear general accounts based on the contemporary records are Boies Penrose, *Travel and Discovery in the Age of the Renaissance, 1420–1620* (1952); J. H. Parry, *The Age of Reconnaissance: Discovery, Exploration, and Settlement, 1450–1650* (1963); and G. V. Scammell, *The World Encompassed: The First European Maritime Empires, c. 800–1650* (1981).

An excellent general introduction to Portuguese exploration is C. R. Boxer, *The Portuguese Seaborne Empire, 1415–1825* (1969). More detail can be found in Bailey W. Diffie and George D. Winius, *Foundations of the Portuguese Empire, 1415–1580*

(1977); A. J. R. Russell-Wood, *The Portuguese Empire: A World on the Move* (1998); and Luc Cuyvers, *Into the Rising Sun: The Journey of Vasco da Gama and the Discovery of the Modern World* (1998). John William Blake, ed., *Europeans in West Africa, 1450–1560* (1942), is an excellent two-volume collection of contemporary Portuguese, Castilian, and English sources. Elaine Sanceau, *The Life of Prester John: A Chronicle of Portuguese Exploration* (1941), is a very readable account of Portuguese relations with Ethiopia. The *Summa Oriental of Tomé Pires: An Account of the East, from the Red Sea to Japan, Written in Malacca and India in 1512–1515*, trans. Armando Cortesão (1944), provides a detailed firsthand account of the Indian Ocean during the Portuguese's first two decades there.

The other Iberian kingdoms' expansion is well summarized by J. H. Parry, *The Spanish Seaborne Empire* (1967). Samuel Eliot Morison's *Admiral of the Ocean Sea: A Life of Christopher Columbus* (1942) is a fine scholarly celebration of the epic mariner, and is also available in an abridged version as *Christopher Columbus, Mariner* (1955). More focused on the shortcomings of Columbus and his Spanish peers is Tzvetan Todorov, *The Conquest of America*, trans. Richard Howard (1985). Marvin Lunenfeld, ed., *1492: Discovery, Invasion, Encounter* (1991), critically examines contemporary sources and interpretations. William D. Phillips and Carla Rhan Phillips, *The Worlds of Christopher Columbus* (1992), examines the mariner and his times in terms of modern concerns. Peggy K. Liss, *Isabel the Queen: Life and Times* (1992), is a sympathetic examination of Queen Isabella of Castile. Detailed individual biographies of all of the individuals in Pizarro's band are the subject of James Lockhart's *Men of Cajamarca: A Social and Biographical Study of the First Conquerors of Peru* (1972). A firsthand account of Magellan's expedition is Antonio Pigafetta, *Magellan's Voyage: A Narrative Account of the First Circumnavigation*, available in a two-volume edition (1969) that includes a facsimile reprint of the manuscript.

Matthew Restall, *Seven Myths of the Spanish Conquests* (2003) uses indigenous sources to challenge traditional interpretations of New World conquests. The trans-Atlantic encounters of Europe and the Americas are described by J. H. Elliott, *The Old World and the New, 1492–1650* (1970). Alfred W. Crosby, *The Columbian Voyages, the Columbian Exchange, and Their Historians* (1987), available as an American Historical Association booklet, provides a brief overview of the first encounters in the Americas and their long-term consequences. The early chapters of Mark A. Burkholder and Lyman L. Johnson, *Colonial Latin America*, 2d ed. (1994), give a clear and balanced account of the Spanish conquest.

The perceptions of the peoples European explorers encountered are not as well documented. David Northrup, *Africa's Discovery of Europe, 1450–1850* (2002) and John Thornton, *Africa and Africans in the Making of the Atlantic World, 1400–1800*, 2d ed. (1998), examine Africans' encounters with Europe and their involvement in the Atlantic economy. *The Broken Spears: The Aztec Account of the Conquest of Mexico*, ed. Miguel Leon-Portilla (1962), presents Amerindian chronicles in a readable package, as does Nathan Wachtel, *The Vision of the Vanquished: The Spanish Conquest of Peru Through Indian Eyes* (1977). Anthony Reid, *Southeast Asia in the Age of Commerce, 1450–1680*, 2 vols. (1988, 1993), deals with events in that region.

◾ Notes

1. Ma Huan, *Ying-yai Sheng-lan: "The Overall Survey of the Ocean's Shores,"* ed. Feng Ch'eng-Chün, trans. J. V. G. Mills (Cambridge, England: Cambridge University Press, 1970), 180.
2. Alvise da Cadamosto in *The Voyages of Cadamosto and Other Documents*, ed. and trans. G. R. Crone (London: Hakluyt Society, 1937), 2.

Climate and Population, to 1500

During the millennia before 1500 human populations expanded in three momentous surges. The first occurred after 50,000 B.C.E. when humans emigrated from their African homeland to all of the inhabitable continents. After that, the global population remained steady for several millennia. During the second expansion, between about 5000 and 500 B.C.E., population rose from about 5 million to 100 million as agricultural societies spread around the world (see Figure 1). Again population growth then slowed for several centuries before a third surge took world population to over 350 million by 1200 C.E. (see Figure 2).

For a long time historians tended to attribute these population surges to cultural and technological advances. Indeed, a great many changes in culture and technology are associated with adaptation to different climates and food supplies in the first surge and with the domestication of plants and animals in the second. However, historians have not found a cultural or technological change to explain the third surge, nor can they explain why creativity would have stagnated for long periods between the surges. Something else must have been at work.

Recently historians have begun to pay more attention to the impact of long-term variations in global climate. By examining ice cores drilled out of glaciers, scientists have been able to compile records of thousands of years of climate change. The comparative width of tree rings from ancient forests has provided additional data on periods of favorable and unfavorable growth. Such evidence shows that cycles of population growth and stagnation followed changes in global climate.

Historians now believe that global temperatures were above normal for extended periods from the late 1100s to the late 1200s C.E. In the temperate lands where most of the world's people lived, above-normal temperatures meant a longer growing season, more bountiful harvests, and thus a more adequate and reliable food supply. The ways in which societies responded to the medieval warm period are as important as the climate change, but it is unlikely that human agency alone would have produced the medieval surge. One notable response was that of the Vikings, who increased the size and range of their settlements in the North Atlantic, although their raids also caused death and destruction.

Some of the complexities involved in the interaction of human agency, climate, and other natural factors are also evident in the demographic changes that followed the medieval warm period. During the 1200s the Mongol invasions caused death and disruption of agriculture across Eurasia. China's population, which had been over 100 million in 1200, declined by a third or more by 1300. The Mongol invasions did not cause harm west of Russia, but climate changes in the 1300s resulted in population losses in Europe. Unusually heavy rains caused crop failures and a prolonged famine in northern Europe from 1315 to 1319.

The freer movement of merchants within the Mongol empire also facilitated the spread of disease across Eurasia, culminating in the great pandemic known as the Black Death in Europe. The demographic recovery underway in China was reversed. The even larger population losses in Europe may have been affected by the decrease in global temperatures to their lowest point in many millennia between 1350 and 1375. Improving economic conditions enabled population to recover more rapidly in Europe after 1400 than in China, where the conditions of rural life remained harsh.

Because many other historical circumstances interact with changing weather patterns, historians have a long way to go in deciphering the role of climate in history. Nevertheless, it is a factor that can no longer be ignored.

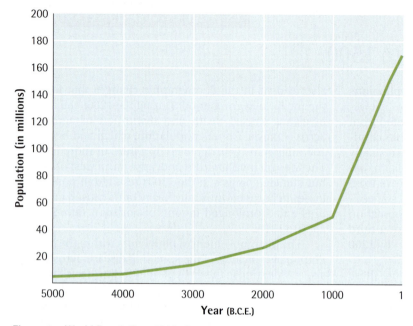

Figure 1   World Population, 5000–1 B.C.E.

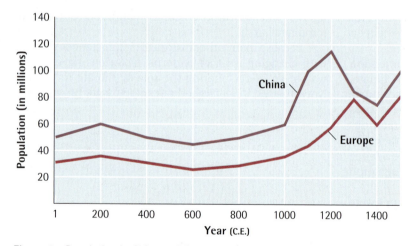

Figure 2   Population in China and Europe, 1–1500 C.E.

PART FIVE

The Globe Encompassed, 1500–1750

CHAPTER 17
Transformations in Europe, 1500–1750

CHAPTER 18
The Diversity of American Colonial Societies, 1530–1770

CHAPTER 19
The Atlantic System and Africa, 1550–1800

CHAPTER 20
Southwest Asia and the Indian Ocean, 1500–1750

CHAPTER 21
Northern Eurasia, 1500–1800

The decades between 1500 and 1750 witnessed a tremendous expansion of commercial, cultural, and biological exchanges around the world. New long-distance sea routes linked Europe with sub-Saharan Africa and the existing maritime networks of the Indian Ocean and East Asia. Spanish and Portuguese voyages ended the isolation of the Americas and created new webs of exchange in the Atlantic and Pacific. Overland expansion of Muslim, Russian, and Chinese empires also increased global interaction.

These expanding contacts had major demographic and cultural consequences. In the Americas, European diseases devastated the Amerindian population, facilitating the establishment of large Spanish, Portuguese, French, and British empires. Europeans introduced enslaved Africans to relieve the labor shortage. Immigrant Africans and Europeans brought new languages, religious practices, music, and forms of personal adornment.

In Asia and Africa, by contrast, the most important changes owed more to internal forces than to European actions. The Portuguese seized control of some important trading ports and networks in the Indian Ocean and pioneered new contacts with China and Japan. In time, the Dutch, French, and English expanded these profitable connections, but in 1750 Europeans were still primarily a maritime force. Asians and Africans generally retained control of their lands and participated freely in overseas trade.

The Islamic world saw the dramatic expansion of the Ottoman Empire in the Middle East and the establishment of the Safavid Empire in Iran and the Mughal Empire in South Asia. In northern Eurasia, Russia and China acquired vast new territories and populations, while a new national government in Japan promoted economic development and stemmed foreign influence.

Ecological change was rapid in areas of rising population and economic activity. Forests were cut down to meet the increasing need for farmland, timber, and fuel. Population growth in parts of Eurasia placed great strain on the environment. On a more positive note, domesticated animals and crops from the Old World transformed agriculture in the Americas, while Amerindian foods such as the potato became staples of the diet of the Old World.

New goods, new wealth, and new tastes from overseas transformed Europe in this period. Global and regional trade promoted urban growth, but conflict was also rife. States spent heavily on warfare in Europe and abroad. The printing press spread new religious and scientific ideas, and challenges to established values and institutions.

By 1750 the balance of power in the world had begun to shift from the East to the West. The Ottoman, Mughal, and Chinese empires had declined in relative strength compared to the much smaller but technologically more sophisticated states of northwestern Europe.

ARCTIC OCEAN

NORTH AMERICA

Quebec

New York

NORTH ATLANTIC OCEAN

New Orleans

Mexico

West Indies

PACIFIC OCEAN

Peru

SOUTH AMERICA

Brazil

Potosi

	1500	1550	1600	1650
Americas	• 1500 Portuguese discover Brazil Viceroyalty of Mexico 1535 •	• 1540 Viceroyalty of Peru • 1545 Silver discovered at Potosi, Bolivia	Brazil is world's main source of sugar 1600 •	Dutch bring sugar and English take slavery to West Indies 1640s • Jamaica 1660 • 1607–1640 England and France found colonies
Europe	1500–1600 Spain's golden century • 1519 Protestant Reformation begins Catholic Reformation begins 1545 •	English defeat Spanish Armada 1588 • • 1550 Scientific Revolution begins		1618–1648 Thirty Years War 1600–1700 Netherlands' golden century
Africa	• 1505 Portuguese begin assault on Swahili cities		• 1591 Morocco conquers Songhai Empire	• 1640s Expansion of transatlantic slave trade
Middle East	1520–1566 Reign of Ottoman sultan Suleiman the Magnificent	• 1571 Ottoman defeat at Lepanto 1588–1629 Reign of Safavid shah Abbas the Great		• 1622 Iranians expel Portuguese from Hormuz
Asia and Oceania	• 1526 Mughal Empire founded in India Russia conquers Sibir Khanate 1582 •	1556–1605 Reign of Mughal emperor Akbar • 1592 Japanese invasion of Korea	"Closing" of Japan 1639 • • 1603 Tokugawa Shogunate founded in Japan	• 1644 Qing Empire begins in China

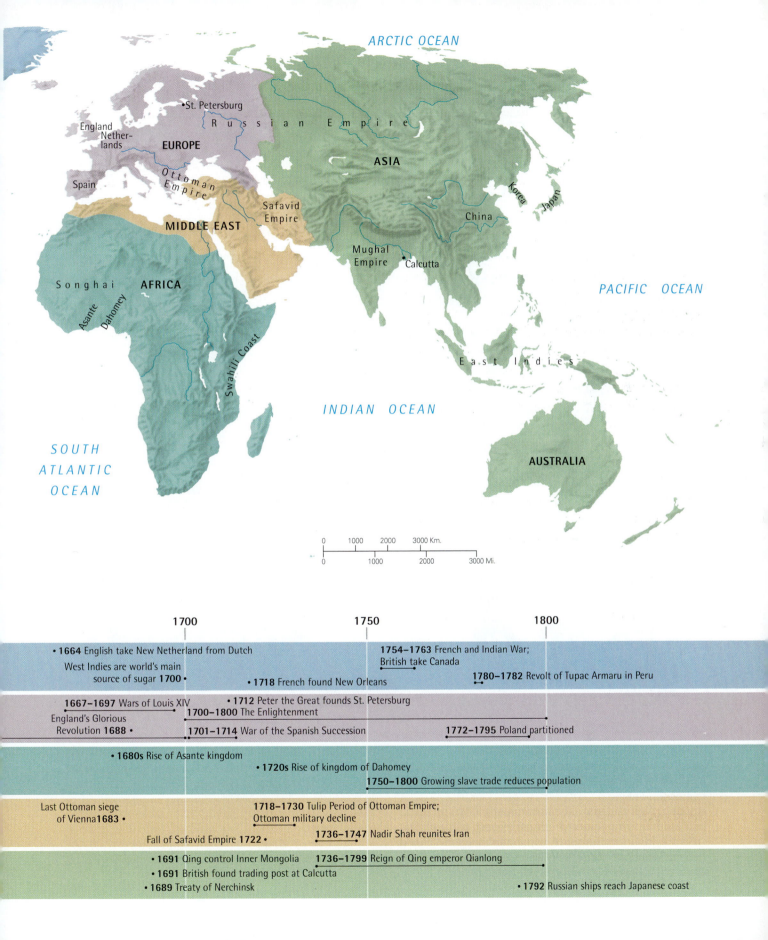

ARCTIC OCEAN

EUROPE

St. Petersburg

R u s s i a n   E m p i r e

England
Nether-
lands

ASIA

Spain

Ottoman
Empire

Korea

Japan

MIDDLE EAST

Safavid
Empire

China

Songhai

AFRICA

Mughal
Empire

Calcutta

PACIFIC OCEAN

Asante

Dahomey

Swahili Coast

East Indies

INDIAN OCEAN

SOUTH
ATLANTIC
OCEAN

AUSTRALIA

0	1000	2000	3000 Km.
0	1000	2000	3000 Mi.

1700   **1750**   **1800**

• **1664** English take New Netherland from Dutch
West Indies are world's main
source of sugar **1700** •
• **1718** French found New Orleans

1754–1763 French and Indian War;
British take Canada
1780–1782 Revolt of Tupac Armaru in Peru

1667–1697 Wars of Louis XIV
England's Glorious
Revolution **1688** •
• **1712** Peter the Great founds St. Petersburg
1700–1800 The Enlightenment
1701–1714 War of the Spanish Succession
1772–1795 Poland partitioned

• **1680s** Rise of Asante kingdom
• **1720s** Rise of kingdom of Dahomey
1750–1800 Growing slave trade reduces population

Last Ottoman siege
of Vienna **1683** •
1718–1730 Tulip Period of Ottoman Empire;
Ottoman military decline
Fall of Safavid Empire **1722** •
1736–1747 Nadir Shah reunites Iran

• **1691** Qing control Inner Mongolia
• **1691** British found trading post at Calcutta
• **1689** Treaty of Nerchinsk
1736–1799 Reign of Qing emperor Qianlong
• **1792** Russian ships reach Japanese coast

17

Transformations in Europe, 1500–1750

Winter in Flanders, 1565 This January scene by the Flemish artist
Pieter Bruegel, the Elder, shows many everyday activities.

CHAPTER OUTLINE

Culture and Ideas

Social and Economic Life

Political Innovations

ENVIRONMENT AND TECHNOLOGY: **Mapping the World**

DIVERSITY AND DOMINANCE: **Political Craft and Craftiness**

As he neared the end of his life in 1575, the French scholar and humanist Loys Le Roy° reflected on the times in which he lived. It was, he believed, a golden age for Europe, and he ticked off the names of more than 130 scholars and translators, writers and poets, artists and sculptors, and explorers and philosophers whose work over the preceding two centuries had restored the standards of ancient learning. Later ages would call this scholarly and artistic revival the European **Renaissance.**

In addition, Le Roy enumerated a series of technological innovations that he believed had also transformed his age: printing, the marine compass, and cannonry. He put printing first because its rapid spread across Europe had done so much to communicate the literary and scholarly revival. The marine compass had made possible the sea voyages that now connected Europe directly to Africa and Asia and had led to the discovery and conquest of the Americas.

Le Roy gave third place to firearms because they had transformed warfare. Cannon and more recently devised hand-held weapons had swept before them all older military instruments. His enthusiasm for this transformation was dampened by the demonstrated capacity of firearms to cause devastation and ruin. Among the other evils of his age Le Roy enumerated syphilis and the spread of religious heresies and sects.

Reading Loys Le Roy's analysis more than four centuries later, one is struck not only by the acuity of his judgment and the beauty and clarity of his prose, but also by the astonishing geographical and historical range of his understanding. He credits both ancient and modern Greeks and Italians for their cultural contributions, the Germans for their role in perfecting printing and cannonry, and the Spanish for their overseas voyages. But his frame of reference is not confined to Europe. He cites the mathematical skills of ancient Egyptians; the military conquests of Mongols, Turks, and Persians (Iranians); Arabs' contributions to science and medicine; and China's contributions to the development of printing.

Loys Le Roy (lwa-EES le-RWAH)

The global framework of Le Roy's analysis led him to conclude that he was living at a turning point in world history. For long centuries, he argued, the military might of the Mongols and Turks had threatened the peoples of Europe, and Safavid Iran and Mamluk Egypt had surpassed any European land in riches. Now the West was in the ascendancy. Europeans' military might equaled that of their Middle Eastern neighbors. They were amassing new wealth from Asian trade and American silver. Most of all, the explosion of learning and knowledge had given Europe intellectual equality and perhaps superiority. Le Roy noted perceptively that while printing presses were in use all across Europe, the Islamic world has closed itself off to the benefits of this new technology, refusing to allow presses to be set up and even forbidding the entry of Arabic works about their lands printed in Europe.

As you read this chapter ask yourself these questions:

- How perceptive was Loys Le Roy about his own age and its place in world history?

- How much did learning, printing, and firearms define early modern Europe? (The marine compass was considered in Chapter 16.)

- Would someone from a lower social station in Europe share Le Roy's optimism about their era?

CULTURE AND IDEAS

One place to observe the conflict and continuity of early modern Europe is in the world of ideas. Theological controversies broke the religious unity of the Latin Church and contributed to violent wars. A huge witch scare showed the power of Christian beliefs about the Devil and traditional folklore about malevolent powers. The influence of classical ideas from Greco-Roman antiquity increased among better-educated people, but some thinkers challenged the authority of the ancients. Their new models of the motion of the planets encouraged others to challenge traditional social and political systems, with important implications for the period after 1750. Each of these events has its own causes, but the technology of the printing press enhanced the impact of all.

Martin Luther This detail of a painting by Lucas Cranach (1547) shows the Reformer preaching in his hometown church at Wittenberg. (Church of St. Marien, Wittenberg, Germany/The Bridgeman Art Library, New York and London)

Religious Reformation

In 1500 the **papacy,** the central government of Latin Christianity, was simultaneously gaining stature and suffering from corruption and dissent. Larger donations and tax receipts let popes fund ambitious construction projects in Rome, their capital city. During the sixteenth century Rome gained fifty-four new churches and other buildings, which showcased the artistic Renaissance then under way. However, the church's wealth and power also attracted ambitious men, some of whose personal lives became the source of scandal.

The jewel of the building projects was the magnificent new Saint Peter's Basilica in Rome. The unprecedented size and splendor of this church were intended to glorify God, display the skill of Renaissance artists and builders, and enhance the standing of the papacy. Such a project required refined tastes and vast sums of money.

The skillful overseer of the design and financing of the new Saint Peter's was Pope Leo X (r. 1513–1521), a member of the wealthy Medici° family of Florence, famous for its patronage of the arts. Pope Leo's artistic taste was superb and his personal life free from scandal, but he was more a man of action than a spiritual leader. One technique that he used to raise funds for the basilica was to authorize an **indulgence**—a forgiveness of the punishment due for past sins, granted by church authorities as a reward for a pious act such as making a pilgrimage, saying a particular prayer, or making a donation to a religious cause.

A young professor of sacred scripture, Martin Luther (1483–1546), objected to the way the new indulgence was preached. As the result of a powerful religious experience, Luther had forsaken money and marriage for a monastic life of prayer, self-denial, and study. He found personal consolation in his own religious quest in passage in Saint Paul's Epistle to the Romans that argued that salvation came not from "doing certain things" but from religious faith. That passage also led Luther to object to the way the indulgence preachers appeared to emphasize giving money more than the faith behind the act. He wrote to Pope Leo, asking him to stop this abuse, and challenged the preachers to a debate on the theology of indulgences.

This theological dispute quickly escalated into a contest between two strong-minded men. Largely ignoring Luther's theological objections, Pope Leo regarded his letter as a challenge to papal power and moved to silence the German monk. During a debate in 1519, a papal representative led Luther into open disagreement with some church doctrines, for which the papacy condemned him. Blocked in his effort to reform the church from within, Luther burned the papal bull (document) of condemnation, rejecting the pope's authority and beginning the movement known as the **Protestant Reformation.**

Accusing those whom he called "Romanists" (Roman Catholics) of relying on "good works," Luther insisted that the only way to salvation was through faith in Jesus Christ. He further declared that Christian belief must be based on the word of God in the Bible and on Christian tradition, not on the authority of the pope, as Catholics held. Eventually his conclusions led him to abandon his monastic prayers and penances and to marry a former nun.

Today Roman Catholics and Lutherans have resolved many of their theological differences, but in the sixteenth century stubbornness on both sides made reconciliation impossible. Moreover, Luther's use of the printing press to promote his ideas won him the support

°Medici (MED-ih-chee)

CHRONOLOGY

	Politics and Culture	Environment and Technology	Warfare
1500	**1500s** Spain's golden century **1519** Protestant Reformation begins **1540s** Scientific Revolution begins **1545** Catholic Reformation begins **Late 1500s** Witch-hunts increase	**Mid-1500s** Improved windmills and increasing land drainage in Holland **1590s** Dutch develop flyboats; Little Ice Age begins	**1526–1571** Ottoman wars **1546–1555** German Wars of Religion **1562–1598** French Wars of Religion **1566–1648** Netherlands Revolt
1600	**1600s** Holland's golden century	**1600s** Depletion of forests growing **1609** Galileo's astronomical telescope **1682** Canal du Midi completed	**1618–1648** Thirty Years War **1642–1648** English Civil War **1652–1678** Anglo-Dutch Wars **1667–1697** Wars of Louis XIV **1683–1697** Ottoman wars
1700	**1700s** The Enlightenment begins	**1750** English mine nearly 5 million tons of coal a year **1755** Lisbon earthquake	**1700–1721** Great Northern War **1701–1714** War of the Spanish Succession

of powerful Germans, who responded to his nationalist portrayal of the dispute as an effort of an Italian pope to beautify his city with German funds.

Inspired by Luther's denunciation of the ostentation and corruption of church leaders, other leaders called for a return to authentic Christian practices and beliefs. John Calvin (1509–1564), a well-educated Frenchman who turned from the study of law to theology after experiencing a religious conversion, became a highly influential Protestant leader. As a young man, Calvin published *The Institutes of the Christian Religion*, a masterful synthesis of Christian teachings, in 1535. Much of the *Institutes* was traditional medieval theology, but Calvin's teaching differed from that of Roman Catholics and Lutherans in two respects. First, while agreeing with Luther's emphasis on faith over works, Calvin denied that even human faith could merit salvation. Salvation, said Calvin, was a gift God gave to those He "predestined" for salvation. Second, Calvin went farther than Luther in curtailing the power of a clerical hierarchy and in simplifying religious rituals. Calvinist congregations elected their own governing committees and in time cre-

ated regional and national synods (councils) to regulate doctrinal issues. Calvinists also displayed simplicity in dress, life, and worship. In an age of ornate garments, they wore simple black clothes, avoided ostentatious living, and worshiped in churches devoid of statues, most musical instruments, stained-glass windows, incense, and vestments.

The Reformers appealed to genuine religious sentiments, but their successes and failures were also due to political circumstances (discussed below) and the social agendas that motivated people to join them. It was no coincidence that Lutheranism had its greatest appeal to German speakers and linguistically related Scandinavians. Peasants and urban laborers sometimes defied their masters by adopting a different faith. Protestants were no more inclined than Roman Catholics to question male dominance in the church and the family, but most Protestants rejected the medieval tradition of celibate priests and nuns and advocated Christian marriage for all adults.

Shaken by the intensity of the Protestant Reformers' appeal, the Catholic Church undertook its own reforms.

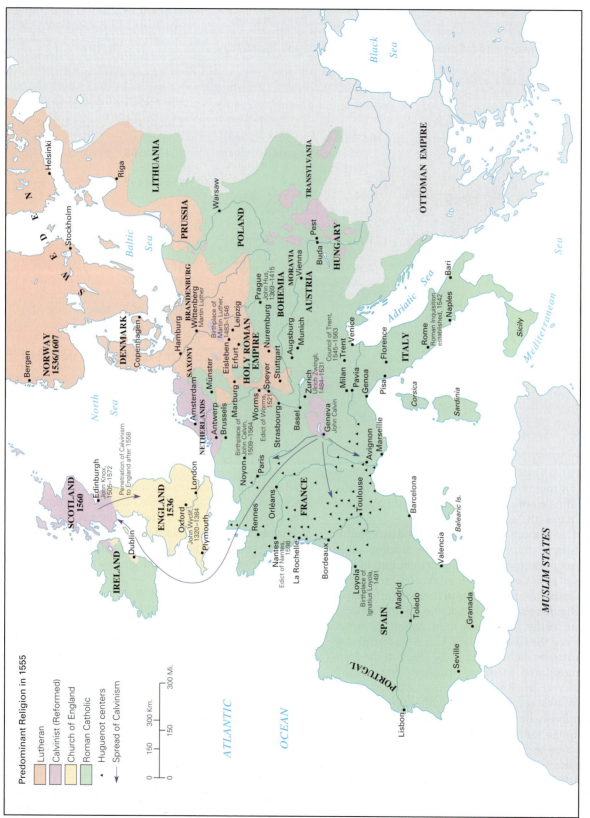

Map 17.1 Religious Reformation in Europe The Reformation brought greater religious freedom but also led to religious conflict and persecution. In many places the Reformation accelerated the trend toward state control of religion and added religious differences to the motives for wars among Europeans.

Death to Witches   This woodcut from 1574 depicts three women convicted of witchcraft being burned alive in Baden, Switzerland. The well dressed townsmen look on stolidly.   (Zentralbibliothek Zurich)

A council that met at the city of Trent, in northern Italy, in three sessions between 1545 and 1563 painstakingly distinguished proper Catholic doctrines from Protestant "errors." The council also reaffirmed the supremacy of the pope and called for a number of reforms, including requiring each bishop to reside in his diocese and each diocese to have a theological seminary to train priests. Also important to this **Catholic Reformation** were the activities of a new religious order—the Society of Jesus, or "Jesuits," that Ignatius of Loyola (1491–1556), a Spanish nobleman, founded in 1540. Well-educated Jesuits helped stem the Protestant tide and win back some adherents by their teaching and preaching (see Map 17.1). Other Jesuits became important missionaries overseas (see Chapters 18 and 21).

Given the complexity of the issues and the intensity of the emotions that the Protestant Reformation stirred, it is not surprising that violence often flared up. Both sides persecuted and sometimes executed those of differing views. Bitter "wars of religion," fought over a mixture of religious and secular issues, continued in parts of western Europe until 1648.

Traditional Thinking and Witch-Hunts

Religious differences among Protestants and between them and Catholics continued to generate animosity long after the first generation of reformers, but from a global perspective European Christians still had much in common both in their theology and in the local folk customs and pre-Christian beliefs that remained powerful everywhere in Europe. The widespread **witch-hunts** that Protestants and Catholics undertook in early modern Europe are a dramatic illustration of those common beliefs and cultural heritage.

Prevailing European ideas about the natural world blended two distinct traditions. One was the folklore about magic and forest spirits passed down orally from pre-Christian times. The second was the biblical teachings of the Christian and Jewish scriptures, heard by all in church and read by growing numbers in vernacular translations. In the minds of most people, Christian teachings about miracles, saints, and devils mixed with folklore.

Like people in other parts of the world, most early modern Europeans believed that natural events could have supernatural causes. When crops failed or domestic animals died unexpectedly, many people blamed unseen spirits. People also attributed human triumphs and tragedies to supernatural causes. When an earthquake destroyed much of Lisbon, Portugal's capital city, in November 1755, for example, both educated and uneducated people saw the event as a punishment sent by God. A Jesuit charged it "scandalous to pretend that the earthquake was just a natural event." An English Protestant leader agreed, comparing Lisbon's fate with that of Sodom, the city that God destroyed because of the sinfulness of its citizens, according to the Hebrew Bible.

The extraordinary fear of the power of witches that swept across northern Europe in the late sixteenth and seventeenth centuries was powerful testimony to belief in the spiritual causes of natural events. It is estimated that secular and church authorities tried over a hundred thousand people—some three-fourths of them women—for practicing witchcraft. Some were acquitted; some recanted; but more than half were executed—most in Protestant lands. Torture and badgering questions persuaded many accused witches to confess to casting spells and to describe in vivid detail their encounters with the Devil and their attendance at nighttime assemblies of witches.

The trial records make it clear that both the accusers and the accused believed that it was possible for angry and jealous individuals to use evil magic and the power of the Devil to cause people and domestic animals to sicken and die or to cause crops to wither in the fields.

Researchers think that at least some of those accused in early modern Europe may really have tried to use witchcraft to harm their enemies. However, it was the Reformation's focus on the Devil—the enemy of God—as the source of evil that made such malevolence so serious a crime and may have helped revive older fears of witchcraft.

Modern historians also argue that many accusations against widows and independent-minded women drew on the widespread belief that women not directly under the control of fathers or husbands were likely to turn to evil. The fact that such women had important roles in tending animals and the sick and in childbirth also made them suspects if death occurred. In parts of the world where belief in witchcraft is still strong, witch-hunts arise at times of social stress, and people who are marginalized by poverty and by the suspicions of others often relish the celebrity that public confession brings. Self-confessed "witches" may even find release from the guilt they feel for wishing evil on their neighbors.

No single reason can explain the rise in witchcraft accusations and fears in early modern Europe, but, for both the accusers and the accused, there are plausible connections between the witch-hunts and rising social tensions, rural poverty, and environmental strains. Far from being a bizarre aberration, witch-hunts reflected the larger social climate of early modern Europe.

The Scientific Revolution

Among the educated, the writings of Greco-Roman antiquity and the Bible were more trusted guides to the natural world than was folklore. The Renaissance had recovered many manuscripts of ancient writers, some of which were printed and widely circulated. The greatest authority on physics was Aristotle, a Greek philosopher who taught that everything on earth was reducible to four elements. The surface of the earth was composed of the two heavy elements, earth and water. The atmosphere was made up of two lighter elements, air and fire, which floated above the ground. Higher still were the sun, moon, planets, and stars, which, according to Aristotelian physics, were so light and pure that they floated in crystalline spheres. This division between the ponderous, heavy earth and the airy, celestial bodies accorded perfectly with the commonsense perception that all heavenly bodies revolved around the earth.

The prevailing conception of the universe was also influenced by the tradition derived from the ancient Greek mathematician Pythagoras, who proved the validity of the famous theorem that still bears his name: in a right triangle, the square of the hypotenuse is equal to the sum of the squares of the other two sides ($a^2 + b^2 = c^2$). Pythagoreans attributed to mystical properties the ability of simple mathematical equations to describe physical objects. They attached special significance to the simplest (to them perfect) geometrical shapes: the circle (a point rotated around another point) and the sphere (a circle rotated on its axis). They believed that celestial objects were perfect spheres orbiting the earth in perfectly circular orbits.

In the sixteenth century, however, the careful observations and mathematical calculations of some daring and imaginative European investigators began to challenge these prevailing conceptions of the physical world. These pioneers of the **Scientific Revolution** demonstrated that the workings of the universe could be explained by natural causes.

Over the centuries, observers of the nighttime skies had plotted the movements of the heavenly bodies, and mathematicians had worked to fit these observations into the prevailing theories of circular orbits. To make all the evidence fit, they had come up with eighty different spheres and some ingenious theories to explain the many seemingly irregular movements. Pondering these complications, a Polish monk and mathematician named Nicholas Copernicus (1473–1543) came up with a mathematically simpler solution: switching the center of the different orbits from the earth to the sun would reduce the number of spheres that were needed.

Copernicus did not challenge the idea that the sun, moon, and planets were light, perfect spheres or that they moved in circular orbits. But his placement of the sun, not the earth, at the center of things began a revolution in understanding about the structure of the heavens and about the central place of humans in the universe. To escape the anticipated controversies, Copernicus delayed the publication of his heliocentric (sun-centered) theory until the end of his life.

Other astronomers, including the Danish Tycho Brahe (1546–1601) and his German assistant Johannes Kepler (1571–1630), strengthened and improved on Copernicus's model, showing that planets actually move in elliptical, not circular orbits. The most brilliant of the Copernicans was the Italian Galileo Galilei° (1564–1642). In 1609 Galileo built a telescope through which he took a closer look at the heavens. Able to magnify distant objects thirty times beyond the power of the naked eye, Galileo saw that heavenly bodies were not the perfectly smooth spheres of the Aristotelians. The moon, he reported in *The Starry Messenger* (1610), had mountains and valleys; the sun had spots; other planets had their own moons. In other words, the earth was not alone in being heavy and changeable.

Galileo Galilei (gal-uh-LAY-oh gal-uh-LAY-ee)

Galileus Galileus Florentinus

Superio̅s
I 6

licentia
2 4.

Eques Octauius Leoni̅ Roman⁰ pictor fecit

Galileo in 1624 This engraving by Ottavio Leone shows the Italian scientist in full vigor at age sixty. (British Museum)

At first, the Copernican universe found more critics than supporters because it so directly challenged not just popular ideas but also the intellectual synthesis of classical and biblical authorities. How, demanded Aristotle's defenders, could the heavy earth move without producing vibrations that would shake the planet apart? Is the Bible wrong, asked the theologians, when the Book of Joshua says that, by God's command, "the sun [not the earth] stood still . . . for about a whole day" to give the ancient Israelites victory in their conquest of Palestine? If Aristotle's physics was wrong, worried other traditionalists, would not the theological synthesis built on other parts of his philosophy be open to question?

Intellectual and religious leaders encouraged political authorities to suppress the new ideas. Most Protestant leaders, following the lead of Martin Luther, condemned the heliocentric universe as contrary to the Bible. Catholic authorities waited longer to act. After all, both Copernicus and Galileo were Roman Catholics. Copernicus had dedicated his book to the pope, and in 1582 another pope, Gregory XIII, had used the latest astronomical findings to issue a new and more accurate calendar (still used today). Galileo ingeniously argued that the conflict between scripture and science was only apparent: the word of God revealed in the Bible was expressed in the imperfect language of ordinary people, but in nature God's truth was revealed more perfectly in a language that could be learned by careful observation and scientific reasoning.

Unfortunately, Galileo also ridiculed those who were slow to accept his findings, charging that Copernican ideas were "mocked and hooted at by an infinite multitude . . . of fools." Smarting under Galileo's stinging sarcasm, some Jesuits and other critics got his ideas condemned by the Roman Inquisition in 1616, which put *The Starry Messenger* on the Index of Forbidden Books and prohibited Galileo from publishing further on the subject. (In 1992 the Catholic Church officially retracted its condemnation of Galileo.)

Despite official opposition, printed books spread the new scientific ideas among scholars across Europe. In England, Robert Boyle (1627–1691) used experimental methods and a trial-and-error approach to examine the inner workings of chemistry. Through the Royal Society, chartered in London in 1662 to promote knowledge of the natural world, Boyle and others became enthusiastic missionaries of mechanical science and fierce opponents of the Aristotelians.

Meanwhile, English mathematician Isaac Newton (1642–1727) was carrying Galileo's demonstration that the heavens and earth share a common physics to its logical conclusion. Newton formulated a set of mathematical laws that all physical objects obeyed. It was the force of gravity—not angels—that governed the elliptical orbits of heavenly bodies. It was gravitation (and the resistance of air) that caused cannonballs to fall back to earth. From 1703 until his death Newton served as president of the Royal Society, using his prestige to promote the new science that came to bear his name.

As the condemnation of Galileo demonstrates, in 1700 most religious and intellectual leaders viewed the new science with suspicion or outright hostility because of the unwanted challenge it posed to established ways of thought. Yet all the principal pioneers of the Scientific Revolution were convinced that scientific discoveries and revealed religion were not in conflict. At the peak of his fame Newton promoted a series of lectures devoted to proving the validity of Christianity. However, by showing that the Aristotelians and biblical writers held ideas about the natural world that were naive and unfactual, these pioneers opened the door to others who used reason to challenge a broader range of unquestioned traditions and superstitions. The world of ideas was forever changed.

The Early Enlightenment

The advances in scientific thought inspired a few brave souls to question the reasonableness of everything from agricultural methods to laws, religion, and social hierarchies. The belief that human reason could discover the laws that governed social behavior and were just as scientific as the laws that governed physics energized a movement known as the **Enlightenment.** Like the Scientific Revolution, this movement was the work of a few "enlightened" individuals, who often faced bitter opposition from the political, intellectual, and religious establishment. Leading Enlightenment thinkers became accustomed to having their books burned or banned and spent long periods in exile to escape being imprisoned.

Influences besides the Scientific Revolution affected the Enlightenment. The Reformation had aroused many to champion one creed or another, but partisan bickering and bloodshed led others to doubt the superiority of any theological position and to recommend toleration of all religions. The killing of suspected witches also shocked many thoughtful people. The leading French thinker Voltaire (1694–1778) declared: "No opinion is worth burning your neighbor for."

Accounts of cultures in other parts of the world also led some European thinkers to question assumptions about the superiority of European political institutions, moral standards, and religious beliefs. Reports of Amerindian life, though romanticized, led some to conclude that those whom they had called savages were in many ways nobler than European Christians. Matteo Ricci, a Jesuit missionary to China whose journals made a strong impression in Europe, contrasted the lack of territorial ambition of the Chinese with the constant warfare in the West and attributed the difference to the fact that China was wisely ruled by educated men whom he called "Philosophers."

Although many circumstances shaped "enlightened" thinking, the new scientific methods and discoveries provided the clearest model for changing European society. Voltaire posed the issues in these terms: "it would be very peculiar that all nature, all the planets, should obey eternal laws" but a human being, "in contempt of these laws, could act as he pleased solely according to his caprice." The English poet Alexander Pope (1688–1774) made a similar point in verse: "Nature and Nature's laws lay hidden in night;/God said, 'Let Newton be' and all was light."

The Enlightenment was more a frame of mind than a coherent movement. Individuals who embraced it drew inspiration from different sources and promoted different agendas. By 1750 its proponents were clearer about what they disliked than about what new institutions should be created. Some "enlightened" thinkers thought society could be made to function with the mechanical orderliness of planets spinning in their orbits. Nearly all were optimistic that—at least in the long run—human beliefs and institutions could be improved. This belief in progress would help foster political and social revolutions after 1750, as Chapter 22 recounts.

Despite the enthusiasm the Enlightenment aroused in some circles, it was decidedly unpopular with many absolutist rulers and with most clergymen. Europe in 1750 was neither enlightened nor scientific. It was a place where political and religious divisions, growing literacy, and the printing press made possible the survival of the new ideas that profoundly changed life in future centuries.

SOCIAL AND ECONOMIC LIFE

From a distance European society seemed quite rigid. At the top of the social pyramid a small number of noble families had privileged access to high offices in the church, government, and military and enjoyed many special privileges, including exemption from taxation. A big step below them were the classes of merchants and professionals, who had acquired wealth but no legal privileges. At the base of the pyramid were the masses, mostly rural peasants and landless laborers, who were exploited by everyone above them. The subordination of women to men seemed equally rigid.

This model of European society is certainly not wrong, but even contemporaries knew that it was too simple. A study of English society in 1688, for example, distinguished twenty-five different social categories and pointed up the shocking inequality among them. It argued that less than half the population contributed to increasing the wealth of the kingdom, while the rest—the majority—were too poor and unskilled to make any substantial contribution.

Some social mobility did occur, particularly in the middle. The principal engine of social change was the economy, and the places where social change occurred most readily were the cities. A secondary means of change was education—for those who could get it.

The Bourgeoisie

Europe's growing cities were the products of a changing economy. In 1500 Paris was the only northern European city with over 100,000 inhabitants. By 1700 both Paris and London had populations over 500,000, and twenty other European cities contained over 60,000 people.

The wealth of the cities came from manufacturing and finance, but especially from trade, both within Europe and overseas. The French called the urban class that dominated these activities the **bourgeoisie**° (burghers, town dwellers). Members of the bourgeoisie devoted long hours to their businesses and poured much of their profits back into them or into new ventures. Even so, they had enough money to live comfortably in large houses with many servants. In the seventeenth and eighteenth centuries wealthier urban classes could buy exotic luxuries imported from the far corners of the earth—Caribbean and Brazilian sugar and rum, Mexican chocolate, Virginia tobacco, North American furs, East Indian cotton textiles and spices, and Chinese tea.

The Netherlands provided many good examples of bourgeois enterprise in the seventeenth century. Manufacturers and skilled craftsmen turned out a variety of goods in the factories and workshops of many cities and towns in the province of Holland. The highly successful Dutch textile industry concentrated on the profitable weaving, finishing, and printing of cloth, leaving the spinning to low-paid workers elsewhere. Along with fine woolens and linens the Dutch were successfully making cheaper textiles for mass markets. Other factories in Holland refined West Indian sugar, brewed beer from Baltic grain, cut Virginia tobacco, and made imitations of Chinese ceramics (see Environment and Technology: East Asian Porcelain in Chapter 21). Free from the censorship imposed by political and religious authorities in neighboring countries, Holland's printers published books in many languages, including manuals with the latest advances in machinery, metallurgy, agriculture, and other technical areas. For a small province barely above sea level, lacking timber and other natural resources, this was a remarkable achievement.

Burgeoning from a fishing village to a metropolis of some 200,000 by 1700, Amsterdam was Holland's largest city and Europe's major port. The bourgeoisie there and in other cities had developed huge commercial fleets that dominated sea trade in Europe and overseas. Dutch ships carried over 80 percent of the trade between Spain and northern Europe, even while Spain and the Netherlands were at war. By one estimate, the Dutch conducted more than half of all the oceangoing commercial shipping in the world in the seventeenth century (for details see Chapters 20 and 21).

Amsterdam also served as Europe's financial center. Seventeenth-century Dutch banks had such a reputation for security that wealthy individuals and governments from all over western Europe entrusted them with their money. The banks in turn invested these funds in

bourgeoisie (boor-zwah-ZEE)

The Fishwife, 1572   Women were essential partners in most Dutch family businesses. This scene by the Dutch artist Adriaen van Ostade shows a woman preparing fish for retail sale. (Rijksmuseum-Amsterdam)

real estate, loaned money to factory owners and governments, and provided capital for big business operations overseas.

The expansion of maritime trade led to new designs for merchant ships. In this, too, the Dutch played a dominant role. Using timber imported from northern Europe, shipyards in Dutch ports built their own vast fleets and other ships for export. Especially successful was the *fluit*, or "flyboat," a large-capacity cargo ship developed in the 1590s. It was inexpensive to build and required only a small crew. Another successful type of merchant ship, the heavily armed "East Indiaman," helped the Dutch establish their supremacy in the Indian Ocean. The Dutch also excelled at mapmaking (see Environment and Technology: Mapping the World).

Like merchants in the Islamic world, Europe's merchants relied on family and ethnic networks. In addition to families of local origin, many northern European cities contained merchant colonies from Venice, Florence, Genoa, and other Italian cities. In Amsterdam and Hamburg lived Jewish merchants who had fled religious persecution in Iberia. Other Jewish communities expanded out of eastern Europe into the German states, especially after the Thirty Years War. Armenian merchants from Iran were moving into the Mediterranean and became important in Russia in the seventeenth century.

Mapping the World

In 1602 in China the Jesuit missionary Matteo Ricci printed an elaborate map of the world. Working from maps produced in Europe and incorporating the latest knowledge gathered by European maritime explorers, Ricci introduced two changes to make the map more appealing to his Chinese hosts. He labeled it in Chinese characters, and he split his map down the middle of the Atlantic so that China lay in the center. This version pleased Chinese elite, who considered China the "Middle Kingdom" surrounded by lesser states. A copy of Ricci's map in six large panels adorned the emperor's Beijing palace.

The stunningly beautiful maps and globes of sixteenth-century Europe were the most complete, detailed, and useful representations of the earth that any society had ever produced. The best mapmaker of the century was Gerhard Kremer, who is remembered as Mercator (the merchant) because his maps were so useful to European ocean traders. By incorporating the latest discoveries and scientific measurements, Mercator could depict the outlines of the major continents in painstaking detail, even if their interiors were still largely unknown to outsiders.

To represent the spherical globe on a flat map, Mercator drew the lines of longitude as parallel lines. Because such lines actually meet at the poles, Mercator's projection greatly exaggerated the size of every landmass and body of water distant from the equator. However, Mercator's rendering offered a very practical advantage: sailors could plot their course by drawing a straight line between their point of departure and their destination. Because of this useful feature, the Mercator projection of the world remained in common use until quite recently. To some extent, its popularity came from the exaggerated size this projection gave to Europe. Like the Chinese, Europeans liked to think of themselves as at the center of things. Europeans also understood their true geographical position better than people in any other part of the world.

Dutch World Map, 1641   It is easy to see why the Chinese would not have liked to see their empire at the far right edge of this widely printed map. Besides the distortions caused by the Mercator projection, geographical ignorance exaggerates the size of North America and Antarctica.   (Courtesy of the Trustees British Museum)

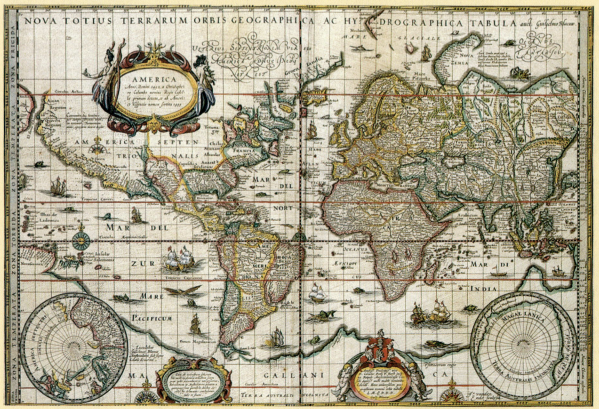

Port of Amsterdam   Ships, barges, and boats of all types are visible in this busy seventeenth-century scene. The large building in the center is the Admiralty House, the headquarters of the Dutch East India Company. (Mansell TimeLife Pictures/Getty Images)

The bourgeoisie sought mutually beneficial alliances with European monarchs, who welcomed economic growth as a means of increasing state revenues. The Dutch government pioneered chartering **joint-stock companies,** giving the Dutch East and West India Companies monopolies over trade to the East and West Indies. France and England chartered companies of their own. The companies then sold shares to individuals to raise large sums for overseas enterprises while spreading the risks (and profits) among many investors (see Chapter 19). Investors could buy and sell shares in specialized financial markets called **stock exchanges,** an Italian innovation transferred to the cities of northwestern Europe in the sixteenth century. The greatest stock market in the seventeenth and eighteenth centuries was the Amsterdam Exchange, founded in 1530. Large insurance companies also emerged in this period, and insuring long voyages against loss became a standard practice after 1700.

Governments also undertook large projects to improve water transport. The Dutch built numerous canals for transport and to drain the lowlands for agriculture. Other governments also financed canals, which included elaborate systems of locks to raise barges up over hills. One of the most important was the 150–mile (240–kilometer) Canal du Midi in France, built by the French government between 1661 and 1682 to link the Atlantic and the Mediterranean. By the seventeenth century

rulers sought the talents of successful businessmen as administrators. Jean Baptiste Colbert° (1619–1683), Louis XIV's able minister of finance, was a notable example.

After 1650 the Dutch faced growing competition from the English, who were developing their own close association of business and government. With government support, the English merchant fleet doubled between 1660 and 1700, and foreign trade rose by 50 percent. As a result, state revenue from customs duties tripled. In a series of wars (1652–1678) the English government used its naval might to break Dutch dominance in overseas trade and to extend England's colonial empire.

Some successful members of the bourgeoisie in England and France chose to use their wealth to raise their social status. By retiring from their businesses and buying country estates, they could become members of the **gentry.** These landowners affected the lifestyle of the old aristocracy. The gentry loaned money to impoverished peasants and to members of the nobility and in time increased their ownership of land. Some families sought aristocratic husbands for their daughters. The old nobility found such alliances attractive because of the large dowries that the bourgeoisie provided. In France a family could gain the exemption from taxation by living in gentility for three generations or, more quickly, by purchasing a title from the king.

Colbert (kohl-BEAR)

Peasants and Laborers

At the other end of society things were bad, but they had been worse. Serfdom, which bound men and women to land owned by a local lord, had been in deep decline since the great plague of the mid-fourteenth century. The institution did not return in western Europe as the population recovered, but competition for work exerted a downward pressure on wages. However, the development of large estates raising grain for the cities led to the rise of serfdom in eastern Europe for the first time. There was also a decline in slavery, which had briefly expanded in southern Europe around 1500 as the result of the Atlantic slave trade from sub-Saharan Africa. After 1600, however, Europeans shipped nearly all African slaves to the Americas.

There is much truth in the argument that western Europe continued to depend on unfree labor but kept it at a distance rather than at home. In any event, legal freedom did little to make a peasant's life safer and more secure. The techniques and efficiency of European agriculture had improved little since 1300. As a result, bad years brought famine; good ones provided only small surpluses. Indeed, the condition of the average person in western Europe may have worsened between 1500 and 1750 as the result of prolonged warfare, environmental problems, and adverse economic conditions. In addition, Europeans felt the adverse effects of a century of relatively cool climate that began in the 1590s. During this **Little Ice Age** average temperatures fell only a few degrees, but the effects were startling (see Issues in World History: The Little Ice Age).

By 1700 high-yielding new crops from the Americas were helping the rural poor avoid starvation. Once grown only as hedges against famine, potatoes and maize (corn) became staples for the rural poor in the eighteenth century. Potatoes sustained life in northeastern and Central Europe and in Ireland, while poor peasants in Italy subsisted on maize. The irony is that all of these lands were major exporters of wheat, but most of those who planted and harvested it could not afford to eat it.

Instead, the grain was put on carts, barges, and ships and carried to the cities of Western Europe. Other fleets brought wine from southern to northern Europe. Parisians downed 100,000 barrels of wine a year at the end of the seventeenth century. Some of the grain was made into beer, which the poor drank because it was cheaper than wine. In 1750 Parisian breweries brewed 23 million quarts (22 million liters) of beer for local consumption.

Other rural men made a living as miners, lumberjacks, and charcoal makers. The expanding iron industry in England provided work for all three, but the high consumption of wood fuel for this and other purposes caused serious **deforestation.** One early-seventeenth-century observer lamented: "within man's memory, it was held impossible to have any want of wood in England. But . . . at present, through the great consuming of wood . . . and the neglect of planting of woods, there is a great scarcity of wood throughout the whole kingdom."[1] The managers of the hundreds of ironworks in England tried to meet the shortages by importing timber and charcoal from more heavily forested Scandinavian countries and Russia. Eventually, the high price of wood and charcoal encouraged smelters to use coal as an alternative fuel. England's coal mining increased twelvefold from 210,000 tons in 1550 to 2,500,000 tons in 1700. From 1709 coke—coal refined to remove impurities—gradually replaced charcoal in the smelting of iron. These new demands drove English coal production to nearly 5 million tons a year by 1750.

France was much more forested than England, but increasing deforestation there prompted Colbert to predict that "France will perish for lack of wood." By the late eighteenth century deforestation had become an issue even in Sweden and Russia, where iron production had become a major industry. New laws in France and England designed to protect the forests were largely inspired by fears of shortages for naval vessels, whose keels required high-quality timbers of exceptional size and particular curvature. Although wood consumption remained high, rising prices encouraged some individuals to plant trees for future harvest.

Everywhere in Europe the rural poor felt the depletion of the forests most strongly. For centuries they had depended on woodlands for abundant supplies of wild nuts and berries, free firewood and building materials, and wild game. Modest improvements in food production in some places were overwhelmed by population growth. Rural women had long supplemented household incomes by spinning yarn. From the mid-1600s rising wages in towns led textile manufacturers to farm more and more textile weaving out to rural areas with high underemployment. This provided men and women with enough to survive on, but the piecework paid very little for long hours of tedious labor.

Throughout this period, many rural poor migrated to the towns and cities in hopes of better jobs, but only some were successful. Even in the prosperous Dutch towns, half of the population lived in acute poverty. Authorities estimated that those permanent city residents who were too poor to tax, the "deserving poor," made up 10 to 20 percent of population. That calculation did not include the large numbers of "unworthy poor"—recent migrants from impoverished rural areas, peddlers traveling from place to place, and beggars (many with horrible deformities and sores) who tried to survive on charity.

Many young women were forced into prostitution to survive. There were also many criminals, usually organized in gangs, ranging from youthful pickpockets to highway robbers.

The pervasive poverty of rural and urban Europe shocked those who were not hardened to it. In about 1580 the mayor of the French city of Bordeaux° asked a group of visiting Amerindian chiefs what impressed them most about European cities. The chiefs are said to have expressed astonishment at the disparity between the fat, well-fed people and the poor, half-starved men and women in rags. Why, the visitors wondered, did the poor not grab the rich by the throat or set fire to their homes?[2]

In fact, misery provoked many rebellions in early modern Europe. For example, in 1525 peasant rebels in the Alps attacked both nobles and clergy as representatives of the privileged and landowning classes. They had no love for merchants either, whom they denounced for lending at interest and charging high prices. Rebellions multiplied as rural conditions worsened. In southwestern France alone some 450 uprisings occurred between 1590 and 1715, many of them set off by food shortages and tax increases. The exemption of the wealthy from taxation was a frequent source of complaint. A rebellion in southern France in 1670 began when a mob of townswomen attacked the tax collector. It quickly spread to the country, where peasant leaders cried, "Death to the people's oppressors!" Authorities dealt severely with such revolts and executed or maimed their leaders.

Women and the Family

Women's status and work were closely tied to their husbands' and families'. In lands that allowed it, a woman in a royal family might inherit a throne (see Table 17.1, page 467 for examples)—in the absence of a male heir. These rare exceptions do not negate the rule that women everywhere ranked below men, but one should also not forget that her class and wealth defined a woman's position in life more than her sex. The wife or daughter of a rich man, for example, had a much better life than any poor man. In special cases, a single woman might be secure and respected, as in the case of women from good families who might head convents of nuns in Catholic countries. But unmarried women and widows were less well off than their married sisters. A good marriage was thus of great importance.

In contrast to the arranged marriages that prevailed in much of the rest of the world, young men and women in early modern Europe most often chose their own

Bordeaux (bor-DOH)

spouses. Ironically, privileged families were more inclined to control marriage plans than poor ones. Royal and noble families carefully plotted the suitability of their children's marriages in furthering the family's status. Bourgeois parents were less likely to force their children into arranged marriages, but the fact that nearly all found spouses within their social class strongly suggests that the bourgeoisie promoted marriages that furthered their business alliances.

Europeans also married later than people in other lands. The sons and daughters of craftworkers and the poor had to delay marriage until they could afford to live on their own. Young men had to serve long apprenticeships to learn trades. Young women also had to work—helping their parents, as domestic servants, or in some other capacity—to save money for the dowry they were expected to bring into the marriage. A dowry was the money and household goods—the amount varied by social class—that enabled a young couple to begin marriage independent of their parents. The typical groom in western and central Europe could not hope to marry before his late twenties, and his bride would be a few years younger—in contrast to the rest of the world, where people usually married in their teens. Marriage also came late in bourgeois families, in part to allow young men to complete their education.

Besides enabling young people to be independent of their parents, the late age of marriage in early modern Europe also held down the birthrate and thus limited family size. Even so, about one-tenth of the births in a city were to unmarried women, often servants, who generally left their infants on the doorsteps of churches, convents, or rich families. Despite efforts to raise such abandoned children, many perished. Delayed marriage also had links to the existence of public brothels, where young men could satisfy their lusts in cheap and impersonal encounters with unfortunate young women, often newly arrived from impoverished rural villages. Nevertheless, rape was a common occurrence, usually perpetrated by gangs of young men who attacked young women rumored to be free with their favors. Some historians believe that such gang rapes reflected poor young men's jealousy at older men's easier access to women.

Bourgeois parents were very concerned that their children have the education and training necessary for success. They promoted the establishment of municipal schools to provide a solid education, including Latin and perhaps Greek, for their sons, who were then sent abroad to learn modern languages or to a university to earn a law degree. Legal training was useful for conducting business and was a prerequisite for obtaining government judgeships and treasury positions. Daughters were less likely to be groomed for business careers, but wives often helped their husbands as bookkeepers and sometimes inherited businesses.

The fact that most schools barred female students, as did most guild and professions, explains why women were not prominent in the cultural Renaissance, the Reformation, the Scientific Revolution, and the Enlightenment. Yet from a global perspective, women in early modern Europe were more prominent in the creation of culture than were women in most other parts of the world. Recent research has brought to light the existence of a number of successful women who were painters, musicians, and writers. Indeed, the spread of learning, the stress on religious reading, and the growth of business likely meant that Europe led the world in female literacy. In a period when most men were illiterate, the number of literate women was small, and only women in wealthier families might have a good education. From the late 1600s some wealthy French women ran intellectual gatherings in their homes. Many more were prominent letter writers. Galileo's daughter, Maria Celeste Galilei, carried on a detailed correspondence with her father from the confinement of her convent, whose walls she had taken a religious vow never to leave.

POLITICAL INNOVATIONS

The monarchs of early modern Europe occupied the apex of the social order, were arbitrators of the intellectual and religious conflicts of their day, and had important influences on the economic life of their realms. For these reasons an overview of political life incorporates all the events previously described in this chapter. In addition, monarchs' political agendas introduced new elements of conflict and change.

The effort to create a European empire failed, but monarchs succeeded in achieving a higher degree of political centralization within their separate kingdoms. The frequent civil and international conflicts of this era sometimes promoted cooperation, but they often encouraged innovation. Leadership and success passed from Spain to the Netherlands and then to England and France. It is hard to avoid the conclusion that the key political technology was cannonry.

State Development

Political diversity characterized Europe. City-states and principalities abounded, either independently or bound into loose federations, of which the **Holy Roman Empire** of the German heartland was the most notable example.

In western Europe the strong monarchies that had emerged were acquiring national identities. Dreams of a European empire comparable to those of Asia remained strong, although efforts to form one were frustrated.

Dynastic ambitions and historical circumstances combined to favor and then block the creation of a powerful empire in the early sixteenth century. In 1519 electors of the Holy Roman Empire chose Charles V (r. 1519–1556) to be the new emperor. Like his predecessors for three generations, Charles belonged to the powerful **Habsburg°** family of Austria, but he had recently inherited the Spanish thrones of Castile and Aragon. With the vast resources of all these offices behind him (see Map 17.2), Charles hoped to centralize his imperial power and lead a Christian coalition to halt the advance into southeastern Europe of the Ottoman Empire, whose Muslim rulers already controlled most of the Middle East and North Africa.

Charles and his Christian allies eventually halted the Ottomans at the gates of Vienna in 1529, although Ottoman attacks continued on and off until 1697. But Charles's efforts to forge his several possessions into Europe's strongest state failed. King Francis I of France, who had lost to Charles in the election for Holy Roman Emperor, openly supported the Muslim Turks to weaken his rival. In addition, the princes of the Holy Roman Empire's many member states were able to use Luther's religious Reformation to frustrate Charles's efforts to reduce their autonomy. Swayed partly by Luther's appeals to German nationalism, many German princes opposed Charles's defense of Catholic doctrine in the imperial Diet (assembly).

After decades of bitter squabbles turned to open warfare in 1546 (the German Wars of Religion), Charles V finally gave up his efforts at unification, abdicated control of his various possessions to different heirs, and retired to a monastery. By the Peace of Augsburg (1555), he recognized the princes' right to choose whether Catholicism or Lutheranism would prevail in their particular states, and he allowed them to keep the church lands they had seized before 1552. The triumph of religious diversity had derailed Charles's plan for centralizing authority in central Europe and put off German political unification for three centuries.

Meanwhile, the rulers of Spain, France, and England were building a more successful program of political unification based on political centralization and religious unity. The most successful rulers reduced the autonomy of the church and the nobility in their states, while making them part of a unified national structure

Habsburg (HABZ-berg)

Map 17.2 The European Empire of Charles V Charles was Europe's most powerful ruler from 1519 to 1556, but he failed to unify the Christian West. In addition to being the elected head of the Holy Roman Empire, he was the hereditary ruler of the Spanish realms of Castile and Aragon and the possessions of the Austrian Habsburgs in Central Europe. The map does not show his extensive holdings in the Americas and Asia.

with the monarch at its head (see Diversity and Dominance: Political Craft and Craftiness). The cooption of the church in the sixteenth century was stormy, but the outcome was clear. Bringing the nobles and other powerful interests into a centralized political system took longer and led to more diverse outcomes.

Religious Policies

The rulers of Spain and France successfully defended the Catholic tradition against Protestant challenges. Following the pattern used by his predecessors to suppress Jewish and Muslim practices, King Philip II of Spain used an ecclesiastical court, the

파운드폭탄 4발 투하… 두 아들과 함께 사망 가

두심진지 구축… 이틀째 시가戰

령이 대중 앞에 나타나거나 애국심
을 고취하는 노래만을 내보내던 방
송마저 중단했다.

라크 전후 대책
의에서는 전후
영국 주도로 히

DIVERSITY AND DOMINANCE

POLITICAL CRAFT AND CRAFTINESS

Political power was becoming more highly concentrated in early modern Europe, but absolute dominance was more a goal than a reality. Whether subject to constitutional checks or not, rulers were very concerned with creating and maintaining good relations with their more powerful subjects. Their efforts to manipulate public opinion and perceptions have much in common with the efforts of modern politicians to manage their "image."

A diplomat and civil servant in the rich and powerful Italian city-state of Florence, Niccolò Machiavelli, is best known for his book The Prince *(1532). This influential essay on the proper exercise of political power has been interpreted as cynical by some and as supremely practical and realistic by others. Because Machiavelli did not have a high opinion of the intelligence and character of most people, he urged rulers to achieve obedience by fear and deception. But he also suggested that genuine mercy, honesty, and piety may be superior to feigned virtue.*

OF CRUELTY AND CLEMENCY, AND WHETHER IT IS BETTER TO BE LOVED THAN FEARED

. . . It will naturally be answered that it would be desirable to be both the one and the other; but, as it is difficult to be both at the same time, it is much safer to be feared than to be loved, when you have to choose between the two. For it may be said of men in general that they are ungrateful and fickle, dissemblers, avoiders of danger, and greedy of gain. So long as you shower benefits on them, they are all yours; they offer you their blood, their substance, their lives, and their children, provided the necessity for it is far off; but when it is near at hand, then they revolt. And the prince who relies on their words, without having otherwise provided for his security is ruined; for friendships that are won by rewards, not by greatness and nobility of soul, although deserved, yet are not real, and cannot be depended upon in time of adversity.

Besides, men have less hesitation in offending one who makes himself beloved than one who makes himself feared; for love holds by a bond of obligation which, as mankind is bad, is broken on every occasion whenever it is for the interest of the obligated party to break it. But fear holds by the apprehension of punishment, which never leaves men. A prince, however, should make himself feared in such a manner that, if he has not won the affection of his people, he shall at least not incur their hatred. . . .

IN WHAT MANNER PRINCES SHOULD KEEP THEIR FAITH

It must be evident to every one that it is more praiseworthy for a prince always to maintain good faith, and practice integrity rather than craft and deceit. And yet the experience of our own times has shown those princes have achieved great things who made small account of good faith, and who understood by cunning to circumvent the intelligence of others; and that in the end they got the better of those whose actions were dictated by loyalty and good faith. You must know, therefore, that there are two ways of carrying on a struggle; one by law and the other by force. The first is practiced by men, and the other by animals; and as the first is often insufficient, it becomes necessary to resort to the second.

. . . If men were altogether good, this advice would be wrong; but since they are bad and will not keep faith with you, you need not keep faith with them. Nor will a prince ever be short of legitimate excuses to give color to his breaches of faith. Innumerable modern examples could be given of this; and it could easily be shown how many treaties of peace, and how many engagements, have been made null and void by the faithlessness of princes; and he who has best known how to play the fox has ever been the most successful.

But it is necessary that the prince should know how to color this nature well, and how to be a great hypocrite and dissembler. For men are so simple, and yield so much to immediate necessity, that the deceiver will never lack dupes. I will mention one of the most recent examples. [Pope] Alexander VI never did nor ever thought of anything but to deceive, and always found a reason for doing so . . . and yet he was always successful in his deceits, because he knew the weakness of men in that particular.

It is not necessary, however, for a prince to possess all the above-mentioned qualities; but it is essential that he should at least seem to have them. I will even venture to say, that to have and practice them constantly is pernicious, but to seem to have them is useful. For instance, a prince should seem to be merciful, faithful, humane, religious, and upright, and should even be so in reality; but he should have his mind so trained that, when occasion requires it, he may know how to change to the opposite. And it must be understood that a prince, and especially one who has but recently acquired his state, cannot perform all those things which cause men to be esteemed as good; he being obligated, for the sake of maintaining his state, to act contrary to humanity, charity, and religion. And therefore, it is necessary that he should have a versatile mind, capable of changing readily, according as the winds and changes of fortune bid him; and, as has been said above, not to swerve from the good if possible, but to know how to resort to evil if necessity demands it.

A prince then should be very careful never to allow anything to escape his lips that does not abound in the above-mentioned five qualities, so that to see and to hear him he may seem all charity, integrity, and humanity, all uprightness and all piety. And more than all else is it necessary for a prince to seem to possess the last quality; for mankind in general judge more by what they see than by what they feel, every one being capable of the former, and few of the latter. Everybody sees what you seem to be, but few really feel what you are; and those few dare not oppose the opinion of the many, who are protected by the majority of the state; for the actions of all men, and especially those of princes, are judged by the result, where there is no other judge to whom to appeal.

A prince should look mainly to the successful maintenance of his state. For the means which he employs for this will always be counted honorable, and will be praised by everybody; for the common people are always taken in by appearances and by results, and it is the vulgar mass that constitutes the world.

*B*ecause, as Machiavelli argued, appearances count for as *much in the public arena as realities, it is difficult to judge whether rulers' statements expressed their real feelings and beliefs or what may have been the most expedient to say at the moment. An example is this speech Queen Elizabeth of England made at the end of November 1601 to Parliament after a particularly difficult year. One senior noble had led a rebellion and was subsequently executed. Parliament was pressing for extended privileges. Having gained the throne in 1558 after many difficulties (including a time in prison), the sixty-eight-year-old queen had much experience in the language and wiles of politics and was well aware of the importance of public opinion. Reprinted many times, the speech became famous as "The Golden Speech of Queen Elizabeth."*

I do assure you, there is no prince that loveth his subjects better, or whose love can countervail our love. There is no jewel, be it of never so rich a price, which I set before this jewel: I mean your love. For I do esteem it more than any treasure or riches; for that we know how to prize, but love and thanks I count unvaluable.

And, though God has raised me high, yet this I count the glory of my crown, that I have reigned with your loves. This makes me that I do not so much rejoice that God hath made me to be a Queen, as to be Queen over so thankful a people.

Therefore, I have cause to wish nothing more than to content the subjects; and that is the duty I owe. Neither do I desire to live longer days than I may see your prosperity; and that is my only desire.

And as I am that person that still (yet under God) has delivered you, so I trust, by the almighty power of God, that I shall be His instrument to preserve you from every peril, dishonour, shame, tyranny, and oppression. . . .

Of myself I must say this: I was never any greedy scraping grasper, nor a straight, fast-holding prince, nor yet a waster. My heart was never set on worldly goods, but only for my subjects' good. What you bestow on me, I will not hoard it up, but receive it to bestow on you again. Yea, mine own properties I count yours, and to be expended for your good. . . .

To be a king and wear a crown is a thing more glorious to them that see it, than it is pleasing to them that bear it. For myself, I was never so much enticed with the glorious name of king, or royal authority of a queen, as delighted that God made me his instrument to maintain his truth and glory, and to defend this Kingdom (as I said) from peril, dishonour, tyranny and oppression.

There will never Queen sit in my seat with more zeal to my country, care for my subjects, and that sooner with willingness will venture her life for your good and safety than myself. For it is not my desire to live nor reign longer than my life and reign shall be for your good. And though you have had and may have many more princes more mighty and wise sitting in this state, yet you never had or shall have any that will be more careful and loving.

Shall I ascribe anything to myself and my sexly weakness? I were not worthy to live then; and of all, most unworthy of the great mercies I have had from God, who has even yet given me a heart, which never feared foreign of home enemy. I speak to give God the praise . . . That I should speak for any glory, God forbid.

QUESTIONS FOR ANALYSIS

1. Do you find Machiavelli's advice to be cynical or realistic?
2. Describe how a member of Parliament might have responded to Queen Elizabeth's declarations of her concern for the welfare of her people above all else.
3. Can a ruler be sincere and manipulative at the same time?

Source: From *The Historical, Political, and Diplomatic Writings of Niccolo Machiavelli,* trans. Christian E. Detmold (Boston: Houghton, Mifflin and Company, 1891), II: 54–59, and Heywood Townshend, *Historical Collections, or an Exact Account of the Proceedings of the Last Four Parliaments of Q. Elizabeth* (London: Basset, Crooke, and Cademan, 1680), 263–266.

Spanish Inquisition, to bring into line those who resisted his authority. Suspected Protestants, as well as critics of the king, found themselves accused of heresy, an offense punishable by death. Even those who were acquitted of the charge learned not to oppose the king again.

In France the Calvinist opponents of the Valois rulers gained the military advantage in the French Wars of Religion (1562–1598), but in the interest of forging lasting unity, their leader Prince Henry of Navarre then embraced the Catholic faith of the majority of his subjects. In their embrace of a union of church and state, the new Bourbon king, Henry IV, his son King Louis XIII, and his grandson King Louis XIV were as supportive of the Catholic Church as their counterparts in Spain. In 1685 Louis XIV even revoked the Edict of Nantes°, by which his grandfather had granted religious freedom to his Protestant supporters in 1598.

In England King Henry VIII had initially been a strong defender of the papacy against Lutheran criticism. But when Henry failed to obtain a papal annulment of his marriage to Catherine of Aragon, who had not furnished him with a male heir, he challenged the papacy's authority over the church in his kingdom. Henry had the English archbishop of Canterbury annul the marriage in 1533. The breach with Rome was sealed the next year when Parliament made the English monarch head of the Church of England.

Like many Protestant rulers, Henry used his authority to disband monasteries and convents and seize their lands. He gave the lands to his powerful allies and sold some to pay for his new navy. However, under Henry and his successors the new Anglican church moved away from Roman Catholicism in ritual and theology much less than was wanted by English Puritans (Calvinists who wanted to "purify" the Anglican church of Catholic practices and beliefs). In 1603 the first Stuart king, James I, dismissed a Puritan petition to eliminate bishops with the statement "No bishops, no king"—a reminder of the essential role of the church in supporting royal power.

Monarchies in England and France

Over the course of the seventeenth century, the rulers of England and France went through some very intense conflicts with their leading subjects over the limits of royal authority. Religion was never absent as an issue in these struggles, but the different constitutional outcomes they produced were of more significance in the long run.

So as to evade any check on his power, King Charles I of England (see Table 17.1) ruled for eleven years without summoning Parliament, his kingdom's representative body. Lacking Parliament's consent to new taxes, he raised funds by coercing "loans" from wealthy subjects and applying existing tax laws more broadly. Then in 1640 a rebellion in Scotland forced him to summon a Parliament to approve new taxes to pay for an army. Noblemen and churchmen sat in the House of Lords. Representatives from the towns and counties sat in the House of Commons. Before it would authorize new taxes, Parliament insisted on strict guarantees that the king would never again ignore the body's traditional rights. These King Charles refused to grant. When he ordered the arrest of his leading critics in the House of Commons in 1642, he plunged the kingdom into the **English Civil War.**

Charles suffered defeat on the battlefield, but still refused to compromise. In 1649 a "Rump" Parliament purged of his supporters ordered him executed and replaced the monarchy with a republic under the Puritan general Oliver Cromwell. During his rule, Cromwell expanded England's presence overseas and imposed firm control over Ireland and Scotland, but he was as unwilling as the Stuart kings to share power with Parliament. After his death Parliament restored the Stuart line, and for a time it was unclear which side had won the war.

However, when King James II refused to respect Parliament's rights and had his heir baptized a Roman Catholic, the leaders of Parliament forced James into exile in the bloodless Glorious Revolution of 1688. The Bill of Rights of 1689 specified that Parliament had to be called frequently and had to consent to changes in laws and to the raising of an army in peacetime. Another law reaffirmed the official status of the Church of England but extended religious toleration to the Puritans.

A similar struggle in France produced a different outcome. There the Estates General represented the traditional rights of the clergy, the nobility, and the towns (that is, the bourgeoisie). The Estates General was able to assert its rights during the sixteenth-century French Wars of Religion, when the monarchy was weak. But thereafter the Bourbon monarchs generally ruled without having to call it into session. They avoided financial crises by more efficient tax collection and by selling appointments to high government offices. In justification they claimed that the monarch had absolute authority to rule in God's name on earth.

Louis XIV's gigantic new palace at **Versailles**° symbolized the French monarch's triumph over the traditional rights of the nobility, clergy, and towns. Capable of hous-

---

Nantes (nahnt)

Versailles (vuhr-SIGH)

Table 17.1   Rulers in Early Modern Western Europe

Spain	France	England/Great Britain
Habsburg Dynasty	**Valois Dynasty**	**Tudor Dynasty**
Charles I (1516–1556) (Holy Roman Emperor Charles V)	Francis I (1515–1547)	Henry VIII (1509–1547)
	Henry II (1547–1559)	Edward VI (1547–1553)
Philip II (1556–1598)	Francis II (1559–1560)	Mary I (1553–1558)
	Charles IX (1560–1574)	Elizabeth I (1558–1603)
	Henry III (1574–1589)	
	Bourbon Dynasty	**Stuart Dynasty**
Philip III (1598–1621)	Henry IV (1589–1610)[a]	James I (1603–1625)
Philip IV (1621–1665)	Louis XIII (1610–1643)	Charles I (1625–1649)[a, b]
Charles II (1665–1700)	Louis XIV (1643–1715)	(Puritan Republic, 1649–1660)
		Charles II (1660–1685)
		James II (1685–1688)[b]
		William III (1689–1702) and Mary II (1689–1694)
Bourbon Dynasty		Anne (1702–1714)
Philip V (1700–1746)		
		Hanoverian Dynasty
	Louis XV (1715–1774)	George I (1714–1727)
Ferdinand VI (1746–1759)		George II (1727–1760)

[a]Died a violent death.   [b]Was overthrown.

ing ten thousand people and surrounded by elaborately landscaped grounds and parks, the palace can be seen as a sort of theme park of royal absolutism. Elaborate ceremonies and banquets centered on the king kept the nobles who lived at Versailles away from plotting rebellion. According to one of them, the duke of Saint-Simon°, "no one was so clever in devising petty distractions" as the king.

The balance of powers in the English model would be widely admired in later times. Until well after 1750 most European rulers admired and imitated the centralized powers and absolutist claims of the French. Some went so far as to build imitations of the Versailles palace. The checks and balances of the English model had a less immediate effect. In his influential *Second Treatise of Civil Government* (1690), the English political philosopher John Locke (1632–1704) disputed monarchial claims to absolute authority by divine right. Rather, he argued, rulers derived their authority from the consent of the governed and, like everyone else, were subject to the law. If monarchs overstepped the law, Locke argued, citizens had not only the right but also the duty to rebel. The later consequences of this idea are considered in Chapter 22.

Saint-Simon (san see-MON)

Warfare and Diplomacy

In addition to the bitter civil wars that pounded the Holy Roman Empire, France, and England, European states engaged in numerous international conflicts. Warfare was almost constant in early modern Europe (see the Chronology at the beginning of the chapter). In their pursuit of power monarchs expended vast sums of money and caused widespread devastation and death. The worst of the international conflicts, the Thirty Years War (1618–1648), caused long-lasting depopulation and economic decline in much of the Holy Roman Empire.

However, the wars also produced dramatic improvements in the skill of European armed forces and in their weaponry that arguably made them the most powerful in the world. The numbers of men in arms increased steadily throughout the early modern period. French forces, for example grew from about 150,000 in 1630 to 400,000 by the early eighteenth century. Even smaller European states built up impressive armies. Sweden, with under a million people, had one of the finest and best-armed military forces in seventeenth-century Europe. Though the country had fewer than 2 million inhabitants in 1700, Prussia's splendid army made it one of Europe's major powers.

Versailles, 1722 This painting by P.-D. Martin shows the east expanse of buildings and courtyards that make up the palace complex built by King Louis XIV. (Giraudon/Art Resource, NY)

Larger armies required more effective command structures. In the words of a modern historian, European armies "evolved . . . the equivalent of a central nervous system, capable of activating technologically differentiated claws and teeth."[3] New signaling techniques improved control of battlefield maneuvers. Frequent marching drills trained troops to obey orders instantly and gave them a close sense of comradeship. To defend themselves cities built new fortifications able to withstand cannon bombardments. Each state tried to outdo its rivals by improvements in military hardware, but battles between evenly matched armies often ended in stalemates that prolonged the wars. Victory increasingly depended on naval superiority.

Only England did not maintain a standing army in peacetime, but England's rise as a sea power had begun under King Henry VIII, who spent heavily on ships and promoted a domestic iron-smelting industry to supply cannon. The Royal Navy also copied innovative ship de-

signs from the Dutch in the second half of the seventeenth century. By the early eighteenth century the Royal Navy surpassed the rival French fleet in numbers. By then, England had merged with Scotland to become Great Britain, annexed Ireland, and built a North American empire.

Although France was Europe's most powerful state, Louis XIV's efforts to expand its borders and dominance were increasingly frustrated by coalitions of the other great powers. In a series of eighteenth-century wars beginning with the War of the Spanish Succession (1701–1714), the combination of Britain's naval strength and the land armies of its Austrian and Prussian allies was able to block French expansionist efforts and prevent the Bourbons from uniting the thrones of France and Spain.

This defeat of the French monarchy's empire-building efforts illustrated the principle of **balance of power** in international relations: the major European states formed

The Spanish Armada   This drawing for a tapestry shows the great warships of the Spanish fleet lined up to face the smaller but faster vessels of the British navy. The ship with oars in the foreground is a galley.   (Eileen Tweedy/The Art Archive)

temporary alliances to prevent any one state from becoming too powerful. Russia emerged as a major power in Europe after its modernized armies defeated Sweden in the Great Northern War (1700–1721). During the next two centuries, though adhering to four different branches of Christianity, the great powers of Europe—Catholic France, Anglican Britain, Catholic Austria, Lutheran Prussia, and Orthodox Russia (see Map 17.3)—maintained an effective balance of power in Europe by shifting their alliances for geopolitical rather than religious reasons. These pragmatic alliances were the first successful efforts at international peacekeeping.

Paying the Piper

To pay the extremely heavy military costs of their wars, European rulers had to increase their revenues. The most successful of them after 1600 promoted mutually beneficial alliances with the rising commercial elite. Both sides understood that trade thrived where government taxation and regulation were not excessive, where courts enforced contracts and collected debts, and where military power stood ready to protect overseas expansion by force when necessary.

Spain, sixteenth-century Europe's mightiest state, illustrates how the financial drains of an aggressive military policy and the failure to promote economic development could lead to decline. Expensive wars against the Ottomans, northern European Protestants, and rebellious Dutch subjects caused the treasury to default on its debts four times during the reign of King Philip II. Moreover, the Spanish rulers' concerns for religious uniformity and traditional aristocratic privilege further undermined the country's economy. In the name of religious uniformity they expelled Jewish merchants, persecuted Protestant dissenters, and forced tens of thousands of skilled farmers and artisans into exile because of their Muslim ancestry. In the name of aristocratic privilege the 3 percent of the population that controlled 97 percent of the land in 1600 was exempt from taxation, while high sales taxes discouraged manufacturing.

For a time, vast imports of silver and gold bullion from Spain's American colonies filled the government treasury. These bullion shipments also contributed to severe inflation (rising prices), worst in Spain but bad throughout the rest of western Europe as well. A Spanish saying captured the problem: American silver was like rain on the roof—it poured down and washed away. Huge debts for foreign wars drained bullion from Spain to its creditors. More wealth flowed out to purchase manufactured goods and even food in the seventeenth century.

The rise of the Netherlands as an economic power stemmed from opposite policies. The Spanish crown had acquired these resource-poor but commercially successful provinces as part of Charles V's inheritance. But King Philip II's decision to impose Spain's ruinously heavy

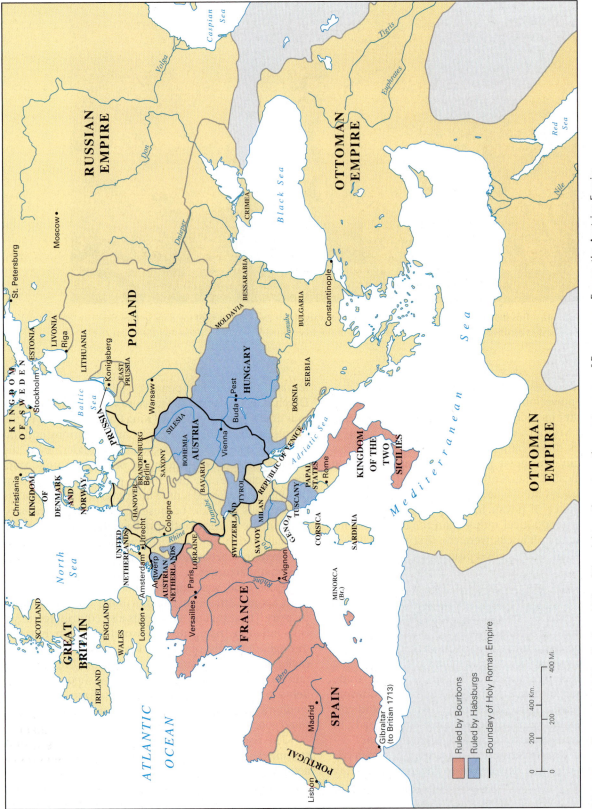

Map 17.3 Europe in 1740 By the middle of the eighteenth century the great powers of Europe were France, the Austrian Empire, Great Britain, Prussia, and Russia. Spain, the Holy Roman Empire, and the Ottoman Empire were far weaker in 1740 than they had been two centuries earlier.

sales tax and enforce Catholic orthodoxy drove the Dutch to revolt in 1566 and again in 1572. If successful, those measures would have discouraged business and driven away the Calvinists, Jews, and others who were essential to Dutch prosperity. The Dutch fought with skill and ingenuity, raising and training an army and a navy that were among the most effective in Europe. By 1609 Spain was forced to agree to a truce that recognized the autonomy of the northern part of the Netherlands. In 1648, after eight decades of warfare, the independence of these seven United Provinces of the Free Netherlands (their full name) became final.

Rather than being ruined by the long war, the United Netherlands emerged as the dominant commercial power in Europe and the world's greatest trading nation. During the seventeenth century, the wealth of the Netherlands multiplied. This economic success owed much to a decentralized government. During the long struggle against Spain, the provinces united around the prince of Orange, their sovereign, who served as commander-in-chief of the armed forces. But in economic matters each province was free to pursue its own interests. The maritime province of Holland grew rich by favoring commercial interests.

After 1650 the Dutch faced growing competition from the English, who were developing their own close association of business and government. In a series of wars (1652–1678) England used its naval might to break Dutch dominance in overseas trade and to extend its own colonial empire. With government support, the English merchant fleet doubled between 1660 and 1700, and foreign trade rose by 50 percent. As a result, state revenue from customs duties tripled. During the eighteenth century Britain's trading position strengthened still more.

The debts run up by the Anglo-Dutch Wars helped persuade the English monarchy to greatly enlarge the government's role in managing the economy. The outcome has been called a "financial revolution." The government increased revenues by taxing the formerly exempt landed estates of the aristocrats and by collecting taxes directly. Previously, private individuals known as tax farmers had advanced the government a fixed sum of money; in return they could keep whatever money they were able to collect from taxpayers. To secure cash quickly for warfare and other emergencies and to reduce the burden of debts from earlier wars, England also followed the Dutch lead in creating a central bank, from which the government was able to obtain long-term loans at low rates.

The French government was also developing its national economy, especially under Colbert. He streamlined tax collection, promoted French manufacturing and shipping by imposing taxes on foreign goods, and improved transportation within France itself. Yet the power of the wealthy aristocrats kept the French government from following England's lead in taxing wealthy landowners, collecting taxes directly, and securing low-cost loans. Nor did France succeed in managing its debt as efficiently as England. (The role of governments in promoting overseas trade is further discussed in Chapter 19.)

CONCLUSION

European historians have used the word *revolution* to describe many different changes taking place in Europe between 1500 and 1750. The expansion of trade has been called a commercial revolution, the reform of state spending a financial revolution, and the changes in weapons and warfare a military revolution. We have also encountered a scientific revolution and the religious revolution of the Reformation.

These important changes in government, economy, society, and thought were parts of a dynamic process that began in the later Middle Ages and led to even bigger industrial and political revolutions before the eighteenth century was over. Yet the years from 1500 to 1750 were not simply—perhaps not even primarily—an age of progress for Europe. For many, the ferocious competition of European armies, merchants, and ideas was a wrenching experience. The growth of powerful states extracted a terrible price in death, destruction, and misery. The Reformation brought greater individual choice in religion but widespread religious persecution as well. Individual women rose or fell with their social class, but few gained equality with men. The expanding economy benefited members of the emerging merchant elite and their political allies, but most Europeans became worse off as prices rose faster than wages. New scientific and enlightened ideas ignited new controversies long before they yielded any tangible benefits.

The historical significance of this period of European history is clearer when viewed in a global context. What stands out are the powerful and efficient European armies, economies, and governments, which larger states elsewhere in the world feared, envied, and sometimes imitated. From a global perspective, the balance of political and economic power was shifting slowly, but inexorably, in the Europeans' favor. In 1500 the Ottomans threatened Europe. By 1750, as the remaining chapters of Part Five detail, Europeans had brought the world's seas and a growing part of its land and people under their control. No single group of Europeans accomplished this. The Dutch eclipsed the pioneering Portuguese and Spanish; then the English and French bested the Dutch. Competition, too, was a factor in European success.

Other changes in Europe during this period had no great overseas significance at the time. The new ideas of the Scientific Revolution and the Enlightenment were still of minor importance. Their full effects in furthering Europeans' global dominion were felt after 1750, as Parts Six and Seven explore.

■ Key Terms

Renaissance (European)	stock exchange
papacy	gentry
indulgence	Little Ice Age
Protestant Reformation	deforestation
Catholic Reformation	Holy Roman Empire
witch-hunt	Habsburg
Scientific Revolution	English Civil War
Enlightenment	Versailles
bourgeoisie	balance of power
joint-stock company	

■ Suggested Reading

Overviews of this period include Euan Cameron, ed., *Early Modern Europe* (1999); H. G. Koenigsberger, *Early Modern Europe: Fifteen Hundred to Seventeen Eighty-Nine* (1987); and Joseph Bergin, *The Short Oxford History of Europe: The Seventeenth Century* (2001). Global perspectives can be found in Fernand Braudel, *Civilization and Capitalism, 15th–18th Century*, trans. Siân Reynolds, 3 vols. (1979), and Immanuel Wallerstein, *The Modern World-System*, vol. 2, *Mercantilism and the Consolidation of the European World-Economy, 1600–1750* (1980).

Technological and environmental changes are the focus of Geoffrey Parker, *Military Revolution: Military Innovation and the Rise of the West, 1500–1800*, 2d ed. (1996); William H. McNeill, *The Pursuit of Power: Technology, Armed Force, and Society Since A.D. 1000* (1982); Robert Greenhalgh Albion, *Forests and Sea Power: The Timber Problem of the Royal Navy, 1652–1862* (1965); Emmanuel Le Roy Ladurie, *Times of Feast, Times of Famine: A History of Climate Since the Year 1000*, trans. Barbara Bray (1971); and Brian Fagan, *The Little Ice Age: How Climate Made History, 1300–1850* (1988). Robert C. Allen, *Enclosure and the Yeoman: The Agricultural Development of the South Midlands, 1450–1850* (1992), focuses on England.

Steven Stapin, *The Scientific Revolution* (1998), and Hugh Kearney, *Science and Change, 1500–1700* (1971) are accessible introductions. Thomas S. Kuhn, *The Structure of Scientific Revolution*, 3d ed. (1996), and A. R. Hall, *The Scientific Revolution, 1500–1800:*

The Formation of the Modern Scientific Attitude, 2d ed. (1962), are classic studies. Carolyn Merchant, *The Death of Nature: Women, Ecology and the Scientific Revolution* (1980), tries to combine several broad perspectives. *The Sciences in Enlightened Europe*, ed. W. Clark, J. Golinski, and S. Schaffer (1999), examines particular topics in a sophisticated way. Dorinda Outram, *The Enlightenment* (1995), provides a recent summary of research.

Excellent introductions to social and economic life are George Huppert, *After the Black Death: A Social History of Early Modern Europe* (1986), and Carlo M. Cipolla, *Before the Industrial Revolution: European Society and Economy, 1000–1700*, 2d ed. (1980). Peter Burke, *Popular Culture in Early Modern Europe* (1978), offers a broad treatment of nonelite perspectives, as does Robert Jütte, *Poverty and Deviance in Early Modern Europe* (1994). For more economic detail see Robert S. DuPlessis, *Transitions to Capitalism in Early Modern Europe* (1997); Myron P. Gutmann, *Toward the Modern Economy: Early Industry in Europe, 1500–1800* (1988); and Carlo M. Cipolla, ed., *The Fontana Economic History of Europe*, vol. 2, *The Sixteenth and Seventeenth Centuries* (1974).

Topics of women's history are examined by Merry Wiesner, *Women and Gender in Early Modern Europe*, 2d ed. (2000); Bonie S. Anderson and Judith Zinsser, *A History of Their Own: Women in Europe*, vol. II, rev. ed. (2000); and Monica Chojnacka and Merry E. Wiesner-Hanks, *Ages of Woman, Ages of Man* (2002). An excellent place to begin examining the complex subject of witchcraft is Brian Levack, *The Witch-Hunt in Early Modern Europe*, 2d ed. (1995); other up-to-date perspectives can be found in J. Barry, M. Hester, and G. Roberts, eds., *Witchcraft in Early Modern Europe: Studies in Culture and Belief* (1998), and Carlo Ginzburg, *The Night Battles: Witchcraft and Agrarian Cults in the Sixteenth and Seventeenth Centuries*, trans. John and Anne Tedechi (1983).

Good single-country surveys are J. A. Sharpe, *Early Modern England: A Social History*, 2d ed. (1997); Emmanuel Le Roy Ladurie, *The Royal French State, 1460–1610* (1994), and *The Ancien Régime: A History of France, 1610–1774* (1998); Jonathan Israel, *The Dutch Republic: Its Rise, Greatness and Fall, 1477–1806* (1995); and James Casey, *Early Modern Spain: A Social History* (1999).

■ Notes

1. Quoted by Carlo M. Cipolla, "Introduction," *The Fontana Economic History of Europe*, vol. 2, *The Sixteenth and Seventeenth Centuries* (Glasgow: Collins/Fontana Books, 1974), 11–12.
2. Michel de Montaigne, *Essais* (1588), ch. 31, "Des Cannibales."
3. William H. McNeill, *The Pursuit of Power: Technology, Armed Force, and Society Since A.D. 1000* (Chicago: University of Chicago Press, 1982), 124.

18

The Diversity of American Colonial Societies, 1530–1770

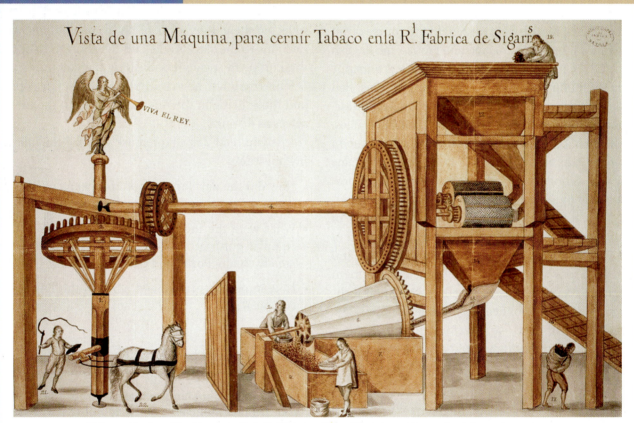

Vista de una Máquina, para cernír Tabáco enla R.^{1} Fabrica de Sigarr^s

VIVA EL REY.

Tobacco Factory Machinery in Colonial Mexico City   The tobacco factory in eighteenth-century Mexico City used a horse-driven mechanical shredder to produce snuff and cigarette tobacco.

CHAPTER OUTLINE

The Columbian Exchange

Spanish America and Brazil

English and French Colonies in North America

Colonial Expansion and Conflict

ENVIRONMENT AND TECHNOLOGY: The Silver Refinery at Potosí, Bolivia, 1700

DIVERSITY AND DOMINANCE: Race and Ethnicity in the Spanish Colonies: Negotiating Hierarchy

Shulush Homa—an eighteenth-century Choctaw leader called "Red Shoes" by the English—faced a dilemma. For years he had befriended the French who had moved into the lower Mississippi Valley, protecting their outlying settlements from other indigenous groups and producing a steady flow of deerskins for trade. In return he received guns and gifts as well as honors previously given only to chiefs. Though born a commoner, he had parlayed his skillful politicking with the French—and the shrewd distribution of the gifts he received—to enhance his position in Choctaw society. Then his fortunes turned. In the course of yet another war between England and France, the English cut off French shipping. Faced with followers unhappy over his sudden inability to supply French guns, Red Shoes decided to make a deal with the English. Unfortunately, the new tactic backfired. His former allies, the French, put a price on his head, which was soon collected. His murder in 1747 launched a Choctaw civil war, a conflict that left French settlements unprotected and the Choctaw people weakened.

The story of Red Shoes reveals a number of themes from the period of European colonization of the Americas. First, although the wars, epidemics, and territorial loss associated with European settlement threatened Amerindians, many adapted the new technologies and new political possibilities to their own purposes and thrived—at least for a time. In the end, though, the best that they could achieve was a holding action. The people of the Old World were coming to dominate the people of the New.

Second, after centuries of isolation, the Americas were being drawn into global events, influenced by the political and economic demands of Europe. The influx of Europeans and Africans resulted in a vast biological and cultural transformation, as the introduction of new plants, animals, diseases, peoples, and technologies fundamentally altered the natural environment of the Western Hemisphere. This was not a one-way transfer, however. The technologies and resources of the New World contributed to profound changes in the Old. Staple crops introduced from the Americas provided highly nutritious foods that helped fuel a population spurt in Europe, Asia, and Africa. As we saw in Chapter 17, riches and products funneled from the Americas changed economic, social, and political relations in Europe.

Third, the fluidity of the Choctaw's political situation reflects the complexity of colonial society, where Amerindians, Europeans, and Africans all contributed to the creation of new cultures. Although similar processes took place throughout the Americas, the particulars varied from place to place, creating a diverse range of cultures. The society that arose in each colony reflected the colony's mix of native peoples, its connections to the slave trade, and the characteristics of the European society establishing the colony. As the colonies matured, new concepts of identity developed, and those living in the Americas began to see themselves as distinct.

As you read this chapter, ask yourself the following questions:

- How did the development of European colonies in the Americas alter the natural environment?

- What were the most important differences in the colonial political institutions and economies created by Spain, Portugal, England, and France?

- How important was forced labor to the European colonies?

THE COLUMBIAN EXCHANGE

The term **Columbian Exchange** refers to the transfer of peoples, animals, plants, and diseases between the New and Old Worlds. The European invasion and settlement of the Western Hemisphere opened a long era of biological and technological transfers that altered American environments. Within a century of first settlement, the domesticated livestock and major agricultural crops of the Old World (the known world before Columbus's voyage) had spread over much of the Americas, and the New World's useful staple crops had enriched the agricultures of Europe, Asia, and Africa. Old World diseases that entered the Americas with European immigrants and African slaves devastated indigenous populations. These dramatic population changes weakened native peoples' capacity for resistance and facilitated the transfer of

C H R O N O L O G Y			
	Spanish America	**Brazil**	**British America**	**French America**

	Spanish America	Brazil	British America	French America
1500	**1518** Smallpox arrives in Caribbean **1535** Creation of Viceroyalty of New Spain **1540s** Creation of Viceroyalty of Peru **1542** New Laws attempt to improve treatment of Amerindians **1545** Silver discovered at Potosí, Bolivia	**1540–1600** Era of Amerindian slavery **After 1540** Sugar begins to dominate the economy		**1524–1554** Jacques Cartier's voyages to explore Newfoundland and Gulf of St. Lawrence
1600	**1625** Population of Potosí reaches 120,000	**By 1620** African slave trade provides majority of plantation workers	**1583** Unsuccessful effort to establish colony on Newfoundland **1607** Jamestown founded **1620** Plymouth founded **1660** Slave population in Virginia begins period of rapid growth **1664** English take New York from Dutch	**1608** Quebec founded
1700	**1700** Last Habsburg ruler of Spain dies **1713** First Bourbon ruler of Spain crowned **1770s and 1780s** Amerindian revolts in Andean region	**1750–1777** Reforms of marquis de Pombal	**1754–1763** French and Indian War	**1699** Louisiana founded **1760** English take Canada

plants, animals, and related technologies. As a result, the colonies of Spain, Portugal, England, and France became vast arenas of cultural and social experimentation.

Demographic Changes

Because of their long isolation from other continents (see Chapter 16), the peoples of the New World lacked immunity to diseases introduced from the Old World. As a result, death rates among Amerindian peoples during the epidemics of the early colonial period were very high. The lack of reliable data has frustrated efforts to measure the deadly impact of these diseases. Scholars disagree about the size of the precontact population but generally agree that, after contact, Old World diseases overwhelmed native populations. According to one estimate, in the century that followed the triumph of Hernán Cortés in 1521, the indigenous population of central Mexico fell from a high somewhere between 13 million and 25 million to approximately 700,000. In this same period nearly 75 percent of the Maya population disappeared. In the region of the Inca Empire, population fell from about 9 million to approximately 600,000. Brazil's native population was similarly ravaged, falling from 2.5 million to under a million within a century of the arrival of the Portuguese. The most conservative estimates of population loss begin with smaller precontact populations but accept that epidemics had a catastrophic effect.

Smallpox, which arrived in the Caribbean in 1518, was the most deadly of the early epidemics. In Mexico and Central America, 50 percent or more of the Amerindian population died during the first wave of smallpox epidemics. The disease then spread to South America with equally devastating effects. Measles arrived in the New World in the 1530s and was followed by diphtheria, typhus, influenza, and, perhaps, pulmonary plague. Mortality was often greatest when two or more diseases struck at the same time. Between 1520 and 1521 influenza, in combination with other ailments, attacked the Cakchiquel of Guatemala. Their chronicle recalls:

> Great was the stench of the dead. After our fathers and grandfathers succumbed, half the people fled to the fields. The dogs and vultures devoured the bodies. . . . So it was that we became orphans, oh my sons! . . . We were born to die![1]

By the mid-seventeenth century malaria and yellow fever were also present in tropical regions. The deadliest form of malaria arrived with the African slave trade. It ravaged the already reduced native populations and afflicted European immigrants as well. Most scholars believe that yellow fever was also brought from Africa, but new research suggests that the disease was present before the conquest in the tropical low country near present-day Veracruz on the Gulf of Mexico. Whatever its origins, yellow fever killed Europeans in the Caribbean Basin and in other tropical regions nearly as efficiently as smallpox had earlier extinguished Amerindians.

The development of English and French colonies in North America in the seventeenth century led to similar patterns of contagion and mortality. In 1616 and 1617 epidemics nearly exterminated many of New England's indigenous groups. French fur traders transmitted measles, smallpox, and other diseases as far as Hudson Bay and the Great Lakes. Although there is very little evidence that Europeans consciously used disease as a tool of empire, the deadly results of contact clearly undermined the ability of native peoples to resist settlement.

The Columbian Exchange   After the conquest, the introduction of plants and animals from the Old World dramatically altered the American environment. Here an Amerindian woman is seen milking a cow. Livestock sometimes destroyed the fields of native peoples, but cattle, sheep, pigs, and goats also provided food, leather, and wool.   (From Martinez Compañon, Trujillo del Perú, V.II, E 79. Photo: Imaging services, Harvard College Library)

Transfer of Plants and Animals

Even as epidemics swept through the indigenous population, the New and the Old Worlds were participating in a vast exchange of plants and animals that radically altered diet and lifestyles in both regions. All the staples of southern European agriculture—such as wheat, olives, grapes, and garden vegetables—were being grown in the Americas in a remarkably short time after contact. African and Asian crops—such as rice, bananas, coconuts, breadfruit, and sugar cane—were soon introduced as well. Native peoples remained loyal to their traditional staples but added many Old World plants to their diet. Citrus fruits, melons, figs, and sugar as well as onions, radishes, and salad greens all found a place in Amerindian cuisines.

In return the Americas offered the Old World an abundance of useful plants. The New World staples—maize, potatoes, and manioc—revolutionized agriculture and diet in parts of Europe, Africa, and Asia (see Environment and Technology: Amerindian Foods in Africa, in Chapter 19). Many experts assert that the rapid growth of world population after 1700 resulted in large measure from the spread of these useful crops, which provided more calories per acre than did any Old World staples other than rice. Beans, squash, tomatoes, sweet potatoes, peanuts, chilies, and chocolate also gained widespread acceptance in the Old World. In addition, the New World provided the Old with plants that provided dyes, medicinal plants, varieties of cotton, and tobacco.

The introduction of European livestock had a dramatic impact on New World environments and cultures. Faced with few natural predators, cattle, pigs, horses, and sheep, as well as pests like rats and rabbits, multiplied rapidly in the open spaces of the Americas. On the vast plains of present-day southern Brazil, Uruguay, and Argentina, herds of wild cattle and horses exceeded 50 million by 1700. Large herds of both animals also appeared in northern Mexico and what became the southwest of the United States.

Where Old World livestock spread most rapidly, environmental changes were most dramatic. Many priests and colonial officials noted the destructive impact of marauding livestock on Amerindian agriculturists. The first viceroy of Mexico, Antonio de Mendoza, wrote to the Spanish king: "May your Lordship realize that if cattle are allowed, the Indians will be destroyed." Sheep, which grazed grasses close to the ground, were also an environmental threat. Yet the viceroy's stark choice misrepresented the complex response of indigenous peoples to these new animals.

Wild cattle on the plains of South America, northern Mexico, and Texas provided indigenous peoples with abundant supplies of meat and hides. In the present-day southwestern United States, the Navajo became sheepherders and expert weavers of woolen cloth. Even in the centers of European settlement, individual Amerindians turned European animals to their own advantage by becoming muleteers, cowboys, and sheepherders.

No animal had a more striking effect on the cultures of native peoples than the horse, which increased the efficiency of hunters and the military capacity of warriors on the plains. The horse permitted the Apache, Sioux, Blackfoot, Comanche, Assiniboine, and others to more efficiently hunt the vast herds of buffalo in North America. The horse also revolutionized the cultures of the Araucanian (or Mapuche) and Pampas peoples in South America.

SPANISH AMERICA AND BRAZIL

The frontiers of conquest and settlement expanded rapidly. Within one hundred years of Columbus's first voyage to the Western Hemisphere, the Spanish Empire in America included most of the islands of the Caribbean, Mexico, the American southwest, Central America, the Caribbean and Pacific coasts of South America, the Andean highlands, and the vast plains of the Rio de la Plata region (a region that includes the modern nations of Argentina, Uruguay, and Paraguay). Portuguese settlement in the New World developed more slowly. But before the end of the sixteenth century, Portugal occupied most of the Brazilian coast.

Early settlers from Spain and Portugal sought to create colonial societies based on the institutions and customs of their homelands. They viewed society as a vertical hierarchy of estates (classes of society), as uniformly Catholic, and as an arrangement of patriarchal extended-family networks. They quickly moved to establish the religious, social, and administrative institutions that were familiar to them.

Despite the imposition of foreign institutions and the massive loss of life caused by epidemics in the sixteenth century, indigenous peoples exercised a powerful influence on the development of colonial societies. Aztec and Inca elite families sought to protect their traditional privileges and rights through marriage or less formal alliances with the Spanish settlers. They also often used colonial courts to defend their claims to land. In Spanish and Portuguese colonies, indigenous military allies and laborers proved crucial to the development of European settlements. Nearly everywhere, Amerindian religious beliefs and practices survived beneath the surface of an imposed Christianity. Amerindian languages, cuisines, medical practices, and agricultural techniques also survived the conquest and influenced the development of Latin American culture.

The African slave trade added a third cultural stream to colonial Latin American society. At first, African slaves were concentrated in plantation regions of Brazil and the Caribbean (see Chapter 19), but by the end of the colonial era, Africans and their descendants were living throughout Latin America, enriching colonial societies with their traditional agricultural practices, music, religious beliefs, cuisine, and social customs.

State and Church

The Spanish crown moved quickly to curb the independent power of the conquistadors and to establish royal authority over both the defeated native populations and the rising tide of European settlers. Created in 1524, the **Council of the Indies** in Spain supervised all government, ecclesiastical, and commercial activity in the Spanish colonies. Geography and technology, however, limited the Council's real power. Local officials could not be controlled too closely, because a ship needed more than two hundred days to make a roundtrip voyage from Spain to Veracruz,

Saint Martín de Porres (1579–1639)   Martín de Porres was the illegitimate son of a Spanish nobleman and his black servant. Eventually recognized by his father, he entered the Dominican Order in Lima, Peru. Known for his generosity, he experienced visions and gained the ability to heal the sick. As was common in colonial religious art, the artist celebrates Martín de Porres's spirituality while representing him doing the type of work assumed most suitable for a person of mixed descent.   (Private Collection)

Mexico, and additional months of travel were required to reach Lima, Peru.

The highest-ranking Spanish officials in the colonies, the viceroys of New Spain and Peru, enjoyed broad power because of their distance from Spain. But the two viceroyalties in their jurisdiction were also vast territories with geographic obstacles to communication. Created in 1535, the Viceroyalty of New Spain, with its capital in Mexico City, included Mexico, the southwest of what is now the United States, Central America, and the islands of the Caribbean. The Viceroyalty of Peru, with its capital in Lima, was formed in the 1540s to govern Span-

ish South America (see Map 18.1). Each viceroyalty was divided into a number of judicial and administrative districts. Until the seventeenth century, almost all of the officials appointed to high positions in Spain's colonial bureaucracy were born in Spain. Eventually, economic mismanagement in Spain forced the Crown to sell appointments to these positions; as a result, local-born members of the colonial elite gained many offices.

In the sixteenth century Portugal concentrated its resources and energies on Asia and Africa. Because early settlers found neither mineral wealth nor rich native empires in Brazil, the Portuguese king hesitated to set up expensive mechanisms of colonial government in the New World. Seeking to promote settlement but limit costs, the king in effect sublet administrative responsibilities in Brazil to court favorites by granting twelve hereditary captaincies in the 1530s. After mismanagement and inadequate investment doomed this experiment, the king appointed a governor-general in 1549 and made Salvador, in the northern province of Bahia, Brazil's capital. In 1720 the first viceroy of Brazil was named.

The government institutions of the Spanish and Portuguese colonies had a more uniform character and were much more extensive and costly than those later established in North America by France and Great Britain. Taxes paid in Spanish America by the silver and gold mines and in Brazil by the sugar plantations and, after 1690, gold mines funded large and intrusive colonial bureaucracies. These institutions made the colonies more responsive to the initiatives of Spain and Portugal, but they also thwarted local economic initiative and political experimentation.

In both Spanish America and Brazil the Catholic Church became the primary agent for the introduction and transmission of Christian belief as well as European language and culture. It undertook the conversion of Amerindians, ministered to the spiritual needs of European settlers, and promoted intellectual life through the introduction of the printing press and formal education.

Spain and Portugal justified their American conquests by assuming an obligation to convert native populations to Christianity. This religious objective was sometimes forgotten, and some members of the clergy were themselves exploiters of native populations. Nevertheless, the effort to convert America's native peoples expanded Christianity on a scale similar to its earlier expansion in Europe at the time of Constantine in the fourth century. In New Spain alone hundreds of thousands of conversions and baptisms were achieved within a few years of the conquest.

The Catholic clergy sought to achieve their evangelical ends by first converting members of the Amerindian elites, in the hope that they could persuade others to fol-

Map 18.1 Colonial Latin America in the Eighteenth Century Spain and Portugal controlled most of the Western Hemisphere in the eighteenth century. In the sixteenth century they had created new administrative jurisdictions—viceroyalties—to defend their respective colonies against European rivals. Taxes assessed on colonial products helped pay for this extension of governmental authority.

low their example. Franciscan missionaries in Mexico hoped to train members of the indigenous elite for the clergy. These idealistic efforts had to be abandoned when church authorities discovered that many converts were secretly observing old beliefs and rituals. The trial and punishment of two converted Aztec nobles for heresy in the 1530s highlighted this problem. Three decades later, Spanish clergy resorted to torture, executions, and the destruction of native manuscripts to eradicate traditional beliefs and rituals among the Maya. Repelled by these events, the church hierarchy ended both the violent repression of native religious practice and efforts to recruit an Amerindian clergy.

Despite its failures, the Catholic clergy did provide native peoples with some protections against the abuse and exploitation of Spanish settlers. The priest **Bartolomé de Las Casas** (1474–1566) was the most influential defender of the Amerindians in the early colonial period. He arrived in Hispaniola in 1502 as a settler and initially lived off the forced labor of Amerindians. Deeply moved by the deaths of so many Amerindians and by the misdeeds of the Spanish, Las Casas gave up this way of life and entered the Dominican Order, later becoming the first bishop of Chiapas, in southern Mexico. For the remainder of his long life Las Casas served as the most important advocate for native peoples, writing a number of books that detailed their mistreatment by the Spanish. His most important achievement was the enactment of the New Laws of 1542—reform legislation that outlawed the enslavement of Amerindians and limited other forms of forced labor.

European clergy arrived in the colonies with the intention of transmitting Catholic Christian belief and ritual without alteration. But the large size of Amerindian populations and their geographic dispersal over a vast landscape thwarted this objective. Linguistic and cultural differences among native peoples also inhibited missionary efforts. These problems frustrated Catholic missionaries and sometimes led to repression and cruelty. The limited success of evangelization permitted the appearance of what must be seen as an Amerindian Christianity that blended Catholic Christian beliefs with important elements of traditional native cosmology and ritual. Most commonly, indigenous beliefs and rituals came to be embedded in the celebration of saints' days or Catholic rituals associated with the Virgin Mary. The Catholic clergy and most European settlers viewed this evolving mixture as the work of the Devil or as evidence of Amerindian inferiority. Instead, it was one component of the process of cultural borrowing and innovation that contributed to a distinct and original Latin American culture.

After 1600 the terrible loss of Amerindian population caused by epidemics and growing signs of resistance to conversion led the Catholic Church to redirect most of its resources from native regions in the countryside to growing colonial cities and towns with large European populations. One important outcome of this altered mission was the founding of universities and secondary schools and the stimulation of urban intellectual life. Over time, the church became the richest institution in the Spanish colonies, controlling ranches, plantations, and vineyards as well as serving as the society's banker.

Colonial Economies

The silver mines of Peru and Mexico and the sugar plantations of Brazil dominated the economic development of colonial Latin America. The mineral wealth of the New World fueled the early development of European capitalism and funded Europe's greatly expanded trade with Asia. Profits produced in these economic centers also promoted the growth of colonial cities, concentrated scarce investment capital and labor resources, and stimulated the development of livestock raising and agriculture in neighboring rural areas (see Map 18.1). Once established, this colonial dependence on mineral and agricultural exports left an enduring social and economic legacy in Latin America.

Gold worth millions of pesos was extracted from mines in Latin America, but silver mines in the Spanish colonies generated the most wealth and therefore exercised the greatest economic influence. The first important silver strikes occurred in Mexico in the 1530s and 1540s. In 1545 the single richest silver deposit in the Americas was discovered at **Potosí°,** in what is now Bolivia, and until 1680 the silver production of Bolivia and Peru dominated the Spanish colonial economy. After this date Mexican silver production greatly surpassed that of the Andean region.

A large labor force was needed to mine silver. The metal was extracted from deep shafts, and the refining process was complex. Silver mines supported farming, livestock raising, and even textile production, which in turn promoted urbanization and the elaboration of regional commercial relations. Silver mining also greatly altered the environment.

At first, silver was extracted from ore by smelting: the ore was crushed in giant stamping mills, then packed with charcoal in a furnace and fired. Within a short time, the wasteful use of forest resources for fuel destroyed forests near the mining centers. Faced with rising fuel costs, Mexican miners developed an efficient method of chemical extraction that relied on mixing mercury with

Potosí (poh-toh-SEE)

A Silver Refinery at Potosí, Bolivia, 1700

The silver refineries of Spanish America were among the largest and most heavily capitalized industrial enterprises in the Western Hemisphere during the colonial period. By the middle of the seventeenth century the mines of Potosí, Bolivia, had attracted a population of more than 120,000.

The accompanying illustration shows a typical refinery (ingenio). Aqueducts carried water from large reservoirs on nearby mountainsides to the refineries. The water wheel shown on the right drove two sets of vertical stamps that crushed ore. Each iron-shod stamp was about the size and weight of a telephone pole. Crushed ore was sorted, dried, and mixed with mercury and other catalysts to extract the silver. The amalgam was then separated by a combination of washing and heating. The end result was a nearly pure ingot of silver that was later assayed and taxed at the mint.

Silver production carried a high environmental cost. Forests were cut to provide fuel and the timbers needed to shore up mine shafts and construct stamping mills and other machinery. Unwanted base metals produced in the refining process poisoned the soil. In addition, the need for tens of thousands of horses, mules, and oxen to drive machinery and transport material led to overgrazing and widespread erosion.

A Bolivian Silver Refinery, 1700   The silver refineries of Spanish America were among the largest industrial establishments in the Western Hemisphere. (From *In Quest of Mineral Wealth: Aboriginal and Colonial Mining and Metallurgy in Spanish America*, edited by Alan K. Craig and Robert C. West, 1994. Vol. 33 of *Geoscience and Man*. Courtesy, Geoscience Publications)

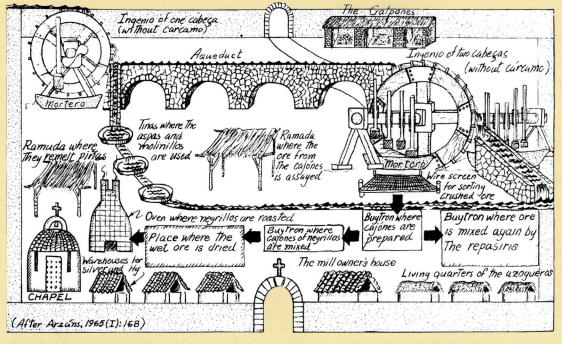

the silver ore (see Environment and Technology: The Silver Refinery at Potosí, Bolivia, 1700). Silver yields and profits increased with the use of mercury amalgamation, but this process, too, had severe environmental costs. Mercury was a poison, and its use contaminated the environment and sickened the Amerindian work force.

From the time of Columbus, indigenous populations had been compelled to provide labor for European settlers in the Americas. Until the 1540s in Spanish colonies, Amerindian peoples were divided among the settlers and were forced to provide them with labor or with textiles, food, or other goods. This form of forced labor was called the **encomienda°**. As epidemics and mistreatment led to the decline in Amerindian population, reforms such as the New Laws sought to eliminate the encomienda. The discovery of silver in both Peru and Mexico, however, led to new forms of compulsory labor. In the mining region of Mexico, Amerindian populations had been greatly reduced by epidemic diseases. Therefore, from early in the colonial period, Mexican silver miners relied on free-wage laborers. Peru's Amerindian population survived in larger numbers, allowing the Spanish to impose a form of labor called the **mita°**. Under this system, one-seventh of adult male Amerindians were compelled to work for six months each year in mines, farms, or textile factories. The most dangerous working conditions existed in the silver mines, where workers were forced to carry heavy bags of ore up fragile ladders to the surface.

This colonial institution was a corrupted version of the Inca-era mit'a, which had been both a labor tax that supported elites and a reciprocal labor obligation that allowed kin groups to produce surpluses of essential goods that provided for the elderly and incapacitated. In the Spanish mita, few Amerindian workers could survive on their wages. Wives and children were commonly forced to join the work force to help meet expenses. Even those who remained behind in the village were forced to send food and cash to support mita workers.

As the Amerindian population fell with each new epidemic, some of Peru's villages were forced to shorten the period between mita obligations. Instead of serving every seven years, many men were forced to return to mines after only a year or two. Unwilling to accept mita service and the other tax burdens imposed on Amerindian villages, large numbers of Amerindians abandoned traditional agriculture and moved permanently to Spanish mines and farms as wage laborers. The long-term result of these individual decisions weakened Amerindian village life and promoted the assimilation of Amerindians into Spanish-speaking Catholic colonial society.

Before the settlement of Brazil, the Portuguese had already developed sugar plantations that depended on slave labor on the Atlantic islands of Madeira, the Azores, the Cape Verdes, and São Tomé. Because of the success of these early experiences, they were able to quickly transfer this profitable form of agriculture to Brazil. After 1550 sugar production expanded rapidly in the northern provinces of Pernambuco and Bahia. By the seventeenth century, sugar dominated the Brazilian economy.

The sugar plantations of colonial Brazil always depended on slave labor. At first the Portuguese sugar planters enslaved Amerindians captured in war or seized from their villages. They used Amerindian men as field hands, although in this indigenous culture women had primary responsibility for agriculture. Any effort to resist or flee led to harsh punishments. Thousands of Amerindian slaves died during the epidemics that raged across Brazil in the sixteenth and seventeenth centuries. This terrible loss of Amerindian life and the rising profits of the sugar planters led to the development of an internal slave trade dominated by settlers from the southern region of São Paulo. To supply the rising labor needs of the sugar plantations of the northeast, slave raiders pushed into the interior, even attacking Amerindian populations in neighboring Spanish colonies. Many of the most prominent slavers were the sons of Portuguese fathers and Amerindian mothers.

Amerindian slaves remained an important source of labor and slave raiding a significant business in frontier regions into the eighteenth century. But sugar planters eventually came to rely more on African than Amerindian slaves. Although African slaves at first cost much more than Amerindian slaves, planters found them to be more productive and more resistant to disease. As profits from the plantations increased, imports of African slaves rose from an average of two thousand per year in the late sixteenth century to approximately seven thousand per year a century later, outstripping the immigration of free Portuguese settlers. Between 1650 and 1750, for example, more than three African slaves arrived in Brazil for every free immigrant from Europe.

Within Spanish America, the mining centers of Mexico and Peru eventually exercised global economic influence. American silver increased the European money supply, promoting commercial expansion and, later, industrialization. Large amounts of silver also flowed across the Pacific to the Spanish colony of the Philippines, where it was exchanged for Asian spices, silks, and pottery. Spain tried to limit this trade, but the desire for Asian goods in the colonies was so strong that there was large-scale trade in contraband goods.

The rich mines of Peru, Bolivia, and Mexico stimulated urban population growth as well as commercial links with distant agricultural and textile producers. The population of the city of Potosí, high in the Andes, reached 120,000 inhabitants by 1625. This rich mining town became the center of a vast regional market that depended on Chilean wheat, Argentine livestock, and Ecuadorian textiles.

The sugar plantations of Brazil played a similar role in integrating the economy of the south Atlantic region. The ports of Salvador and Rio de Janeiro in Brazil exchanged sugar, tobacco, and reexported slaves from

---

encomienda (in-co-mee-EN-dah)   **mita** (MEE-tah)

Brazilian Sugar Plantation Sugar was the most important agricultural product exported from Europe's Western Hemisphere colonies. The African slave trade was developed in large measure to supply the labor needs of sugar plantations and refineries in the Americas. Brazil's economy was dominated by sugar and slavery in the colonial period. In this illustration slaves unload sugar cane from a cart before crushing it in the horizontal mill to extract the juice to process into molasses and sugar. (From Johann Mority Rugendas, *Viagem Pitoresca Atraves di Brasil* (São Paolo: Livraria Martins Editora, 1954). Harvard College Library Imaging Services)

Brazil for yerba (Paraguayan tea), hides, livestock, and silver produced in neighboring Spanish colonies. Portugal's increasing openness to British trade also allowed Brazil to become a conduit for an illegal trade between Spanish colonies and Europe. At the end of the seventeenth century the discovery of gold in Brazil helped overcome this large region's currency shortage and promoted further economic integration.

Both Spain and Portugal attempted to control the trade of their American colonies. Spain's efforts were more ambitious, granting first Seville and then Cádiz monopoly trade rights. Similar monopoly privileges were then awarded to the merchant guilds of Lima, Peru, and Mexico City. Because ships returning to Spain with silver and gold were often attacked by foreign naval forces and pirates, Spain came to rely on convoys escorted by warships to supply the colonies and return with silver and gold. By 1650 Portugal had instituted a similar system of monopoly trade and fleets. The combination of monopoly commerce and convoy systems protected shipping and facilitated the collection of taxes, but these measures also slowed the flow of European goods to the colonies and kept prices high. Frustrated by these restraints, colonial populations established illegal commercial relations with the English, French, and Dutch. By the middle of the seventeenth century a majority of European imports were arriving in Latin America illegally.

Society in Colonial Latin America

With the exception of some early viceroys, few members of Spain's great noble families came to the New World. *Hidalgos°*—lesser nobles—were well represented, as were Spanish merchants, artisans, miners, priests, and lawyers. Small numbers of criminals, beggars, and prostitutes also found their way to the colonies. This flow of immigrants from Spain was never large, and Spanish settlers were always a tiny minority in a colonial society numerically dominated by Amerindians and rapidly growing populations of Africans, **creoles** (whites born in America to European parents), and people of mixed ancestry (see Diversity and Dominance: Race and Ethnicity in the Spanish Colonies: Negotiating Hierarchy).

Conquistadors and early settlers who received from the Crown grants of labor and tribute goods (encomienda) from Amerindian communities as rewards for service to Spain dominated colonial society in early Spanish America. These encomenderos sought to create a hereditary social and political class comparable to the nobles of Europe. But their systematic abuse of Amerindian communities and the catastrophic loss of Amerindian life during the epidemics of the sixteenth century undermined their position. They also confronted the

hidalgos (ee-DAHL-goes)

DIVERSITY AND DOMINANCE

RACE AND ETHNICITY IN THE SPANISH COLONIES: NEGOTIATING HIERARCHY

Many European visitors to colonial Latin America were interested in the mixing of Europeans, Amerindians, and Africans in the colonies. Many also commented on the treatment of slaves. The passages that follow allow us to examine two colonial societies.

The first selection was written by two young Spanish naval officers and scientists, Jorge Juan and Antonio de Ulloa, who arrived in the colonies in 1735 as members of a scientific expedition. They visited the major cities of the Pacific coast of South America and traveled across some of the most difficult terrain in the hemisphere. In addition to their scientific chores, they described architecture, local customs, and the social order. In this section they describe the ethnic mix in Quito, now the capital of Ecuador.

The second selection was published in Lima under the pseudonym Concolorcorvo around 1776. We now know that the author was Alonso Carrío de la Vandera. Born in Spain, he traveled to the colonies as a young man. He served in many minor bureaucratic positions, one of which was the inspection of the postal route between Buenos Aires and Lima. Carrío turned his long and often uncomfortable trip into an insightful, and sometimes highly critical, examination of colonial society. The selection that follows describes Córdoba, Argentina.

Juan and Ulloa and Carrío seem perplexed by colonial efforts to create and enforce a racial taxonomy that stipulated and named every possible mixture of European, Amerindian, and African, noting the vanity and social presumptions of the dominant white population. We are fortunate to have these contemporary descriptions of the diversity of colonial society, but it is important to remember that these authors were clearly rooted in their time and confident in the superiority of Europe. Although they noted many of the abuses of Amerindian, mixed, and African populations while puncturing the pretensions of the colonial elites, they were also quick to assume the inferiority of the nonwhite population.

QUITO

This city is very populous, and has, among its inhabitants, some families of high rank and distinction; though their number is but small considering its extent, the poorer class bearing here too great a proportion. The former are the descendants either of the original conquerors, or of presidents, auditors, or other persons of character [high rank], who at different times came over from Spain invested with some lucrative post, and have still preserved their luster, both of wealth and descent, by intermarriages, without intermixing with meaner families though famous for their riches. The commonalty may be divided into four classes; Spaniards or Whites, Mestizos, Indians or Natives, and Negroes, with their progeny. These last are not proportionally so numerous as in the other parts of the Indies; occasioned by it being something inconvenient to bring Negroes to Quito, and the different kinds of agriculture being generally performed by Indians.

The name of Spaniard here has a different meaning from that of Chapitone [sic] or European, as properly signifying a person descended from a Spaniard without a mixture of blood. Many Mestizos, from the advantage of a fresh complexion, appear to be Spaniards more than those who are so in reality; and from only this fortuitous advantage are accounted as such. The Whites, according to this construction of the word, may be considered as one sixth part of the inhabitants.

The Mestizos are the descendants of Spaniards and Indians, and are to be considered here in the same different degrees between the Negroes and Whites, as before at Carthagena [sic]; but with this difference, that at Quito the degrees of Mestizos are not carried so far back; for, even in the second or third generations, when they acquire the European color, they are considered as Spaniards. The complexion of the Mestizos is swarthy and reddish, but not of that red common in the fair Mulattos. This is the first degree, or the immediate issue of a Spaniard and Indian. Some are, however, equally tawny with the Indians themselves, though they are distinguished from them by their beards: while others, on the contrary, have so fine a complexion that they might pass for Whites, were it not for some signs which betray them, when viewed attentively. Among these, the most remarkable is the lowness of the forehead, which often leaves but a small space between their hair and eye-brows; at the same time the hair grows remarkably forward on the temples, extending to the lower part of the ear. Besides, the hair itself is harsh, lank, coarse, and very black; their nose very small, thin, and has a little rising on the middle, from whence it forms a small curve, terminating in a point, bending towards the upper lip. These marks, besides some dark spots on the body, are so constant and invariable, as to make it very difficult to conceal the fallacy of their complexion. The Mestizos may be reckoned a third part of the inhabitants.

The next class is the Indians, who form about another third; and the others, who are about one sixth, are the Castes [mixed]. These four classes, according to the most authentic accounts taken from the parish register, amount to between 50 and 60,000 persons, of all ages, sexes, and ranks. If among these classes the Spaniards, as is natural to think, are the most eminent for riches, rank, and power, it must at the same time be owned, however melancholy the truth may appear, they are in proportion the most poor, miserable and distressed; for they refuse to apply themselves to any mechanic business, considering it as a disgrace to that quality they so highly value themselves upon, which consists in not being black, brown, or of a copper color. The Mestizos, whose pride is regulated by prudence, readily apply themselves to arts and trades, but chose those of the greatest repute, as painting, sculpture, and the like, leaving the meaner sort to the Indians.

CÓRDOBA

There was not a person who would give me even an estimate of the number of residents comprising this city, because neither the secular nor the ecclesiastical council has a register, and I know not how these colonists prove the ancient and distinguished nobility of which they boast; it may be that each family has its genealogical history in reserve. In my computation, there must be within the city and its limited common lands around 500 to 600 residents, but in the principal houses there are a very large number of slaves, most of them Creoles [native born] of all conceivable classes, because in this city and in all of Tucumán there is no leniency about granting freedom to any of them. They are easily supported since the principal aliment, meat, is of such moderate price, and there is a custom of dressing them only in ordinary cloth which is made at home by the slaves themselves, shoes being very rare. They aid their masters in many profitable ways and under this system do not think of freedom, thus exposing themselves to a sorrowful end, as is happening in Lima.

As I was passing through Córdoba, they were selling 2,000 Negroes, all Creoles from Temporalidades [property confiscated from the Jesuit order in 1767], from just the two farms of the [Jesuit] colleges of this city. I have seen the lists, for each one has its own, and they proceed by families numbering from two to eleven, all pure Negroes and Creoles back to the fourth generation, because the priests used to sell all of those born with a mixture of Spanish, mulatto, or Indian blood. Among this multitude of Negroes were many musicians and many of other crafts; they proceeded with the sale by families. I was assured that the nuns of Santa Teresa alone had a group of 300 slaves of both sexes, to whom they give

their just ration of meat and dress in the coarse cloth which they make, while these good nuns content themselves with what is left from other ministrations. The number attached to other religious establishments is much smaller, but there is a private home which has 30 or 40, the majority of whom are engaged in various gainful activities. The result is a large number of excellent washerwomen whose accomplishments are valued so highly that they never mend their outer skirts in order that the whiteness of their undergarments may be seen. They do the laundry in the river, in water up to the waist, saying vaingloriously that she who is not soaked cannot wash well. They make ponchos [hand-woven capes], rugs, sashes, and sundries, and especially decorated leather cases which the men sell for 8 reales each, because the hides have no outlet due to the great distance to the port; the same thing happens on the banks of the Tercero and Cuarto rivers, where they are sold at 2 reales and frequently for less.

The principal men of the city wear very expensive clothes, but this is not true of the women, who are an exception in both Americas and even in the entire world, because they dress decorously in clothing of little cost. They are very tenacious in preserving the customs of their ancestors. They do not permit slaves, or even freedmen who have a mixture of Negro blood, to wear any cloth other than that made in this country, which is quite coarse. I was told recently that a certain bedecked mulatto [woman] who appeared in Córdoba was sent word by the ladies of the city that she should dress according to her station, but since she paid no attention to this reproach, they endured her negligence until one of the ladies, summoning her to her home under some other pretext, had the servants undress her, whip her, burn her finery before her eyes, and dress her in the clothes befitting her class; despite the fact that the [victim] was not lacking in persons to defend her, she disappeared lest the tragedy be repeated.

QUESTIONS FOR ANALYSIS

1. What do the authors of these selections seem to think about the white elites of the colonies? Are there similarities in the ways that Juan and Ulloa and Carrío describe the mixed population of Quito and the slave population of Córdoba?

2. Are there differences in the way that the authors characterize the relationship between color and class?

3. What does the humiliation of the mixed-race woman in Córdoba tell us about ideas of race and class in the Spanish colony?

Sources: Jorge Juan and Antonio de Ulloa, *A Voyage to South America,* The John Adams translation (abridged), Introduction by Irving A. Leonard (New York: Alfred A. Knopf, 1964), 135–137, copyright © 1964 by Alfred A. Knopf, Inc. Used by permission of Alfred A. Knopf, a division of Random House, Inc.; Concolorcorvo, *El Lazarillo, A Guide for Inexperienced Travelers between Buenos Aires and Lima,* 1773, translated by Walter D. Kline, (Bloomington: Indiana University Press, 1965), 78–80. Used with permission of Indiana University Press.

growing power of colonial viceroys, judges, and bishops appointed by the king.

By the end of the sixteenth century, the elite of Spanish America included both European immigrants and creoles. Europeans dominated the highest levels of the church and government as well as commerce. Creoles commonly controlled colonial agriculture and mining. Wealthy creole families with extensive holdings in land and mines often sought to increase their family prestige by arranging for their daughters to marry successful Spanish merchants and officials. Often richer in reputation than in wealth, immigrants from Spain welcomed the opportunity to forge these connections. Although tensions between Spaniards and creoles were inevitable, most elite families included members of both groups.

Before the Europeans arrived in the Americas, the native peoples were members of a large number of distinct cultural and linguistic groups. Cultural diversity and class distinctions were present even in the highly centralized Aztec and Inca empires. The loss of life provoked by the European conquest undermined this rich social and cultural complexity, and the imposition of Catholic Christianity further eroded ethnic boundaries among native peoples. Colonial administrators and settlers broadly applied the racial label "Indian," which facilitated the imposition of special taxes and labor obligations while at the same time erasing long-standing class and ethnic differences.

Amerindian elites struggled to survive in the new political and economic environments created by military defeat and European settlement. Crucial to this survival was the maintenance of hereditary land rights and continued authority over indigenous commoners. Some elite families sought to protect their positions by forging links with conquistadors and early settlers through marriage or less formal relations. As a result, indigenous and colonial elite families were often tied together by kinship, particularly in the sixteenth century. Both self-interest and a desire to protect their communities led them to quickly gain familiarity with colonial legal systems and establish political alliances with judges and other members of the colonial administrative classes. In many cases they were successful. For example, in New Spain many representatives of the indigenous elite gained both recognition of their nobility and new hereditary land rights from Spanish authorities. As this successful minority of elite families solidified their position in the new order, they became essential intermediaries between the indigenous masses and colonial administrators, collecting Spanish taxes and organizing the labor of their dependents for colonial enterprises.

Indigenous commoners suffered the heaviest burdens. Tribute payments, forced labor obligations, and the loss of traditional land rights were common. European domination dramatically changed the indigenous world. The old connections between peoples and places were weakened or, in some cases, lost. Religious life, marriage practices, diet, and material culture were altered profoundly. The survivors of these terrible shocks learned to adapt to the new colonial environment. They embraced some elements of the dominant colonial culture and its technologies. They found ways to enter the market economies of the cities. They learned to produce new products, such as raising sheep and growing wheat. Most importantly, they learned new forms of resistance, like using colonial courts to protect community lands or to resist the abuses of corrupt officials.

Thousands of blacks participated in the conquest and settlement of Spanish America. The majority were European-born Catholic slaves who came to the New World with their masters. Some free blacks immigrated voluntarily. More than four hundred blacks, most of them slaves, participated in the conquest of Peru and Chile. In the fluid social environment of the conquest era, many slaves gained their freedom. Some simply fled from their masters. Juan Valiente escaped his master in Mexico, participated in Francisco Pizarro's conquest of the Inca Empire, and later became one of the most prominent early settlers of Chile, where he was granted Amerindian laborers in an encomienda.

The status of the black population of colonial Latin America declined with the opening of a direct slave trade with Africa (for details, see Chapter 19). Africans were culturally different from the Afro-Iberian slaves and freedmen who accompanied the conquerors. Afro-Iberians commonly had deep roots in Spain or Portugal; their language was Spanish or Portuguese; and their religion was Catholicism. African slaves had different languages, religious beliefs, and cultural practices, and these differences were viewed by settlers as signs of inferiority, ultimately serving as a justification for slavery. By 1600 people with black ancestry were barred from positions in church and government as well as from many skilled crafts.

The rich mosaic of African identities was retained in colonial Latin America. Enslaved members of many cultural groups struggled to retain their languages, religious beliefs, and marriage customs. But in regions with large slave majorities, these cultural and linguistic barriers often divided slaves and made resistance more difficult. Over time, elements from many African traditions blended and mixed with European (and in some cases Amerindian) language and beliefs to forge distinct local cultures. The rapid growth of an American-born slave population accelerated this process of cultural change.

Slave resistance took many forms, including sabotage, malingering, running away, and rebellion. Although many slave rebellions occurred, colonial authorities were always able to reestablish control. Groups of runaway slaves, however, were sometimes able to defend themselves for years. In both Spanish America and Brazil, communities of runaways (called quilombos° in Brazil and palenques° in Spanish colonies) were common. The largest quilombo was Palmares, where thousands of slaves defended themselves against Brazilian authorities for sixty years until they were finally overrun in 1694.

Slaves were skilled artisans, musicians, servants, artists, cowboys, and even soldiers. However, the vast majority worked in agriculture. Conditions for slaves were worst on the sugar plantations of Brazil and the Caribbean, where harsh discipline, brutal punishments, and backbreaking labor were common. Because planters preferred to buy male slaves, there was always a gender imbalance on plantations. As a result, neither the traditional marriage and family patterns of Africa nor those of Europe developed. The disease environment of the tropics, as well as the poor housing, diet, hygiene, and medical care offered to slaves, also weakened slave families.

The colonial development of Brazil was distinguished from that of Spanish America by the absence of rich and powerful indigenous civilizations such as those of the Aztecs and Inca and by lower levels of European immigration. Nevertheless, Portuguese immigrants came to exercise the same domination in Brazil as the Spanish exercised in their colonies. The growth of cities and the creation of imperial institutions eventually duplicated in outline the social structures found in Spanish America, but with an important difference. By the early seventeenth century, Africans and their American-born descendants were the largest racial group in Brazil. As a result, Brazilian colonial society (unlike Spanish Mexico and Peru) was influenced more by African culture than by Amerindian culture.

Both Spanish and Portuguese law provided for manumission, the granting of freedom to individual slaves. The majority of those gaining their liberty had saved money and purchased their own freedom. This was easiest to do in cities, where slave artisans and market women had the opportunity to earn and save money. Only a tiny minority of owners freed slaves without demanding compensation. Household servants were the most likely beneficiaries of this form of manumission. Only about 1 percent of the slave population gained freedom each year through manumission. However, because slave women received the majority of manumissions and because children born subsequently were considered free, the free black population grew rapidly.

Painting of Castas   This is an example of a common genre of colonial Spanish American painting. In the eighteenth century there was increased interest in ethnic mixing, and wealthy colonials as well as some Europeans commissioned sets of paintings that showed mixed families. The paintings commonly also indicated what the artist believed was an appropriate class setting. In this painting a richly dressed Spaniard is depicted with his Amerindian wife dressed in European clothing. Notice that the painter has the mestiza daughter look to her European father for guidance.   (Private Collection. Photographer: Camilo Garza/Fotocam, Monterrey, Mexico)

Within a century of settlement, groups of mixed descent were in the majority in many regions. There were few marriages between Amerindian women and European men, but less formal relationships were common. Few European or creole fathers recognized their mixed offspring, who were called **mestizos°.** Nevertheless, this rapidly expanding group came to occupy a middle position in colonial society, dominating urban artisan trades and small-scale agriculture and ranching. In frontier regions many members of the elite were mestizos, some proudly asserting their descent from the Amerindian

---

quilombos (key-LOM-bos)   **palenques** (pah-LEN-kays)

mestizo (mess-TEE-zoh)

elite. The African slave trade also led to the appearance of new American ethnicities. Individuals of mixed European and African descent—called **mulattos**—came to occupy intermediate position in the tropics similar to the social position of mestizos in Mesoamerica and the Andean region. In Spanish Mexico and Peru and in Brazil, mixtures of Amerindians and Africans were also common.

All these mixed-descent groups were called castas° in Spanish America. Castas dominated small-scale retailing and construction trades in cities. In the countryside, many small ranchers and farmers as well as wage laborers were castas. Members of mixed groups who gained high status or significant wealth generally spoke Spanish or Portuguese, observed the requirements of Catholicism, and, whenever possible, lived the life of Europeans in their residence, dress, and diet.

ENGLISH AND FRENCH COLONIES IN NORTH AMERICA

The North American colonial empires of England and France and the colonies of Spain and Portugal had many characteristics in common (see Map 18.1). The governments of England and France hoped to find easily extracted forms of wealth or great indigenous empires like those of the Aztecs or Inca. Like the Spanish and Portuguese, English and French settlers responded to native peoples with a mixture of diplomacy and violence. African slaves proved crucial to the development of all four colonial economies.

Important differences, however, distinguished North American colonial development from the Latin American model. The English and French colonies were developed nearly a century after Cortés's conquest of Mexico and initial Portuguese settlement in Brazil. The intervening period witnessed significant economic and demographic growth in Europe. It also witnessed the Protestant Reformation, which helped propel English and French settlement in the Americas. By the time England and France secured a foothold in the Americas, the regions of the world were also more interconnected by trade. Distracted by ventures elsewhere and by increasing military confrontation in Europe, neither England nor France imitated the large and expensive colonial bureaucracies established by Spain and Portugal. As a result, private companies and individual proprietors played a much larger role in the development of English and French colonies. Particularly in the English colonies, this prac-

---

castas (CAZ-tahs)

tice led to greater regional variety in economic activity, political institutions and culture, and social structure than was evident in the colonies of Spain and Portugal.

Early English Experiments

England's first efforts to gain a foothold in the Americas produced more failures than successes. The first attempt was made by a group of West Country gentry and merchants led by Sir Humphrey Gilbert. Their effort in 1583 to establish a colony in Newfoundland, off the coast of Canada, quickly failed. After Gilbert's death in 1584, his half-brother, Sir Walter Raleigh, organized private financing for a new colonization scheme. A year later 108 men attempted a settlement on Roanoke Island, off the coast of present-day North Carolina. Afflicted with poor leadership, undersupplied, and threatened by Amerindian groups, the colony was abandoned within a year. Another effort to settle Roanoke was made in 1587. Because the Spanish Armada was threatening England, no relief expedition was sent to Roanoke until 1590. When help finally arrived, there was no sign of the 117 men, women, and children who had attempted settlement. Raleigh's colonial experiment was abandoned.

In the seventeenth century England renewed its effort to establish colonies in North America. England continued to rely on private capital to finance settlement and continued to hope that the colonies would become sources of high-value products such as silk, citrus, and wine. New efforts to establish American colonies were also influenced by English experience in colonizing Ireland after 1566. In Ireland land had been confiscated, cleared of its native population, and offered for sale to English investors. The city of London, English guilds, and wealthy private investors all purchased Irish "plantations" and then recruited "settlers." By 1650 investors had sent nearly 150,000 English and Scottish immigrants to Ireland. Indeed, Ireland attracted six times as many colonists in the early seventeenth century as did New England.

The South

London investors, organized as the privately funded Virginia Company, took up the challenge of colonizing Virginia in 1606. A year later 144 settlers disembarked at Jamestown, an island 30 miles (48 kilometers) up the James River in the Chesapeake Bay region. Additional settlers arrived in 1609. The investors and settlers hoped for immediate profits, but these unrealistic dreams were soon dashed. Although the location was easily defended, it was a swampy and unhealthy place; in the first fifteen years nearly 80 percent of all settlers in Jamestown died from disease or Amerindian attacks. There was no mineral wealth, no passage to Asia, and no docile and exploitable native population. By concentrating their energies on the illusion of easy wealth, settlers failed to grow enough food and were saved on more than one occasion by the generosity of neighboring Amerindian peoples.

In 1624 the English crown was forced to dissolve the Virginia Company because of its mismanagement of the colony. Freed from the company's commitment to Jamestown's unhealthy environment, colonists pushed deeper into the interior, developing a sustainable economy based on furs, timber, and, increasingly, tobacco. The profits from tobacco soon attracted new immigrants and new capital. Along the shoreline of Chesapeake Bay and the rivers that fed it, settlers spread out, developing plantations and farms. Colonial Virginia's population remained dispersed. In Latin America large and powerful cities dominated by viceroys and royal courts and networks of secondary towns flourished. In contrast, no city of any significant size developed in colonial Virginia.

Colonists in Latin America had developed systems of forced labor to develop the region's resources. Encomienda, mita, and slavery were all imposed on indigenous peoples, and later the African slave trade compelled the migration of millions of additional forced laborers to the colonies of Spain and Portugal. The English settlement of the Chesapeake Bay region added a new system of compulsory labor to the American landscape: **indentured servants.** Ethnically indistinguishable from free settlers, indentured servants eventually accounted for approximately 80 percent of all English immigrants to Virginia and the neighboring colony of Maryland. A young man or woman unable to pay for transportation to the New World accepted an indenture (contract) that bound him or her to a term ranging from four to seven years of labor in return for passage and, at the end of the contract, a small parcel of land, some tools, and clothes.

During the seventeenth century approximately fifteen hundred indentured servants, mostly male, arrived each year (see Chapter 19 for details on the indentured labor system). Planters were less likely to lose money if they purchased the cheaper limited contracts of indentured servants instead of purchasing African slaves during the period when both groups suffered high mortality rates. As life expectancy in the colony improved, planters began to purchase more slaves. They calculated that greater profits could be secured by paying the higher initial cost of slaves owned for life than by purchasing the contracts of indentured servants bound for short periods of time. As a result, Virginia's slave population grew rapidly from 950 in 1660 to 120,000 by 1756.

By the 1660s many of the elements of the mature colony were in place in Virginia. Colonial government was administered by a Crown-appointed governor and his council, as well as by representatives of towns meeting together as the **House of Burgesses.** When these representatives began to meet alone as a deliberative body, they initiated a form of democratic representation that distinguished the English colonies of North America from the colonies of other European powers. Ironically, this expansion in colonial liberties and political rights occurred along with the dramatic increase in the colony's slave population. The intertwined evolution of American freedom and American slavery gave England's southern colonies a unique and conflicted political character that endured even after independence.

At the same time, the English colonists were expanding settlements in the South. The Carolinas at first prospered from the profits of the fur trade. Fur traders pushed into the interior, eventually threatening the French trading networks based in New Orleans and Mobile. Native peoples eventually provided over 100,000 deerskins annually to this profitable commerce. The environmental and cultural costs of the fur trade were little appreciated at the time. As Amerindian peoples hunted more intensely, the natural balance of animals and plants was disrupted in southern forests. The profits of the fur trade altered Amerindian culture as well, leading villages to place less emphasis on subsistence hunting and fishing and traditional agriculture. Amerindian life was profoundly altered by deepening dependencies on European products, including firearms, metal tools, textiles, and alcohol.

Although increasingly brought into the commerce and culture of the Carolina colony, indigenous peoples were being weakened by epidemics, alcoholism, and a rising tide of ethnic conflicts generated by competition for hunting grounds. Conflicts among indigenous peoples—who now had firearms—became more deadly. Many Amerindians captured in these wars were sold as slaves to local colonists, who used them as agricultural workers or exported them to the sugar plantations of the Caribbean islands. Dissatisfied with the terms of trade imposed by fur traders and angered by this slave trade, Amerindians launched attacks on English settlements in the early 1700s. Their defeat by colonial military forces inevitably led to new seizures of Amerindian land by European settlers.

The northern part of the Carolinas had been settled from Virginia and followed that colony's mixed economy of tobacco and forest products. Slavery expanded slowly in this region. Charleston and the interior of South Carolina followed a different path. Settled first by planters from the Caribbean island of Barbados in 1670, this colony soon developed an economy based on plantations and slavery in imitation of the colonies of the Caribbean and Brazil. In 1729 North and South Carolina became separate colonies.

Despite an unhealthy climate, the prosperous rice and indigo plantations near Charleston attracted a diverse array of immigrants and an increasing flow of African slaves. African slaves were present from the founding of Charleston. They were instrumental in introducing irrigated rice agriculture along the coastal lowlands and in developing indigo (a plant that produced a blue dye) plantations at higher elevations away from the coast. Slaves were often given significant responsibilities. As one planter sending two slaves and their families to a frontier region put it: "[They] are likely young people, well acquainted with Rice & every kind of plantation business, and in short [are] capable of the management of a plantation themselves."[2]

As profits from rice and indigo rose, the importation of African slaves created a black majority in South Carolina. African languages, as well as African religious beliefs and diet, strongly influenced this unique colonial culture. Gullah, a dialect with African and English roots, evolved as the common idiom of the Carolina coast. African slaves were more likely than American-born slaves to rebel or run away. Africans played a major role in South Carolina's largest slave uprising, the Stono Rebellion of 1739. After a group of about twenty slaves, many of them African Catholics who sought to flee south to Spanish Florida, seized firearms, about a hundred slaves from nearby plantations joined them. The colonial militia soon defeated the rebels and executed many of them, but the rebellion shocked slave owners throughout England's southern colonies and led to greater repression.

Colonial South Carolina was the most hierarchical society in British North America. Planters controlled the economy and political life. The richest families maintained impressive households in Charleston, the largest city in the southern colonies, as well as on their plantations in the countryside. Small farmers, cattlemen, artisans, merchants, and fur traders held an intermediate but clearly subordinate social position. Native peoples remained influential participants in colonial society through commercial contacts and alliances, but they were increasingly marginalized. As had occurred in colonial Latin America, the growth of a large mixed population blurred racial and cultural boundaries. On the frontier, the children of white men and Amerindian women held an important place in the fur trade. In the plantation regions and Charleston, the offspring of white men and black women often held preferred positions within the slave work force or, if they had been freed, as carpenters, blacksmiths, or in other skilled trades.

New England

The colonization of New England by two separate groups of Protestant dissenters, Pilgrims and Puritans, put the settlement of this region on a different course. The **Pilgrims,** who came first, wished to break completely with the Church of England, which they believed was still essentially Catholic. Unwilling to confront the power of the established church and the monarch, they sought an opportunity to pursue their spiritual ends in a new land. As a result, in 1620 approximately one hundred settlers—men, women, and children—established the colony of Plymouth on the coast of present-day Massachusetts. Although nearly half of the settlers died during the first winter, the colony survived. Plymouth benefited from strong leadership and the discipline and cooperative nature of the settlers. Nevertheless, this experiment in creating a church-directed community failed. The religious enthusiasm and purpose that at first sustained the Pilgrims was dissipated by new immigrants who did not share the founders' religious beliefs, and by geographic dispersal to new towns. In 1691 Plymouth was absorbed into the larger Massachusetts Bay Colony of the Puritans.

The **Puritans** wished to "purify" the Church of England, not break with it. They wanted to abolish its hierarchy of bishops and priests, free it from governmental interference, and limit membership to people who shared their beliefs. Subjected to increased discrimination in England for their efforts to transform the church, large numbers of Puritans began emigrating from England in 1630.

The Puritan leaders of the Massachusetts Bay Company—the joint-stock company that had received a royal charter to finance the Massachusetts Bay Colony—carried the company charter, which spelled out company rights and obligations as well as the direction of company government, with them from England to Massachusetts. By bringing the charter, they limited Crown efforts to control them; the Crown could revoke but not alter the terms of the charter. By 1643 more than twenty thousand Puritans had settled in the Bay Colony.

Immigration to Massachusetts differed from immigration to the Chesapeake and to South Carolina. Most newcomers to Massachusetts arrived with their families. Whereas 84 percent of Virginia's white population in 1625 was male, Massachusetts had a normal gender balance in its population almost from the beginning. It was also the healthiest of England's colonies. The result was a rapid natural increase in population. The population of Massachusetts quickly became more "American" than the population of the colonies to the south or in the Caribbean, whose survival depended on a steady flow of new English immigrants to counter high mortality rates.

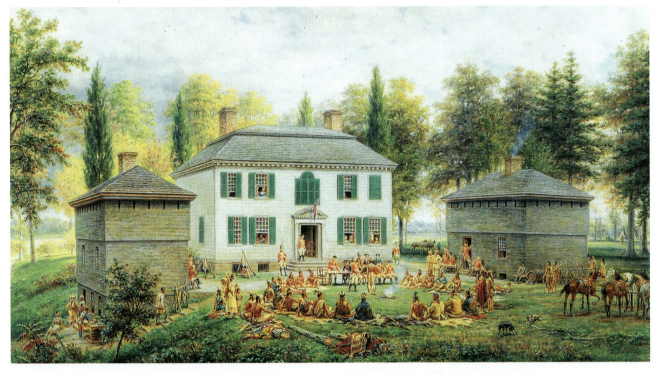

The Home of Sir William Johnson, British Superintendent for Indian Affairs, Northern District   As the colonial era drew to a close, the British attempted to limit the cost of colonial defense by negotiating land settlements between native peoples and settlers. These agreements were doomed by the growing tide of western migration. William Johnson (1715–1774) maintained a fragile peace along the northern frontier by building strong personal relations with influential leaders of the Mohawk and other members of the Iroquois Confederacy. His home in present-day Johnstown, New York, shows the mixed nature of the frontier—the relative opulence of the main house offset by the two defensive blockhouses built for protection.   ("Johnson Hall," by E. L. Henry. Courtesy, Albany Institute of History and Art)

Massachusetts also was more homogeneous and less hierarchical than the southern colonies.

Political institutions evolved out of the terms of the company charter. A governor was elected, along with a council of magistrates drawn from the board of directors of the Massachusetts Bay Company. Disagreements between this council and elected representatives of the towns led, by 1650, to the creation of a lower legislative house that selected its own speaker and began to develop procedures and rules similar to those of the House of Commons in England. The result was greater autonomy and greater local political involvement than in the colonies of Latin America.

Economically, Massachusetts differed dramatically from the southern colonies. Agriculture met basic needs, but poor soils and harsh climate offered no opportunity to develop cash crops like tobacco or rice. To pay for imported tools, textiles, and other essentials, the colonists needed to discover some profit-making niche in the growing Atlantic market. Fur, timber and other forest products, and fish provided the initial economic foundation, but New England's economic well-being soon depended on providing commercial and shipping services in a dynamic and far-flung commercial arena that included the southern colonies, the smaller Caribbean islands, Africa, and Europe.

In Spanish and Portuguese America, heavily capitalized monopolies (companies or individuals given exclusive economic privileges) dominated international trade. In New England, by contrast, merchants survived by discovering smaller but more sustainable profits in diversified trade across the Atlantic. The colony's commercial success rested on market intelligence, flexibility, and streamlined organization. The success of this development strategy is demonstrated by urban population growth. With sixteen thousand inhabitants in 1740, Boston, the capital of Massachusetts Bay Colony, was the largest city in British North America. This coincided with the decline of New England's once-large indigenous population, which had been dramatically

Canadian Fur Trader The fur trade provided the economic foundation of early Canadian settlement. The trade depended on a mix of native and European skills and resources. Fur traders were cultural intermediaries. They transmitted European skills and resources. Fur traders were cultural intermediaries. They transmitted European technologies and products like firearms and machine-made textiles to native peoples and native technologies and products to the canoe and furs to European settlements. Many were the sons of native women and nearly all were fluent in native languages.   (National Archives of Canada)

reduced by a combination of epidemics and brutal military campaigns.

Lacking a profitable agricultural export like tobacco, New England did not develop the extreme social stratification of the southern plantation colonies. Slaves and indentured servants were present, but in very small numbers. New England was ruled by the richest colonists and shared the racial attitudes of the southern colonies, but it also was the colonial society with fewest differences in wealth and status and with the most uniformly British and Protestant population in the Americas.

The Middle Atlantic Region

Much of the future success of English-speaking America was rooted in the rapid economic development and remarkable cultural diversity that appeared in the Middle Atlantic colonies. In 1624 the Dutch West India Company established the colony of New Netherland and located its capital on Manhattan Island. The colony was poorly managed and underfinanced from the start, but its location commanded the potentially profitable and strategically important Hudson River. Dutch merchants established trading relationships with the **Iroquois Confederacy**—an alliance among the Mohawk, Oneida, Onondaga, Cayuga, and Seneca peoples—and with other native peoples that gave them access to the rich fur trade of Canada. When confronted by an English military expedition in 1664, the Dutch surrendered without a fight. James, duke of York and later King James II of England, became proprietor of the colony, which was renamed New York.

New York was characterized by tumultuous politics and corrupt public administration. The colony's success was guaranteed in large measure by the development of New York City as a commercial and shipping center. Located at the mouth of the Hudson River, the city played an essential role in connecting the region's grain farmers to the booming markets of the Caribbean and southern Europe. By the early eighteenth century New York Colony had a diverse population that included English colonists; Dutch, German, and Swedish settlers; and a large slave community.

Pennsylvania began as a proprietary colony and as a refuge for Quakers, a persecuted religious minority. In 1682 William Penn secured an enormous grant of territory (nearly the size of England) because the English king Charles II was indebted to Penn's father. As proprietor (owner) of the land, Penn had sole right to establish a government, subject only to the requirement that he provide for an assembly of freemen.

Penn quickly lost control of the colony's political life, but the colony enjoyed remarkable success. By 1700 Pennsylvania had a population of more than 21,000, and Philadelphia, its capital, soon passed Boston to become the largest city in the British colonies. Healthy climate, excellent land, relatively peaceful relations with native peoples (prompted by Penn's emphasis on negotiation rather than warfare), and access through Philadelphia to good markets led to rapid economic and demographic growth in the colony.

Both Pennsylvania and South Carolina were grain-exporting colonies, but they were very different societies. South Carolina's rice plantations required large numbers of slaves. In Pennsylvania free workers, including a large number of German families, produced the bulk of the colony's grain crops on family farms. As a result, Pennsylvania's economic expansion in the late seventeenth century occurred without reproducing South Carolina's hierarchical and repressive social order. By the early eighteenth century, however, the prosperous city of Philadelphia did have a large population of black slaves and freedmen. Many were servants in the homes of wealthy merchants, but the fast-growing economy offered many opportunities in skilled trades as well.

French America

Patterns of French settlement more closely resembled those of Spain and Portugal than of England. The French were committed to missionary activity among Amerindian peoples and emphasized the extraction of natural resources—furs rather than minerals. The navigator and promoter Jacques Cartier first stirred France's interest in North America. In three voyages between 1524 and 1542, he explored the region of Newfoundland and the Gulf of St. Lawrence. A contemporary of Cortés and Pizarro, Cartier also hoped to find mineral wealth, but the stones he brought back to France turned out to be quartz and iron pyrite, "fool's gold."

The French waited more than fifty years before establishing settlements in North America. Coming to Canada after spending years in the West Indies, Samuel de Champlain founded the colony of **New France** at Quebec°, on the banks of the St. Lawrence River, in 1608. This location provided ready access to Amerindian trade routes, but it also compelled French settlers to take sides in the region's ongoing warfare. Champlain allied New France with the Huron and Algonquin peoples, traditional enemies of the powerful Iroquois Confederacy. Although French firearms and armor at first tipped the balance of power to France's native allies, the members of the Iroquois Confederacy proved to be resourceful and persistent enemies.

The European market for fur, especially beaver, fueled French settlement. Young Frenchmen were sent to live among native peoples to master their languages and customs. These **coureurs de bois°,** or runners of the woods, often began families with indigenous women, and they and their children, who were called métis°, helped direct the fur trade, guiding French expansion to the west and south. Amerindians actively participated in the trade because they quickly came to depend on the goods they received in exchange for furs—firearms, metal tools and utensils, textiles, and alcohol. This change in

the material culture of the native peoples led to overhunting, which rapidly transformed the environment and led to the depletion of beaver and deer populations. It also increased competition among native peoples for hunting grounds, thus promoting warfare.

The proliferation of firearms made indigenous warfare more deadly. The Iroquois Confederacy responded to the increased military strength of France's Algonquin allies by forging commercial and military links with Dutch and later English settlements in the Hudson River Valley. Well armed by the Dutch and English, the Iroquois Confederacy nearly eradicated the Huron in 1649 and inflicted a series of humiliating defeats on the French. At the high point of their power in the early 1680s, Iroquois hunters and military forces gained control of much of the Great Lakes region and the Ohio River Valley. A large French military expedition and a relentless attack focused on Iroquois villages and agriculture finally checked Iroquois power in 1701.

Spain had effectively limited the spread of firearms in its colonies. But the fur trade, together with the growing military rivalry between Algonquin and Iroquois peoples and their respective French and English allies, led to the rapid spread of firearms in North America. Use of firearms in hunting and warfare moved west and south, reaching indigenous plains cultures that had previously adopted the horse introduced by the Spanish. This intersection of horse and gun frontiers in the early eighteenth century dramatically increased the military power and hunting efficiency of the Sioux, Comanche, Cheyenne, and other indigenous peoples, and slowed the pace of European settlement in the North American west.

In French Canada, the Jesuits led the effort to convert native peoples to Christianity. Building on earlier evangelical efforts in Brazil and Paraguay, French Catholic missionaries mastered native languages, created boarding schools for young boys and girls, and set up model agricultural communities for converted Amerindians. The Jesuits' greatest successes coincided with a destructive wave of epidemics and renewed warfare among native peoples in the 1630s. Eventually, churches were established throughout Huron and Algonquin territories. Nevertheless, local culture persisted. In 1688 a French nun who had devoted her life to instructing Amerindian girls expressed the frustration of many missionaries with the resilience of indigenous culture:

> We have observed that of a hundred that have passed through our hands we have scarcely civilized one. . . . When we are least expecting it, they clamber over our wall and go off to run with their kinsmen in the woods, finding more to please them there than in all the amenities of our French house.[3]

Quebec (kwuh-BEC)   **coureurs de bois** (koo-RUHR day BWA)
métis (may-TEES)

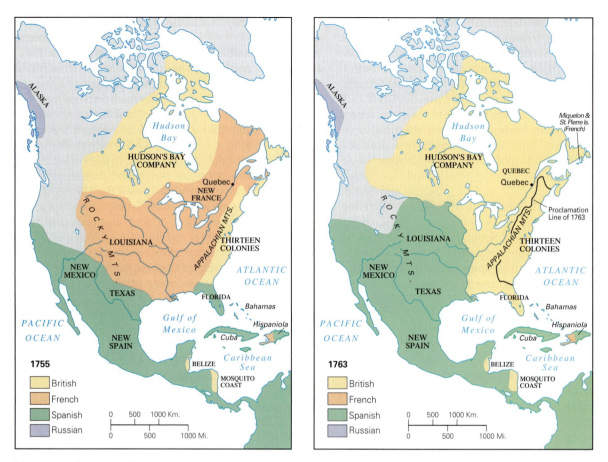

Map 18.2   European Claims in North America, 1755–1763   The results of the French and Indian War dramatically altered the map of North America. France's losses precipitated conflicts between Amerindian peoples and the rapidly expanding population of the British colonies.

As epidemics undermined conversion efforts in mission settlements and evidence of indigenous resistance to conversion mounted, the church redirected some of its resources from the evangelical effort to the larger French settlements, founding schools, hospitals, and churches.

Responsibility for finding settlers and supervising the colonial economy was first granted to a monopoly company chartered in France. Even though the fur trade flourished, population growth was slow. Founded at about the same time as French Canada, Virginia had twenty times more European residents by 1627. After the establishment of royal authority in the 1660s, Canada's French population increased but remained at only seven thousand in 1673. Although improved fiscal management and more effective colonial government did promote a limited agricultural expansion, the fur trade remained important. It is clear that Canada's small settler population and the fur trade's dependence on the

voluntary participation of Amerindians allowed indigenous peoples to retain greater independence and more control over their traditional lands than was possible in the colonies of Spain, Portugal, or England. Unlike these colonial regimes, which sought to transform ancient ways of life or force the transfer of native lands, the French were compelled to treat indigenous peoples as allies and trading partners. This permitted indigenous peoples to more gradually adapt to new religious, technological, and market realities.

Despite Canada's small population, limited resources, and increasing vulnerability to attack by the English and their indigenous allies, the French aggressively expanded to the west and south. Louisiana was founded in 1699, but by 1708 there were fewer than three hundred soldiers, settlers, and slaves in the territory. Like Canada, Louisiana depended on the fur trade, exporting more than fifty thousand deerskins in 1726. Also as in Canada,

Amerindians, driven by a desire for European goods, eagerly embraced this trade. In 1753 a French official reported a Choctaw leader as saying, "[The French] were the first . . . who made [us] subject to the different needs that [we] can no longer now do without."[4]

France's North American colonies were threatened by a series of wars fought by France and England and by the population growth and increasing prosperity of neighboring English colonies. The "French and Indian War" (which led to a broader conflict, the Seven Years War, 1756–1763), however, proved to be the final contest for North American empire (see Map 18.2). England committed a larger military force to the struggle and, despite early defeats, took the French capital of Quebec in 1759. Although resistance continued briefly, French forces in Canada surrendered in 1760. The peace agreement forced France to yield Canada to the English and cede Louisiana to Spain. The differences between French and English colonial realities were suggested by the petition of one Canadian indigenous leader to a British officer after the French surrender. "[W]e learn that our lands are to be given away not only to trade thereon but also to them in full title to various [English] individuals. . . . We have always been a free nation, and now we will become slaves, which would be very difficult to accept after having enjoyed our liberty so long."[5] With the loss of Canada the French concentrated their efforts on their sugar-producing colonies in the Caribbean (see Chapter 19).

COLONIAL EXPANSION AND CONFLICT

In the last decades of the seventeenth century, all of the European colonies in the Americas began to experience a long period of economic and demographic expansion. The imperial powers responded by strengthening their administrative and economic controls in the colonies. They also sought to force colonial populations to pay a larger share of the costs of administration and defense. These efforts at reform and restructuring coincided with a series of imperial wars fought along Atlantic trade routes and in the Americas. France's loss of its North American colonies was one of the most important results of these struggles. Equally significant, colonial populations throughout the Americas became more aware of separate national identities and more aggressive in asserting local interests against the will of distant monarchs.

Imperial Reform in Spanish America and Brazil

Spain's Habsburg dynasty ended when the Spanish king Charles II died without an heir in 1700 (see Table 17.1, page 467). After thirteen years of conflict involving the major European powers and factions within Spain, Philip of Bourbon, grandson of Louis XIV of France, gained the Spanish throne. Under Philip V and his Bourbon heirs, Spain's colonial administration and tax collection were reorganized. Spain's reliance on convoys protected by naval vessels was abolished; more colonial ports were permitted to trade with Spain; and intercolonial trade was expanded. Spain also created new commercial monopolies to produce tobacco, some alcoholic beverages, and chocolate. The Spanish navy was strengthened, and trade in contraband was more effectively policed.

For most of the Spanish Empire, the eighteenth century was a period of remarkable economic expansion associated with population growth. Amerindian populations began to recover from the early epidemics; the flow of Spanish immigrants increased; and the slave trade to the plantation colonies was expanded. Mining, the heart of the Spanish colonial economy, increased as silver production in Mexico and Peru rose steadily into the 1780s. Agricultural exports also expanded: tobacco, dyes, hides, chocolate, cotton, and sugar joined the flow of goods to Europe.

But these reforms carried unforeseen consequences that threatened the survival of the Spanish Empire. Despite expanded silver production, the economic growth of the eighteenth century was led by the previously minor agricultural and grazing economies of Cuba, the Rio de la Plata region, Venezuela, Chile, and Central America. These export economies were less able than the mining economies of Mexico and Peru to weather breaks in trade caused by imperial wars. Each such disruption forced landowning elites in Cuba and the other regions to turn to alternative, often illegal, trade with English, French, or Dutch merchants. By the 1790s the wealthiest and most influential sectors of Spain's colonial society had come to view the Spanish Empire as an impediment to prosperity and growth.

Bourbon political and fiscal reforms also contributed to a growing sense of colonial grievance by limiting creoles' access to colonial offices and by imposing new taxes and monopolies on colonial production. Consumer and producer resentment, for example, led to rioting when the Spanish established monopolies on tobacco, cacao (chocolate), and brandy. Because these reforms produced a more intrusive and expensive colonial government that interfered with established business practices,

Market in Rio de Janeiro In many of the cities of colonial Latin America female slaves and black free women dominated retail markets. In this scene from late colonial Brazil Afro-Brazilian women sell a variety of foods and crafts. (Sir Henry Chamberlain, Views and Costumes of the City and Neighborhoods of Rio de Janeiro, London, 1822)

many colonists saw the changes as an abuse of the informal constitution that had long governed the empire. Only in the Bourbon effort to expand colonial militias in the face of English threats did creoles find opportunity for improved status and greater responsibility.

In addition to tax rebellions and urban riots, colonial policies also provoked Amerindian uprisings. Most spectacular was the rebellion initiated in 1780 by the Peruvian Amerindian leader José Gabriel Condorcanqui. Once in rebellion, he took the name of his Inca ancestor Tupac Amaru°, who had been executed as a rebel in 1572. **Tupac Amaru II** was well connected in Spanish colonial society. He had been educated by the Jesuits and was actively involved in trade with the silver mines at Potosí. Despite these connections, he still resented the abuse of Amerindian villagers.

Historians still debate the objectives of this rebellion. Tupac Amaru's own pronouncements did not clearly state whether he sought to end local injustices or overthrow Spanish rule. It appears that a local Spanish judge who challenged Tupac Amaru's hereditary rights provided the initial provocation, but that Tupac Amaru was ultimately driven by the conviction that colonial authorities were oppressing the indigenous people. As thousands joined him, he dared to contemplate the overthrow of Spanish rule.

Amerindian communities suffering under the mita and tribute obligations provided the majority of Tupac Amaru's army. He also received some support from creoles, mestizos, and slaves. After his capture, he was brutally executed, as were his wife and fifteen other family members and allies. Even after his execution, Amerindian rebels continued the struggle for more than two years. By the time Spanish authority was firmly reestablished, more than 100,000 lives had been lost and enormous amounts of property destroyed.

Brazil experienced a similar period of expansion and reform after 1700. Portugal created new administrative positions and gave monopoly companies exclusive rights to little-developed regions. Here, too, a more intrusive colonial government led to rebellions and plots, including open warfare in 1707 between "sons of the soil" and "outsiders" in São Paulo. The most aggressive period of reform occurred during the ministry of the marquis of Pombal (1750–1777). The Pombal reforms were made possible by an economic expansion fueled by the discovery of gold in the 1690s and diamonds after 1720 as well as by the development of markets for coffee and cotton. This new wealth paid for the importation of nearly 2 million African slaves. In Spanish America, a reinvigorated Crown sought to eliminate contraband trade. Portugal, however, had fallen into the economic orbit of England, and Brazil's new prosperity fueled a new wave of English imports.

Tupac Amaru (TOO-pack a-MAH-roo)

Reform and Reorganization in British America

England's efforts to reform and reorganize its North American colonies began earlier than the Bourbon initiative in Spanish America. After the period of Cromwell's Puritan Republic (see Chapter 17), the restored Stuart king, Charles II, undertook an ambitious campaign to establish greater Crown control over the colonies. Between 1651 and 1673 a series of Navigation Acts sought to severely limit colonial trading and colonial production that competed directly with English manufacturers. James II also attempted to increase royal control over colonial political life. Royal governments replaced original colonial charters as in Massachusetts and proprietorships as in the Carolinas. Because the New England colonies were viewed as centers of smuggling, the king temporarily suspended their elected assemblies. At the same time, he appointed colonial governors and granted them new fiscal and legislative powers.

James II's overthrow in the Glorious Revolution of 1688 ended this confrontation, but not before colonists were provoked to resist and, in some cases, rebel. They overthrew the governors of New York and Massachusetts and removed the Catholic proprietor of Maryland. William and Mary restored relative peace, but these conflicts alerted the colonists to the potential for aggression by the English government. Colonial politics would remain confrontational until the American Revolution.

During the eighteenth century the English colonies experienced renewed economic growth and attracted a new wave of European immigration, but social divisions were increasingly evident. The colonial population in 1770 was more urban, more clearly divided by class and race, and more vulnerable to economic downturns. Crises were provoked when imperial wars with France and Spain disrupted trade in the Atlantic, increased tax burdens, forced military mobilizations, and provoked frontier conflicts with the Amerindians. On the eve of the American Revolution, England defeated France and weakened Spain. The cost, however, was great. Administrative, military, and tax policies imposed to gain empirewide victory alienated much of the American colonial population.

CONCLUSION

The New World colonial empires of Spain, Portugal, France, and England had many characteristics in common. All subjugated Amerindian peoples and introduced large numbers of enslaved Africans. Within all four empires forests were cut down, virgin soils were turned with the plow, and Old World animals and plants were introduced. Colonists in all four applied the technologies of the Old World to the resources of the New, producing wealth and exploiting the commercial possibilities of the emerging Atlantic market.

Each of the New World empires also reflected the distinctive cultural and institutional heritages of its colonizing power. Mineral wealth allowed Spain to develop the most centralized empire. Political and economic power was concentrated in the great capital cities of Mexico City and Lima. Portugal and France pursued objectives similar to Spain's in their colonies. However, neither Brazil's agricultural economy nor France's Canadian fur trade produced the financial resources that made possible the centralized control achieved by Spain. Nevertheless, all three of these Catholic powers were able to impose and enforce significant levels of religious and cultural uniformity, relative to the British.

Greater cultural and religious diversity characterized British North America. Colonists were drawn from throughout the British Isles and included participants in all of Britain's numerous religious traditions. They were joined by German, Swedish, Dutch, and French Protestant immigrants. British colonial government varied somewhat from colony to colony and was more responsive to local interests. Thus colonists in British North America were better able than those in the areas controlled by Spain, Portugal, and France to respond to changing economic and political circumstances. Most importantly, the British colonies attracted many more European immigrants than did the other New World colonies. Between 1580 and 1760 French colonies received 60,000 immigrants, Brazil 523,000, and the Spanish colonies 678,000. Within a shorter period—between 1600 and 1760—the British settlements welcomed 746,000. Population in British North America—free and slave combined—reached an extraordinary 2.5 million by 1775.

By the eighteenth century, colonial societies across the Americas had matured as wealth increased, populations grew, and contacts with the rest of the world became more common (see Chapter 19). Colonial elites were more confident of their ability to define and defend local interests. Colonists in general were increasingly aware of their unique and distinctive cultural identities and willing to defend American experience and practice in the face of European presumptions of superiority. Moreover, influential groups in all the colonies were drawn toward the liberating ideas of Europe's Enlightenment. In the open and less inhibited spaces of the Western Hemisphere, these ideas (as Chapter 22 examines) soon provided a potent intellectual basis for opposing the continuation of empire.

■ Key Terms

Columbian Exchange	indentured servant
Council of the Indies	House of Burgesses
Bartolomé de Las Casas	Pilgrims
Potosí	Puritans
encomienda	Iroquois Confederacy
creoles	New France
mestizo	coureurs de bois
mulatto	Tupac Amaru II

■ Suggested Reading

Alfred W. Crosby, Jr., is justifiably the best-known student of the Columbian Exchange. See his *The Columbian Exchange: Biological and Cultural Consequences of 1492* (1972) and *Ecological Imperialism* (1986). William H. McNeill, *Plagues and Peoples* (1976), puts the discussion of the American exchange in a world history context. Elinor G. K. Melville, *A Plague of Sheep: Environmental Consequences of the Spanish Conquest of Mexico* (1994), is the most important recent contribution to this field.

Colonial Latin America, 4th ed. (2001), by Mark A. Burkholder and Lyman L. Johnson, provides a good introduction to colonial Latin American history. *Early Latin America* (1983) by James Lockhart and Stuart B. Schwartz and *Spain and Portugal in the New World, 1492–1700* (1984) by Lyle N. McAlister are both useful introductions as well.

The specialized historical literature on the American colonial empires is extensive and deep. A sampling of useful works follows. For the early colonial period see Inga Clendinnen, *Ambivalent Conquests* (1987); James Lockhart, *The Nahuas After the Conquest* (1992); and John Hemming, *Red Gold: The Conquest of the Brazilian Indians* (1978). Nancy M. Farriss, *Maya Society Under Spanish Rule: The Collective Enterprise of Survival* (1984), is also one of the most important books on colonial Spanish America. For the Catholic Church see William Taylor, *Magistrates of the Sacred: Priests and Parishioners in Eighteenth-Century Mexico* (1996). Lyman L. Johnson and Sonya Lipsett-Rivera, eds., *The Faces of Honor* (1999), provides a good introduction to the culture of honor. For the place of women see Asunción Lavrin, ed., *Sexuality and Marriage in Colonial Latin America* (1989). On issues of class R. Douglas Cope, *The Limits of Racial Domination* (1994), is recommended. On the slave trade Herbert S. Klein, *The Middle Passage* (1978), and Philip D. Curtin, *The Atlantic Slave Trade: A Census* (1969), are indispensable. Frederick P. Bowser, *The African Slave in Colonial Peru, 1524–1650* (1973); Mary C. Karasch, *Slave Life and Culture in Rio de Janeiro, 1808–1850* (1986); and Stuart B. Schwartz, *Sugar Plantations in the Formation of Brazilian Society: Bahia, 1550–1835* (1985), are excellent introductions to the African experience in two very different Latin American societies.

Among the useful general studies of the British colonies are Charles M. Andrews, *The Colonial Period of American History: The Settlements,* 3 vols. (1934–1937); David Hackett Fischer, *Albion's Seed: Four British Folkways in America* (1989); and Gary B. Nash, *Red, White, and Black: The Peoples of Early America,* 2d ed. (1982). On the economy see John J. McCusker and Russell R. Menard, *The Economy of British America, 1607–1789* (1979). For slavery see David Brion Davis, *The Problem of Slavery in Western Culture* (1966); Allan Kulikoff, *Tobacco and Slaves: The Development of Southern Cultures in the Chesapeake, 1680–1800* (1986); and Peter H. Wood, *Black Majority: Negroes in Colonial South Carolina from 1670 Through the Stono Rebellion* (1974). Two very useful works on the relations between Europeans and Indians are James Merrill, *The Indians' New World: Catawbas and Their Neighbors from European Contact Through the Era of Removal* (1989); and Daniel H. Usner, Jr., *Indians, Settlers, and Slaves in a Frontier Exchange Economy: The Lower Mississippi Valley Before 1783* (1992).

For late colonial politics see Gary B. Nash, *Urban Crucible: Social Change, Political Consciousness, and the Origins of the American Revolution* (1979); Bernard Bailyn, *The Origins of American Politics* (1986); Jack P. Greene, *The Quest for Power: The Lower Houses of Assembly in the Southern Royal Colonies* (1963); and Richard Bushman, *King and People in Provincial Massachusetts* (1985). On immigration see Bernard Bailyn, *The Peopling of British North America* (1986).

On French North America, William J. Eccles, *France in America,* rev. ed. (1990), is an excellent overview; see also his *The Canadian Frontier, 1534–1760* (1969). G. F. G. Stanley, *New France, 1701–1760* (1968), is also an important resource. R. Cole Harris, *The Seigneurial System in Canada: A Geographical Study* (1966), provides an excellent analysis of the topic. Harold Innis, *The Fur Trade in Canada: An Introduction to Canadian Economic History* (1927), remains indispensable. Also of value are Cornelius Jaenen, *The Role of the Church in New France* (1976), Carole Blackburn, *Harvest of Souls: The Jesuit Missions and Colonialism in North America, 1632–1650* (2000); and Alison L. Prentice, *Canadian Women: A History* (1988).

■ Notes

1. Quoted in Alfred W. Crosby, Jr., *The Columbian Exchange: Biological and Cultural Consequences of 1492* (Westport, CT: Greenwood, 1972), 58.
2. Ibid.
3. Quoted in R. Douglas Francis, Richard Jones, and Donald B. Smith, *Origins: Canadian History to Confederation* (Toronto: Holt, Rinehart, and Winston of Canada, 1992), 52.
4. Quoted in Daniel H. Usner, Jr., *Indians, Settlers and Slaves in a Frontier Exchange Economy: The Lower Mississippi Valley Before 1783,* Institute of Early American History and Culture Series (Chapel Hill: University of North Carolina Press, 1992), 96.
5. Quoted in Cornelius J. Jaenen, "French and Native Peoples in New France," in J. M. Bumsted, *Interpreting Canada's Past,* vol. 1, 2d ed. (Toronto: Oxford University Press, 1993), 73.

19

The Atlantic System and Africa, 1550–1800

Caribbean Sugar Mill   The wind mill crushes sugar cane whose juice is boiled down in the smoking building next door.

CHAPTER OUTLINE

Plantations in the West Indies

Plantation Life in the Eighteenth Century

Creating the Atlantic Economy

Africa, the Atlantic, and Islam

ENVIRONMENT AND TECHNOLOGY: Amerindian Foods in Africa

DIVERSITY AND DOMINANCE: Slavery in West Africa and the Americas

In 1694 the English ship *Hannibal* called at the West African port of Whydah° to purchase slaves. The king of Whydah welcomed Captain Thomas Phillips and others of the ship's officers and invited them to his residence. Phillips gave the African ruler the rich presents required for Europeans to trade there and negotiated an agreement on the prices for slaves.

The ship's doctor carefully inspected the naked captives to be sure they were of sound body, young, and free of disease. After their purchase, the slaves were branded with an H (for *Hannibal*) to establish ownership. Once they were loaded on the ship, the crew put shackles on the men to prevent their escape. Phillips recorded that the shackles were removed once the ship was out of sight of land and the risk of a slave revolt had passed. In all, the *Hannibal* purchased 692 slaves, of whom about a third were women and girls.

This was not a private venture. The *Hannibal* had been hired by the **Royal African Company** (RAC), an association of English investors that in 1672 had received a charter from the English monarchy giving them exclusive rights to trade along the Atlantic coast of Africa. Besides slaves, the RAC purchased ivory and other products.

Under the terms of their agreement, the RAC would pay the owners of the *Hannibal* £10.50 for each slave brought to Barbados—but only for those delivered alive. To keep the slaves healthy, Captain Phillips had the crew feed them twice a day on boiled corn meal and beans brought from Europe flavored with hot peppers and palm oil purchased in Africa. Each slave received a pint (half a liter) of water with every meal. In addition, the slaves were made to "jump and dance for an hour or two to our bagpipe, harp, and fiddle" every evening to keep them fit. Despite the incentives and precautions for keeping the cargo alive, deaths were common among the hundreds of people crammed into every corner of a slave ship. The *Hannibal*'s experience was worse than most, losing 320 slaves and 14 crew members during the seven-week voyage to Barbados. One hundred slaves came down with smallpox, an infection one must have brought on board. Only a dozen died of that disease, but, the captain lamented, "what the small-pox spar'd, the flux [dysentery] swept off, to our great regret, after all our pains and care to give them their messes [meals] in due order and season, keeping their lodgings as clean as possible, and enduring so much misery and stench so long among a parcel of creatures nastier than swine." One wonders what one of the Africans might have written about the nasty creatures who put them in these conditions.

The *Hannibal*'s high losses, nearly double the average losses of an English slaver during the passage to Barbados in the last quarter of the seventeenth century, destroyed the profitability of the voyage. The 372 Africans who were landed alive netted the RAC about £7,000, but the purchase price of 692 slaves at Whydah and the costs of their transportation on the *Hannibal* amounted to about £10,800.

As the *Hannibal*'s experience suggests, the Atlantic slave trade took a devastating toll in African lives and was far from a sure-fire money maker for European investors. Nevertheless, the slave trade and plantation slavery were crucial pieces of a booming new **Atlantic system** that moved goods and wealth, as well as people and cultures, around the Atlantic.

As you read this chapter, ask yourself the following questions:

- How did the Atlantic system affect Europe, Africa, and the Americas?

- How and why did European businessmen, with the help of their governments, put this trading system together?

- How and why did the West Indies and other places in the Americas become centers of African population and culture?

- How did sub-Saharan Africa's expanding contacts in the Atlantic compare with its contacts with the Islamic world?

Whydah (WEE-duh)

C H R O N O L O G Y

	West Indies	Atlantic	Africa
1500	**ca. 1500** Spanish settlers introduce sugar-cane cultivation	**1530** Amsterdam Exchange opens	**1500–1700** Gold trade predominates
			1591 Morocco conquers Songhai
1600	**1620s and 1630s** English and French colonies in Caribbean **1640s** Dutch bring sugar plantation system from Brazil **1655** English take Jamaica	**1621** Dutch West India Company chartered	**1638** Dutch take Elmina
	1670s French occupy western half of Hispaniola	**1660s** English Navigation Acts **1672** Royal African Company chartered **1698** French *Exclusif*	**1680s** Rise of Asante
1700	**1700** West Indies surpass Brazil in sugar production	**1700 to present** Atlantic system flourishing	**1700–1830** Slave trade predominates **1720s** Rise of Dahomey **1730** Oyo makes Dahomey pay tribute
	1760 Tacky's rebellion in Jamaica		
	1795 Jamaican Maroon rebellion		

PLANTATIONS IN THE WEST INDIES

The West Indies was the first place in the Americas reached by Columbus and the first part of the Americas where native populations collapsed. It took a long time to repopulate these islands from abroad and forge new economic links between them and other parts of the Atlantic. But after 1650 sugar plantations, African slaves, and European capital made these islands a major center of the Atlantic economy.

Colonization Before 1650

Spanish settlers introduced sugar-cane cultivation into the West Indies shortly after 1500, but these colonies soon fell into neglect as attention shifted to colonizing the American mainland. After 1600 the West Indies revived as a focus of colonization, this time by northern Europeans interested in growing tobacco and other crops. In the 1620s and 1630s English colonization societies founded small European settlements on Montserrat°, Barbados°, and other Caribbean islands, while the French colonized Martinique°, Guadeloupe°, and some other islands. Because of greater support from their government, the English colonies prospered first, largely by growing tobacco for export.

This New World leaf, long used by Amerindians for recreation and medicine, was finding a new market among seventeenth-century Europeans. Despite the opposition of individuals like King James I of England, who condemned tobacco smoke as "dangerous to the eye, hateful to the nose, harmful to the brain, and dangerous to the lungs," the habit spread. By 1614 tobacco was reportedly being sold in seven thousand shops in and around London, and some English businessmen were dreaming of a tobacco trade as valuable as Spain's silver fleets.

Turning such pipe dreams into reality was not easy. Diseases, hurricanes, and attacks by the Carib and the Spanish scourged the early French and English West

Montserrat (mont-suh-RAHT)   **Barbados** (bahr-BAY-dohs)
Martinique (mahr-tee-NEEK)   **Guadeloupe** (gwah-duh-LOOP)

Indies colonists. They also suffered from shortages of supplies from Europe and shortages of labor sufficient to clear and plant virgin land with tobacco. Two changes improved the colonies' prospects. One was the formation of **chartered companies.** To promote national claims without government expense, France and England gave groups of private investors monopolies over trade to their West Indies colonies in exchange for the payment of annual fees. The other change was that the companies began to provide free passage to the colonies for poor Europeans. These indentured servants paid off their debt by working three or four years for the established colonists (see Chapter 18).

Under this system the French and English population on several tobacco islands grew rapidly in the 1630s and 1640s. By the middle of the century, however, the Caribbean colonies were in crisis because of stiff competition from milder Virginia-grown tobacco, also cultivated by indentured servants. The cultivation of sugar cane, introduced in the 1640s by Dutch investors expelled from Brazil, provided a way out of this crisis. In the process, the labor force changed from mostly European to mostly African.

The Portuguese had introduced sugar cultivation into Brazil from islands along the African coast after 1550 and had soon introduced enslaved African labor as well (see Chapter 18). By 1600 Brazil was the Atlantic world's greatest sugar producer. Some Dutch merchants invested in Brazilian sugar plantations so that they might profit from transporting the sugar across the Atlantic and distributing it in Europe. However, in the first half of the seventeenth century the Dutch were fighting for their independence from the Spanish crown, which then ruled Portugal and Brazil. As part of that struggle, the Dutch government chartered the **Dutch West India Company** in 1621 to carry the conflict to Spain's overseas possessions.

Not just a disguised form of the Dutch navy, the Dutch West India Company was a private trading company. Its investors expected the company's profits to cover its expenses and pay them dividends. After the capture of a Spanish treasure fleet in 1628, the company used some of the windfall to pay its stockholders a huge dividend and the rest to finance an assault on Brazil's valuable sugar-producing areas. By 1635 the Dutch company controlled 1,000 miles (1,600 kilometers) of northeastern Brazil's coast. Over the next fifteen years the new Dutch owners improved the efficiency of the Brazilian sugar industry, and the company prospered by supplying the plantations with enslaved Africans and European goods and carrying the sugar back to Europe.

Like its assault on Brazil, the Dutch West India Company's entry into the African slave trade combined economic and political motives. It seized the important West African trading station of Elmina from the Portuguese in 1638 and took their port of Luanda° on the Angolan coast in 1641. From these coasts the Dutch shipped slaves to Brazil and the West Indies. Although the Portuguese were able to drive the Dutch out of Angola after a few years, Elmina remained the Dutch West India Company's headquarters in West Africa.

Once free of Spanish rule in 1640, the Portuguese crown turned its attention to reconquering Brazil. By 1654 Portuguese armies had driven the last of the Dutch sugar planters from Brazil. Some of the expelled planters transplanted their capital and knowledge of sugar production to small Caribbean colonies, which the Dutch had founded earlier as trading bases with Spanish colonies; others introduced the Brazilian system into English and French Caribbean islands. This was a momentous turning point in the history of the Atlantic economy.

Sugar and Slaves

The Dutch infusion of expertise and money revived the French colonies of Guadeloupe and Martinique, but the English colony of Barbados best illustrates the dramatic transformation that sugar brought to the seventeenth-century Caribbean. In 1640 Barbados's economy depended largely on tobacco, mostly grown by European settlers, both free and indentured. By the 1680s sugar had become the colony's principal crop, and enslaved Africans were three times as numerous as Europeans. Exporting up to 15,000 tons of sugar a year, Barbados had become the wealthiest and most populous of England's American colonies. By 1700 the West Indies had surpassed Brazil as the world's principal source of sugar.

The expansion of sugar plantations in the West Indies required a sharp increase in the volume of the slave trade from Africa (see Figure 19.1). During the first half of the seventeenth century about ten thousand slaves a year had arrived from Africa. Most were destined for Brazil and the mainland Spanish colonies. In the second half of the century the trade averaged twenty thousand slaves a year. More than half were intended for the English, French, and Dutch West Indies and most of the rest for Brazil. A century later the volume of the Atlantic slave trade was three times larger.

The shift in favor of African slaves was a product of many factors. Recent scholarship has cast doubt on the once-common assertion that Africans were more suited than Europeans to field labor, since newly arrived Africans

Luanda (loo-AHN-duh)

Figure 19.1   Transatlantic Slave Trade from Africa, 1551–1850

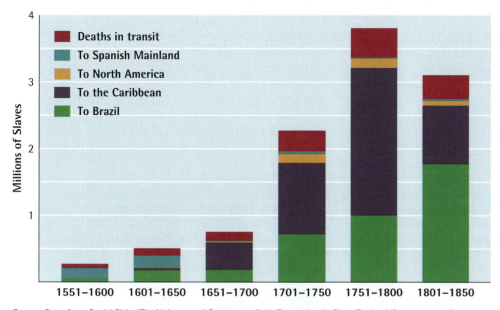

Source: Data from David Eltis, "The Volume and Structure of the Transatlantic Slave Trade: A Reassessment," *William and Mary Quarterly*, 3d Series, 58 (2001), tables II and III.

and Europeans both died in large numbers in the American tropics. Africans' slightly higher survival rate was not decisive because mortality was about the same among later generations of blacks and whites born in the West Indies and acclimated to its diseases.

The West Indian historian Eric Williams also refuted the idea that the rise of African slave labor was primarily motivated by prejudice. Citing the West Indian colonies' prior use of enslaved Amerindians and indentured Europeans, along with European convicts and prisoners of war, he argued that "Slavery was not born of racism: rather, racism was the consequence of slavery."[1] Williams suggested that the shift was due to the lower cost of African labor.

Yet slaves were far from cheap. Cash-short tobacco planters in the seventeenth century preferred indentured Europeans because they cost half as much as African slaves. Poor European men and women were willing to work for little in order to get to the Americas, where they could acquire their own land cheaply at the end of their terms of service. However, as the cultivation of sugar spread after 1750, rich speculators drove the price of land in the West Indies so high that end-of-term indentured servants could not afford to buy it. As a result, poor Europeans chose to indenture themselves in the mainland North American colonies, where cheap land was still available. Rather than raise wages to attract European laborers, Caribbean sugar planters switched to slaves.

Rising sugar prices helped the West Indian sugar planters afford the higher cost of African slaves. The fact that the average slave lived seven years, while the typical indentured labor contract was for only three or four years, also made slaves a better investment. The planters could rely on the Dutch and other traders to supply them with enough new slaves to meet the demands of the expanding plantations. Rising demand for slaves (see Figure 19.1) drove their sale price up steadily during the eighteenth century. These high labor costs were one more factor favoring large plantations over smaller operations.

PLANTATION LIFE IN THE EIGHTEENTH CENTURY

To find more land for sugar plantations, France and England founded new Caribbean colonies. In 1655 the English had wrested the island of Jamaica from the Spanish (see Map 18.1). The French seized the western half of the large Spanish island of Hispaniola in the 1670s. During the eighteenth century this new French colony of Saint Domingue° (present-day Haiti) became the greatest producer of sugar in the Atlantic world,

Saint Domingue (san doh-MANGH)

Plantation Scene, Antigua, British West Indies   The sugar made at the mill in the background was sealed in barrels and loaded on carts that oxen and horses drew to the beach. By means of a succession of vessels the barrels were taken to the ship that hauled the cargo to Europe. The importance of African labor is evident from the fact that only one white person appears in the painting. (Courtesy of the John Carter Brown Library at Brown University)

while Jamaica surpassed Barbados as England's most important sugar colony. The technological, environmental, and social transformation of these island colonies illustrates the power of the new Atlantic system.

Technology and Environment

The cultivation of sugar cane was fairly straightforward. From fourteen to eighteen months after planting, the canes were ready to be cut. The roots continued to produce new shoots that could be harvested about every nine months. Only simple tools were needed: spades for planting, hoes to control the weeds, and sharp machetes to cut the canes. What made the sugar plantation a complex investment was that it had to be a factory as well as a farm. Freshly cut canes needed to be crushed within a few hours to extract the sugary sap. Thus, for maximum efficiency, each plantation needed its own expensive crushing and processing equipment.

At the heart of the sugar works was the mill where canes were crushed between sets of heavy rollers. Small mills could be turned by animal or human power, but larger, more efficient mills needed more sophisticated sources of power. Eighteenth-century Barbados went in heavily for windmills, and the French sugar islands and Jamaica used costly water-powered mills, often fed by elaborate aqueducts.

From the mill, lead-lined wooden troughs carried the cane juice to a series of large copper kettles in the boiling shed, where the excess water boiled off, leaving a thick syrup. Workers poured the syrup into conical molds in the drying shed. The sugar crystals that formed in the molds were packed in wooden barrels for shipment to Europe. The dark molasses that drained off was made into rum in yet another building, or it was barreled for export.

To make the operation more efficient and profitable, investors gradually increased the size of the typical West Indian plantation from around 100 acres (40 hectares) in the seventeenth century to at least twice that size in the eighteenth century. Some plantations were even larger. In 1774 Jamaica's 680 sugar plantations averaged 441 acres (178 hectares) each; some spread over 2,000 acres

(800 hectares). Jamaica specialized so heavily in sugar production that the island had to import most of its food. Saint Domingue had a comparable number of plantations of smaller average size but generally higher productivity. The French colony was also more diverse in its economy. Although sugar production was paramount, some planters raised provisions for local consumption and crops such as coffee and cacao for export.

In some ways the mature sugar plantation was environmentally responsible. The crushing mill was powered by water, wind, or animals, not fossil fuels. The boilers were largely fueled by burning the crushed canes, and the fields were fertilized by manure from the cattle. In two respects, however, the plantation was very damaging to the environment: soil exhaustion and deforestation.

Repeated cultivation of a single crop removes more nutrients from the soil than animal fertilizer and fallow periods can restore. Instead of rotating sugar with other crops in order to restore the nutrients naturally, planters found it more profitable to clear new lands when yields declined too much in the old fields. When land close to the sea was exhausted, planters moved on to new islands. Many of the English who first settled Jamaica were from Barbados, and the pioneer planters on Saint Domingue came from older French sugar colonies. In the second half of the eighteenth century, Jamaican sugar production began to fall behind that of Saint Domingue, which still had access to virgin land. Thus the plantations of this period were not a stable form of agriculture but rather gradually laid waste to the landscape.

Deforestation, the second form of environmental damage, continued a trend begun in the sixteenth century. The Spanish had cut down some forests in the Caribbean to make pastures for the cattle they introduced. Sugar cultivation rapidly accelerated land clearing. Forests near the coast were the first to disappear, and by the end of the eighteenth century only land in the interior of the islands retained dense forests.

Combined with soil exhaustion and deforestation, other changes profoundly altered the ecology balance of the West Indies. By the eighteenth century nearly all of the domesticated animals and cultivated plants in the Caribbean were ones that Europeans had introduced. The Spanish had brought cattle, pigs, and horses, all of which multiplied so rapidly that no new imports had been necessary after 1503. They had also introduced new plants. Of these, bananas and plantain from the Canary Islands were a valuable addition to the food supply, and sugar and rice formed the basis of plantation agriculture, along with native tobacco. Other food crops arrived with the slaves from Africa, including okra, black-eyed peas, yams, grains such as millet and sorghum, and mangoes. Many of these new animals and plants were useful additions to the islands,

but they crowded out indigenous species. New World foods also found their way to Africa (see Environment and Technology: Amerindian Foods in Africa).

The most tragic and dramatic transformation in the West Indies occurred in the human population. Chapter 16 detailed how the indigenous Arawak peoples of the large islands were wiped out by disease and abuse within fifty years of Columbus's first voyage. As the plantation economy spread, the Carib surviving on the smaller islands were also pushed to the point of extinction. Far earlier and more completely than in any mainland colony, the West Indies were repeopled from across the Atlantic—first from Europe and then from Africa.

Slaves' Lives

During the eighteenth century West Indian plantation colonies were the world's most polarized societies. On most islands 90 percent or more of the inhabitants were slaves. Power resided in the hands of a **plantocracy,** a small number of very rich men who owned most of the slaves and most of the land. Between the slaves and the masters might be found only a few others—some estate managers and government officials and, in the French islands, small farmers, both white and black. Thus it is only a slight simplification to describe eighteenth-century Caribbean society as being made up of a large, abject class of slaves and a small, powerful class of masters.

The profitability of a Caribbean plantation depended on extracting as much work as possible from the slaves. Their long workday might stretch to eighteen hours or more when the cane harvest and milling were in full swing. Sugar plantations achieved exceptional productivity through the threat and use of force. As Table 19.1 shows (see page 507), on a typical Jamaican plantation about 80 percent of the slaves actively engaged in productive tasks; the only exceptions were infants, the seriously ill, and the very old. Everyone on the plantation, except those disabled by age or infirmity, had an assigned task.

Table 19.1 also illustrates how slave labor was organized by age, sex, and ability. As in other Caribbean colonies, only 2 or 3 percent of the slaves were house servants. About 70 percent of the able-bodied slaves worked in the fields, generally in one of three labor gangs. A "great gang," made up of the strongest slaves in the prime of life, did the heaviest work, such as breaking up the soil at the beginning of the planting season. A second gang of youths, elders, and less fit slaves did somewhat lighter work. A "grass gang," composed of children under the supervision of an elderly slave, was responsible for weeding and other simple work, such as collecting grass

Amerindian Foods in Africa

The migration of European plants and animals across the Atlantic to the New World was one side of the Columbian Exchange (see Chapter 18). The Andean potato, for example, became a staple crop of the poor in Europe, and cassava (a Brazilian plant cultivated for its edible roots) and maize (corn) moved across the Atlantic to Africa.

Maize was a high-yielding grain that could produce much more food per acre than many grains indigenous to Africa. The varieties of maize that spread to Africa were not modern high-bred "sweet corn" but starchier types found in white and yellow corn meal. Cassava—not well known to modern North Americans except perhaps in the form of tapioca—became the most important New World food in Africa. Truly a marvel, cassava had the highest yield of calories per acre of any staple food and thrived even in poor soils and during droughts. Both the leaves and the root could be eaten. Ground into meal, the root could be made into a bread that would keep for up to six months, or it could be fermented into a beverage.

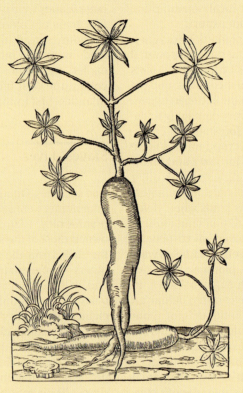

Cassava Plant Both the leaves and the starchy root of the cassava plant could be eaten. (Engraving from André Thevet, *Les Singularitez de la France Antarctique.* Paris: Maurice de la Porte, 1557. Courtesy of the James Bell Library, University of Minnesota)

Cassava and maize were probably accidentally introduced into Africa by Portuguese ships from Brazil that discarded leftover supplies after reaching Angola. It did not take long for local Africans to recognize the food value of these new crops, especially in drought-prone areas. As the principal farmers in Central Africa, women must have played an important role in learning how to cultivate, harvest, and prepare these foods. By the eighteenth century Lunda rulers hundreds of miles from the Angolan coast were actively promoting the cultivation of maize and cassava on their royal estates in order to provide a more secure food supply.

Some historians of Africa believe that in the inland areas these Amerindian food crops provided the nutritional base for a population increase that partially offset losses due to the Atlantic slave trade. By supplementing the range of food crops available and by enabling populations to increase in once lightly settled or famine-prone areas, cassava and maize, along with peanuts and other New World legumes, permanently altered Africans' environmental prospects.

---

for the animals. Women formed the majority of the field laborers, even in the great gang. Nursing mothers took their babies with them to the fields. Slaves too old for field labor tended the toddlers.

Because slave ships brought twice as many males as females from Africa, men outnumbered women on Caribbean plantations. As Table 19.1 shows, a little over half of the adult males were employed in nongang work. Some tended the livestock, including the mules and oxen that did the heavy carrying work; others were skilled tradesmen, such as blacksmiths and carpenters. The most important artisan slave was the head boiler, who oversaw the delicate process of reducing the cane sap to crystallized sugar and molasses.

Skilled slaves received rewards of food and clothing or time off for good work, but the most common reason for working hard was to escape punishment. A slave gang was headed by a privileged male slave, appropriately called the **"driver,"** whose job was to ensure that the gang completed its work. Since production quotas

Table 19.1 Slave Occupations on a Jamaican Sugar Plantation, 1788

Occupations and Conditions	Men	Women	Boys and Girls	Total
Field laborers	62	78		140
Tradesmen	29			29
Field drivers	4			4
Field cooks		4		4
Mule-, cattle-, and stablemen	12			12
Watchmen	18			18
Nurse		1		1
Midwife		1		1
Domestics and gardeners		5	3	8
Grass-gang			20	20
Total employed	**125**	**89**	**23**	**237**
Infants			23	23
Invalids (18 with yaws)				32
Absent on roads				5
Superannuated [elderly]				7
Overall total				**304**

Source: Adapted from "Edward Long to William Pitt," in Michael Craton, James Walvin, and David Wright, eds., *Slavery, Abolition, and Emancipation* (London: Longman, 1976), 103. © Michael Craton, James Walvin, and David Wright, reprinted by permission of Pearson Education Limited.

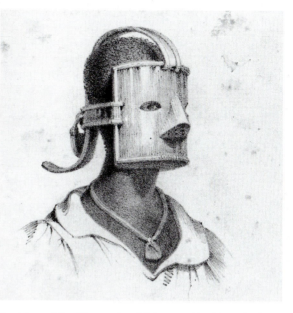

Punishment for Slaves   In addition to whipping and other cruel punishments, slave owners devised other ways to shame and intimidate slaves into obedience. This metal face mask prevented the wearer from eating or drinking.   (By permission of the Syndics of Cambridge University Library)

were high, slaves toiled in the fields from sunup to sunset, except for meal breaks. Those who fell behind due to fatigue or illness soon felt the sting of the whip. Openly rebellious slaves who refused to work, disobeyed orders, or tried to escape were punished with flogging, confinement in irons, or mutilation. Sometimes slaves were punished with an "iron muzzle," which covered their faces and kept them from eating and drinking.

Even though slaves did not work in the fields on Sunday, it was no day of rest, for they had to farm their own provisioning grounds, maintain their dwellings, and do other chores, such as washing and mending their rough clothes. Sunday markets, where slaves sold small amounts of produce or animals they had raised to get a little spending money, were common in the British West Indies.

Except for occasional holidays—including the Christmas-week revels in the British West Indies—there

was little time for recreation and relaxation. Slaves might sing in the fields, but singing was simply a way to distract themselves from their fatigue and the monotony of the work. There was certainly no time for schooling, nor was there willingness to educate slaves beyond skills useful to the plantation.

Time for family life was also inadequate. Although the large proportion of young adults in plantation colonies ought to have had a high rate of natural increase, the opposite occurred. Poor nutrition and overwork lowered fertility. A woman who did become pregnant found it difficult to carry a child to term while continuing heavy fieldwork or to ensure her infant's survival. As a result of these conditions along with disease and accidents from dangerous mill equipment, deaths heavily outnumbered births on West Indian plantations (see Table 19.2). Life expectancy for slaves in nineteenth-century Brazil was only 23 years of age for males and 25.5 years for females. The figures were probably similar for the eighteenth-century Caribbean. A callous opinion, common among slave owners in the Caribbean and in parts of Brazil, held that it was cheaper to import a youthful new slave from Africa than to raise one to the same age on a plantation.

The harsh conditions of plantation life played a major role in shortening slaves' lives, but the greatest killer

Table 19.2   Birth and Death on a Jamaican Sugar Plantation, 1779–1785

Year	Born Males	Born Females	Purchased	Died Males	Died Females	Proportion of Deaths
1779	5	2	6	7	5	1 in 26
1780	4	3	—	3	2	1 in 62
1781	2	3	—	4	2	1 in 52
1782	1	3	9	4	5	1 in 35
1783	3	3	—	8	10	1 in 17
1784	2	1	12	9	10	1 in 17
1785	2	3	—	0	3	1 in 99
Total	19	18	27	35	37	
	Born 37			Died 72		

Source: From "Edward Long to William Pitt," in Michael Craton, James Walvin, and David Wright, eds., *Slavery, Abolition, and Emancipation* (London: Longman, 1976), 105. © Michael Craton, James Walvin, and David Wright, reprinted by permission of Pearson Education Limited.

was disease. The very young were carried off by dysentery caused by contaminated food and water. Slaves newly arrived from Africa went through the period of adjustment to a new environment known as **seasoning,** during which one-third, on average, died of unfamiliar diseases. Slaves also suffered from diseases brought with them, including malaria. On the plantation profiled in Table 19.1, for example, more than half of the slaves incapacitated by illness had yaws, a painful and debilitating skin disease common in Africa. As a consequence, only slave populations in the healthier temperate zones of North America experienced natural increase; those in tropical Brazil and the Caribbean had a negative rate of growth.

Such high mortality greatly added to the volume of the Atlantic slave trade, since plantations had to purchase new slaves every year or two just to replace those who died (see Table 19.2). The additional imports of slaves to permit the expansion of the sugar plantations meant that the majority of slaves on most West Indian plantations were African-born. As a result, African religious beliefs, patterns of speech, styles of dress and adornment, and music were prominent parts of West Indian life.

Given the harsh conditions of their lives, it is not surprising that slaves in the West Indies often sought to regain the freedom into which most had been born. Individual slaves often ran away, hoping to elude the men and dogs who would track them. Sometimes large groups of plantation slaves rose in rebellion against their bondage and abuse. For example, a large rebellion in Jamaica in 1760 was led by a slave named Tacky, who had been a chief on the Gold Coast of Africa. One night his followers broke into a fort and armed themselves. Joined by slaves from nearby plantations, they stormed several plantations, setting them on fire and killing the planter families. Tacky died in the fighting that followed, and three other rebel leaders stoically endured cruel deaths by torture that were meant to deter others from rebellion.

Because they believed rebellions were usually led by slaves with the strongest African heritage, European planters tried to curtail African cultural traditions. They required slaves to learn the colonial language and discouraged the use of African languages by deliberately mixing slaves from different parts of Africa. In French and Portuguese colonies, slaves were encouraged to adopt Catholic religious practices, though African deities and beliefs also survived. In the British West Indies, where only Quaker slave owners encouraged Christianity among their slaves before 1800, African herbal medicine remained strong, as did African beliefs concerning nature spirits and witchcraft.

Free Whites and Free Blacks

The lives of the small minority of free people were very different from the lives of slaves. In the French colony of Saint Domingue, which had nearly half of the slaves in the Caribbean in the eighteenth century, free people fell into three distinct groups. At the top of free society were the wealthy owners of large sugar plantations (the *grands*

The Unknown Maroon of Saint-Domingue This modern sculpture by Albert Mangonès celebrates the brave but perilous life of a runaway slave, who is shown drinking water from a seashell. (Albert Mangonès, "The Unknown Maroon of Saint-Domingue." From Richard Price, *Maroon Societies,* Johns Hopkins University Press. Reproduced with permission.)

blancs°, or "great whites"), who dominated the economy and society of the island. Second came less-well-off Europeans (*petits blancs*°, or "little whites"). Most of them raised provisions for local consumption and crops such as coffee, indigo, and cotton for export, relying on their own and slave labor. Third came the free blacks. Though nearly as numerous as the free whites and engaged in similar occupations, they ranked below whites socially. A few free blacks became wealthy enough to own their own slaves.

The dominance of the plantocracy was even greater in British colonies. Whereas sugar constituted about half of Saint Domingue's exports, in Jamaica the figure was over 80 percent. Such concentration on sugar cane left much less room for small cultivators, white or black, and confined most landholding to a few larger owners. At midcentury three-quarters of the farmland in Jamaica belonged to individuals who owned 1,000 acres (400 hectares) or more.

One source estimated that a planter had to invest nearly £20,000 ($100,000) to acquire even a medium-size Jamaican plantation of 600 acres (240 hectares) in 1774. A third of this money went for land on which to grow sugar and food crops, pasture animals, and cut timber and firewood. A quarter of the expense was for the sugar works and other equipment. The largest expense was to purchase 200 slaves at about £40 ($200) each. In comparison, the wage of an English rural laborer at this time was about £10 ($50) a year (one-fourth the price of a slave), and the annual incomes in 1760 of the ten wealthiest noble families in Britain averaged only £20,000 each.

Reputedly the richest Englishmen of this time, West Indian planters often translated their wealth into political power and social prestige. The richest planters put their plantations under the direction of managers and lived in Britain, often on rural estates that once had been the preserve of country gentlemen. Between 1730 and 1775 seventy of these absentee planters secured election to the British Parliament, where they formed an influential voting bloc. Those who resided in the West Indies had political power as well, for the British plantocracy controlled the colonial assemblies.

Most Europeans in plantation colonies were single males. Many of them took advantage of slave women for sexual favors or took slave mistresses. A slave owner who fathered a child by a female slave often gave both mother and child their freedom. In some colonies such **manumission** (a legal grant of freedom to an individual slave) produced a significant free black population. By the late eighteenth century free blacks were more numerous than slaves in most of the Spanish colonies. They made up almost 30 percent of the black population of Brazil, and they existed in significant numbers in the French colonies. Free blacks were far less common in the British colonies and the United States, where manumission was rare.

As in Brazil (see Chapter 18), escaped slaves constituted another part of the free black population. In the Caribbean runaways were known as **maroons.** Maroon communities were especially numerous in the mountainous interiors of Jamaica and Hispaniola as well as in the island parts of the Guianas°. Jamaican maroons, after withstanding several attacks by the colony's militia, signed a treaty in 1739 that recognized their independence in return for their cooperation in stopping new runaways and suppressing slave revolts. Similar treaties with the large maroon population in the Dutch colony of Surinam (Dutch Guiana) recognized their possession of large inland regions.

---

grands blancs (grawn blawnk)   **petits blancs** (pay-TEE blawnk)

Guianas (guy-AHN-uhs)

CREATING THE ATLANTIC ECONOMY

At once archaic in their cruel system of slavery and oddly modern in their specialization in a single product, the West Indian plantation colonies were the bittersweet fruits of a new Atlantic trading system. Changes in the type and number of ships crossing the Atlantic illustrate the rise of this new system. The Atlantic trade of the sixteenth century calls to mind the treasure fleet, an annual convoy of from twenty to sixty ships laden with silver and gold bullion from Spanish America. Two different vessels typify the far more numerous Atlantic voyages of the late seventeenth and eighteenth centuries. One was the sugar ship, returning to Europe from the West Indies or Brazil crammed with barrels of brown sugar destined for further refinement. At the end of the seventeenth century an average of 266 sugar ships sailed every year just from the small island of Barbados. The second type of vessel was the slave ship. At the trade's peak between 1760 and 1800, some 300 ships, crammed with an average of 250 African captives each, crossed the Atlantic to the Americas each year.

Many separate pieces went into the creation of the new Atlantic economy. Besides the plantation system itself, three other elements merit further investigation: new economic institutions, new partnerships between private investors and governments in Europe, and new working relationships between European and African merchants. The new trading system is a prime example of how European capitalist relationships were reshaping the world.

Capitalism and Mercantilism

The Spanish and Portuguese voyages of exploration in the fifteenth and sixteenth centuries were government ventures, and both countries tried to keep their overseas trade and colonies royal monopolies (see Chapters 16 and 18). Monopoly control, however, proved both expensive and inefficient. The success of the Atlantic economy in the seventeenth and eighteenth centuries owed much to private enterprise, which made trading venues more efficient and profitable. European private investors were attracted by the profits they could make from an established and growing trading and colonial system, but their successful participation in the Atlantic economy depended on new institutions and a significant measure of government protection that reduced the likelihood of catastrophic loss.

Two European innovations enabled private investors to fund the rapid growth of the Atlantic economy. One was the ability to manage large financial resources through mechanisms that modern historians have labeled **capitalism.** The essence of early modern capitalism was a system of large financial institutions—banks, stock exchanges, and chartered trading companies—that enabled wealthy investors to reduce risks and increase profits. Originally developed for business dealings within Europe, the capitalist system expanded overseas in the seventeenth century, when slow economic growth in Europe led many investors to seek greater profits abroad.

Banks were a central capitalist institution. By the early seventeenth century Dutch banks had developed such a reputation for security that individuals and governments from all over western Europe entrusted them with large sums of money. To make a profit, the banks invested these funds in real estate, local industries, loans to governments, and overseas trade.

Individuals seeking returns higher than the low rate of interest paid by banks could purchase shares in a joint-stock company, a sixteenth-century forerunner of the modern corporation. Shares were bought and sold in specialized financial markets called stock exchanges. The Amsterdam Exchange, founded in 1530, became the greatest stock market in the seventeenth and eighteenth centuries. To reduce risks in overseas trading, merchants and trading companies bought insurance on their ships and cargoes from specialized companies that agreed to cover losses.

The capitalism of these centuries was buttressed by **mercantilism,** policies adopted by European states to promote their citizens' overseas trade and accumulate capital in the form of precious metals, especially gold and silver. Mercantilist policies strongly discouraged citizens from trading with foreign merchants and used armed force when necessary to secure exclusive relations.

Chartered companies were one of the first examples of mercantilist capitalism. A charter issued by the government of the Netherlands in 1602 gave the Dutch East India Company a legal monopoly over all Dutch trade in the Indian Ocean. This privilege encouraged private investors to buy shares in the company. They were amply rewarded when Dutch East India Company captured control of long-distance trade routes in the Indian Ocean from the Portuguese (see Chapter 20). As we have seen, a sister firm, the Dutch West India Company, was chartered in 1621 to engage in the Atlantic trade and to seize sugar-producing areas in Brazil and African slaving ports from the Portuguese.

Such successes inspired other governments to set up their own chartered companies. In 1672 a royal charter placed all English trade with West Africa in the hands of a new Royal African Company, which established its headquarters at Cape Coast Castle, just east of Elmina on the Gold Coast. The French government also played an active role in chartering companies and promoting overseas trade and colonization. Jean Baptiste Colbert°, King Louis XIV's minister of finance from 1661 to 1683, chartered French East India and French West India Companies to reduce French colonies' dependence on Dutch and English traders.

French and English governments also used military force in pursuit of commercial dominance, especially to break the trading advantage of the Dutch in the Americas. Restrictions on Dutch access to French and English colonies provoked a series of wars with the Netherlands between 1652 and 1678 (see Chapter 18), during which the larger English and French navies defeated the Dutch and drove the Dutch West India Company into bankruptcy.

With Dutch competition in the Atlantic reduced, the French and English governments moved to revoke the monopoly privileges of their chartered companies. England opened trade in Africa to any English subject in 1698 on the grounds that ending monopolies would be "highly beneficial and advantageous to this kingdom." It was hoped that such competition would also cut the cost of slaves to West Indian planters, though the demand for slaves soon drove the prices up again.

Such new mercantilist policies fostered competition among a nation's own citizens, while using high tariffs and restrictions to exclude foreigners. In the 1660s England had passed a series of Navigation Acts that confined trade with its colonies to English ships and cargoes. The French called their mercantilist legislation, first codified in 1698, the *Exclusif*°, highlighting its exclusionary intentions. Other mercantilist laws defended manufacturing and processing interests in Europe against competition from colonies, imposing prohibitively high taxes on any manufactured goods and refined sugar imported from the colonies.

As a result of such mercantilist measures, the Atlantic became Britain, France, and Portugal's most important overseas trading area in the eighteenth century. Britain's imports from its West Indian colonies in this period accounted for over one-fifth of the value of total British imports. The French West Indian colonies played an even larger role in France's overseas trade. Only the Dutch, closed out of much of the American trade, found Asian trade of greater importance (see Chapter 20). Profits from the Atlantic economy, in turn, promoted further economic expansion and increased the revenues of European governments.

Colbert (kohl-BEAR)   *Exclusif* (ek-skloo-SEEF)

The Atlantic Circuit

At the heart of this trading system was a clockwise network of sea routes known as the **Atlantic Circuit** (see Map 19.1). It began in Europe, ran south to Africa, turned west across the Atlantic Ocean to the Americas, and then swept back to Europe. Like Asian sailors in the Indian Ocean, Atlantic mariners depended on the prevailing winds and currents to propel their ships. What drove the ships as much as the winds and currents was the desire for the profits that each leg of the circuit was expected to produce.

The first leg, from Europe to Africa, carried European manufactures—notably metal bars, hardware, and guns—as well as great quantities of cotton textiles brought from India. Some of these goods were traded for West African gold, timber, and other products, which were taken back to Europe. More goods went to purchase slaves, who were transported across the Atlantic to the plantation colonies in the part of the Atlantic Circuit known as the **Middle Passage.** On the third leg, plantation goods from the colonies returned to Europe. Each leg carried goods from where they were abundant and relatively cheap to where they were scarce and therefore more valuable. Thus, in theory, each leg of the Atlantic Circuit could earn much more than its costs, and a ship that completed all three legs could return a handsome profit to its owners. In practice, shipwrecks, deaths, piracy, and other risks could turn profit into loss.

The three-sided Atlantic Circuit is only the simplest model of Atlantic trade. Many other trading voyages supplemented the basic circuit. Cargo ships made long voyages from Europe to the Indian Ocean, passed southward through the Atlantic with quantities of African gold and American silver, and returned with the cotton textiles necessary to the African trade. Other sea routes brought the West Indies manufactured goods from Europe or foodstuffs and lumber from New England. In addition, some Rhode Island and Massachusetts merchants participated in a "Triangular Trade" that carried rum to West Africa, slaves to the West Indies, and molasses and rum back to New England. There was also a considerable two-way trade between Brazil and Angola that exchanged Brazilian liquor and other goods for slaves. On another route, Brazil and Portugal exchanged sugar and gold for European imports.

European interests dominated the Atlantic system. The manufacturers who supplied the trade goods and the investors who provided the capital were all based in Europe, but so too were the principal consumers of the plantation products. Before the seventeenth century, sugar had been rare and fairly expensive in western Europe. By 1700 annual consumption of sugar in England had risen to about 4 pounds (nearly 2 kilograms) per

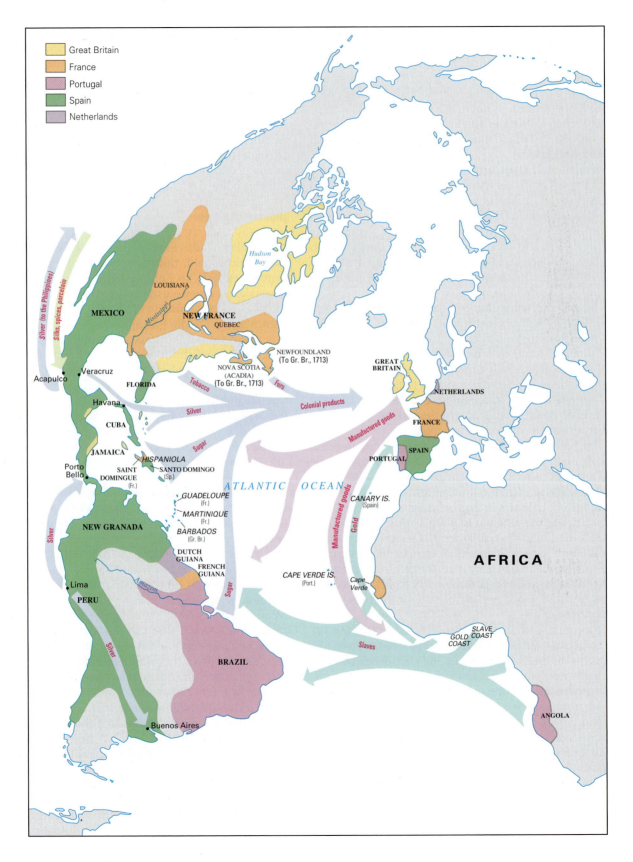

Great Britain
France
Portugal
Spain
Netherlands

Silver (to the Philippines)
Silks, spices, porcelain

Hudson Bay

LOUISIANA

MEXICO

Mississippi

NEW FRANCE
QUEBEC

NEWFOUNDLAND
(To Gr. Br., 1713)

NOVA SCOTIA
(ACADIA)
(To Gr. Br., 1713)

GREAT BRITAIN

NETHERLANDS

Acapulco
Veracruz

FLORIDA

Tobacco

Furs

FRANCE

Havana

Silver

Colonial products

Manufactured goods

CUBA

Sugar

SPAIN

JAMAICA

PORTUGAL

Porto Bello

HISPANIOLA
SAINT
DOMINGUE
(Fr.)

SANTO DOMINGO
(Sp.)

GUADELOUPE
(Fr.)

ATLANTIC OCEAN

CANARY IS.
(Spain)

Manufactured goods

Gold

MARTINIQUE
(Fr.)

NEW GRANADA

BARBADOS
(Gr. Br.)

DUTCH
GUIANA
FRENCH
GUIANA

Amazon

Silver

Lima

PERU

Sugar

CAPE VERDE IS.
(Port.)

Cape
Verde

AFRICA

Silver

BRAZIL

Slaves

SLAVE
COAST
GOLD
COAST

Buenos Aires

ANGOLA

Slave Ship   This model of the English vessel *Brookes* shows the specially built section of the hold where enslaved Africans were packed together during the Middle Passage. Girls, boys, and women were confined separately.   (Wilberforce House Museum, Hull, Humberside, UK/The Bridgeman Art Library, London and New York)

person. Rising western European prosperity and declining sugar prices promoted additional consumption, starting with the upper classes and working its way down the social ladder. People spooned sugar into popular new beverages imported from overseas—tea, coffee, and chocolate—to overcome the beverages' natural bitterness. By 1750 annual sugar consumption in Britain had doubled, and it doubled again to about 18 pounds (8 kilograms) per person by the early nineteenth century (well below the American average of about 100 pounds [45 kilograms] a year in 1960).

The flow of sugar to Europe depended on another key component of the Atlantic trading system: the flow of slaves from Africa (see Map 19.2). The rising volume of the Middle Passage also measures the Atlantic system's expansion. During the first 150 years after the European discovery of the Americas, some 800,000 Africans had begun the journey across the Atlantic. During the boom in sugar production between 1650 and 1800, the slave trade amounted to nearly 7.5 million. Of the survivors,

Map 19.1   The Atlantic Economy   By 1700 the volume of maritime exchanges among the Atlantic continents had begun to rival the trade of the Indian Ocean basin. Notice the trade in consumer products, slave labor, precious metals, and other goods. Silver trade to East Asia laid the basis for a Pacific Ocean economy.

over half landed in the West Indies and nearly a third in Brazil. Plantations in North America imported another 5 percent, and the rest went to other parts of Spanish America (see Figure 19.1).

In these peak decades, the transportation of slaves from Africa was a highly specialized trade, although it regularly attracted some amateur traders hoping to make a quick profit. Most slaves were carried in ships that had been specially built or modified for the slave trade by the construction between the ships' decks of additional platforms on which the human cargo was packed as tightly as possible.

Seventeenth-century mercantilist policies placed much of the Atlantic slave trade in the hands of chartered companies. During their existence the Dutch West India Company and the English Royal African Company each carried about 100,000 slaves across the Atlantic. In the eighteenth century private English traders from Liverpool and Bristol controlled about 40 percent of the slave trade. The French, operating out of Nantes and Bordeaux, handled about half as much, but the Dutch hung on to only 6 percent. The Portuguese supplying Brazil and other places had nearly 30 percent of the Atlantic slave trade, in contrast to the 3 percent carried in North American ships.

To make a profit, European slave traders had to buy slaves in Africa for less than the cost of the goods they traded in return. Then they had to deliver as many

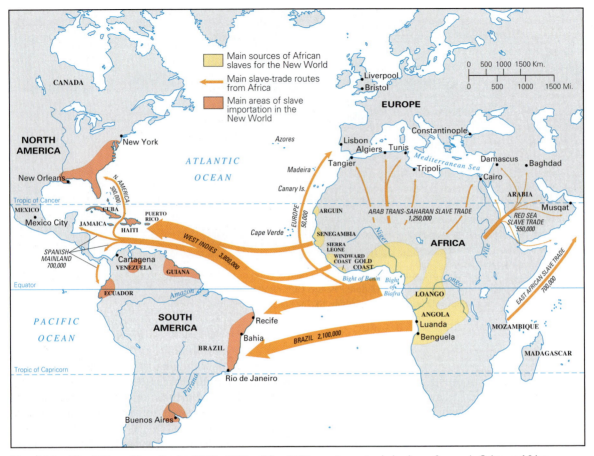

Map 19.2   The African Slave Trade, 1500–1800   After 1500 a vast new trade in slaves from sub-Saharan Africa to the Americas joined the ongoing slave trade to the Islamic states of North Africa, the Middle East, and India. The West Indies were the major destination of the Atlantic slave trade, followed by Brazil.

healthy slaves as possible across the Atlantic for resale in the plantation colonies. The treacherous voyage to the Americas lasted from six to ten weeks. Some ships completed it with all of their slaves alive, but large, even catastrophic, losses of life were common (see Figure 19.1). On average, however, slave transporters succeeded in lowering mortality during the Middle Passage from about 23 percent on voyages before 1700 to half that in the last half of the eighteenth century.

Some deaths resulted from the efforts of the captives to escape. As on the voyage of the *Hannibal* recounted at the beginning of the chapter, male slaves were shackled together to prevent them from trying to escape while they were still in sight of land. Because some still managed to jump overboard in pairs, slave ships were outfitted with special netting around the outside. Some slaves developed deep psychological depression, known to

contemporaries as "fixed melancholy." Crews force-fed slaves who refused to eat, but some successfully willed themselves to death.

When opportunities presented themselves (nearness to land, illness among the crew), some enslaved Africans tried to overpower their captors. To inhibit such mutinies, African men were confined below deck during most of the voyage, except at mealtimes when they were brought up in small groups under close supervision. In any event, "mutinies" were rarely successful and were put down with brutality that occasioned further losses of life.

Other deaths during the Middle Passage were due to ill treatment. Although it was in the interests of the captain and crew to deliver their slave cargo in good condition, whippings, beatings, and even executions were used to maintain order or force captives to take nourishment. Moreover, the dangers and brutalities of the slave trade were so notorious that many ordinary seamen shunned such work. As a consequence, cruel and brutal officers and crews abounded on slave ships.

Although examples of unspeakable cruelties are common in the records, most deaths in the Middle Passage were the result of disease rather than abuse, as the voyage of the *Hannibal* illustrated. Dysentery spread by contaminated food and water caused many deaths. Other slaves died of contagious diseases such as smallpox carried by persons whose infections were not detected during medical examinations prior to boarding. Such maladies spread quickly in the crowded and unsanitary confines of the ships, claiming the lives of many slaves already physically weakened and mentally traumatized by their ordeals.

Crew members in close contact with the slaves were exposed to the same epidemics and also died in great numbers. Moreover, sailors often fell victim to tropical diseases, such as malaria, to which Africans had acquired resistance. It is a measure of the callousness of the age, as well as the cheapness of European labor, that over the course of a round-trip voyage from Europe the proportion of crew deaths could be as high as the slave deaths.

AFRICA, THE ATLANTIC, AND ISLAM

The Atlantic system took a terrible toll in African lives both during the Middle Passage and under the harsh conditions of plantation slavery. Many other Africans died while being marched to African coastal ports for sale overseas. The overall effects on Africa of these losses and of other aspects of the slave trade have been the subject of considerable historical debate. It is clear that the trade's impact depended on the intensity and terms of different African regions' involvement.

Any assessment of the Atlantic system's effects in Africa must also take into consideration the fact that some Africans profited from the trade by capturing and selling slaves. They chained the slaves together or bound them to forked sticks for the march to the coast, then bartered them to the European slavers for trade goods. The effects on the enslaver were different from the effects on the enslaved. Finally, a broader understanding of the Atlantic system's effects in sub-Saharan Africa comes from comparisons with the effects of Islamic contacts.

The Gold Coast and the Slave Coast

As Chapter 16 showed, early European visitors to Africa's Atlantic coast were interested more in trading than in colonizing or controlling the continent. As the Africa trade mushroomed after 1650, this pattern continued. African kings and merchants sold slaves and goods at many new coastal sites, but the growing slave trade did not lead to substantial European colonization.

The transition to slave trading was not sudden. Even as slaves were becoming Atlantic Africa's most valuable export, goods such as gold, ivory, and timber remained a significant part of the total trade. For example, during its eight decades of operation from 1672 to 1752, the Royal African Company made 40 percent of its profits from dealings in gold, ivory, and forest products. In some parts of West Africa, such nonslave exports remained predominant even at the peak of the trade.

African merchants were very discriminating about what merchandise they received in return for slaves or goods. A European ship that arrived with goods of low quality or not suited to local tastes found it hard to purchase a cargo at a profitable price. European guidebooks to the African trade carefully noted the color and shape of beads, the pattern of textiles, the type of guns, and the sort of metals that were in demand on each section of the coast. In the early eighteenth century the people of Sierra Leone had a strong preference for large iron kettles; brass pans were preferred on the Gold Coast; and iron and copper bars were in demand in the Niger Delta, where smiths turned them into useful objects (see Map 19.3).

Although preferences for merchandise varied, Africans' greatest demands were for textiles, hardware, and guns. Of the goods the Royal African Company traded in West Africa in the 1680s, over 60 percent were Indian and European textiles and 30 percent were hardware and weaponry. Beads and other jewelry made up 3 percent. The rest consisted of cowrie shells that were used as money. In the eighteenth century, tobacco and rum from the Americas became welcome imports.

Both Europeans and Africans attempted to drive the best bargain for themselves and sometimes engaged in deceitful practices. The strength of the African bargaining position, however, may be inferred from the fact that as the demand for slaves rose, so too did their price in Africa. In the course of the eighteenth century the goods needed to purchase a slave on the Gold Coast doubled and in some places tripled or quadrupled.

West Africans' trading strengths were reinforced by African governments on the Gold and Slave Coasts that made Europeans observe African trading customs and

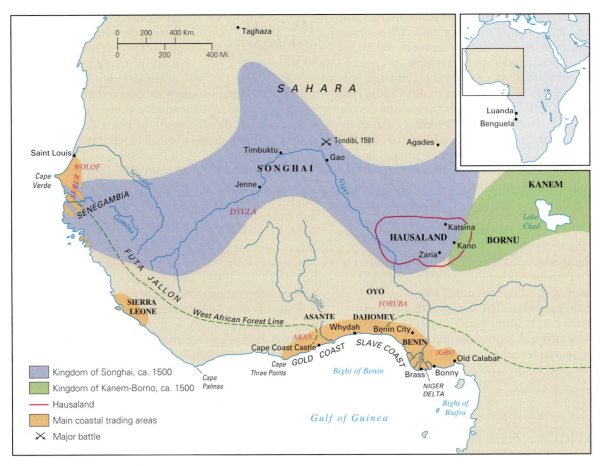

Map 19.3   West African States and Trade, 1500–1800   The Atlantic and the trans-Saharan trade brought West Africans new goods and promoted the rise of powerful states and trading communities. The Moroccan invasion of Songhai and Portuguese colonization of the Angolan ports of Luanda and Benguela showed the political dangers of such relations.

prevented them from taking control of African territory. Rivalry among European nations, each of which established its own trading "castles" along the Gold Coast, also reduced Europeans' bargaining strength. In 1700 the head of the Dutch East India Company in West Africa, Willem Bosman°, bemoaned the fact that, to stay competitive against the other European traders, his company had to include large quantities of muskets and gunpowder in the goods it exchanged, thereby adding to Africans' military power.

Bosman also related that before being allowed to buy slaves at Whydah on the Slave Coast, his agents first had to pay the king a substantial customs duty and then pay a premium price for whatever slaves the king had to sell. By African standards, Whydah was a rather small kingdom controlling only that port and its immediate hinterland. In 1727 it was annexed by the larger kingdom of Dahomey°, which maintained a strong trading position with Europeans at the coast. Dahomey's rise in the 1720s depended heavily on the firearms that the slave trade supplied for its well-trained armies of men and women.

In the cases of two of Dahomey's neighbors, the connections between state growth and the Atlantic trade were more complex. One was the inland Oyo° kingdom to the northeast. Oyo cavalry overran Dahomey in 1730 and forced it to pay an annual tribute to keep its independence. The other was the newer kingdom of Asante°,

---

Willem Bosman (VIL-uhm boos-MAHN)

Dahomey (dah-HOH-mee)   **Oyo** (aw-YOH)
Asante (uh-SHAN-tee)

west of Dahomey along the Gold Coast, which expanded rapidly after 1680. Both Oyo and Asante participated in the Atlantic trade, but neither kingdom was as dependent on it as Dahomey. Overseas trade formed a relatively modest part of the economies of these large and populous states and was balanced by their extensive overland trade with their northern neighbors and with states across the Sahara. Like the great medieval empires of the western Sudan, Oyo and Asante were stimulated by external trade but not controlled by it.

How did African kings and merchants obtain slaves for sale? Bosman dismissed misconceptions prevailing in Europe in his day. "Not a few in our country," he wrote to a friend in 1700, "fondly imagine that parents here sell their children, men their wives, and one brother the other. But those who think so, do deceive themselves; for this never happens on any other account but that of necessity, or some great crime; but most of the slaves that are offered to us are prisoners of war, which are sold by the victors as their booty."[2] Other accounts agree that prisoners taken in war were the greatest source of slaves for the Atlantic trade, but it is difficult to say how often capturing slaves for export was the main cause of warfare. "Here and there," conclude two respected historians of Africa, "there are indications that captives taken in the later and more peripheral stages of these wars were exported overseas, but it would seem that the main impetus of conquest was only incidentally concerned with the slave-trade in any external direction."[3]

An early-nineteenth-century king of Asante had a similar view: "I cannot make war to catch slaves in the bush, like a thief. My ancestors never did so. But if I fight a king, and kill him when he is insolent, then certainly I must have his gold, and his slaves, and his people are mine too. Do not the white kings act like this?"[4] English rulers had indeed sentenced seventeenth-century Scottish and Irish prisoners to forced labor in the West Indies. One may imagine that the African and the European prisoners did not share their kings' view that such actions were legitimate.

The Bight of Biafra and Angola

In the eighteenth century the slave trade expanded eastward to the Bight° of Biafra. In contrast to the Gold and Slave Coasts, where strong kingdoms predominated, the densely populated interior of the Bight of Biafra contained no large states. Even so, the powerful merchant princes of the coastal ports made European traders give them rich presents. Because of the absence of sizable states, there were no large-scale wars and consequently few prisoners of war. Instead, kidnapping was the major source of slaves.

Through a network of markets and inland routes, some inland African merchants supplied European slave traders at the coast with debtors, victims of kidnapping, and convicted criminals. The largest inland traders of the Bight of Biafra were the Aro of Arochukwu, who used their control of a famous religious oracle to enhance their prestige. The Aro cemented their business links with powerful inland families and the coastal merchants through gifts and marriage alliances.

As the volume of the Atlantic trade along the Bight of Biafra expanded in the late eighteenth century, some inland markets evolved into giant fairs with different sections specializing in slaves and imported goods. In the 1780s an English ship's doctor reported that slaves were "bought by the black traders at fairs, which are held for that purpose, at a distance of upwards of two hundred miles from the sea coast." He reported seeing between twelve hundred and fifteen hundred enslaved men and women arriving at the coast from a single fair.[5]

The local context of the Atlantic trade was different south of the Congo estuary at Angola, the greatest source of slaves for the Atlantic trade (see Map 19.2). This was also the one place along the Atlantic coast where a single European nation, Portugal, controlled a significant amount of territory. Except when overrun by the Dutch for a time in the seventeenth century, Portuguese residents of the main coastal ports of Luanda and Benguela° served as middlemen between the caravans that arrived from the far interior and the ships that crossed from Brazil. From the coastal cities Afro-Portuguese traders guided large caravans of trade goods inland to exchange for slaves at special markets. Some markets met in the shadow of Portuguese frontier forts; powerful African kings controlled others.

Many of the slaves sold at these markets were prisoners of war captured by expanding African states. By the late eighteenth century slaves sold from Angolan ports were prisoners of wars fought as far as 600 to 800 miles (1,000 to 1,300 kilometers) inland. Many were victims of wars of expansion fought by the giant federation of Lunda kingdoms. As elsewhere in Africa, such prisoners usually seem to have been a byproduct of African wars rather than the purpose for which the wars were fought.

Research has linked other enslavement with environmental crises in the hinterland of Angola.[6] During

---

Bight (bite)

Benguela (ben-GWAY-luh)

Queen Nzinga of Angola, 1622   This formidable African woman went to great lengths to maintain her royal dignity when negotiating a treaty for her brother with the Portuguese governor of Luanda. To avoid having to stand in his presence, she had one of her women bend herself into a human seat. Nzinga later ruled in her own name and revolted against the Portuguese with the aid of Dutch and African allies.   (Jean-Loup Charmet)

the eighteenth century these southern grasslands periodically suffered severe droughts, which drove famished refugees to better-watered areas. Powerful African leaders gained control of such refugees in return for supplying them with food and water. These leaders built up their followings by assimilating refugee children, along with adult women, who were valued as food producers and for reproduction. However, they often sold into the Atlantic trade the adult male refugees, who were more likely than the women and children to escape or challenge the ruler's authority. Rising Angolan leaders parceled out the Indian textiles, weapons, and alcohol they received in return for such slaves as gifts to attract new followers and to cement the loyalty of their established allies.

The most successful of these inland Angolan leaders became heads of powerful new states that stabilized areas devastated by war and drought and repopulated them with the refugees and prisoners they retained. The slave frontier then moved farther inland. This cruel system worked to the benefit of a few African rulers and merchants at the expense of the many thousands of Africans who were sent to death or perpetual bondage in the Americas.

Although the organization of the Atlantic trade in Africa varied, it was based on a partnership between European and African elites. To obtain foreign textiles, metals, and weapons, African rulers and merchants sold slaves and many products. Most of the exported slaves were prisoners taken in wars associated with African state growth. But strong African states also helped offset the Europeans' economic advantage and hindered them from taking control of African territory. Even in the absence of strong states, powerful African merchant communities everywhere dominated the movement of goods and people. The Africans who gained from these exchanges were the rich and powerful few. Many more Africans were losers in the exchanges.

Africa's European and Islamic Contacts

The ways in which sub-Saharan Africans were establishing new contacts with Europe paralleled their much older pattern of relations with the Islamic world. There were striking similarities and differences in Africans' political, commercial, and cultural interactions with these two external influences between 1500 and 1800.

Traders Approaching Timbuktu   As they had done for centuries, traders brought their wares to this ancient desert-edge city. Timbuktu's mosques tower above the ordinary dwellings of the fabled city.   (The Art Archive)

During the three and a half centuries of contact up to 1800, Africans ceded very little territory to Europeans. Local African rulers kept close tabs on the European trading posts they permitted along the Gold and Slave Coasts and collected lucrative rents and fees from the traders who came there. Aside from some uninhabited islands off the Atlantic coast, Europeans established colonial beachheads in only two places. One was the Portuguese colony of Angola; the other was the Dutch East India Company's Cape Colony at the southern tip of the continent, which was tied to the Indian Ocean trade, not to the Atlantic trade. Unlike Angola, the Cape Colony did not export slaves; rather, most of the 25,750 slaves in its population in 1793 were imported from Madagascar, South Asia, and the East Indies.

North Africa had become a permanent part of the Islamic world in the first century of Islamic expansion. Sub-Saharan Africans had learned of Muslim beliefs and practices more gradually from the traders who crossed the Sahara from North Africa or who sailed from the Middle East to the Swahili trading cities of East Africa. However, the geography, trading skills, and military prowess of sub-Saharan Africans had kept them from

being conquered by expansive Middle Eastern empires. During the sixteenth century all of North Africa except Morocco was annexed to the new Ottoman Islamic empire, and Ethiopia lost extensive territory to other Muslim conquerors, but until 1590 the Sahara was an effective buttress against invasion.

The great **Songhai**° Empire of West Africa was pushing its dominion into the Sahara from the south. Like its predecessor Mali, Songhai drew its wealth from the trans-Saharan trade and was ruled by an indigenous Muslim dynasty (see Map 19.3). However, Songhai's rulers faced a challenge from the northwestern kingdom of Morocco, whose Muslim rulers sent a military expedition of four thousand men and ten thousand camels across the desert. Half the men perished on their way across the desert. Songhai's army of forty thousand cavalry and foot soldiers faced the survivors in 1591, but could not withstand the Moroccans' twenty-five hundred muskets. Although Morocco was never able to annex the western Sudan, for the next two centuries the occupying troops extracted a massive tribute of slaves

---

Songhai (song-GAH-ee)

DIVERSITY AND DOMINANCE

SLAVERY IN WEST AFRICA AND THE AMERICAS

Social diversity was common in Africa and the domination of masters over slaves was a feature of many societies. Ahmad Baba (1556–1627) was an outstanding Islamic scholar in the city of Timbuktu. He came from an old Muslim family of the city. In about 1615 he replied to some questions that had been sent to him. His answers reveal a great deal about the official and unofficial condition of slavery in the Sudan of West Africa, especially in the Hausa states of Kano and Katsina (see Map 19.3).

You asked: What have you to say concerning the slaves imported from the lands of the Sudan whose people are acknowledged to be Muslims, such as Bornu, . . . Kano, Goa, Songhay, Katsina and others among whom Islam is widespread? Is it permissible to possess them [as slaves] or not?

Know—may God grant us and you success—that these lands, as you have stated are Muslim. . . . But close to each of them are lands in which are unbelievers whom the Muslim inhabitants of these lands raid. Some of these unbelievers are under the Muslims' protection and pay them [taxes]. . . . Sometimes there is war between the Muslim sultans of some of these lands and one attacks the other, taking as many prisoners as he can and selling the captive though he is a free-born Muslim. . . . This is a common practice among them in Hausaland; Katsina raids Kano, as do others, though their language is one and their situations parallel; the only difference they recognize among themselves is that so-and-so is a born Muslim and so-and-so is a born unbeliever. . . .

Whoever is taken prisoner in a state of unbelief may become someone's property, whoever he is, as opposed to those who have become Muslims of their own free will . . . and may not be possessed at all.

A little over a century later another African provided information about enslavement practices in the Western Sudan. Ayuba Suleiman Diallo (ah-YOO-bah SOO-lay-mahn JAH-loh) (1701–?) of the state of Bondu some 200 miles from the Gambia River was enslaved and transported to Maryland, where he was a slave from 1731 to 1733. When an Englishman learned of Ayuba's literacy in Arabic, he recorded his life story, anglicizing his name to Job Solomon. According to the account, slaves in Bondu did much of the hard work, while men of Ayuba's class were free to devote themselves to the study of Islamic texts.

In February, 1730, Job's father hearing of an English ship at Gambia River, sent him, with two servants to attend him, to sell two Negroes, and to buy paper, and some other necessaries; but desired him not to venture over the river, because the country of the Mandingoes, who are enemies to the people of Futa, lies on the other side. Job not agreeing with Captain Pike (who commanded the ship, lying then at Gambia, in the service of Captain Henry Hunt, brother to Mr. William Hunt, merchant, in Little Tower-street, London) sent back the two servants to acquaint his father with it, and to let him know that he intended to go no farther. Accordingly . . . he crossed the River Gambia, and disposed of his Negroes for some cows. As he was returning home, he stopped for some refreshment at the house of an old acquaintance; and the weather being hot, he hung up his arms in the house, while he refreshed himself. . . . It happened that a company of the Mandingoes, . . . passing by at that time, and observing him unarmed, rushed in, to the number of seven or eight at once, at a back door, and pinioned Job, before he could get his arms, together with his interpreter, who is a slave in Maryland still. They then shaved their heads and beards, which Job and his man resented as the highest indignity; tho' the Mandingoes meant no more by it, than to make them appear like slaves taken in war. On the 27th of February, 1730, they carried them to Captain Pike at Gambia, who purchased them; and on the first of March they were put on board. Soon after Job found means to acquaint Captain Pike that he was the same person that came to trade with him a few days before, and after what manner he had been taken. Upon this Captain Pike gave him free leave to redeem himself and his man; and Job sent to an acquaintance of his father's, near Gambia, who promised to send to Job's father, to inform him of what had happened, that he might take some course to have him set at liberty. But it being a fortnight's [two weeks'] journey between that friend's house and his father's, and the ship sailing in about a week after, Job was brought with the rest of the slaves to Annapolis in Maryland, and delivered to Mr. Vachell Denton. . . .

Mr. Vachell Denton sold Job to one Mr. Tolsey in Kent Island in Maryland, who put him to work in making tobacco; but he was soon convinced that Job had never been used to such labour. He every day showed more and more uneasiness under this exercise, and at last grew sick, being no way able to bear it; so his master was obliged to find easier work for him, and therefore put him to tend the cattle. Job would often leave the cattle, and withdraw into the woods to pray; but a white boy frequently watched him, and whilst he was at his devotion would mock him and throw dirt in his face. This very much disturbed Job, and added considerably to his other misfortunes; all which were increased by his ignorance of the English language, which prevented his complaining, or telling his case to any person about him. Grown in some measure desperate, by reason of his present hardships, he resolved to travel at a venture; thinking he might possibly be taken up by some master, who would use him better, or otherwise meet with some lucky accident, to divert or abate his grief. Accordingly, he travelled thro' the woods, till he came to the County of Kent, upon Delaware Bay. . . . There is a law in force, throughout the [mid-Atlantic] colonies . . . as far as Boston in New England, viz. that any Negroe, or white servant who is not known in the county, or has no pass, may be secured by any person, and kept in the common [jail], till the master of such servant shall fetch him. Therefore Job being able to give no account of himself, was put in prison there.

This happened about the beginning of June 1731, when I, who was attending the courts there, and heard of Job, went with several gentlemen to the [jailer's] house, being a tavern, and desired to see him. He was brought into the tavern to us, but could not speak one word of English. Upon our talking and making signs to him, he wrote a line to two before us, and when he read it, pronounced the words Allah and Mahommed; by which, and his refusing a glass of wine we offered him, we perceived he was a Mahometan [Muslim], but could not imagine of what country he was, or how he got thither; for by his affable carriage, and the easy composure of his countenance, we could perceive he was no common slave.

When Job had been some time confined, an old Negroe man, who lived in that neighborhood, and could speak the Jalloff [Wolof] language, which Job also understood, went to him, and conversed with him. By this Negroe the keeper was informed to whom Job belonged, and what was the cause of his leaving his master. The keeper thereupon wrote to his master, who soon after fetched him home, and was much kinder to him than before; allowing him place to pray in, and in some other conveniences, in order to make his slavery as easy as possible. Yet slavery and confinement was by no means agreeable to Job, who had never been used to it; he therefore wrote a letter in Arabick to his father, acquainting him with his misfortunes, hoping he might yet find means to redeem him. . . . It happened that this letter was seen by James Oglethorpe, Esq. [founder of the colony of Georgia and

Ayuba Suleiman Diallo (1701–??) (British Library)

director of the Royal African Company]; who, according to his usual goodness and generosity, took compassion on Job, and [bought him from his master]; his master being very willing to part with him, as finding him no ways fit for his business.

In spring 1733 Job's benefactors took him to England, teaching him passable English during the voyage, and introduced him to the English gentry. Job attracted such attention that local men took up a collection to buy his freedom and pay his debts, and introduced him at the royal court. In 1735 Job returned to Gambia in a Royal African Company ship, richly clothed and accompanied by many gifts.

QUESTIONS FOR ANALYSIS

1. Since Ahmad Baba points out that Islamic law permitted a Muslim to raid and enslave non-Muslims, do you think that the non-Mulsim Mandinka (Mandingos) would have considered it justifiable to enslave Ayuba, since he was a Muslim?

2. What aspects of Ayuba Suleiman's experiences of enslavement were normal, and which unusual?

3. How different might Ayuba's experiences of slavery have been had he been sold to Jamaica rather than Maryland?

4. How strictly was the ban against enslaving Muslims observed in Hausaland?

Source: Thomas Hodgkin, ed., *Nigerian Perspectives: An Historical Anthology*, 2d ed. (London: Oxford University Press, 1975), 154–156; Thomas Bluett, *Some Memoirs of the Life of Job, the Son of Solomon the High Priest of Boonda in Africa* (London: Richard Ford, 1734), 16–24.

and goods from the local population and collected tolls from passing merchants.

Morocco's destruction of Songhai weakened the trans-Saharan trade in the western Sudan. The **Hausa** trading cities in the central Sudan soon attracted most of the caravans bringing textiles, hardware, and weapons across the Sahara. The goods the Hausa imported and distributed through their trading networks were similar to those coastal African traders commanded from the Atlantic trade, except for the absence of alcohol (which was prohibited to Muslims). The goods they sent back in return also resembled the major African exports into the Atlantic: gold and slaves. One unique export to the north was the caffeine-rich kola nut, a stimulant that was much in demand among Muslims in North Africa. The Hausa also exported cotton textiles and leather goods.

Few statistics of the slave trade to the Islamic north exist, but the size of the trade seems to have been substantial, if smaller than the transatlantic trade at its peak. Between 1600 and 1800, by one estimate, about 850,000 slaves trudged across the desert's various routes (see Map 19.2). A nearly equal number of slaves from sub-Saharan Africa entered the Islamic Middle East and India by way of the Red Sea and the Indian Ocean.

In contrast to the plantation slavery of the Americas, most African slaves in the Islamic world were soldiers and servants. In the late seventeenth and eighteenth centuries Morocco's rulers employed an army of 150,000 African slaves obtained from the south, whose loyalty they trusted more than the loyalty of recruits from their own lands. Other slaves worked for Moroccans on sugar plantations, as servants, and as artisans. Unlike the case in the Americas, the majority of African slaves in the Islamic world were women who served wealthy households as concubines, servants, and entertainers. The trans-Saharan slave trade also included a much higher proportion of children than did the Atlantic trade, including eunuchs meant for eventual service as harem guards. It is estimated that only one in ten of these boys survived the surgical removal of their genitals.

The central Sudanese kingdom of **Bornu** illustrates several aspects of trans-Saharan contacts. Ruled by the same dynasty since the ninth century, this Muslim state had grown and expanded in the sixteenth century as the result of guns imported from the Ottoman Empire. Bornu retained many captives from its wars or sold them as slaves to the north in return for the firearms and horses that underpinned the kingdom's military power. One Bornu king, Mai Ali, conspicuously displayed his kingdom's new power and wealth while on four pilgrimages to Mecca between 1642 and 1667. On the last, an enormous entourage of slaves—said to number fifteen thousand—accompanied him.

Like Christians of this period, Muslims saw no moral impediment to owning or trading in slaves. Indeed, Islam considered enslaving "pagans" to be a meritorious act because it brought them into the faith. Although Islam forbade the enslavement of Muslims, Muslim rulers in Bornu, Hausaland, and elsewhere were not strict observers of that rule (see Diversity and Dominance: Slavery in West Africa and the Americas).

Sub-Saharan Africans had much longer exposure to Islamic cultural influences than to European cultural influences. Scholars and merchants learned to use the Arabic language to communicate with visiting North Africans and to read the Quran. Islamic beliefs and practices as well as Islamic legal and administrative systems were influential in African trading cities on the southern edge of the Sahara and on the Swahili coast. In some places Islam had extended its influence among rural people, but in 1750 it was still very much an urban religion.

European cultural influence in Africa was even more limited. Some coastal Africans had shown an interest in Western Christianity during the first century of contact with the Portuguese, but in the 1700s only Angola had a significant number of Christians. Coastal African traders found it useful to learn one or more European languages, but African languages dominated inland trade routes. A few African merchants sent their sons to Europe to learn European ways. One of these young men, Philip Quaque°, who was educated in England, was ordained as a priest in the Church of England and became the official chaplain of the Cape Coast Castle from 1766 until his death in 1816. A few other Africans learned to write in a European language, such as the Old Calabar trader Antera Duke who kept a diary in English in the late eighteenth century.

Overall, how different and similar were the material effects of Islam and Europe in sub-Saharan Africa by 1800? The evidence is incomplete, but some assessment is possible with regard to population and possessions.

Although both foreign Muslims and Europeans obtained slaves from sub-Saharan Africa, there was a significant difference in the numbers they obtained. Between 1550 and 1800 some 8 million Africans were exported into the Atlantic trade, compared to perhaps 2 million in the Islamic trade to North Africa and the Middle East. What effect did these losses have on Africa's population? Scholars who have looked deeply into the question generally agree on three points: (1) even at the

---

Quaque (KWAH-kay)

peak of the trade in the 1700s sub-Saharan Africa's overall population remained very large; (2) localities that contributed heavily to the slave trade, such as the lands behind the Slave Coast, suffered acute losses; (3) the ability of a population to recover from losses was related to the proportion of fertile women who were shipped away. The fact that Africans sold fewer women than men into the larger Atlantic trade somewhat reduced its long-term effects.

Many other factors played a role. Angola, for example, supplied more slaves over a longer period than any other part of Africa, but the trade drew upon different parts of a vast and densely populated hinterland. Moreover, the periodic population losses due to famine in this region may have been reduced by the increasing cultivation of high-yielding food plants from the Americas (see Environment and Technology: Amerindian Foods in Africa).

The impact of the goods received in sub-Saharan Africa from these trades is another topic of research. Africans were very particular about what they received, and their experience made them very adept at assessing the quality of different goods. Economic historians have questioned the older idea that the imports of textiles and metals undermined African weavers and metalworkers. First, they point out that on a per capita basis the volume of these imports was too small to have idled many African artisans. Second, the imports are more likely to have supplemented rather than replaced local production. The goods received in sub-Saharan Africa were intended for consumption and thus did not serve to develop the economy. Likewise, the sugar, tea, and chocolate Europeans consumed did little to promote economic development in Europe. However, both African and European merchants profited from trading these consumer goods. Because they directed the whole Atlantic system, Europeans gained far more wealth than Africans.

Historians disagree in their assessment of how deeply European capitalism dominated Africa before 1800, but Europeans clearly had much less political and economic impact in Africa than in the West Indies or on the mainland of the Americas. Still, it is significant that Western capitalism was expanding rapidly in the seventeenth century, while the Ottoman Empire, the dominant state of the Middle East, was entering a period of economic and political decline (see Chapter 20). The tide of influence in Africa was thus running in the Europeans' direction.

CONCLUSION

The new Atlantic trading system had great importance in and momentous implications for world history. In the first phase of their expansion Europeans had conquered and colonized the Americas and captured major Indian Ocean trade routes. The development of the Atlantic system showed their ability to move beyond the conquest and capture of existing systems to create a major new trading system that could transform a region almost beyond recognition.

The West Indies felt the transforming power of capitalism more profoundly than did any other place outside Europe in this period. The establishment of sugar plantation societies was not just a matter of replacing native vegetation with alien plants and native peoples with Europeans and Africans. More fundamentally, it made these once-isolated islands part of a dynamic trading system controlled from Europe. To be sure, the West Indies was not the only place affected. Parts of northern Brazil were touched as deeply by the sugar revolution, and other parts of the Americas were yielding to the power of European colonization and capitalism.

Africa played an essential role in the Atlantic system, importing trade goods and exporting slaves to the Americas. Africa, however, was less dominated by the Atlantic system than were Europe's American colonies. Africans remained in control of their continent and interacted culturally and politically with the Islamic world more than with the Atlantic.

Historians have seen the Atlantic system as a model of the kind of highly interactive economy that became global in later centuries. For that reason the Atlantic system was a milestone in a much larger historical process, but not a monument to be admired. Its transformations were destructive as well as creative, producing victims as well as victors. Yet one cannot ignore that the system's awesome power came from its ability to create wealth. As the next chapter describes, southern Asia and the Indian Ocean basin were also beginning to feel the effects of Europeans' rising power.

■ Key Terms

Royal African Company	maroon
Atlantic system	capitalism
chartered company	mercantilism
Dutch West India Company	Atlantic Circuit
plantocracy	Middle Passage
driver	Songhai
seasoning	Hausa
manumission	Bornu

Suggested Reading

The global context of early modern capitalism is examined by Immanuel Wallerstein, *The Modern World-System,* 3 vols. (1974–1989); by Fernand Braudel, *Civilization and Capitalism, 15th–18th Century,* 3 vols. (1982–1984); and in two volumes of scholarly papers edited by James D. Tracy, *The Rise of Merchant Empires* (1990) and *The Political Economy of Merchant Empires* (1991). Especially relevant are the chapters in *The Rise of Merchant Empires* by Herbert S. Klein, summarizing scholarship on the Middle Passage, and by Ralph A. Austen, on the trans-Saharan caravan trade between 1500 and 1800.

The best general introductions to the Atlantic system are Philip D. Curtin, *The Rise and Fall of the Plantation Complex* (1990); David Ellis, *The Rise of African Slavery in the Americas* (2000); and Robin Blackburn, *The Making of New World Slavery* (1997). Recent scholarly articles on subjects considered in this chapter are available in *The Atlantic Slave Trade: Effects on Economies, Societies, and Peoples in Africa, the Americas and Europe,* ed. Joseph E. Inikori and Stanley L. Engerman (1992); in *Slavery and the Rise of the Atlantic System,* ed. Barbara L. Solow (1991); and in *Africans in Bondage: Studies in Slavery and the Slave Trade,* ed. Paul Lovejoy (1986). Pieter Emmer has edited a valuable collection of articles on *The Dutch in the Atlantic Economy, 1580–1880: Trade, Slavery, and Emancipation* (1998).

Herbert S. Klein's *The Atlantic Slave Trade* (1999) provides a brief overview of research on that subject. A useful collection of debates is David Northrup, ed., *The Atlantic Slave Trade,* 2d ed. (2002). Hugh Thomas's *The Slave Trade: The Story of the Atlantic Slave Trade, 1440–1870* (1999) and Basil Davidson's *The Atlantic Slave Trade,* rev. ed. (1980) are other useful historical narratives. More global in its conception is Patrick Manning, *Slave Trades, 1500–1800: Globalization of Forced Labor* (1996).

The connections of African communities to the Atlantic are explored by David Northrup, *Africa's Discovery of Europe, 1450–1850* (2002); John Thornton, *Africa and Africans in the Making of the Atlantic World, 1400–1800,* 2d ed. (1998); and the authors of *Captive Passage: The Transatlantic Slave Trade and the Making of the Americas* (2002). Still valuable are Margaret E. Crahan and Franklin W. Knight, eds., *Africa and the Caribbean: The Legacies of a Link* (1979), and Richard Price, ed., *Maroon Societies: Rebel Slave Communities in the Americas,* 2d ed. (1979).

Herbert S. Klein's *African Slavery in Latin America and the Caribbean* (1986) is an exceptionally fine synthesis of recent research on New World slavery. The larger context of Caribbean history is skillfully surveyed by Eric Williams, *From Columbus to Castro: The History of the Caribbean* (1984), and more simply surveyed by William Claypole and John Robottom, *Caribbean Story,* vol. 1, *Foundations,* 2d ed. (1990). A useful collection of sources and readings is Stanley Engerman, Seymour Drescher, and Robert Paquette, eds., *Slavery* (2001).

Roland Oliver and Anthony Atmore, *The African Middle Ages, 1400–1800,* 2d ed. (2003), summarize African history in this period. Students can pursue specific topics in more detail in Richard Gray, ed., *The Cambridge History of Africa,* vol. 4 (1975), and B. A. Ogot, ed., *UNESCO General History of Africa,* vol. 5 (1992). For recent research on slavery and the African, Atlantic, and Muslim slave trades with Africa, see Paul Lovejoy, *Transformations in Slavery: A History of Slavery in Africa,* 2d ed. (2000); Claire C. Robertson and Martin A. Klein, eds., *Women and Slavery in Africa* (1983); and Patrick Manning, *Slavery and African Life: Occidental, Oriental, and African Slave Trades* (1990). See also Philip D. Curtin, ed., *Africa Remembered: Narratives by West Africans from the Era of the Slave Trade* (1968, 1997).

Those interested in Islam's cultural and commercial contacts with sub-Saharan Africa will find useful information in James L. A. Webb, Jr., *Desert Frontier: Ecological and Economic Change Along the Western Sahel, 1600–1850* (1995); Elizabeth Savage, ed., *The Human Commodity: Perspectives on the Trans-Saharan Slave Trade* (1992); and J. Spencer Trimingham, *The Influence of Islam upon Africa* (1968).

Notes

1. Eric Williams, *Capitalism and Slavery* (Charlotte: University of North Carolina Press, 1944), 7.
2. Willem Bosman, *A New and Accurate Description of Guinea, etc.* (London, 1705), quoted in David Northrup, ed., *The Atlantic Slave Trade* (Lexington, MA: D. C. Heath, 1994), 72.
3. Roland Oliver and Anthony Atmore, *The African Middle Ages, 1400–1800* (Cambridge, England: Cambridge University Press, 1981), 100.
4. King Osei Bonsu, quoted in Northrup, ed., *The Atlantic Slave Trade,* 93.
5. Alexander Falconbridge, *Account of the Slave Trade on the Coast of Africa* (London: J. Phillips, 1788), 12.
6. Joseph C. Miller, "The Significance of Drought, Disease, and Famine in the Agriculturally Marginal Zones of West-Central Africa," *Journal of African History* 23 (1982), 17–61.

Southwest Asia and the Indian Ocean, 1500–1750

20

Building a Palace This miniature painting from the reign of the Mughal emperor Akbar illustrates the building techniques of seventeenth-century India.

CHAPTER OUTLINE

The Ottoman Empire, to 1750

The Safavid Empire, 1502–1722

The Mughal Empire, 1526–1761

Trade Empires in the Indian Ocean, 1600–1729

DIVERSITY AND DOMINANCE: **Islamic Law and Ottoman Rule**

ENVIRONMENT AND TECHNOLOGY: **Metal Currency and Inflation**

Anthony Jenkinson, merchant-adventurer for the Muscovy Company, which was founded in 1555 to develop trade with Russia, became the first Englishman to set foot in Iran. In 1561 he sailed to Archangel in Russia's frigid north, and from there found his way down the Volga River and across the Caspian Sea. The local ruler he met in northwestern Iran was an object of wonder:

> richly appareled with long garments of silk, and cloth of gold, embroidered with pearls of stone; upon his head was a *tolipane* [headdress shaped like a tulip] with a sharp end pointing upwards half a yard long, of rich cloth of gold, wrapped about with a piece of India silk of twenty yards long, wrought in gold richly enameled, and set with precious stones; his earrings had pendants of gold a handful long, with two rubies of great value, set in the ends thereof.

Moving on to Qazvin°, Iran's capital, Jenkinson met the shah, whom the English referred to as the "Great Sophie" (apparently from Safavi°, the name of the ruling family). "In lighting from my horse at the Court gate, before my feet touched the ground, a pair of the Sophie's own shoes . . . were put upon my feet, for without the same shoes I might not be suffered to tread upon his holy ground."[1] Finding no one capable of reading a letter he carried from Queen Elizabeth, written in Latin, English, Hebrew, and Italian, he nevertheless managed to propose trade between England and Iran. The shah, who was in the midst of negotiations with the Ottoman sultan to end a half-century of hostilities, rejected the idea of diverting Iranian silk from Ottoman markets.

Though Jenkinson and later merchants discovered that Central Asia's bazaars were only meagerly supplied with goods, the idea of bypassing the Ottomans in the eastern Mediterranean and trading directly with Iran through Russia remained tempting. The Ottomans, too, dreamed of outflanking Safavid Iran. In 1569 an Ottoman army unsuccessfully tried to dig a 40-mile (64-kilometer) canal between the Don

River, which opened into the Black Sea, and the Volga, which flowed into the Caspian. Putting Ottoman ships in the Caspian would have facilitated an attack on Iran from the north.

Russia, then ruled by Tsar Ivan IV (r. 1533–1584), known as Ivan the Terrible or Awesome, stood in the Ottoman path. Ivan transformed his principality from a second-rate power into the sultan's primary competitor in Central Asia. In the river-crossed steppe, where Turkic nomads had long enjoyed uncontested sway, Slavic Christian Cossacks from the region of the Don and Dnieper Rivers used armed wagon trains and river craft fitted with small cannon to push southward and establish a Russian presence.

A contest for trade with or control of Central Asia, and beyond that with the Muslim Mughal empire in India, grew out of the centrality conferred on the region by three centuries of Mongol and Turkic conquest. Nevertheless, changes in the organization of world trade were sapping the vitality of the Silk Road, and power was shifting to European seafaring empires linking the Atlantic with the Indian Ocean. For all their naval power in the Mediterranean, neither the Ottomans, the Safavid shahs in Iran, nor the Mughal emperors of India deployed more than a token navy in the southern seas.

As you read this chapter, ask yourself the following questions:

- What were the advantages and disadvantages of a land empire as opposed to a maritime empire?
- What role did religion play in political alliances and rivalries and in the formation of states?
- How did trading patterns change between 1500 and 1750?
- How did imperial rulers maintain dominance over their diverse populations?

THE OTTOMAN EMPIRE, TO 1750

The most long-lived of the post-Mongol Muslim empires, the **Ottoman Empire** grew from a tiny nucleus in 1300 to encompass most of southeastern Europe by

---

Qazvin (kaz-VEEN)   **Safavi** (SAH-fah-vee)

C H R O N O L O G Y			
	Ottoman Empire	**Safavid Empire**	**Mughal Empire**	**Europeans in the Indian Ocean States**

	Ottoman Empire	Safavid Empire	Mughal Empire	Europeans in the Indian Ocean States
1500	**1514** Selim I defeats Safavid shah at Chaldiran; conquers Egypt and Syria (1516–1517) **1520–1566** Reign of Suleiman the Magnificent; peak of Ottoman Empire **1529** First Ottoman siege of Vienna	**1502–1524** Shah Ismail establishes Safavid rule in Iran **1514** Defeat by Ottomans at Chaldiran limits Safavid growth		**1511** Portuguese seize Malacca from local Malay ruler
	1571 Ottoman naval defeat at Lepanto	**1587–1629** Reign of Shah Abbas the Great; peak of Safavid Empire	**1526** Babur defeats last sultan of Delhi at Panipat **1539** Death of Nanak, founder of Sikh religion **1556–1605** Akbar rules in Agra; peak of Mughal Empire	**1565** Spanish establish their first fort in the Philippines
1600				**1600** English East India company founded **1602** Dutch East India Company founded **1606** Dutch reach Australia **1641** Dutch seize Malacca from Portuguese **1650** Omani Arabs capture Musqat from Portuguese
	1610 End of Anatolian revolts	**1622** Iranians oust Portuguese from Hormuz after 108 years	**1658–1707** Aurangzeb imposes conservative Islamic regime **1690** British found city of Calcutta	
1700	**1718–1730** Tulip Period; military decline apparent to Austria and Russia	**1722** Afghan invaders topple last Safavid shah **1736–1747** Nadir Shah temporarily reunites Iran; invades India (1739)	**1739** Iranians under Nadir Shah sack Delhi	**1698** Omani Arabs seize Mombasa from Portuguese **1742** Expansion of French Power in India

the late fifteenth century. Mamluk Syria and Egypt succumbed in the early sixteenth century, leaving the Ottomans with the largest Muslim empire since the original Islamic caliphate in the seventh century. However, the empire resembled the new centralized monarchies of France and Spain (see Chapter 17) more than any medieval model.

Enduring more than five centuries until 1922, the Ottoman Empire survived several periods of wrenching change, some caused by internal problems, others by the growing power of European adversaries. These periods of change reveal the problems faced by huge, land-based empires around the world.

Expansion and Frontiers

At first a tiny state in northwestern Anatolia built by Turkish nomad horsemen, zealous Muslim warriors, and a few Christian converts to Islam (see Map 20.1), the empire grew because of three factors: (1) the shrewdness of its founder Osman (from which the name "Ottoman" comes) and his descendants, (2) control of a strategic link between Europe and Asia at Gallipoli° on the Dardanelles strait, and (3) the creation of an army that took advantage of the traditional skills of the Turkish cavalryman and new military possibilities presented by gunpowder and Christian prisoners of war.

At first, Ottoman armies concentrated on Christian enemies in Greece and the Balkans, conquering a strong Serbian kingdom at the Battle of Kosovo° (in present-day Yugoslavia) in 1389. Much of southeastern Europe and Anatolia was under the control of the sultans by 1402, when Bayazid° I, "the Thunderbolt," confronted Timur's challenge from Central Asia. After Timur defeated and captured Bayazid at the Battle of Ankara (1402), a generation of civil war followed, until Mehmed° I reunified the sultanate.

During a century and a half of fighting for territory both east and west of Constantinople, the sultans repeatedly eyed the heavily fortified capital of the slowly dying Byzantine Empire. In 1453 Sultan Mehmed II, "the Conqueror," laid siege to Constantinople, using enormous cannon to bash in the city's walls, dragging warships over a high hill from the Bosporus strait to the city's inner harbor to avoid its sea defenses, and finally penetrating the city's land walls through a series of infantry assaults. The fall of Constantinople—henceforth commonly known as Istanbul—brought over eleven hundred years of Byzantine rule to an end and made the Ottomans seem invincible.

In 1514, at the Battle of Chaldiran (in Armenia), Selim° I, "the Inexorable," ended a potential threat on his eastern frontier from the new and expansive realm of the Safavid shah in Iran (see below). Although warfare between the two recurred, the general border between the Ottomans and their eastern neighbor dates to this battle. Iraq became a contested and repeatedly ravaged frontier zone.

When Selim conquered the Mamluk Sultanate of Egypt and Syria in 1516 and 1517, the Red Sea became the Ottomans' southern frontier. In the west, the rulers of the major port cities of Algeria and Tunisia, some of them Greek or Italian converts to Islam, voluntarily joined the empire in the early sixteenth century, thereby strengthening its Mediterranean fleets.

The son of Selim I, **Suleiman° the Magnificent** (r. 1520–1566), known to his subjects as Suleiman Kanuni, "the Lawgiver," commanded the greatest Ottoman assault on Christian Europe. Suleiman seemed unstoppable as he conquered Belgrade in 1521, expelled the Knights of the Hospital of St. John from the island of Rhodes the following year, and laid siege to Vienna in 1529. Only the lateness of the season and the need to retreat before the onset of winter saved Vienna's overmatched Christian garrison. In later centuries, Ottoman historians looked back on Suleiman's reign as a golden age when the imperial system worked to perfection.

While Ottoman armies pressed deeper and deeper into eastern Europe, the sultans also sought to control the Mediterranean. Between 1453 and 1502 the Ottomans fought the opening rounds of a two-century war with Venice, the most powerful of Italy's commercial city-states. From the Fourth Crusade of 1204 onward, Venice had assembled a profitable maritime empire that included major islands such as Crete and Cyprus along with strategic coastal strongpoints in Greece. Venice thereby became more than just a trading nation. Its island sugar plantations, exploiting cheap slave labor, competed favorably with Egypt in the international trade of the fifteenth century. With their rivals the Genoese, who traded through the strategic island of Chios, the Venetians stifled Ottoman maritime activities in the Aegean Sea.

The initial fighting left Venice with reduced military power and subject to an annual tribute payment, but it controlled its lucrative islands for another century. The Ottomans, like the Chinese, were willing to let other nations carry trade to and from their ports; they preferred trade of this sort as long as the other nations acknowledged Ottoman authority. It never occurred to them that a sea empire held together by flimsy ships could rival a great land empire fielding an army of a hundred thousand.

In the south Muslims of the Red Sea and Indian Ocean region customarily traded by way of Egypt and Syria. In the early sixteenth century merchants from southern India and Sumatra sent emissaries to Istanbul requesting naval support against the Portuguese. The Ottomans responded vigorously to Portuguese threats close to their territories, such as at Aden at the southern entrance to the Red Sea, but their efforts farther afield fell short of stopping the Portuguese.

So long as eastern luxury products still flowed to Ottoman markets, why commit major resources to subduing an enemy whose main threat was a demand that merchant vessels, mostly belonging to non-Ottoman

---

Gallipoli (gah-LIP-po-lee)   **Kosovo** (KO-so-vo)
Bayazid (BAY-yah-zeed)   **Mehmed** (MEH-met)
Selim (seh-LEEM)

Suleiman (SOO-lay-man)

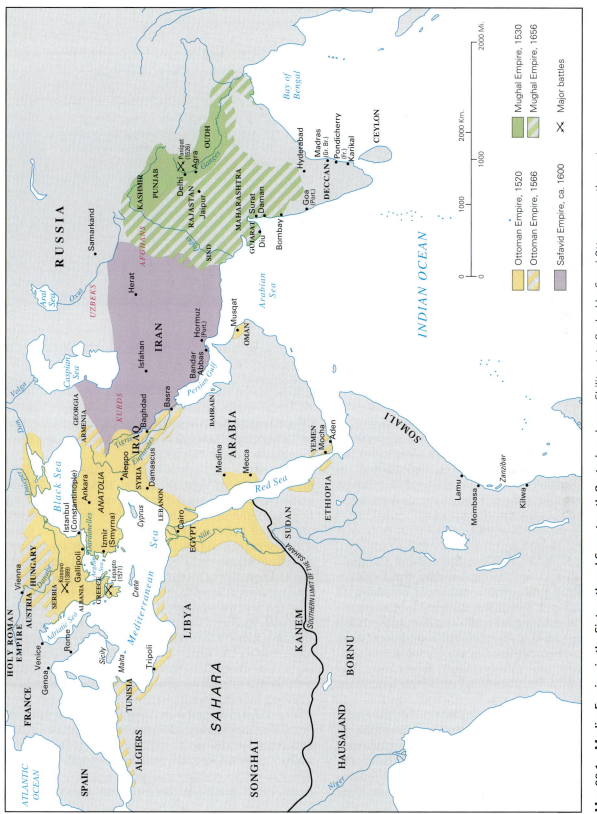

Map 20.1   Muslim Empires in the Sixteenth and Seventeenth Centuries   Iran, a Shi'ite state flanked by Sunni Ottomans on the west and Sunni Mughals on the east, had the least exposure to European influences. Ottoman expansion across the southern Mediterranean Sea intensified European fears of Islam. The areas of strongest Mughal control dictated that Islam's spread into southeast Asia would be heavily influenced by merchants and religious figures from Gujarat instead of from eastern India.

Aya Sofya Mosque in Istanbul   Orginally a Byzantine cathedral, Aya Sofya (in Greek, Hagia Sophia) was transformed into a mosque after 1453, and four minarets were added. It then became a model for subsequent Ottoman mosques. To the right behind it is the Bosporus strait dividing Europe and Asia, to the left the Golden Horn inlet separating the old city of Istanbul from the newer parts. The gate to the Ottoman sultan's palace is to the right of the mosque. The pointed tower to the left of the dome is part of the palace.   (Robert Frerck/Woodfin Camp & Associates)

Muslims, buy protection from Portuguese attack? Portuguese power was territorially limited to fortified coastal points, such as Hormuz at the entrance to the Persian Gulf, Goa in western India, and Malacca in Malaya (see Chapter 16). The Ottomans did send a small naval force to Indonesia, but they never acted consistently or aggressively in the Indian Ocean.

Central Institutions

Heirs of the military traditions of Central Asia, the Ottoman army originally consisted of lightly armored mounted warriors skilled at shooting short bows made of compressed layers of bone, wood, and leather. The conquest of Christian territories in the Balkans in the late fourteenth century, however, gave the Ottomans access to a new military resource: Christian prisoners of war induced to serve as military slaves.

Slave soldiery had a long history in Islamic lands. The Mamluk Sultanate of Egypt and Syria was built on that practice. The Mamluks, however, acquired their new blood from slave markets in Central Asia and the Caucasus. Enslaving Christian prisoners, an action of questionable legality in Islamic law, was an Ottoman innovation.

Converted to Islam, these "new troops," called yeni cheri in Turkish and **"Janissary"°** in English, gave the Ottomans great military flexibility.

Christians by upbringing, the Janissaries had no misgivings about fighting against Turks and Muslims when the sultans attacked in western Asia. Not coming from a culture of horse nomads, they readily accepted the idea of fighting on foot and learning to use guns, which were then still too heavy and awkward for a horseman to load and fire. The Janissaries lived in barracks and trained all year round. Until the mid-sixteenth century, they were barred from holding jobs or marrying.

Selection for Janissary training changed early in the fifteenth century. The new system, called the **devshirme°** (literally "selection"), imposed a regular levy of male children on Christian villages in the Balkans and occasionally elsewhere. Devshirme children were placed with Turkish families to learn their language before commencing military training. The most promising of them received their education at the sultan's palace in Istanbul, where they studied Islam and what we might call the liberal arts in addition to military matters. This regime, sophisticated for its time, produced not only the Janis-

Janissary (JAN-nih-say-ree)   **devshirme** (dev-sheer-MEH)

sary soldiers but also, from among the few who received special training in the inner service of the palace, senior military commanders and heads of government departments up to the rank of grand vizier.

The Ottoman Empire became cosmopolitan in character. The sophisticated court language, Osmanli° (the Turkish form of Ottoman), shared basic grammar and vocabulary with the Turkish spoken by Anatolia's nomads and villagers, but Arabic and Persian elements made it as distinct from that language as the Latin of educated Europeans was from the various Latin-derived Romance languages. People who served in the military or the bureaucracy and conversed in Osmanli belonged to the askeri°, or "military," class, which made them exempt from taxes and dependent on the sultan for their well-being. The mass of the population, whether Muslims, Christians, or Jews—Jews flooded into Ottoman territory after their expulsion from Spain in 1492 (see Chapter 17)—constituted the raya°, literally "flock of sheep."

By the beginning of the reign of Sultan Suleiman, the Ottoman Empire was the most powerful and best-organized state in Europe and the Islamic world. Its military balanced mounted archers, primarily Turks supported by grants of land in return for military service, with Janissaries—Turkified Albanians, Serbs, and Macedonians paid from the central treasury and trained in the most advanced weaponry. Greek, Turkish, Algerian, and Tunisian sailors manned the galley-equipped navy, usually under the command of an admiral from one of the North African ports.

The balance of the Ottoman land forces brought success to Ottoman arms in recurrent wars with the Safavids, who were much slower to adopt firearms, and in the inexorable conquest of the Balkans. In naval matters, a major expedition against Malta that would have given the Ottomans a foothold in the western Mediterranean failed in 1565. Combined Christian forces also achieved a massive naval victory at the Battle of Lepanto, off Greece, in 1571. In a year's time, however, the sultan had replaced all of the galleys sunk in that battle.

Under the land-grant system, resident cavalrymen administered most rural areas in Anatolia and the Balkans. They maintained order, collected taxes, and reported for each summer's campaign with their horses, retainers, and supplies, all paid for from the taxes they collected. When not campaigning, they stayed at home. Some historians maintain that these cavalrymen, who did not own their land, had little interest in encouraging production or introducing new technologies; but since a

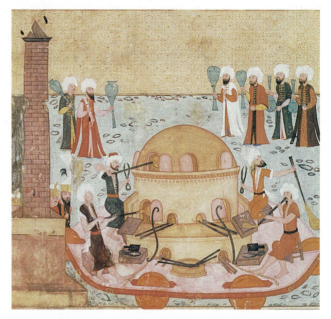

Ottoman Glassmakers on Parade   Celebrations of the circumcisions of the sultan's sons featured parades organized by the craft guilds of Istanbul. This float features glassmaking, a common craft in Islamic realms. The most elaborate glasswork included oil lamps for mosques and colored glass for the small stained-glass windows below mosque domes.   (Topkapi Saray Museum)

militarily able son usually succeeded his father, the grant holders did have some interest in productivity.

The Ottoman conception of the world saw the sultan providing justice for his raya and the military protecting them. In return, the raya paid the taxes that supported both the sultan and the military. In reality, the central government, like most large territorial governments in premodern times, seldom intersected the lives of most subjects. Arab, Turkish, and Balkan townsfolk sought justice in religious law courts and depended on local notables and religious leaders to represent them before Ottoman provincial officials. Balkan regions such as Albania and Bosnia had large numbers of converts, and Islam gradually became the majority religion. Thus the law of Islam (the Shari'a°), as interpreted by local ulama° (religious scholars), conditioned urban institutions and social life (see Diversity and Dominance: Islamic Law and Ottoman Rule). Local customs prevailed among non-Muslims and in many rural areas. Non-Muslims also looked to their own religious leaders for guidance in family and spiritual matters.

Osmanli (os-MAHN-lee)   **askeri** (AS-keh-ree)   **raya** (RAH-yah)

Shari'a (sha-REE-ah)   **ulama** (oo-leh-MAH)

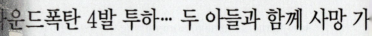

DIVERSITY AND DOMINANCE

ISLAMIC LAW AND OTTOMAN RULE

Ebu's-Su'ud was the Mufti of Istanbul from 1545 to 1574, serving under the sultans Suleiman the Magnificent (1520–1566) and his son Selim II (1566–1574). Originally one of many city-based religious scholars giving opinions on matters of law, the mufti of Istanbul by Ebu's-Su'ud's time had become the top religious official in the empire and the personal adviser to the sultan on religious and legal matters. The position would later acquire the title Shaikh al-Islam.

Historians debate the degree of independence these muftis had. Since the ruler, as a Muslim, was subject to the Shari'a, the mufti could theoretically veto his policies. On important matters, however, the mufti more often seemed to come up with the answer that best suited the sultan who appointed him. This bias is not apparent in more mundane areas of the law.

The collection of Ebu's-Su'ud's fatwas, or legal opinions, from which the examples below are drawn shows the range of matters that came to his attention. They are also an excellent source for understanding the problems of his time, the relationship between Islamic law and imperial governance, and the means by which the state asserted its dominance over the common people. Some opinions respond directly to questions posed by the sultan. Others are hypothetical, using the names Zeyd, 'Amr, and Hind the way police today use John Doe and Jane Doe. While qadis, or Islamic judges, made findings of fact in specific cases on trial, muftis issued only opinions on matters of law. A qadi as well as a plaintiff or defendant might ask a question of a mufti. Later jurists consulted collections of fatwas for precedents, but the fatwas had no permanent binding power.

On the plan of Selim II to attack the Venetians in Crete in 1570   A land was previously in the realm of Islam. After a while, the abject infidels overran it, destroyed the colleges and mosques, and left them vacant. They filled the pulpits and the galleries with the tokens of infidelity and error, intending to insult the religion of Islam with all kinds of vile deeds, and by spreading their ugly acts to all corners of the earth.

His Excellency the Sultan, the Refuge of Religion, has, as zeal for Islam requires, determined to take the aforementioned land from the possession of the shameful infidels and to annex it to the realm of Islam.

When peace was previously concluded with the other lands in the possession of the said infidels, the aforenamed land was included. An explanation is sought as to whether, in accordance with the Pure shari'a, this is an impediment to the Sultan's determining to break the treaty.

Answer: There is no possibility that it could ever be an impediment. For the Sultan of the People of Islam (may God glorify his victories) to make peace with the infidels is legal only when there is a benefit to all Muslims. When there is no benefit, peace is never legal. When a benefit has been seen, and it is then observed to be more beneficial to break it, then to break it becomes absolutely obligatory and binding.

His Excellency [Muhammad] the Apostle of God (may God bless him and give him peace) made a ten-year truce with the Meccan infidels in the sixth year of the Hegira. His Excellency 'Ali (may God ennoble his face) wrote a document that was corroborated and confirmed. Then, in the following year, it was considered more beneficial to break it and, in the eighth year of the Hegira, [the Prophet] attacked [the Meccans], and conquered Mecca the Mighty.

On war against the Shi'ite Muslim Safavids of Iran   Is it licit according to the shari'a to fight the followers of the Safavids? Is the person who kills them a holy warrior, and the person who dies at their hands a martyr?

Answer: Yes, it is a great holy war and a glorious martyrdom.

Assuming that it is licit to fight them, is this simply because of their rebellion and enmity against the [Ottoman] Sultan of the People of Islam, because they drew the sword against the troops of Islam, or what?

Answer: They are both rebels and, from many points of view, infidels.

Can the children of Safavid subjects captured in the Nakhichevan campaign be enslaved?

Answer: No.

The followers of the Safavids are killed by order of the Sultan. If it turns out that some of the prisoners, young and old, are [Christian] Armenian[s], are they set free?

Answer: Yes. So long as the Armenians have not joined the Safavid troops in attacking and fighting against the troops of Islam, it is illegal to take them prisoner.

On the Holy Land   Are all the Arab realms Holy Land, or does it have specific boundaries, and what is the difference between the Holy Land and other lands?

Answer: Syria is certainly called the Holy Land. Jerusalem, Aleppo and its surroundings, and Damascus belong to it.

On land-grants   What lands are private property, and what lands are held by feudal tenure [i.e., assignment in exchange for military service]?

Answer: Plots of land within towns are private property. Their owners may sell them, donate them or convert them to trust. When [the owner] dies, [the land] passes to all the heirs. Lands held by feudal tenure are cultivated lands around villages, whose occupants bear the burden of their services and pay a portion of their [produce in tax]. They cannot sell the land, donate it or convert it to trust. When they die, if they have sons, these have the use [of the land]. Otherwise, the cavalryman gives [it to someone else] by *tapu* [title deed].

On the consumption of coffee   Zeyd drinks coffee to aid concentration or digestion. Is this licit?

Answer: How can anyone consume this reprehensible [substance], which dissolute men drink when engaged in games and debauchery?

The Sultan, the Refuge of Religion, has on many occasions banned coffee-houses. However, a group of ruffians take no notice, but keep coffee-houses for a living. In order to draw the crowds, they take on unbearded apprentices, and have ready instruments of entertainment and play, such as chess and backgammon. The city's rakes, rogues and vagabond boys gather there to consume opium and hashish. On top of this, they drink coffee and, when they are high, engage in games and false sciences, and neglect the prescribed prayers. In law, what should happen to a judge who is able to prevent the said coffee-sellers and drinkers, but does not do so?

Answer: Those who perpetrate these ugly deeds should be prevented and deterred by severe chastisement and long imprisonment. Judges who neglect to deter them should be dismissed.

On matters of theft   How are thieves to be "carefully examined"?

Answer: His Excellency 'Ali (may God ennoble his face) appointed Imam Shuraih as judge. It so happened that, at that time, several people took a Muslim's son to another district. The boy disappeared and, when the people came back, the missing boy's father brought them before Judge Shuraih. [When he brought] a claim [against them on account of the

loss of his son], they denied it, saying: "No harm came to him from us." Judge Shuraih thought deeply and was perplexed.

When the man told his tale to His Excellency 'Ali, [the latter] summoned Judge Shuraih and questioned him. When Shuraih said; "Nothing came to light by the shari'a," ['Ali] summoned all the people who had taken the man's son, separated them from one another, and questioned them separately. For each of their stopping places, he asked: "What was the boy wearing in that place? What did you eat? And where did he disappear?" In short, he made each of them give a detailed account, and when their words contradicted each other, each of their statements was written down separately. Then he brought them all together, and when the contradictions became apparent, they were no longer able to deny [their guilt] and confessed to what had happened.

This kind of ingenuity is a requirement of the case.

[This fatwa appears to justify investigation of crimes by the state instead of by the qadi. Judging from court records, which contain very few criminal cases, it seems likely that in practice, many criminal cases were dealt with outside the jurisdiction of the qadi's court.]

Zeyd takes 'Amr's donkey without his knowledge and sells it. Is he a thief?

Answer: His hand is not cut off.

Zeyd mounts 'Amr's horse as a courier and loses it. Is compensation necessary?

Answer: Yes

In which case: What if Zeyd has a Sultanic decree [authorising him] to take horses for courier service?

Answer: Compensation is required in any case. He was not commanded to lose [the horse]. Even if he were commanded, it is the person who loses it who is liable.

On homicides   Zeyd enters Hind's house and tries to have intercourse forcibly. Since Hind can repel him by no other means, she strikes and wounds him with an axe. If Zeyd dies of the wound, is Hind liable for anything?

Answer: She has performed an act of Holy War.

QUESTIONS FOR ANALYSIS

1. **What do these fatwas indicate with regard to the balance between practical legal reasoning and religious dictates?**

2. **How much was the Ottoman government constrained by the Shari'a?**

3. **What can be learned about day-to-day life from materials of this sort?**

Source: Excerpts from Colin Imber, *Ebu's-Su'ud: The Islamic Legal Tradition* (Stanford, CA: University Press, 1997), 84–88, 93–94, 223–226, 250, 257. Copyright © 1997 Colin Imber, originating publisher Edinburgh University Press. Used with permission of Stanford University Press, www.sup.org.

Crisis of the Military State, 1585–1650

As military technology evolved, cannon and lighter-weight firearms played an ever-larger role on the battlefield. Accordingly, the size of the Janissary corps—and its cost to the government—grew steadily, and the role of the Turkish cavalry, which continued to disdain firearms, diminished. In the mid-sixteenth century, to fill state coffers and pay the Janissaries, the sultan started reducing the number of landholding cavalrymen. Revenues previously spent on their living expenses and military equipment went directly into the imperial treasury. Some of the displaced cavalrymen, armed and unhappy, became a restive element in rural Anatolia.

In the late sixteenth century, inflation caused by a flood of cheap silver from the New World (see Environment and Technology: Metal Currency and Inflation), affected many of the remaining landholders, who collected taxes according to legally fixed rates. Some saw their purchasing power decline so much that they could not report for military service. This delinquency played into the hands of the government, which wanted to reduce the cavalry and increase the Janissary corps. As the central government recovered control of the land, more and more cavalrymen joined the ranks of dispossessed troopers. Students and professors in madrasas (religious colleges) similarly found it impossible to live on fixed stipends from madrasa endowments.

Constrained by religious law from fundamentally reforming the tax system, the government levied emergency surtaxes to obtain enough funds to pay the Janissaries and bureaucrats. For additional military strength, particularly in wars with Iran, the government reinforced the Janissaries with partially trained, salaried soldiers hired for the duration of a campaign. Once the summer campaign season ended, these soldiers found themselves out of work and short on cash.

This complicated situation resulted in revolts that devastated Anatolia between 1590 and 1610. Former landholding cavalrymen, short-term soldiers released at the end of a campaign, peasants overburdened by emergency taxes, and even impoverished students of religion formed bands of marauders. Anatolia experienced the worst of the rebellions and suffered greatly from emigration and loss of agricultural production. Banditry, made worse by the government's inability to stem the spread of muskets among the general public, beset other parts of the empire as well.

In the meantime, the Janissaries took advantage of their growing influence to gain relief from prohibitions on marrying and engaging in business. Janissaries who involved themselves in commerce lessened the burden on the state budget. Married Janissaries who enrolled sons or relatives in the corps made it possible in the seventeenth century for the government to save state funds by abolishing the devshirme system with its traveling selection officers. However, the increase in the total number of Janissaries and their steady deterioration as a military force more than offset these savings.

Economic Change and Growing Weakness, 1650–1750

A very different Ottoman Empire emerged from this period of crisis. The sultan once had led armies. Now he mostly resided in his palace and had little experience of the real world. This manner of living resulted from a gradually developed policy of keeping the sultan's male relatives confined to the palace to prevent them from plotting coups or meddling in politics. The sultan's mother and the chief eunuch overseeing the private quarters of the palace thus became important arbiters of royal favor, and even of succession to the sultanate, while the chief administrators—the grand viziers—oversaw the affairs of government. (Ottoman historians draw special attention to the negative influence of women in the palace after the time of Suleiman, but to some degree they reflect stereotypical male, and Muslim, fears about women in politics.)

The devshirme had been discontinued, and the Janissaries had taken advantage of their increased power and privileges to make membership in their corps hereditary. Together with several other newly prominent infantry regiments, they involved themselves in crafts and trading, both in Istanbul and in provincial capitals such as Cairo, Aleppo, and Baghdad. This activity took a toll on their military skills, but they continued to be a powerful faction in urban politics that the sultans could neither ignore nor reform.

Land grants in return for military service also disappeared. Tax farming arose in their place. Tax farmers paid specific taxes, such as customs duties, in advance in return for the privilege of collecting greater amounts from the actual taxpayers. In one instance, two tax farmers advanced the government 18 million akches° (small silver coins) for the customs duties of the Aegean port of Izmir° and collected a total of 19,169,203 akches, for a profit of 6.5 percent.

Rural administration, already disrupted by the rebellions, suffered from the transition to tax farms. The military landholders had kept order on their lands to maintain their incomes. Tax farmers seldom lived on the land, and their tax collection rights could vary from year to year. The imperial government, therefore, faced

---

akches (ahk-CHEH) **Izmir** (IZ-meer)

Metal Currency and Inflation

Inflation occurs when the quantity of goods and services available for purchase remains stable while the quantity of money in circulation increases. With more money in their pockets, people are willing to pay more to get what they want. Prices go up, and what people think of as the value of money goes down.

Today, with paper money and electronic banking, governments try to control inflation by regulating the printing of money or by other means. Prior to the nineteenth century, money consisted of silver and gold coins, and governments did not keep track of how much money was in circulation. As long as the annual production of gold and silver mines was quite small, inflation was not a worry. In the sixteenth and seventeenth centuries, however, precious metal poured into Spain from silver and gold mines in the New World, but there was no increase in the availability of goods and services. The resulting inflation triggered a "price revolution" in Europe—a general tripling of prices between 1500 and 1650. In Paris in 1650 the price of wheat and hay was fifteen times higher than the price had been in 1500.

This wave of inflation worked its way east, contributing to social disorder in the Ottoman Empire. European traders had more money available than Ottoman merchants and could outbid them for scarce commodities. Lacking silver and gold mines, the Ot-

toman government reduced the amount of precious metal in Ottoman coins. This made the problem worse. Hit hardest were people who had fixed incomes. Cavalrymen holding land grants worth a set amount each year were unable to equip themselves for military campaigns. Students living on fixed scholarships went begging.

Safavid Iran needed silver and gold to pay for imports from Mughal India, which imported few Iranian goods. Iranians sold silk to the Ottoman Empire for silver and gold, worsening the Ottoman situation, and then passed the precious metal on to India. Everyday life in Iran depended on barter or locally minted copper coinage, both more resistant to inflation. Copper for coins was sometimes imported from China.

Though no one then grasped the connection between silver production in Mexico and the trade balance between Iran and India, the world of the sixteenth and seventeenth centuries was becoming more closely linked economically than it had ever been before.

Set of Coin Dies   The lower die, called the anvil die, was set in a piece of wood. A blank disk of gold, silver or copper was placed on top of it. The hammer die was placed on top of the blank and struck with a hammer to force the coin's image onto it.   (Courtesy, Israel Museum, Jerusalem)

greater administrative burdens and came to rely heavily on powerful provincial governors or on wealthy men who purchased lifelong tax collection rights that prompted them to behave more or less as private landowners.

Rural disorder and decline in administrative control sometimes opened the way for new economic opportunities. The port of Izmir, known to Europeans by the ancient name "Smyrna," had a population of around two thousand in 1580. By 1650 the population had increased to between thirty thousand and forty thousand. Along with refugees from the Anatolian uprisings and from European pirate attacks along the coast came European merchants and large colonies of Armenians, Greeks, and

Jews. A French traveler in 1621 wrote: "At present, Izmir has a great traffic in wool, beeswax, cotton, and silk, which the Armenians bring there instead of going to Aleppo . . . because they do not pay as many dues."[2]

Izmir transformed itself between 1580 and 1650 from a small Muslim Turkish town into a multiethnic, multireligious, multilinguistic entrepôt because of the Ottoman government's inability to control trade and the slowly growing dominance of European traders in the Indian Ocean. Spices from the East, though still traded in Aleppo and other long-established Ottoman centers, were not to be found in Izmir. Aside from Iranian silk brought in by caravan, European traders at Izmir purchased local agricultural products—dried fruits, sesame seeds, nuts, and olive oil. As a consequence, local farmers who previously had grown grain for subsistence shifted their plantings more and more to cotton and other cash crops, including, after its introduction in the 1590s, tobacco, which quickly became popular in the Ottoman Empire despite government prohibitions. In this way, the agricultural economy of western Anatolia, the Balkans, and the Mediterranean coast—the Ottoman lands most accessible to Europe (see Map 20.1)—became enmeshed in a growing European commercial network.

At the same time, military power slowly ebbed. The ill-trained Janissaries sometimes resorted to hiring substitutes to go on campaign, and the sultans relied on partially trained seasonal recruits and on armies raised by the governors of frontier provinces. By the middle of the eighteenth century it was obvious to the Austrians and Russians that the Ottoman Empire was weakening. On the eastern front, however, Ottoman exhaustion after many wars was matched by the demise in 1722 of their perennial adversary, the Safavid state of Iran.

The Ottoman Empire lacked both the wealth and the inclination to match European economic advances. Overland trade from the east dwindled as political disorder in Safavid Iran cut deeply into Iranian silk production (see below). Coffee from the highlands of Yemen, a product that rose from obscurity in the fifteenth century to become the rage first in the Ottoman Empire and then in Europe, traditionally reached the market by way of Egypt. By 1770, however, Muslim merchants trading in the Yemeni port of Mocha° (literally "the coffee place") paid 15 percent in duties and fees. But European traders, benefiting from long-standing trade agreements with the sultans, paid little more than 3 percent.

Such trade agreements, called capitulations, led to European domination of Ottoman seaborne trade. Nevertheless, the Europeans did not control strategic ports in the Mediterranean comparable to Malacca in the Indian Ocean and Hormuz on the Persian Gulf, so their economic power stopped short of colonial settlement or direct control in Ottoman territories.

A few astute Ottoman statesmen observed the growing disarray of the empire and advised the sultans to reestablish the land-grant and devshirme systems of Suleiman's reign. Most people, however, could not perceive the downward course of imperial power, much less the reasons behind it. Ottoman historians named the period between 1718 and 1730 the **"Tulip Period"** because of the craze for high-priced tulip bulbs that swept Ottoman ruling circles. The craze echoed a Dutch tulip mania that had begun in the mid-sixteenth century,

when the flower was introduced into Holland from Istanbul, and had peaked in 1636 with particularly rare bulbs going for 2,500 florins apiece—the value of twenty-two oxen. Far from seeing Europe as the enemy that would eventually dismantle the empire, the Istanbul elite experimented with European clothing and furniture styles and purchased printed books from the empire's first (and short-lived) press.

In 1730, however, the gala soirees, at which guests watched turtles with candles on their backs wander in the dark through massive tulip beds, gave way to a conservative Janissary revolt with strong religious overtones. Sultan Ahmed III abdicated, and the leader of the revolt, Patrona Halil°, an Albanian former seaman and stoker of the public baths, swaggered around the capital for several months dictating government policies before he was seized and executed.

The Patrona Halil rebellion confirmed the perceptions of a few that the Ottoman Empire was facing severe difficulties. Yet decay at the center spelled benefit elsewhere. In the provinces, ambitious and competent governors, wealthy landholders, urban notables, and nomad chieftains took advantage of the central government's weakness. By the middle of the eighteenth century groups of Mamluks had regained a dominant position in Egypt, and Janissary commanders had become virtually independent rulers in Baghdad. In central Arabia a conservative Sunni movement inspired by Muhammad ibn Abd al-Wahhab began a remarkable rise beyond the reach of Ottoman power. Although no region declared full independence, the sultan's power was slipping away to the advantage of a broad array of lower officials and upstart chieftains in all parts of the empire while the Ottoman economy was reorienting itself toward Europe.

THE SAFAVID EMPIRE, 1502–1722

The **Safavid Empire** of Iran (see Map 20.1) resembled its longtime Ottoman foe in many ways: it initially used land grants to support its all-important cavalry; its population spoke several languages; it focused on land rather than sea power; and urban notables, nomadic chieftains, and religious scholars served as intermediaries between the people and the government. Certain other qualities, such as a royal tradition rooted in pre-Islamic legends and adoption of Shi'ism, continue to the present day to set Iran off from its neighbors.

Mocha (MOH-kuh)

Patrona Halil (pa-TROH-nuh ha-LEEL)

Safavid Shah with Attendants and Musicians   This painting by Ali-Quli Jubbadar, a European convert to Islam working for the Safavid armory, reflects Western influences. Notice the use of light and shadow to model faces and the costume of the attendant to the shah's right. The shah's waterpipe indicates the spread of tobacco, a New World crop, to the Middle East.   (Courtesy of Oriental Institute, Academy of Sciences, Leningrad. Reproduced from Album of Persian and Indian Miniatures [Moscow, 1962], ill. no. 98)

The Rise of the Safavids

Timur had been a great conqueror, but his children and grandchildren contented themselves with modest realms in Afghanistan and Central Asia, while a number of would-be rulers vied for control elsewhere. In Iran itself, the ultimate victor in a complicated struggle for power among Turkish chieftains was a boy of Kurdish, Iranian, and Greek ancestry named Ismail°, the hereditary leader of a militant Sufi brotherhood called the "Safaviya" for his ancestor Safi al-Din. In 1502, at age sixteen, Ismail proclaimed himself shah of Iran. At around the same time, he declared that henceforward his realm would practice **Shi'ite Islam** and revere the family of Muhammad's son-in-law Ali. He called on his subjects to abandon their Sunni beliefs.

Most of the members of the Safaviya spoke Turkish and belonged to nomadic groups known as qizilbash°, or "redheads," because of their distinctive turbans. Many considered Ismail god incarnate and fought ferociously on his behalf. If Ismail wished his state to be Shi'ite, his word was law to the qizilbash. The Iranian subject population, however, resisted. Neighboring lands gave asylum to Sunni refugees whose preaching and intriguing helped stoke the fires that kept Ismail (d. 1524) and his son Tahmasp° (d. 1576) engaged in war after war. It took a century and a series of brutal persecutions to make Iran an overwhelmingly Shi'ite land. The transformation also involved the importation of Arab Shi'ite scholars from Lebanon and Bahrain to institute Shi'ite religious education at a high level.

Society and Religion

Although Ismail's reasons for compelling Iran's conversion are unknown, the effect was to create a deep chasm between Iran and its neighbors, all of which were Sunni. Iran's distinctiveness had been long in the making, however. Persian, written in the Arabic script from the tenth century onward, had emerged as the second language of Islam. By 1500 an immense library of legal and theological writings; epic, lyric, and mystic poetry; histories; and drama and fiction had come into being. Iranian scholars and writers normally read Arabic as well as Persian and sprinkled their writings with Arabic phrases, but their Arab counterparts were much less inclined to learn Persian. Even handwriting styles differed, Iranians preferring highly cursive forms of the Arabic script.

This divergence between the two language areas had intensified after 1258 when the Mongols destroyed Baghdad, the capital of the Islamic caliphate, and thereby diminished the importance of Arabic-speaking Iraq. Syria and Egypt, under Mamluk rule, had become the heartland of the Arab world, while Iran developed largely on its own, building extensive contacts with India, whose Muslim rulers favored the Persian language.

Where cultural styles had radiated in all directions from Baghdad during the heyday of the Islamic

---

Ismail (IS-ma-eel)   **qizilbash** (KIH-zil-bahsh)
Tahmasp (tah-MAHSP)

caliphate in the seventh through ninth centuries, now Iraq separated an Arab zone from a Persian zone. The post-Mongol period saw an immense burst of artistic creativity and innovation in Iran, Afghanistan, and Central Asia. Painted and molded tiles and tile mosaics, often in vivid turquoise blue, became the standard exterior decoration of mosques in Iran. Architects in Syria and Egypt never used them. The Persian poets Hafez (1319–1389?) and Sa'di (1215–1291) raised morally instructive and mystical-allegorical verse to a peak of perfection. Arabic poetry languished.

The Turks, who steadily came to dominate the political scene from Bengal to Istanbul, generally preferred Persian as a vehicle for literary and religious expression. The Mamluks in Egypt and Syria, however, showed greatest respect for Arabic. The Turkish language, which had a vigorous tradition of folk poetry, developed only slowly, primarily in the Ottoman Empire, as a language of literature and administration. Ironically, Ismail Safavi was a noted religious poet in the Turkish language of his qizilbash followers, while his mortal adversary, the Ottoman Selim I (r. 1512–1520), composed elegant poetry in Persian.

To be sure, Islam itself provided a tradition that crossed ethnic and linguistic borders. Mosque architecture differed, but Iranians, Arabs, and Turks, as well as Muslims in India, all had mosques. They also had madrasas that trained the ulama to sustain and interpret the Shari'a as the all-encompassing law of Islam. Yet local understandings of the common tradition differed substantially.

Each Sufi brotherhood had distinctive rituals and concepts of mystical union with God, but Iran stood out as the land where Sufism most often fused with militant political objectives. The Safaviya was not the first brotherhood to deploy armies and use the point of a sword to promote love of God. The later Safavid shahs, however, banned (somewhat ineffectively) all Sufi orders from their domain.

Even prior to Shah Ismail's imposition of Shi'ism, therefore, Iran had become a distinctive society. Nevertheless, the impact of Shi'ism was significant. Shi'ite doctrine says that all temporal rulers, regardless of title, are temporary stand-ins for the **"Hidden Imam,"** the twelfth descendant of Ali, who was the prophet Muhammad's cousin and son-in-law. Shi'ites believe that leadership of the Muslim community rests solely with divinely appointed Imams from Ali's family, that the twelfth descendant (the Hidden Imam) disappeared as a child in the ninth century, and that the Shi'ite community will lack a proper religious authority until he returns. Some Shi'ite scholars concluded that the faithful should calmly accept the world as it was and wait quietly for the Hidden Imam's

return. Others maintained that they themselves should play a stronger role in political affairs because they were best qualified to know the Hidden Imam's wishes. These two positions, which still play a role in Iranian Shi'ism, tended to enhance the self-image of the ulama as independent of imperial authority and slowed the trend of religious scholars' becoming subordinate government functionaries, as happened with many Ottoman ulama.

Shi'ism also affected the psychological life of the people. Commemoration of the martyrdom of Imam Husayn (d. 680), Ali's son and the third Imam, during the first two weeks of every lunar year regularized an emotional outpouring with no parallel in Sunni lands. Day after day for two weeks (as they do today) preachers recited the woeful tale to crowds of weeping believers, and chanting and self-flagellating men paraded past crowds of reverent onlookers in elaborate street processions, often organized by craft guilds. Passion plays in which Husayn and his family are mercilessly killed by the Sunni caliph's general became a unique form of Iranian public theater.

Of course, Shi'ites elsewhere observed some of the same rites of mourning for Imam Husayn, particularly in the Shi'ite pilgrimage cities of Karbala and Najaf° in Ottoman Iraq. But Iran, with over 90 percent of its population professing Shi'ism, felt the impact of these rites most strongly. Over time, the subjects of the Safavid shahs came to feel more than ever a people apart, even though many of them had been Shi'ite for only two or three generations.

A Tale of Two Cities: Isfahan and Istanbul

Isfahan° became Iran's capital in 1598 by decree of **Shah Abbas I** (r. 1587–1629). Outwardly, Istanbul and Isfahan looked quite different. Built on seven hills on the south side of the narrow Golden Horn inlet, Istanbul boasted a skyline punctuated by the gray stone domes and thin, pointed minarets of the great imperial mosques. Their design derived from Hagia Sophia, the Byzantine cathedral converted to a mosque and renamed Aya Sofya° after 1453. By contrast, the mosques surrounding the royal plaza in Isfahan featured brightly tiled domes rising to gentle peaks and unobtrusive minarets. High walls surrounded the sultan's palace in Istanbul. Shah Abbas focused Isfahan on the giant royal plaza, which was large enough for his army to play polo, and he used an airy palace overlooking the plaza to receive dignitaries and review his troops. This public image contributed to Shah Abbas' being called "the Great."

Najaf (NAH-jaf) **Isfahan** (is-fah-HAHN)
Aya Sofya (AH-yah SOAF-yah)

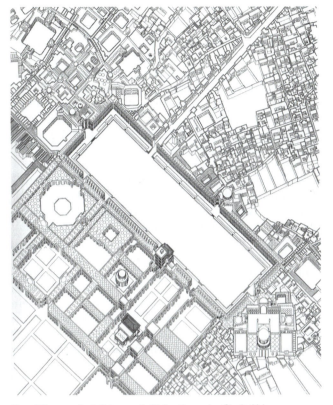

Royal Square in Isfahan   Built by the order Shah Abbas over a period of twenty years starting in 1598, the open space is as long as five football fields (555 by 172 yards). At the upper left end of the square in this drawing is the entrance to the covered bazaar, at the bottom the immense Royal Mosque. The left hand side adjoins the Shah's palace and state administrative office. A multi-story pavilion for reviewing troops and receiving guests overlooks the square across from the smaller domed personal mosque of the Shah.   [Reproduced with permission from Klaus Herdeg, *Formal Structure in Islamic Architecture of Iran and Turkestan* (New York: Rizzoli, 1990)]

The harbor of Istanbul, the primary Ottoman seaport, teemed with sailing ships and smaller craft, many of them belonging to a colony of European merchants perched on a hilltop on the north side of the Golden Horn. Isfahan, far from the sea, only occasionally received European visitors. Along with Jews and Hindus, a colony of Armenian Christians brought in by Shah Abbas who settled in a suburb of the city handled most of its trade.

Beneath these superficial differences, the two capitals had much in common. Wheeled vehicles were scarce in hilly Istanbul and nonexistent in Isfahan, which was within the broad zone where camels supplanted wheeled transport after the rise of the Arab caravan cities in the pre-Islamic centuries. In size and layout both cities favored walking and, aside from the royal plaza in Isfahan, lacked the open spaces common in contemporary European cities. Away from the major mosque complexes, streets were narrow and irregular. Houses crowded against each other in dead-end lanes. Residents enjoyed the privacy of interior courtyards. Artisans and merchants organized themselves into guilds that had strong social and religious as well as economic bonds. The shops of the guilds adjoined each other in the markets.

Women seldom appeared in public, even in Istanbul's mazelike covered market or in Isfahan's long, serpentine bazaar. At home, the women's quarters—called anderun°, or "interior," in Iran and harem, or "forbidden area," in Istanbul—were separate from the public rooms where the men of the family received visitors. Low cushions, charcoal braziers for warmth, carpets, and small tables constituted most of the furnishings. In Iran and the Arab provinces, shelves and niches for books could be cut into thick, mud-brick walls. Residences in Istanbul were usually built of wood. Glazed tile in geometric or floral patterns covered the walls of wealthy men's reception areas.

The private side of family life has left few traces, but it is apparent that women's society—consisting of wives, children, female servants, and sometimes one or more eunuchs (castrated male servants)—had some connections with the outside world. Ottoman court records reveal that women using male agents bought and sold urban real estate, often dealing with inherited shares of their fathers' estates. Some even established religious endowments for pious purposes. The fact that Islamic law, unlike most European codes, permitted a wife to retain her property after marriage gave some women a stake in the general economy and a degree of independence from their spouses. Women also appeared in other types of court cases, where they often testified for themselves, for Islamic courts did not recognize the role of attorney. Although comparable Safavid court records do not survive, historians assume that a parallel situation prevailed in Iran.

European travelers commented on the veiling of women outside the home, but miniature paintings indicate that ordinary female garb consisted of a long, ample dress with a scarf or long shawl pulled tight over the forehead to conceal the hair. Lightweight trousers, either close-fitting or baggy, were worn under the dress. This mode of dress differed little from that of men. Poor men wore light trousers, a long shirt, a jacket, and a brimless cap or turban. Wealthier men wore ankle-length caftans, often closely fitted around the chest, over their trousers. The norm for both sexes was complete coverage of arms, legs, and hair.

anderun (an-deh-ROON)

Istanbul Family on the Way to a Bath House Public baths, an important feature of Islamic cities, set different hours for men and women. Young boys, such as the lad in the turban shown here, went with their mothers and sisters. Notice that the children wear the same styles as the adults. (Osterreichische Nationalbibliothek)

Men monopolized public life. Poetry and art, both somewhat more elegantly developed in Isfahan than in Istanbul, centered as much on the charms of beardless boys as of pretty maidens. Despite religious disapproval of homosexuality, attachments to adolescent boys were neither unusual nor hidden. Women on city streets included non-Muslims, the aged, the very poor, and slaves. Miniature paintings frequently depict female dancers, musicians, and even acrobats in attitudes and costumes that range from decorous to decidedly erotic.

Despite social similarities, the overall flavors of Isfahan and Istanbul were not the same. Isfahan had a prosperous Armenian quarter across the river from the city's center, but it was not a truly cosmopolitan capital. Like other rulers of extensive land empires, Shah Abbas located his capital toward the center of his domain, within comparatively easy reach of any threatened frontier. Istanbul, in contrast, was a great seaport and crossroads located on the straits separating the sultan's European and Asian possessions. People of all sorts lived or spent time in Istanbul—Venetians, Genoese, Arabs, Turks, Greeks, Armenians, Albanians, Serbs, Jews, Bulgarians, and more. In this respect, Istanbul conveyed the cosmopolitan character of major seaports from London to Canton (Guangzhou) and belied the fact that its prosperity rested on the vast reach of the sultan's territories rather than on the voyages of its merchants.

Economic Crisis and Political Collapse

The silk fabrics of northern Iran, monopolized by the shahs, provided the mainstay of the Safavid Empire's foreign trade. However, the manufacture that eventually became most powerfully associated with Iran was the deep-pile carpet made by knotting colored yarns around stretched warp threads. Different cities produced distinctive carpet designs. Women and girls did much of the actual knotting work.

Carpets with geometrical or arabesque designs appear in Timurid miniature paintings, but no knotted "Persian rug" survives from the pre-Safavid era. One of the earliest dated carpets was produced in 1522 to adorn the tomb of Shaikh Safi al-Din, the fourteenth-century founder of the Safaviya. This use indicates the high value accorded these products within Iran. One German visitor to Isfahan remarked: "The most striking adornment of the banqueting hall was to my mind the carpets laid out over all three rostra [platforms to sit on for eating] in a most extravagant fashion, mostly woolen rugs from Kirman with animal patterns and woven of the finest wool."[3]

Overall, Iran's manufacturing sector was neither large nor notably productive. Most of the shah's subjects, whether Iranians, Turks, Kurds, or Arabs, lived by subsistence farming or herding. Neither area of activity recorded significant technological advances during the Safavid period. The shahs granted large sections of the country to the qizilbash nomads in return for mounted warriors for the army. Nomad groups held these lands in common, however, and did not subdivide them into individual landholdings as in the Ottoman Empire. Thus, many people in rural areas lived according to the will of a nomad chieftain who had little interest in building the agricultural economy.

The Safavids, like the Ottomans, had difficulty finding the money to pay troops armed with firearms. This crisis occurred somewhat later in Iran because of its greater distance from Europe. By the end of the sixteenth century, it was evident that a more systematic adoption of cannon and firearms in the Safavid Empire would be needed to hold off the Ottomans and the Uzbeks° (Turkish rulers who had succeeded the Timurids on Iran's Central Asian frontier; see Map 20.1). Like the Ottoman cavalry a century earlier, however, the nomad warriors refused to trade in their bows for firearms. Shah Abbas responded by establishing a slave corps of year-round soldiers and arming them with guns.

The Christian converts to Islam who initially provided the manpower for the new corps came mostly

Uzbeks (UHZ-bex)

from captives taken in raids on Georgia in the Caucasus°. Some became powerful members of the court. They formed a counterweight to the nomad chiefs just as the Janissaries had earlier challenged the landholding Turkish cavalry in the Ottoman Empire. The strong hand of Shah Abbas kept the inevitable rivalries and intrigues between the factions under control. His successors showed less skill.

In the late sixteenth century the inflation caused by cheap silver spread into Iran; then overland trade through Safavid territory declined because of mismanagement of the silk monopoly after Shah Abbas's death in 1629. As a result, the country faced the unsolvable problem of finding money to pay the army and bureaucracy. Trying to remove the nomads from their lands to regain control of taxes proved more difficult and more disruptive militarily than the piecemeal dismantling of the land-grant system in the Ottoman Empire. Demands from the central government caused the nomads, who were still a potent military force, to withdraw to their mountain pastures until the pressure subsided. By 1722 the government had become so weak and commanded so little support from the nomadic groups that an army of marauding Afghans was able to capture Isfahan and effectively end Safavid rule.

Despite Iran's long coastline, the Safavids never possessed a navy. The Portuguese seized the strategic Persian Gulf island of Hormuz in 1517 and were expelled only in 1622, when the English ferried Iranian soldiers to the attack. Entirely land-oriented, the shahs relied on the English and Dutch for naval support and never considered confronting them at sea. Nadir Shah, a general who emerged from the confusion of the Safavid fall to reunify Iran briefly between 1736 and 1747, purchased some naval vessels from the English and used them in the Persian Gulf. But his navy decayed after his death, and Iran did not have a navy again until the twentieth century.

THE MUGHAL EMPIRE, 1526–1761

As a land of Hindus ruled by a Muslim minority, the realm of the Mughal° sultans of India differed substantially from the empires of the Ottomans and Safavids. To be sure, the Ottoman provinces in the Balkans, except for Albania and Bosnia, remained mostly Christian; but the remainder of the Ottoman Empire was overwhelmingly Muslim with small Christian and Jewish minorities. The Ottoman sultans made much of their control of Mecca and Medina and resulting supervision of the annual pilgrimage caravans just as the Safavids fostered pilgrimages to a shrine in Mashhad in northeastern Iran for their overwhelmingly Shi'ite subjects.

India, in contrast, lay far from the Islamic homelands (see Map 20.1). Muslim dominion in northern India began with repeated military campaigns in the early eleventh century, and the Mughals had to contend with the Hindus' long-standing resentment of the destruction of their culture. Unlike the Balkan peoples who had struggled to maintain their separate identities in relation to the Byzantines, the crusaders, and one another before arrival of the Turks, the peoples of the Indian subcontinent had used centuries of freedom from foreign intrusion to forge a distinctive Hindu civilization that could not easily accommodate the worldview of Islam. Thus, the Mughals faced the challenge not just of conquering and organizing a large territorial state but also of finding a formula for Hindu-Muslim coexistence.

Political Foundations

Babur° (1483–1530), the founder of the **Mughal Empire,** descended from Timur. Though Mughal means "Mongol" in Persian, the Timurids were of Turkic rather than Mongol origin. Timur's marriage to a descendant of Genghis Khan had earned him the Mongol designation "son-in-law," but like the Ottomans, his family did not enjoy the political legitimacy that came with Genghisid decent experienced by lesser rulers in Central Asia and in the Crimea north of the Black Sea.

Invading from Central Asia, Babur defeated the last Muslim sultan of Delhi at the Battle of Panipat in 1526. Even though this victory marked the birth of a brilliant and powerful state in India, Babur's descendants continued to think of Central Asia as their true home, from time to time expressing intentions of recapturing Samarkand and referring to its Uzbek ruler—a genuine descendant of Genghis Khan—as a governor rather than an independent sovereign.

India proved to be the primary theater of Mughal accomplishment, however. Babur's grandson **Akbar** (r. 1556–1605), a brilliant but mercurial man whose illiteracy betrayed his upbringing in the wilds of Afghanistan, established the central administration of the expanding state. Under him and his three successors—the last of whom died in 1707—all but the southern tip of India

---

Caucasus (CAW-kuh-suhs)   Mughal (MOH-guhl)

Babur (BAH-bur)

Elephants Breaking Bridge of Boats   This illustration of an incident in the life of Akbar illustrates the ability of Mughal miniature painters to depict unconventional action scenes. Because the flow of rivers in India and the Middle East varied greatly from dry season to wet season, boat bridges were much more common than permanent constructions.   (Victoria and Albert Museum, London/Bridgeman Art Library)

administration, India under Akbar enjoyed great prosperity in the sixteenth century. Akbar and his successors faced few external threats and experienced generally peaceful conditions in their northern Indian heartland. Nevertheless, they were capable of squandering immense amounts of blood and treasure fighting Hindu kings and rebels in the Deccan region or Afghans on their western frontier (see Map 20.1).

Foreign trade boomed at the port of Surat in the northwest, which also served as an embarkation point for pilgrims headed for Mecca. Like the Safavids, the Mughals had no navy or merchant ships. The government saw the Europeans—now primarily Dutch and English, the Portuguese having lost most of their Indian ports—less as enemies than as shipmasters whose naval support could be procured as needed in return for trading privileges. It never questioned the wisdom of selling Indian cottons for European coin—no one understood how cheap silver had become in Europe—and shipping them off to European customers in English and Dutch vessels.

Hindus and Muslims

India had not been dominated by a single ruler since the time of Harsha Vardhana (r. 606– 647). Muslim destruction of Hindu cultural monuments, the expansion of Muslim territory, and the practice, until Akbar's time, of enslaving prisoners of war and compelling them to convert to Islam horrified the Hindus. But the politically divided Hindus did not put up a combined resistance. The Mughal state, in contrast, inherited traditions of unified imperial rule from both the Islamic caliphate and the more recent examples of Genghis Khan and Timur.

Those Mongol-based traditions did not necessarily mean religious intolerance. Seventy percent of the mansabdars° (officials holding land grants) appointed under Akbar were Muslim soldiers born outside India, but 15 percent were Hindus, mostly warriors from the north called **Rajputs°**. One of them rose to be a powerful revenue minister. Their status as mansabdars confirmed the policy of religious accommodation adopted by Akbar and his successors.

Akbar, the most illustrious Mughal ruler, differed from his Ottoman and Safavid counterparts—Suleiman the Magnificent and Shah Abbas the Great—in his striving for social harmony and not just for more territory and revenue. He succeeded to the throne at age thirteen, and his actions were dominated at first by a regent and then by his strong-minded childhood nurse. On reach-

fell under Mughal rule, administered first from Agra and then from Delhi°.

Akbar granted land revenues to military officers and government officials in return for their service. Ranks called **mansabs°,** some high and some low, entitled their holders to revenue assignments. As in the other Islamic empires, the central government kept careful track of these nonhereditary grants.

With a population of 100 million, a thriving trading economy based on cotton cloth, and a generally efficient

Delhi (DEL-ee)   **mansabs** (MAN-sabz)

mansabdars (man-sab-DAHRZ)   **Rajputs** (RAHJ-putz)

ing twenty, Akbar took command of the government. He married a Hindu Rajput princess, whose name is not recorded, and welcomed her father and brother to the court in Agra.

Other rulers might have used such a marriage as a means of humiliating a subject group, but Akbar signaled his desire for Muslim-Hindu reconciliation. A year later he rescinded the head tax that Muslim rulers traditionally levied on tolerated non-Muslims. This measure was more symbolic than real because the tax had not been regularly collected, but the gesture helped cement the allegiance of the Rajputs.

Akbar longed for an heir. Much to his relief, his Rajput wife gave birth to a son in 1569, ensuring that future rulers would have both Muslim and Hindu ancestry.

Akbar ruled that in legal disputes between two Hindus, decisions would be made according to village custom or Hindu law as interpreted by local Hindu scholars. Muslims followed Shari'a law. Akbar made himself the legal court of last resort in a 1579 declaration that he was God's infallible earthly representative. Thus, appeals could be made to Akbar personally, a possibility not usually present in Islamic jurisprudence.

He also made himself the center of a new "Divine Faith" incorporating Muslim, Hindu, Zoroastrian, Sikh°, and Christian beliefs. Sufi ideas attracted him and permeated the religious rituals he instituted at his court. To promote serious consideration of his religious principles, he monitored, from a high catwalk, debates among scholars of all religions assembled in his private octagonal audience chamber. When courtiers uttered the Muslim exclamation "Allahu Akbar"—"God is great"—its second grammatical meaning, "God is Akbar," was not lost on them. Akbar's religious views did not survive him, but the court culture he fostered, reflecting a mixture of Muslim and Hindu traditions, flourished until his zealous great-grandson Aurangzeb° (r. 1658–1707) reinstituted many restrictions on Hindus.

Mughal and Rajput miniature portraits of political figures and depictions of scantily clad women brought frowns to the faces of pious Muslims, who deplored the representation of human beings in art. Most of the leading painters were Hindus. In literature, in addition to the florid style of Persian verse favored at court, a new taste developed for poetry and prose in the popular language of the Delhi region. The modern descendant of this language is called Urdu in Pakistan, from the Turkish word *ordu*, meaning "army" (in India it is called Hindi).

Akbar's policy of toleration does not explain the pattern of conversion in Mughal India, most of which

was to Sunni Islam. Some scholars maintain that most converts came from the lowest Hindu social groups, or castes, who hoped to improve their lot in life, but little data confirm this theory. Others argue that Sufi brotherhoods, which developed strongly in India, led the way in converting people to Islam, but this proposition has not been proved. The most heavily Muslim regions developed in the valley of the Indus River and in Bengal. The Indus center dates from the isolated establishment of Muslim rule there as early as the eighth century.

A careful study of local records and traditions from east Bengal indicates that the eastward movement of the delta of the Ganges River, caused by silting, and the spread of rice cultivation into forest clearings played the primary role in conversions to Islam there. Mansabdars (mostly Muslims) with land grants in east Bengal contracted with local entrepreneurs to collect a labor force, cut down the forest, and establish rice paddies. Though some entrepreneurs were Hindu, most were non-Sufi Muslim religious figures. The latter centered their farming communities on mosques and shrines, using religion as a social cement. Most natives of the region were accustomed to worshiping local forest deities rather than the main Hindu gods. So the shift to Islam represented a move to a more sophisticated, literate culture appropriate to their new status as farmers producing for the commercial rice market. Gradual religious change of this kind often produced Muslim communities whose social customs differed little from those in neighboring non-Muslim communities. In east Bengal, common Muslim institutions, such as madrasas, the ulama, and law courts, were little in evidence.

The emergence of **Sikhism** in the Punjab region of northwest India constituted another change in Indian religious life in the Mughal period. Nanak (1469–1539), the religion's first guru (spiritual teacher), stressed meditation as a means of seeking enlightenment and drew upon both Muslim and Hindu imagery in his teachings. His followers formed a single community without differences of caste. However, after Aurangzeb ordered the ninth guru beheaded in 1675 for refusing to convert to Islam, the tenth guru dedicated himself to avenging his father's death and reorganized his followers into "the army of the pure," a religious order dedicated to defending Sikh beliefs. These devotees signaled their faith by leaving their hair uncut beneath a turban; carrying a comb, a steel bracelet, and a sword or dagger; and wearing military-style breeches. By the eighteenth century, the Mughals were encountering fierce opposition from the Sikhs as well as from Hindu guerrilla forces in the rugged and ravine-scarred province of Maharashtra on India's west coast.

Sikh (sick) **Aurangzeb** (ow-rang-ZEB)

Central Decay and Regional Challenges, 1707–1761

Mughal power did not long survive Aurangzeb's death in 1707. Some historians consider the land-grant system a central element in the rapid decline of imperial authority, but other factors played a role as well. Aurangzeb failed to effectively integrate new Mughal territories in southern India into the imperial structure, and a number of strong regional powers challenged Mughal military supremacy. The Marathas proved a formidable enemy as they carved out a swath of territory across India's middle, and Sikhs, Hindu Rajputs, and Muslim Afghans exerted intense pressure from the northwest. A climax came in 1739 when Nadir Shah, the general who had seized power in Iran after the fall of the Safavids, invaded the subcontinent and sacked Delhi, which Akbar's grandson had rebuilt and beautified as the Mughal capital some decades before. He carried off to Iran, as part of the booty, the priceless, jewel-encrusted "peacock throne," symbol of Mughal grandeur. The later Mughals found another throne to sit on; but their empire, which survived in name to 1857, was finished.

In 1723 Nizam al-Mulk°, the powerful vizier of the Mughal sultan, gave up on the central government and established his own nearly independent state at Hyderabad in the eastern Deccan. Other officials bearing the title nawab° (from Arabic *na'ib* meaning "deputy" and Anglicized as "nabob") became similarly independent in Bengal and Oudh° in the northeast, as did the Marathas farther west. In the northwest, simultaneous Iranian and Mughal weakness allowed the Afghans to establish an independent kingdom.

Some of these regional powers and smaller princely states flourished with the removal of the sultan's heavy hand. Linguistic and religious communities, freed from the religious intolerance instituted during the reign of Aurangzeb, similarly enjoyed greater opportunity for political expression. However, this disintegration of central power favored the intrusion of European adventurers.

Joseph François Dupleix° took over the presidency of the east coast French stronghold of Pondicherry° in 1741 and began a new phase of European involvement in India. He captured the English trading center of Madras and used his small contingent of European and European-trained Indian troops to become a power broker in southern India. Though offered the title nawab, Dupleix preferred to operate behind the scenes, using

Indian princes as puppets. His career ended in 1754 when he was called home. Deeply involved in European wars, the French government declined to pursue further adventures in India. Dupleix's departure cleared the way for the British, whose ventures in India are described in Chapter 25.

TRADE EMPIRES IN THE INDIAN OCEAN, 1600–1729

It is no coincidence that the Mughal, Safavid, and Ottoman Empires declined simultaneously in the seventeenth and eighteenth centuries. Complex changes in military technology and in the world economy, along with the increasing difficulty of basing an extensive land empire on military forces paid through land grants, affected them all adversely. The opposite held for seafaring countries intent on turning trade networks into maritime empires. Improvements in ship design, navigation accuracy, and the use of cannon gave an ever-increasing edge to European powers competing with local seafaring peoples. Moreover, the development of joint-stock companies, in which many merchants pooled their capital, provided a flexible and efficient financial instrument for exploiting new possibilities. The English East India Company was founded in 1600, the Dutch East India Company in 1602.

Although the Ottomans, Safavids, and Mughals did not effectively contest the growth of Portuguese and then Dutch, English, and French maritime power, the majority of non-European shipbuilders, captains, sailors, and traders were Muslim. Groups of Armenian, Jewish, and Hindu traders were also active, but they remained almost as aloof from the Europeans as the Muslims did. The presence in every port of Muslims following the same legal traditions and practicing their faith in similar ways cemented the Muslims' trading network. Islam, from its very outset in the life and preaching of Muhammad (570–632), had favored trade and traders. Unlike Hinduism, it was a proselytizing religion, a factor that encouraged the growth of coastal Muslim communities as local non-Muslims associated with Muslim commercial activities converted and intermarried with Muslims from abroad.

Although European missionaries, particularly the Jesuits, tried to extend Christianity into Asia and Africa (see Chapters 16 and 21), most Europeans, the Portuguese excepted, did not treat local converts or the offspring of mixed marriages as full members of their communities. Islam was generally more welcoming. As a

---

Nizam al-Mulk (nee-ZAHM al-MULK)   **nawab** (NAH-wab)
Oudh (OW-ad)   **Dupleix** (doo-PLAY)
Pondicherry (pon-dir-CHEH-ree)

consequence, Islam spread extensively into East Africa and Southeast Asia during precisely the time of rapid European commercial expansion. Even without the support of the Muslim land empires, Islam became a source of resistance to growing European domination.

Muslims in the East Indies

Historians disagree about the chronology and manner of Islam's spread in Southeast Asia. Arab traders appeared in southern China as early as the eighth century, so Muslims probably reached the East Indies at a similarly early date. Nevertheless, the dominance of Indian cultural influences in the area for several centuries thereafter indicates that early Muslim visitors had little impact on local beliefs. Clearer indications of conversion and the formation of Muslim communities date from roughly the fourteenth century, with the strongest overseas linkage being to the port of Cambay in India (see Map 20.2) rather than to the Arab world. Islam first took root in port cities and in some royal courts and spread inland only slowly, possibly transmitted by itinerant Sufis.

Although appeals to the Ottoman sultan for support against the Europeans ultimately proved futile, Islam strengthened resistance to Portuguese, Spanish, and Dutch intruders. When the Spaniards conquered the Philippines during the decades following the establishment of their first fort in 1565, they encountered Muslims on the southern island of Mindanao° and the nearby Sulu archipelago. They called them "Moros," the Spanish term for their old enemies, the Muslims of North Africa. In the ensuing Moro wars, the Spaniards portrayed the Moros as greedy pirates who raided non-Muslim territories for slaves. In fact, they were political, religious, and commercial competitors whose perseverance enabled them to establish the Sulu Empire based in the southern Philippines, one of the strongest states in Southeast Asia from 1768 to 1848.

Other local kingdoms that looked on Islam as a force to counter the aggressive Christianity of the Europeans included the actively proselytizing Brunei° Sultanate in northern Borneo and the **Acheh° Sultanate** in northern Sumatra. At its peak in the early seventeenth century, Acheh succeeded Malacca as the main center of Islamic expansion in Southeast Asia. It prospered by trading pepper for cotton cloth from Gujarat in India. Acheh declined after the Dutch seized Malacca from Portugal in 1641.

How well Islam was understood in these Muslim kingdoms is open to question. In Acheh, for example, a series of women ruled between 1641 and 1699. This practice ended when local Muslim scholars obtained a ruling from scholars in Mecca and Medina that Islam did not approve of female rulers. After this ruling scholarly understandings of Islam gained greater prominence in the East Indies.

Historians have looked at merchants, Sufi preachers, or both as the first propagators of Islam in Southeast Asia. The scholarly vision of Islam, however, took root in the sixteenth century by way of pilgrims returning from years of study in Mecca and Medina. Islam promoted the dissemination of writing in the region. Some of the returning pilgrims wrote in Arabic, others in Malay or Javanese. As Islam continued to spread, adat ("custom"), a form of Islam rooted in pre-Muslim religious and social practices, retained its preeminence in rural areas over practices centered on the Shari'a, the religious law. But the royal courts in the port cities began to heed the views of the pilgrim teachers. Though different in many ways, both varieties of Islam provided believers with a firm basis of identification in the face of the growing European presence. Christian missionaries gained most of their converts in regions that had not yet converted to Islam, such as the northern Philippines.

Muslims in East Africa

Muslim rulers also governed the East African ports that the Portuguese began to visit in the fifteenth century, though they were not allied politically (see Map 20.2). People living in the millet and rice lands of the Swahili Coast—from the Arabic sawahil° meaning "coasts"—had little contact with those in the dry hinterlands. Throughout this period, the East African lakes region and the highlands of Kenya witnessed unprecedented migration and relocation of peoples because of drought conditions that persisted from the late sixteenth through most of the seventeenth century.

Cooperation among the trading ports of Kilwa, Mombasa, and Malindi was hindered by the thick bush country that separated the cultivated tracts of coastal land and by the fact that the ports competed with one another in the export of ivory; ambergris° (a whale byproduct used in perfumes); and forest products such as beeswax, copal tree resin, and wood. Kilwa also exported gold. In the eighteenth century slave trading, primarily to Arabian ports but also to India, increased in

---

Mindanao (min-duh-NOW)   **Brunei** (BROO-nie)
Acheh (AH-cheh)

---

sawahil (suh-WAH-hil)   ambergris (AM-ber-grees)

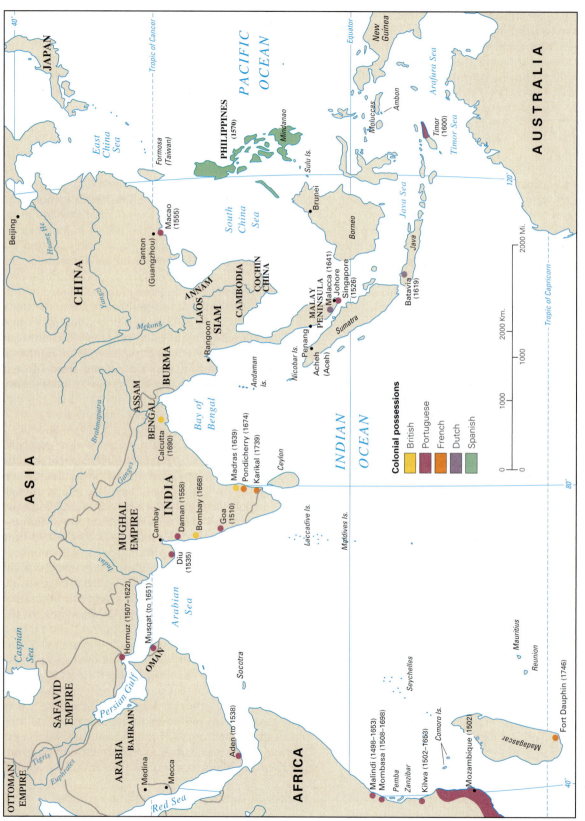

Map 20.2 **European Colonization in the Indian Ocean to 1750** Since Portuguese explorers were the first Europeans to reach India by rounding Africa, Portugal gained a strong foothold in both areas. Rival Spain was barred from colonizing the region by the Treaty of Tordesillas in 1494, which limited Spanish efforts to lands west of a line drawn through the mid-Atlantic Ocean. The line carried around the globe provided justification of Spanish colonization in the Philippines. French, British, and Dutch colonies date from after 1600, when joint-stock companies provided a new stimulus for overseas commerce.

Portuguese Fort Guarding Musqat Harbor   Musqat in Oman and Aden in Yemen, the best harbors in southern Arabia, were targets for imperial navies trying to establish dominance in the Indian Ocean. Musqat's harbor is small and circular, with one narrow entrance overlooked by this fortress. The palace of the sultan of Oman is still located at the opposite end of the harbor.   (Robert Harding Picture Library)

importance. Because Europeans—the only peoples who kept consistent records of slave-trading activities—played a minor role in this slave trade, few records have survived to indicate its extent. Perhaps the best estimate is that 2.1 million slaves were exported between 1500 and 1890, a little over 12.5 percent of the total traffic in African slaves during that period (see Chapter 19).

The Portuguese conquered all the coastal ports from Mozambique northward except Malindi, with whose ruler Portugal cooperated. A Portuguese description of the ruler names some of the cloth and metal goods that Malindi imported, as well as some local manufactures:

> The King wore a robe of damask trimmed with green satin and a rich [cap]. He was seated on two cushioned chairs of bronze, beneath a rough sunshade of crimson satin attached to a pole. An old man, who attended him as a page, carried a short sword in a silver sheath. There were many players on [horns], and two trumpets of ivory richly carved and of the size of a man, which were blown through a hole in the side, and made sweet harmony with the [horns].[4]

Initially, the Portuguese favored the port of Malindi, which caused the decline of Kilwa and Mombasa. Repeatedly plagued by local rebellion, Portuguese power suffered severe blows when the Arabs of **Oman** in southeastern Arabia captured their south Arabian stronghold at Musqat (1650) and then went on to seize Mombasa

(1698), which had become the Portuguese capital in East Africa. The Portuguese briefly retook Mombasa but lost control permanently in 1729. From then on, the Portuguese had to content themselves with Mozambique in East Africa and a few remaining ports in India (Goa) and farther east (Macao and Timor).

The Omanis created a maritime empire of their own, one that worked in greater cooperation with the African populations. The Bantu language of the coast, broadened by the absorption of Arabic, Persian, and Portuguese loanwords, developed into **Swahili°,** which was spoken throughout the region. Arabs and other Muslims who settled in the region intermarried with local families, giving rise to a mixed population that played an important role in developing a distinctive Swahili culture.

Islam also spread in the southern Sudan in this period, particularly in the dry areas away from the Nile River. This growth coincided with a waning of Ethiopian power as a result of Portugal's stifling of trade in the Red Sea. Yet no significant contact developed between the emerging Muslim Swahili culture and that of the Muslims in the Sudan to the north.

The Dutch played a major role in driving the Portuguese from their possessions in the East Indies. They were better organized than the Portuguese through the Dutch East India Company. Just as the Portuguese had tried to dominate the trade in spices, so the Dutch

---

Swahili (swah-HEE-lee)

concentrated at first on the spice-producing islands of Southeast Asia. The Portuguese had seized Malacca, a strategic town on the narrow strait at the end of the Malay Peninsula, from a local Malay ruler in 1511 (see Chapter 16). The Dutch took it away from them in 1641, leaving Portugal little foothold in the East Indies except the islands of Ambon° and Timor (see Map 20.2).

Although the United Netherlands was one of the least autocratic countries of Europe, the governors-general appointed by the Dutch East India Company deployed almost unlimited powers in their efforts to maintain their trade monopoly. They could even order the execution of their own employees for "smuggling"—that is, trading on their own. Under strong governors-general, the Dutch fought a series of wars against Acheh and other local kingdoms on Sumatra and Java. In 1628 and 1629 their new capital at **Batavia,** now the city of Jakarta on Java, was besieged by a fleet of fifty ships belonging to the sultan of Mataram°, a Javanese kingdom. The Dutch held out with difficulty and eventually prevailed when the sultan was unable to get effective help from the English.

Suppressing local rulers, however, was not enough to control the spice trade once other European countries adopted Dutch methods, learned more about where goods might be acquired, and started to send more ships to Southeast Asia. In the course of the eighteenth century, therefore, the Dutch gradually turned from being middlemen between Southeast Asian producers and European buyers to producing crops in areas they controlled, notably in Java. Javanese teak forests yielded high-quality lumber, and coffee, transplanted from Yemen, grew well in the western hilly regions. In this new phase of colonial export production, Batavia developed from being the headquarters town of a far-flung enterprise to being the administrative capital of a conquered land.

Beyond the East Indies, the Dutch utilized their discovery of a band of powerful eastward-blowing winds (called the "Roaring Forties" because they blow throughout the year between 40 and 50 degrees south latitude) to reach Australia in 1606. In 1642 and 1643 Abel Tasman became the first European to set foot on Tasmania and New Zealand and to sail around Australia, signaling European involvement in that region (see Chapter 25).

Ambon (am-BOHN)   Mataram (MAH-tah-ram)

CONCLUSION

Asians and Africans ruled by the Ottoman and Mughal sultans and the Safavid shahs did not perceive that a major shift in world economic and political alignments was under way by the late seventeenth century. The rulers focused their efforts on conquering more and more land, sometimes at the expense of Christian Europe and Hindu India, but also at one another's expense, since the Sunni-Shi'ite division justified Iranian attacks on its neighbors and vice versa.

To be sure, more and more trade was being carried in European vessels, particularly after the advent of joint-stock companies in 1600; and Europeans had enclaves in a handful of port cities and islands. But the age-old tradition of Asia was that imperial wealth came from control of broad expanses of agricultural land. Except for state monopolies, such as Iranian silk, governments did not greatly concern themselves with what farmers did. They relied mostly on land taxes, usually indirectly collected via holders of land grants or tax farmers, rather than on customs duties or control of markets to fill the government coffers.

With ever-increasing military expenditures, these taxes fell short of the rulers' needs. Few people realized, however, that this problem was basic to the entire economic system rather than a temporary revenue shortfall. Imperial courtiers pursued their luxurious ways; poetry and the arts continued to flourish; and the quality of manufacturing and craft production remained generally high. Eighteenth-century European observers, luxuriating in the prosperity gained from their ever-increasing control of the Indian Ocean, marveled no less at the riches and industry of these eastern lands than at the fundamental weakness of their political and military systems.

■ Key Terms

Ottoman Empire	Mughal Empire
Suleiman the Magnificent	Akbar
Janissary	mansabs
devshirme	Rajputs
Tulip Period	Sikhism
Safavid Empire	Acheh Sultanate
Shi'ite Islam	Oman
Hidden Imam	Swahili
Shah Abbas I	Batavia

■ Suggested Reading

The best comprehensive and comparative account of the post-Mongol Islamic land empires, with an emphasis on social history, is Ira Lapidus, *A History of Islamic Societies* (1988). For a work of similar scope concentrating on intellectual history see Marshall G. S. Hodgson, *The Venture of Islam*, vol. 3, *The Gunpowder Empires and Modern Times* (1974).

On the Ottoman Empire in its prime see Colin Imber, *The Ottoman Empire, 1300–1650: The Structure of Power* (2002). Daniel Goffman, *The Ottoman Empire and Early Modern Europe* (2002), compares the Ottomans with contemporary European kingdoms. Jason Goodwin, *Lords of the Horizons: A History of the Ottoman Empire* (1999), offers a brief journalistic account. Ottoman origins are well covered in Cemal Kafadar, *Between Two Worlds* (1995). For a collection of articles on non-political matters see Halil Inalcik and Donald Quataert, eds., *An Economic and Social History of the Ottoman Empire, 1300–1914* (1994). For a sociological analysis of change in the seventeenth century see Karen Barkey, *Bandits and Bureaucrats* (1994).

Some specialized studies of cities and regions give a sense of the major changes in Ottoman society and economy after the sixteenth century: Daniel Goffman, *Izmir and the Levantine World, 1550–1650* (1990); Abraham Marcus, *The Middle East on the Eve of Modernity: Aleppo in the Eighteenth Century* (1989); Bruce McGowan, *Economic Life in the Ottoman Empire: Taxation, Trade, and the Struggle for Land, 1600–1800* (1981); and Dina Rizk Khoury, *State and Provincial Society in the Ottoman Empire: Mosul, 1540–1834* (1997).

Articles in Benjamin Braude and Bernard Lewis, eds., *Christians and Jews in the Ottoman Empire: The Functioning of a Plural Society* (1982), deal with questions relating to religious minorities. Leslie Pierce skillfully treats the role of women in the governance of the empire in *The Imperial Harem: Women and Sovereignty in the Ottoman Empire* (1993). Ralph S. Hattox, *Coffee and Coffeehouses: The Origins of a Social Beverage in the Medieval Near East* (1988), is an excellent contribution to Ottoman social history.

The most comprehensive treatment of the history of Safavid Iran is in the articles in Peter Jackson and Laurence Lockhart, eds., *The Cambridge History of Iran*, vol. 6, *The Timurid and Safavid Periods* (1986). The articles by Hans Roemer in this volume provide solid political narratives of the pre-Safavid and Safavid periods. Roger Savory's important article on the structure of the Safavid state is available in a more extensive form in his *Iran Under the Safavids* (1980).

For the artistic side of Safavid history, abundantly illustrated, see Anthony Welch, *Shah Abbas and the Arts of Isfahan* (1973). Said Amir Arjomand, *The Shadow of God and the Hidden Imam: Religion, Political Order, and Societal Change in Shiite Iran from the Beginning to 1890* (1984), contains the best analysis of the complicated relationship between Shi'ism and monarchy. For Safavid economic history see Willem Floor, *A Fiscal History of Iran in the Safavid and Qajar Periods, 1500–1925* (1998); and Rudoph Matthee, *The Politics of Trade in Safavid Iran: Silk for Silver, 1600–1730* (1999).

A highly readable work that situates the Mughal Empire within the overall history of the subcontinent is Stanley Wolpert, *A New History of India*, 6th ed. (1999). For a broad treatment of the entire development of Islamic society in India with emphasis on the Mughal period, see S. M. Ikram, *History of Muslim Civilization in India and Pakistan* (1989). Wheeler Thackston has made a lively translation of Babur's autobiography in *The Baburnama: Memoirs of Babur, Prince and Emperor* (1996). For a comprehensive history of the Mughals see John F. Richards, *The Mughal Empire* (1993). See also Richard Foltz, *Mughal India and Central Asia* (1999). Irfan Habib has edited an extensive collection of articles on the Mughal Empire in its prime entitled *Akbar and His India* (1997). For the history of the Sikhs see W. H. McLeod, *The Sikhs: History, Religion, and Society* (1989). Two specialized works on the economic and trading history of India are Ashin Das Gupta and M. N. Pearson, eds., *India and the Indian Ocean, 1500–1800* (1987), and Stephen Frederic Dale, *Indian Merchants and Eurasian Trade, 1600–1750* (1994).

The history of East Africa in this period is not well documented, but B. A. Ogot, ed., *UNESCO General History of Africa*, vol. 5, *Africa from the Sixteenth to the Eighteenth Century* (1992), provides a useful collection of articles. See also Tom Spear, *The Swahili* (1984), and James de Vere Allen, *Swahili Origins* (1993).

For a brief, general introduction to the relations between the Muslim land empires and the development of Indian Ocean trade, see Patricia Risso, *Merchants and Faith: Muslim Commerce and Culture in the Indian Ocean* (1995). Esmond Bradley Martin and Chryssee Perry Martin have written a popular and well-illustrated work on the western Indian Ocean entitled *Cargoes of the East: The Ports, Trade and Culture of the Arabian Seas and Western Indian Ocean* (1978). C. R. Boxer, *The Dutch Seaborne Empire, 1600–1800* (1973), is a classic account of all aspects of Dutch maritime expansion.

■ Notes

1. Quoted in Sarah Searight, *The British in the Middle East* (New York: Atheneum 1970), 36.
2. Daniel Goffman, *Izmir and the Levantine World, 1550–1650* (Seattle: University of Washington Press, 1990), 52.
3. Quoted in Peter Jackson and Laurence Lockhart, eds., *The Cambridge History of Iran*, vol. 6, *The Timurid and Safavid Periods* (New York: Cambridge University Press, 1986), 703.
4. Esmond Bradley Martin and Chryssee Perry Martin, *Cargoes of the East: The Ports, Trade and Culture of the Arabian Seas and Western Indian Ocean* (1978), 17.

21

Northern Eurasia,
1500–1800

Russian Ambassadors to Holland Display Their Furs, 1576 Representatives from Muscovy impressed the court of King Maximilian II of Bohemia with their sable coats and caps.

CHAPTER OUTLINE
Japanese Reunification
The Later Ming and Early Qing Empires
The Russian Empire
Comparative Perspectives
ENVIRONMENT AND TECHNOLOGY: East Asian Porcelain
DIVERSITY AND DOMINANCE: Gendered Violence: The Yangzhou Massacre

Li Zicheng° was an apprentice ironworker in a barren northern Chinese province. His dreams for the future were dashed when, in a desperate effort to save money, the Hanli emperor ordered the elimination of Li's job and those of many other government employees. The savings went to fund more troops to defend the capital city of Beijing° against attacks by **Manchu** armies from Manchuria in the northeast. By 1630 Li Zicheng had found work as a soldier, but he and his fellow soldiers mutinied when the government failed to provide them with needed supplies. A natural leader, Li soon headed a group of several thousand Chinese rebels. In 1635 he and other rebel leaders were strong enough to control much of north central China.

Wedged between the armies of the Manchu pressing from the north and the rebels to the southwest, the Ming government grew ever weaker. Taking advantage of the weakness, Li Zicheng's forces began to move toward Beijing. Along the way they captured towns and conscripted young men into their army. The rebels also won popular support with promises to end the abuses of the Ming and restore peace and prosperity. In April 1644 Li's armies were able to take over Beijing without a fight. The last Ming emperor hanged himself in the palace garden, bringing to an end the dynasty that had ruled China since 1368.

The rebels' success was short-lived. Believing there was more to fear from uneducated, violent men like Li, the Ming general Wu Sangui joined forces with the Manchu. Wu may have been influenced by the fact that Li had captured one of the general's favorite concubines and taken her for himself. Together Wu and the Manchu retook Beijing in June. Li's forces scattered, and a year later he was dead, either a suicide or beaten to death by peasants whose food he tried to steal.[1]

Meanwhile, the Manchu were making it clear that they intended to be the new masters of China. They installed their young sovereign as the new emperor and over the next two decades hunted down the last of the Ming loyalists and heirs to the throne.

China was not the only state in Northern Eurasia facing uprisings from within and foreign threats. In the period from 1500 to 1800 Japan and Russia experienced turbulence as they underwent massive political change and economic growth. Besides challenges from nearby neighbors, the three also faced new contacts and challenges from the commercially and militarily powerful European states.

As you read this chapter, ask yourself the following questions:

- How did Japan, China, and Russia respond to internal social, economic, and political pressures?

- How did China and Russia deal with military challenges from their immediate neighbors?

- How did Japan, China, and Russia differ in the ways they reacted to western European commercial and cultural contacts?

JAPANESE REUNIFICATION

Like China and Russia in the centuries between 1500 and 1800, Japan experienced three major changes: internal and external military conflicts, political growth and strengthening, and expanded commercial and cultural contacts. Along with its culturally homogenous population and natural boundaries, Japan's smaller size made the process of political unification shorter than in the great empires of China and Russia. Japan also differed in its responses to new contacts with western Europeans.

Civil War and the Invasion of Korea, 1500–1603

In the twelfth century Japan's imperial unity had disintegrated, and the country fell under the rule of numerous warlords known as *daimyo*°. Each of the daimyo had his own castle town, a small bureaucracy, and an army of warriors, the *samurai*°. Daimyo pledged a loose allegiance to the hereditary commander of the armies, the shogun, as well as to the Japanese emperor residing in the capital city of Kyoto°. The emperor and shogun were symbols of national unity but lacked political power.

Warfare among the different daimyo was common. In the late 1500s Japan experienced a prolonged civil war

---

Li Zicheng (lee ZUH-cheng) **Beijing** (bay-JING)

daimyo (DIE-mee-oh) **samurai** (SAH-moo-rye)
Kyoto (KYOH-toh)

that brought the separate Japanese islands under powerful warlords. The most successful of these warlords was Hideyoshi°. In 1592, buoyed with his success in Japan, the supremely confident Hideyoshi launched an invasion of the Asian mainland with 160,000 men. His apparent intention was not just to conquer the Korean peninsula but to make himself emperor of China as well.

The Korean and Japanese languages are closely related, but the dominant influence on Korean culture had long been China. Korea generally accepted a subordinate relationship with its giant neighbor and paid tribute to the Chinese dynasty in power. In many ways the Yi dynasty that ruled Korea from 1392 to 1910 was a model Confucian state. Although Korea had developed its own system of writing in 1443 and made extensive use of printing with movable type from the fifteenth century, most printing continued to use Chinese characters.

Against Hideyoshi's invaders the Koreans employed all the technological and military skill for which the Yi period was renowned. Ingenious covered warships, or "turtle boats," intercepted a portion of the Japanese fleet. The mentally unstable Hideyoshi countered with brutal punitive measures. The Koreans and their Chinese allies could not stop the Japanese conquest of the peninsula and into the Chinese province of Manchuria. However, after Hideyoshi's death in 1598, the other Japanese military leaders withdrew their forces, and the Japanese government made peace in 1606.

Korea was severely devastated by the invasion. In the confusion after the Japanese withdrawal, the Korean *yangban* (nobility) and lesser royals were able to lay claim to so much tax-paying land that royal revenues may have fallen by two-thirds. But the most dramatic consequences of the Japanese invasion were in China. The battles in Manchuria weakened Chinese garrisons there, permitting Manchu opposition to consolidate. Manchu forces invaded Korea in the 1620s and eventually compelled the Yi to become a tributary state. As already related, the Manchu would be in possession of Beijing, China's capital, by 1644.

The Tokugawa Shogunate, to 1800

After Hideyoshi's demise, Japanese leaders brought the civil wars to an end, and in 1603 they established a more centralized government. A new shogun, Tokugawa Ieyasu° (1543–1616), had gained the upper hand in the conflict and established a new military government known as the **Tokugawa Shogunate.**

The shoguns created a new administrative capital at Edo° (now Tokyo). Trade along the well-maintained road between Edo and the imperial capital of Kyoto promoted the development of the Japanese economy and the formation of other trading centers (see Map 26.3).

Although the Tokugawa Shogunate gave Japan more political unity than the islands had seen in centuries, the regional lords, the daimyo, still had a great deal of power and autonomy. Ieyasu and his successor shoguns had to work hard to keep this decentralized political system from disintegrating.

In some ways, economic integration was more a feature of Tokugawa Japan than was political centralization. Because Tokugawa shoguns required the daimyo to visit Edo frequently, good roads and maritime transport linked the city to the castle towns on three of the four main islands of Japan. Commercial traffic also developed along these routes. The shogun paid the lords in rice, and the lords paid their followers in rice. To meet their personal expenses, recipients of rice had to convert much of it into cash. This transaction stimulated the development of rice exchanges at Edo and at Osaka°, where merchants speculated in rice prices. By the late seventeenth century Edo was one of the largest cities in the world, with nearly a million inhabitants.

The domestic peace of the Tokugawa era forced the warrior class to adapt itself to the growing bureaucratic needs of the state. As the samurai became better educated, more attuned to the tastes of the civil elite, and more interested in conspicuous consumption, they became important customers for merchants dealing in silks, *sake*° (rice wine), fans, porcelain, lacquer ware, books, and moneylending. The state attempted—unsuccessfully—to curb the independence of the merchants when the economic well-being of the samurai was threatened, particularly when rice prices went too low or interest rates on loans were too high.

The 1600s and 1700s were centuries of high achievement in artisanship, and Japanese skills in steel making, pottery, and lacquer ware were joined by excellence in the production and decoration of porcelain (see Environment and Technology: East Asian Porcelain), thanks in no small part to Korean experts brought back to Japan after the invasion of 1592. In the early 1600s manufacturers and merchants amassed enormous family fortunes. Several of the most important industrial and financial companies—for instance, the Mitsui° companies—had their origins in sake breweries of the early Tokugawa period, then branched out into manufacturing, finance, and transport.

Hideyoshi (HEE-duh-YOH-shee)
Tokugawa Ieyasu (TOH-koo-GAH-wah ee-ay-YAH-soo)

Edo (ED-oh) **Osaka** (OH-sah-kah) **sake** (SAH-kay)
Mitsui (MIT-soo-ee)

CHRONOLOGY

	Korea and Japan	China and Central Asia	Russia
1500	1543 First Portuguese contacts	1517 Portuguese embassy to China	1547 Ivan IV tsar
	1592 Japanese invasion of Korea		1582 Russians conquer Khanate of Sibir
1600	1603 Tokugawa Shogunate formed	1601 Matteo Ricci allowed to reside in Beijing	1613–1645 Rule of Mikhail, the first Romanov tsar
	1633–1639 Edicts close down trade with Europe	1644 Qing conquest of Beijing	1649 Subordination of serfs complete
		1662–1722 Rule of Emperor Kangxi	
		1689 Treaty of Nerchinsk with Russia	1689–1725 Rule of Peter the Great
1700	1702 Trial of the Forty-Seven Ronin	1691 Qing control of Inner Mongolia	1712 St. Petersburg becomes Russia's capital
		1736–1795 Rule of Emperor Qianlong	1762–1796 Rule of Catherine the Great
	1792 Russian ships first spotted off the coast of Japan		1799 Alaska becomes a Russian colony

Wealthy merchant families usually cultivated close alliances with their regional daimyo and, if possible, with the shogun himself. In this way they could weaken the strict control of merchant activity that was an official part of Tokugawa policy. By the end of the 1700s the merchant families of Tokugawa Japan held the key to future modernization and the development of heavy industry, particularly in the prosperous provinces.

Japan and the Europeans

Direct contacts with Europeans from the mid-sixteenth century presented Japan with new opportunities and problems. The first major impact was on Japanese military technology. Within thirty years of the arrival of the first Portuguese in 1543, the daimyo were fighting with Western-style firearms, copied and improved upon by Japanese armorers. Japan's civil conflicts of the late sixteenth century launched the first East Asian "gunpowder revolution."

The Japanese also welcomed new trade with merchants from distant Portugal, Spain, the Netherlands, and England, but the government closely regulated their activities. Aside from the brief boom in porcelain exports in the seventeenth century, few Japanese goods went to Europe, and not much from Europe found a market in Japan. The Japanese sold the Dutch copper and silver, which the Dutch exchanged in China for silks that they then resold in Japan. The Japanese, of course, had their own trade with China.

Portuguese and Spanish merchant ships also brought Catholic missionaries. One of the first, Francis Xavier, went to India in the mid-sixteenth century looking for converts and later traveled throughout Southeast and East Asia. He spent two years in Japan and died in 1552, hoping to gain entry to China.

Japanese responses were decidedly mixed to Xavier and other Jesuits (members of the Catholic religious order the Society of Jesus). Large numbers of ordinary Japanese found the new faith deeply meaningful, but

East Asian Porcelain

By the 1400s artisans in China, Korea, and Japan were all producing high-quality pottery with lustrous surface glazes. The best quality, intended for the homes of the wealthy and powerful, was made of pure white clay and covered with a hard translucent glaze. Artisans often added intricate decorations in cobalt blue and other colors. Cheaper pottery found a huge market in East Asia.

Such pottery was also exported to Southeast Asia, the Indian Ocean, and the Middle East. Little found its way to Europe before 1600, but imports soared once the Dutch established trading bases in East Asia. Europeans called the high-quality ware "porcelain." Blue and white designs were especially popular.

One of the great centers of Chinese production was at the large artisan factory at Jingdezhen (JING-deh-JUHN). No sooner had the Dutch tapped into this source than the civil wars and Manchu conquests disrupted production in the middle 1600s. Desperate for a substitute source, the Dutch turned to porcelain from Japanese producers at Arita and Imari, near Nagasaki. Despite Japan's restriction of European trade, the Dutch East India Company transported some 190,000 pieces of Japanese ceramic ware to the Netherlands between 1653 and 1682.

In addition to a wide range of Asian designs, Chinese and Japanese artisans made all sorts of porcelain for the European market. These included purely decorative pottery birds, vases, and pots as well as utilitarian vessels and dishes intended for table use. The serving dish illustrated here came from dinnerware sets the Japanese made especially for the Dutch East India Company. The VOC logo at the center represents the first letters of the company's name in Dutch. It is surrounded by Asian design motifs.

After the return of peace in China, the VOC imported tens of thousands of Chinese porcelain pieces a year. The Chinese artisans sometimes produced imitations of Japanese designs that had become popular in Europe. Meanwhile, the Dutch were experimenting with making their own imitations of East Asian porcelain, right down to the Asian motifs and colors that had become so fashionable in Europe.

Japanese Export Porcelain   Part of a larger set made for the Dutch East India Company (Photograph courtesy Peabody Essex Museum, #83830).

members of the Japanese elite were inclined to oppose it as disruptive and foreign. By 1580 more than 100,000 Japanese had become Christians, and one daimyo gave Jesuit missionaries the port city of Nagasaki°. In 1613 Date Masamune°, the fierce and independent daimyo of northern Honshu°, sent his own embassy to the Vatican, by way of the Philippines (where there were significant communities of Japanese merchants and pirates) and Mexico City. Some daimyo converts ordered their subjects to become Christians as well. Other Japanese were won over by the Jesuit, Dominican, and Franciscan missionaries.

By the early seventeenth century there were some 300,000 Japanese Christians and a few newly ordained Japanese priests. But these extraordinary events could not stand apart from the fractious politics of the day and suspicions about the larger intentions of the Europeans and their well-armed ships. The new shogunate in Edo became the center of hostility to Christianity. In 1614 a decree charging the Christians with seeking to overthrow true doctrine, change the government, and seize

Nagasaki (NAH-guh-SAHK-kee)   Date Masamune (DAH-tay mah-suh-MOO-nay)   Honshu (HOHN-shoo)

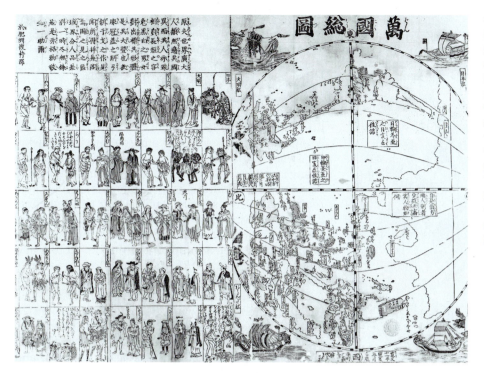

万国総図

Comprehensive Map of the Myriad Nations Thanks to the "Dutch studies" scholars and to overseas contacts, many Japanese were well informed about the cultures, technologies, and political systems of various parts of the world. This combination map and ethnographic text of 1671 enthusiastically explores the differences among the many peoples living or traveling in Asia. The map of the Pacific hemisphere has the north pole on the left and the south pole on the extreme right of the drawing. (British Museum/Fotomas Index)

the land ordered the movement eliminated. Some missionaries left Japan, but others took their movement underground. The government began its persecutions in earnest in 1617, and the beheadings, crucifixions, and forced recantations over the next several decades destroyed almost the entire Christian community.

A series of decrees issued between 1633 and 1639 went much farther, ordering an end to European trade as the price to be paid for eliminating Christian influences. Europeans who entered illegally faced the death penalty. A new government office made sure Christianity did not reemerge; people were required to produce certificates from Buddhist temples attesting to their religious orthodoxy and thus their loyalty to the regime.

The closing of Japan to European influence was not total. A few Dutch were permitted to reside on a small artificial island in Nagasaki's harbor, and a few Japanese were licensed to supply their needs. The information these intermediaries acquired about European weapons technology, shipbuilding, mathematics and astronomy, anatomy and medicine, and geography was known as "Dutch studies."

The Tokugawa government also placed restrictions on the number of Chinese ships that could trade in Japan, but these were harder to enforce. Regional lords in northern and southern Japan not only pursued overseas trade and piracy but also claimed dominion over islands between Japan and Korea to the east and between Japan and Taiwan to the south, including present-day Okinawa.

Despite such evasions, the larger lesson is the substantial success of the new shogunate in exercising its authority.

Elite Decline and Social Crisis

During the 1700s population growth put a great strain on the well-developed lands of central Japan. In more remote provinces, where the lords promoted new settlements and agricultural expansion, the rate of economic growth far outstripped the growth rate in central Japan.

Also destabilizing the Tokugawa government in the 1700s was the shogunate's inability to stabilize rice prices and halt the economic decline of the samurai. To finance their living, the samurai had to convert their rice to cash in the market. The Tokugawa government realized that the rice brokers might easily enrich themselves at the expense of the samurai if the price of rice and the rate of interest were not strictly controlled. Laws designed to regulate both had been passed early in the Tokugawa period, and laws requiring moneylenders to forgive samurai debts were added later. But these laws were not always enforced, sometimes because neither the lords nor the samurai wished them to be. By the early 1700s members of both groups were dependent on the willingness of merchants to provide credit.

The Tokugawa shoguns sought to protect the samurai from decline while curbing the growing power of the

Woodblock Print of the "Forty-Seven Ronin" Story   The saga of the forty-seven ronin and the avenging of their fallen leader has fascinated the Japanese public since the event occurred in 1702. This watercolor from the Tokugawa period shows the leaders of the group pausing on the snowy banks of the Sumida River in Edo (Tokyo) before storming their enemy's residence.   (Jean-Pierre Hauchecorne Collection)

merchant class. Their legitimacy rested on their ability to reward and protect the interests of the lords and samurai who had supported the Tokugawa conquest. But the Tokugawa government, like the governments of China, Korea, and Vietnam, accepted the Confucian idea that agriculture should be the basis of state wealth and that merchants should occupy lowly positions in society because of their reputed lack of moral character.

Governments throughout East Asia used Confucian philosophy to attempt to limit the influence and power of merchants. The Tokugawa government, however, was at a special disadvantage. Its decentralized system limited its ability to regulate merchant activities and actually stimulated the growth of commercial activities. From the founding of the Tokugawa Shogunate in 1603 until 1800, the economy grew faster than the population. Household amenities and cultural resources that in China were found only in the cities were common in the Japanese countryside. Despite official disapproval, merchants and

others involved in the growing economy enjoyed relative freedom and influence in eighteenth-century Japan. They produced a vivid culture of their own, fostering the development of *kabuki* theater, colorful woodblock prints and silk-screened fabrics, and restaurants.

The ideological and social crisis of Tokugawa Japan's transformation from a military to a civil society is captured in the "Forty-Seven Ronin°" incident of 1701–1703. A senior minister provoked a young daimyo into drawing his sword at the shogun's court. For this offense the young lord was sentenced to commit *seppuku°*, the ritual suicide of the samurai. His own followers then became *ronin*, "masterless samurai," obliged by the traditional code of the warrior to avenge their deceased master. They broke into the house of the senior minister who had provoked their own lord, and they killed him and others in his household. Then they withdrew to a temple in Edo and notified the shogun of what they had done out of loyalty to their lord and to avenge his death.

A legal debate began in the shogun's government. To deny the righteousness of the ronin would be to deny samurai values. But to approve their actions would create social chaos, undermine laws against murder, and deny the shogunal government the right to try cases of samurai violence. The shogun ruled that the ronin had to die but would be permitted to die honorably by committing *seppuku*. Traditional samurai values had to surrender to the supremacy of law. The purity of purpose of the ronin is still celebrated in Japan, but since then Japanese writers, historians, and teachers have recognized that the self-sacrifice of the ronin for the sake of upholding civil law was necessary.

The Tokugawa Shogunate put into place a political and economic system that fostered innovation, but the government itself could not exploit it. Thus, during the Tokugawa period the government remained quite traditional while other segments of society developed new methods of productivity and management.

THE LATER MING AND EARLY QING EMPIRES

Like Japan, China after 1500 experienced civil and foreign wars, an important change in government, and new trading and cultural relations with Europe and its neighbors. The internal and external forces at work in China were different in detail and operated on a much larger scale, but they led in similar directions. By 1800

ronin (ROH-neen)   **seppuku** (SEP-poo-koo)

China had a greatly enhanced empire, an expanding economy, and growing doubts about the importance of European trade and Christianity.

The Ming Empire, 1500–1644

The brilliant economic and cultural achievements of the early **Ming Empire** continued during the 1500s. Ming manufacturers had transformed the global economy with their techniques for the assembly-line production of porcelain. An international market eager for Ming porcelain, as well as for silk and lacquered furniture, stimulated the commercial development of East Asia, the Indian Ocean, and Europe. But this golden age was followed by many decades of political weakness, warfare, and rural woes until a new dynasty, the Qing° from Manchuria, guided China back to peace and prosperity.

The Europeans whose ships began to seek out new contacts with China in the early sixteenth century left many accounts of their impressions. Like others before them, they were astonished at Ming China's imperial power, exquisite manufactures, and vast population. European merchants bought such large quantities of the high-grade blue-on-white porcelain commonly used by China's upper classes that in English all fine dishes became known simply as "china."

The growing integration of China into the world economy stimulated rapid growth in the silk, cotton, and porcelain industries. Agricultural regions that supplied raw materials to these industries and food for the expanding urban populations also prospered. In exchange for Chinese porcelain and textiles, tens of thousands of tons of silver from Japan and Latin America flooded into China in the century before 1640. The influx of silver led many Chinese to substitute payments in silver for various land taxes, labor obligations, and other kinds of dues.

Ming cities had long been culturally and commercially vibrant. Many large landowners and absentee landlords lived in the cities, as did officials, artists, and rich merchants who had purchased ranks or prepared their sons for the examinations. The elite classes had created a brilliant culture in which novels, operas, poetry, porcelain, and painting were all closely interwoven. Owners of small businesses catering to the urban elites could make money through printing, tailoring, running restaurants, or selling paper, ink, ink-stones, and writing brushes. The imperial government operated factories for the production of ceramics and silks. Enormous government complexes at Jingdezhen and elsewhere invented

Qing (ching)

assembly-line techniques and produced large quantities of high-quality ceramics for sale in China and abroad.

Despite these achievements, serious problems were developing that left the Ming Empire economically exhausted, politically deteriorating, and technologically lagging behind both its East Asian neighbors and some European countries. Some of these problems were the result of natural disasters associated with climate change and disease. There is evidence that the climate changes known as the Little Ice Age in seventeenth-century Europe affected the climate in China as well (see Issues in World History: The Little Ice Age). Annual temperatures dropped, reached a low point about 1645, and remained low until the early 1700s. The resulting agricultural distress and famine fueled large uprisings that speeded the end of the Ming Empire. The devastation caused by these uprisings and the spread of epidemic disease resulted in steep declines in local populations.

Along with many benefits, the rapid growth in the trading economy also led to such problems as rapid urban growth and business speculation. Some provinces suffered from price inflation that the flood of silver caused. In contrast to the growing involvement of European governments in promoting economic growth, the Ming government showed little interest in developing the economy and pursued some policies that were inimical to it. Despite the fact that paper currency had failed to find general acceptance as far back as the 1350s, Ming governments persisted in issuing new paper money and promoting copper coins, even after abundant supplies of silver had won the approval of the markets. Corruption was also a serious government problem. By the end of the Ming period the factories were plagued by disorder and inefficiency. The situation became so bad during the late sixteenth and seventeenth centuries that workers held strikes with increasing frequency. During a labor protest at Jingdezhen in 1601, workers threw themselves into the kilns to protest working conditions.

Yet the urban and industrial sectors of later Ming society fared much better than the rural, agricultural sector. After a period of economic growth and recovery from the population decline of the thirteenth century, the rural Ming economy did not maintain strong growth. After the beginning of the sixteenth century, China had knowledge, gained from European traders, of new crops from Africa and America. But they were introduced very slowly, and neither rice-growing regions in southern China nor wheat-growing regions in northern China experienced a meaningful increase in productivity under the later Ming. After 1500 economic depression in the countryside, combined with recurring epidemics in central and southern China, kept rural population growth in check.

Ming Collapse and the Rise of the Qing

Rising environmental, economic, and administrative problems weakened the Ming Empire but did not cause its fall. That was the result of growing rebellion within and the rising power of the Manchu outside the borders.

Insecure boundaries are an indication of the later Ming Empire's difficulties. The Ming had long been under pressure from the powerful Mongol federations of the north and west. In the late 1500s large numbers of Mongols were unified by their devotion to the Dalai Lama°, or universal teacher, of Tibetan Buddhism, whom they regarded as their spiritual leader. Building on this spiritual unity, a brilliant leader named Galdan restored Mongolia as a regional military power around 1600. The Manchu, an agriculturally based people who controlled the region north of Korea, grew stronger in the northeast.

In the southwest, there were repeated uprisings among native peoples crowded by the immigration of Chinese farmers. Pirates, many Japanese, based in Okinawa and Taiwan frequently looted the southeastern coastal towns. Ming military resources, concentrated against the Mongols and the Manchu in the north, could not be deployed to defend the coasts. As a result, many southern Chinese migrated to Southeast Asia to profit from the sea-trading networks of the Indian Ocean.

As the previous section related, the Japanese invasion of 1592 to 1598 set the Ming collapse in motion. To stop the Japanese the Ming brought Manchu troops into an international force and eventually paid a high price for that invitation. Weakened by the strain of repelling the Japanese, Chinese defenses in the northeast could not stop the advance of Manchu troops, who had already brought Korea under their sway.

Taking advantage of this situation, as the opening of this chapter related, the Chinese rebel leader Li Zicheng advanced and captured Beijing. With the emperor dead by his own hand and the imperial family in flight, a Ming general invited Manchu leaders to help his forces take Beijing from the rebels. The Manchu did so in the summer of 1644. Rather than restoring the Ming, they claimed China for their own and began a forty-year conquest of the rest of the Ming territories (see Diversity and Dominance: Gendered Violence: The Yangzhou Massacre). By the end of the century, the Manchu had gained control of south China and incorporated the island of Taiwan into imperial China for the first time (see Map 21.1). They also conquered parts of Mongolia and Central Asia.

A Manchu family headed the new **Qing Empire,** and Manchu generals commanded the military forces. But Manchu were a very small portion of the population, and one of several minority populations. The overwhelming majority of Qing officials, soldiers, merchants, and farmers were ethnic Chinese. Like other successful invaders of China, the Qing soon adopted Chinese institutions and policies.

Trading Companies and Missionaries

For the European mariners who braved the long voyages to Asia, the China trade was second in importance only to the spice trade of southern Asia. China's vast population and manufacturing skills drew a steady supply of ships from western Europe, but enthusiasm for the trade developed more slowly, especially at the imperial court.

A Portuguese ship reached China at the end of 1513, but was not permitted to trade. A formal Portuguese embassy in 1517 got bogged down in Chinese protocol and procrastination, and China expelled the Portuguese in 1522. Finally, in 1557 the Portuguese gained the right to trade from a base in Macao°. Spain's Asian trade was conducted from Manila in the Philippines, which served as the terminus of trans-Pacific trade routes from South America. For a time, the Spanish and the Dutch both maintained outposts for trade with China and Japan on the island of Taiwan, but in 1662 they were forced to concede control over the island to the Qing, who incorporated Taiwan for the first time as a part of China.

By then, the Dutch East India Company (VOC) had displaced the Portuguese as the major European trader in the Indian Ocean and, despite the setback on Taiwan, was establishing itself as the main European trader in East Asia. VOC representatives courted official favor in China by acknowledging the moral superiority of the emperor. They performed the ritual kowtow (in which the visitor knocked his head on the floor while crawling toward the throne) to the Ming emperor.

Catholic missionaries accompanied the Portuguese and Spanish merchants to China, just as they did to Japan. While the Franciscans and Dominicans sought to replicate the conversion efforts at the bottom of society that had worked so well in Japan, the Jesuits concentrated their efforts among China's intellectual and political elite. In this they were far more successful than they had been in Japan—at least until the eighteenth century.

The outstanding Jesuit of late Ming China, Matteo Ricci° (1552–1610), became expert in the Chinese language and an accomplished scholar of the Confucian

---

Dalai Lama (DAH-lie LAH-mah)

Macao (muh-KOW)   **Matteo Ricci** (mah-TAY-oh REE-chee)

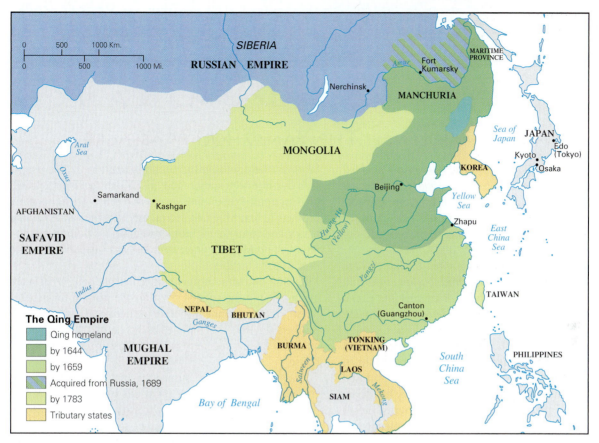

Map 21.1 The Qing Empire, 1644–1783 The Qing Empire began in Manchuria and captured north China in 1644. Between 1644 and 1783 the Qing conquered all the former Ming territories and added Taiwan, the lower Amur River basin, Inner Mongolia, eastern Turkestan, and Tibet. The resulting state was more than twice the size of the Ming Empire.

classics. Under Ricci's leadership, the Jesuits sought to adapt Catholic Christianity to Chinese cultural traditions while enhancing their status by introducing the Chinese to the latest science and technology from Europe. From 1601 Ricci was allowed to reside in Beijing on an imperial stipend as a Western scholar. Later Jesuits headed the office of astronomy that issued the official calendar.

Emperor Kangxi (r. 1662–1722)

The seventeenth and eighteenth centuries—particularly the reigns of the **Kangxi**° (r. 1662–1722) and Qianlong° (r. 1736–1796) emperors—were a period of great economic, military, and cultural achievement in China. The early Qing emperors wished to foster economic and demographic recovery in China. They repaired the roads

Kangxi (KAHNG-shee)   Qianlong (chee-YEN-loong)

and waterworks, lowered transit taxes, mandated comparatively low rents and interest rates, and established economic incentives for resettlement of the areas devastated during the peasant rebellions of the late Ming period. Foreign trade was encouraged. Vietnam, Burma, and Nepal sent regular embassies to the Qing tribute court and carried the latest Chinese fashions back home. Overland routes of communication from Korea to Central Asia were revived, and through its conquests the Qing Empire gained access to the superior horses of Afghanistan.

The early Qing conquest of Beijing and north China was carried out under the leadership of a group of Manchu aristocrats who dominated the first Qing emperor based in China and were regents for his young son, who was declared emperor in 1662. This child-emperor, Kangxi, spent several years doing political battle with his regents, and in 1669 he gained real as well as formal control of the government by executing his chief regent.

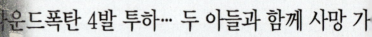

DIVERSITY AND DOMINANCE

GENDERED VIOLENCE: THE YANGZHOU MASSACRE

After the fall of Beijing to the Manchu, the rest of China felt the dominance of the conquerors. The Qing were not eager for reminders of their brutal takeover to circulate. This rare eyewitness account, which survived because it was smuggled out of China, reveals not just the violence of the conquest but also the diversity of its impact on men and women.

The account begins in 1645 as rumors of approaching Manchu soldiers spread through Yangzhou, an important city near the juncture of the Yangzi River and the Grand Canal, and the soldiers charged with its defense begin to flee.

Crowds of barefoot and disheveled refugees were flocking into the city. When questioned, they were too distraught to reply. At that point dozens of mounted soldiers in confused waves came surging south looking as though they had given up all hope. Along them appeared a man who turned out to be the commandant himself. It seems he had intended to leave by the east gate but could not because the enemy soldiers outside the wall were drawing too near; he was therefore forced to cut across this part of town to reach the south gate. This is how we first learned for sure that the enemy troops would enter the city. . . .

My house backed against the city wall, and peeping through the chinks in my window, I saw the soldiers on the wall marching south then west, solemn and in step. Although the rain was beating down, it did not seem to disturb them. This reassured me because I gathered that they were well disciplined units.

. . . For a long time no one came. I retreated again to the back window and found that the regiment on the wall had broken ranks; some soldiers were walking about, others standing still.

All of a sudden I saw some soldiers escorting a group of women dressed in Yangzhou fashion. This was my first real shock. Back in the house, I said to my wife, "Should things go badly when the soldiers enter the city, you may need to end your life."

"Yes," she replied, "Whatever silver we have you should keep. I think we women can stop thinking about life in this world." She gave me all the silver, unable to control her crying. . . .

Soon my younger brother arrived, then my two older brothers. We discussed the situation and I said, "The people who live in our neighborhood are all rich merchants. It will be disastrous if they think we are rich too." I then urged my brothers to brave the rain and quickly take the women by the back route to my older brother's house. His home was situated behind Mr. He's graveyard and was surrounded by the huts of poor families. . . .

Finally, my eldest brother reappeared and said, "People are being killed in the streets! What are we waiting for here? It doesn't matter so much whether we live or die, as long as we brothers stay together." Immediately I gathered together our ancestral tablets and went with him to our second brother's house. . . .

The cunning soldiers, suspecting that many people were still hidden, tried to entice them out by posting a placard promising clemency. About fifty to sixty people, half of them women, emerged. My elder brother said, "We four by ourselves will never survive if we run into these vicious soldiers, so we had better join the crowd. Since there are so many of them, escape will be easier. Even if things do not turn out well, as long as we are together, we will have no cause for regret." In our bewilderment we could think of no other way to save our lives. Thus agreed, we went to join the group.

The leaders were three Manchu soldiers. They searched my brothers and found all the silver they were carrying, but left me untouched. At that point some women appeared, two of whom called out to me. I recognized them as the concubines of my friend Mr. Zhu Shu and stopped them anxiously. They were disheveled and partly naked, their feet bare and covered with mud up to the ankles. One was holding a girl whom the soldiers hit with a whip and threw into the mud. Then we were immediately driven on. One soldier, sword in hand, took the lead; another drove us from behind with a long spear; and a third walked along on our right and left flanks alternately, making sure no one escaped. In groups of twenty or thirty we were herded along like sheep and cattle. If we faltered we were struck, and some people were even killed on the spot. The women were tied together with long chains around their necks, like a clumsy string of pearls. Stumbling at every step, they were soon covered with mud. Here and there on the ground lay babies, trampled by people or horses. Blood and gore soaked the fields, which were filled with the sound of sobbing. We passed gutters and ponds piled high with corpses; the blood had turned the water to a deep greenish-red color and filled the ponds to the brim.

. . . We then entered the house of [a] merchant, . . . which had been taken over by the three soldiers. Another soldier was already there. He had seized several attractive women and was rifling their trunks for fancy silks, which he piled in a heap. Seeing the three soldiers arrive, he laughed and pushed several dozen of us into the back hall. The women he led into a side chamber. . . .

The three soldiers stripped the women of their wet clothing all the way to their underwear, then ordered the seamstress to measure them and give them new garments. The women, thus coerced, had to expose themselves and stand naked. What shame they endured! Once they had changed, the soldiers grabbed them and forced them to join them in eating and drinking, then did whatever they pleased with them, without any regard for decency.

[The narrator escapes and hides atop a wooden canopy over a bed.] Later on a soldier brought a woman in and wanted her to sleep with him in the bed below me. Despite her refusal he forced her to yield. "This is too near the street. It is not a good place to stay," the woman said. I was almost discovered, but after a time the soldier departed with the woman. . . . [The narrator flees again and is reunited with his wife and relatives.]

At length, however, there came a soldier of the "Wolf Men" tribe, a vicious-looking man with a head like a mouse and eyes like a hawk. He attempted to abduct my wife. She was obliged to creep forward on all fours, pleading as she had with the others, but to no avail. When he insisted that she stand up, she rolled on the ground and refused. He then beat her so savagely with the flat of his sword that the blood flowed out in streams, totally soaking her clothes. Because my wife had once admonished me, "If I am unlucky I will die no matter what; do not plead for me as a husband or you will get caught too," I acted as if I did not know she was being beaten and hid far away in the grass, convinced she was about to die. Yet the depraved soldier did not stop there; he grabbed her by the hair, cursed her, struck her cruelly, and then dragged her away by the leg. . . . Just then they ran into a body of mounted soldiers. One of them said a few words to the soldier in Manchu. At this he dropped my wife and departed with them. Barely able to crawl back, she let out a loud sob, every part of her body injured. . . .

Unexpectedly there appeared a handsome looking man of less than thirty, a double-edged sword hung by his side, dressed in Manchu-style hat, red coat, and a pair of black boots. His follower, in a yellow jacket, was also very gallant in appearance. Immediately behind them were several residents of Yangzhou. The young man in red, inspecting me closely, said, "I would

judge from your appearance that you are not one of these people. Tell me honestly, what class of person are you?"

I remembered that some people had obtained pardons and others had lost their lives the moment they said that they were poor scholars. So I did not dare come out at once with the truth and instead concocted a story. He pointed to my wife and son and asked who they were, and I told him the truth. "Tomorrow the prince will order that all swords be sheathed and all, of you will be spared," he said and then commanded his followers to give us some clothes and an ingot of silver. He also asked me, "How many days have you been without food?"

"Five days," I replied.

"Then come with me," he commanded. Although we only half trusted him, we were afraid to disobey. He led us to a well-stocked house, full of rice, fish, and other provisions. "Treat these four people well," he said to a woman in the house and then left. . . .

The next day was [April 30]. Killing and pillaging continued, although not on the previous scale. Still the mansions of the rich were thoroughly looted, and almost all the teenage girls were abducted. . . . every grain of rice, every inch of silk now entered these tigers' mouths. The resulting devastation is beyond description.

[May 2]. Civil administration was established in all the prefectures and counties; proclamations were issued aimed at calming the people, and monks from each temple were ordered to burn corpses. The temples themselves were clogged with women who had taken refuge, many of whom had died of fright or starvation. The "List of Corpses Burned" records more than eight hundred thousand, and this list does not include those who jumped into wells, threw themselves into the river, hanged themselves, were burned to death inside houses, or were carried away by the soldiers. . . .

When this calamity began there had been eight of us: my two elder brothers, my younger brother, my elder brother's wife, their son, my wife, my son, and myself. Now only three of us survived for sure, though the fate of my wife's brother and sister-in-law was not yet known. . . .

From the 25th of the fourth month to the 5th of the fifth month was a period of ten days. I have described here only what I actually experienced or saw with my own eyes; I have not recorded anything I picked up from rumor or hearsay.

QUESTIONS FOR ANALYSIS

1. What accounts for the soldiers' brutal treatment of the women.
2. What did different women do to protect themselves?
3. Having conquered, what did the Manchu do to restore order?

Source: Reprinted with permission of the Free Press, a division of Simon and Schuster Adult Publishing Group, from *Chinese Civilization: A Sourcebook,* Second Edition, edited by Patricia Buckley Ebrey. Copyright ©1993 by Patricia Buckley Ebrey.

Emperor Kangxi   In a portrait from about 1690, the young Manchu ruler is portrayed as a refined scholar in the Confucian tradition. He was a scholar and had great intellectual curiosity, but this portrait would not suggest that he was also capable of leading troops in battle.   (The Palace Museum, Beijing)

Kangxi was then sixteen. He was an intellectual prodigy who mastered classical Chinese, Manchu, and Mongolian at an early age and memorized the Chinese classics. His reign, lasting until his death in 1722, was marked not only by great expansion of the empire but by great stability as well.

The Qing rulers were as anxious as the Ming to consolidate their northern frontiers, especially as they feared an alliance between Galdan's Mongol state and the expanding Russian presence along the **Amur° River.** In the 1680s the Kangxi sent forces to attack the wooden forts on the northern bank of the Amur that hardy Russian scouts had built. Neither empire sent large forces into the Amur territories, and the contest was partly a struggle for the goodwill of the local Evenk and Dagur

Amur (AH-moor)

peoples. The Qing emperor emphasized the importance of treading lightly in the struggle and well understood the principles of espionage:

> Upon reaching the lands of the Evenks and the Dagurs you will send to announce that you have come to hunt deer. Meanwhile, keep a careful record of the distance and go, while hunting, along the northern bank of the Amur until you come by the shortest route to the town of Russian settlement at Albazin. Thoroughly reconnoiter its location and situation. I don't think the Russians will take a chance on attacking you. If they offer you food, accept it and show your gratitude. If they do attack you, don't fight back. In that case, lead your people and withdraw into our own territories. For I have a plan of my own.[2]

That delicacy gives a false impression of the intensity of the struggle between these two great empires. Qing forces twice attacked Albazin. The Qing were worried about Russian alliances with other frontier peoples, while Russia wished to protect its access to the furs, timber, and metals concentrated in Siberia, Manchuria, and Yakutsk. The Qing and Russians were also rivals for control of northern Asia's Pacific coast. Continued conflict would benefit neither side. In 1689 the Qing and Russian Empires negotiated the Treaty of Nerchinsk, using Jesuit missionaries as interpreters. The treaty fixed the border along the Amur River and regulated trade across it. Although this was a thinly settled area, the treaty proved important since the frontier it demarcated has long endured.

The next step was to settle the Mongolian frontier. Kangxi personally led troops in the great campaigns that defeated Galdan and brought Inner Mongolia under Qing control by 1691.

Kangxi was distinguished by his openness to new ideas and technologies from different regions. Unlike the rulers of Japan, who drove Christian missionaries out, he welcomed Jesuit advisers and put them in important offices. Jesuits helped create maps in the European style as practical guides to newly conquered regions and as symbols of Qing dominance. Kangxi considered introducing the European calendar, but protests from the Confucian elite were so strong that the plan was dropped. The emperor frequently discussed scientific and philosophical issues with the Jesuits. When he fell ill with malaria in the 1690s, Jesuit medical expertise (in this case, the use of quinine) aided his recovery. Kangxi also ordered the creation of illustrated books in Manchu detailing European anatomical and pharmaceutical knowledge.

To gain converts among the Chinese elite, the Jesuits made important compromises in their religious teaching. The most important was their toleration of Confucian ancestor worship. The matter caused great controversy

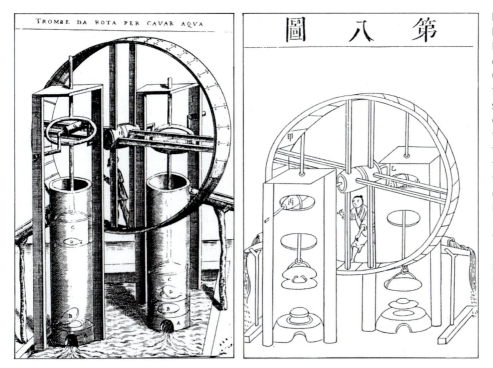

TROMBE DA ROTA PER CAVAR AQVA

圖 八 第

From the Jesuit Library at Beijing Jesuits such as Matteo Ricci were willing to share books on technology and science with Chinese scholars. But without firsthand experience it was impossible for Chinese translators to convey how the devices actually worked. Here, a man walking in a wheel drives a shaft that changes the pressure inside two pumps. In the Chinese translation of the drawing, the mechanisms were all lost. (Left: From Zonca, *Trombe da Rota per Cavar Aqua* [1607]. Right: "Diagram Number Eight" from *Qi tushuo* [*Illustrations on Energy*] [1627]. Both courtesy of Joseph Needham, *Science and Civilization in China*, vol. 4)

between the Jesuits and their Catholic rivals in China, the Franciscans and Dominicans, and also between the Jesuits and the pope. In 1690 the disagreement reached a high pitch. Kangxi wrote to Rome supporting the Jesuit position. Further disagreement with a papal legate to China led Kangxi to order the expulsion of all missionaries who refused to sign a certificate accepting his position. Most of the Jesuits signed, but relations with the imperial court were irreparably harmed. Jesuit presence in China declined in the eighteenth century, and later Qing emperors persecuted Christians rather than naming them to high offices.

Chinese Influences on Europe

The exchange of information between the Qing and the Europeans that Kangxi had fostered was never one-way. When the Jesuits informed the Qing court on matters of anatomy, for instance, the Qing were able to demonstrate an early form of inoculation, called "variolation," that had been used to stem the spread of smallpox after the Qing conquest of Beijing. The technique helped inspire the development of other vaccines later in Europe.

Similarly, Jesuit writings about the intellectual and cultural achievements of China excited admiration in Europe. The wealthy and the aspiring middle classes of Europe demanded Chinese things—or things that looked to Europeans as if they could be Chinese. Not only silk, porcelain, and tea were avidly sought, but also cloisonné jewelry, tableware and decorative items, lacquered and jeweled room dividers, painted fans, and carved jade and ivory (which originated in Africa and was finished in China). One of the most striking Chinese influences on European interior life in this period was wallpaper—an adaptation of the Chinese practice of covering walls with enormous loose-hanging watercolors or calligraphy scrolls. By the mid-1700s special workshops throughout China were producing wallpaper and other consumer items according to the specifications of European merchants. The items were shipped to Canton for export to Europe.

In political philosophy, too, the Europeans felt they had something to learn from the early Qing emperors. In the late 1770s poems supposedly written by Emperor Qianlong were translated into French and disseminated through the intellectual circles of western Europe. These works depicted the Qing emperors as benevolent despots who campaigned against superstition and ignorance, curbed the excesses of the aristocracy, and patronized science and the arts. European intellectuals who were questioning their own political systems found the image of a practical, secular, compassionate ruler intriguing. The French thinker Voltaire proclaimed the

Qing emperors model philosopher-kings and advocated such rulership as a protection against the growth of aristocratic privilege.

Tea and Diplomacy

The Qing were eager to expand China's economic influence but were determined to control the trade very strictly. To make trade easier to tax and to limit piracy and smuggling, the Qing permitted only one market point for each foreign sector. Thus Europeans were permitted to trade only at Canton.

This system worked well enough for European traders until the late 1700s, when Britain became worried about its massive trade deficit with China. From bases in India and Singapore, British traders moved eastward to China and eventually displaced the Dutch as China's leading European trading partner. The directors of the East India Company (EIC) believed that China's technological achievements and gigantic potential markets made it the key to limitless profit. China had tea, rhubarb, porcelain, and silk to offer. By the early 1700s the EIC dominated European trading in Canton.

Tea from China had spread overland on Eurasian routes in medieval and early modern times to become a prized import in Russia, Central Asia, and the Middle East, all of which know it by its northern Chinese name, *cha*—as do the Portuguese. Other western Europeans acquired tea from the sea routes and thus know it by its name in the Fujian province of coastal China and Taiwan: *te*. In much of Europe, tea competed with chocolate and coffee as a fashionable drink by the mid-1600s.

Great fortunes were being made in the tea trade, but the English had not found a product to sell to China. They believed that China was a vast unexploited market, with hundreds of millions of potential consumers of lamp oil made from whale blubber, cotton grown in India or the American South, or guns manufactured in London or Connecticut. Particularly after the loss of the thirteen American colonies, Britain feared that its markets would diminish, and the EIC and other British merchants believed that only the Qing trade system—the "Canton system," as the British called it—stood in the way of opening new paths for commerce.

The British government also worried about Britain's massive trade deficit with China. Because the Qing Empire rarely bought anything from Britain, British silver poured into China to pay for imported tea and other products. The Qing government, whose revenues were declining in the later 1700s while its expenses rose, needed the silver. But in Britain the imbalance of payments stirred anxiety and anger over the restrictions that the Qing placed on imported foreign goods. To make matters worse, the East India Company had managed its worldwide holdings badly, and as it teetered on bankruptcy, its attempts to manipulate Parliament became increasingly intrusive. In 1792 the British government dispatched Lord George Macartney, a well-connected peer with practical experience in Russia and India, to China. Including scientists, artists, and translators as well as guards and diplomats, the **Macartney mission** showed Britain's great interest in the Qing Empire as well as the EIC's desire to revise the trade system.

China was not familiar with the European system of ambassadors, and Macartney struggled to portray himself in Chinese terms as a "tribute emissary" come to salute the Qianlong emperor's eightieth birthday. He steadfastly refused to perform the kowtow to the emperor, but did agree to bow on one knee as he would to his own monarch, King George III. The Qianlong emperor received Macartney courteously in September 1793, but refused to alter the Canton trading system, open new ports of trade, or allow the British to establish a permanent mission in Beijing, The Qing had no interest in changing a system that provided revenue to the imperial family and lessened serious piracy problems. Qianlong sent a letter to King George explaining that China had no need to increase its foreign trade, had no use for Britain's ingenious devices and manufacturers, and set no value on closer diplomatic ties.

Dutch, French, and Russian embassies soon attempted to achieve what Macartney had failed to do. When they also failed, European frustration with the Qing mounted. The great European admiration for China faded, and China was considered despotic, self-satisfied, and unrealistic. Political solutions seemed impossible because the Qing court would not communicate with foreign envoys or observe the simplest rules of the diplomatic system familiar to Europeans. In Macartney's view, China was like a venerable old warship, well maintained and splendid to look at, but obsolete and no longer up to the task.

Population and Social Stress

The Chinese who escorted Macartney and his entourage in 1792–1793 took them through China's prosperous cities and productive farmland. The visitors did not see evidence of the economic and environmental decline that had begun to affect China in the last decades of the 1700s. The population explosion had intensified demand for rice and wheat, for land to be opened for the planting of crops imported from Africa and the Americas, and for more thorough exploitation of land already in use.

East Meets West In a large procession, sixteen men carry the seated Qianlong emperor to a meeting with the English ambassador Lord Macartney at the emperor's extensive summer palace on 14 September 1793. The British are on the right. (British Museum, Department of Prints and Drawings)

In the peaceful decades of Qing rule, China's population had grown to three times its size in 1500. If one accepts an estimate of some 350 million in the late 1700s, China had twice the population of all of Europe. Despite the efficiency of Chinese agriculture and the gradual adoption of New World crops such as corn and sweet potatoes, population growth led to social and environmental problems. More people meant less land per person for farming. Increased demand for building materials and firewood sharply reduced China's remaining woodlands. Deforestation, in turn, accelerated wind and water erosion and increased the danger of flooding. Dams and dikes were not maintained, and silted-up river channels were not dredged. By the end of the eighteenth century parts of the thousand-year-old Grand Canal linking the rivers of north and south China were nearly unusable, and the towns that bordered it were starved for commerce.

The result was misery in many parts of interior China. Some districts responded by increasing production of cash crops such as tea, cotton, and silk that were tied to the export market. Some peasants sought seasonal jobs in better-off agricultural areas or worked in low-status jobs such as barge puller, charcoal burner, or night soil carrier. Many drifted to the cities to make their way by begging, prostitution, or theft. In central and southwestern China, where serious floods had impoverished many farmers, rebellions became endemic. Often joining in revolt were various indigenous peoples, who were largely concentrated in the less fertile lands in the south and in the northern and western borderlands of the empire (see Map 21.2).

The Qing government was not up to controlling its vast empire. The Qing Empire was twice the size of the Ming geographically, but employed about the same number of officials. The government's dependence on working alliances with local elites had led to widespread corruption and shrinking government revenues. As was the case with other empires, the Qing's spectacular rise had ended, and decline had set in.

THE RUSSIAN EMPIRE

From modest beginnings in 1500, Russia expanded rapidly during the next three centuries to create an empire that stretched from eastern Europe across northern Asia and into North America. Russia also became one of the major powers of Europe by 1750, with armies capable of mounting challenges to its Asian and European neighbors.

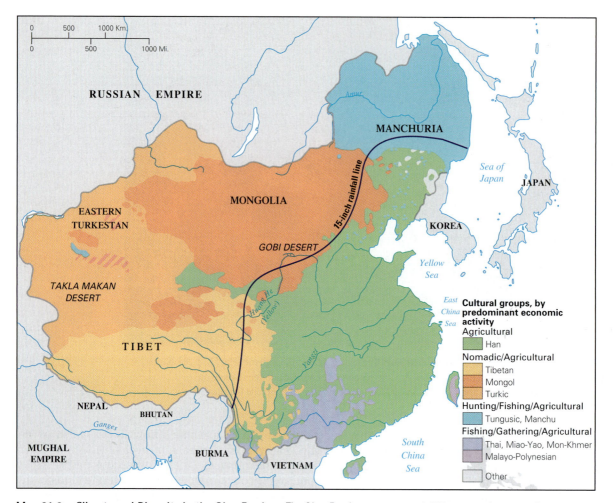

Map 21.2   Climate and Diversity in the Qing Empire   The Qing Empire encompassed different environmental zones, and the climate differences corresponded to population density and cultural divisions. Wetter regions to the east of the 15-inch rainfall line also contained the most densely populated 20 percent of Qing land. The drier, less densely populated 80 percent of the empire was home to the greatest portion of peoples who spoke languages other than Chinese. Many were nomads, fishermen, hunters, and farmers who raised crops other than rice.

The Drive Across Northern Asia

The Russians were a branch of the Slavic peoples of eastern Europe, and most were Orthodox Christians like the Greeks. During the centuries just before 1500, their history had been dominated by Asian rule. The Mongol Khanate of the Golden Horde had ruled the Russians and their neighbors from the 1240s until 1480.

Under the Golden Horde Moscow became the most important Russian city and the center of political power. Moscow lay in the forest that stretched across northern Eurasia, in contrast to the treeless steppe (plains) fa-vored by Mongol horsemen for pasture. The princes of **Muscovy°**, the territory surrounding the city of Moscow, led the movement against the Golden Horde and ruthlessly annexed the great territories of the neighboring Russian state of Novgorod in 1478.

Once free from Mongol domination, the princes of Moscovy set out on conquests that in time made them masters of the old dominions of the Golden Horde and then of a far greater empire. Prince Ivan IV (r. 1533–1584) pushed the conquests south and east, expanding Rus-

Muscovy (MUSS-koe-vee)

sia's borders far to the east through the conquest of the Khanates of Kazan and Astrakhan and the northern Caucasus region (see Map 21.3).

At the end of the sixteenth century, Russians ruled the largest state in Europe and large territories on the Asian side of the **Ural Mountains** as well. Since 1547 the Russian ruler used the title **tsar°** (from the Roman imperial title "caesar"), the term Russians had used for the rulers of the Mongol Empire. The Russian church promoted the idea of Moscow as the "third Rome," successor to the Roman Empire's second capital, Constantinople, which had fallen to the Ottoman Turks in 1453. But such foreign titles were a thin veneer over a very Russian pattern of expansion.

These claims to greatness were also exaggerated: in 1600 the Russian Empire was poor, backward, and landlocked. Only the northern city of Arkangelsk was connected by water to the rest of the world—when its harbor was not frozen. The independent Crimean peoples to the south were powerful enough to sack Moscow in 1571. Beyond them, the still vigorous Ottoman Empire controlled the shores of the Black Sea, while the Safavid rulers of Iran dominated the trade routes of southern Central Asia. The powerful kingdoms of Sweden and Poland-Lithuania to the west turned back Russian forces trying to gain access to the warmer waters of the Baltic Sea and pummeled them badly.

A path of less resistance lay to the east across **Siberia,** and it had much to recommend it. Many Russians felt more at home in the forested northern part of Siberia than on the open steppes, and the thinly inhabited region teemed with valuable resources. Most prominent of these resources was the soft, dense fur that forest animals grew to survive the long winter cold. Like their counterparts in Canada (see Chapter 18), hardy Russian pioneers in Siberia made a living from animal pelts. The merchants from western Europe and other lands who came to buy these furs in Moscow provided the tsars with revenues and access to European technology.

Early Russian exploration of Siberia was not the work of the state but of the Strogonovs, a wealthy Russian trading family. The small bands of hunting and fishing peoples who inhabited this cold and desolate region had no way of resisting the armed adventurers hired by the Strogonovs. Their troops attacked the only political power in the region, the Khanate of Sibir, and they used their rifles to destroy the khanate in 1582. Taking advantage of rivers to move through the almost impenetrable forests, Russian fur trappers reached the Pacific during the seventeenth century and soon crossed over into

tsar (zahr)

Alaska. Russian political control followed at a much slower pace. In the seventeenth century Siberia was a frontier zone with widely scattered forts, not a province under full control. Native Siberian peoples continued to resist Russian control fiercely, and the Russians had to placate local leaders with gifts and acknowledge their rights and authority. From the early seventeenth century the tsar also used Siberia as a penal colony for criminals and political prisoners.

The trade in furs and forest products helped ease Russian isolation and fund further conquests. The eastward expansion of the Russian state took second place during the seventeenth century to the tsars' efforts to build political and military power and establish control over the more numerous peoples of Siberia and the steppe.

In the 1640s Russian settlers had begun to move into the valley of the Amur River east of Mongolia in order to grow grain. The government's wooden forts aroused the concerns of the Ming about yet another threat on their northern frontier. As seen already, by the time the Qing were in a position to deal with the Russian presence, the worrisome threat of Galdan's Mongol military power had arisen. Equally concerned about the Mongols, the Russians were pleased to work out a frontier agreement with China. The 1689 Treaty of Nerchinsk recognized Russian claims west of Mongolia but required the Russians to withdraw their settlements east. Moreover, the negotiations showed China's recognition of Russia as an important and powerful neighbor.

Russian Society and Politics to 1725

Russian expansion produced far-reaching demographic changes and more gradual changes in the relations of the tsar with the elite classes. A third transformation was in the freedom and mobility of the Russian peasantry.

As the empire expanded, it incorporated people with different languages, religious beliefs, and ethnic identities. The emerging Russian Empire included peoples who spoke Asian languages and who were not Christians. Language differences were not hard to overcome, but religious and other cultural differences often caused tensions, especially when differences were manipulated for political purposes. Orthodox missionaries made great efforts to turn people in Siberia into Christians, in much the same way that Catholic missionaries did in Canada. But among the more populous steppe peoples, Islam eventually replaced Christianity as the dominant religion. More fundamental than language, ethnicity, or religion were the differences in how people made their living. Russians tended to live as

Map 21.3   The Expansion of Russia, 1500–1800   Sweden and Poland initially blocked Russian expansion in Europe, while the Ottoman Empire blocked the southwest. In the sixteenth century, Russia began to expand east, toward Siberia and the Pacific Ocean. By the end of the rule of Catherine the Great in 1796, Russia encompassed all of northern and northeastern Eurasia.

farmers, hunters, builders, scribes, or merchants, while those newly incorporated into the empire were mostly herders, caravan workers, and soldiers.

As people mixed, individual and group identities could become quite complex. Even among Russian speakers who were members of the Russian Orthodox Church there was wide diversity of identity. The **Cossacks** are a revealing example. The name probably came from a Turkic word for a warrior or mercenary soldier and referred to bands of people living on the steppes between Moscovy and the Caspian and Black Seas. In practice, Cossacks became highly diverse in their origins and beliefs. What mattered was that they belonged to close-knit bands, were superb riders and fighters, and were feared by both the villagers and the legal authorities. Cossacks made temporary allegiances with many rulers but were most loyal to their bands and to whoever was currently paying for their military services.

Many Cossacks were important allies in the expansion of the Russian Empire. They formed the majority of the soldiers and early settlers employed by the Strogonovs in the penetration of Siberia. Most historians believe that Cossacks founded all the major towns of Russian Siberia. They also manned the Russian camps on the Amur River. The Cossacks west of the Urals performed distinctive service for Russia in defending against Swedish and Ottoman incursions, but they also resisted any efforts to undermine their own political autonomy. Those in the rich and populous lands of the Ukraine, for example, rebelled when the tsar agreed to a division of their lands with Poland-Lithuania in 1667.

In the early seventeenth century Swedish and Polish forces briefly occupied Moscow on separate occasions. In the midst of this "Time of Troubles" the old line of Muscovite rulers was finally deposed, and the Russian aristocracy—the boyars°—allowed one of their own, Mikhail Romanov°, to become tsar (r. 1613–1645). The early Romanov rulers saw a close connection between the consolidation of their own authority and successful competition with neighboring powers. They tended to represent conflicts between Slavic Russians and Turkic peoples of Central Asia as being between Christians and "infidels" or between the civilized and the "barbaric." Despite this rhetoric, it is important to understand that these cultural groups were defined less by blood ties than by the way in which they lived.

The political and economic transformations of the Russian Empire had serious repercussions for the peasants who tilled the land in European Russia. As centralized power rose, the freedom of the peasants fell. The

boyar (BOY-ar)
Romanov (ROH-man-off or roh-MAN-off)

process was longer and more complex than the rise of slavery in the Americas. The Moscovy rulers and early tsars rewarded their loyal nobles with grants of land that included obligations of the local peasants to work for these lords. Law and custom permitted peasants to change masters during a two-week period each year, which encouraged lords to treat their peasants well, but the rising commercialization of agriculture also raised the value of these labor obligations.

The long periods of civil and foreign warfare in the late sixteenth and early seventeenth centuries caused such disruption and economic decline that many peasants fled to the Cossacks or across the Urals to escape. Some who couldn't flee sold themselves into slavery to ensure a steady supply of food. When peace returned, landlords sought to recover these runaway peasants and bind them more firmly to their land. A law change in 1649 completed the transformation of peasants into **serfs** by eliminating the period when they could change masters and removing limitations on the length of the period during which runaways could be forced to return to their masters.

Like slavery, serfdom was a hereditary status, but in theory the serf was tied to a piece of land, not owned by a master. In practice, the difference between serfdom and slavery grew finer as the laws regulating selfdom became stricter. By 1723 all Russian slaves were transformed into serfs. In the Russian census of 1795, serfs made up over half the population of Russia. The serfs were under the control of landowners who made up only 2 percent of Russia's population, similar to the size of the slave-owning class in the Caribbean.

Peter the Great

The greatest of the Romanovs was Tsar **Peter the Great** (r. 1689–1725), who made major changes to reduce Russia's isolation and increase the empire's size and power. Tsar Peter is remembered for his efforts to turn Russia away from its Asian cultural connections and toward what he deemed the civilization of the West. In fact, he accelerated trends under way for some time. By the time he ascended the throne, there were hundreds of foreign merchants in Moscow; western European soldiers had trained a major part of the army in new weapons and techniques; and Italian architects had made an impression on the city's churches and palaces. It was on this substantial base that Peter erected a more rapid transformation of Russia.

Peter matured quickly both physically and mentally. In his youth the government was in the hands of his half-sister Sophia, who was regent on behalf of him and her sickly brother Ivan. Living on an estate near the foreigners' quarter outside Moscow, Peter learned what he could of life outside Russia and busied himself with gaining practical skills in blacksmithing, carpentry, shipbuilding, and the arts of war. He organized his own military drill unit among other young men. When Princess Sophia tried to take complete control of the government in 1689, Peter rallied enough support to send her to a monastery, secure the abdication of Ivan, and take charge of Russia. He was still in his teens.

Peter concerned himself with Russia's expansion and modernization. To secure a warm-water port on the Black Sea, he constructed a small but formidable navy that could blockade Ottoman ports. Describing his wars with the Ottoman Empire as a new crusade to liberate Constantinople from the Muslim sultans, Peter also saw himself as the legal protector of Orthodox Christians living under Ottoman rule. Peter's forces had seized the port of Azov in 1696, but the fortress was lost again in 1713, and Russian expansion southward was blocked for the rest of Peter's reign.

In the winter of 1697–1698, after his Black Sea campaign, Peter traveled in disguise across Europe to discover how western European societies were becoming so powerful and wealthy. The young tsar paid special attention to ships and weapons, even working for a time as a ship's carpenter in the Netherlands. With great insight, he perceived that western European success owed as much to trade and toleration as to technology. Trade generated the money to spend on weapons, while toleration attracted talented persons fleeing persecution. Upon his return to Russia, Peter resolved to expand and reform his vast and backward empire.

In the long and costly Great Northern War (1700–1721), his modernized armies broke Swedish control of the Baltic Sea, establishing more direct contacts between Russia and Europe. Peter's victory forced the European powers to recognize Russia as a major power for the first time.

On land captured from Sweden at the eastern end of the Baltic, Peter built St. Petersburg, a new city that was to be his window on the West. In 1712 the city became Russia's capital. To demonstrate Russia's new sophistication, Peter ordered architects to build St. Petersburg's houses and public buildings in the baroque style then fashionable in France.

Peter also pushed the Russian elite to imitate western European fashions. He personally shaved off his noblemen's long beards to conform to Western styles and ordered them to wear Western clothing. To end the traditional seclusion of upper-class Russian women, Peter required officials, officers, and merchants to bring their wives to the social gatherings he organized in the capital. He also directed the nobles to educate their children.

Another of Peter's strategies was to reorganize Rus-

Peter the Great This portrait from his time as a student in Holland in 1697 shows Peter as ruggedly masculine and practical, quite unlike most royal portraits of the day that posed rulers in foppish elegance and haughty majesty. Peter was a popular military leader as well as an autocratic ruler. (Collection, Countess Bobrinskoy/Michael Holford)

sian government along the lines of the powerful German state of Prussia. To break the power of the boyars he sharply reduced their traditional roles in government and the army. The old boyar council of Moscow was replaced by a group of advisers in St. Petersburg whom the tsar appointed. Members of the traditional nobility continued to serve as generals and admirals, but officers in Peter's modern, professional army and navy were promoted according to merit, not birth.

The goal of Peter's westernization strategy was to strengthen the Russian state and increase the power of the tsar. A decree of 1716 proclaimed that the tsar "is not obliged to answer to anyone in the world for his doings, but possesses power and authority over his kingdom and land, to rule them at his will and pleasure as a Christian ruler." Under this expansive definition of his role, Peter brought the Russian Orthodox Church more firmly under state control, built factories and iron and copper foundries to provide munitions and supplies for the military, and increased the burdens of taxes and forced labor on the serfs. Peter was an absolutist ruler of the sort then popular in western Europe, and he had no more intention of improving the conditions of the serfs, on whose labors the production of basic foodstuffs depended, than did the European slave owners of the Americas.

The Fontanka Canal in St. Petersburg in 1753   The Russian capital continued to grow as a commercial and administrative center. As in Amsterdam, canals were the city's major arteries. On the right is a new summer palace built by Peter's successor.   (Engraving, after M. I. Makhaiev, from the official series of 1753, British Museum)

Consolidation of the Empire

Russia's eastward expansion also continued under Peter the Great and his successors. The frontier settlement with China and Qianlong's quashing of Inner Mongolia in 1689 freed Russians to concentrate on the northern Pacific. The Pacific northeast was colonized, and in 1741 an expedition led by Captain Vitus Bering crossed the strait (later named for him) into North America. In 1799 a Russian company of merchants received a monopoly over the Alaskan fur trade, and its agents were soon active along the entire northwestern coast of North America.

Far more important than these immense territories in the cold and thinly populated north were the populous agricultural lands to the west acquired during the reign of Catherine the Great (r. 1762–1796). A successful war with the Ottoman Empire gave Russia control of the rich north shore of the Black Sea by 1783. As a result of three successive partitions of the once powerful kingdom of Poland between 1772 and 1795, Russia's frontiers advanced 600 miles (nearly 1,000 km.) to the west (see Map 21.3). When Catherine died, the Russian Empire extended from Poland in the west to Alaska in the east,

from the Barents Sea in the north to the Black Sea in the south.

Catherine also made important additions to Peter's policies of promoting industry and building a canal system to improve trade. Besides furs, the Russians had also become major exporters of gold, iron, and timber. Catherine implemented administrative reforms and showed a special talent for diplomacy. Through her promotion of the ideas of the Enlightenment, she expanded Peter's policies of westernizing the Russian elite.

COMPARATIVE PERSPECTIVES

Looked at separately, the histories of Japan, China, and Russia seem to have relatively little in common. Contacts with each other and with other parts of the world appear far less important than forces within each state. However, when examined comparatively these separate histories reveal similarities and differences that help explain the global dynamics of this period and the larger historical patterns of which it is a part.

Political Comparisons

China and Russia are examples of the phenomenal flourishing of empires in Eurasia between 1500 and 1800. Already a vast empire under the Ming, China doubled in size under the Qing, mostly through westward expansion into less densely populated areas. In expanding from a modestly sized principality into the world's largest land empire, Russia added rich and well-populated lands to the west and south and far larger but less populous lands to the east. Russia and China were land based, just like the Ottoman and Mughal Empires, with the strengths and problems of administrative control and tax collection that size entailed.

Although western Europe is often seen as particularly imperialist in the centuries after 1500, only Spain's empire merits comparison with Russia's in the speed of its growth, its land size, and its presence on three continents. The more typical western European empires of this era, the new seaborne trading empires of the Portuguese, Dutch, French, and English, had much less territory, far tighter administration, and a much more global sweep.

Japan was different. Though nominally headed by an emperor, Japan's size and ethnic homogeneity do not support calling it an empire in the same breath with China and Russia. Tokugawa Japan was similar in size and population to France, the most powerful state of western Europe, but its political system was much more decentralized. Japan's efforts to add colonies on the East Asian mainland had failed.

China had once led the world in military innovation (including the first uses of gunpowder), but the modern "gunpowder revolution" of the fifteenth and sixteenth centuries was centered in the Ottoman Empire and western European states. Although the centuries after 1500 were full of successful military operations, Chinese armies continued to depend on superior numbers and tactics for their success, rather than on new technology. As in the past, infantrymen armed with guns served alongside others armed with bows and arrows, swords, and spears.

The military forces of Japan and Russia underwent more innovative changes than those of China, in part through Western contacts. In the course of its sixteenth-century wars of unification, Japan produced its own gunpowder revolution but thereafter lacked the motivation and the means to stay abreast of the world's most advanced military technology. By the eighteenth century Russia had made greater progress in catching up with its European neighbors, but its armies still relied more on their size than on the sophistication of their weapons.

Naval power provides the greatest military contrast among the three. Eighteenth-century Russia constructed modern fleets of warships in the Baltic and the Black Seas, but neither China nor Japan developed navies commensurate with their size and coastlines. China's defenses against pirates and other sea invaders were left to its maritime provinces, whose small war junks were armed with only a half-dozen cannon. Japan's naval capacity was similarly decentralized. In 1792, when Russian ships exploring the North Pacific turned toward the Japanese coast, the local daimyo used his own forces to chase them away. All Japanese daimyo understood that they would be on their own if foreign incursions increased.

Cultural, Social, and Economic Comparisons

The expansion of China and Russia incorporated not just new lands but also diverse new peoples. Both empires pursued policies that tolerated diversity along with policies to promote cultural assimilation. In contrast, Japan remained more culturally homogeneous, and the government reacted with great intolerance to the growing influence of converts to western Christianity.

Chinese society had long been diverse, and its geographical, occupational, linguistic, and religious differences grew as the Qing expanded (see Map 21.2). China had also long used Confucian models, imperial customs, and a common system of writing to transcend such differences. These techniques were most effective in assimilating elites. It is striking how quickly and thoroughly the Manchu conquerors adopted Chinese imperial ways of thinking and acting as well as of dressing, speaking, and writing.

Kangxi's reign is a notable example of how tolerant the Chinese elite could be of new ideas from the Jesuits and other sources. Yet it is important to note that the Jesuits' success owed much to their portraying themselves as supporters of Confucian values and learning. Although Chinese converts to Catholicism were instrumental in introducing European techniques of crop production and engineering, influential members of China's government were highly suspicious of the loyalties of these converts, persecuted them, and eventually moved to prohibit or severely limit missionary activity.

Russia likewise approached its new peoples with a mixture of pragmatic tolerance and a propensity for seeing Russian ways and beliefs as superior. Religion was a particular sore point. With the support of the tsars, Russian Orthodox missionaries encouraged conversion of Siberian peoples. In the new lands of Eastern Europe, Orthodoxy was a common bond for some new subjects, but the Roman Catholic Poles incorporated in the late 1700s would soon suffer greatly for their divergent beliefs and practices. The Russian language was strongly promoted. Russia was also notable for its absorption of new ideas and styles from western Europe, especially under the leadership of its eighteenth-century rulers, although even among the elite, these influences often overlay Russian cultural traditions in a very superficial way

Social structures in China and Russia were as hierarchical and oppressive as in the Islamic states of southern Asia, and in the case of Russia have invited comparisons with the slave plantation societies of the Americas. Rulers were nearly absolute in their powers in theory, though more limited in practice by the size of their empires and by layers of bureaucracy and corruption.

Forced labor remained common in the Russian and Chinese Empires. Serfdom grew more brutal and widespread in Russia in the seventeenth and eighteenth centuries, although the expansion of the frontier eastward across Siberia also opened an escape route for many peasants and serfs. Some Chinese peasants also improved their lot by moving to new territories, but population growth increased overall misery in the eighteenth century. China was also notable for the size of its popular insurrections, especially the one that toppled the Ming.

In striking contrast to the rising importance of commercial interests in the West, private merchants in China and Japan occupied more precarious positions. Confucian thought ranked merchants below peasants in their contributions to society. In Japan a line between maritime traders and pirates would be very difficult to draw, and Chinese sea trade was not much different. Governments conducted diplomatic and strategic missions but had no interest in encouraging overseas voyages or colonies. Instead both Japan and China moved to restrict overseas trade. In the end, commercial contacts were far more important to Europe than to East Asia.

CONCLUSION

As the world has grown more interconnected, it has become increasingly difficult to sort out the degree to which major historical changes were due to forces within a society or to outside forces acting upon it. The histories of Japan, China, and Russia between 1500 and 1800 reveal how internal forces operated separately from external ones and the degree to which they were intertwined.

The formation of the Tokugawa in Japan is a clear example of a society changing from within. The decisions

of government to suppress the Christianity that some Japanese had adopted from European missionaries and to severely curtail commercial and intellectual contacts with distant Europe illustrate how readily even the smallest of the three states could control its dealings with outsiders.

China's history illustrates a more complex interplay of internal and external forces. In the world's most populous state, the already faltering Ming dynasty was greatly weakened by Hideyoshi's Japanese invasion through Korea, overthrown by Li Zicheng's rebels from within, and replaced by the conquering armies of the Manchu from across the northern frontier. The Qing's settlement of the Amur frontier with Russia illustrates how diplomacy and compromise could serve mutual interests. Finally, the Chinese added new European customers to already extensive internal and external markets and developed both positive and problematic cultural relations with the Jesuits and some other Europeans. From a Chinese perspective, European contacts could be useful but were neither essential nor of great importance.

The internal and external factors in Russia's history are the hardest to sort out. Especially problematic is assessing the rising importance of the West in light of Russia's growing trade in that direction, Russia's emergence as a European Great Power, and the stated policies of both Peter the Great and Catherine the Great to westernize their people. Clearly, Western influences were very important, but just as clearly their importance can easily be exaggerated. The impetus for Muscovy's expansion came out of its own history and domination by the Mongols. Trade with western Europe was not the center of the Russian economy. Tsar Peter was primarily interested in imitating Western technology, not in the full range of Western culture. The Russian church was quite hostile to the Catholics and Protestants to their west, whom it regarded as heretics. Peter the Great banned the Jesuits from Russia, considering them a subversive and backward influence.

Looking at each country separately and from within, the influence of western Europeans seems clearly inferior to a host of internal and regional influences. Yet when one looks at what happened in Japan, China, and Russia in the decades after 1800, it is hard to avoid the conclusion that their relationship with the West was a common factor that, when combined with unresolved internal problems, would have a tremendous impact on the course of their history. Qianlong might tell Macartney and the British that he had no use for expanded contacts, but the sentiment was not mutual. As the next part details, after the increasingly powerful Western societies got over dealing with their own internal problems, they would be back, and they would be impossible to dismiss or resist.

◾ Key Terms

Manchu

daimyo

samurai

Tokugawa Shogunate

Ming Empire

Qing Empire

Kangxi

Amur River

Macartney Mission

Muscovy

Ural Mountains

tsar

Siberia

Cossacks

serfs

Peter the Great

◾ Suggested Reading

A fascinating place to begin is with John E. Wills, Jr., *1688: A Global History* (2001), Part III, "Three Worlds Apart: Russia, China, and Japan."

On Japan in this period see Andrew Gordon, *A Modern History of Japan: From Tokugawa Times to the Present* (2003); *The Cambridge History of Japan,* vol. 4: *Early Modern Japan,* ed. John Whitney Hall (1991); Chie Nakane and Shinzaburo Oishi, *Tokugawa Japan: The Social and Economic Antecedents of Modern Japan,* trans. Conrad Totman (1990); and Tessa Morris-Suzuki, *The Technological Transformation of Japan from the Seventeenth to the Twenty-First Century* (1994). Mary Elizabeth Berry, *Hideyoshi* (1982), is an account of the reunification of Japan at the end of the sixteenth century and the invasion of Korea. See also Michael Cooper, ed., *They Came to Japan: An Anthology of European Reports on Japan, 1543–1640* (1965).

For China during the transition from the Ming to Qing periods, see Jonathan D. Spence, *The Search for Modern China* (1990); James W. Tong, *Disorder Under Heaven: Collective Violence in the Ming Dynasty* (1991); Frederic Wakeman, *The Great Enterprise* (1985); and Lynn Struve, *Voices from the Ming-Qing Cataclysm: In Tiger's Jaws* (1993). The latest work on the late Ming is summarized in *The Cambridge History of China,* vol. 8, *The Ming Dynasty, 1368–1644, Part 2* (1998). On the history of the Manchu and of the Qing Empire see Evelyn Sakakida Rawski, *The Last Emperors* (1999), and Pamela Kyle Crossley, *The Manchus* (1997).

On Chinese society generally in this period, see two classic (though slightly dated) works by Ping-ti Ho, *The Ladder of Success in Imperial China: Aspects of Social Mobility, 1368–1911* (1962), and *Studies in the Population of China 1368–1953* (1959); and see the general study by Susan Naquin and Evelyn S. Rawski, *Chinese Society in the Eighteenth Century* (1987). On the two greatest of the Qing emperors and their times, see Jonathan D. Spence, *Emperor of China; Self Portrait of K'ang Hsi, 1654–1722* (1974). For a more scholarly treatment see Lawrence D. Kessler, *K'ang-hsi and the Consolidation of Ch'ing Rule, 1661–1684* (1976); Jonathan D. Spence, *Ts'ao Yin and the K'ang-hsi Emperor: Bondservant and Master* (1966); and Harold Kahn, *Monarchy in the Emperor's Eyes: Image and Reality in the Ch'ien-lung Reign* (1971).

On the Qing trade systems see John E. Wills, *Embassies and Illusions: Dutch and Portuguese Envoys to K'ang-hsi, 1666–1687* (1984), and Craig Clunas, *Chinese Export Art and Design* (1987).

There is a great deal published on the Macartney mission, much of it originating in the diaries and memoirs of the participants. See the exhaustively detailed Alain Peyrefitte, *The Immobile Empire,* trans. Jon Rothschild (1992). For a more theoretical discussion see James L. Hevia, *Cherishing Men from Afar: Qing Guest Ritual and the Macartney Embassy of 1793* (1995).

On early modern Russian history, see Robert O. Crummey, *Aristocrats and Servitors: The Boyar Elite in Russia, 1613–1689* (1983), and Andreas Kappeler, *The Russian Empire: A Multiethnic History* (2001). Western perceptions of Russia are examined in Marshall T. Poe, *"A People Born to Slavery": Russia in Early Modern European Ethnography* (2000), and Lloyd E. Berry and Robert O. Crummey, ed., *Rude and Barbarous Kingdom: Russia in the Accounts of Sixteenth-Century English Voyagers* (1968). Among the best-known recent books on Tsar Peter are Matthew Smith Anderson, *Peter the Great,* 2d ed. (1995); Robert K. Massie, *Peter the Great: His Life and World* (1980); and Lindsey Hughes, *Russia in the Age of Peter the Great: 1682–1725* (1998). For Russian naval development and Russian influence in the Pacific and in America, see Glynn Barratt, *Russia in Pacific Waters, 1715–1825: A Survey of the Origins of Russia's Naval Presence in the North and South Pacific* (1981), and Howard I. Kushner, *Conflict on the Northwest Coast: American-Russian Rivalry in the Pacific Northwest, 1790–1867* (1975).

For Jesuits in East Asia in the sixteenth and seventeenth centuries, see Michael Cooper, S.J., *Rodrigues the Interpreter: An Early Jesuit in Japan and China* (1974); David E. Mungello, *Curious Land: Jesuit Accommodation and the Origins of Sinology* (1985); and Jonathan D. Spence, *The Memory Palace of Matteo Ricci* (1984). Still useful are C. R. Boxer, *The Christian Century in Japan, 1549–1650* (1951), and Cornelius Wessels, *Early Jesuit Travellers in Central Asia, 1603–1721* (1924). On European images of and interactions with China connected to the Jesuits, see the relevant portions of Jonathan D. Spence, *The Chan's Great Continent: China in Western Minds* (1998); Joanna Waley-Cohen, *The Sextants of Beijing: Global Currents in Chinese History* (1999); and David E. Mungello, *The Great Encounter of China and the West, 1500–1800* (1999).

On the East India companies see John E. Wills, *Pepper, Guns, and Parleys: The Dutch East India Company and China, 1662–1681* (1974); Dianne Lewis, *Jan Compagnie in the Straits of Malacca, 1641–1795* (1995); and John Keay, *The Honourable Company: A History of the English East India Company* (1991). On the development of global commerce in tea, coffee, and cocoa, see the relevant chapters in Roy Porter and Mikuláš Teich, *Drugs and Narcotics in History* (1995).

◾ Notes

1. Adapted from Jonathan D. Spence, *The Search for Modern China* (New York: W. W. Norton, 1990), 21–25.
2. Adapted from G. V. Melikhov, "Manzhou Penetration into the Basin of the Upper Amur in the 1680s," in S. L. Tikhvinshii, ed., *Manzhou Rule in China* (Moscow: Progress Publishers, 1983).

The Little Ice Age

A giant volcanic eruption in the Peruvian Andes in 1600 affected the weather in many parts of the world for several years. When volcanic ash from the eruption of Mount Huanyaputina (hoo-AHN-yah-poo-TEE-nuh) shot into the upper atmosphere and spread around the world, it screened out sunlight. As a result, the summer of 1601 was the coldest in two hundred years in the northern hemisphere.

Archaeologist Brian Fagan has pointed out that Mount Huanyaputina's chilling effects were a spectacular event in a much longer pattern of climate change that has been called the Little Ice Age.[1] Although global climate had been cooling since the late 1200s, in the northern temperate regions the 1590s had been exceptionally cold. Temperatures remained cooler than normal throughout the seventeenth century.

The most detailed information on the Little Ice Age comes from Europe. Glaciers in the Alps grew much larger. Trade became difficult when rivers and canals that had once been navigable in winter froze solid from bank to bank. In the coldest years, the growing season in some places was as much as two months shorter than normal. Unexpectedly late frosts withered the tender shoots of newly planted crops in spring. Wheat and barley ripened more slowly during cooler summers and were often damaged by early fall frosts.

People could survive a smaller-than-average harvest in one year by drawing on food reserves, but when cold weather damaged crops in two or more successive years, the consequences were devastating. Deaths due to malnutrition and cold increased sharply when summer temperatures in northern Europe registered 2.7°F (1.5°C) lower than average in 1674 and 1675 and again in 1694 and 1695. The cold spell of 1694 and 1695 caused a famine in Finland that carried off a quarter to a third of the population.

At the time people had no idea what was causing the unusual cold of the Little Ice Age. Advances in climate history make it clear that the cause was not a single terrestrial event such as the eruption of Mount Huanyaputina. Nor was the Little Ice Age the product of human actions, unlike some climate changes such as today's global warming.

Ultimately, the earth's weather is governed by the sun. In the seventeenth century astronomers in Europe reported seeing fewer sunspots, dark spots on the sun's surface that are indicative of solar activity and thus the sun's warming power. Diminished activity in the sun was primarily responsible for the Little Ice Age.

If the sun was the root cause, the effects of global cooling should not have been confined to northern Europe. Although contemporary accounts are much scarcer in other parts of the world, there is evidence of climate changes around the world in this period. Observations of sunspots in China, Korea, and Japan drop to zero between 1639 and 1700. China experienced unusually cool weather in the seventeenth century, but the warfare and disruption accompanying the fall of the Ming and the rise of the Qing probably were much more to blame for the famines and rural distress of that period.

By itself, a relatively slight decrease in average annual temperature would not have a serious effect on human life outside the northern temperate areas. However, evidence suggests that there was also a significant rise in humidity in this period in other parts of the world. Ice cores drilled into ancient glaciers in the Arctic and Antarctic show increased snowfall. Information compiled by historian James L. A. Webb, Jr., shows that lands south of the Sahara received more rainfall between 1550 and 1750 than they had during the previous era.[2] Increased rainfall would have been favorable for pastoral people, whose herds found new pasture in what had once been desert, and for the farmers farther south whose crops got more rain.

In the eighteenth century the sun's activity began to return to normal. Rising temperatures led to milder winters and better harvests in northern Eurasia. Falling rainfall allowed the Sahara to advance southward, forcing the agricultural frontier to retreat.

■ Notes

1. Brian Fagan, *The Littlest Ice Age: How Climate Made History, 1300–1850* (New York: Basic Books, 2000).
2. James L. A. Webb, Jr., *Desert Frontier: Ecological Change Along the Western Sahel, 1600–1850* (Madison: University of Wisconsin Press, 1995).

PART SIX

Revolutions Reshape the World, 1750–1870

CHAPTER 22
Revolutionary Changes in the
Atlantic World, 1750–1850

CHAPTER 23
The Early Industrial
Revolution, 1760–1851

CHAPTER 24
Nation Building and Economic
Transformation in the
Americas, 1800–1890

CHAPTER 25
Africa, India, and the New
British Empire, 1750–1870

CHAPTER 26
Land Empires in the Age of
Imperialism, 1800–1870

B etween 1750 and 1870, nearly every part of the world experienced dramatic political, economic, and social change. The beginnings of industrialization, the American and French Revolutions, and the revolutions for independence in Latin America transformed political and economic life in Europe and the Americas. The most powerful nations challenged existing borders and ethnic boundaries. European nations expanded into Africa, Asia, and the Middle East while Russia and the United States acquired vast new territories.

The American, French, and Latin American revolutions created new political institutions and unleashed the forces of nationalism and social reform. The Industrial Revolution introduced new technologies and patterns of work that made industrial societies wealthier, more fluid socially, and militarily more powerful. Western intellectual life became more secular as the practical benefits of science and technology became evident. Reformers led successful efforts to abolish the Atlantic slave trade and, later, slavery itself in the Western Hemisphere. Efforts to expand voting rights and improve the status of women also gained support in Europe and the Americas.

European empires in the Western Hemisphere were largely dismantled by 1825. But the Industrial Revolution led to a new wave of economic and imperial expansion. France conquered the North African state of Algeria, while Great Britain expanded its colonial rule in India and established new colonies in Australia and New Zealand. Of these, India alone had a larger population than that of all the colonies Europe had lost in the Americas.

Throughout Africa, European economic influence greatly expanded, deepening the region's connection to the Atlantic economy and generating new political forces. Some African states were invigorated by this era of intensified cultural exchange, creating new institutions and developing new products for export. The Ottoman Empire and the Qing Empire were also deeply influenced by Western expansionism. Both empires met this challenge by implementing reform programs that preserved traditional structures while adopting elements of Western technology and organization. The Ottoman court introduced reforms in education, the military, and law and created the first constitution in an Islamic state. The Qing Empire survived the period of European expansion, but a series of military defeats and a prolonged civil war severely weakened the authority of the central government. Russia lagged behind Western Europe in transforming its economy and political institutions, but military weakness and internal reform pressures led to modernization efforts, including the abolition of serfdom.

The economic, political, and social revolutions that began in the mid-eighteenth century shook the foundations of European culture and led to the expansion of Western power around the globe. Some of the nations of Asia, Africa, and Latin America resisted foreign intrusions by reforming and strengthening their own institutions, forms of production, and military technologies. Others pushed for more radical change, adopting Western commercial policies, industrial technologies, and government institutions. But after 1870, all these states would face even more aggressive Western imperialism, which few of them were able to resist.

Region	1750	1775	1800
Americas	1754–1763 French and Indian War	U.S. Declaration of Independence 1776 •	Louisiana Purchase by United States 1803 • • 1789 U.S. Constitution ratified • 1791 Slaves revolt in Haiti 1809–1825 Wars for independence in Spanish America
Europe	• ca. 1750 Industrial Revolution begins in Britain 1756–1763 Seven Years War		1789–1799 French Revolution 1814–1815 Congress of Vienna 1799–1815 Rule of Napoleon in France
Africa	1750–1800 Growing slave trade reduces population	Britain takes Cape Colony 1795 •	Sokoto Caliphate founded 1809 • Shaka founds Zulu kingdom 1818 •
Middle East		1769–1772 High point of restored Mamluk influence in Egypt	1789–1807 Reign of Ottoman sultan Selim III • 1798 Napoleon invades Egypt Muhammad Ali founds dynasty in Egypt 1805 •
Asia and Oceania	• 1755 Qing conquest of Turkestan East India Company rule of Bengal begins 1765 •	1769–1778 Captain Cook's exploration of Australia, New Zealand	White Lotus Rebellion in China 1796–1804 Britain takes Ceylon 1798 • East India Company creates Bombay presidency 1818 •

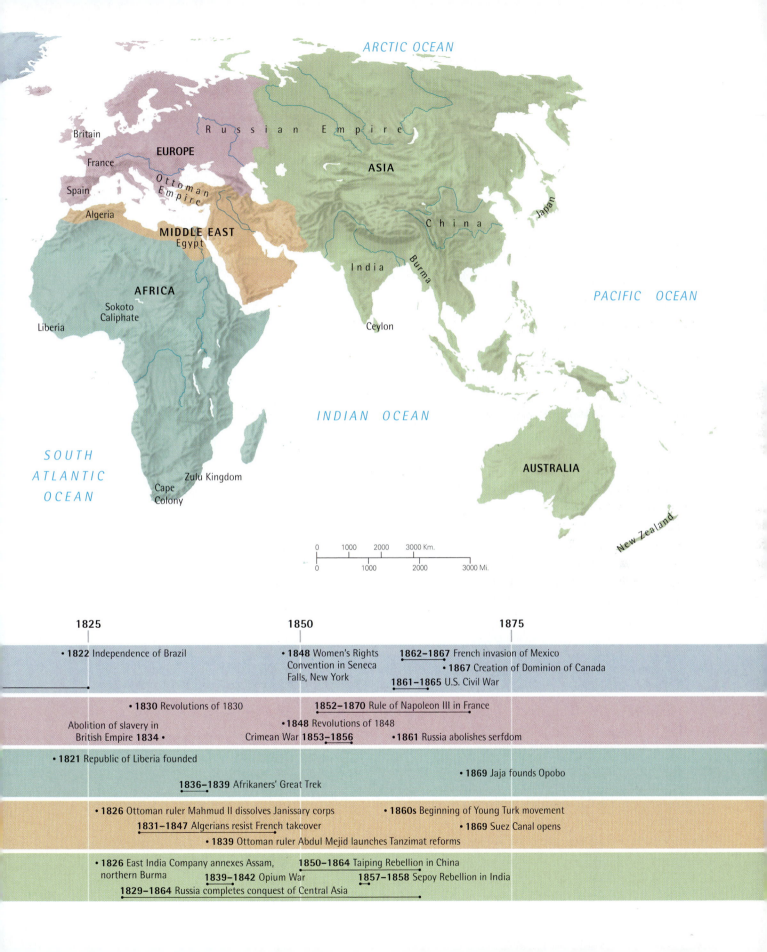

ARCTIC OCEAN

Britain

EUROPE

Russian Empire

ASIA

France

Ottoman Empire

Spain

Algeria

MIDDLE EAST

Egypt

China

Japan

AFRICA

India

Burma

Sokoto Caliphate

Liberia

Ceylon

PACIFIC OCEAN

INDIAN OCEAN

SOUTH ATLANTIC OCEAN

AUSTRALIA

Zulu Kingdom

Cape Colony

New Zealand

| 0 | 1000 | 2000 | 3000 Km. |
| 0 | 1000 | 2000 | 3000 Mi. |

1825   1850   1875

• **1822** Independence of Brazil

• **1848** Women's Rights Convention in Seneca Falls, New York

1862–1867 French invasion of Mexico

• **1867** Creation of Dominion of Canada

1861–1865 U.S. Civil War

• **1830** Revolutions of 1830

1852–1870 Rule of Napoleon III in France

Abolition of slavery in British Empire **1834** •

• **1848** Revolutions of 1848

Crimean War **1853–1856**

• **1861** Russia abolishes serfdom

• **1821** Republic of Liberia founded

• **1869** Jaja founds Opobo

1836–1839 Afrikaners' Great Trek

• **1826** Ottoman ruler Mahmud II dissolves Janissary corps

• **1860s** Beginning of Young Turk movement

1831–1847 Algerians resist French takeover

• **1869** Suez Canal opens

• **1839** Ottoman ruler Abdul Mejid launches Tanzimat reforms

• **1826** East India Company annexes Assam, northern Burma

1850–1864 Taiping Rebellion in China

1839–1842 Opium War

1857–1858 Sepoy Rebellion in India

1829–1864 Russia completes conquest of Central Asia

22 Revolutionary Changes in the Atlantic World, 1750–1850

Burning of Cap Français, St. Domingue in 1793   In 1791, the slaves of St. Domingue, France's richest colony, began a rebellion that, after years of struggle, ended slavery and created the Western Hemisphere's second independent nation, Haiti.

CHAPTER OUTLINE

Prelude to Revolution: The Eighteenth-Century Crisis

The American Revolution, 1775–1800

The French Revolution, 1789–1815

Revolution Spreads, Conservatives Respond, 1789–1850

ENVIRONMENT AND TECHNOLOGY: The Pencil

DIVERSITY AND DOMINANCE: Robespierre and Wollstonecraft Defend and Explain the Terror

On the evening of August 14, 1791, more than two hundred slaves and black freedmen met in secret in the plantation district of northern Saint Domingue° (present-day Haiti) to set the date for an armed uprising against local slave owners. Although the delegates agreed to delay the attack for a week, violence began almost immediately. During the following decade, slavery was abolished; military forces from Britain and France were defeated; and Haiti achieved independence.

The meeting was provoked by news and rumors about revolutionary events in France that had spread through the island's slave community. Events in France had also divided the island's white population into competing camps of royalists (supporters of France's King Louis XVI) and republicans (who sought an end to monarchy). The free mixed-race population initially gained some political rights from the French Assembly but was then forced to rebel when the local slave-owning elite reacted violently.

A black freedman named François Dominique Toussaint eventually became leader of the insurrection. He proved to be one of the most remarkable representatives of the revolutionary era, later taking the name Toussaint L'Ouverture°. He organized the rebels into a potent military force, negotiated with the island's royalist and republican factions and with representatives of Great Britain and France, and wrote his nation's first constitution. Commonly portrayed as a fiend by slave owners throughout the Western Hemisphere, to the slaves Toussaint became a towering symbol of resistance to oppression.

The Haitian slave rebellion was an important episode in the long and painful political and cultural transformation of the modern Western world. Economic expansion and the growth of trade were creating unprecedented wealth. The first stage of the Industrial Revolution (see Chapter 23) increased manufacturing productivity and led to greater global interdependence, new patterns of consumerism, and altered social structures. At the same time, intellectuals were questioning the traditional place of monarchy and religion in society. An increasingly powerful class of merchants, professionals, and manufacturers created by the emerging economy provided an audience for these new intellectual currents and began to press for a larger political role.

This revolutionary era turned the Western world "upside down." The *ancien régime*°, the French term for Europe's old order, rested on medieval principles: politics dominated by powerful monarchs, intellectual and cultural life dominated by religion, and economics dominated by a hereditary agricultural elite. In the West's new order, politics was opened to vastly greater participation; science and secular inquiry took the place of religion in intellectual life; and economies were increasingly opened to competition.

This radical transformation did not take place without false starts and temporary setbacks. Imperial powers resisted the loss of colonies; monarchs and nobles struggled to retain their ancient privileges; and the church fought against the claims of science. Revolutionary steps forward were often matched by reactionary steps backward. The liberal and nationalist ideals of the eighteenth-century revolutionary movements were only imperfectly realized in Europe and the Americas in the nineteenth century. Despite setbacks, belief in national self-determination and universal suffrage and a passion for social justice continued to animate reformers into the twentieth century.

As you read this chapter, ask yourself the following questions:

- How did imperial wars among European powers provoke revolution?
- In what ways were the revolutions, expanded literacy, and new political ideas linked?
- How did revolution in one country help incite revolution elsewhere?
- Why were the revolutions in France and Haiti more violent than the American Revolution?

Saint Domingue (san doe-MANG)   **Toussaint L'Ouverture** (too-SAN loo-ver-CHORE)

ancien régime (ahn-see-EN ray-ZHEEM)

PRELUDE TO REVOLUTION: THE EIGHTEENTH-CENTURY CRISIS

In large measure, the cost of wars fought among Europe's major powers over colonies and trade precipitated the revolutionary era that began in 1775 with the American Revolution. Britain, France, and Spain were the central actors in these global struggles, but other imperial powers were affected as well. Unpopular and costly wars had been fought earlier and paid for with new taxes. But changes in the Western intellectual and political environments led to a much more critical response. Any effort to extend the power of a monarch or impose new taxes now raised questions about the rights of individuals and the authority of political institutions.

Colonial Wars and Fiscal Crises

The rivalry among European powers intensified in the early 1600s when the newly independent Netherlands began an assault on the American and Asian colonies of Spain and Portugal. The Dutch attacked Spanish treasure fleets in the Caribbean and Pacific and seized parts of Portugal's colonial empire in Brazil and Angola. Europe's other emerging sea power, Great Britain, also attacked Spanish fleets and seaports in the Americas. By the end of the seventeenth century expanding British sea power had checked Dutch commercial and colonial ambitions and ended the Dutch monopoly of the African slave trade.

As Dutch power ebbed, Britain and France began a long struggle for political preeminence in western Europe and for territory and trade outlets in the Americas and Asia. Both the geographic scale and the expense of this conflict expanded during the eighteenth century. Nearly all of Europe's great powers were engaged in the War of the Spanish Succession (1701–1714). In 1739 a war between Britain and Spain over smuggling in the Americas quickly broadened into a generalized European conflict, the War of the Austrian Succession (1740–1748). Conflict between French and English settlers in North America then helped ignite a long war that altered the colonial balance of power. War began along the American frontier between French and British forces and their Amerindian allies. Known as the French and Indian War, this conflict helped lead to a wider struggle, the Seven Years War (1756–1763). British victory led to undisputed control of North America east of the Mississippi River while also forcing France to surrender most of its holdings in India.

The enormous costs of these conflicts distinguished them from earlier wars. Traditional taxes collected in traditional ways no longer covered the obligations of governments. For example, at the end of the Seven Years War in 1763, Britain's war debt reached £137 million. Britain's total budget before the war had averaged only £8 million. With the legacy of war debt, Britain's interest payments alone came to exceed £5 million. Even as European economies expanded because of increased trade and the early stages of the Industrial Revolution, fiscal crises overtook one European government after another. In an intellectual environment transformed by the Enlightenment, the need for new revenues provoked debate and confrontation within a vastly expanded and more critical public.

The Enlightenment and the Old Order

The complex and diverse intellectual movement called the **Enlightenment** applied the methods and questions of the Scientific Revolution of the seventeenth century to the study of human society. Dazzled by Copernicus's ability to explain the structure of the solar system and Newton's representation of the law of gravity, European intellectuals began to apply the logical tools of scientific inquiry to other questions. Some labored to systematize knowledge or organize reference materials. For example, Carolus Linnaeus° (a Swedish botanist known by the Latin form of his name) sought to categorize all living organisms, and Samuel Johnson published a comprehensive English dictionary with over forty thousand definitions. In France Denis Diderot° worked with other Enlightenment thinkers to create a compendium of human knowledge, the thirty-five-volume *Encyclopédie*.

Other thinkers pursued lines of inquiry that challenged long-established religious and political institutions. Some argued that if scientists could understand the laws of nature, then surely similar forms of disciplined investigation might reveal laws of human nature. Others wondered whether society and government might be better regulated and more productive if guided by science rather than by hereditary rulers and the church. These new perspectives and the intellectual optimism that fed them were to help guide the revolutionary movements of the late eighteenth century.

The English political philosopher John Locke (1632–1704) argued in 1690 that governments were created to

---

Carolus Linnaeus (kar-ROLL-uhs lin-NEE-uhs)   **Denis Diderot** (duh-nee DEE-duh-roe)

C H R O N O L O G Y

	The Americas	Europe
1750	**1754–1763** French and Indian War	**1756–1763** Seven Years War
1775	**1770** Boston Massacre **1776** American Declaration of Independence **1778** United States alliance with France **1781** British surrender at Yorktown **1783** Treaty of Paris ends American Revolution **1791** Slaves revolt in Saint Domingue (Haiti)	**1778** Death of Voltaire and Rousseau **1789** Storming of Bastille begins French Revolution; Declaration of Rights of Man and Citizen in France **1793–1794** Reign of Terror in France **1795–1799** The Directory rules France
1800	**1798** Toussaint L'Ouverture defeats British in Haiti **1804** Haitians defeat French invasion and declare independence	**1799** Napoleon overthrows the Directory **1804** Napoleon crowns himself emperor **1814** Napoleon abdicates; Congress of Vienna opens **1815** Napoleon defeated at Waterloo **1830** Greece gains independence; revolution in France overthrows Charles X **1848** Revolutions in France, Austria, Germany, Hungary, and Italy

protect life, liberty, and property and that the people had a right to rebel when a monarch violated these natural rights. Locke's closely reasoned theory began with the assumption that individual rights were the foundation of civil government. In *The Social Contract*, published in 1762, the French-Swiss intellectual Jean-Jacques Rousseau° (1712–1778) asserted that the will of the people was sacred and that the legitimacy of the monarch depended on the consent of the people. Although both men believed that government rested on the will of the people rather than on divine will, Locke emphasized the importance of individual rights, and Rousseau envisioned the people acting collectively because of their shared historical experience.

All Enlightenment thinkers were not radicals like Rousseau. There was never a uniform program for political and social reform, and the era's intellectuals often disagreed about principles and objectives. The Enlightenment is commonly associated with hostility toward religion and monarchy, but few European intellectuals openly expressed republican or atheist sentiments. The church was most commonly attacked when it attempted to censor ideas or ban books. Critics of monarchial au-

thority were as likely to point out violations of ancient custom as to suggest democratic alternatives. Even Voltaire, one of the Enlightenment's most critical intellects and great celebrities, believed that Europe's monarchs were likely agents of political and economic reform and even wrote favorably of China's Qing° emperors.

Indeed, sympathetic members of the nobility and reforming European monarchs such as Charles III of Spain (r. 1759–1788), Catherine the Great of Russia (r. 1762–1796), Joseph II of Austria (r. 1780–1790), and Frederick the Great of Prussia (r. 1740–1786) actively sponsored and promoted the dissemination of new ideas, providing patronage for many intellectuals. They recognized that elements of the Enlightenment critique of the ancien régime buttressed their own efforts to expand royal authority at the expense of religious institutions, the nobility, and regional autonomy. Goals such as the development of national bureaucracies staffed by civil servants selected on merit, the creation of national legal systems, and the modernization of tax systems united many of Europe's monarchs and intellectuals. Monarchs also understood that the era's passion for science and technology held the potential of fattening

---

Jean-Jacques Rousseau (zhah-zhock roo-SOE)

Qing (ching)

The Pencil

From early times Europeans had used sharp points, lead, and other implements to sketch, make marks, and write brief notes. At the end of the seventeenth century a source of high-quality graphite was discovered at Borrowdale in northwestern England. Borrowdale graphite gained acceptance among artists, artisans, and merchants. At first, pure graphite was simply wrapped in string. By the eighteenth century, pieces of graphite were being encased in wooden sheaths and resembled modern pencils. Widespread use of this useful tool was retarded by the limited supply of high-quality graphite from the English mines.

The English crown periodically closed the Borrowdale mines or restricted production to keep prices high and maintain adequate supplies for future needs. As a result, artisans in other European nations developed alternatives that used lower-quality graphite or, most commonly, graphite mixed with sulfur and glues.

The major breakthrough occurred in 1793 in France when war with England ruptured trade links. The government of revolutionary France responded to the shortage of graphite by assigning a thirty-nine-year-old scientist, Nicolas-Jacques Conté, to find an alternative. Conté had earlier promoted the military use of balloons and conducted experiments with hydrogen. He had also used graphite alloys in the development of crucibles for melting metal.

Within a short period, Conté produced a graphite that is the basis for most lead pencils today. He mixed finely ground graphite with potter's clay and water. The resulting paste was dried in a long mold, sealed in a ceramic box, and fired in an oven. The graphite strips were then placed in wooden cases. Although some believed the Conté pencils were inferior to the pencils made from Borrowdale graphite, Conté produced

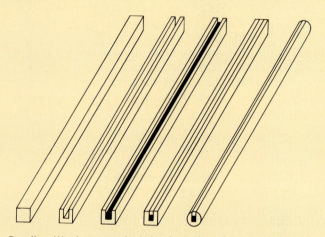

Pencils Wartime necessity led to invention of the modern pencil in France. (Drawing by Fred Avent for Henry Petroski. Reproduced by permission)

a very serviceable pencil that could be produced in uniform quality and unlimited amounts.

Summarizing the achievement of Conté in *The Pencil*, Henry Petroski wrote: "The laboratory is really the modern workshop. And modern engineering results when the scientific method is united with experience with the tools and products of craftsmen. . . . Modern engineering, in spirit if not in name, would come to play a more and more active role in turning the craft tradition into modern technology, with its base of research and development."

Source: This discussion depends on Henry Petroski, *The Pencil: A History of Design and Circumstance* (New York: Knopf, 1990); the quotation is from pp. 50–78. Drawing by Fred Avent for Henry Petroski. Reproduced by permission.

national treasuries and improving economic performance (see Environment and Technology: The Pencil). Periodicals disseminating new technologies often gained the patronage of these reforming monarchs.

Though willing to embrace reform proposals when they served royal interests, Europe's monarchs moved quickly to suppress or ban radical ideas that promoted republicanism or directly attacked religion. However, too many channels of communication were open to permit a thoroughgoing suppression of ideas. In fact, censorship tended to enhance intellectual reputations, and persecuted intellectuals generally found patronage in the courts of foreign rivals.

Many of the major intellectuals of the Enlightenment maintained extensive correspondence with each other as well as with political leaders. This communication led to numerous firsthand contacts among the intellectuals of different nations and helped create a coherent assault on what was typically called ignorance—beliefs and values associated with the ancien régime. Rousseau, for example, briefly sought refuge in Britain, where the Scottish philosopher David Hume befriended him. Similarly, Voltaire sought patronage and protection in England and later in Prussia.

Women were instrumental in the dissemination of the new ideas. In England educated middle-class women purchased and discussed the books and pamphlets of the era. Some were important contributors to intellectual life as writers and commentators, raising by example and in argument the issue of the rights of women. In Paris wealthy women made their homes centers of debate, intellectual speculation, and free inquiry. Their salons brought together philosophers, social critics, artists, and members of the aristocracy and commercial elite. Unlike their contemporaries in England, the women of the Parisian salons used their social standing more to direct the conversations of men than to give vent to their own opinions.

The intellectual ferment of the era deeply influenced the expanding middle class in Europe and the Western Hemisphere. Members of this class were eager consumers of books and the inexpensive newspapers and journals that were widely available. This broadening of the intellectual audience overwhelmed traditional institutions of censorship. Scientific discoveries, new technologies, and controversial work on human nature and politics also were discussed in the thousands of coffeehouses and teashops opening in major cities and market towns.

Many European intellectuals were interested in the Americas. Some Europeans continued to dismiss the New World as barbaric and inferior, but others used idealized accounts of the New World to support their critiques of European society. These thinkers looked to Britain's North American colonies for confirmation of their belief that human nature unconstrained by the corrupted practices of Europe's old order would quickly produce material abundance and social justice. More than any other American, the writer and inventor **Benjamin Franklin** came to symbolize both the natural genius and the vast potential of America.

Born in 1706 in Boston, the young Franklin was apprenticed to his older brother, a printer. At seventeen he ran away to Philadelphia, where he succeeded as a printer and publisher and was best known for his *Poor Richard's Almanac*. By age forty-two he was a wealthy man. He retired from active business to pursue writing, science, and public affairs. In Philadelphia Franklin was instrumental in the creation of the organizations that later became the Philadelphia Free Library, the American Philosophical Society, and the University of Pennsylvania.

Franklin's contributions were both practical and theoretical. He was the inventor of bifocal glasses, the lightning rod, and an efficient wood-burning stove. In 1751 he published a scientific work, *Experiments and Observations on Electricity*, that established his intellectual reputation in Europe. Intellectuals heralded the book as proof that the simple and unsophisticated world of America was a particularly hospitable environment for genius.

Franklin was also an important political figure. He served Pennsylvania as a delegate to the Albany (New York) Congress in 1754, which sought to coordinate colonial defense against attacks by the French and their Amerindian allies. Later he was a Pennsylvania delegate to the Continental Congress that issued the Declaration of Independence in 1776. His service in England as colonial lobbyist and later as the Continental Congress's ambassador to Paris allowed him to cultivate his European reputation. Franklin's wide achievement, witty conversation, and careful self-promotion make him a symbol of the era. In him the Enlightenment's most radical project, the freeing of human potential from the inhibitions of inherited privilege, found its most agreeable confirmation.

As Franklin's career demonstrates, the Western Hemisphere shared in the debates of Europe. New ideas penetrated the curricula of many colonial universities and appeared in periodicals and books published in the New World. As scientific method was applied to economic and political questions, colonial writers, scholars, and artists on both sides of the Atlantic were drawn into a debate that eventually was to lead to the rejection of colonialism itself. This radicalization of the colonial intellectual community was provoked by the European monarchies' efforts to reform colonial policies. As European authorities swept away colonial institutions and long-established political practices without consultation, colonial residents had to acknowledge that their status as colonies meant perpetual subordination to European rulers. Among people compelled to recognize this structural dependence and inferiority, the idea that government authority ultimately rested on the consent of the governed was potentially explosive.

In Europe and the colonies, many intellectuals resisted the Enlightenment, seeing it as a dangerous assault on the authority of the church and monarchy. This Counter Enlightenment was most influential in France and other Catholic nations. Its adherents argued the importance of faith to human happiness and social well-being. They also emphasized duty and obligation to the community of believers in opposition to the concern for

Beer Street (1751)   This engraving by William Hogarth shows an idealized London street scene where beer drinking is associated with manly strength, good humor, and prosperity. The self-satisfied corpulent figure in the left foreground has been reading a copy of the king's speech to Parliament. We can imagine him offering a running commentary to his drinking companions as he reads.   (The Art Archive)

individual rights and individual fulfillment common in the works of the Enlightenment. Most importantly for the politics of the era, they rejected their enemies' enthusiasm for change and utopianism, reminding their readers of human fallibility and the importance of history. While the central ideas of the Enlightenment gained strength across the nineteenth century, the Counter Enlightenment provided the ideological roots of both conservatism and popular antidemocratic movements.

Folk Cultures and Popular Protest

While intellectuals and the reforming royal courts of Europe debated the rational and secular enthusiasms of the Enlightenment, most people in Western society remained loyal to competing cultural values grounded in the preindustrial past. These regionally distinct folk cultures were framed by the memory of shared local historical experi-ence and nourished by religious practices encouraging emotional release. They emphasized the obligations that people had to each other and local, rather than national, loyalties. Though never formally articulated, these cultural traditions composed a coherent expression of the mutual rights and obligations connecting the people and their rulers. Rulers who violated the constraints of these understandings were likely to face violent opposition.

In the eighteenth century, European monarchs sought to increase their authority and to centralize power by reforming tax collection, judicial practice, and public administration. Although monarchs viewed these changes as reforms, the common people often saw them as violations of sacred customs and sometimes expressed their outrage in bread riots, tax protests, and attacks on royal officials. These violent actions were not efforts to overturn traditional authority but were instead efforts to preserve custom and precedent. In Spain and the Spanish colonies, for example, protesting mobs commonly asserted the apparently contradictory slogan "Long live the King. Death to bad government." They expressed loyalty to and love for their monarch while at the same time assaulting his officials and preventing the implementation of changes to long-established customs.

Folk cultures were threatened by other kinds of reform as well. Rationalist reformers of the Enlightenment sought to bring order and discipline to the citizenry by banning or by altering the numerous popular cultural traditions—such as harvest festivals, religious holidays, and country fairs—that enlivened the drudgery of everyday life. These events were popular celebrations of sexuality and individuality as well as opportunities for masked and costumed celebrants to mock the greed, pretension, and foolishness of government officials, the wealthy, and the clergy. Hard drinking, gambling, and blood sports like cockfighting and bearbaiting were popular in this preindustrial mass culture. Because these customs were viewed as corrupt and decadent by reformers influenced by the Enlightenment, governments undertook efforts to substitute civic rituals, patriotic anniversaries, and institutions of self-improvement. These challenges to custom—like the efforts at political reform—often provoked protests, rebellions, and riots.

The efforts of ordinary men and women to resist the growth of government power and the imposition of new cultural forms provide an important political undercurrent to much of the revolutionary agitation and conflict between 1750 and 1850. Spontaneous popular uprisings and protests punctuated nearly every effort at reform in the eighteenth century. But these popular actions gained revolutionary potential only when they coincided with ideological divisions and conflicts within the governing class itself. In America and France the old order was swept away when the protests and rebellions of the rural and urban poor coincided with the appearance of revolutionary leaders who followed Enlightenment ideals in efforts to create secular republican states. Likewise, the slave rebellion in Saint Domingue (Haiti) achieved revolutionary potential when it attracted the support of black freedmen and disaffected poor whites radicalized by news of the French Revolution.

THE AMERICAN REVOLUTION, 1775–1800

In British North America, clumsy efforts to reform colonial tax policy to cover rising defense expenditures and to diminish the power of elected colonial legislatures outraged a populace accustomed to greater local auton-

omy. Once begun, the American Revolution ushered in a century-long process of political and cultural transformation in Europe and the Americas. By the end of this revolutionary century the authority of monarchs had been swept away or limited by constitutions, and religion had lost its dominating place in Western intellectual life. Moreover, the medieval idea of a social order determined by birth had been replaced by a capitalist vision that emphasized competition and social mobility.

Frontiers and Taxes

After defeating the French in 1763, the British government faced two related problems in its North American colonies. As settlers pushed west into Amerindian lands, the government saw the likelihood of renewed conflict and rising military expenses. Already burdened with heavy debts from the French and Indian War, Britain tried to limit settler pressure on Amerindian lands and get colonists to shoulder more of the costs of imperial defense and colonial administration.

In the Great Lakes region the British tried to contain costs by reducing the prices paid for furs and refusing to honor the French practice of giving gifts and paying rent for frontier forts to Amerindian communities that had become dependent on European trade goods, especially firearms, gunpowder, textiles, and alcohol. When the British forced down the trade value of furs, Amerindians had to hunt more aggressively to get the volume of commodities they required, putting new pressures on the environment and endangering some species. The situation got worse as settlers and white trappers pushed across the Appalachians to compete with indigenous hunters.

At the end of the Seven Years War (see Chapter 18), Pontiac, an Ottawa chief, led a broad alliance of native peoples that drove the British military from western outposts and raided settled areas of Virginia and Pennsylvania. Although this Amerindian alliance was defeated within a year, the potential for new violence existed all along the frontier.

The British government's panicked reaction was the Proclamation of 1763, which sought to establish an effective western limit for settlement, throwing into question the claims of thousands of established farmers without effectively protecting Amerindian land. No one was satisfied. In 1774 the British government annexed disputed western territory to the province of Quebec, thus denying eastern colonies the authority to distribute additional lands.

Frontier issues increased hostility and suspicion between the British government and many of the colonists but did not directly lead to a breach. However, when the British government sought relief from the cost of imperial wars with a campaign of fiscal reforms and new taxes, it sparked a political confrontation that would lead to rebellion. New commercial regulations increased the cost of foreign molasses and endangered New England's profitable trade with Spanish and French Caribbean sugar colonies. The colonial practice of issuing paper money, a custom made necessary by the colonies' chronic balance-of-payments deficits, was outlawed. Colonial legislatures formally protested these measures, and angry colonists organized boycotts of British goods.

The Stamp Act of 1765, which imposed a tax, to be paid in scarce coin, on all legal documents, newspapers, pamphlets, and nearly all other printed material, proved incendiary. Propertied colonists, including holders of high office and members of the colonial elite, now assumed leading roles in protests, using fiery political language that identified Britain's rulers as "parricides" and "tyrants." Women from many of the most prominent colonial families organized boycotts of British goods. The production of homespun textiles by colonial women now became a patriotic enterprise. A young girl in Boston proclaimed that she was a "daughter of liberty" because she had learned to spin.[1] Organizations such as the Sons of Liberty held public meetings, intimidated royal officials, and developed committees to enforce the boycotts. The combination of violent protest and trade boycott forced the repeal of the Stamp Act, but new taxes and duties were soon imposed, and Parliament sent British troops to quell urban riots. One indignant woman later sent her poignant perception of this injustice to a British officer:

> [T]he most ignorant peasant knows, and [it] is clear to the weakest capacity, that no man has the right to take their money without their consent. The supposition is ridiculous and absurd, as none but highwaymen and robbers attempt it. Can you, my friend, reconcile it with your own good sense, that a body of men in Great Britain, who have little intercourse with America . . . shall invest themselves with a power to command our lives and properties [?][2]

New colonial boycotts cut the importation of British goods by two-thirds. Angry colonists also destroyed property and bullied or attacked royal officials. British authorities reacted by threatening traditional liberties, even dissolving the colonial legislature of Massachusetts, and by dispatching two regiments of soldiers to reestablish control of Boston's streets. Support for a

The Tarring and Feathering of a British Official, 1774 This illustration from a British periodical shows the unfortunate John Malcomb, commissioner of customs at Boston. By the mid-1770s British periodicals were focusing public opinion on mob violence and the breakdown of public order in the colonies. British critics of colonial political protests viewed the demand for liberty as little more than an excuse for mob violence. (The Granger Collection, New York)

complete break with Britain grew after March 5, 1770, when a British force fired on an angry Boston crowd, killing five civilians. This "Boston Massacre," which seemed to expose the naked force on which colonial rule rested, radicalized public opinion throughout the colonies.

Parliament attempted to calm public opinion by repealing some taxes and duties, but then stumbled into another crisis by granting a monopoly for importing tea to the colonies to the British East India Company, raising anew the constitutional issue of Parliament's right to tax the colonies. The crisis came to a head when protesters dumped tea worth £10,000 into Boston harbor. Britain responded by appointing a military man, Thomas Gage, as governor of Massachusetts and by closing the port of Boston. Public order in Boston now depended on British troops, and public administration was in the hands of a general. This militarization of colonial government in Boston undermined Britain's constitutional authority and made a military test of strength inevitable.

The Course of Revolution, 1775–1783

As the crisis mounted, patriot leaders created new governing bodies that made laws, appointed justices, and even took control of colonial militias, thus effectively deposing many British governors, judges, and customs officers. Simultaneously, radical leaders organized crowds to intimidate loyalists—people who were pro-British—and organized women to enforce boycotts of British goods.

When representatives elected to the Continental Congress met in Philadelphia in 1775, patriot militia had met British troops at Lexington and Concord, Massachusetts (see Map 22.1), and blood had already been shed. Events were propelling the colonies toward revolution. Congress assumed the powers of government, creating a currency and organizing an army led by **George Washington** (1732–1799), a Virginia planter who had served in the French and Indian War.

Popular support for independence was given a hard edge by the angry rhetoric of thousands of street-corner speakers and the inflammatory pamphlet *Common Sense*, written by Thomas Paine, a recent immigrant from England. Paine's pamphlet sold 120,000 copies. On July 4, 1776, Congress approved the Declaration of Independence, the document that proved to be the most enduring statement of the revolutionary era's ideology:

> We hold these truths to be self evident: That all men are created equal; that they are endowed by their creator with certain unalienable rights; that among these are life, liberty and the pursuit of happiness; that, to secure these rights, governments are instituted among men, deriving their just powers from the consent of the governed.

The Declaration's affirmation of popular sovereignty and individual rights would influence the language of revolution and popular protest around the world.

Hoping to shore up British authority, Great Britain sent additional military forces to pacify the colonies. By 1778 British land forces numbered 50,000 and were supported by 30,000 German mercenaries. This military commitment proved futile. Despite the existence of a large loyalist community, the British army found it difficult to control the countryside. Although British forces won most of the battles, Washington slowly built a competent Continental army as well as the civilian support networks that provided supplies and financial resources.

The real problem for the British government was its inability to discover a compromise solution that would satisfy colonial grievances. Half-hearted efforts to resolve the bitter conflict over taxes failed, and a later offer to roll back the clock and reestablish the administrative arrangements of 1763 made little headway. Overconfidence and poor leadership prevented the British from finding a political solution before revolutionary institutions were in place and the armies engaged. By allowing confrontation to occur, the British government lost the opportunity to mobilize and give direction to the large numbers of loyalists and pacifists in the colonies.

Along the Canadian border, both sides solicited Amerindians as potential allies and feared them as potential enemies. For over a hundred years, members of the powerful Iroquois Confederacy—Mohawk, Oneida, Onondaga, Cayuga, Seneca, and (after 1722) Tuscarora—had protected their traditional lands with a combination of diplomacy and warfare, playing a role in all the colonial wars of the eighteenth century. Just as the American Revolution forced neighbors and families to join the rebels or remain loyal, it divided the Iroquois, who fought on both sides.

The Mohawk proved to be the most valuable British allies among the Iroquois. Their loyalist leader **Joseph Brant** (Thayendanegea°) organized Britain's most potent fighting force along the Canadian border. His raids along the northern frontier earned him the title "Monster" Brant, but he was actually a man who moved easily between European and Amerindian cultures. Educated by missionaries, he was fluent in English and helped translate Protestant religious tracts into Mohawk. He was tied to many of the wealthiest loyalist families through his sister, formerly the mistress of Sir William Johnson, Britain's superintendent of Indian affairs for North America. Brant had traveled to London, had an audience with George III, (r. 1760–1820) and had been embraced by London's aristocratic society.

The defeat in late 1777 of Britain's general John Burgoyne by General Horatio Gates at Saratoga, New York, put the future of the Mohawk at risk. This victory, which gave heart to patriot forces that had recently suffered a string of defeats, led to destructive attacks on Iroquois villages. Brant's supporters fought on to the end of the war, but patriot victories along the frontier curtailed their political and military power. Brant eventually joined the loyalist exodus to Canada. For these Ameri-

---

Thayendanegea (ta YEHN dah NEY geh ah)

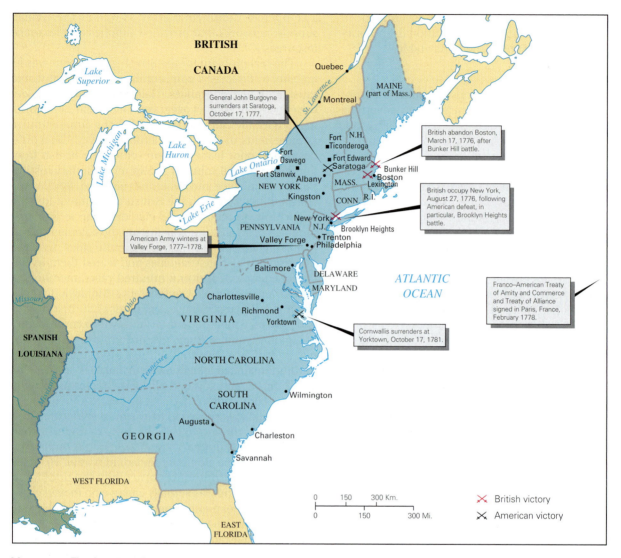

Map 22.1   The American Revolutionary War   The British army won most of the major battles, and British troops held most of the major cities. Even so, the American revolutionaries eventually won a comprehensive military and political victory.

cans the revolution did not mean the protection of life and property.

The British defeat at Saratoga also convinced France to enter the war as an ally of the United States in 1778. French military help proved crucial, supplying American forces and forcing the British to defend their colonies in the Caribbean. The French contribution was most clear in the final decisive battle, fought at Yorktown, Virginia (see Map 22.1). With the American army supported by French soldiers and a French fleet, General Charles Cornwallis surrendered to Washington as

the British military band played "The World Turned Upside-Down."

This victory effectively ended the war. The Continental Congress sent representatives to the peace conference that followed with instructions to work in tandem with the French. Believing that France was more concerned with containing British power than with guaranteeing a strong United States, America's peace delegation chose to negotiate directly with Britain and gained a generous settlement. The Treaty of Paris (1783) granted unconditional independence and established generous boundaries for the former colonies. In return the United States promised to repay prewar debts due to British merchants and to allow loyalists to recover property confiscated by patriot forces. In the end, loyalists were poorly treated, and thousands of them decided to leave for Canada.

The Construction of Republican Institutions, to 1800

Even before the Declaration of Independence, many colonies had created new governments independent of British colonial authorities. After independence leaders in each of the new states (as the former colonies were called) summoned constitutional conventions to draft formal charters and submitted the results to voters for ratification. Europeans were fascinated by the drafting of written constitutions and by the formal ratification of these constitutions by a vote of the people. Many of these documents were quickly translated and published in Europe. Remembering conflicts between royal governors and colonial legislatures, the authors of state constitutions placed severe limits on executive authority but granted legislatures greater powers than in colonial times. Many state constitutions also included bills of rights to provide further protection against government tyranny.

An effective constitution for the new national government was developed with difficulty. The Second Continental Congress sent the Articles of Confederation—the first constitution of the United States—to the states for approval in 1777, but it was not accepted by all the states until 1781. It created a one-house legislature in which each state was granted a single vote. A simple majority of the thirteen states was sufficient to pass minor legislation, but nine votes were necessary for declaring war, imposing taxes, and coining or borrowing money. Executive power was exercised by committees, not by a president. Given the intended weakness of this government, it is remarkable that it successfully organized the human and material resources to defeat Great Britain.

With the coming of peace, many of the most powerful political figures in the United States recognized that the Confederation was unable to enforce unpopular requirements of the peace treaty such as the recognition of loyalist property claims, the payment of prewar debts, and even the payment of military salaries and pensions to veterans. In September 1786 Virginia invited the other states to discuss the government's failure to deal with trade issues. This led to a call for a new convention to meet in Philadelphia nine months later. A rebellion led by Revolutionary War veterans in western Massachusetts gave the assembling delegates a sense of urgency.

The **Constitutional Convention,** which began meeting in May 1787, achieved a nonviolent second American Revolution. The delegates pushed aside the announced purpose of the convention—"to render the constitution of the federal government adequate to the exigencies of the union"—and secretly undertook the creation of a new constitution. George Washington was elected presiding officer. His reputation and popularity provided a solid foundation on which the delegates could contemplate an alternative political model.

Debate focused on representation, electoral procedures, executive powers, and the relationship between the federal government and the states. Compromise solutions included distribution of political power among the executive, legislative, and judicial branches and the division of authority between the federal government and the states. The final compromise provided for a two-house legislature: the lower house (the House of Representatives) to be elected directly by voters and the upper house (the Senate) to be elected by state legislatures. The chief executive—the president—was to be elected indirectly by "electors" selected by ballot in the states.

Although the U.S. Constitution created the most democratic government of the era, only a minority of the adult population was given full rights. In some northern states where large numbers of free blacks had fought with patriot forces, there was some hostility to the continuation of slavery, but southern leaders were able to protect the institution. Although slaves were denied participation in the political process, slave states were permitted to count three-fifths of the slave population in the calculations that determined the number of congressional representatives, thus multiplying the political power of the slave-owning class. Southern delegates also gained a twenty-year continuation of the slave trade to 1808 and a fugitive slave clause that required all states to return runaway slaves to their masters.

Women were powerfully affected by their participation in revolutionary politics and by the changes in the economy brought on by the break with Britain. They had led prewar boycotts and had organized relief and charitable organizations during the war. Some had served in the military as nurses, and a smaller number had joined the ranks disguised as men. Nevertheless, they were denied political rights in the new republic. Only New Jersey did not specifically bar women from voting, granting the right to vote to all free residents who met modest property-holding requirements. As a result, women and

African-Americans who met property requirements were able to vote in New Jersey until 1807, when lawmakers eliminated this right.

THE FRENCH REVOLUTION, 1789–1815

The French Revolution undermined traditional monarchy as well as the power of the Catholic Church and the hereditary aristocracy but, unlike the American Revolution, did not create an enduring form of representative democracy. The colonial revolution in North America, however, did not confront so directly the entrenched privileges of an established church, monarchy, and aristocracy, and the American Revolution produced no symbolic drama comparable to the public beheading of the French king Louis XVI in early 1793. Among its achievements, the French Revolution expanded mass participation in political life and radicalized the democratic tradition inherited from the English and American experiences. But in the end, the passions unleashed by revolutionary events in France could not be sustained, and popular demagogues and the dictatorship of Napoleon stalled democratic reform.

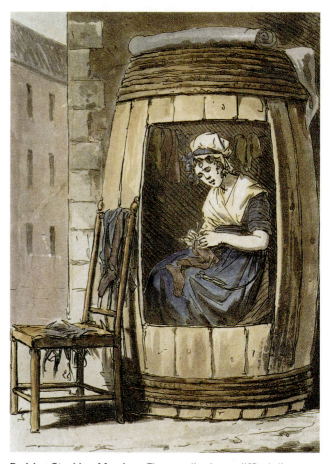

Parisian Stocking Mender　The poor lived very difficult lives. This woman uses a discarded wine barrel as a shop where she mends socks.　(Private collection)

French Society and Fiscal Crisis

French society was divided into three groups. The clergy, called the First Estate, numbered about 130,000 in a nation of 28 million. The Catholic Church owned about 10 percent of the nation's land and extracted substantial amounts of wealth from the economy in the form of tithes and ecclesiastical fees. Despite its substantial wealth, the church was exempted from nearly all taxes. The clergy was organized hierarchically, and members of the hereditary nobility held almost all the upper positions in the church.

The 300,000 members of the nobility, the Second Estate, controlled about 30 percent of the land and retained ancient rights on much of the rest. Nobles held the vast majority of high administrative, judicial, military, and church positions. Though traditionally barred from some types of commercial activity, nobles were important participants in wholesale trade, banking, manufacturing, and mining. Like the clergy, this estate was hierarchical: important differences in wealth, power, and outlook separated the higher from the lower nobility. The nobility was also a highly permeable class: the Second Estate in the eighteenth century saw an enormous infusion of wealthy commoners who purchased administrative and judicial offices that conferred noble status.

The Third Estate included everyone else, from wealthy financier to homeless beggar. The bourgeoisie°, or middle class, grew rapidly in the eighteenth century. There were three times as many members of this class in 1774, when Louis XVI took the throne, as there had been in 1715, at the end of Louis XIV's reign. Commerce, finance, and manufacturing accounted for much of the wealth of the Third Estate. Wealthy commoners also owned nearly a third of the nation's land. This literate and socially ambitious class supported an expanding publishing industry, subsidized the fine arts, and purchased many of the extravagant new homes being built in Paris and other cities.

bourgeoisie (boor-zwah-ZEE)

Peasants accounted for 80 percent of the French population. Artisans and other skilled workers, small shopkeepers and peddlers, and small landowners held a more privileged position in society. They owned some property and lived decently when crops were good and prices stable. By 1780 poor harvests had increased their cost of living and led to a decline in consumer demand for their products. They were rich enough to fear the loss of their property and status, well educated enough to be aware of the growing criticism of the king, but too poor and marginalized to influence policy.

The nation's poor were a large, growing, and troublesome sector. The poverty and vulnerability of peasant families forced younger children to seek seasonal work away from home and led many to crime and beggary. That raids by roving vagabonds threatened isolated farms was one measure of this social dislocation. In Paris and other French cities the vile living conditions and unhealthy diet of the working poor were startling to visitors from other European nations. Urban streets swarmed with beggars and prostitutes. Paris alone had 25,000 prostitutes in 1760. The wretchedness of the French poor is perhaps best indicated by the growing problem of child abandonment. On the eve of the French Revolution at least 40,000 children a year were given up by their parents. The convenient fiction was that these children would be adopted; in reality the majority died of neglect.

Unable to afford decent housing, obtain steady employment, or protect their children, the poor periodically erupted in violent protest and rage. In the countryside violence was often the reaction when the nobility or clergy increased dues and fees. In towns and cities an increase in the price of bread often provided the spark, for bread prices largely determined the quality of life of the poor. These explosive episodes, however, were not revolutionary in character. The remedies sought were conventional and immediate rather than structural and long-term. That was to change when the Crown tried to solve its fiscal crisis.

The expenses of the War of the Austrian Succession began the crisis. Louis XV (r. 1715–1774) first tried to impose new taxes on the nobility and on other groups that in the past had enjoyed exemptions. This effort failed in the face of widespread protest and the refusal of the Parlement of Paris, a court that heard appeals from local courts throughout France, to register the new tax. The crisis deepened when debts from the Seven Years War compelled the king to impose emergency fiscal measures. Again, the king met resistance from the Parlement of Paris. In 1768 frustrated authorities exiled the members of that Parlement and pushed through a series of unpopular fiscal measures. When the twenty-two-year-old Louis XVI assumed the throne in 1774, he attempted to gain popular support by recalling the exiled members of the Parlement of Paris, but he soon learned that provincial parlements had also come to see themselves as having a constitutional power to check any growth in monarchial authority.

In 1774 Louis's chief financial adviser warned that the government could barely afford to operate; as he put it, "the first gunshot [act of war] will drive the state to bankruptcy." Despite this warning, the French took on the heavy burden of supporting the American Revolution, delaying collapse by borrowing enormous sums and disguising the growing debt in misleading fiscal accounts. By the end of the war with Britain, more than half of France's national budget was required to service the resulting debt. It soon became clear that fiscal reforms and new taxes, not new loans, were necessary.

In 1787 the desperate king called an Assembly of Notables to approve a radical and comprehensive reform of the economy and fiscal policy. Despite the fact that the members of this assembly were selected by the king's advisers from the high nobility, the judiciary, and the clergy, it proved unwilling to act as a rubber stamp for the proposed reforms or new taxes. Instead, these representatives of France's most privileged classes sought to protect their interests by questioning the competence of the king and his ministers to supervise the nation's affairs.

Protest Turns to Revolution, 1789–1792

In frustration, the king dismissed the Notables and attempted to implement some reforms on his own, but his effort was met by an increasingly hostile judiciary and by popular demonstrations. Because the king was unable to extract needed tax concessions from the French elite, he was forced to call the **Estates General,** the French national legislature, which had not met since 1614. The narrow self-interest and greed of the rich—who would not tolerate an increase in their taxes—rather than the grinding poverty of the common people had created the conditions for political revolution.

In late 1788 and early 1789 members of the three estates came together throughout the nation to discuss grievances and elect representatives who would meet at Versailles°. The Third Estate's representatives were mostly men of property, but there was anger directed against the king's ministers and an inclination to move France toward constitutional monarchy with an elected

Versailles (vuhr-SIGH)

Parisians Storm the Bastille　This depiction of the storming of the Bastille on July 14, 1789, was painted by an artist who witnessed the epochal event still celebrated by the French as a national holiday.　(Photos12.com-ARJ)

legislature. Many nobles and members of the clergy sympathized with the reform agenda of the Third Estate, but deep internal divisions over procedural and policy issues limited the power of the First and the Second Estates.

Traditionally, the three estates met separately, and a positive vote by two of the three was required for action. Tradition, however, was quickly overturned when the Third Estate refused to conduct business until the king ordered the other two estates to sit with it in a single body. During a six-week period of stalemate, many parish priests from the First Estate began to meet with the commoners. When this expanded Third Estate declared itself the **National Assembly,** the king and his advisers recognized that the reformers intended to force them to accept a constitutional monarchy.

After being locked out of their meeting place, the Third Estate appropriated an indoor tennis court and pledged to write a constitution. The Oath of the Tennis Court ended Louis's vain hope that he could limit the agenda to fiscal reform. The king's effort to solve the nation's fiscal crisis was being connected in unpredictable ways to the central ideas of the era: the people were sovereign, and the legitimacy of political institutions and individual rulers ultimately depended on their carrying out the people's will. Louis prepared for a confrontation with the National Assembly by moving military forces to Versailles. Before he could act, the people of Paris intervened.

A succession of bad harvests beginning in 1785 had propelled bread prices upward throughout France and provoked an economic depression as demand for nonessential goods collapsed. By the time the Estates General met, nearly a third of the Parisian work force was unemployed. Hunger and anger marched hand in hand through working-class neighborhoods.

When the people of Paris heard that the king was massing troops in Versailles to arrest the representatives, crowds of common people began to seize arms and mobilize. On July 14, 1789, a crowd searching for military supplies attacked the Bastille, a medieval fortress used as a prison. The futile defense of the Bastille° cost ninety-eight lives before its garrison surrendered. Enraged, the attackers hacked the commander to death and then paraded through the city with his head and that of Paris's chief magistrate stuck on pikes.

These events coincided with uprisings by peasants in the country. Peasants sacked manor houses and destroyed documents that recorded their traditional obligations. They refused to pay taxes and dues to landowners and seized common lands. Forced to recognize the fury raging through rural areas, the National Assembly voted to end traditional obligations and to reform the tax system. Having forced acceptance of their narrow agenda, the peasants ceased their revolt.

These popular uprisings strengthened the hand of the National Assembly in its dealings with the king. One manifestation of this altered relationship was passage of the **Declaration of the Rights of Man.** There were clear similarities between the language of this declaration and the U.S. Declaration of Independence. Indeed, Thomas Jefferson, who had written the American document, was U.S. ambassador to Paris and offered his opinion to those drafting the French statement. The French declaration, however, was more sweeping in its language than the American. Among the enumerated natural rights were "liberty, property, security, and resistance to oppression." The Declaration of the Rights of Man also guaranteed free expression of ideas, equality before the law, and representative government.

While delegates debated political issues in Versailles, the economic crisis worsened in Paris. Women employed in the garment industry and in small-scale retail businesses were particularly hard hit. Because the working women of Paris faced high food prices everyday as they struggled to feed their families, their anger had a hard edge. Public markets became political arenas where the urban poor met daily in angry assembly. Here the revolutionary link between the material deprivation of the French poor and the political aspirations of the French bourgeoisie was forged.

On October 5, market women organized a crowd of thousands to march the 12 miles (19 kilometers) to Versailles. Once there, they forced their way into the National Assembly to demand action from the frightened representatives: "the point is that we want bread." The crowd then entered the royal apartments, killed some of the king's guards, and searched for Queen Marie Antoinette°, whom they loathed as a symbol of extrava-

---

Bastille (bass-TEEL)   **Antoinette** (ann twah-NET)

gance. Eventually, the crowd demanded that the royal family return to Paris. Preceded by the heads of two aristocrats carried on pikes and hauling away the palace's supply of flour, the triumphant crowd escorted the royal family to Paris.

With the king's ability to resist democratic change overcome by the Paris crowd, the National Assembly achieved a radically restructured French society in the next two years. It passed a new constitution that dramatically limited monarchial power and abolished the nobility as a hereditary class. Economic reforms swept away monopolies and trade barriers within France. The Legislative Assembly (the new constitution's name for the National Assembly) seized church lands to use as collateral for a new paper currency, and priests—who were to be elected—were put on the state payroll. When the government tried to force priests to take a loyalty oath, however, many Catholics joined a growing counterrevolutionary movement.

At first, many European monarchs had welcomed the weakening of the French king, but by 1791 Austria and Prussia threatened to intervene in support of the monarchy. The Legislative Assembly responded by declaring war. Although the war went badly at first for French forces, people across France responded patriotically to foreign invasions, forming huge new volunteer armies and mobilizing national resources to meet the challenge. By the end of 1792 French armies had gained a stalemate with the foreign forces.

The Terror, 1793–1794

In this period of national crisis and foreign threat, the French Revolution entered its most radical phase. A failed effort by the king and queen to escape from Paris and find foreign allies cost the king any remaining popular support. As foreign armies crossed into France, his behavior was increasingly viewed as treasonous. On August 10, 1792, a crowd similar to the one that had marched on Versailles invaded his palace in Paris and forced the king to seek protection in the Legislative Assembly. The Assembly suspended the king, ordered his imprisonment, and called for the formation of a new National Convention to be elected by the vote of all men.

Rumors of counterrevolutionary plots kept working-class neighborhoods in an uproar. In September mobs surged through the city's prisons, killing nearly half the prisoners. Swept along by popular passion, the newly elected National Convention convicted Louis XVI of treason, sentencing him to death and proclaiming France a republic. The guillotine ended the king's life in January

Playing Cards from the French Revolution Even playing cards could be used to attack the aristocracy and Catholic Church. In this pack of cards, "Equality" and "Liberty" replaced kings and queens. (Jean-Loup Charmet/The Bridgeman Art Library)

1793. Invented in the spirit of the era as a more humane way to execute the condemned, this machine was to become the bloody symbol of the revolution. These events helped by February 1793 to precipitate a wider war with France now confronting nearly all of Europe's major powers.

The National Convention—the new legislature of the new First Republic of France—convened in September. Almost all of its members were from the middle class, and nearly all were **Jacobins°**—the most uncompromising democrats. Deep political differences, however, separated moderate Jacobins—called "Girondists°," after a region in southern France—and radicals known as "the Mountain." Members of the Mountain—so named because their seats were on the highest level in the assembly hall—were more sympathetic than the Girondists to the demands of the Parisian working class and more impatient with parliamentary procedure and constitutional constraints on government action. The Mountain came to be dominated by **Maximilien Robespierre°,** a young, little-known lawyer from the provinces who had been influenced by Rousseau's ideas.

With the French economy still in crisis and Paris suffering from inflation, high unemployment, and scarcity, Robespierre used the popular press and political clubs to forge an alliance with the volatile Parisian working class. His growing strength in the streets allowed him to purge the National Convention of his enemies and to restructure the government. Executive power was placed in the hands of the newly formed Committee of Public Safety, which created special courts to seek out and punish domestic enemies.

Among the groups that lost ground were the active feminists of the Parisian middle class and the working-class women who had sought the right to bear arms in defense of the Revolution. These women had provided decisive leadership at crucial times, helping propel the Revolution toward widened suffrage and a more democratic structure. Armed women had actively participated in every confrontation with conservative forces. It is ironic that the National Convention—the revolutionary era's most radical legislative body, elected by universal male suffrage—chose to repress the militant feminist forces that had prepared the ground for its creation.

Faced with rebellion in the provinces and foreign invasion, Robespierre and his allies unleashed a period of repression called the Reign of Terror (1793–1794) (see Diversity and Dominance: Robespierre and Wollstonecraft Defend and Explain the Terror). During the Terror, approximately 40,000 people were executed or died in prison, and another 300,000 were imprisoned. New actions against the clergy were also approved, including the provocative measure of forcing priests to marry. Even time was subject to revolutionary change. A new republican calendar created twelve thirty-day months divided into ten-day weeks. Sunday, with its Christian meanings, disappeared from the calendar.

By spring 1794 the Revolution was secure from foreign and domestic enemies, but repression, now institutionalized, continued. Among the victims were some who had been Robespierre's closest political collaborators during the early stage of the Terror. The execution of these former allies prepared the way for Robespierre's own fall by undermining the sense of invulnerability that had secured the loyalty of his remaining partisans in the National Convention. After French victories eliminated the immediate foreign threat, conservatives in the

---

Jacobin (JAK-uh-bin) **Girondist** (juh-RON-dist) **Robespierre** (ROBES-pee-air)

Convention felt secure enough to vote for the arrest of Robespierre on July 27, 1794. Over the next two days, Robespierre and nearly a hundred of his remaining allies were executed by guillotine.

Reaction and Dictatorship, 1795–1815

Purged of Robespierre's collaborators, the Convention began to undo the radical reforms. It removed many of the emergency economic controls that had been holding down prices and protecting the working class. Gone also was toleration for violent popular demonstrations. When the Paris working class rose in protest in 1795, the Convention approved the use of overwhelming military force. Another retreat from radical objectives was signaled when the Catholic Church was permitted to regain much of its former influence. The church's confiscated wealth, however, was not returned. A more conservative constitution was also ratified. It protected property, established a voting process that reduced the power of the masses, and created a new executive authority, the Directory. Once installed in power, however, the Directory proved unable to end the foreign wars or solve domestic economic problems.

After losing the election of 1797 the Directory suspended the results. The republican phase of the Revolution was clearly dead. Legitimacy was now based on coercive power rather than on elections. Two years later, **Napoleon Bonaparte** (1769–1821), a brilliant young general in the French army, seized power. Just as the American and French Revolutions had been the start of the modern democratic tradition, the military intervention that brought Napoleon to power in 1799 marked the advent of another modern form of government: popular authoritarianism.

The American and French Revolutions had resulted in part from conflicts over representation. If the people were sovereign, what institutions best expressed popular will? In the United States the answer was to expand the electorate and institute representative government. The French Revolution had taken a different direction with the Reign of Terror. Interventions on the floor of the National Convention by market women and soldiers, the presence of common people at revolutionary tribunals and at public executions, and expanded military service were all forms of political communication that temporarily satisfied the French people's desire to influence their government. Napoleon tamed these forms of political expression to organize Europe's first popular dictatorship. He succeeded because his military reputation promised order to a society exhausted by a decade of crisis, turmoil, and bloodshed.

In contrast to the National Convention, Napoleon proved capable of realizing France's dream of dominating Europe and providing effective protection for persons and property at home. Negotiations with the Catholic Church led to the Concordat of 1801. This agreement gave French Catholics the right to freely practice their religion, and it recognized the French government's authority to nominate bishops and retain priests on the state payroll. In his comprehensive rewriting of French law, the Civil Code of 1804, Napoleon won the support of the peasantry and of the middle class by asserting two basic principles inherited from the moderate first stage of the French Revolution: equality in law and protection of property. Even some members of the nobility became supporters after Napoleon declared himself emperor and France an empire in 1804. However, the discrimination against women that had begun during the Terror was extended by the Napoleonic Civil Code. Women were denied basic political rights and were able to participate in the economy only with the guidance and supervision of their fathers and husbands.

While providing personal security, the Napoleonic system denied or restricted many individual rights. Free speech and free expression were limited. Criticism of the government, viewed as subversive, was proscribed, and most opposition newspapers disappeared. Spies and informers directed by the minister of police enforced these limits to political freedom. Thousands of the regime's enemies and critics were questioned or detained in the name of domestic tranquility.

Ultimately, the Napoleonic system depended on the success of French arms and French diplomacy (see Map 22.2). From Napoleon's assumption of power until his fall, no single European state could defeat the French military. Even powerful alliances like that of Austria and Prussia were brushed aside with humiliating defeats and forced to become allies of France. Only Britain, protected by its powerful navy, remained able to thwart Napoleon's plans to dominate Europe. His effort to mobilize forces for an invasion of Britain failed in late 1805 when the British navy defeated the French and allied Spanish fleets off the coast of Spain at the Battle of Trafalgar.

Desiring to again extend French power to the Americas, Napoleon invaded Portugal in 1807 and Spain in 1808. French armies soon became tied down in a costly conflict with Spanish and Portuguese patriots who had forged an alliance with the only available European power, Great Britain. Frustrated by events on the Iberian Peninsula and faced with a faltering economy, Napoleon made the fateful decision to invade Russia. In June 1812

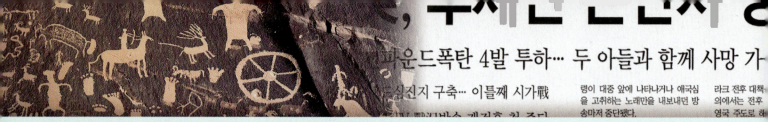

DIVERSITY AND DOMINANCE

ROBESPIERRE AND WOLLSTONECRAFT DEFEND AND EXPLAIN THE TERROR

Many Europeans who had initially been sympathetic to the French Revolution were repelled by the Terror. In 1793 and 1794 while France was at war with Austria, Prussia, Great Britain, Holland, and Spain about 2,600 people were executed in Paris, including the king and queen, members of the nobility, and Catholic clergy. The public nature of the judicial procedures and executions outraged many. Critics of the Revolution asked if these excesses were not worse than those committed by the French monarchy. Others defended the violence as necessary, arguing that the Terror had been provoked by enemies of the Revolution or was the consequence of earlier injustices.

The following two opinions date from 1794. Maximilien Robespierre was the head of the Committee of Public Safety, the effective head of the revolutionary government. Robespierre was a provincial lawyer who rose to power in Paris as the Revolution was radicalized. In the statement that follows he is unrepentant, arguing that violence was necessary in the defense of liberty. He made this statement on the eve of his political demise; in 1794 he was driven from power and executed by the revolutionary movement he had helped create.

Mary Wollstonecraft, an English intellectual and advocate for women's rights who was living in Paris at the time of the execution of Louis XVI, was troubled by the violence, and her discussion of these events is more an apology than a defense. She had published her famous A Vindication of the Rights of Woman in 1792, after which she left for Paris. Wollstonecraft left Paris after war broke out between France and Britain. She remained an important force in European intellectual life until her death from complications of childbirth in 1797.

MAXIMILIEN ROBESPIERRE, "ON THE MORAL AND POLITICAL PRINCIPLES OF DOMESTIC POLICY"

[L]et us deduce a great truth: the characteristic of popular government is confidence in the people and severity towards itself.

The whole development of our theory would end here if you had only to pilot the vessel of the Republic through calm waters; but the tempest roars, and the revolution imposes on you another task.

This great purity of the French revolution's basis, the very sublimity of its objective, is precisely what causes both our strength and our weakness. Our strength, because it gives to us truth's ascendancy over imposture, and the rights of the public interest over private interests; our weakness, because it rallies all vicious men against us, all those who in their hearts contemplated despoiling the people and all those who intend to let it be despoiled with impunity, both those who have rejected freedom as a personal calamity and those who have embraced the revolution as a career and the Republic as prey. Hence the defection of so many ambitious or greedy men who since the point of departure have abandoned us along the way because they did not begin the journey with the same destination in view. The two opposing spirits that have been represented in a struggle to rule nature might be said to be fighting in this great period of human history to fix irrevocably the world's destinies, and France is the scene of this fearful combat. Without, all the tyrants encircle you; within, all tyranny's friends conspire; they will conspire until hope is wrested from crime. We must smother the internal and external enemies of the Republic or perish with it; now in this situation, the first maxim of your policy ought to be to lead the people by reason and the people's enemies by terror.

If the spring of popular government in time of peace is virtue, the springs of popular government in revolution are at once virtue and terror: virtue, without which terror is fatal; terror, without which virtue is powerless. Terror is nothing other than justice, prompt, severe, inflexible; it is therefore an emanation of virtue; it is not so much a special principle as it is a consequence of the general principle of democracy applied to our country's most urgent needs.

It has been said that terror is the principle of despotic government. Does your government therefore resemble despotism? Yes, as the sword that gleams in the hands of the heroes of liberty resembles that with which the henchmen of tyranny are armed. Let the despot govern by terror his brutalized subjects; he is right, as a despot. Subdue by terror the enemies of liberty, and you will be right, as founders of the Republic. The government of the revolution is liberty's despotism against tyranny. Is force made only to protect crime? And is the thunderbolt not destined to strike the heads of the proud?

. . . Society owes protection only to peaceable citizens; the only citizens in the Republic are the republicans. For it, the royalists, the conspirators are only strangers or, rather, enemies. This terrible war waged by liberty against tyranny-is it not indivisible? Are the enemies within not the allies of the enemies without? The assassins who tear our country apart, the intriguers who buy the consciences that hold the people's mandate; the traitors who sell them; the mercenary pamphleteers hired to dishonor the people's cause, to kill public virtue, to stir up the fire of civil discord, and to prepare political counterrevolution by moral counterrevolution—are all those men less guilty or less dangerous than the tyrants whom they serve?

MARY WOLLSTONECRAFT, "AN HISTORICAL AND MORAL VIEW OF THE ORIGIN AND PROGRESS OF THE FRENCH REVOLUTION"

Weeping scarcely conscious that I weep, O France! Over the vestiges of thy former oppression, which, separating man from man with a fence of iron, sophisticated [complicated] all, and made many completely wretched; I tremble, lest I should meet some unfortunate being, fleeing from the despotism of licentious freedom, hearing the snap of the guillotine at his heels, merely because he was once noble, or has afforded an asylum to those whose only crime is their name—and, if my pen almost bound with eagerness to record the day that leveled the Bastille [an abbey used as a prison before the Revolution] with the dust, making the towers of despair tremble to their base, the recollection that still the abbey is appropriated to hold the victims of revenge and suspicion [she means that the Bastille remained a prison for those awaiting revolutionary justice]. . . .

Excuse for the Ferocity of the Parisians The deprivation of natural, equal, civil, and political rights reduced the most cunning the lower orders to practice fraud, and the rest to habits of stealing, audacious robberies, and murders. And why? Because the rich and poor were separated into bands of tyrants and slaves, and the retaliation of slaves is always terrible. In short, every sacred feeling, moral and divine, has been obliterated, and the dignity of man sullied, by a system of policy and jurisprudence as repugnant to reason as at variance with humanity.

The only excuse that can be made for the ferocity of the Parisians is then simply to observe that they had not any

confidence in the laws, which they had always found to be merely cobwebs to catch small flies [the poor]. Accustomed to be punished themselves for every trifle, and often for only being in the way of the rich, or their parasites, when, in fact, had the Parisians seen the execution of a noble, or priest, though convicted of crimes beyond the daring of vulgar minds? When justice, or the law, is so partial, the day of retribution will come with the red sky of vengeance, to confound the innocent with the guilty. The mob were barbarous beyond the tiger's cruelty.

. . .

Let us cast our eyes over the history of man, and we shall scarcely find a page that is not tarnished by some foul deed or bloody transaction. Let us examine the catalogue of the vices of men in a savage state, and contrast them with those of men civilized; we shall find that a barbarian, considered as a moral being, is an angel, compared with the refined villain of artificial life. Let us investigate the causes which have produced this degeneracy, and we shall discover that they are those unjust plans of government which have been formed by peculiar circumstances in every part of the globe.

Then let us coolly and impartially contemplate the improvements which are gaining ground in the formation of principles of policy; and I flatter myself it will be allowed by every humane and considerate being that a political system more simple than has hitherto existed would effectually check those aspiring follies, which, by imitation, leading to vice, have banished from governments the very shadow of justice and magnanimity.

Thus had France grown up and sickened on the corruption of a state diseased. . . . it is only the philosophical eye, which looks into the nature and weighs the consequences of human actions, that will be able to discern the cause, which has produced so many dreadful effects.

QUESTIONS FOR ANALYSIS

1. Why does Robespierre believe that revolution cannot tolerate diversity of opinion? Are his reasons convincing?
2. How does Robespierre distinguish the terror of despots from the terror of liberty?
3. How does Wollstonecraft explain the "ferocity" of the Parisians?
4. What does Wollstonecraft believe will come from this period of violence?

Sources: Maximilien Robespierre, "On the Moral and Political Principles of Domestic Policy," February 5, 1794, *Modern History Sourcebook: Robespierre: Terror and Virtue, 1794, http://www.fordham.edu/halsall/mod/robespierre-terror.html*; Mary Wollstonecraft, "An Historical and Moral View of the Origin and Progress of the French Revolution," *A Mary Wollstonecraft Reader,* ed. Barbara H. Solomon and Paula S. Berggren (New York: New American Library, 1983), 374–375, 382–383.

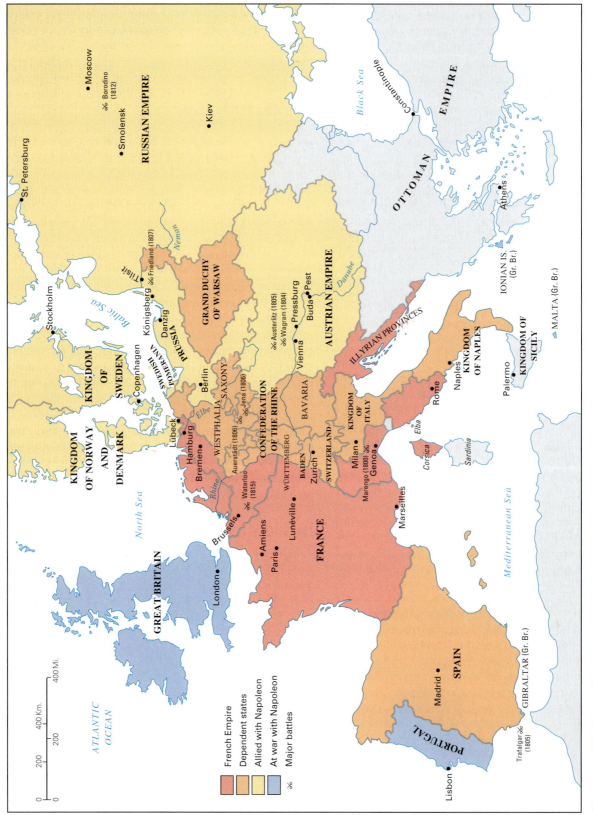

Map 22.2   Napoleon's Europe, 1810   By 1810 Great Britain was the only remaining European power at war with Napoleon. Because of the loss of the French fleet at the Battle of Trafalgar in 1805, Napoleon was unable to threaten Britain with invasion, and Britain was able to actively assist the resistance movements in Spain and Portugal, thereby helping weaken French power.

he began his campaign with the largest army ever assembled in Europe, approximately 600,000 men. After fighting an inconclusive battle at Borodino, Napoleon pressed on to Moscow. Five weeks after occupying Moscow, he was forced to retreat by Russian patriots who set the city on fire and by approaching armies. During the retreat, the brutal Russian winter and attacks by Russian forces destroyed his army. A broken and battered fragment of 30,000 men returned home to France.

After the debacle in Russia, Austria and Prussia deserted Napoleon and entered an alliance with England and Russia. Unable to defend Paris, Napoleon was forced to abdicate the French throne in April 1814. The allies exiled Napoleon to the island of Elba off the coast of Italy and restored the French monarchy. The next year Napoleon escaped from Elba and returned to France. But his moment had passed. He was defeated by an allied army at Waterloo, in Belgium, after only one hundred days in power. His final exile was on the distant island of St. Helena in the South Atlantic, where he died in 1821.

REVOLUTION SPREADS, CONSERVATIVES RESPOND, 1789–1850

Even as the dictatorship of Napoleon eliminated the democratic legacy of the French Revolution, revolutionary ideology was spreading and taking hold in Europe and the Americas. In Europe the French Revolution promoted nationalism and republicanism. In the Americas the legacies of the American and French Revolutions led to a new round of struggles for independence. News of revolutionary events in France destabilized the colonial regime in Saint Domingue (present-day Haiti), a small French colony on the western half of the island of Hispaniola, and resulted in the first successful slave rebellion. In Europe, however, the spread of revolutionary fervor was checked by reaction as monarchs formed an alliance to protect themselves from further revolutionary outbreaks.

The Haitian Revolution, 1789–1804

In 1789 the French colony of Saint Domingue was among the richest European colonies in the Americas. Its plantations produced sugar, cotton, indigo, and coffee. The colony produced two-thirds of France's tropical imports and generated nearly one-third of all French foreign trade. This impressive wealth depended on a brutal slave regime. Saint Domingue's harsh punishments and poor living conditions were notorious throughout the Caribbean. The colony's high mortality and low fertility rates created an insatiable demand for African slaves. As a result, in 1790 the majority of the colony's 500,000 slaves were African-born.

In 1789, when news of the calling of France's Estates General arrived on the island, wealthy white planters sent a delegation to Paris charged with seeking more home rule and greater economic freedom for Saint Domingue. The free mixed-race population, the **gens de couleur°**, also sent representatives. These nonwhite delegates were mostly drawn from the large class of slave-owning small planters and urban merchants. They focused on ending race discrimination and achieving political equality with whites. They did not seek freedom for slaves; the most prosperous gens de couleur were slave owners themselves. As the French Revolution became more radical, the gens de couleur forged an alliance with sympathetic French radicals, who came to identify the colony's wealthy planters as royalists and aristocrats.

The political turmoil in France weakened the ability of colonial administrators to maintain order. The authority of colonial officials was no longer clear, and the very legitimacy of slavery was being challenged in France. In the vacuum that resulted, rich planters, poor whites, and the gens de couleur pursued their narrow interests, engendering an increasingly bitter and confrontational struggle. Given the slaves' hatred of the brutal regime that oppressed them and the accumulated grievances of the free people of color, there was no way to limit the violence once the control of the slave owners slipped. When Vincent Ogé°, leader of the gens de couleur mission to France, returned to Saint Domingue in 1790 to organize a military force, the planters captured, tortured, and executed him. This cruelty was soon repaid in kind.

By 1791 whites, led by the planter elite, and the gens de couleur were engaged in open warfare. This breach between the two groups of slave owners gave the slaves an opening. A slave rebellion began on the plantations of the north and spread throughout the colony (see Map 22.3). Plantations were destroyed, masters and overseers killed, and crops burned. An emerging rebel leadership that combined elements of African political culture with revolutionary ideology from France mobilized and directed the rebelling slaves.

The rebellious slaves eventually gained the upper hand under the leadership of **François Dominique Toussaint L'Ouverture,** a former domestic slave, who created a disciplined military force. Toussaint was politically

gens de couleur (zhahn deh koo-LUHR)   **Ogé** (oh-ZHAY)

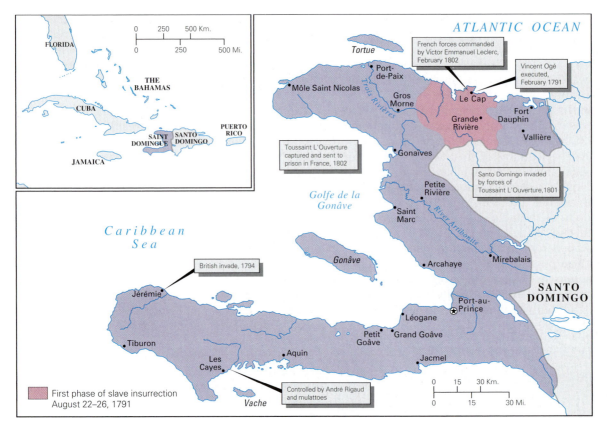

Map 22.3   The Haitian Revolution   On their way to achieving an end to slavery and gaining national independence, the Haitian revolutionaries were forced to defeat British and French military interventions as well as the local authority of the slave masters.

strengthened in 1794 when the radical National Convention in Paris abolished slavery in all French possessions. He overcame his rivals in Saint Domingue, defeated a British expeditionary force in 1798, and then led an invasion of the neighboring Spanish colony of Santo Domingo, freeing the slaves there. Toussaint continued to assert his loyalty to France but gave the French government no effective role in local affairs.

As reaction overtook revolution in France, both the abolition of slavery and Toussaint's political position were threatened. When the Directory contemplated the reestablishment of slavery, Toussaint protested:

> Do they think that men who have been able to enjoy the blessing of liberty will calmly see it snatched away? They supported their chains only so long as they did not know any condition of life more happy than slavery. But today when they have left it, if they had a thousand lives they would sacrifice them all rather than be forced into slavery again.[3]

In 1802 Napoleon sent a large military force to Saint Domingue to reestablish both French colonial authority and slavery (see Map 22.3). At first the French forces were successful. Toussaint was captured and sent to France, where he died in prison. Eventually, however, the loss of thousands of lives to yellow fever and the resistance of the revolutionaries turned the tide. Visible in the resistance to the French were small numbers of armed women. During the early stages of the Haitian Revolution, very few slave women had taken up arms, although many had aided Toussaint's forces in support roles. But after a decade of struggle and violence, more Haitian women were politically aware and willing to join the armed resistance. In 1804 Toussaint's successors declared independence, and the free republic of Haiti joined the United States as the second independent nation in the Western Hemisphere. But independence and emancipation were achieved at a terrible price. Tens of thousands had died; the economy was destroyed; and public administration was corrupted by more than a decade of vio-

Haiti's Former Slaves Defend Their Freedom   In this representation, a veteran army sent by Napoleon to reassert French control in Haiti battles with Haitian forces in a tropical forest. The combination of Haitian resistance and yellow fever defeated the French invasion.   (Bettmann/Corbis)

lence. Political violence and economic stagnation were to trouble Haiti throughout the nineteenth century.

The Congress of Vienna and Conservative Retrenchment, 1815–1820

From 1814 to 1815 representatives of Britain, Russia, Austria, and Prussia met as the **Congress of Vienna** to reestablish political order in Europe. While they were meeting, Napoleon escaped from Elba, then was defeated at Waterloo. The French Revolution and Napoleon's imperial ambitions had threatened the very survival of Europe's old order. Ancient monarchies had been overturned and dynasties replaced with interlopers. Long-established political institutions had been tossed aside, and long-recognized international borders had been ignored. The very existence of the nobility and church had been put at risk. Under the leadership of the Austrian foreign minister, Prince Klemens von Metternich° (1773–1859), the allies worked together in Vienna

Metternich (MET-uhr-nik)

to create a comprehensive peace settlement that they hoped would safeguard the conservative order.

The central objective of the Congress of Vienna was to roll back the clock in France. Because the participants believed that a strong and stable France was the best guarantee of future peace, the French monarchy was reestablished, and France's 1792 borders were recognized. Most of the continental European powers received some territorial gains, for Metternich sought to offset French strength with a balance of power. In addition, Austria, Russia, and Prussia formed a separate alliance to more actively confront the revolutionary and nationalist energies that the French Revolution had unleashed. In 1820 this "Holy Alliance" acted decisively to defeat liberal revolutions in Spain and Italy. By repressing republican and nationalist ideas in universities and the press, the Holy Alliance also attempted to meet the potential challenge posed by subversive ideas. Metternich's program of conservative retrenchment succeeded in the short term, but powerful ideas associated with liberalism and nationalism remained a vital part of European political life throughout the nineteenth century.

Nationalism, Reform, and Revolution, 1821–1850

Despite the power of the conservative monarchs, popular support for national self-determination and democratic reform grew throughout Europe. Greece had been under Ottoman control since the fifteenth century. In 1821 Greek patriots launched an independence movement. Metternich and other conservatives opposed Greek independence, but European artists and writers enamored with the cultural legacy of ancient Greece rallied political support for intervention. After years of struggle, Russia, France, and Great Britain forced the Ottoman Empire to recognize Greek independence in 1830.

Louis XVIII, brother of the executed Louis XVI, had been placed on the throne of France by the victorious allies in 1814. He ruled as a constitutional monarch until his death in 1824 and was followed to the throne by his brother Charles X. Charles attempted to rule in the pre-revolutionary style of his ancestors, repudiating the constitution in 1830. Unwilling to accept this reactionary challenge, the people of Paris rose up and forced Charles to abdicate. His successor was his cousin Louis Philippe° (r. 1830–1848), who accepted the reestablished constitution and extended voting privileges.

At the same time democratic reform movements appeared in both the United States and Great Britain. In the United States after 1790 the original thirteen states were joined by new states with constitutions granting voting rights to most free males. After the War of 1812 the right to vote was expanded in the older states as well. This broadening of the franchise led to the election of the populist president Andrew Jackson in 1828 (see Chapter 24).

However, revolutionary violence in France made the British aristocracy and the conservative Tory Party fearful of expanded democracy and mass movements of any kind. In 1815 the British government passed the Corn Laws, which limited the importation of foreign grains. The laws favored the profits of wealthy landowners who produced grain at the expense of the poor who were forced to pay more for their bread. When poor consumers organized to overturn these laws, the government outlawed most public meetings, using troops to crush protest in Manchester. Reacting against these policies, reformers gained the passage of laws that increased the power of the House of Commons, redistributed votes from agricultural to industrial districts, and increased the number of voters by nearly 50 percent. Although the most radical demands of these reformers, called

Chartists, were defeated, new labor and economic reforms addressing the grievances of workers were passed (see Chapter 23).

Despite the achievement of Greek independence and limited political reform in France and Great Britain, conservatives continued to hold the upper hand in Europe. Finally, in 1848 the desire for democratic reform and national self-determination and the frustrations of urban workers led to upheavals across Europe. The **Revolutions of 1848** began in Paris, where members of the middle class and workers united to overthrow the regime of Louis Philippe and create the Second French Republic. Adult men were given voting rights; slavery was abolished in French colonies; the death penalty was ended; and a ten-hour workday was legislated for Paris. But Parisian workers' demands for programs to reduce unemployment and prices provoked conflicts with the middle class, which wanted to protect property rights. When workers rose up against the government, French troops were called out to crush them. Desiring the reestablishment of order, the French elected Louis Napoleon, nephew of the former emperor, president in December 1848. Three years later, he overturned the constitution as a result of popular plebiscite and, after ruling briefly as dictator, became Emperor Napoleon III. He remained in power until 1871.

Reformers in Hungary, Italy, Bohemia, and elsewhere pressed for greater national self-determination in 1848. When the Austrian monarchy did not meet their demands, students and workers in Vienna took to the streets to force political reforms similar to those sought in Paris. With revolution spreading throughout the Austrian Empire, Metternich, the symbol of reaction, fled Vienna in disguise. Little lasting change occurred, however, because the new Austrian emperor, Franz Joseph (r. 1848–1916) was able to use Russian military assistance and loyal Austrian troops to reestablish central authority.

Middle-class reformers and workers in Berlin joined forces in an attempt to compel the Prussian king to accept a liberal constitution and seek unification of the German states. But the Constituent Assembly called to write a constitution and arrange for national integration became entangled in diplomatic conflicts with Austria and Denmark. As a result, Frederick William IV (r. 1840–1861) was able to reassert his authority, thwarting both constitutional reform and unification.

Despite their heroism on the barricades of Paris, Vienna, Rome, and Berlin, the revolutionaries of 1848 failed to gain either their nationalist or their republican objectives. Monarchs retained the support not only of aristocrats but also of professional militaries, largely re-

---

Louis Philippe (loo-EE-fee-LEEP)

The Revolution of 1830 in Belgium   After the 1830 uprising that overturned the restored monarchy in France, Belgians rose up to declare their independence from Holland. In Poland and Italy, similar uprisings combining nationalism and a desire for self-governance failed. This painting by Baron Gustaf Wappers romantically illustrates the popular nature of the Belgian uprising by bringing to the barricades men, women, and children drawn from both the middle and the working classes.   (Musées royaux des Beaux-Arts de Belgique, Brussels)

cruited from among peasants who had little sympathy for urban workers. Revolutionary coalitions, in contrast, were fragile and lacked clear objectives. Workers' demands for higher wages, lower prices, and labor reform often drove their middle-class allies into the arms of the reactionaries.

CONCLUSION

This era of revolution was, in large measure, the product of a long period of costly warfare among the imperial nations of Europe. Using taxes and institutions inherited from the past, England and France found it increasingly difficult to fund distant wars in the Americas or in Asia. Royal governments attempting to impose new taxes met with angry resistance. The spread of literacy and the greater availability of books helped create a European culture more open to reform or the revolutionary change of existing institutions. The ideas of Locke and Rousseau guided critics of monarchy toward a new political culture of elections and representative institutions. Each new development served as example and provocation for new revolutionary acts. French officers who took part in the American Revolution helped ignite the French Revolution. Black freemen from Haiti traveled to France to seek their rights and returned to spread revolutionary passions. Each revolution had its own character. The revolutions in France and Haiti proved to be more violent and destructive than the American Revolution. Revolutionaries in France and Haiti, facing a more strongly entrenched and more powerful opposition and greater social inequalities, responded with greater violence.

The conservative retrenchment that followed the defeat of Napoleon succeeded in the short term. Monarchy, multinational empires, and the established church retained their hold on the loyalty of millions of Europeans and could count on the support of many of Europe's wealthiest and most powerful individuals. But liberalism and nationalism continued to stir revolutionary sentiment. The contest between adherents of the old order and partisans of change was to continue well into the nineteenth century. In the end, the nation-state, the Enlightenment legacy of rational inquiry, broadened political participation, and secular intellectual culture prevailed. This outcome was determined in large measure by the old order's inability to satisfy the new social classes that appeared with the emerging industrial economy. The material transformation produced by industrial capitalism could not be contained in the narrow confines of a hereditary social system, nor could the rapid expansion of scientific learning be contained within the doctrines of traditional religion.

The revolutions of the late eighteenth century began the transformation of Western society, but they did not complete it. Only a minority gained full political rights. Women did not achieve full political rights until the twentieth century. Democratic institutions, as in revolutionary France, often failed. Moreover, as Chapter 24 discusses, slavery endured in the Americas past the mid-1800s, despite the revolutionary era's enthusiasm for individual liberty.

■ Key Terms

Enlightenment
Benjamin Franklin
George Washington
Joseph Brant
Constitutional Convention
Estates General
National Assembly
Declaration of the Rights of Man
Jacobins
Maximilien Robespierre
Napoleon Bonaparte
gens de couleur
François Dominique Toussaint L'Ouverture
Congress of Vienna
Revolutions of 1848

■ Suggested Reading

The American Revolution has received a great amount of attention from scholars. Colin Bonwick, *The American Revolution* (1991), and Edward Countryman, *The American Revolution* (1985), provide excellent introductions. Edmund S. Morgan, *The Challenge of the American Revolution* (1976), remains a major work of interpretation. Gordon S. Wood, *The Radicalism of the American Revolution* (1992), is a brilliant examination of the ideological and cultural meanings of the Revolution. A contrarian view is offered by Francis Jennings, *The Creation of America Through Revolution to Empire* (2003). See also William Howard Adams, *The Paris Years of Thomas Jefferson* (1997). Lance Banning, *The Sacred Fire of Liberty: James Madison and the Founding of the Federal Republic* (1995), is a convincing revision of the story of Madison and his era. For the role of women in the American Revolution see Linda K. Kerber, *Women of the Republic: Intellect and Ideology in Revolutionary America* (1980), and Mary Beth Norton, *Liberty's Daughters: The Revolutionary Experience of American Women, 1750–1800* (1980). Also recommended is Norton's *Founding Mothers and Fathers: Gendered Power and the Forming of American Society* (1996). Among the many works that deal with African-Americans and Amerindians during the era, see Sylvia Frey, *Water from Rock: Black Resistance in a Revolutionary Age* (1991); Barbara Graymont, *The Iroquois in the American Revolution* (1972); and William N. Fenton, *The Great Law and the Longhouse: A Political History of the Iroquois Confederacy* (1998).

For intellectual life in the era of the French Revolution see Anne Goldgar, *Impolite Learning: Conduct and Community in the Republic of Letters, 1680–1750* (1995); Dena Goodman, *The Republic of Letters: A Cultural History of the Enlightenment* (1994); and James Swenson, *On Jean-Jacques Rousseau Considered as One of the First Authors of the Revolution* (2002). For the Counter Enlightenment see Darrin M. McMahon, *Enemies of the Enlightenment, The French Counter-Enlightenment and the Making of Modernity* (2001). For the "underside" of this era see the discussion of "folk culture" in *Shaping History: Ordinary People in European Politics, 1500–1700* (1998), by Wayne Te Brake. François Furet, *Interpreting the French Revolution* (1981), breaks with interpretations that emphasize class and ideology. Georges Lefebve, *The Coming of the French Revolution*, trans. R. R. Palmer (1947), presents the classic class-based analysis. George Rudé, *The Crowd in History: Popular Disturbances in France and England* (1981), remains the best introduction to the role of mass protest in the period. Lynn Hunt, *The Family Romance of the French Revolution* (1992), examines the gender content of revolutionary politics. For the role of women see Joan Landes, *Women and the Public Sphere in the Age of the French Revolution* (1988), and the recently published *The Women of Paris and Their French Revolution* (1998) by Dominique Godineau. Felix Markham, *Napoleon* (1963), and Robert B. Holtman, *The Napoleonic Revolution* (1967), provide reliable summaries of the period.

The Haitian Revolution has received less extensive coverage than the revolutions in the United States and France. C. L. R.

James, *The Black Jacobins*, 2d ed. (1963), is the classic study. Anna J. Cooper, *Slavery and the French Revolutionists, 1788–1805* (1988), also provides an overview of this important topic. Carolyn E. Fick, *The Making of Haiti: The Saint Domingue Revolution from Below* (1990), is the best recent synthesis. David P. Geggus, *Slavery, War, and Revolution* (1982), examines the British role in the revolutionary period. See also David Barry Gaspar and David Patrick Geggus, eds., *A Turbulent Time: The French Revolution and the Greater Caribbean* (1997).

For the revolutions of 1830 and 1848 see Arthur J. May's brief survey in *The Age of Metternich, 1814–48*, rev. ed. (1963). Henry Kissinger's *A World Restored* (1957) remains among the most interesting discussions of the Congress of Vienna. Eric Hobsbawm's *The Age of Revolution* (1962) provides a clear analysis of the class issues that appeared during this era. Paul Robertson's *Revolutions of 1848: A Social History* (1960) remains a valuable introduction. See also Peter Stearns and Herrick Chapman, *European Society in Upheaval* (1991). For the development of European social reform movements see Albert Lindemann, *History of European Socialism* (1983).

For national events in Hungary see István Deák's examination of Hungary, *The Lawful Revolution: Louis Kossuth and the Hungarians, 1848–49* (1979). On Germany see Theodore S. Hamerow, *Restoration, Revolution, and Reaction, 1815–1871* (1966). For French events see Roger Price, *A Social History of Nineteenth-Century France* (1987). Barbara Taylor, *Eve and the New Jerusalem: Socialism and Feminism in the Nineteenth Century* (1983), analyzes connections between workers' and women's rights issues in England.

■ Notes

1. Quoted in Ray Raphael, *A People's History of the American Revolution* (New York: Perenial, 2001), 142.
2. Ibid., 141.
3. Quoted in C. L. R. James, *The Black Jacobins,* 2d ed., (New York: Vintage Books, 1963), 196.

23 The Early Industrial Revolution, 1760–1851

Mr. Watt's Engine   This drawing shows the functioning parts of a Watt engine used to pump water from a mine: the boiler, cylinder Q, condenser N, rocking horse, and pump S.

CHAPTER OUTLINE

Causes of the Industrial Revolution

The Technological Revolution

The Impact of the Early Industrial Revolution

New Economic and Political Ideas

Industrialization and the Nonindustrial World

ENVIRONMENT AND TECHNOLOGY: The Origin of Graphs

DIVERSITY AND DOMINANCE: Adam Smith and the Division of Labor

From 1765 until the 1790s a small group of men calling themselves the Lunar Society met once a month in Birmingham, England. They gathered on nights when the moon was full, so they could find their way home in the dark. Among them were the pottery manufacturer Josiah Wedgwood, the engine designer James Watt, the chemist Joseph Priestley, the iron manufacturer Matthew Boulton, and the naturalist Erasmus Darwin. They did not leave a record of what they discussed, but the fact that businessmen, craftsmen, and scientists had interests in common was something new in the history of the world. Though members of very different professions, they were willing to exchange ideas and discoveries in an atmosphere of experimentation and innovation. They invited experts in industry, science, and engineering to speak at their meetings in order to obtain the latest information in their fields.

Meanwhile, similar societies throughout Britain were creating a vogue for science and were giving the word *progress* a new meaning: "change for the better." By focusing on the practical application of knowledge, groups like the Lunar Society laid the groundwork for the economic and social transformations that historians call the **Industrial Revolution.** This revolution involved dramatic innovations in manufacturing, mining, transportation, and communications and equally rapid changes in society and commerce. New relationships between social groups created an environment that was conducive to technical innovation and economic growth. New technologies and new social and economic arrangements allowed the industrializing countries—first Britain, then western Europe and the United States—to unleash massive increases in production and productivity, exploit the world's natural resources as never before, and transform the environment and human life in unprecedented ways.

The distribution of power and wealth generated by the Industrial Revolution was very uneven, for industrialization widened the gap between rich and poor. The people who owned and controlled the innovations amassed wealth and power over nature and over other people. Some of them lived lives of spectacular luxury. Workers, including children, worked long hours in dangerous factories and lived crowded together in unsanitary tenements.

The effect of the Industrial Revolution around the world was also very uneven. The first countries to industrialize grew rich and powerful. In Egypt and India, the economic and military power of the European countries stifled the tentative beginnings of industrialization. Regions that had little or no industry were easily taken advantage of. The disparity between the industrial and the developing countries that exists today has its origins in the early nineteenth century.

As you read this chapter, ask yourself the following questions:

- What caused the Industrial Revolution?

- What were the key innovations that increased productivity and drove industrialization?

- What was the impact of these changes on the society and environment of the industrializing countries?

- How did the Industrial Revolution affect the relations between the industrialized and the nonindustrialized parts of the world?

CAUSES OF THE INDUSTRIAL REVOLUTION

What caused the Industrial Revolution, and why did it begin in England in the late eighteenth century? These are two of the great questions of history. The basic preconditions of this momentous event seem to have been economic development propelled by population growth, an agricultural revolution, the expansion of trade, and an openness to innovation.

Population Growth

The population of Europe rose in the eighteenth century—slowly at first, faster after 1780, then even faster in the early nineteenth century. The fastest growth took place in England and Wales. Population there rose from 5.5 million in 1688 to 9 million in 1801 and 18 million by 1851—increases never before experienced in European history.

The growth of population resulted from more widespread resistance to disease and more reliable food supplies, thanks to the new crops that originated in the Americas (see Chapter 17). More dependable food supplies and better job opportunities led people to marry at earlier ages and have more children. A high birthrate meant a large percentage of children in the general population. In the early nineteenth century some 40 percent of the population of Britain was under fifteen years of age. This high proportion of youths explains both the vitality of the British people in that period and the widespread use of child labor. People also migrated at an unprecedented rate—from the countryside to the cities, from Ireland to England, and, more generally, from Europe to the Americas. Thanks to immigration, the population of the United States rose from 4 million in 1791 to 9.6 million in 1820 and 31.5 million in 1860—faster growth than in any other part of the world at the time.

The Agricultural Revolution

Innovations in manufacturing could only have taken place alongside a simultaneous revolution in farming that provided food for city dwellers and forced poorer peasants off the land. This **agricultural revolution** had begun long before the eighteenth century. One important aspect was the acceptance of the potato, introduced from South America in the sixteenth century. In the cool and humid regions of Europe from Ireland to Russia, potatoes yielded two or three times more food per acre than did the wheat, rye, and oats they replaced. Maize (American corn) was grown across Europe from northern Iberia to the Balkans. Turnips, legumes, and clover did not deplete the soil and could be fed to cattle, which were sources of milk and meat. Manure from cattle in turn fertilized the soil for other crops.

The security of small-scale tenant farmers and sharecroppers depended on traditional methods and rural customs such as collecting plants left over in the fields after the harvest, pasturing their animals on common village lands, and gathering firewood in common woods. Only prosperous landowners with secure titles to their land could afford to bear the risk of trying new methods and new crops. Rich landowners therefore "enclosed" the land—that is, consolidated their holdings—and got Parliament to give them title to the commons that in the past had been open to all. Once in control of the land, they could drain and improve the soil, breed better livestock, and introduce crop rotation. This "enclosure movement" turned tenants and sharecroppers into landless farm laborers. Many moved to the cities to seek work; others became homeless migrants and vagrants; and still others emigrated to Canada, Australia, and the United States.

In eastern Europe, as in Britain, large estates predominated, and aristocratic landowners used such improvements to increase their wealth and political influence. In western Europe enclosure was hampered by the fact that the law gave secure property rights to numerous small farmers.

Trade and Inventiveness

In most of Europe the increasing demand that accompanied the growth of population was met by increasing production in traditional ways. Roads were improved so stagecoaches could travel faster. Royal manufacturers trained additional craftsmen to produce fine china, silks, and carpets by hand. In rural areas much production was carried out through cottage industries. Merchants delivered fibers, leather, and other raw materials to craftspeople (often farmers in the off-season) and picked up the finished products. The growth of the population and food supply was accompanied by the growth of trade. Most of it was local trade in traditional goods and services. But a growing share consisted of simple goods that even middle-class people could afford: sugar, tea, cotton textiles, iron hardware, pottery. Products from other parts of the world like tea and sugar required extensive networks of shipping and finance.

As the story of the Lunar Society demonstrates, scientific discoveries, commercial enterprise, and technical skills became closely connected. Technology and innovation fascinated educated people throughout Europe and eastern North America. The French *Encyclopédie* contained thousands of articles and illustrations of crafts and manufacturing (see Diversity and Dominance: Adam Smith and the Division of Labor). The French and British governments sent expeditions around the world to collect plants that could profitably be grown in their colonies. They also offered prizes to anyone who could find a method of determining the longitude of a ship at sea to avoid the shipwrecks that had cost the lives of thousands of sailors. The American Benjamin Franklin, like many others, experimented with electricity. In France, the Montgolfier brothers invented a hot-air balloon. Claude Chappe° created the first semaphore telegraph. French artillery officers proposed making guns with interchangeable parts. The American Eli Whitney and his associate John Hall invented machine tools, that

Chappe (SHAPP)

CHRONOLOGY

	Technology	Economy, Society, and Politics
1750		
	1759 Josiah Wedgwood opens pottery factory	
	1764 Spinning jenny	
	1769 Richard Arkwright's water frame; James Watt patents steam engine	**1776** Adam Smith's *Wealth of Nations*
	1779 First iron bridge	**1776–1783** American Revolution
	1785 Boulton and Watt sell steam engines; Samuel Crompton's mule	**1789–1799** French Revolution
	1793 Eli Whitney's cotton gin	
1800	**1800** Alessandro Volta's battery	
	1807 Robert Fulton's *Clermont*	**1804–1815** Napoleonic Wars
	1820s Construction of Erie Canal	**1820s** U.S. cotton industry begins
	1829 *Rocket,* first steam-powered locomotive	
	1837 Wheatstone and Cooke's telegraph	**1833** Factory Act in Britain
	1838 First ships steam across the Atlantic	**1834** German Zollverein; Robert Owen's Grand National Consolidated Trade Union
	1840 *Nemesis* sails to China	
	1843 Samuel Morse's Baltimore-to-Washington telegraph	**1846** Repeal of British Corn Laws
		1847–1848 Irish famine
		1848 Collapse of Chartist movement; Revolutions in Europe
1850	**1851** Crystal Palace opens in London	**1854** First cotton mill in India

is, machines capable of making other machines. These machines greatly increased the productivity of manufacturing.

Britain and Continental Europe

Economic growth was evident throughout the North Atlantic area, yet industrialization did not take place everywhere at once. To understand why, we must look at the peculiar role of Great Britain. Britain enjoyed a rising standard of living during the eighteenth century, thanks to good harvests, a growing population, and a booming overseas trade. Britain was the world's leading exporter of tools, guns, hardware, clocks, and other craft goods (see Map 23.1). Its mining and metal industries employed engineers willing to experiment with new ideas. It had the largest merchant marine and produced more ships, naval supplies, and navigation instruments than other countries.

Until the mid-eighteenth century the British were better known for their cheap imitations than for their innovations or quality products. But they put inventions into practice more quickly than other people, as the engineer John Farey told a parliamentary committee in 1829: "The prevailing talent of English and Scotch people is to apply new ideas to use and to bring such applications to perfection, but they do not imagine as much as foreigners" (see Environment and Technology: The Origin of Graphs).

Before 1790 Britain had a more fluid society than did the rest of Europe. The English royal court was less ostentatious than the courts of France, Spain, and Austria. Its aristocracy was less powerful, and the lines separating the social classes were not as sharply drawn. Political power was not as centralized as on the European continent, and the government employed fewer bureaucrats and officials. Members of the gentry, and even some aristocrats, married into merchant families. Intermarriage among the families of petty merchants, yeoman farmers, and town craftsmen was common. Guilds, which resisted innovation, were relatively weak. Ancestry remained important, but wealth also commanded respect. A businessman with enough money could buy a landed estate,

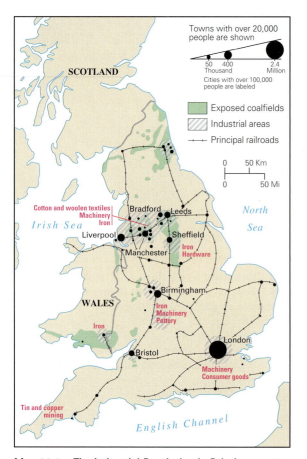

Map 23.1   The Industrial Revolution in Britain, ca. 1850
The first industries arose in northern and western England. These regions had abundant coal and iron-ore deposits for the iron industry and moist climate and fast-flowing rivers, factors imporant for the cotton textile industry.

ance institutions able to support growing business enterprises and a patent system that offered inventors the hope of rich rewards. The example of men who became wealthy and respected for their inventions—such as Richard Arkwright, the cotton magnate, and James Watt, the steam engine designer—stimulated others.

In the eighteenth century, the economies of continental Europe also underwent a dynamic expansion, thanks to the efforts of individual entrepreneurs and investors. Yet growth was still hampered by high transportation costs, misguided government regulations, and rigid social structures. The Low Countries were laced with canals, but the terrain elsewhere in Europe made canal building costly and difficult. The ruling monarchies made some attempts to import British techniques and organize factory production, but they all foundered for lack of markets or management skills. From 1789 to 1815 Europe was scarred by revolutions and wars. War created opportunities for suppliers of weapons, uniforms, and horses produced by traditional methods. But the interruption of trade between Britain and continental Europe slowed the diffusion of new techniques, and the insecurity of countries at war discouraged businessmen from investing in factories and machinery.

The political revolutions swept away the restrictions of the old regimes. After 1815 the economies of western Europe were ready to begin industrializing. Industrialization took hold in Belgium and northern France, as businessmen visited Britain to observe the changes and spy out industrial secrets. In spite of British laws forbidding the emigration of skilled workers and the export of textile machinery, many workers slipped through. By the 1820s several thousand Britons were at work on the continent of Europe setting up machines, training workers in the new methods, and even starting their own businesses.

Acutely aware of Britain's head start and the need to stimulate their own industries, European governments took action. They created technical schools. They eliminated internal tariff barriers, tolls, and other hindrances to trade. They encouraged the formation of joint-stock companies and banks to channel private savings into industrial investments. On the European continent, as in Britain, cotton cloth was the first industry. The mills of France, Belgium, and the German states served local markets but could not compete abroad with the more advanced British industry. By 1830 the political climate in western Europe was as favorable to business as Britain's had been a half-century earlier.

Abundant coal and iron-ore deposits determined the concentration of industries in a swath of territories running from northern France through Belgium and the

a seat in Parliament, and the social status that accompanied them.

At a time when transportation by land was very costly, Great Britain had good water transportation thanks to its indented coastline, navigable rivers, and growing network of canals. It had a unified internal market with none of the duties and tolls that goods had to pay every few miles in France. This encouraged regional specialization, such as tin mining in Cornwall and cotton manufacturing in Lancashire, and a growing trade between regions.

Britain was highly commercial; more people were involved in production for export and in trade and finance than in any other major country. It was especially active in overseas trade with the Americas, West Africa, the Middle East, and India. It had financial and insur-

The Origin of Graphs

Not all technologies involve hardware. There are also information technologies, such as graphs, the visual representation of numerical tables. We see graphs so often in textbooks, magazines, and newspapers that we take them for granted. But they too have a history.

Scientists in France and England created the first graphs in the seventeenth century to illustrate natural phenomena. Some represented tables of data, such as the movements of stars and atmospheric pressure. Until the late eighteenth century few people outside of scientific circles knew or cared about such graphs. This changed with the growing public interest in economic data, population statistics, and other secular subjects that were so much a part of the Enlightenment.

The first person to publish graphs of interest to the general public was William Playfair (1729–1823), an Englishman who started his career as a draftsman for the engine manufacturing firm of Boulton and Watt. In 1786 he published *The Commercial and Political Atlas*, a book that was widely read and went though several editions. All but one of the forty-four graphs in it were line graphs with the vertical axis showing economic data and the horizontal axis representing time. Playfair explained to skeptical readers how a line could represent money:

> This method has struck several persons as being fallacious, because geometrical measurement has not any relation to money or to time; yet here it is made to represent both. The most familiar and simple answer to this objection is by giving an example. Suppose the money received by a man in trade were all in guineas, and that every evening he made a single pile of all the guineas received during the day, each pile would represent a day, and its height would be proportioned to the receipts of that day; so that by this plain operation, time, proportion, and amount *would all be physically combined.*
>
> Lineal arithmetic then, it may be averred, is nothing more than those piles of guineas represented on paper, and on a small scale, in which an inch (suppose) represents the thickness of five millions of guineas, as in geography it does the breadth of a river, or any other extent of country.

As for why it was necessary to show economic data in the form of a graph, Playfair explained:

> Men of high rank, or active business, can only pay attention to general outlines; nor is attention to particulars of use, any further than they give a general information; it is hoped that, with the Assistance of these Charts, such information will be got, without the fatigue and trouble of studying the particulars of which it is composed.

Today, graphs are an indispensable means of conveying information in business and finance, in the sciences, and in government. We need graphs because they give us information quickly and efficiently, "without the fatigue and trouble of studying the particulars."

Source: William Playfair, *The Commercial and Political Atlas,* 3rd ed. (London: J. Wallis, 1801), ix, xiv–xv.

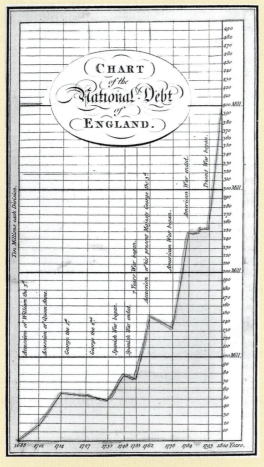

Line Graph of National Debt of England 1803
This graph by William Playfair is designed to shock the viewer by showing the national debt of Britain skyrocketing out of control, especially during the country's many wars. (British Library)

Ruhr district of western Germany to Silesia in Prussia (now part of Poland). By the 1850s France, Belgium, and the German states were in the midst of an industrial boom like that of Britain, based on iron, cotton, steam engines, and railroads.

THE TECHNOLOGICAL REVOLUTION

Five innovations spurred industrialization: (1) mass production through the division of labor, (2) new machines and mechanization, (3) a great increase in the manufacture of iron, (4) the steam engine and the changes it made possible in industry and transportation, and (5) the electric telegraph. China had achieved the first three of these during the Song dynasty (960–1279), but had not developed the steam engine or electricity. The continued success of Western industrialization depended heavily on these new forms of energy.

Wedgwood's Potteries   In Staffordshire, England, Josiah Wedgwood established a factory to mass-produce beautiful and inexpensive china. The bottle-shaped buildings are kilns in which thousands of pieces of china could be fired at one time. Kilns, factories, and housing were all mixed together in pottery towns, and smoke from burning coal filled the air.   (Mary Evans Picture Library)

Mass Production: Pottery

The pottery industry offers a good example of **mass production,** the making of many identical items by breaking the process into simple repetitive tasks. East Asian potters had long known how to make fine glazed porcelain, or "china," but the high cost of transporting it to Europe before the mid-eighteenth century meant that only the wealthy could afford fine Chinese porcelain. Middle-class people used pewter tableware, and the poor ate from wooden or earthenware bowls. Several royal manufactures—Meissen° in Saxony, Delft in Holland, and Sèvres° in France—produced exquisite handmade products for the courts and aristocracy, but their products were much too expensive for mass consumption. Meanwhile, more and more Europeans acquired a taste for Chinese tea as well as for cocoa and coffee, and they wanted porcelain that would not spoil the flavor of hot beverages. This demand created opportunities for inventive entrepreneurs.

Like other countries, Britain had many small pottery workshops where craftsmen made a few plates and cups at a time. Much of this activity took place in a part of the Midlands that possessed good clay, coal for firing, and lead for glazing. There **Josiah Wedgwood,** the son of a potter, started his own pottery business in 1759. He had a scientific bent and invented the pyrometer, a device to measure the extremely high temperatures that are found

Meissen (MY-sen)   Sèvres (SEV-ruh)

in kilns during the firing of pottery, for which he was elected a member of the Royal Society. Today the name Wedgwood is associated with expensive, highly decorated china. But Wedgwood's most important contribution lay in producing ordinary porcelain cheaply by means of the **division of labor** (see Diversity and Dominance: Adam Smith and the Division of Labor).

Wedgwood subdivided the work into highly specialized and repetitive tasks, such as unloading the clay, mixing it, pressing flat pieces, dipping the pieces in glaze, putting handles on cups, packing kilns, and carrying things from one part of his plant to another. To prevent interruptions in production, he instituted strict discipline among his workers. He substituted the use of molds for the potter's wheel wherever possible, a change that not only saved labor but also created identical plates and bowls that could be stacked. He invested in toll roads and canals so that special pottery clay found in southwestern England could be economically shipped to his factories in the Midlands.

Wedgwood's interest in applying technology to manufacturing was sparked by his membership in the Lunar Society. In 1782 the naturalist Erasmus Darwin encouraged him to purchase a steam engine from Boulton and Watt, the firm founded by two other members of the society. The engine that Wedgwood bought to mix clay and grind flint was one of the first to be installed in a factory.

These were radical departures from the age-old methods of craftsmanship. But the division of labor and new machinery allowed Wedgwood to lower the cost of his products while improving their quality, and to offer his wares for sale at lower prices. His factory grew far larger than his competitors' factories and employed several hundred workers. His salesmen traveled throughout England touting his goods, and his products were sold on the European continent as well.

Mechanization: The Cotton Industry

The cotton industry, the largest industry in this period, illustrates the role of **mechanization,** the use of machines to do work previously done by hand. Cotton cloth had long been the most common fabric in China, India, and the Middle East, where it was spun and woven by hand. The cotton plant did not grow in Europe, but the cloth was so much cooler, softer, and cleaner than wool that wealthy Europeans developed a liking for the costly import. When the powerful English woolen industry persuaded Parliament to forbid the import of cotton cloth into England, that prohibition stimulated attempts to import cotton fiber and make the cloth locally. Here was an opportunity for enterprising inventors to reduce costs with labor-saving machinery.

To turn inventions into successful businesses, inventors had to link up with entrepreneurs or become businessmen themselves. Making a working prototype often took years, even decades, and many inventions led to dead ends. History remembers the successful, but even they struggled against great odds.

Beginning in the 1760s a series of inventions revolutionized the spinning of cotton thread. The first was the spinning jenny, invented in 1764, which mechanically drew out the cotton fibers and twisted them into thread. The jenny was simple, cheap to build, and easy for one person to operate. Early models spun six or seven threads at once, later ones up to eighty. The thread, however, was soft and irregular and could be used only in combination with linen, a strong yarn derived from the flax plant.

In 1769 **Richard Arkwright** invented another spinning machine, the water frame, which produced thread strong enough to be used without linen. Arkwright was both a gifted inventor and a successful businessman. His machine was larger and more complex than the jenny and required a source of power such as a water wheel, hence the name "water frame." To obtain the necessary energy he installed dozens of machines in a building next to a fast-flowing river. The resemblance to a flour mill gave such enterprises the name cotton mill.

In 1785 Samuel Crompton patented a machine that combined the best features of the jenny and the water frame. This device, called a mule, produced a strong thread that was thin enough to be used to make a better type of cotton cloth called muslin. The mule could make a finer, more even thread than could any human being, and at a lower cost. At last British industry could undersell high-quality handmade cotton cloth from India, and British cotton output increased tenfold between 1770 and 1790.

The boom in thread production and the soaring demand for cloth created bottlenecks in weaving, stimulating inventors to mechanize the rest of textile manufacturing. The first power loom was introduced in 1784 but was not perfected until after 1815. Other inventions of the period included carding machines, chlorine bleach, and cylindrical presses to print designs on fabric. By the 1830s large English textile mills powered by steam engines were performing all the steps necessary to turn raw cotton into printed cloth. This was a far cry from the cottage industries of the previous century.

Mechanization offered two advantages: (1) increased productivity for the manufacturer and (2) lower prices for the consumer. Whereas in India it took five hundred hours to spin a pound of cotton, the mule of 1790 could do so in three person-hours, and the self-acting mule—an improved version introduced in 1830—required only eighty minutes. Cotton mills needed very few skilled workers, and managers often hired children to tend the spinning machines. The same was true of power looms, which gradually replaced handloom weaving: the number of power looms rose from 2,400 in 1813 to 500,000 by 1850. Meanwhile, the price of cloth fell by 90 percent between 1782 and 1812 and kept on dropping.

The industrialization of Britain made cotton America's most valuable crop. In the 1790s most of Britain's cotton came from India, as the United States produced a mere 750 tons (729 metric tons), mostly from South Carolina. In 1793 the American Eli Whitney patented his cotton gin, a simple device that separated the bolls or seed pods from the fiber and made cotton growing economical. This invention permitted the spread of cotton

DIVERSITY AND DOMINANCE

ADAM SMITH AND THE DIVISION OF LABOR

*A*dam Smith (1723–1790), a Scottish social philosopher, is famous for one book, An Inquiry into the Nature and Causes of the Wealth of Nations, *which was first published in 1776 and has been reprinted many times and translated into many languages. It was the first work to explain the economy of a nation as a system. In it, Smith criticized the notion, common in the eighteenth century, that a nation's wealth was synonymous with the amount of gold and silver in the government's coffers. Instead, he defined* wealth *as the amount of goods and services produced by a nation's people. By this definition, labor and its products are an essential element in a nation's prosperity.*

In the passage that follows, Smith discusses the increase in productivity (to use a modern term) that results from dividing a craft into separate tasks, each of which is performed over and over by one worker. He contrasts two methods of making pins. In one a team of workers divided up the job of making pins and produced a great many every day; in the other pin-workers "wrought separately and independently" and produced very few pins per day. It is clear that the division of labor produces more pins per worker per day. But who benefits? Left unsaid is that a pin factory had to be owned and operated by a manufacturer who hired workers and assigned a task to each one. Thus did industrialization reduce the diversity of self-employed craftsmen by replacing them with a system of dominance.

The illustration shows a pin-makers' workshop in late eighteenth-century France. Each worker is performing a specific task on a few pins at once, and all the energy comes from human muscles. These are the characteristics of a proto-industrial workshop.

To take an example, therefore, from a very trifling manufacture—but one in which the division of labour has been very often taken notice of—the trade of the pin-maker: a workman not educated to this business (which the division of labour has rendered a distinct trade), nor acquainted with the use of machinery employed in it (to the invention of which the same division of labour has probably given occasion), could scarce, perhaps, with his utmost industry, make one pin in a day, and certainly could not make twenty. But in the way in which this business is now carried on, not only the whole work is a peculiar trade, but it is divided into a number of branches, of which the greater part are likewise peculiar trades. One man draws out the wire, another straights it, a third cuts it, a fourth points it, a fifth grinds it at the top for receiving the head; to make the head requires two or three distinct operations, to put it on, is a peculiar business, to whiten the pins is another; it is even a trade by itself to put them into the paper; and the important business of making a pin is, in this manner, divided into about eighteen distinct operations, which, in some manufactories, are all performed by distinct hands, though in others the same man will sometimes perform two or three of them. I have seen a small manufactory of this kind where ten men only were employed, and where some of them, conse-

farming into Georgia, then into Alabama, Mississippi, and Louisiana, and finally as far west as Texas. By the late 1850s the southern states were producing a million tons of cotton a year, five-sixths of the world's total.

With the help of British craftsmen who introduced jennies, mules, and power looms, Americans developed their own cotton industry in the 1820s. By 1840 the United States had twelve hundred cotton mills, two-thirds of them in New England, that served the booming domestic market.

The Iron Industry

Iron making also was transformed during the Industrial Revolution. Throughout Eurasia and Africa, iron had been in use for thousands of years for tools, swords and other weapons, and household items such as knives, pots, hinges, and locks. In the eleventh century, during the Song period, Chinese forges had produced cast iron in large quantities. Production declined after the Song, but iron continued to be common and inexpensive in China. Wherever iron was pro-

A Pin-Makers Workshop The man in the middle (Figure 2) is pulling wire off a spindle (G) and through a series of posts (HK in Figure 17). This ensures that the wire will be perfectly straight. The worker seated on the lower right (Figure 3) takes the long pieces of straightened wire and cuts them into shorter lengths. The man in the lower left-hand corner (Figure 5) sharpens twelve to fifteen wires at a time by holding them against a grindstone turned by the worker in Figure 6. Figure 16 shows a close-up of this operation. The men in Figures 7 and 8 put the finishing touches on the points. The one in Figure 4 cuts the sharpened pins using the tool shown in Figures 21. Other operations—such as forming the wire to the proper thickness, cleaning and coating it with tin, attaching the heads—are depicted in other engravings in the same encyclopedia. (Division of Rare and Manuscript Collections, Cornell University Library).

quently, performed two or three distinct operations. But though they were very poor, and therefore but indifferently accommodated with the necessary machinery, they could, when they exerted themselves, make among them about twelve pounds of pins in a day. There are in a pound upwards of four thousand pins of a middling size. Those ten persons, therefore, could make among them upwards of forty-eight thousand pins in a day. Each person, therefore, making a tenth part of forty-eight thousand pins, might be considered as making four thousand eight hundred pins a day. But if they had all wrought separately and independently, and without any of them having been educated to this peculiar business, they certainly could not each of them have made twenty, perhaps not one pin in a day; that is, certainly, not the two hundred and fortieth, perhaps not the four thousand eight hundredth part of what they are at present capable of performing, in consequence of a proper division and combination of their different operations.

QUESTIONS FOR ANALYSIS

1. Why does dividing the job of pin-making into ten or more operations result in the production of more pins per worker? How much more productive are these workers than if each one made complete pins from start to finish?

2. How closely does the picture of a pin-maker's workshop illustrate Smith's verbal description?

3. What disadvantage would there be to working in a pin manufacture where the job was divided as in Smith's example, compared to making entire pins from start to finish?

4. What other examples can you think of, from Adam Smith's day or from more recent times, of the advantages of the division of labor?

Source: Adam Smith, *An Inquiry into the Nature and Causes of the Wealth of Nations,* ed. Edward Gibbon Wakefield (London: Charles Knight & Co., 1843), 7–9.

duced, however, deforestation eventually drove up the cost of charcoal (used for smelting) and restricted output. Furthermore, iron had to be repeatedly heated and hammered to drive out impurities, a difficult and costly process. Because of limited wood supplies and the high cost of skilled labor, iron was a rare and valuable metal outside China before the eighteenth century.

A first breakthrough occurred in 1709 when Abraham Darby discovered that coke (coal from which the impurities have been cooked out) could be used in place of charcoal. The resulting metal was of lower quality than charcoal-smelted iron but much cheaper to produce, for coal was plentiful. Just as importantly, in 1784 Henry Cort found a way to remove some of the impurities in coke-iron by puddling—stirring the molten iron with long rods. Cort's process made it possible to turn high-sulfur English coal into coke to produce wrought iron (a soft and malleable form of iron) very cheaply. By 1790 four-fifths of Britain's iron was made with coke, while other countries still used charcoal. Coke-iron was cheaper and

Pit Head of a Coal Mine This is a small coal mine. In the center of this picture stands a Newcomen engine used to pump water. The work of hauling coal out of the mine was still done by horses and mules. The smoke coming out of the smokestack is a trademark of the early industrial era. (National Museums and Galleries on Merseyside, Walker Art Gallery [WAG 659])

less destructive of forests, and it allowed a great expansion in the size of individual blast furnaces, substantially reducing the cost of iron. There seemed almost no limit to the quantity of iron that could be produced with coke. Britain's iron production began rising fast, from 17,000 tons in 1740 to 3 million tons in 1844, as much as in the rest of the world put together.

In turn, there seemed no limit to the amount of iron that an industrializing society would purchase or to the novel applications for this cheap and useful material. In 1779 the iron manufacturer Abraham Darby III (grandson of the first Abraham Darby) built a bridge of iron across the Severn River. In 1851 Londoners marveled at the **Crystal Palace,** a huge greenhouse made entirely of iron and glass and large enough to enclose the tallest trees.

The availability of cheap iron made the mass production of objects such as guns, hardware, and tools appealing. However, fitting together the parts of these products required a great deal of labor. To reduce labor costs, manufacturers turned to the idea of interchangeable parts. This idea originated in the eighteenth century when French army officers attempted, without success, to persuade gun makers to produce precisely identical parts. Craftsmen continued to use traditional methods to make gun parts that had to be fitted together by hand. By the mid-nineteenth century, however, interchangeable-parts manufacturing had been adopted in the manufacture of firearms, farm equipment, and sewing machines. At the Crystal Palace exhibition of 1851, Euro-peans called it the "American system of manufactures." In the next hundred years the use of machinery to mass-produce consumer items was to become the hallmark of American industry.

The Steam Engine

In the history of the world, there had been a number of periods of great technological inventiveness and economic growth. But in all previous cases, the dynamism eventually faltered for various reasons, such as the Mongol invasions that overthrew the Song dynasty in China and the Abassid Caliphate (750–1258) in the Middle East.

The Industrial Revolution that began in the eighteenth century, in contrast, has never slowed down but has instead only accelerated. One reason has been increased interactions between scientists, technicians, and businesspeople. Another has been access to an inexhaustible source of cheap energy, namely fossil fuels.

The first machine to transform fossil fuel into mechanical energy was the **steam engine,** a substitute for human and animal power as well as for wind and water power. Although the mechanization of manufacturing was very important, the steam engine was what set the Industrial Revolution apart from all previous periods of growth and innovation.

Before the eighteenth century, many activities had been limited by the lack of energy. For example, deep

Transatlantic Steamship Race   In 1838, two ships equipped with steam engines, the *Sirius* and the *Great Western*, steamed from England to New York. Although the *Sirius* left a few days earlier, the *Great Western*—shown here arriving in New York harbor—almost caught up with it, arriving just four hours after the *Sirius*. This race inaugurated regular transatlantic steamship service.   (Courtesy of the Mariners' Museum, Newport News, VA)

mines filled with water faster than horses could pump it out. Scientists understood the concept of atmospheric pressure and had created experimental devices to turn heat into motion, but they had not found a way to put those devices to practical use. Then, between 1702 and 1712 Thomas Newcomen developed the first practical steam engine, a crude but effective device. One engine could pump water out of mines as fast as four horses, and it could run day and night without getting tired.

The Newcomen engine's voracious appetite for fuel mattered little in coal mines, where fuel was cheap, but made the engine too costly for other uses. In 1764 **James Watt,** a maker of scientific instruments at Glasgow University in Scotland, was asked to repair the university's model Newcomen engine. Watt realized that the engine wasted fuel because the cylinder had to be alternately heated and cooled. He developed a separate condenser—a vessel into which the steam was allowed to escape after it had done its work, leaving the cylinder always hot and the condenser always cold. Watt patented his idea in 1769. He enlisted the help of the iron manufacturer Matthew Boulton to turn his invention into a commercial product. Their first engines were sold to pump water out of copper and tin mines, where fuel was too costly for Newcomen engines. In 1781 Watt invented the sun-and-planet gear, which turned the back-and-forth action of the piston into rotary motion. This allowed steam en-

gines to power machinery in flour and cotton mills, pottery manufactures, and other industries. Watt's steam engine was the most celebrated invention of the eighteenth century. Because there seemed almost no limit to the amount of coal in the ground, steam-generated energy appeared to be an inexhaustible source of power, and steam engines could be used where animal, wind, and water power were lacking.

Inspired by the success of Watt's engine, inventors in France in 1783, in the United States in 1787, and in England in 1788 put steam engines on boats. The need to travel great distances in the United States explains why the first commercially successful steamboat was Robert Fulton's *North River*, which steamed up and down the Hudson River between New York City and Albany, New York, in 1807.

Soon steamboats were launched on other American rivers, especially the Ohio and the Mississippi, gateways to the Midwest. In the 1820s the Erie Canal linked the Atlantic seaboard with the Great Lakes and opened Ohio, Indiana, and Illinois to European settlement. Steamboats proliferated west of the Appalachian Mountains; by 1830 some three hundred plied the Mississippi and its tributaries. To counter the competition from New York State, Pennsylvania built a thousand miles of canals by 1840. The United States was fast becoming a nation that moved by water.

Oceangoing steam-powered ships were much more difficult to build than river boats, for the first steam engines used so much coal that no ship could carry more than a few days' supply. The *Savannah*, which crossed the Atlantic in 1819, was a sailing ship with an auxiliary steam engine that was used for only ninety hours of its twenty-nine-day trip. Engineers soon developed more efficient engines, and in 1838 two steamers, the *Great Western* and the *Sirius*, crossed the Atlantic on steam power alone. Elsewhere, sailing ships held their own until late in the century. World trade was growing so fast that there was enough business for ships of every kind.

The De Witt Clinton Locomotive, 1835–1840   The De Witt Clinton was the first steam locomotive built in the United States. The high smokestack let the hot cinders cool so they would not set fire to nearby trees, an important consideration at a time when eastern North America was still covered with forest. The three passenger cars are clearly horse carriages fitted with railroad wheel.   (Corbis)

Railroads

On land as on water, the problem was not imagining uses for steam-powered vehicles but building ones that worked, for steam engines were too heavy and weak to pull any weight. After Watt's patent expired in 1800, inventors experimented with lighter, more powerful high-pressure engines—an idea Watt had rejected as too dangerous. In 1804 the engineer Richard Trevithick built an engine that consumed twelve times less coal than Newcomen's and three times less than Watt's. With it, he built several steam-powered vehicles able to travel on roads or rails.

By the 1820s England had many railways on which horses pulled heavy wagons. On one of them, the Stockton and Darlington Railway, chief engineer George Stephenson began using steam locomotives in 1825. Four years later the owners of the Liverpool and Manchester Railway organized a contest between steam-powered locomotives and horse-drawn wagons. Stephenson and his son Robert easily won the contest with their locomotive *Rocket*, which pulled a 20-ton train at up to 30 miles (48 kilometers) per hour. After that triumph, a railroad-building mania that lasted for twenty years swept Britain. The first lines linked towns and mines with the nearest harbor or waterway. In the late 1830s passenger traffic soared, and entrepreneurs built lines between the major cities and then to small towns as well. Railroads were far cheaper, faster, and more comfortable than stagecoaches, and millions of people got in the habit of traveling.

In the United States entrepreneurs built railroads as quickly and cheaply as possible with an eye to fast profits, not long-term durability. By the 1840s, 6,000 miles (10,000 kilometers) of track connected and radiated westward from Boston, New York, Philadelphia, and Baltimore. The boom of the 1840s was dwarfed by the mania of the 1850s, when 21,000 miles (34,000 kilometers) of new track were laid, much of it westward across the Ap-

palachians to Memphis, St. Louis, and Chicago. After 1856 the trip from New York to Chicago, which had once taken three weeks by boat and on horseback, could be made in forty-eight hours. More than anything else, it was the railroads that opened up the Midwest, turning the vast prairie into wheat fields and pasture for cattle to feed the industrial cities of the eastern United States.

Railways triggered the industrialization of Europe (see Map 23.2). Belgium, independent since 1830, quickly copied the British railways. In France and Prussia, the state planned and supervised railroad construction from the start. This delayed construction until the mid-1840s. When it began, however, it had an even greater impact than in Britain, for it not only satisfied the long-standing need for transportation, but also stimulated the iron, machinery, and construction industries.

Communication over Wires

After the Italian scientist Alessandro Volta invented the battery in 1800, making it possible to produce an electric current, many inventors tried to apply electricity to communication. The first practical **electric telegraph** systems were developed almost simultaneously in England and Amer-

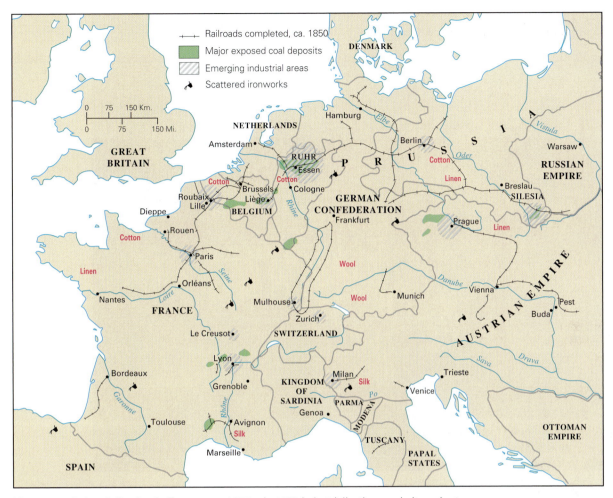

Map 23.2   Industrialization in Europe, ca. 1850   In 1850 industrialization was in its early stages on the European continent. The first industrial regions were comparatively close to England and possessed rich coal deposits: Belgium and the Ruhr district of Germany. Politics determined the location of railroads. Notice the star-shaped French network of rail lines emanating from Paris and the lines linking the different parts of the German Confederation.

ica. In 1837 in England Charles Wheatstone and William Cooke introduced a five-wire telegraph that remained in use until the early twentieth century. That same year, the American Samuel Morse introduced a code of dots and dashes that could be transmitted with a single wire; in 1843 he erected a telegraph line between Washington and Baltimore.

The railroad companies were among the first users of the new electric telegraph. They allowed telegraph companies to string wires along the tracks in exchange for the right to send telegrams from station to station announcing the departure and arrival of trains. Such

messages made railroads much safer as well as more efficient.

By the late 1840s telegraph wires were being strung throughout the eastern United States and western Europe. In 1851 the first submarine telegraph cable was laid across the English Channel from England to France; it was the beginning of a network that eventually connected the entire globe. The world was rapidly shrinking, to the applause of Europeans and Americans for whom speed was a clear measure of progress. No longer were communications limited to the speed of a sailing ship, a galloping horse, or a fast-moving train.

Overcrowded London   The French artist Gustave Doré depicted the tenements of industrial London where workers and their families lived. This drawing shows crowded and unsanitary row houses, each one room wide, with tiny back yards, and a train steaming across a viaduct overhead.   (Prints Division, New York Public Library, Astor, Lenox, and Tilden Foundations)

THE IMPACT OF THE EARLY INDUSTRIAL REVOLUTION

The Industrial Revolution led to profound changes in society, politics, and the economy. At first, the changes were local. While some people became wealthy and built beautiful mansions, others lived in slum neighborhoods with polluted water and smoke-filled air. By the mid-nineteenth century, the worst local effects were being alleviated and cities became cleaner and healthier. Replacing them on a national scale were more complex problems: business cycles, labor conflicts, and the transformation of entire regions into industrial landscapes. At the international and global level, industrialization empowered the nations of western Europe and North America at the expense of the rest of the world.

The New Industrial Cities

The most dramatic environmental changes brought about by industrialization occurred in the towns. Never before had towns grown so fast. London, one of the largest cities in Europe in 1700 with 500,000 inhabitants, grew to 959,000 by 1800 and to 2,363,000 by 1850; it was then the largest city the world had ever known. Smaller towns grew even faster. Manchester, a small town of 20,000 in 1758, reached 400,000 a century later, a twentyfold increase. Liverpool grew sixfold in sixty years, from 82,000 in 1801 to 472,000 in 1861. New York City, already 100,000 strong in 1815, reached 600,000 (including Brooklyn) in 1850. European cities also grew, but more slowly; their fastest growth occurred after 1850 with increasing industrialization. In some areas, towns merged and formed megalopolises, such as Greater London, the English Midlands, central Belgium, and the Ruhr district of western Germany.

Industrialization made some people very prosperous. A great deal of this new wealth went into the building of fine homes, churches, museums, and theaters in wealthy neighborhoods in London, Berlin, and New York. Much of the beauty of London dates from the time of the Industrial Revolution. Yet, by all accounts, the industrial cities grew much too fast, and much of the growth occurred in the poorest neighborhoods. As poor migrants streamed in from the countryside, developers built cheap, shoddy row houses for them to rent. These tenements were dangerously overcrowded. Often, several families had to live in one small room.

Sudden population growth, overcrowding, and inadequate municipal services conspired to make urban problems more serious than in earlier times. Town dwellers recently arrived from the country brought country ways with them. People threw their sewage and trash out the windows to be washed down the gutters in the streets. The poor kept pigs and chickens; the rich kept horses; and pedestrians stepped into the street at their own risk. Factories and workers' housing were mixed together. Air pollution from burning coal, a problem since the sixteenth century, got steadily worse. Londoners in particular breathed dense and noxious coal smoke. People drank water drawn from wells and rivers contaminated by sewage and industrial runoff. The River Irwell, which ran through Manchester, was, in the words of one visitor, "considerably less a river than a flood of liquid manure."[1]

"Every day that I live," wrote an American visitor to Manchester, "I thank Heaven that I am not a poor man with a family in England."[2] In his poem "Milton," William Blake (1757–1827) expressed the revulsion of sensitive people at the spoliation of England's "mountains green" and "pleasant pastures":

> And did the Countenance Divine
> Shine forth upon our clouded hills?
> And was Jerusalem builded here
> Among these dark Satanic Mills?

Railroads invaded the towns, bringing noise and smoke into densely populated neighborhoods. Railroad companies built their stations as close to the heart of cities as they could. On the outskirts of cities, railroad yards, sidings, and repair shops covered acres of land,

Paris Apartment at Night   This cutaway drawing in a French magazine shows the vertical segregation by social class that prevailed in the 1840s. The lower level is occupied by the concierge and her family. The first floor belongs to a wealthy family throwing a party for high-society friends. Middle-class people living on the next floor seem annoyed by the noise coming from below. Above them, a thief has entered an artist's studio. A poor seamstress and her child live in the garret under the roof. When elevators were introduced in the late nineteenth century, people of different income levels became segregated by neighborhoods instead of by floors.   (Bibliothèque nationale de France)

surrounded by miles of warehouses and workers' housing. Farther out, far from the dangerous and polluted cities where their factories were located, newly rich industrialists created an environment halfway between country homes and townhouses: the first suburbs.

Under these conditions, diseases proliferated. To the long list of preindustrial urban diseases such as smallpox, dysentery, and tuberculosis, industrialization added new ailments. Rickets, a bone disease caused by lack of sunshine, became endemic in dark and smoky industrial cities. Steamships brought cholera from India, causing great epidemics that struck poor neighborhoods especially hard. In the 1850s, when the average life expectancy in England was forty years, it was only twenty-four years in Manchester, and around seventeen years in Manchester's poorest neighborhoods, because of high rates of infant mortality. Observers of nineteenth-century industrial cities documented the horrors of slum life in vivid detail. Their shocking reports led to municipal reforms, such as garbage removal, water and sewage systems, and parks and schools. These measures began to alleviate the ills of urban life after the mid-nineteenth century.

Rural Environments

Long before the Industrial Revolution began, practically no wilderness areas were left in Britain and very few in western Europe. Almost every piece of land was covered with fields, forests, or pastures shaped by human activity, or by towns; yet humans continued to alter the environment. The most serious problem was deforestation. As they had been doing for centuries, people cut timber to build ships and houses, to heat homes, and to manufacture bricks, iron, glass, beer, bread, and many other items (see Chapter 17).

Americans transformed their environment even faster than Europeans. In North America, the Canadian and American governments seized land from the Indians and made it available at low cost to white farmers and logging companies. After shipbuilding and construction had depleted the British forests in the early nineteenth century, Britain relied heavily on imports of Canadian lumber. East of the Appalachian Mountains, settlers viewed forests not as a valuable resource but as a hindrance to development. In their haste to "open up the West," pioneers felled trees and burned them, built houses and abandoned them, and moved on. The cultivation of cotton in the southern United States was especially harmful. Planters cut down forests, grew cotton for a few years until it depleted the soil, then moved west, abandoning the land to scrub pines. This was slash-and-burn agriculture on an industrial scale.

At that time, America seemed immune to human depredations. Americans thought of nature as an obstacle to be overcome and dominated. This mindset persisted long after the entire continent was occupied and the environment truly endangered.

Paradoxically, in some ways industrialization relieved pressures on the environment in Europe. Raw materials once grown on the land—such as wood, hay, and wool—were replaced by materials found underground, like iron ore and coal, or obtained overseas, like cotton. While Russia, Sweden, the United States, and other forested countries continued to smelt iron with charcoal, the British and western Europeans substituted coke made from coal. As the population increased and land grew scarcer, the cost of growing feed for horses rose, creating incentives to find new, less land-hungry means of transportation. Likewise, as iron became cheaper and wood more expensive, ships and many other objects formerly made of wood began to be made of iron.

To contemporaries, the most obvious changes in rural life were brought about by the new transportation systems. In the eighteenth century France had a national network of quality roads, which Napoleon extended into Italy and Germany. In Britain local governments' neglect of the roads that served long-distance traffic led to the formation of private enterprises—"Turnpike Trusts"—that built numerous toll roads. For heavy goods, horse-drawn wagons were costly even on good roads because of the need to feed the horses. The growing volume of heavy freight triggered canal-building booms in Britain, France, and the Low Countries in the late eighteenth century. Some canals, like the duke of Bridgewater's canal in England, connected coal mines to towns or navigable rivers. Others linked navigable rivers and created national transportation networks.

Canals were marvels of construction, with deep cuts, tunnels, and even aqueducts that carried barges over rivers. They also were a sort of school where engineers learned skills they were able to apply to the next great transportation system: the railroads. They laid track across rolling country by cutting deeply into hillsides and erecting daringly long bridges of stone and iron across valleys. Lesser lines snaked their way to small towns hidden in remote valleys. Soon, clanking trains pulled by puffing, smoke-belching locomotives were invading long-isolated districts.

Thus, in the century after industrialization began, the landscape of industrializing countries was transformed more rapidly than ever before. But the ecological changes, like the technological and economic changes that caused them, were only beginning.

Working Conditions

Industrialization offered new opportunities to the enterprising. Carpenters, metalworkers, and machinists were in great demand. Since industrial machines were fairly simple, some workers became engineers or went into business for themselves. The boldest in England moved to the European continent, the Americas, or India, using their skills to establish new industries.

The successful, however, were a minority. Most industrial jobs were unskilled, repetitive, and boring. Factory work did not vary with the seasons or the time of day but began and ended by the clock. Workdays were long; there were few breaks; and foremen watched constantly. Workers who performed one simple task over and over had little sense of achievement or connection to the final product. Industrial accidents were common and could ruin a family. Unlike even the poorest preindustrial farmer or artisan, factory workers had no control over their tools, jobs, or working hours.

Industrial work, by definition, was physically removed from the home. This had a major impact on women and family life. Women workers were concentrated in textile mills, partly because of ancient traditions, partly because textile work required less strength than metalworking, construction, or hauling. On average, women earned one-third to one-half as much as men. Young unmarried women worked to support themselves or to save for marriage. Married women took factory jobs when their husbands were unable to support the family. Mothers of infants faced a hard choice: whether to leave their babies with wet-nurses at great expense and danger or bring them to the factory and keep them drugged. Rather than working together as family units, husbands and wives increasingly worked in different places.

In the early years of industrialization, even where factory work was available, it was never the main occupation of working women. Most young women who sought paid employment became domestic servants in spite of the low pay, drudgery, and risk of sexual abuse by male employers. Women with small children tried hard to find work they could do at home, such as laundry, sewing, embroidery, millinery, or taking in lodgers.

Even with both parents working, poor families found it hard to make ends meet. As in preindustrial societies, parents thought children should contribute to their upkeep as soon as they were able to. The first generation of workers brought children as young as five or six with them to the factories and mines; they had little choice, since there were no public schools or daycare centers. Employers encouraged the practice and even hired orphans. They preferred children because they were cheaper and more docile than adults and were better able to tie broken threads or crawl under machines to sweep the dust.

In Arkwright's cotton mills two-thirds of the workers were children. In another mill 17 percent were under ten years of age, and 53 percent were between ten and seventeen; they worked fourteen to sixteen hours a day and

"Love Conquers Fear"   This is a sentimental Victorian drawing of children in a textile mill. Child labor was common in the first half of the nineteenth century, and workers were exposed to dangerous machines and moving belts, as well as to dust and dirt.   (British Library)

were beaten if they made mistakes or fell asleep. Mine operators used children to pull coal carts along the low passageways from the coal face to the mine shaft. In the mid-nineteenth century, when the British government began restricting child labor, mill owners increasingly recruited adult immigrants from Ireland.

American industry began on a somewhat different note than the British. In the early nineteenth century Americans still remembered their revolutionary ideals. When Francis Cabot Lowell built a cotton mill in Massachusetts, he hired the unmarried daughters of New England farmers, promising them decent wages and housing in dormitories under careful moral supervision. Other manufacturers eager to combine profits with morality followed his example. Soon the profit motive won out, and manufacturers imposed longer hours, harsher working conditions, and lower wages. The young women protested: "As our fathers resisted with blood the lordly avarice of the British ministry, so we, their daughters, never will wear the yoke which has been prepared for us."[3] When they went on strike, the mill owners replaced them with Irish immigrant women willing to accept lower pay and worse conditions.

While the cotton boom enriched planters, merchants, and manufacturers, African-Americans paid for it with their freedom. In the 1790s, 700,000 slaves of African descent lived in the United States. The rising demand for cotton and the British and American prohibition of the African slave trade in 1808 caused an increase in the price of slaves. As the "Cotton Kingdom" expanded, the number of slaves rose through natural increase and the reluctance of slave owners to free their slaves. By 1850 there were 3.2 million slaves in the United States, 60 percent of whom grew cotton. Similarly, Europe's and North America's surging demand for tea and coffee prolonged slavery in the sugar plantations of the West Indies and caused it to spread to the coffee-growing regions of southern Brazil. In the British West Indies slavery was abolished in 1833, but elsewhere in the Americas it persisted for another thirty to fifty years.

Slavery was not, as white American southerners maintained, a "peculiar institution"—a consequence of biological differences, biblical injunctions, or African traditions. Slavery was just as much part and parcel of the Industrial Revolution as child labor in Britain, the clothes that people wore, and the beverages they drank.

Changes in Society

Industrialization accentuated the polarization of society and income disparities. In his novel *Sybil; or, The Two Nations*, the British politician Benjamin Disraeli° (1804–1881) spoke of "Two nations between whom there is no intercourse and no sympathy, who are as ignorant of each other's habits, thoughts, and feelings as if they were dwellers in different zones, or inhabitants of different planets . . . the rich and the poor."

In Britain the worst-off were those who clung to an obsolete skill or craft. The cotton-spinning boom of the 1790s briefly brought prosperity to weavers. Their high wages and low productivity, however, induced inventors to develop power looms. As a result, by 1811 the wages of handloom weavers had fallen by a third; by 1832, by two-thirds. Even by working longer hours, they could not escape destitution.

Disraeli (diz-RAY-lee)

In the industrial regions of Britain and continental Europe, the wages and standard of living of factory workers did not decline steadily like those of handloom weavers; they fluctuated wildly. During the war years of 1792 to 1815, the price of food, on which the poor spent most of their income, rose faster than wages. The result was widespread hardship. Then, in the 1820s real wages and public health began to improve. Industrial production grew at over 3 percent a year, pulling the rest of the economy along. Prices fell and wages rose. Even the poor could afford comfortable, washable cotton clothes and underwear.

Improvement, however, was not steady. One reason was the effect of **business cycles**—recurrent swings from economic hard times to recovery and growth, then back to hard times. When demand fell, businesses contracted or closed, and workers found themselves unemployed. Most had few or no savings, and no government at the time provided unemployment insurance. Hard times returned in the "hungry forties." In 1847–1848 the potato crop failed in Ireland. One-quarter of the Irish population died in the resulting famine, and another quarter emigrated to England and North America. On the European continent the negative effects of economic downturns were tempered by the existence of small family farms to which urban workers could return when they were laid off.

Only in the 1850s did the benefits of industrialization—cheaper food, clothing, and utensils—begin to improve workers' standard of living. The real beneficiary of the early Industrial Revolution was the middle class. In Britain landowning gentry and merchants had long shared wealth and influence. In the late eighteenth century a new group arose: entrepreneurs whose money came from manufacturing. Most, like Arkwright and Wedgwood, were the sons of middling shopkeepers, craftsmen, or farmers. Their enterprises were usually self-financed, for little capital was needed to start a cotton-spinning or machine-building business. Many tried and some succeeded, largely by plowing their profits back into the business. A generation later, in the nineteenth century, some newly rich industrialists bought their way into high society. The same happened in western Europe after 1815.

Before the Industrial Revolution, wives of merchants had often participated in the family business; widows occasionally managed sizable businesses on their own. With industrialization came a "cult of domesticity" to justify removing middle-class women from contact with the business world. Instead, they became responsible for the home, the servants, the education of children, and the family's social life (see Chapter 27).

Middle-class people who attributed their success, often correctly, to their own efforts and virtues believed in individual responsibility: if some people could succeed through hard work, thrift, and temperance, then those who did not succeed had no one but themselves to blame. Many workers, however, were newly arrived from rural districts and earned too little to save for the long stretches of unemployment they experienced. The squalor and misery of life in factory towns led to a noticeable increase in drunkenness on paydays. While the life of the poor remained hard, the well-to-do attributed their own success to sobriety, industriousness, thrift, and responsibility. The moral position of the middle-class mingled condemnation with concern, coupled with feelings of helplessness in the face of terrible social problems, such as drunkenness, prostitution, and child abandonment.

New Economic and Political Ideas

Changes as profound as the Industrial Revolution triggered political ferment and ideological conflict. So many other momentous events took place during those years—the American Revolution (1776–1783), the French Revolution (1789–1799), the Napoleonic Wars (1804–1815), the reactions and revolts that periodically swept over Europe after 1815—that we cannot neatly separate out the consequences of industrialization from the rest. But it is clear that by undermining social traditions and causing a growing gap between rich and poor, the Industrial Revolution strengthened the ideas of laissez faire° and socialism and sparked workers' protests.

Laissez Faire and Its Critics

The most celebrated exponent of **laissez faire** ("let them do") was Adam Smith (1723–1790), a Scottish economist. In *The Wealth of Nations* (1776) Smith argued that if individuals were allowed to seek personal gain, the effect, as though guided by an "invisible hand," would be to increase the general welfare. The government should refrain from interfering in business, except to protect private property; it should even allow duty-free trade with foreign countries. By advocating free-market capitalism, Smith was challenging the prevailing economic doctrine of earlier centuries, **mercantilism,** which argued that governments should regulate trade in order to maximize their hoard of precious metals (see Chapter 19).

Persuaded by Adam Smith's arguments, governments dismantled many of their regulations in the decades after 1815. Britain even lowered its import duties, though other countries kept theirs. Nonetheless, it was obvious that industrialization was not improving the general welfare but was instead causing widespread misery. Two other thinkers, Thomas Malthus (1766–1834) and David Ricardo (1772–1832), attempted to explain the poverty they saw without challenging the basic premises of laissez faire. The cause of the workers' plight, Malthus and Ricardo said, was the population boom, which outstripped the food supply and led to falling wages. The workers' poverty, they claimed, was as much a result of "natural law" as the wealth of successful businessmen, and the only way the working class could avoid mass famine was to delay marriage and practice self-restraint and sexual abstinence.

Laissez faire provided an ideological justification for a special kind of capitalism: banks, stock markets, and chartered companies allowed investors to obtain profits with reasonable risks but with much less government control and interference than in the past. In particular, removing guild and other restrictions allowed businesses to employ women and children and keep wages low.

Businesspeople in Britain eagerly adopted laissez-faire ideas that justified their activities and kept the government at bay. But not everyone accepted the grim conclusions of the "dismal science," as economics was then known. The British philosopher Jeremy Bentham (1748–1832) believed that it was possible to maximize "the greatest happiness of the greatest number," if only a Parliament of enlightened reformers would study the social problems of the day and pass appropriate legislation.

The German economist Friedrich List (1789–1846) rejected laissez faire and free trade as a British trick "to make the rest of the world, like the Hindus, its serfs in all industrial and commercial relations." To protect their "infant industries" from British competition, he argued, the German states had to eliminate tariff barriers between them but erect high barriers against imports from Britain. On the European continent, List's ideas were as influential as those of Smith and Ricardo and led in 1834 to the formation of the Zollverein,° a customs union of most of the German states.

---

laissez faire (LAY-say fair)

Zollverein (TSOLL-feh-rine)

Positivists and Utopian Socialists

Bentham optimistically advocated gradual improvements. In contrast, three French social thinkers, moved by sincere concern for the poor, offered a radically new vision of a just civilization. Espousing a philosophy called **positivism,** the count of Saint-Simon (1760–1825) and his disciple Auguste Comte° (1798–1857) argued that the scientific method could solve social as well as technical problems. They recommended that the poor, guided by scientists and artists, form workers' communities under the protection of benevolent business leaders. These ideas found no following among workers, but they attracted the enthusiastic support of bankers and entrepreneurs, for whom positivism provided a rationale for investing in railroads, canals, and other symbols of modernity. The third French thinker, Charles Fourier° (1768–1837), loathed capitalists and imagined an ideal society in which groups of sixteen hundred workers would live in dormitories and work together on the land and in workshops where music, wine, and pastries would soften the hardships of labor. Critics called his ideas **utopian° socialism,** from the Greek word *utopia* meaning "nowhere." Fourier's ideas are now considered a curiosity, but positivism resonates to this day among liberal thinkers, especially in Latin America.

The person who came closest to creating a utopian community was the Englishman Robert Owen (1771–1858), a successful cotton manufacturer who believed that industry could provide prosperity for all. Conscience-stricken by the plight of British workers, Owen took over the management of New Lanark, a mill town south of Glasgow. He improved the housing and added schools, a church, and other amenities. He also testified in Parliament against child labor and for government inspection of working conditions, angering his fellow industrialists, but helping bring about long-overdue reforms.

Protests and Reforms

Workers benefited little from the ideas of these middle-class philosophers. Instead, they resisted the harsh working conditions in their own ways. They changed jobs frequently. They were often absent, especially on Mondays. When they were not closely watched, the quality of their work was likely to be poor.

Periodically, workers rioted or went on strike, especially when food prices were high and when downturns in the business cycle left many unemployed. In some places, craftsmen broke into factories and destroyed the machines that threatened their livelihoods. Such acts of resistance did nothing to change the nature of industrial work. Not until workers learned to act together could they hope to have much influence.

Gradually, workers formed benevolent societies and organizations to demand universal male suffrage and shorter workdays. In 1834 Robert Owen organized the Grand National Consolidated Trade Union to lobby for an eight-hour workday; it quickly gained half a million members but collapsed a few months later in the face of government prosecution of trade-union activities. A new movement called Chartism arose soon thereafter. It was led by the London cabinetmaker William Lovett and the Irish landlord Fergus O'Connor and appealed to miners and industrial workers. It demanded universal male suffrage, equal electoral districts, the secret ballot, salaries for members of Parliament, and annual elections. It gathered 1.3 million signatures on a petition, but Parliament rejected it. Chartism collapsed in 1848, but left a legacy of labor organizing.

Eventually, mass movements persuaded political leaders to look into the abuses of industrial life, despite the prevailing laissez-faire philosophy. In the 1820s and 1830s the British Parliament began investigating conditions in factories and mines. The Factory Act of 1833 prohibited the employment of children younger than nine in textile mills. It also limited the working hours of children between the ages of nine and thirteen to eight hours a day and of fourteen- to eighteen-year-olds to twelve hours. The Mines Act of 1842 prohibited the employment of women and boys under age ten underground. Several decades passed before the government appointed enough inspectors to enforce the new laws.

Most important was the struggle over the Corn Laws—tariffs on imported grain. Their repeal in 1846, in the name of "free trade," was designed to lower the cost of food for workers and thereby allow employers to pay lower wages. A victory for laissez faire, the repeal also represented a victory for the rising class of manufacturers and other employers over the conservative landowners who had long dominated politics and whose harvests faced competition from cheaper imported food.

The British learned to seek reform through accommodation. On the European continent, in contrast, the revolutions of 1848 revealed widespread discontent with repressive governments but failed to soften the hardships of industrialization (see Chapter 27).

Comte (COME-tuh)   **Fourier** (FOOR-yeh)   **utopian** (you-TOE-pee-uhn)

INDUSTRIALIZATION AND THE NONINDUSTRIAL WORLD

The spread of the Industrial Revolution in the early nineteenth century transformed the relations of western Europe and North America with the rest of the world. For most of the world, trade with the industrial countries meant exporting raw materials, not locally made handicraft products. China was defeated and humiliated by the products of industrial manufacture. In Egypt and India cheap industrial imports, backed by the power of Great Britain, delayed industrialization for a century or more. In these three cases, we can discern the outlines of the Western domination that has characterized the history of the world since the late nineteenth century.

In January 1840 a shipyard in Britain launched a radically new ship. The *Nemesis* had an iron hull, a flat bottom that allowed it to navigate in shallow waters, and a steam engine to power it upriver and against the wind. The ship was heavily armed. In November it arrived off the coast of China. Though ships from Europe had been sailing to China for three hundred years, the *Nemesis* was the first steam-powered iron gunboat seen in Asian waters. A Chinese observer noted: "Iron is employed to make it strong. The hull is painted black, weaver's shuttle fashion. On each side is a wheel, which by the use of coal fire is made to revolve as fast as a running horse. . . . At the vessel's head is a Marine God, and at the head, stern, and sides are cannon, which give it a terrific appearance. Steam vessels are a wonderful invention of foreigners, and are calculated to offer delight to many."[4]

Instead of offering delight, the *Nemesis* and other steam-powered warships that soon joined it steamed up the Chinese rivers, bombarded forts and cities, and transported troops and supplies from place to place along the coast and up rivers far more quickly than Chinese soldiers could move on foot. With this new weapon, Britain, a small island nation half a world away, was able to defeat the largest and most populated country in the world (see Chapter 26).

Egypt, strongly influenced by European ideas since the French invasion of 1798, began to industrialize in the early nineteenth century. The driving force was its ruler, Muhammad Ali (1769–1849), a man who was to play a major role not only in the history of Egypt but in the Middle East and East Africa as well (see Chapter 25). He wanted to build up the Egyptian economy and military in order to become less dependent on the Ottoman sul-

Steam Tractor in India   Power machinery was introduced into India because of the abundance of skilled low-cost labor. In this scene, a steam tractor fords a shallow stream to the delight of onlookers. The towerlike construction on the right is probably a pier for a railroad bridge.   (Billie Love Historical Society)

tan, his nominal overlord. To do so, he imported advisers and technicians from Europe and built cotton mills, foundries, shipyards, weapons factories, and other industrial enterprises. To pay for all this, he made the peasants grow wheat and cotton, which the government bought at a low price and exported at a profit. He also imposed high tariffs on imported goods in order to force the pace of industrialization.

Muhammad Ali's efforts fell afoul of the British, who did not want a powerful country threatening to interrupt the flow of travelers and mail across Egypt, the shortest route between Europe and India. When Egypt went to war against the Ottoman Empire in 1839, Britain intervened and forced Muhammad Ali to eliminate all import duties in the name of free trade. Unprotected, Egypt's fledgling industries could not compete with the flood of cheap British products. Thereafter, Egypt exported raw cotton, imported manufactured goods, and became, in effect, an economic dependency of Britain.

Until the late eighteenth century, India had been the world's largest producer and exporter of cotton textiles, handmade by skilled spinners and weavers. The British

East India Company took over large parts of India just as the Industrial Revolution was beginning in Britain (see Chapter 25 and Map 25.2). It allowed cheap British factory-made yarn and cloth to flood the Indian market duty-free, putting spinners and later handloom weavers out of work. Unlike Britain, India had no factories to which displaced handicraft workers could turn for work. Most of them became landless peasants, eking out a precarious living.

Like other tropical regions, India became an exporter of raw materials and an importer of British industrial goods. To hasten the process, British entrepreneurs and colonial officials introduced railroads into the subcontinent. The construction of India's railroad network began in the mid-1850s, along with coal mining to fuel the locomotives and the installation of telegraph lines to connect the major cities.

Some Indian entrepreneurs saw opportunities in the atmosphere of change that the British created. In 1854 the Bombay merchant Cowasjee Nanabhoy Davar imported an engineer, four skilled workers, and several textile machines from Britain and started India's first textile mill. This was the beginning of India's mechanized cotton industry. Despite many gifted entrepreneurs, India's industrialization proceeded at a snail's pace, for the government was in British hands and the British did nothing to encourage Indian industry.

The cases of Egypt, India, and China show how the demands of Western nations and the military advantage that industrialization gave them led them to interfere in the internal affairs of nonindustrial societies. As we shall see in Chapter 28, this was the start of a new age of Western dominance.

CONCLUSION

The great change we call the Industrial Revolution began in Great Britain, a society that was open to innovation, commercial enterprise, and the cross-fertilization of science, technology, and business. New machines and processes in the cotton and iron industries were instrumental in launching the Industrial Revolution, but what made industrialization an ongoing phenomenon was a new source of energy, the steam engine.

In the period from 1760 to 1851 the new technologies of the Industrial Revolution greatly increased humans' power over nature. Goods could be manufactured in vast quantities at low cost. People and messages could travel at unprecedented speeds. Most important, hu-

mans gained access to the energy stored in coal and used it to power machinery and propel ships and trains faster than vehicles had ever traveled before. With their new-found power, humans turned woodland into farmland, dug canals and laid tracks, bridged rivers and cut through mountains, and covered the countryside with towns and cities.

The ability to command nature, far from benefiting everyone, increased the disparities between individuals and societies. Industrialization brought forth entrepreneurs—whether in the mills of England or on plantations in the American South—with enormous power over their employees or slaves, a power that they found easy and profitable to abuse. Some people acquired great wealth, while others lived in poverty and squalor. While middle-class women were restricted to caring for their homes and children, many working-class women had to leave home to earn wages in factories or as domestic servants. These changes in work and family life provoked intense debates among intellectuals. Some defended the disparities in the name of laissez faire; others criticized the injustices that industrialization brought. Society was slow to bring these abuses under control.

By the 1850s the Industrial Revolution had spread from Britain to western Europe and the United States, and its impact was being felt around the world. To make a product that was sold on every continent, the British cotton industry used African slaves, American land, British machines, and Irish workers. As we shall see in Chapter 24, industrialization brought even greater changes to the Americas than it did to the Eastern Hemisphere.

■ Key Terms

Industrial Revolution
agricultural revolution
mass production
Josiah Wedgwood
division of labor
mechanization
Richard Arkwright
Crystal Palace
steam engine
James Watt
electric telegraph
business cycles
laissez faire
mercantilism
positivism
utopian socialism

Suggested Reading

General works on the history of technology give pride of place to industrialization. For an optimistic overview see Joel Mokyr, *The Lever of Riches: Technological Creativity and Economic Progress* (1990). Other important recent works include James McClellan III and Harold Dorn, *Science and Technology in World History* (1999); David Landes, *The Wealth and Poverty of Nations* (1998); and Ian Inkster, *Technology and Industrialization: Historical Case Studies and International Perspectives* (1998).

There is a rich literature on the British industrial revolution, beginning with T. S. Ashton's classic *The Industrial Revolution, 1760–1830*, published in 1948 and often reprinted. The interactions between scientists, technologists, and businessmen are described in Jenny Uglow, *The Lunar Men: Five Friends Whose Curiosity Changed the World* (2002), but see also Joel Mokyr, *The Gifts of Athena: Historical Origins of the Knowledge Economy* (2002). The importance of the steam engine is the theme of Jack Goldstone, "Efflorescences and Economic Growth in World History: Rethinking the 'Rise of the West' and the Industrial Revolution," in *Journal of World History* (Fall 2002).

The impact of industrialization on workers is the theme of E. P. Thompson's classic work *The Making of the English Working Class* (1963), but see also E. R. Pike, *"Hard Times": Human Documents of the Industrial Revolution* (1966). The role of women is most ably revealed in Lynn Y. Weiner, *From Working Girl to Working Mother: The Female Labor Force in the United States, 1820–1980* (1985), and in Louise Tilly and Joan Scott, *Women, Work, and Family* (1978).

European industrialization is the subject of J. Goodman and K. Honeyman, *Gainful Pursuits: The Making of Industrial Europe: 1600–1914* (1988); John Harris, *Industrial Espionage and Technology Transfer: Britain and France in the Eighteenth Century* (1998); and David Landes, *The Unbound Prometheus: Technological Change and Industrial Development in Western Europe from 1750 to the Present* (1972). On the beginnings of American industrialization see David Jeremy, *Artisans, Entrepreneurs and Machines: Essays on the Early Anglo-American Textile Industry, 1770–1840* (1998).

On the environmental impact of industrialization see Richard Wilkinson, *Poverty and Progress: An Ecological Perspective on Economic Development* (1973), and Richard Tucker and John Richards, *Global Deforestation in the Nineteenth-Century World Economy* (1983).

The first book to treat industrialization as a global phenomenon is Peter Stearns, *The Industrial Revolution in World History* (1993); see also Louise Tilly's important article "Connections" in *American Historical Review* (February 1994).

Notes

1. Quoted in Lewis Mumford, *The City in History* (New York: Harcourt Brace, 1961), 460.
2. Quoted in F. Roy Willis, *Western Civilization: An Urban Perspective*, vol. II (Lexington, MA: D.C. Heath, 1973), 675.
3. Alice Kessler-Harris, *Women Have Always Worked: A Historical Overview* (Old Westbury, New York: The Feminist Press, 1981), 59.
4. *Nautical Magazine* 12 (1843): 346.

24 Nation Building and Economic Transformation in the Americas, 1800–1890

The Train Station in Orizaba, Mexico, 1877   In the last decades of the nineteenth century Mexico's political leaders actively promoted economic development. The railroad became the symbol of this ideal.

CHAPTER OUTLINE

Independence in Latin America, 1800–1830

The Problem of Order, 1825–1890

The Challenge of Social and Economic Change

DIVERSITY AND DOMINANCE: The Afro-Brazilian Experience, 1828

ENVIRONMENT AND TECHNOLOGY: Constructing the Port of Buenos Aires, Argentina

Between 1836 and 1848 Mexico lost 50 percent of its territory to the United States. In the political crisis that followed, reformers, called liberals, fought conservatives for control of the nation. The liberal Benito Juárez° dominated this era as a war leader and a symbol of Mexican nationalism. Many have compared him to his contemporary, Abraham Lincoln. Juárez began his life in poverty. An Amerindian orphan, he became a lawyer and political reformer. He helped drive the dictator Antonio López de Santa Anna from power in 1854 and helped lead efforts to reduce the power of the Catholic Church and the military. He later served as chief justice of the Supreme Court and as president.

When conservatives rebelled against the Constitution of 1857, Juárez assumed the presidency and led liberal forces to victory. Mexico's conservatives turned to Napoleon III of France, who sent an army that suspended the constitution and imposed Archduke Maximilian of Habsburg, brother of Emperor Franz Joseph of Austria, as emperor. But the French army could not defeat Juárez, and Mexican resistance was eventually supported by U.S. diplomatic pressure. When the French left, Maximilian was captured and executed. This victory over a powerful foreign enemy redeemed a nation that had earlier been humiliated by the United States. But the creation of democracy proved more elusive than the protection of Mexican sovereignty. Despite the Mexican constitution's prohibition of presidential reelection, Juárez would serve as president until his death in 1872.

Despite cycles of political violence like that experienced by Mexico, the nineteenth century witnessed a radical transformation of the Western Hemisphere. Spurred by the American and French revolutions see Chapter 22) and encouraged by nationalism and the ideal of political freedom, most of the region's nations achieved independence, although Mexico and others faced foreign interventions.

Throughout the nineteenth century the new nations in the Western Hemisphere wrestled with the difficult questions that independence raised. If colonies could reject submission to imperial powers, could not regions with distinct cultures, social structures, and economies refuse to accept the political authority of the newly formed nation-states? How could nations born in revolution accept the political strictures of written constitutions—even those they wrote themselves? How could the ideals of liberty and freedom expressed in those constitutions be reconciled with the denial of rights to Amerindians, slaves, recent immigrants, and women?

While trying to resolve these political questions, the new nations also attempted to promote economic growth. But colonial economic development, with its emphasis on agricultural and mining exports, inhibited efforts to promote diversification and industrialization, just as the legacy of class and racial division thwarted the realization of political ideals.

As you read this chapter, ask yourself the following questions:

- What were the causes of the revolutions for independence in Latin America?

- What major political challenges did Western Hemisphere nations face in the nineteenth century?

- How did abolitionism, the movement for women's rights, and immigration change the nations of the Western Hemisphere?

- How did industrialization and new agricultural technologies affect the environment?

INDEPENDENCE IN LATIN AMERICA, 1800–1830

As the eighteenth century drew to a close, Spain and Portugal held vast colonial possessions in the Western Hemisphere, although their power had declined relative to that of their British and French rivals. Both Iberian empires had reformed their colonial administration and strengthened their military forces in the eighteenth century. Despite these efforts, the same economic and political forces that had undermined British

---

Benito Juárez (beh-NEE-toh WAH-rez)

rule in the colonies that became the United States were present in Spanish America and Brazil.

Roots of Revolution, to 1810

The great works of the Enlightenment as well as revolutionary documents like the Declaration of Independence and the Declaration of the Rights of Man circulated widely in Latin America by 1800, but very few colonial residents desired to follow the examples of the American and French Revolutions (see Chapter 22). Local-born members of Latin America's elites and middle classes were frustrated by the political and economic power of colonial officials and angered by high taxes and imperial monopolies. But it was events in Europe that first pushed the colonies towards independence. Napoleon's decision to invade Portugal (1807) and Spain (1808), not revolutionary ideas, created the crisis of legitimacy that undermined the authority of colonial officials, and ignited Latin America's struggle for independence.

In 1808 as a French army neared Lisbon, the royal family of Portugal fled to Brazil. King John VI maintained his court there for over a decade. In Spain, in contrast, Napoleon forced King Ferdinand VII to abdicate and placed his own brother, Joseph Bonaparte, on the throne. Spanish patriots fighting against the French created a new political body, the Junta° Central, to administer the areas they controlled. Most Spaniards viewed the Junta as a temporary patriotic institution created to govern Spain while the king remained a French prisoner. The Junta, however, claimed the right to exercise the king's powers over Spain's colonies, and this claim provoked a crisis.

Large numbers of colonial residents in Spanish America, perhaps a majority, favored obedience to the Junta Central. A vocal minority, which included many wealthy and powerful individuals, objected. The dissenters argued that they were subjects of the king, not dependents of the Spanish nation. They wanted to create local juntas and govern their own affairs until Ferdinand regained the throne. Spanish loyalists in the colonies resisted this tentative assertion of local autonomy and thus provoked armed uprisings. In late 1808 and 1809 popular movements overthrew Spanish colonial officials in Venezuela, Mexico, and Alto Peru (modern Bolivia) and created local juntas. In each case, Spanish officials quickly reasserted control and punished the leaders. Their harsh repression, however, further polarized public opinion in the colonies and gave rise to a greater sense of a separate American nationality. By 1810 Spanish colonial authorities were facing a new round of revolutions more clearly focused on the achievement of independence.

Spanish South America, 1810–1825

In Caracas (the capital city of modern Venezuela) a revolutionary Junta led by creoles (colonial-born whites) declared independence in 1811. Although this group espoused popular sovereignty and representative democracy, its leaders were large landowners who defended slavery and opposed full citizenship for the black and mixed-race majority. Their aim was to expand their own privileges by eliminating Spaniards from the upper levels of Venezuela's government and from the church. The junta's narrow agenda spurred loyalists in the colonial administration and church hierarchy to rally thousands of free blacks and slaves to defend the Spanish Empire. Faced with this determined resistance, the revolutionary movement placed overwhelming political authority in the hands of its military leader **Simón Bolívar**° (1783–1830), who later became the preeminent leader of the independence movement in Spanish South America.

The son of wealthy Venezuelan planters, Bolívar had studied both the classics and the works of the Enlightenment. He used the force of his personality to mobilize political support and to hold the loyalty of his troops. Defeated on many occasions, Bolívar successfully adapted his objectives and policies to attract new allies and build coalitions. Although initially opposed to the abolition of slavery, for example, he agreed to support emancipation in order to draw slaves and freemen to his cause and to gain supplies from Haiti. Bolívar was also capable of using harsh methods to ensure victory. Attempting to force resident Spaniards to join the rebellion in 1813 he proclaimed: "Any Spaniard who does not . . . work against tyranny in behalf of this just cause will be considered an enemy and punished; as a traitor to the nation, he will inevitably be shot by a firing squad."[1]

Between 1813 and 1817 military advantage shifted back and forth between the patriots and loyalists. Bolívar's ultimate success was aided by his decision to enlist demobilized English veterans of the Napoleonic Wars and by a military revolt in Spain in 1820. The English veterans, hardened by combat, helped improve the battlefield performance of Bolívar's army. The revolt in Spain forced Ferdinand VII—restored to the throne in 1814 after the defeat of Napoleon—to accept a constitution that

---

Junta (HUN-tah)

Simón Bolívar (see-MOAN bow-LEE-varh)

CHRONOLOGY

	United States and Canada	Mexico and Central America	South America
	1789 U.S. Constitution ratified		
1800	**1803** Louisiana Purchase		**1808** Portuguese royal family arrives in Brazil
	1812–1815 War of 1812	**1810–1821** Mexican movement for independence	**1808–1809** Revolutions for independence begin in Spanish South America
1825	**1836** Texas gains independence from Mexico		**1822** Brazil gains independence
	1845 Texas admitted as a state	**1846–1848** War between Mexico and the United States	
		1847–1870 Caste War	
1850	**1848** Women's Rights Convention in Seneca Falls, New York	**1857** Mexico's new constitution limits power of Catholic church and military	**1850** Brazilian slave trade ends
	1861–1865 Civil War	**1862–1867** French invade Mexico	**1865–1870** Argentina, Uruguay, and Brazil wage war against Paraguay
	1867 Creation of Dominion of Canada	**1867** Emperor Maximilian executed	**1870s** Governments of Argentina and Chile begin final campaigns against indigenous peoples
1875	**1876** Sioux and allies defeat U.S. Army in Battle of Little Bighorn		
	1879 Thomas Edison develops incandescent lamp		**1879–1881** Chile wages war against Peru and Bolivia; telegraph, barbed wire, and refrigeration introduced in Argentina
	1890 "Jim Crow" laws enforce segregation in South		**1888** Abolition of slavery in Brazil
	1890s United States becomes world's leading steel producer		

limited the powers of both the monarch and the church. Colonial loyalists who for a decade had fought to maintain the authority of monarch and church viewed those reforms as unacceptably liberal.

With the king's supporters divided, momentum swung to the patriots. After liberating present-day Venezuela, Colombia, and Ecuador, Bolívar's army occupied the area that is now Peru and Bolivia (named for Bolívar). Finally defeating the last Spanish armies in 1824, Bolívar and his closest supporters attempted to draw the former Spanish colonies into a formal confederation. The first step was to forge Venezuela, Colombia, and Ecuador into the single nation of Gran Colombia

(see Map 24.1). With Bolívar's encouragement, Peru and Bolivia also experimented with unification. Despite his prestige, however, all of these initiatives had failed by 1830.

Buenos Aires (the capital city of modern Argentina) was the second important center of revolutionary activity in Spanish South America. In Buenos Aires news of Ferdinand VII's abdication led to the creation of a junta organized by militia commanders, merchants, and ranchers, which overthrew the viceroy in 1810. To deflect the opposition of loyalists and Spanish colonial officials, the junta claimed loyalty to the imprisoned king. After Ferdinand regained the Spanish throne, however, junta

OREGON COUNTRY (Joint U.S.-British occupation)

BRITISH NORTH AMERICA (Gr. Br.)

UNITED STATES

Colorado

Mississippi

Rio Grande

MEXICO 1821

San Antonio

Mexico City

Veracruz

Gulf of Mexico

Havana

CUBA (Spain)

BAHAMA IS. (Gr. Br.)

HAITI 1804

PUERTO RICO (Spain)

ATLANTIC OCEAN

BRITISH HONDURAS (Gr. Br.)

GUATEMALA
Guatemala City

JAMAICA (Gr. Br.)

Caribbean Sea

UNITED PROVINCES OF CENTRAL AMERICA 1823—1839

Panama

Caracas

TRINIDAD (Gr. Br.)

VENEZUELA

Magdalena

Socorro

Bogotá

BR. GUIANA (Gr. Br.)

DUTCH GUIANA (Neth.)

FRENCH GUIANA (France)

GRAN COLOMBIA 1819—1830

Galápagos Islands

Quito

ECUADOR

Amazon

EMPIRE OF BRAZIL 1822

PACIFIC OCEAN

PERU 1824

Lima

BOLIVIA 1825

La Paz

Sucre

Salvador

PARAGUAY 1811

São Paulo

Rio de Janeiro

Paraná

CHILE 1817

UNITED PROVINCES OF THE RÍO DE LA PLATA 1816

Valparaíso

Santiago

ARGENTINA
Buenos Aires
Bahía Blanca

URUGUAY 1828

Montevideo

1811 Year independence gained

Colony

0   500   1000 Km.

0   500   1000 Mi.

PATAGONIA (Disputed between Argentina and Chile)

Islas Malvinas (Falkland Islands)

Map 24.1   Latin America by 1830   By 1830 patriot forces had overturned the Spanish and Portuguese Empires of the Western Hemisphere. Regional conflicts, local wars, and foreign interventions challenged the survival of many of these new nations following independence.

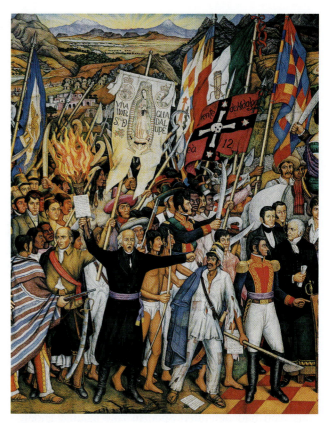

Padre Hidalgo   The first stage of Mexico's revolution for independence was led by Padre Miguel Hidalgo y Costilla, who rallied the rural masses of central Mexico to his cause. His defeat, trial, and execution made him one of Mexico's most important political martyrs.   (Schaalkwijk/Art Resource, NY)

leaders dropped this pretense. In 1816 they declared independence as the United Provinces of the Río de la Plata.

Patriot leaders in Buenos Aires at first sought to retain control over the territory of the Viceroyalty of Río de la Plata, which had been created in 1776 and included modern Argentina, Uruguay, Paraguay, and Bolivia. But Spanish loyalists in Uruguay and Bolivia and a separatist movement in Paraguay defeated these ambitions. Even within the territory of Argentina, the government in Buenos Aires was unable to control regional rivalries and political differences. As a result, the region rapidly descended into political chaos.

A weak succession of juntas, collective presidencies, and dictators soon lost control over much of the interior of Argentina. However, in 1817 the government in Buenos Aires did manage to support a mixed force of Chileans and Argentines led by José de San Martín° (1778–1850), who crossed the Andes Mountains to attack Spanish military forces in Chile and Peru. During this campaign San Martín's most effective troops were former slaves, who had gained their freedom by enlisting in the army, and gauchos, the cowboys of the Argentine pampas (prairies). After gaining victory in Chile San Martín pushed on to Peru in 1820, but failed to gain a clear victory there. The violent and destructive uprising of Tupac Amaru II in 1780 had traumatized the Andean region and made colonists fearful that support for independence might unleash another Amerindian uprising (see Chapter 18). Unable to make progress, San Martín surrendered command of patriot forces in Peru to Simón Bolívar, who overcame final Spanish resistance in 1824.

Mexico, 1810–1823

In 1810 Mexico was Spain's wealthiest and most populous colony. Its silver mines were the richest in the world, and the colony's capital, Mexico City, was larger than any city in Spain. Mexico also had the largest population of Spanish immigrants among the colonies. Spaniards dominated the government, church, and economy. When news of Napoleon's invasion of Spain reached Mexico, conservative Spaniards in Mexico City overthrew the local viceroy because he was too sympathetic to the creoles. This action by Spanish loyalists underlined the new reality: with the king of Spain removed from his throne by the French, colonial authority now rested on brute force.

The first stage of the revolution against Spain occurred in central Mexico. In this region wealthy ranchers and farmers had aggressively forced many Amerindian communities from their traditional agricultural lands. Crop failures and epidemics further afflicted the region's rural poor. Miners and the urban poor faced higher food prices and rising unemployment. With the power of colonial authorities weakened by events in Spain, anger and fear spread through towns and villages in central Mexico.

On September 16, 1810, **Miguel Hidalgo y Costilla°**, parish priest of the small town of Dolores, rang the

---

José de San Martín (hoe-SAY deh san mar-TEEN)

Miguel Hidalgo y Costilla (mee-GEHL ee-DAHL-go ee cos-TEA-ah)

church bells, attracting thousands. In a fiery speech he urged the crowd to rise up against the oppression of Spanish officials. Tens of thousands of the rural and urban poor joined his movement. They lacked military discipline and adequate weapons but knew who their oppressors were, spontaneously attacking the ranches and mines that had been exploiting them. Many Spaniards and colonial-born whites were murdered or assaulted. At first wealthy Mexicans were sympathetic to Hidalgo's objectives, but they eventually supported Spanish authorities when they recognized the threat that the angry masses following Hidalgo posed to them. The military tide quickly turned against Hidalgo and he was captured, tried, and executed in 1811.

The revolution continued under the leadership of another priest, **José María Morelos**°, a former student of Hidalgo's. A more adept military and political leader than his mentor, Morelos created a formidable fighting force and, in 1813, convened a congress that declared independence and drafted a constitution. Despite these achievements, loyalist forces also proved too strong for Morelos. He was defeated and executed in 1815.

Although small numbers of insurgents continued to wage war against Spanish forces, colonial rule seemed secure in 1820. However, news of the military revolt in Spain unsettled the conservative groups and church officials who had defended Spanish rule against Hidalgo and Morelos. In 1821 Colonel Agustín de Iturbide° and other loyalist commanders forged an alliance with remaining insurgents and declared Mexico's independence. The conservative origins of Mexico's transition to independence were highlighted by the decision to create a monarchial form of government and crown Iturbide as emperor. In early 1823, however, the army overthrew Iturbide and Mexico became a republic.

Brazil, to 1831

The arrival of the Portuguese royal family in Brazil in 1808 helped maintain the loyalty of the colonial elite and stimulate the local economy. After the defeat of Napoleon in Europe, the Portuguese government called for King John VI to return to Portugal. He at first resisted this pressure. Then in 1820 the military uprising in Spain provoked a sympathetic liberal revolt in Portugal, and the Portuguese military garrison in Rio de Janeiro forced the king to permit the creation of juntas. John recognized that he needed to take dramatic ac-

José María Morelos (hoe-SAY mah-REE-ah moh-RAY-los)
Agustín de Iturbide (ah-goos-TEEN deh ee-tur-BEE-deh)

tion to protect his throne. In 1821 he returned to Portugal. Hoping to protect his claims to Brazil, he left his son Pedro in Brazil as regent.

By 1820 the Spanish colonies along Brazil's borders had experienced ten years of revolution and civil war, and some, like Argentina and Paraguay, had gained independence. Unable to ignore these struggles, some Brazilians began to reevaluate Brazil's relationship with Portugal. Many Brazilians resented their homeland's economic subordination to Portugal. The arrogance of Portuguese soldiers and bureaucrats led others to talk openly of independence. Rumors circulated that Portuguese troops were being sent to discipline Brazil and force the regent Pedro to join his father in Lisbon.

Unwilling to return to Portugal and committed to maintaining his family's hold on Brazil, Pedro aligned himself with the rising tide of independence sentiment. In 1822 he declared Brazilian independence. Pedro's decision launched Brazil into a unique political trajectory. Unlike its neighbors, which became constitutional republics, Brazil gained independence as a constitutional monarchy with Pedro I, heir to the throne of Portugal, as emperor.

Pedro I was committed to both monarchy and many liberal principles. He directed the writing of the constitution of 1824, which provided for an elected assembly and granted numerous protections for political opposition. But he made powerful enemies by attempting to protect the Portuguese who remained in Brazil from arbitrary arrest and seizure of their property. More dangerously still, he opposed slavery in a nation dominated by a slave-owning class. In 1823 Pedro I anonymously published an article that characterized slavery as a "cancer eating away at Brazil" (see Diversity and Dominance: The Afro-Brazilian Experience, 1828). Despite opposition, in 1830 he concluded a treaty with Great Britain to end Brazilian participation in the slave trade. The political elite of Brazil's slave-owning regions opposed the treaty and for nearly two decades worked tirelessly to prevent enforcement. Pedro also continued his father's costly commitment of military forces to control neighboring Uruguay. As military losses and costs rose, the Brazilian public grew impatient. A small but vocal minority that opposed the monarchy and sought the creation of a democracy used these issues to rally public opinion against the emperor.

Confronted by street demonstrations and violence between Brazilians and Portuguese, Pedro I abdicated the throne in 1831 in favor of his five-year-old son Pedro II. After a nine-year regency, Pedro II assumed full powers as emperor of Brazil. He reigned until he was overthrown by republicans in 1889.

THE PROBLEM OF ORDER, 1825–1890

All the newly independent nations of the Western Hemisphere had difficulties establishing stable political institutions. The idea of popular sovereignty found broad support across the hemisphere. As a result, written constitutions and elected assemblies were put in place, often before the actual achievement of independence. Even in the hemisphere's two monarchies, Mexico and Brazil, the emperors sought to legitimize their rule by accepting constitutional limits on their authority and by the creation of representative assemblies. Nevertheless, widespread support for constitutional order and for representative government failed to prevent bitter factional conflict, regionalism, and the appearance of charismatic political leaders and military uprisings.

Constitutional Experiments

In reaction to the arbitrary and tyrannical authority of colonial rulers, revolutionary leaders in both the United States and Latin America espoused constitutionalism. They believed that the careful description of political powers in written constitutions offered the best protection for individual rights and liberties. In practice, however, many new constitutions proved unworkable. In the United States George Washington, James Madison, and other leaders became dissatisfied with the nation's first constitution, the Articles of Confederation. They led the effort to write a new constitution, which was put into effect in 1789. In Latin America few constitutions survived the rough-and-tumble of national politics. Between 1811 and 1833 Venezuela and Chile ratified and then rejected a combined total of nine constitutions.

Important differences in colonial political experience influenced later political developments in the Americas. The ratification of a new constitution in the United States was the culmination of a long historical process that had begun with the development of English constitutional law and continued under colonial charters. Many more residents of the British North American colonies had had the experience of voting and holding political office than did people in Portuguese and Spanish colonies. The British colonies provided opportunities for holding elective offices in town governments and colonial legislatures, and, by the time of independence, citizens had grown accustomed to elections, political parties, and factions. In contrast, constitutional government and elections were only briefly experienced in Spanish America between 1812 and 1814—while Ferdinand VII was a prisoner of Napoleon—and this short period was disrupted by the early stages of the revolutions for independence. Brazil had almost no experience with popular politics before independence. Despite these differences in experience and constitutional forms, every new republic in the Americas initially limited the right to vote to free men of property.

Democratic passions and the desire for effective self-rule led to significant political reform in the Americas, even in some of the region's remaining colonies. British Canada was divided into separate colonies and territories, each with a separate and distinct government. Political life in each colony was dominated by a provincial governor and appointed advisory councils drawn from the local elite. Elected assemblies existed within each province, but they exercised limited power. Agitation to end oligarchic rule and make government responsive to the will of the assemblies led to armed rebellion in 1837. In the 1840s Britain responded by establishing responsible government in each of the Canadian provinces, allowing limited self-rule. By the 1860s regional political leaders interested in promoting economic development realized that railroads and other internal improvements required a government with a "national" character. Both the U.S. Civil War and raids from U.S. territory into Canada by Irish nationalists attempting to force an end to British control of Ireland gave the reform movement a sense of urgency and focused attention on the need to protect the border. Negotiations led to the **Confederation of 1867,** which included the provinces of Ontario, Quebec, New Brunswick, and Nova Scotia. The Confederation that created the new Dominion of Canada with a central government in Ottawa (see Map 24.2) was hailed by one observer as the "birthday of a new nationality."[2] The path to effective constitutional government was rockier to the south. Because neither Spain nor Portugal had permitted anything like the elected legislatures and municipal governments of colonial North America, the drafters of Latin American constitutions were less constrained by practical political experience. As a result, many of the new Latin American nations experimented with untested political institutions. For example, Simón Bolívar, who wrote the first constitutions of five South American republics, included in Bolivia's constitution a fourth branch of government that had "jurisdiction over the youth, the hearts of men, public spirit, good customs, and republican ethics."

Most Latin American nations found it difficult to define the political role of the Catholic Church after independence. In the colonial period the Catholic Church

DIVERSITY AND DOMINANCE

THE AFRO-BRAZILIAN EXPERIENCE, 1828

Brazil was the most important destination for the Atlantic slave trade. From the sixteenth century to the 1850s more than 2 million African slaves were imported by Brazil, roughly twice the number of free European immigrants who arrived in the same period. Beginning in the 1820s Great Britain, Brazil's main trading partner, began to press for an end to the slave trade. British visitors to Brazil became an important source of critical information for those who sought to end the trade.

The following opinions were provided by a British clergyman, Robert Walsh, who traveled widely in Brazil in 1828 and 1829. Walsh's account reflects the racial attitudes of his time, but his testimony is valuable because of his ability to recognize the complex and sometime unexpected ways that slaves and black freedmen were integrated into Brazilian society.

[At the Alfandega, or custom house,] . . . for the first time I saw the Negro population under circumstances so striking to a stranger. The whole labour of bearing and moving burdens is performed by these people, and the state in which they appear is revolting to humanity. Here were a number of beings entirely naked, with the exception of a covering of dirty rags tied about their waists. Their skins, from constant exposure to the weather, had become hard, crusty, and seamed, resembling the coarse black covering of some beast, or like that of an elephant, a wrinkled hide scattered with scanty hairs. On contemplating their persons, you saw them with a physical organization resembling beings of a grade below the rank of man . . . . Some of these beings were yoked to drays, on which they dragged heavy burdens. Some were chained by the necks and legs, and moved with loads thus encumbered. Some followed each other in ranks, with heavy weights on their heads, chattering the most inarticulate and dismal cadence as they moved along. Some were munching young sugar-canes, like beasts of burden eating green provender [animal feed], and some were seen near water, lying on the bare ground among filth and offal, coiled up like dogs, and seeming to expect or require no more comfort or accommodation, exhibiting a state and conformation so unhuman,

that they not only seemed, but actually were, far below the inferior animals around them. Horses and mules were not employed in this way; they were used only for pleasure, and not for labour. They were seen in the same streets, pampered, spirited, and richly caparisoned, enjoying a state far superior to the negroes, and appearing to look down on the fettered and burdened wretches they were passing, as on beings of an inferior rank in the creation to themselves. . . .

The first impression of all this on my mind, was to shake the conviction I had always felt, of the wrong and hardship inflicted on our black fellow creatures, and that they were only in that state which God and nature had assigned them; that they were the lowest grade of human existence, and the link that connected it with the brute, and that the gradation was so insensible, and their natures so intermingled, that it was impossible to tell where one had terminated and the other commenced; and that it was not surprising that people who contemplated them every day, so formed, so employed, and so degraded, should forget their claims to that rank in the scale of beings in which modern philanthropists are so anxious to place them. I did not at the moment myself recollect, that the white man, made a slave on the coast of Africa, suffers not only a similar mental but physical deterioration from hardships and emaciation, and becomes in time the dull and deformed beast I now saw yoked to a burden.

A few hours only were necessary to correct my first impressions of the negro population, by seeing them under a different aspect. We were attracted by the sound of military music, and found it proceeded from a regiment drawn up in one of the streets. Their colonel had just died, and they attended to form a procession to celebrate his obsequies. They were all of different shades of black, but the majority were negroes. Their equipment was excellent; they wore dark jackets, white pantaloons, and black leather caps and belts, all which, with their arms, were in high order. Their band produced sweet and agreeable music, of the leader's own composition, and the men went through some evolutions with regularity and dexterity. They were only a militia regiment, yet were as well appointed and disciplined as one of our regiments of the line. Here then was the first step in that gradation by which the black population of this country ascend in the scale of humanity; he advances from the state below that of a beast of burden into a military rank, and he shows himself as capable of discipline and improvement as a human being of any other colour.

Our attention was next attracted by negro men and women bearing about a variety of articles for sale; some in baskets, some on boards and cases carried on their heads. They belonged to a class of small shopkeepers, many of whom vend their wares at home, but the greater number send them about in this way, as in itinerant shops. A few of these people were still in a state of bondage, and brought a certain sum every evening to their owners, as the produce of their daily labour. But a large proportion, I was informed, were free, and exercised this little calling on their own account. They were all very neat and clean in their persons, and had a decorum and sense of respectability about them, superior to whites of the same class and calling. All their articles were good in their kind, and neatly kept, and they sold them with simplicity and confidence, neither wishing to take advantage of others, nor suspecting that it would be taken of themselves. I bought some confectionary from one of the females, and I was struck with the modesty and propriety of her manner; she was a young mother, and had with her a neatly dressed child, of which she seemed very fond. I gave it a little comfit [candy covered nut], and it turned up its dusky countenance to her and then to me, taking my sweetmeat, and at the same time kissing my hand. As yet unacquainted with the coin of the country, I had none that was current about me, and was leaving the articles; but the poor young woman pressed them on me with a ready confidence, repeating in broken Portuguese, outo tempo, I am sorry to say, the "other time" never came, for I could not recognize her person afterwards to discharge her little debt, though I went to the same place for the purpose.

It soon began to grow dark, and I was attracted by a number of persons bearing large lighted wax tapers, like torches, gathering before a house. As I passed by, one was put into my hand by a man who seemed in some authority, and I was requested to fall into a procession that was forming. It was the preparation for a funeral, and on such occasions, I learned that they always request the attendance of a passing stranger, and feel hurt if they are refused. I joined the party, and proceeded with them to a neighbouring church. When we entered we ranged ourselves on each side of a platform which stood near the choir, on which was laid an open coffin, covered with pink silk and gold borders. The funeral service was chanted by a choir of priests, one of whom was a negro, a large comely man, whose jet black visage formed a strong and striking contrast to his white vestments. He seemed to perform his part with a decorum and sense of solemnity, which I did not observe in his brethren. After scattering flowers on the coffin, and fumigating it with incense, they retired, the procession dispersed, and we returned on board. I had been but a few hours on shore, for the first time, and I saw an African negro under four aspects of society; and it appeared to me, that in every one his character depended on the state in which he was placed, and the estimation in which he was held. As a despised slave, he was far lower than other animals of burthen that surrounded him; more miserable in his look, more revolting in his nakedness, more distorted in his person, and apparently more deficient in intellect than the horses and mules that passed him by. Advanced to the grade of a soldier, he was clean and neat in his person, amenable to discipline, expert at his exercises, and showed the port [sic.] and being of a white man similarly placed. As a citizen, he was remarkable for the respectability of his appearance, and the decorum of his manners in the rank assigned him; and as a priest, standing in the house of God, appointed to instruct society on their most important interests, and in a grade in which moral and intellectual fitness is required, and a certain degree of superiority is expected, he seemed even more devout in his impressions, and more correct in his manners, than his white associates. I came, therefore, to the irresistible conclusion in my mind, that colour was an accident affecting the surface of a man, and having no more to do with his qualities than his clothes—that God had equally created an African in the image of his person, and equally given him an immortal soul; and that an European had no pretext but his own cupidity, for impiously thrusting his fellow man from that rank in the creation which the Almighty had assigned him, and degrading him below the lot of the brute beasts that perish.

QUESTIONS FOR ANALYSIS

1. What was the author's first impression of the Brazilian slave population?
2. How does slavery dehumanize slaves?
3. What does the author later observe that changes this opinion?
4. What circumstances or opportunities permitted Brazil's free blacks to improve their lives?

Source: Robert Edgar Conrad, *Children of God's Fire, A Documentary History of Black Slavery in Brazil* (Princeton, NJ: Princeton University Press, 1983), 216–220. Reprinted by permission of the author.

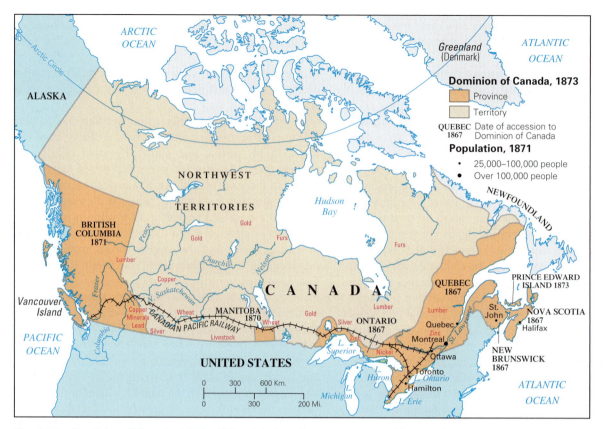

Map 24.2 Dominion of Canada, 1873 Although independence was not yet achieved and settlement remained concentrated along the U.S. border, Canada had established effective political and economic control over its western territories by 1873.

was a religious monopoly that controlled all levels of education, and dominated intellectual life. Many early constitutions aimed to reduce this power by making education secular and by permitting the practice of other religions. The church reacted by organizing its allies and financing conservative political movements. In Mexico, Colombia, Chile, and Argentina conflicts between liberals who sought the separation of church and state and supporters of the church's traditional powers dominated political life until late in the nineteenth century.

Limiting the power of the military proved to be another significant stumbling block to the creation of constitutional governments in Latin America. The wars for independence elevated the prestige of military leaders. When the wars were over, Bolívar and other military commanders seldom proved willing to subordinate themselves to civilian authorities. At the same time, frustrated by the often-chaotic workings of constitutional democracy, few citizens were willing to support civilian politicians in any contest with the military. As a result,

many Latin American militaries successfully resisted civilian control. Brazil, ruled by Emperor Pedro I, was the principal exception to this pattern.

Personalist Leaders

Successful patriot leaders in both the United States and Latin America gained mass followings during the wars for independence. They recruited and mobilized popular support by using patriotic symbols and by carefully associating their actions with national objectives. After independence, many patriot military leaders were able to use their personal followings to gain national political leadership. George Washington's ability to dominate the political scene in the early republican United States anticipated the later political ascendancy of revolutionary heroes such as Iturbide in Mexico and Bolívar in Gran Colombia. In each case, military reputation provided the foundation for personal political power. Washington was distinguished from most other early leaders by his willingness to surrender power. More commonly, **personalist leaders** relied on their ability to mobilize and direct the masses of these new nations rather than on the authority of constitutions and laws. Their model was Napoleon, who rose from the French army to become emperor, not James Madison, the primary author of the U.S. Constitution. In Latin America, a personalist leader who gained and held political power without constitutional sanction was called a *caudillo*°.

Latin America's slow development of stable political institutions made personalist politics more influential than they were in the United States. Nevertheless, charismatic politicians in the United States such as Andrew Jackson did sometimes challenge constitutional limits to their authority, as did the *caudillos* of Latin America.

Throughout the Western Hemisphere charismatic military men played key roles in attracting mass support for independence movements that were commonly dominated by colonial elites. Although this popular support was often decisive in the struggle for independence, the first constitutions of nearly all the American republics excluded large numbers of poor citizens from full political participation. But nearly everywhere in the Americas marginalized groups found populist leaders to articulate their concerns and challenge limits on their participation. Using informal means, these leaders sought to influence the selection of officeholders and to place their concerns in the public arena. Despite their success in overturning the deference-based politics of the colonial past, this populist political style at times threatened constitutional order and led to dictatorship.

Powerful personal followings allowed **Andrew Jackson** of the United States and **José Antonio Páez**° of Venezuela to challenge constitutional limits to their authority. During the independence wars in Venezuela and Colombia, Páez (1790–1873) organized and led Bolívar's most successful cavalry force. Like most of his followers, Páez was uneducated and poor, but his physical strength, courage, and guile made him a natural guerrilla leader and helped him build a powerful political base in Venezuela. Páez described his authority in the following manner: "[The soldiers] resolved to confer on me the supreme command and blindly to obey my will, confident . . . that I was the only one who could save them."[3] Able to count on the personal loyalty of his followers, Páez was seldom willing to accept the constitutional authority of a distant president.

After defeating the Spanish armies, Bolívar pursued his dream of forging a permanent union of former Spanish colonies modeled on the federal system of the United States. But he underestimated the strength of nationalist sentiment unleashed during the independence wars. Páez and other Venezuelan leaders resisted the surrender of their hard-won power to Bolívar's Gran Colombian government in distant Bogotá (the capital city of modern Colombia). When Bolívar's authority was challenged by political opponents in 1829 Páez declared Venezuela's independence. Merciless to his enemies and indulgent with his followers, Páez ruled the country as president or dictator for the next eighteen years. Despite implementing an economic program favorable to the elite, Páez remained popular with the masses by skillfully manipulating popular political symbols. Even as his personal wealth grew through land acquisitions and commerce, Páez took care to present himself as a common man.

Andrew Jackson (1767–1845) was the first U.S. president born in humble circumstances. A self-made man who eventually acquired substantial property and owned over a hundred slaves, Jackson was extremely popular among frontier residents, urban workers, and small farmers. Although he was notorious for his untidy personal life as well as for dueling, his courage, individualism, and willingness to challenge authority helped attain political success as judge, general, congressman, senator, and president.

During his military career, Jackson proved to be impatient with civilian authorities. Widely known because of his victories over the Creek and Seminole peoples, he was elevated to the pinnacle of American politics by his celebrated defeat of the British at the Battle of New Orleans in 1815 and by his seizure of Florida from the Spanish in 1818. In 1824 he received a plurality of the popular votes cast for the presidency, but he failed to win a majority of the electoral votes and was denied the presidency when the House of Representatives chose John Quincy Adams.

Jackson's followers viewed his landslide election victory in 1828 and reelection in 1832 as the triumph of democracy over the entrenched aristocracy. In office Jackson challenged constitutional limits on his authority, substantially increasing presidential power at the expense of Congress and the Supreme Court. Like Páez, Jackson was able to dominate national politics by blending a populist political style that celebrated the virtues and cultural enthusiasms of common people with support for policies that promoted the economic interests of some of the nation's most powerful propertied groups.

Personalist leaders were common in both Latin America and the United States, but Latin America's

---

caudillo (kouh-DEE-yoh)   **José Antonio Páez** (hoe-SAY an-TOE-nee-oh PAH-ays)

weaker constitutional tradition, more limited protection of property rights, lower literacy levels, and less-developed communications systems provided fewer checks on the ambitions of popular politicians. The Constitution of the United States was never suspended, and no national election result in the United States was ever successfully overturned by violence. Latin America's personalist leaders, however, often ignored constitutional restraints on their authority, and election results seldom determined access to presidential power. As a result, by 1900 every Latin American nation had experienced periods of dictatorship.

The Threat of Regionalism

After independence, new national governments were generally weaker than the colonial governments they replaced. In debates over tariffs, tax and monetary policies, and, in many nations, slavery and the slave trade, regional elites often were willing to lead secessionist movements or to provoke civil war rather than accept laws that threatened their interests. Some of the hemisphere's newly independent nations did not survive these struggles; others lost territories to aggressive neighbors.

In Spanish America all of the postindependence efforts to forge large multistate federations failed. Central America and Mexico had been united in the Viceroyalty of New Spain and briefly maintained their colonial-era administrative ties following independence in 1821. After the overthrow of Iturbide's imperial rule in Mexico in 1823, however, regional politicians split with Mexico and created the independent Republic of Central America. Regional rivalries and civil wars during the 1820s and 1830s forced the breakup of that entity as well and led to the creation of five separate nations. Bolívar attempted to maintain the colonial unity of Venezuela, Colombia, and Ecuador by creating the nation of Gran Colombia with a capital in Bogotá. But even before his death in 1830 Venezuela and Ecuador had become independent states.

During colonial times Argentina, Uruguay, Paraguay, and Bolivia had been united in a single viceroyalty with its capital in Buenos Aires. With the defeat of Spain, political leaders in Paraguay, Uruguay, and Bolivia declared their independence from Buenos Aires. Argentina, the area that remained after this breakup, was itself nearly overwhelmed by these powerful centrifugal forces. After independence, Argentina's liberals took power in Buenos Aires. They sought a strong central government to promote secular education, free trade, and immigration from Europe. Conservatives dominated the interior provinces. They supported the Catholic Church's traditional control of education as well as the protection of local textile and winemaking industries from European imports. In 1819, when political leaders in Buenos Aires imposed a national constitution that ignored these concerns, the conservatives of the interior rose in rebellion.

After a decade of civil war and rebellions a powerful local *caudillo*, Juan Manuel de Rosas°, came to power. For more than two decades he dominated Argentina, running the nation as if it were his private domain. The economy expanded under Rosas, but his use of intimidation, mob violence, and assassination created many enemies. In 1852 an alliance of foreign and domestic enemies overthrew him, but a new cycle of provincial rivalry and civil war prevented the creation of a strong central government until 1861.

Regionalism threatened the United States as well. The defense of state and regional interests played an important role in the framing of the U.S. Constitution. Many important constitutional provisions represented compromises forged among competing state and regional leaders. The creation of a Senate with equal representation from each state, for example, was an attempt to calm small states, which feared they might be dominated by larger states. The formula for representation in the House of Representatives was also an effort to compromise the divisions between slave and free states. Yet, despite these constitutional compromises, the nation was still threatened by regional rivalries.

Slavery increasingly divided the nation into two separate and competitive societies. A rising tide of immigration to the northern states in the 1830s and 1840s began to move the center of political power in the House of Representatives away from the south. Many southern leaders sought to protect slavery by expanding it to new territories. They supported the Louisiana Purchase in 1803 (see Map 24.3), an agreement with France that transferred to the United States a vast territory extending from the Gulf of Mexico to Canada. Southern leaders also supported statehood for Texas and war with Mexico (discussed later in the chapter).

The territorial acquisitions proved a mixed blessing to the defenders of slavery because they forced a national debate about slavery itself. Should slavery be allowed to expand into new territories? Could slavery be protected if new territories eligible for statehood were overwhelmingly free?

In 1860 Abraham Lincoln (1809–1865), who was committed to checking the spread of slavery, was elected president of the United States. In response, the planter elite in the southern states chose the dangerous course

---

Juan Manuel de Rosas (huan man-WELL deh ROH-sas)

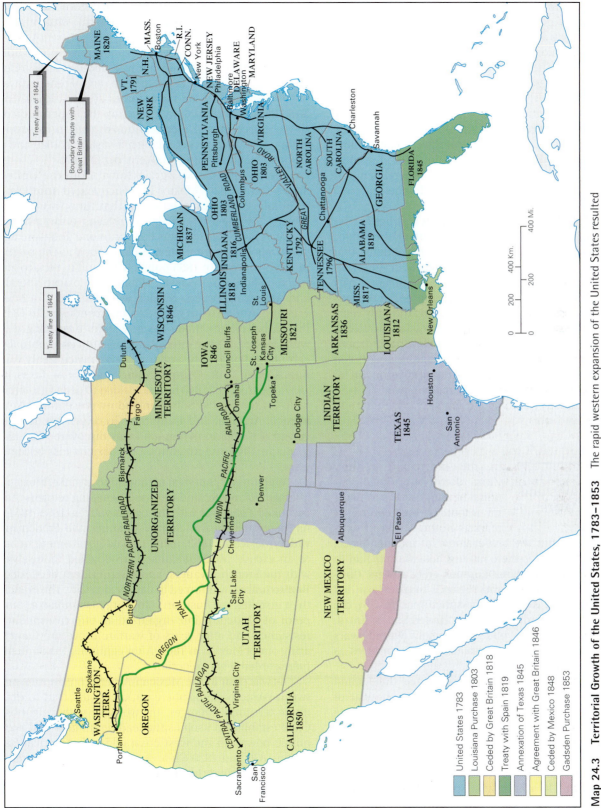

Map 24.3 Territorial Growth of the United States, 1783–1853 The rapid western expansion of the United States resulted from aggressive diplomacy and warfare against Mexico and Amerindian peoples. Railroad development helped integrate the trans-Mississippi west and promote economic expansion.

of secession from the federal Union. The seceding states formed a new government, the Confederate States of America, known as the Confederacy. Lincoln was able to preserve the Union, but his victory was purchased at an enormous cost. The U.S. Civil War (1861–1865), waged by southern Confederate forces and northern Union (U.S.) forces, was the most destructive conflict in the history of the Western Hemisphere. More than 600,000 lives were lost before the Confederacy surrendered in 1865. The Union victory led to the abolition of slavery. It also transferred national political power to a northern elite committed to industrial expansion and federal support for the construction of railroads and other internal improvements.

The Confederate States of America was better prepared politically and economically for independence than were the successful secessionist movements that broke up Gran Colombia and other Spanish American federations. Nevertheless, the Confederacy failed, in part because of poor timing. The new nations of the Western Hemisphere were most vulnerable during the early years of their existence; indeed, all the successful secessions occurred within the first decades following independence. In the case of the United States, southern secession was defeated by an experienced national government legitimated and strengthened by more than seven decades of relative stability reinforced by dramatic economic and population growth.

Foreign Interventions and Regional Wars

In the nineteenth century wars often determined national borders, access to natural resources, and control of markets in the Western Hemisphere. Even after the achievement of independence, some Western Hemisphere nations, like Mexico, had to defend themselves against Europe's great powers. Contested national borders and regional rivalries also led to wars between Western Hemisphere nations. By the end of the nineteenth century the United States, Brazil, Argentina, and Chile had successfully waged wars against their neighbors and established themselves as regional powers.

Within thirty years of independence the United States fought a second war with England—the War of 1812 (1812–1815). The weakness of the new republic was symbolized by the burning of the White House and Capitol by British troops in 1814. This humiliation was soon overcome, however, and by the end of the nineteenth century the United States was the hemisphere's greatest military power. Its war against Spain in 1898–1899 cre-

ated an American empire that reached from the Philippines in the Pacific Ocean to Puerto Rico in the Caribbean Sea (see Chapter 28).

Europe also challenged the sovereignty of Latin American nations. During the first decades after independence Argentina faced British and French naval blockades, and British naval forces systematically violated Brazil's territorial waters to stop the importation of slaves. Mexico faced more serious threats to its sovereignty, defeating a weak Spanish invasion in 1829 and a French assault on the city of Veracruz in 1838.

Mexico also faced a grave threat from the United States. In the 1820s Mexico had encouraged Americans to immigrate to Texas, which at that time was part of Mexico. By the early 1830s Americans outnumbered Mexican nationals in Texas by four to one and were aggressively challenging Mexican laws such as the prohibition of slavery. In 1835 political turmoil in Mexico led to a rebellion in Texas by an alliance of Mexican liberals and American settlers. Mexico was defeated in a brief war, and in 1836 Texas gained its independence. In 1845 the United States made Texas a state, provoking war with Mexico a year later. American forces eventually captured Mexico City, and a punitive peace treaty was imposed in 1848. Compounding the loss of Texas in 1837, the treaty of 1848 forced Mexico to cede vast territories to the United States, including present-day New Mexico, Arizona, and California. In return Mexico received $15 million. When gold was discovered in California in 1848, the magnitude of Mexico's loss became clear.

With the very survival of the nation at stake, Mexico's liberals took power and imposed sweeping reforms that provoked a civil war with the conservatives (1858–1861). As mentioned in the chapter opening, the French invaded Mexico in 1862, using unpaid government debts as an excuse. Mexico's conservatives allied themselves with the French invaders, and the president of Mexico, **Benito Juárez,** was forced to flee Mexico City. The French then installed the Austrian Habsburg Maximilian as emperor of Mexico. Juárez organized an effective military resistance and after years of warfare drove the French army out of Mexico in 1867. After capturing Maximilian, Juárez ordered his execution.

As was clear in the Mexican-American War, wars between Western Hemisphere nations could lead to dramatic territorial changes. In two wars with neighbors Chile established itself as the leading military and economic power on the west coast of South America. Between 1836 and 1839 Chile defeated the Confederation of Peru and Bolivia. In 1879 Chilean and British investors in nitrate mines located in the Atacama Desert, a dis-

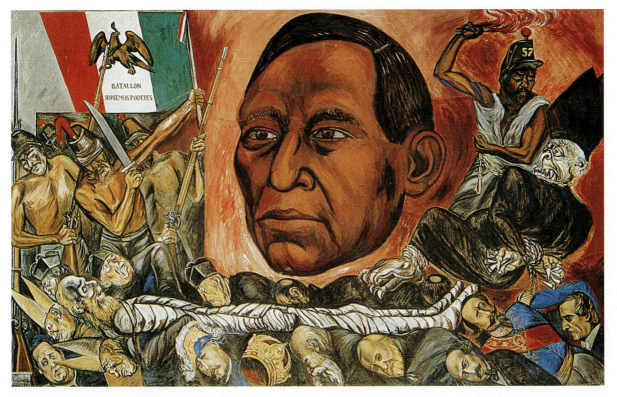

Benito Juárez's Triumph over the French   Benito Juárez overcame humble origins to lead the overthrow of Emperor Maximilian and the defeat of French imperialism. He remains a powerful symbol of secularism and republican virtue in Mexico. In this 1948 mural by José Clemente Orozco, Juárez's face dominates a scene of struggle that pits Mexican patriots against the allied forces of the Catholic Church, Mexican conservatives, and foreign invaders. The artist also celebrates the struggle of Mexico's Amerindians and mestizos against the white elite.   (Museo Nacional de Historia/CENIDIAP-INBA)

puted border region, provoked a new war with Peru and Bolivia (War of the Pacific). The Chilean army and navy won a crushing victory in 1881, forcing Bolivia to cede its only outlet to the sea and Peru to yield the rich mining districts.

Argentina and Brazil fought over control of Uruguay in the 1820s, but a military stalemate eventually forced them to recognize Uruguayan independence. In 1865 Argentina and Uruguay joined Brazil to wage war against Paraguay (War of the Triple Alliance, or Paraguayan War). After five years of warfare the Paraguayan dictator Francisco Solano López° and more than 20 percent of the population of Paraguay had died. Paraguay suffered military occupation, lost territory to the victors, and was forced to open its markets to foreign trade.

Francisco Solano López (fran-CEES-co so-LAN-oh LOH-pehz)

Native Peoples and the Nation-State

Both diplomacy and military action shaped relations between the Western Hemisphere's new nation-states and the indigenous peoples living within them. During late colonial times, to avoid armed conflict and to limit the costs of frontier defense, Spanish, Portuguese, and British imperial governments attempted to restrict the expansion of settlements into territories already occupied by Amerindians. With independence, the colonial powers' role as mediator for and protector of native peoples ended.

Still-independent Amerindian peoples posed a significant military challenge to many Western Hemisphere republics. Weakened by civil wars and constitutional crises, many of the new nations were less able to maintain frontier peace than the colonial governments had been. After independence Amerindian peoples in Argentina, the United States, Chile, and Mexico succeeded

Navajo Leaders Gathered in Washington to Negotiate   As settlers, ranchers, and miners pushed west in the nineteenth century, leaders of Amerindian peoples were forced to negotiate territorial concessions with representatives of the U.S. government. In order to impress Amerindian peoples with the wealth and power of the United States, many of their leaders were invited to Washington, D.C. This photo shows Navajo leaders and their Anglo translators in Washington, D.C., in 1874.   (#5851 Frank McNill Collection, State Records Center & Archives, Sante Fe, NM)

in pushing back some frontier settlements. But despite these early victories, by the end of the 1880s native military resistance was finally overcome in both North and South America.

After the American Revolution, the rapid expansion of agricultural settlements threatened native peoples in North America. Between 1790 and 1810 tens of thousands of settlers entered territories guaranteed to Amerindians in treaties with the United States. More than 200,000 white settlers were present in Ohio alone by 1810. Indigenous leaders responded by seeking the support of British officials in Canada and by forging broad indigenous alliances. American forces decisively defeated one such Amerindian alliance in 1794 at the Battle of Fallen Timbers in Ohio. After 1800 two Shawnee leaders, the brothers **Tecumseh**° and Prophet (Tenskwatawa), created a larger and better-

organized alliance among Amerindian peoples in the Ohio River Valley and gained some support from Great Britain. In 1811 American military forces attacked and destroyed the ritual center of the alliance, Prophet Town. The final blow came during the War of 1812 when Tecumseh, fighting alongside his British allies, was killed in battle.

In the 1820s white settlers forced native peoples living in Ohio, southern Indiana and Illinois, southwestern Michigan, most of Missouri, central Alabama, and southern Mississippi to cede their land. The 1828 presidential election of Andrew Jackson, a veteran of wars against native peoples, brought matters to a head. In 1830 Congress passed the Indian Removal Act, forcing the re-settlement of the Cherokee, Creek, Choctaw, and other eastern peoples to land west of the Mississippi River. The removal was carried out in the 1830s, and nearly half of the forced migrants died on this journey, known as the Trail of Tears.

Tecumseh (teh-CUM-sah)

Amerindians living on the Great Plains offered formidable resistance to the expansion of white settlement. By the time substantial numbers of white buffalo hunters, cattlemen, and settlers reached the American west, indigenous peoples were skilled users of horses and firearms. These technologies had transformed the cultures of the Sioux, Comanche, Pawnee, Kiowa, and other Plains peoples. The improved efficiency of the buffalo hunt reduced their dependence on agriculture. As a result, women, whose primary responsibility had been raising crops, lost prestige and social power to male hunters. Living arrangements also changed as the single-family tepees of migratory buffalo hunters replaced the multigenerational lodges of the traditional farming economy.

During the U.S. Civil War, native peoples experienced a disruption of their trade with Eastern merchants and the suspension of payments pledged by previous treaties. After the war ever more settlers pushed onto the plains. Buffalo herds were hunted to near extinction for their hides, and land was lost to farmers and ranchers. During nearly four decades of armed conflict with the United States Army, Amerindian peoples were forced to give up their land and their traditional ways. The Comanche, who had dominated the southern plains during the period of Spanish and Mexican rule, were forced by the U.S. government to cede most of their land in Texas in 1865. The Sioux and their allies resisted. In 1876 they overwhelmed General George Armstrong Custer and the Seventh Cavalry in the Battle of Little Bighorn (in the southern part of the present-day state of Montana). But finally the Sioux were also forced to accept reservation life. Military campaigns in the 1870s and 1880s then broke the resistance of the Apache.

The indigenous peoples of Argentina and Chile experienced a similar trajectory of adaptation, resistance, and defeat. Herds of wild cattle provided indigenous peoples with a limitless food supply, and horses and metal weapons increased their military capacities. Thus, for a while, the native peoples of Argentina and Chile effectively checked the southern expansion of agriculture and ranching. Amerindian raiders operated within 100 miles (160 kilometers) of Buenos Aires into the 1860s. Unable to defeat these resourceful enemies, the governments of Argentina and Chile relied on an elaborate system of gift giving and prisoner exchanges to maintain peace on the frontier. By the 1860s, however, population increase, political stability, and military modernization allowed Argentina and Chile to take the offensive.

In the 1870s the government of Argentina used overwhelming military force to crush native resistance. Thousands of Amerindians were killed, and survivors were driven onto marginal land. In Chile the story was the same. When civil war and an economic depression weakened the Chilean government at the end of the 1850s, the Mapuches° (called "Araucanians" by the Spanish) attempted to push back frontier settlements. Despite early successes the Mapuches were defeated in the 1870s by modern weaponry. In Chile, as in Argentina and the United States, government authorities justified military campaigns against native peoples by demonizing them. Newspaper editorials and the speeches of politicians portrayed Amerindians as brutal and cruel, and as obstacles to progress. In April 1859 a Chilean newspaper commented:

> The necessity, not only to punish the Araucanian race, but also to make it impotent to harm us, is well recognized . . . as the only way to rid the country of a million evils. It is well understood that they are odious and prejudicial guests in Chile . . . conciliatory measures have accomplished nothing with this stupid race—the infamy and disgrace of the Chilean nation.[4]

Political divisions and civil wars within the new nations sometimes provided an opportunity for long-pacified native peoples to rebel. In the Yucatán region of Mexico, the owners of henequen (the agave plant that produces fiber used for twine) and sugar plantations had forced many Maya° communities off their traditional agricultural lands, reducing thousands to peonage. This same regional elite declared itself independent of the government in Mexico City that was convulsed by civil war in the late 1830s. The Mexican government was unable to reestablish control because it faced the greater threat of invasion by the United States. Seeing their oppressors divided, the Maya rebelled in 1847. This well-organized and popular uprising, known as the **Caste War,** nearly returned the Yucatán to Maya rule. Grievances accumulated over more than three hundred years led to great violence and property destruction. The Maya were not defeated until the war with the United States ended. Even then Maya rebels retreated to unoccupied territories and created an independent state, which they called the "Empire of the Cross." Organized around a mix of traditional beliefs and Christian symbols, this indigenous state resisted Mexican forces to 1870. A few defiant Maya strongholds survived until 1901.

Mapuches (mah-POO-chez)
Maya (MY-ah)

THE CHALLENGE OF SOCIAL AND ECONOMIC CHANGE

During the nineteenth century the newly independent nations of the Western Hemisphere struggled to realize the Enlightenment ideals of freedom and individual liberty that had helped ignite the revolutions for independence. The achievement of these objectives was slowed by the persistence of slavery and other oppressive colonial-era institutions. Cultural and racial diversity also presented obstacles to reform. Nevertheless, by century's end reform movements in many of the hemisphere's nations had succeeded in ending the slave trade, abolishing slavery, expanding voting rights, and assimilating immigrants from Asia and Europe.

Increased industrialization and greater involvement in the evolving world economy challenged the region's political stability and social arrangements. A small number of nations embraced industrialization, but most Western Hemisphere economies became increasingly dependent on the export of agricultural goods and minerals during the nineteenth century. While the industrializing nations of the hemisphere became richer than the nations that remained exporters of raw materials, all the region's economies became more vulnerable and volatile as a result of greater participation in international markets. Like contemporary movements for social reform, efforts to assert national economic control produced powerful new political forces.

The Abolition of Slavery

In both the United States and Latin America strong antislavery sentiments were expressed during the struggles for independence. Revolutionary leaders of nearly all the new nations of the Western Hemisphere asserted ideals of universal freedom and citizenship that contrasted sharply with the reality of slavery. Men and women who wanted to outlaw slavery were called **abolitionists.** Despite their efforts, slavery survived in much of the hemisphere until the 1850s. In regions where the export of plantation products was most important—such as the United States, Brazil, and Cuba—the abolition of slavery was achieved with great difficulty.

In the United States slavery was weakened by abolition in some northern states and by the termination of the African slave trade in 1808. But this progress was stalled by the profitable expansion of cotton agriculture after the War of 1812. In Spanish America tens of thousands of slaves gained freedom by joining revolutionary armies during the wars for independence. After independence, most Spanish American republics prohibited the slave trade. Counteracting that trend was the growing international demand for sugar and coffee, products traditionally produced on plantations by slaves. As prices rose for plantation products in the first half of the nineteenth century, Brazil and Cuba (the island remained a Spanish colony until 1899) increased their imports of slaves.

During the long struggle to end slavery in the United States, American abolitionists argued that slavery offended both morality and the universal rights asserted in the Declaration of Independence. Abolitionist Theodore Weld articulated the religious objection to slavery in 1834:

> No condition of birth, no shade of color, no mere misfortune of circumstance, can annul the birth-right charter, which God has bequeathed to every being upon whom he has stamped his own image, by making him a free *moral agent* [emphasis in original], and that he who robs his fellow man of this tramples upon right, subverts justice, outrages humanity . . . and sacrilegiously assumes the prerogative of God.[5]

Two groups denied full rights of citizenship under the Constitution, women and free African-Americans, played important roles in the abolition of slavery. Women served on the executive committee of the American Anti-Slavery Society and produced some of the most effective propaganda against slavery. Eventually, thousands of women joined the abolitionist cause, where they provided leadership and were effective speakers and propagandists. When social conservatives attacked this highly visible public role, many women abolitionists responded by becoming public advocates of female suffrage as well.

Frederick Douglass, a former slave, became one of the most effective abolitionist speakers and writers. Other, more radical black leaders pushed the abolitionist movement to accept the inevitability of violence. They saw civil war or slave insurrection as necessary for ending slavery. In 1843 Henry Highland Garnet stirred the National Colored Convention when he demamded, "Brethren, arise, arise, arise! . . . Let every slave in the land do this and the days of slavery are numbered."[6] In the 1850s the growing electoral strength of the newly formed Republican Party forced a confrontation between slave and free states. After the election of Abraham Lincoln in 1860, the first of the eleven southern states that formed the Confederacy seceded from the Union. During the Civil War pressure for emancipation rose as tens of thousands of black freemen and escaped slaves joined the Union army. Hundreds of thousands of other slaves fled their masters' plantations and farms for the protection of advancing northern armies. In 1863, in the midst of the Civil War and two years after the abolition of serfdom in Russia (see Chapter 26), President Lincoln began the abolition of slavery by issuing the Emancipation Proclamation, which ended slavery in rebel states not occupied by the Union army. Final abolition was accomplished after the war, in 1865, by the Thirteenth Amendment to the Constitution. By the 1880s, however, most African-Americans lived in harsh conditions as sharecroppers, and by the end of the century nearly all southern states had instituted "Jim Crow" laws that segregated blacks in public transportation, jobs, and schools. This coincided with increased racial violence that saw an average of fifty blacks lynched each year.

In Brazil slavery survived for more than two decades after it was abolished in the United States. Progress toward abolition was not only slower but also depended on foreign pressure. In 1830 Brazil signed a treaty with the British ending the slave trade. Despite this agreement, Brazil illegally imported over a half-million more African slaves before the British navy finally forced compliance in the 1850s. In the 1850s and 1860s the Brazilian emperor, Pedro II, and many liberals worked to abolish slavery, but their desire to find a form of gradual emancipation acceptable to slave owners slowed progress.

During the war with Paraguay (1865–1870) large numbers of slaves joined the Brazilian army in exchange for freedom. Their loyalty and heroism undermined the military's support for slavery. Educated Brazilians increasingly viewed slavery as an obstacle to economic development and an impediment to democratic reform. In the 1870s, as abolitionist sentiment grew, reformers forced the passage of laws providing for the gradual emancipation of slaves. When political support for slavery weakened in the 1880s, growing numbers of slaves forced the issue by fleeing from bondage. By then army leaders were resisting demands to capture and return runaway slaves. Legislation abolishing slavery finally was passed by the Brazilian parliament and accepted by the emperor in 1888.

The plantations of the Caribbean region received almost 40 percent of all African slaves shipped to the New World. Throughout the region tiny white minorities lived surrounded by slave and free colored majorities. At the end of the eighteenth century the slave rebellion in Saint Domingue (see Chapter 22) spread terror among slave owners across the Caribbean. Because of fear that any effort to overthrow colonial rule might unleash new slave rebellions, there was little enthusiasm among free

A Former Brazilian Slave Returns from Military Service   The heroic participation of black freemen and slaves in the Paraguayan War (1865–1870) led many Brazilians to advocate the abolition of slavery. The original caption for this drawing reads: "On his return from the war in Paraguay: Full of glory, covered with laurels, after having spilled his blood in defense of the fatherland and to free a people from slavery, the volunteer sees his own mother bound and whipped! Awful reality!"   (Courtesy, Fundacao Biblioteca Nacional, Brazil)

settlers in Caribbean colonies for independence. Nor did local support for abolition appear among white settlers or free colored populations. Thus abolition in most Caribbean colonies commonly resulted from political decisions made in Europe by colonial powers.

Nevertheless, like slaves in Brazil, the United States, and Spanish America, slaves in the Caribbean helped propel the movement toward abolition by rebelling, running away, and resisting in more subtle ways. Although initially unsuccessful, the rebellions that threatened other French Caribbean colonies after the Haitian Revolution (1789–1804)) weakened France's support for slavery. Jamaica and other British colonies also experienced rebellions and saw the spread of communities of runaways. In Spanish Cuba as well, slave resistance forced increases in expenditures for police forces in the nineteenth century.

After 1800 the profitability of sugar plantations in the British West Indian colonies declined with increased competition from Cuba, and a coalition of labor groups, Protestant dissenters, and free traders in Britain pushed for the abolition of slavery. Britain, the major participant in the eighteenth-century expansion of slavery in the Americas, ended its participation in the slave trade in 1807. It then negotiated a series of treaties with Spain, Brazil, and other importers of slaves to eliminate the slave trade to the Americas. Once these treaties were in place, British naval forces acted to force compliance.

Slavery in British colonies was abolished in 1833. However, the law compelled "freed" slaves to remain with former masters as "apprentices." Abuses by planters and resistance to apprenticeship by former slaves led to complete abolition in 1838. A decade later slavery in the French Caribbean was abolished after upheavals in France led to the overthrow of the government of Louis Philippe (see Chapter 22). The abolition of slavery in the Dutch Empire in 1863 freed 33,000 slaves in Surinam and 12,000 in the Antilles. Slave owners were compensated for their loss, and the freedmen of Surinam were required to provide ten years of compensated labor to their former owners.

In the Caribbean, slavery lasted longest in Cuba and Puerto Rico, Spain's remaining colonies. Britain's use of diplomatic pressure and naval force to limit the arrival of African slaves weakened slavery after 1820. More important, however, was the growth of support for abolition in these colonies. Both Cuba and Puerto Rico had larger white and free colored populations than did the Caribbean colonies of Britain and France. As a result, there was less fear in Cuba and Puerto Rico that abolition would lead to the political ascendancy of former slaves (as had occurred in Haiti). In Puerto Rico, where slaves numbered approximately thirty thousand, local reformers secured the abolition of slavery in 1873. In the midst of a decade-long war to defeat forces seeking the independence of Cuba, the Spanish government gradually moved toward abolition. Initially, slave children born after September 18, 1868, were freed but obligated to work for their former masters for eighteen years. In 1880 all other slaves were freed on the condition that they serve their masters for eight additional years. Finally, in 1886 these conditions were eliminated; slavery was abolished; and Cuban patriots forged the multiracial alliance that was to initiate a war for Cuban independence in 1895 (see Chapter 28).

Immigration

During the colonial period free Europeans were a minority among immigrants to the Western Hemisphere. Between 1500 and 1760 African slaves entering the Western Hemisphere outnumbered European immigrants by nearly two to one. Another 4 million or so African slaves were imported before the effective end of the slave trade at the end of the 1850s. As the African slave trade came to an end, the arrival of millions of immigrants from Europe and Asia contributed to the further transformation of the Western Hemisphere. This nineteenth-century wave of immigration fostered rapid economic growth and the occupation of frontier regions in the United States, Canada, Argentina, Chile, and Brazil. It also promoted urbanization. By century's end nearly all of the hemisphere's fastest-growing cities (Buenos Aires, Chicago, New York, and São Paulo, for example) had large immigrant populations.

Europe provided the majority of immigrants to the Western Hemisphere during the nineteenth century. For much of the century they came primarily from western Europe, but after 1870 most came from southern and eastern Europe. The scale of immigration increased dramatically in the second half of the century. The United States received approximately 600,000 European immigrants in the 1830s, 1.5 million in the 1840s, and then 2.5 million per decade until 1880. In the 1890s an astonishing total of 5.2 million immigrants arrived. This helped push the national population from 39 million in 1871 to 63 million in 1891, an increase of 62 percent. Most of the immigrants ended up in cities. Chicago, for example, grew from 444,000 in 1870 to 1.7 million in 1900.

European immigration to Latin America also increased dramatically after 1880. Combined immigration to Argentina and Brazil rose from just under 130,000 in the 1860s to 1.7 million in the 1890s. By 1910, 30 percent of the Argentine population was foreign-born, more than twice the proportion in the U.S. population. Argentina was an extremely attractive destination for European immigrants, receiving more than twice as many immigrants as Canada between 1870 and 1930. Even so, immigration to Canada increased tenfold during this period.

Asian immigration to the Western Hemisphere increased after 1850. Between 1849 and 1875 approximately 100,000 Chinese immigrants arrived in Peru and another 120,000 entered Cuba. Canada attracted about 50,000 Chinese in the second half of the century. The United States, however, was the primary North American destination for Chinese immigrants, receiving 300,000 between 1854 and 1882. India also contributed to the social transformation of the Western Hemisphere, sending more than a half-million immigrants to the Caribbean region. British Guiana alone received 238,000 immigrants, mostly indentured laborers, from the Asian subcontinent.

Despite the obvious economic benefits that accompanied this inflow of people, hostility to immigration mounted in many nations. Nativist political movements

Chinese Funeral in Vancouver, Canada   In the 1890s Vancouver was an important Western Hemisphere destination for Chinese immigrants. This photo shows how an important element of traditional Chinese culture thrived among the storefronts and streetcar lines of the late-Victorian Canadian city. (Vancouver Public Library, Special Collections, VPL1234)

argued that large numbers of foreigners could not be successfully integrated into national political cultures. By the end of the century fear and prejudice led many governments in the Western Hemisphere to limit immigration or to distinguish between "desirable" and "undesirable" immigrants, commonly favoring Europeans over Asians.

Asians faced more obstacles to immigration than did Europeans and were more often victims of violence and extreme forms of discrimination in the New World. In the 1870s and 1880s anti-Chinese riots erupted in many western cities in the United States. Congress responded to this wave of racism by passing the Chinese Exclusion Act in 1882, which eliminated most Chinese immigration. In 1886 fears that Canada was being threatened by "inferior races" led to the imposition of a head tax that made immigration to Canada more difficult for Chinese families. During this same period strong anti-Chinese prejudice surfaced in Peru, Mexico, and Cuba. Japanese immigrants in Brazil and East Indians in the English-speaking Caribbean faced similar prejudice.

Immigrants from Europe also faced prejudice and discrimination. In the United States, Italians were commonly portrayed as criminals or anarchists. In Argentina, social scientists attempted to prove that Italian immigrants were more violent and less honest than the native-born population. Immigrants from Spain were widely stereotyped in Argentina as miserly and dishonest. Eastern European Jews seeking to escape pogroms and discrimination at home found themselves barred from many educational institutions and professional careers in both the United States and Latin America. Negative stereotypes were invented for Irish, German, Swedish, Polish, and Middle Eastern immigrants as well. The perceived grievances used to justify these common prejudices were remarkably similar from Canada to Argentina. Immigrants, it was argued, threatened the well-being of native-born workers by accepting low wages, and they threatened national culture by resisting assimilation.

Many intellectuals and political leaders wondered if the evolving mix of culturally diverse populations could sustain a common citizenship. As a result, efforts were directed toward compelling immigrants to assimilate. Schools became cultural battlegrounds where language, cultural values, and patriotic feelings were transmitted to the children of immigrants. Across the hemisphere, school curricula were revised to promote national culture. Ignoring Canada's large French-speaking population, an English-speaking Canadian reformer commented on recent immigration: "If Canada is to become in a real sense a nation, if our people are to become one people, we must have one language."[7] Fear and prejudice were among the emotions promoting the singing of patriotic songs, the veneration of national flags and other symbols, and the writing of national histories that emphasized patriotism and civic virtue. Nearly everywhere in the Americas schools worked to create homogeneous national cultures.

American Cultures

Despite discrimination, immigrants continued to stream into the Western Hemisphere, introducing new languages, living arrangements, technologies, and work customs. Immigrants altered the politics of many of the hemisphere's nations as they sought to influence government policies. Where immigrants arrived in the greatest numbers, they put enormous pressure on housing, schools, and social welfare services. To compensate for their isolation from home, language, and culture, immigrants often created ethnically based mutual aid societies, sports and leisure clubs, and neighborhoods. Ethnic organizations and districts provided valuable social and economic support for recent arrivals while sometimes worsening the fears of the native-born that immigration posed a threat to national culture.

Immigrants were changed by their experiences in their adopted nations and by programs that forced them to accept new cultural values through education or, in some cases, service in the military. Similar efforts to forge national cultures were put in place in Europe by modernizing governments at the same time. The modification of the language, customs, values, and behaviors of a group as a result of contact with people from another culture is called **acculturation.**

Immigrants and their children, in turn, made their mark on the cultures of their adopted nations in the Americas. They learned the language spoken in their adopted countries as fast as possible in order to improve their earning capacity. At the same time, words and phrases from their languages entered the vocabularies of the host nations. Languages as diverse as Yiddish and Italian strongly influenced American English, Argentine Spanish, and Brazilian Portuguese. Dietary practices introduced from Europe and Asia altered the cuisine of nearly every American nation. In turn, immigrants commonly added native foods to their diets, especially the hemisphere's abundant and relatively cheap meats.

Throughout the hemisphere culture and popular music changed as well. For example, the Argentine tango, based on African-Argentine rhythms, was transformed by new instrumentation and orchestral arrangements brought by Italian immigrants. Mexican ballads blended

Arrest of Labor Activist in Buenos Aires   The labor movement in Buenos Aires grew in numbers and became more radical with the arrival of tens of thousands of Italian and Spanish immigrants. Fearful of socialist and anarchist unions, the government of Argentina used an expanded police force to break strikes by arresting labor leaders.   (Archivo General de la Nación, Buenos Aires)

with English folk music in the U.S. southwest, and Italian operas played to packed houses in Buenos Aires. Sports, games of chance, and fashion also experienced this process of borrowing and exchange.

Union movements and electoral politics in the hemisphere also felt the influence of new arrivals who aggressively sought to influence government and improve working conditions. The labor movements of Mexico, Argentina, and the United States, in particular, were influenced by the anarchist and socialist beliefs of European immigrants. Mutual benevolent societies and less-formal ethnic associations pooled resources to help immigrants open businesses, aid the immigration of relatives, or bury family members. They also established links with political movements, sometimes exchanging votes for favors.

Women's Rights and the Struggle for Social Justice

The abolition of slavery in the Western Hemisphere did not end racial discrimination or provide full political rights for every citizen. Not only blacks but also women, new immigrants, and native peoples in nearly every Western Hemisphere nation suffered the effects of political and economic discrimination. During the second half of the nineteenth century reformers struggled to remove these limits on citizenship while also addressing the welfare needs of workers and the poor.

In 1848 a group of women angered by their exclusion from an international antislavery meeting issued a call for a meeting to discuss women's rights. The **Women's Rights Convention** at Seneca Falls, New York, issued a statement that said, in part, "We hold these truths to be self-evident: that all men and women are equal." While moderates focused on the issues of greater economic independence and full legal rights, increasing numbers of women demanded the right to vote. Others lobbied to provide better conditions for women working outside the home, especially in textile factories. Sarah Grimké responded to criticism of women's activism:

> This has been the language of man since he laid aside the whip as a means to keep woman in subjection. He spares her body, but the war he has waged against her mind, her heart, and her soul, has been no less destructive to her as a moral being. How monstrous is the doctrine that woman is to be dependent on man![8]

Progress toward equality between men and women was equally slow in Canada and Latin America. Canada's first women doctors received their training in the United States because no woman was able to receive a medical degree in Canada until 1895. Full enfranchisement occurred in Canada in the twentieth century, but Canadian women did gain the right to vote in some provincial and municipal elections before 1900. Like women in the United States, Canadian women provided leadership in temperance, child welfare, and labor reform movements.

Argentina and Uruguay were among the first Latin American nations to provide public education for women. Both nations introduced coeducation in the 1870s. Chilean women gained access to some careers in medicine and law in the 1870s. In Argentina the first woman doctor graduated from medical school in 1899. In Brazil, where many women were active in the abolitionist movement, four women graduated in medicine by 1882. Throughout the hemisphere more rapid progress was achieved in lower-status careers that threatened male economic power less directly, and by the end of the century women dominated elementary school teaching throughout the Western Hemisphere.

From Canada to Argentina and Chile, the majority of working-class women had no direct involvement in these reform movements, but they succeeded in transforming gender relations in their daily lives. By the end of the nineteenth century, large numbers of poor women worked outside the home on farms, in markets, and, increasingly, in factories. Many bore full responsibility for providing for their children. Whether men thought women should remain in the home or not, by the end of the century women were unambiguously present in the economy (see also Chapter 27).

Throughout the hemisphere there was little progress toward eliminating racial discrimination. Blacks were denied the vote throughout the southern United States. They also were subjected to the indignity of segregation—consigned to separate schools, hotels, restaurants, seats in public transportation, and even water fountains. Racial discrimination against men and women of African descent was also common in Latin America, though seldom spelled out in legal codes. Unlike the southern states of the United States, Latin American nations did not insist on formal racial segregation or permit lynching. Nor did they enforce a strict color line. Many men and women of mixed background were able to enter the skilled working class or middle class. Latin Americans tended to view racial identity across a continuum of physical characteristics rather than in the narrow terms of black and white that defined race relations in the United States.

The abolition of slavery in Latin America did not lead to an end to racial discrimination. Some of the participants in the abolition struggles later organized to promote racial integration. They demanded access to education, the right to vote, and greater economic opportunity, pointing out the economic and political costs of denying full rights to all citizens. Their success depended on effective political organization and on forging alliances with sympathetic white politicians. Black intellectuals also struggled to overturn racist stereotypes. In Brazil, Argentina, and Cuba, as in the United States, political and literary magazines celebrating black cultural achievement became powerful weapons in the struggle against racial discrimination. Although men and women of African descent continued to experience prejudice and discrimination everywhere in the Americas, successful men and women of mixed descent in Latin America confronted fewer obstacles to their advancement than did similar groups in the United States.

Development and Under-development

The Atlantic economy experienced three periods of economic contraction during the nineteenth century, but nearly all the nations of the Western Hemisphere were richer in 1900 than in 1800. The Industrial Revolution, worldwide population growth, and an increasingly integrated world market stimulated economic expansion (see Environment and Technology: Constructing the Port of Buenos Aires, Argentina). Wheat, corn, wool, meats, and nonprecious minerals joined the region's earlier exports of silver, sugar, dyes, coffee, and cotton. During the nineteenth century the United States was the only Western Hemisphere nation to industrialize, but nearly every government promoted new economic activities. Governments and private enterprises invested in roads, railroads, canals, and telegraphs to better serve distant markets. Most governments adopted tariff and monetary policies to foster economic diversification and growth. Despite these efforts, by 1900 only three Western Hemisphere nations—the United States, Canada, and Argentina—achieved individual income levels similar to those of western Europe. All three nations had open land, temperate climates, diverse resources, and large inflows of immigrants.

New demands for copper, zinc, lead, coal, and tin unleashed by the Industrial Revolution led to mining booms in the western United States, Mexico, and Chile. Unlike the small-scale and often short-term gold- and silver-mining operations of the colonial era, the mining companies of the late nineteenth century were heavily capitalized international corporations that could bully governments and buy political favors. During this period, European and North American corporations owned most new mining enterprises in Latin America. Petroleum development, which occurred at the end of the century in Mexico and elsewhere, would follow this pattern as well (see the discussion of the Mexican economy during the Díaz dictatorship in Chapter 31).

New technology accelerated economic integration, but the high cost of this technology often increased dependence on foreign capital. Many governments promoted railroads by granting tax benefits, free land, and monopoly rights to both domestic and foreign investors. By 1890 vast areas of the Great Plains in the United States, the Canadian prairie, the Argentine pampas, and parts of northern Mexico were producing grain and livestock for foreign markets opened by the development of railroads. Steamships also lowered the cost of transportation to distant markets, and the telegraph stimulated expansion by speeding information about the demand for and availability of products.

The simultaneous acquisition of several new technologies multiplied the effects of individual technologies. In Argentina the railroad, the telegraph, barbed wire, and refrigeration all appeared in the 1870s and 1880s. Although Argentina had had abundant livestock herds since the colonial period, the distance from Europe's markets prevented Argentine cattle raisers from exporting fresh meat or live animals. Technology overcame these obstacles. The combination of railroads and the telegraph lowered freight costs and improved information about markets. Steamships shortened trans-Atlantic crossings. Refrigerated ships made it possible to sell meat in the markets of Europe. As land values rose and livestock breeding improved, new investments were protected by barbed wire, the first inexpensive fencing available on the nearly treeless plains.

Growing interdependence and increased competition produced deep structural differences among Western Hemisphere economies by 1900. Two distinct economic tracks became clearly visible. One led to industrialization and prosperity, what is now called **development.** The other continued colonial dependence on exporting raw materials and on low-wage industries, now commonly called **underdevelopment.** By 1900 material prosperity was greater and economic development more diversified in English-speaking North America than in the nations of Latin America. With a temperate climate, vast fertile prairies, and an influx of European immigrants, Argentina was the only Latin American nation to approach the prosperity of the United States and Canada.

The Introduction of New Technologies Changes the Mining Industry Powerful hydraulic technologies were introduced in western mining sites in the United States. This early photo shows how high-power water jets could transform the natural environment. (Colorado Historical Society)

Changes in the performance of international markets helped determine the trajectory of Western Hemisphere economies as new nations promoted economic development. When the United States gained independence the world capitalist economy was in a period of rapid growth. With a large merchant fleet, a diversified economy that included some manufacturing, and adequate banking and insurance services, the United States benefited from the expansion of the world economy. Rapid population growth due in large measure to immigration, high levels of individual wealth, widespread landownership, and relatively high literacy rates also fostered rapid economic development in the United States. The rapid expansion of railroad mileage suggests this success. In 1865 the United States had the longest network in the world. By 1915 it had multiplied eleven-fold (see Map 24.4). Steel production grew rapidly as well, with the United States overtaking Britain and Germany in the 1890s. One cost of the nation's industrialization

was the vastly expanded power of monopolies, like Standard Oil, over political life.

Canada's struggle for greater political autonomy led to the Confederation of 1867, which coincided with a second period of global economic expansion. Canada also benefited from a special trading relationship with Britain, the world's preeminent industrial nation, and from a rising tide of immigrants after 1850. Nevertheless, some regions within each of these prosperous North American nations—Canada's Maritime Provinces and the southern part of the United States, for example— demonstrated the same patterns of underdevelopment found in Latin America.

Latin American nations gained independence in the 1820s, when the global economy was contracting due to the end of the Napoleonic Wars and market saturation provoked by the early stages of European industrialization. In the colonial period Spain and Portugal had promoted the production of agricultural and mining

Constructing the Port of Buenos Aires, Argentina

Located on the banks of the Río de la Plata, Buenos Aires had been a major commercial center and port since the late eighteenth century. But Buenos Aires was not a natural harbor. Because of the shallowness of the river, the largest oceangoing ships were forced to anchor hundreds of yards offshore while goods and passengers were unloaded by small boats or by specially built ox carts with huge wheels. Smaller vessels docked at a river port to the city's south.

By the 1880s the Argentine economy was being transformed by the growing demands of European consumers for meat and grain. As exports surged and land values exploded, the wages of Argentines rose, and the nation became a favored destination for European immigrants. Argentina was becoming the wealthiest nation in Latin America.

The nation's political and economic elites decided that future growth required the modernization and expansion of port facilities. Two competing plans were debated. The first emphasized the incremental expansion and dredging of the river port. This was supported by local engineers and political groups suspicious of foreign economic interests. The second, and ultimately successful, plan involved dredging a port and deep-water channel from the low mud flats near the city center. This plan was more expensive, relying on British engineering firms, British banks, and British technology. It was supported by Argentine economic interests most closely tied to the European export trade and by national political leaders who believed progress and prosperity required the imitation of European models. Already the British were the nation's primary creditors as well as leaders in the development of the nation's railroads, streetcar lines, and gas works in Buenos Aires.

The photograph below shows the construction of Puerto Madero, the new port of Buenos Aires, in the 1890s. The work force was almost entirely recruited from recent immigrants. The engineering staff was dominated by British experts. Most of the profits were culled by the local elite through real estate deals and commissions associated with construction. Puerto Madero, named after its local promoter, was opened in stages beginning in 1890. Cost overruns and corruption stretched out completion to 1898. By 1910 arrivals and departures reached thirty thousand ships and 18 million tons. But the project was poorly designed, and "improvements" were still being made in the 1920s.

Why had the government of Argentina chosen the costliest and most difficult design? Argentine politicians were seduced by the idea of modernity; they chose the most complex and technologically sophisticated solution to the port problem. And they believed that British engineering and British capital were guarantees of modernity. The new port facilities did facilitate a boom in exports and imports, and the huge public works budget did provide incomes for thousands of laborers. However, debts, design flaws, and the increased influence of foreign capital in Argentina left a legacy of problems that Argentina would be forced to deal with in the future. (See the discussion of Juan Perón in Chapter 31.)

Excavation of Port of Buenos Aires, Argentina   Relying on foreign capital and engineering, the government of Argentina improved the port to facilitate the nation's rapidly expanding export economy.   (Courtesy, Hack Hoffenburg, South American Resources)

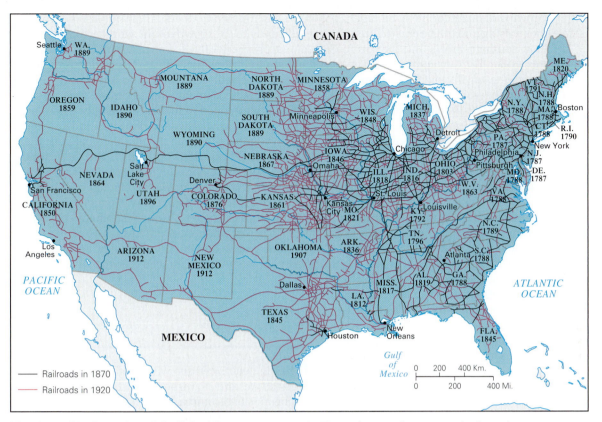

Map 24.4   The Expansion of the United States, 1850–1920.   The settlement of western territories and their admission as states depended on migration, the exploitation of natural resources and important new technologies like railroads and telegraphs that facilitated economic and political integration.

exports. After independence those raw-material exports faced increased competition. Although these sectors experienced periods of great prosperity in the nineteenth century, they also faced stiff competition and falling prices as new regions began production or new products captured markets. Sugar, coffee, nitrates, and copper all followed this pattern.

The history of the specialized Latin American economies, subject to periodic problems of oversupply and low prices, was one of boom and bust. Many Latin American governments sought to promote exports in the face of increased competition and falling prices by resisting union activity and demands for higher wages and by opening domestic markets to foreign manufactures. Resulting low wages and an abundance of foreign manufactured goods, in turn, undermined efforts to promote industrialization in Latin America.

Weak governments, political instability, and, in some cases, civil war also slowed Latin American economic development. A comparative examination of Western Hemisphere economic history makes clear that stable

and reliable public administration is a necessary part of the development process. Because Latin America was dependent on capital and technology from abroad, Great Britain and, by the end of the century, the United States were often able to impose unfavorable trade conditions or even intervene militarily to protect investments. The combined impact of these domestic and international impediments to development became clear when Mexico, Chile, and Argentina failed to achieve high levels of domestic investment in manufacturing late in the nineteenth century, despite a rapid accumulation of wealth derived from traditional exports.

Altered Environments

Population growth, economic expansion, new technologies, and the introduction of plants and animals to new regions dramatically altered the environment of the Western Hemisphere. Cuba's planters cut down many of the island's forests in the early nineteenth century to expand sugar production. Growing demand for meat led ranchers to expand livestock-raising into fragile environments in Argentina, Uruguay, southern Brazil, and the southwestern United States. Other forms of commercial agriculture also threatened the environment. Farmers in South Carolina and Georgia gained a short-term increase in cotton production by abandoning crop rotation after 1870, but this practice quickly led to soil exhaustion and erosion. The use of steel plows on North American prairies and Argentine pampas eliminated many native grasses and increased the threat of soil erosion. Coffee planters in Brazil exhausted soil fertility with a destructive cycle of overplanting followed by expansion onto forest reserves cleared by cutting and burning. Similarly massive transfers of land from public to private ownership occurred in Argentina and Brazil in order to promote livestock-raising and agriculture.

Rapid urbanization also put heavy pressure on the environment. New York, Chicago, Rio de Janeiro, Buenos Aires, and Mexico City were among the world's fastest-growing cities in the nineteenth century. Governments strained to provide adequate sewers, clean water, and garbage disposal. Timber companies clear-cut large areas of Michigan, Wisconsin, and the Appalachian Mountains to provide lumber for railroad ties and frame houses, pulp for paper, and fuel for locomotives and foundries. Under the Timber and Stone Act of 1878, the U.S. government sold more than 3.5 million additional acres (1.4 million hectares) of public land to individual and corporations at low cost by 1900. At the same time, the forest industries of British Honduras (now Belize), Nicaragua, and Guatemala grew rapidly in response to demand in Europe and North America for tropical hardwoods like mahogany. As forest throughout the hemisphere was cleared, animal habitats and native plant species disappeared.

The scale of mining operation grew in Nevada, Montana, and California, accelerating erosion and pollution. Similar results occurred in other mining areas. The expansion of nitrate mining and, later, open-pit copper mining in Chile scarred and polluted the environment. The state of Minas Gerais° in Brazil experienced a series of mining booms that began with gold in the late seventeenth century and continued with iron ore in the nineteenth. By the end of the nineteenth century its red soil was ripped open, its forests were depleted, and erosion was uncontrolled. Similar devastation afflicted parts of Bolivia and Mexico.

Efforts to meet increasing domestic demand for food and housing and to satisfy foreign demands for exports

led to environmental degradation but also contributed significantly to the growth of the world economy and to regional prosperity. By the end of the nineteenth century small-scale conservation efforts were under way in many nations, and the first national parks and nature reserves had been created. In the United States large areas remained undeveloped. A few particularly beautiful areas were preserved in a national park system. In 1872 Yellowstone in Wyoming became the first national park. President Theodore Roosevelt (1901–1909) and the naturalist John Muir played major roles in preserving large areas of the western states. In Canada the first national park was created at Banff in 1885 and was expanded from 10 to 260 square miles (26 to 673 square kilometers) two years later. However, when confronted by a choice between economic growth and environmental protection, all the hemisphere's nations embraced growth.

CONCLUSION

The nineteenth century witnessed enormous changes in the Western Hemisphere. Except in Canada, many Caribbean islands, and a handful of mainland colonies like Surinam, the Guyanas, and Belize, colonial controls were removed by century's end. The powerful new political ideas of the Enlightenment and an increased sense of national identity contributed to the desire for independence and self-rule. The success of the American and Haitian Revolutions began the assault on the colonial order, transforming the hemisphere's politics. Napoleon's invasion of Portugal and Spain then helped initiate the movement toward independence in Latin America.

Once colonial rule was overturned, the creation of stable and effective governments proved difficult. Powerful personalist leaders resisted the constraints imposed by constitutions. National governments often confronted divisive regional political movements. From Argentina in the south to the United States in the north, regional political rivalries provoked civil wars that challenged the very survival of the new nations. Foreign military interventions and wars with native peoples also consumed resources and determined national boundaries. The effort to fulfill the promise of universal citizenship led to struggles to end slavery, extend civil and political rights to women and minorities, and absorb new immigrants. These objectives were only partially achieved.

Industrialization had a transforming effect on the hemisphere as well. Wealth, political power, and population were increasingly concentrated in urban areas. In

---

Minas Gerais (ME-nas JER-aize)

most countries, bankers and manufacturers, rather than farmers and plantation owners, directed national destinies. The United States, the most industrialized nation in the Americas, played an aggressive economic role in the region's affairs and used its growing military power as well. Industrialization altered the natural environment in dramatic ways. Modern factories consumed huge amounts of raw materials and energy. Copper mines in Chile and Mexico, Cuban sugar plantations, Brazilian coffee plantations, and Canadian lumber companies all left their mark on the natural environment, and all had ties to markets in the United States. The concentration of people in cities in the United States and Latin America put pressure on water supplies, sewage treatment, and food supplies.

By 1900, however, the hemisphere's national governments were much stronger than they had been at independence. Latin America lagged behind the United States and Canada in institutionalizing democratic political reforms, but Latin American nations in 1900 were stronger and more open than they had been in 1850. By 1900 all the hemisphere's nations also were better able to meet the threats of foreign intervention and regionalism. Among the benefits resulting from the increased strength of national governments were the abolition of slavery and the extension of political rights to formerly excluded citizens.

Serious challenges remained. Amerindian peoples were forced to resettle on reservations, were excluded from national political life, and, in some countries, remained burdened with special tribute and tax obligations. Women began to enter occupations previously reserved to men but still lacked full citizenship rights. The baneful legacy of slavery and colonial racial stratification remained a barrier to many men and women. The benefits of economic growth were not equitably distributed among the nations of the Western Hemisphere or within individual nations. In 1900 nearly every American nation was wealthier, better educated, more democratic, and more populous than at independence. But these nations were also more vulnerable to distant economic forces, more profoundly split between haves and have-nots, and more clearly divided into a rich north and a poorer south.

■ Key Terms

Simón Bolívar
Miguel Hidalgo y Costilla
José María Morelos
Confederation of 1867
personalist leaders
Andrew Jackson
José Antonio Páez
Benito Juárez
Tecumseh
Caste War
abolitionists
acculturation
Women's Rights Convention
development
underdevelopment

■ Suggested Reading

For the independence era in Latin America see John Lynch, *The Spanish American Revolutions, 1808–1826*, 2d ed. (1986); Jay Kinsbruner, *Independence in Spanish America* (1994); and A. J. R. Russell-Wood, ed., *From Colony to Nation: Essays on the Independence of Brazil* (1976).

The postindependence political and economic struggles in Latin America can be traced in David Bushnell and Neil Macaulay, *The Emergence of Latin America in the Nineteenth Century* (1988). Tulio Halperin-Donghi, *The Contemporary History of Latin America* (1993), and E. Bradford Burns, *The Poverty of Progress: Latin America in the Nineteenth Century* (1980), argue in different ways that Latin America's economic and social problems originated in unfavorable trade relationships with more-developed nations. See also an excellent collection of essays, Leslie Bethell, ed., *The Cambridge History of Latin America*, vol. 3, *From Independence to c. 1870* (1985).

There is an enormous literature on politics and nation building in the United States and Canada. Among the many worthy studies of the United States are John Lauritz Larson, *Internal Improvement: National Public Works and the Promise of Popular Government in the Early United States* (2001); William J. Cooper, *The South and the Politics of Slavery, 1828–1856* (1978); Kenneth M. Stampp, *America in 1857* (1991); and Lawrence Frederick Kohl, *The Politics of Individualism: Parties and the American Character in the Jacksonian Era* (1989). For Canada see J. M. S. Careless, *The Union of the Canadas: The Growth of Canadian Institutions, 1841–1857* (1967); Ged Martin, ed., *The Causes of Canadian Confederation* (1990); and Arthur I. Silver, *The French-Canadian Idea of Confederation, 1864–1900* (1982).

The social and cultural issues raised in this chapter are also the subject of a vast literature. For an excellent history of the immigration era see Walter Nugent, *Crossing: The Great Transatlantic*

Migrations, 1870–1914 (1992). See also Gunther Barth, *Bitter Strength: A History of Chinese in the United States, 1850–1870* (1964), and Nicolás Sánchez-Albornoz, *The Population of Latin America: A History* (1974).

On the issue of slavery see David Brion Davis, *Slavery and Human Progress* (1984), and George M. Frederickson, *The Black Image in the White Mind: The Debate on Afro-American Character and Destiny, 1817–1914* (1971). Among the many fine studies of abolition see Benjamin Quarles, *Black Abolitionists* (1969), and John Stauffer, *The Black Hearts of Men* (2001). For the women's rights movement see Ellen C. Du Bois, *Feminism and Suffrage: The Emergence of an Independent Woman's Movement in the Nineteenth Century* (1984), and Lori D. Ginzberg, *Women and the Work of Benevolence: Morality, Politics, and Class in the Nineteenth-Century United States* (1990). Among numerous excellent studies of Indian policies see Robert M. Utley, *The Indian Frontier of the American West, 1846–1890* (1984), and the recent *Andrew Jackson and His Indian Wars* (2001) by Robert V. Remini. On those topics for Canada see J. R. Miller, *Skyscrapers Hide the Heavens: A History of Indian White Relations in Canada* (1989); Olive Patricia Dickason, *Canada's First Nations* (1993); and Alison Prentice, *Canadian Women: A History* (1988).

For abolition in Latin America and the Caribbean see Rebecca Scott, *Slave Emancipation in Cuba: The Transition to Free Labor, 1860–1899* (1985); Robert Conrad, *The Destruction of Brazilian Slavery, 1850–1888* (1973); and William A. Green, *British Slave Emancipation: The Sugar Colonies and the Great Experiment, 1830–1865* (1973). An introduction to the place of women in Latin American society is found in Francesca Miller, *Latin American Women and the Search for Social Justice* (1991), and Jane Jaquette, ed., *The Women's Movement in Latin America* (1989). See also David Barry Gaspar and Darlene Clark Hine, eds., *More Than Chattel: Black Women and Slavery in the Americas* (1996).

An introduction to environmental consequence of North American development is provided by William Cronon, *Nature's Metropolis: Chicago and the Great West* (1991); Joseph M. Petulla, *American Environmental History* (1973); and Donald Worster, *Rivers of Empire: Water, Aridity, and the Growth of the American West* (1985). For Brazil see Warren Dean, *With Broadax and Firebrand: The Destruction of the Brazilian Atlantic Forest* (1995); and for Argentina, Uruguay, and Chile, Alfred Crosby, *Ecological Imperialism: The Biological Expansion of Europe, 900–1900* (1986).

■ Notes

1. Quoted in Lyman L. Johnson, "Spanish American Independence and Its Consequences," in *Problems in Modern Latin American History: A Reader,* ed. John Charles Chasteen and Joseph S. Tulchin (Wilmington, DE: Scholarly Resources, 1994), 21.
2. Quoted in Margaret Conrad, Alvin Finkel, and Cornelius Jaenen, *History of the Canadian Peoples*, vol. 1 (Toronto: Copp Clark Pittman Ltd., 1993), 606–607.
3. José Antonio Páez, *Autobiografía del General José Antonio Páez*, vol. 1 (New York: Hallety Breen, 1869), 83.
4. Quoted in Brian Loveman, *Chile: The Legacy of Hispanic Capitalism* (New York: Oxford University Press, 1979), 170.
5. Quoted in Bernard Bailyn, David Brion Davis, David Herbert Donald, John L. Thomas, Robert H. Wiebe, and Gordon S. Wood, *The Great Republic: A History of the American People* (Lexington, MA: D. C. Heath, 1981), 398.
6. Quoted in Mary Beth Norton, et al, A People and a Nation. A History of the United States, 6th edition (Boston, MA: Houghton Mifflin Company, 2001), 284.
7. J. S. Woodsworth in 1909, quoted in R. Douglas Francis, Richard Jones, and Donald B. Smith, *Destinies: Canadian History Since Confederation,* 2d ed. (Toronto: Holt, Rinehart and Winston, 1992), 141.
8. Sarah Grimké, "Reply to the Massachusetts Clergy," in Nancy Woloch, ed., *Early American Women: A Documentary History, 1600–1900* (Belmont, CA: Wadsworth, 1992), 343.

25

Africa, India, and the New British Empire, 1750–1870

Indian Railroad Station, 1866 British India built the largest network of railroads in Asia. People of every social class traveled by train.

CHAPTER OUTLINE

Changes and Exchanges in Africa

India Under British Rule

Britain's Eastern Empire

DIVERSITY AND DOMINANCE: Ceremonials of Imperial Domination

ENVIRONMENT AND TECHNOLOGY: Whaling

In 1782 Tipu Sultan inherited the throne of the state of Mysore°, which his father had made the most powerful state in South India. The ambitious and talented new ruler also inherited a healthy distrust of the territorial ambitions of Great Britain's East India Company. In 1785, before the company could invade Mysore, Tipu Sultan launched his own attack. He then sent an embassy to France in 1788, seeking an alliance against Britain. Neither of these ventures was immediately successful.

Not until a decade later did the French agree to a loose alliance with Tipu Sultan as part of their plan to challenge Britain's colonial and commercial supremacy in the Indian Ocean. General Napoleon Bonaparte invaded Egypt in 1798 to threaten British trade routes to India and hoped to use the alliance with Tipu Sultan to drive the British out of India. The French invasion of Egypt went well enough at first, but a British naval blockade and the ravages of disease crippled the French force. When the French withdrew, another military adventurer, Muhammad Ali, commander of the Ottoman army in Egypt, took advantage of the situation to revitalize Egypt and expand its rule.

Meanwhile, Tipu's struggle with the East India Company was going badly. A military defeat in 1792 forced him to surrender most of his coastal lands. Despite the loose alliance with France, he was unable to stop further British advances. Tipu lost his life in 1799 while defending his capital against a British assault. Mysore was divided between the British and their Indian allies.

As these events illustrate, talented local leaders and European powers were all vying to expand their influence in South Asia and Africa between 1750 and 1870. Midway through that period, it was by no means clear who would gain the upper hand. Britain and France were as likely to fight each other as they were to fight an Asian or African state. In 1800 the two nations were engaged in their third major war for overseas supremacy since 1750. By 1870, however, Britain had gained a decisive advantage over France.

The new British Empire in the East included the subcontinent of India, settler colonies in Australia and New Zealand, and a growing network of trading outposts. By 1870 Britain had completed the campaign to replace the overseas slave trade from Africa with "legitimate" trade and had spearheaded new Asian and South Pacific labor migrations into a rejuvenated string of tropical colonies.

As you read this chapter, ask yourself the following questions:

- Why were the British able to gain decisive advantages in distant lands?

- Why were Asians and Africans so divided, some choosing to cooperate with the Europeans and others resisting their advances?

- How important an advantage were Britain's weapons, ships, and economic motives?

- How much of the outcome was the result of advance planning, and how much was due to particular individuals or to chance?

- By 1870, how much had the British and the different peoples of Africa and Asia gained or lost?

CHANGES AND EXCHANGES IN AFRICA

In the century before 1870 Africa underwent dynamic political changes and a great expansion of foreign trade. Indigenous African leaders as well as Middle Eastern and European imperialists built powerful new states and expanded old ones. As the continent's external slave trades to the Americas and to Islamic lands died slowly under British pressure, trade in goods such as palm oil, ivory, timber, and gold grew sharply. In return Africans imported large quantities of machine-made textiles and firearms. These complex changes are best understood by looking at African regions separately.

Mysore (my-SORE)

664

C H R O N O L O G Y

	Empire	Africa	India
1750	**1763** End of Seven Years War **1769–1778** Captain James Cook explores New Zealand and eastern Australia **1795** End of Dutch East India Company		**1756** Black Hole of Calcutta **1765** East India Company (EIC) rule of Bengal begins
1800	**1808** Britain outlaws slave trade	**1795** Britain takes Cape Colony **1798** Napoleon invades Egypt **1805** Muhammad Ali seizes Egypt **1808** Britain takes over Sierra Leone **1809** Sokoto Caliphate founded **1818** Shaka founds Zulu kingdom **1821** Foundation of Republic of Liberia; Egypt takes control of Sudan	**1798** Britain annexes Ceylon **1799** EIC defeats Mysore **1818** EIC creates Bombay Presidency **1826** EIC annexes Assam and northern Burma **1828** Brahmo Samaj founded
	1834 Britain abolishes slavery	**1831–1847** Algerians resist French takeover **1836–1839** Afrikaners' Great Trek	**1834** Indentured labor migrations begin
1850	**1867** End of Atlantic slave trade **1877** Queen Victoria becomes Empress of India	**1840** Omani sultan moves capital to Zanzibar **1869** Jaja founds Opobo **1889** Menelik unites modern Ethiopia	**1857–1858** Sepoy Rebellion leads to end of EIC rule and Mughal rule **1885** First Indian National Congress

New Africa States

Internal forces produced clusters of new states in two parts of sub-Saharan Africa between 1750 and 1870. In southern Africa changes in warfare gave rise to a powerful Zulu kingdom and other new states. In inland West Africa Islamic reformers created the gigantic Sokoto° Caliphate and companion states (see Map 25.1).

For many centuries the Nguni° peoples had pursued a life based on cattle and agriculture in the fertile coastlands of southeastern Africa (in modern South Africa). Small independent chiefdoms suited their political needs until a serious drought hit the region at the beginning of the nineteenth century. Out of the conflict for grazing and farming lands, an upstart military genius named Shaka (r. 1818–1828) created the **Zulu** kingdom in 1818. Strict military drill and close-combat warfare featuring ox-hide shields and lethal stabbing spears made the Zulu the most powerful and most feared fighters in southern Africa.

Shaka expanded his kingdom by raiding his African neighbors, seizing their cattle, and capturing their women and children. Breakaway military bands spread this system of warfare and state building inland to the high plateau country, across the Limpopo River (in modern Zimbabwe°), and as far north as Lake Victoria. As the power and population of these new kingdoms increased, so too did the number of displaced and demoralized refugees around them.

To protect themselves from the Zulu, some neighboring Africans created their own states. The Swazi kingdom consolidated north of the Zulu, and the kingdom of

---

Sokoto (SOH-kuh-toh)   **Nguni** (ng-GOO-nee)

Zimbabwe (zim-BAH-bway)

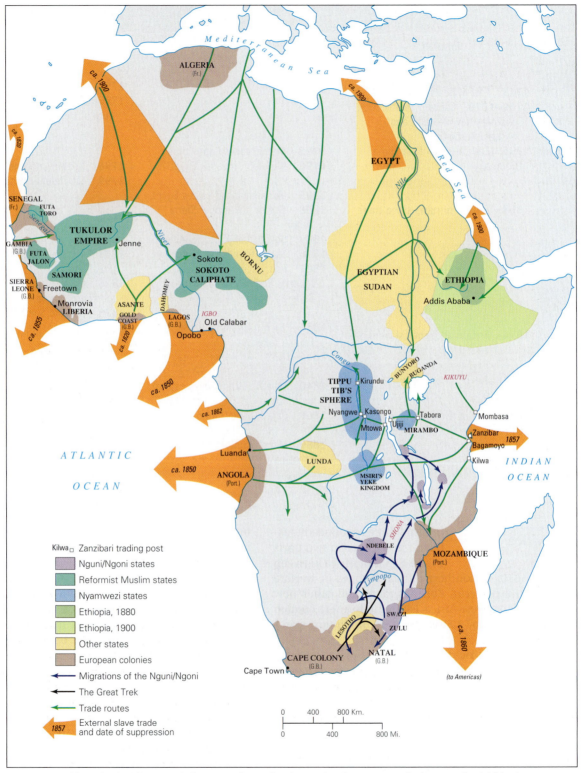

Map 25.1   Africa in the Nineteenth Century   Expanding internal and overseas trade drew much of Africa into global networks, but foreign colonies in 1870 were largely confined to Algeria and southern Africa. Growing trade, Islamic reform movements, and other internal forces created important new states throughout the continent.

Lesotho° grew by attracting refugees to strongholds in southern Africa's highest mountains. Both Lesotho and Swaziland survive as independent states to this day.

Although Shaka ruled for little more than a decade, he succeeded in creating a new national identity as well as a new kingdom. He grouped all the young people in his domains by age into regiments. Regiment members lived together and immersed themselves in learning Zulu lore and customs, including fighting methods for the males. A British trader named Henry Francis Fynn expressed his "astonishment at the order and discipline" he found everywhere in the Zulu kingdom. He witnessed public festivals of loyalty to Shaka at which regiments of young men and women numbering in the tens of thousands danced around the king for hours. Parades showed off the king's enormous herds of cattle, a Zulu measure of wealth.

Meanwhile, Islamic reform movements were creating another cluster of powerful states in the savannas of West Africa. Islam had been a force in the politics and cities of this region for centuries, but it had made only slow progress among most rural people. As a consequence, most Muslim rulers had found it prudent to tolerate the older religious practices of their rural subjects. In the 1770s local Muslim scholars began preaching the need for a vigorous reform of Islamic practices. They condemned the accommodations Muslim rulers had made with older traditions and called for a forcible conquest of rural "pagans." The reformers followed a classic Muslim pattern: a *jihad* (holy war) added new lands, where governments enforced Islamic laws and promoted the religion's spread among conquered people.

The largest of the new Muslim reform movements occurred in the Hausa° states (in what is now northern Nigeria) under the leadership of Usuman dan Fodio° (1745–1817), a Muslim cleric of the Fulani° people. He charged that the Hausa kings, despite their official profession of Islam, were "undoubtedly unbelievers . . . because they practice polytheistic rituals and turn people away from the path of God." Distressed by the lapses of a former pupil, the king of Gobir, Usuman issued a call in 1804 for a jihad to overthrow him. Muslims unhappy with their social or religious position spread the movement to other Hausa states. The successful armies united the conquered Hausa states and neighboring areas under a caliph (sultan) who ruled from the city of Sokoto. The **Sokoto Caliphate** (1809–1906) was the largest state

Lesotho (luh-SOO-too)   Hausa (HOW-suh)
Usuman dan Fodio (OO-soo-mahn dahn FOH-dee-oh)
Fulani (foo-LAH-nee)

Zulu in Battle Dress, 1838   Elaborate costumes helped impress opponents with the Zulu's strength. Shown here are long-handled spears and thick leather shields. The stabbing spear is not shown. (Killie Campbell Africana Library. Photo: Jane Taylor/Sonia Halliday)

in West Africa since the fall of Songhai in the sixteenth century.

As in earlier centuries, these new Muslim states became centers of Islamic learning and reform. Schools for training boys in Quranic subjects spread rapidly, and the great library at Sokoto attracted many scholars. Although officials permitted non-Muslims within the empire to follow their religions in exchange for paying a special tax, they suppressed public performances of dances and ceremonies associated with traditional religions. During the jihads, many who resisted the expansion of Muslim rule were killed, enslaved, or forced to convert.

Sokoto's leaders sold some captives into the Atlantic slave trade and many more into the trans-Saharan slave trade, which carried ten thousand slaves a year, mostly women and children, across the desert to North Africa and the Middle East. Slavery also increased greatly within the Sokoto Caliphate and other new Muslim states. It is estimated that by 1865 there were more slaves in the Sokoto Caliphate than in any remaining slave-holding state in the Americas.[1] Most of the enslaved persons raised food, making possible the seclusion of free women in their homes in accordance with reformed Muslim practice.

Modernization in Egypt and Ethiopia

While new states were arising elsewhere, in northeastern Africa the ancient states of Egypt and Ethiopia were undergoing growth and **modernization.** Napoleon's invading army had withdrawn from Egypt by 1801, but the shock of this display of European strength and Egyptian weakness was long-lasting. The successor to Napoleon's rule was **Muhammad Ali** (1769–1849), who eliminated his rivals and ruled Egypt from 1805 to 1848. He began the political, social, and economic reforms that created modern Egypt.

Muhammad Ali's central aim was to give Egypt sufficient military strength to prevent another European conquest, but he was pragmatic enough to make use of European experts and techniques to achieve that goal. His reforms transformed Egyptian landholding, increased agricultural production, and created a modern administration and army. To train candidates for the army and administration, Muhammad Ali set up a European-style state school system and opened a military college at Aswan°. To pay for these ventures and for the European experts and equipment he imported, he required Egyptian peasants to cultivate cotton and other crops for export.

In the 1830s Muhammad Ali headed the strongest state in the Islamic world and the first to employ Western methods and technology for modernization. The process was far from blind imitation of the West. Rather, the technical expertise of the West was combined with Islamic religious and cultural traditions. For example, the Egyptian printing industry, begun to provide Arabic translations of technical manuals, turned out critical editions of Islamic classics and promoted a revival of Arabic writing and literature later in the century.

By the end of Muhammad Ali's reign in 1848, the modernization of Egypt was well underway. The population had nearly doubled; trade with Europe had expanded by almost 600 percent; and a new class of educated Egyptians had begun to replace the old ruling aristocracy. Egyptians were replacing many of the foreign experts, and the fledgling program of industrialization was providing the country with its own textiles, paper, weapons, and military uniforms. The demands on peasant families for labor and military service, however, were acutely disruptive.

Ali's grandson Ismail° (r. 1863–1879) placed even more emphasis on westernizing Egypt. "My country is no longer in Africa," Ismail declared, "it is in Europe."[2] His efforts increased the number of European advisers in Egypt—and Egypt's debts to French and British banks. In the first decade of his reign, revenues increased thirty-fold and exports doubled (largely because of a huge increase in cotton exports during the American Civil War). By 1870 Egypt had a network of new irrigation canals, 800 miles (1,300 kilometers) of railroads, a modern postal service, and the dazzling new capital city of Cairo. When the market for Egyptian cotton collapsed after the American Civil War, however, Egypt's debts to British and French investors led to the country's partial occupation.

From the middle of the century, state building and reform also were underway in the ancient kingdom of Ethiopia, whose rulers had been Christian for fifteen hundred years. Weakened by internal divisions and the pressures of its Muslim neighbors, Ethiopia was a shadow of what it had been in the sixteenth century, but under Emperor Téwodros° II (r. 1833–1868) and his successor Yohannes° IV (r. 1872–1889) most highland regions were brought back under imperial rule. The only large part of ancient Ethiopia that remained outside Emperor Yohannes's rule was the Shoa kingdom, ruled by King Menelik° from 1865. When Menelik succeeded Yohannes as emperor in 1889, the merger of their separate realms created the modern boundaries of Ethiopia.

Beginning in the 1840s Ethiopian rulers purchased modern weapons from European sources and created strong armies loyal to the ruler. Emperor Téwodros also encouraged the manufacture of weapons locally. With the aid of Protestant missionaries his craftsmen even constructed a giant cannon capable of firing a half-ton shell. However, his efforts to coerce more technical aid by holding some British officials captive backfired when the British invaded instead. As the British forces advanced, Téwodros committed suicide to avoid being taken prisoner. Satisfied that their honor was avenged, the British withdrew. Later Ethiopian emperors kept up the program of reform and modernization.

Aswan (AS-wahn)

Ismail (is-MAH-eel)   **Téwodros** (tay-WOH-druhs)
Yohannes (yoh-HAHN-nehs)   **Menelik** (MEN-uh-lik)

Téwodros's Mighty Cannon   Like other modernizers in the nineteenth century, Emperor Téwodros of Ethiopia sought to reform his military forces. In 1861 he forced resident European missionaries and craftsmen to build guns and cannon, including this 7-ton behemoth nicknamed "Sebastapol" after the Black Sea port that had been the center of the Crimean War. It took five hundred men to haul the cannon across Ethiopia's hilly terrain.   (From Hormuzd Rassam, *Narrative of the British Mission to Theodore, King of Abyssinia, II*, London 1869, John Murray)

European Penetration

More lasting than Britain's punitive invasion of Ethiopia was France's conquest of Algeria, a move that anticipated the general European "scramble" for Africa after 1870. Equally pregnant with future meaning was the Europeans' exploration of the inland parts of Africa in the middle decades of the century.

Long an exporter of grain and olive oil to France, the North African state of Algeria had even supplied Napoleon with grain for his 1798 invasion of Egypt. The failure of French governments to repay this debt led to many disputes between Algeria and France and eventually to a severing of diplomatic relations in 1827 after the ruler of Algeria, annoyed with the French ambassador, allegedly struck him with a fly whisk. Three years later an unpopular French government, hoping to stir French

nationalism with an easy overseas victory, attacked Algeria on the pretext of avenging this insult.

The invasion of 1830 proved a costly mistake. The French government was soon overthrown, but the war in Algeria dragged on for eighteen years. The attack by an alien Christian power united the Algerians behind 'Abd al-Qadir°, a gifted and resourceful Muslim holy man. To achieve victory, the French built up an army of over 100,000 that broke Algerian resistance by destroying farm animals and crops and massacring villagers by the tens of thousands. After 'Abd al-Qadir was captured and exiled in 1847, the resistance movement fragmented, but the French occupiers faced resistance in the mountains for another thirty years. Poor European settlers,

---

'Abd al-Qadir (AHB-dahl-KAH-deer)

who rushed in to take possession of Algeria's rich coastlands, numbered 130,000 by 1871.

Meanwhile, a more peaceful European intrusion was penetrating Africa's geographical secrets. Small expeditions of adventurous explorers, using their own funds or financed by private geographical societies, were seeking to uncover the mysteries of inner Africa that had eluded Europeans for four centuries. Besides discovering more about the course of Africa's mighty rivers, these explorers wished to assess the continent's mineral wealth or convert the African millions to Christianity.

Many of the explorers were concerned with tracing the course of Africa's great rivers. Explorers learned in 1795 that the Niger River in West Africa flowed from west to east (not the other way, as had often been supposed) and in 1830 that the great morass of small streams entering the Gulf of Guinea was in fact the Niger Delta.

The north-flowing Nile, whose annual floods made Egypt bloom, similarly attracted explorers bent on finding the headwaters of the world's longest river. In 1770 Lake Tana in Ethiopia was established as a major source, and in 1861–1862 Lake Victoria (named for the British sovereign) was found to be the other main source.

In contrast to the heavily financed expeditions with hundreds of African porters that searched the Nile, the Scottish missionary David Livingstone (1813–1873) organized modest treks through southern and Central Africa. The missionary doctor's primary goal was to scout out locations for Christian missions, but he was also highly influential in tracing the course of the Zambezi River between 1853 and 1856. He named its greatest waterfall for the British monarch Queen Victoria. Livingstone also traced the course of the upper Congo River, where in 1871 he was met by the Welsh-American journalist Henry Morton Stanley (1841–1904) on a publicity-motivated search for the "lost" missionary doctor. On an expedition from 1874 to 1877, Stanley descended the Congo River to its mouth.

One of the most remarkable features of the explorers' experiences in Africa was their ability to move unmolested from place to place. The strangers were seldom harmed without provocation. Stanley preferred large expeditions that fought their way across the continent, but Livingstone's modest expeditions, which posed no threat to anyone, regularly received warm hospitality.

Abolition and Legitimate Trade

No sooner was the mouth of the Niger River discovered than eager entrepreneurs began to send expeditions up the river to scout out its potential for trade. Along much of coastal West Africa, commercial relations with Europeans remained dominant between 1750 and 1870. The value of trade between Africa and the other Atlantic continents more than doubled between the 1730s and the 1780s, then doubled again by 1870.[3] Before about 1825 the slave trade accounted for most of that increase, but thereafter African exports of vegetable oils, gold, ivory, and other goods drove overseas trade to new heights.

Europeans played a critical role in these changes in Africa's overseas trade. The Atlantic trade had arisen to serve the needs of the first European empires, and its transformation was linked to the ideas and industrial needs of Britain's new economy and empire.

One step in the Atlantic slave trade's extinction was the successful slave revolt in Saint Domingue in the 1790s (see Chapter 22). It ended slavery in the largest plantation colony in the West Indies, and elsewhere in the Americas it inspired slave revolts that were brutally repressed. As news of the slave revolts and their repression spread, humanitarians and religious reformers called for an end to the trade. Since it was widely believed that African-born slaves were more likely to rebel than were persons born into slavery, support for abolition of the slave trade was found even among Americans wanting to preserve slavery. In 1808 both Great Britain and the United States made carrying and importing slaves from Africa illegal for their citizens. Most other Western countries followed suit by 1850, but few enforced abolition with the vigor of the British.

Once the world's greatest slave traders, the British became the most aggressive abolitionists. Britain sent a naval patrol to enforce the ban along the African coast and negotiated treaties allowing the patrol to search other nations' vessels suspected of carrying slaves. During the half-century after 1815, Britain spent some $60 million (£12 million) to end the slave trade, a sum equal to the profits British slave traders had made in the fifty years before 1808.

Although British patrols captured 1,635 slave ships and liberated over 160,000 enslaved Africans, the trade proved difficult to stop. Cuba and Brazil continued to import huge numbers of slaves, which drove prices up and persuaded some African rulers and merchants to continue to sell slaves and to help foreign slavers evade the British patrols. After British patrols quashed the slave trade along the Gold Coast, the powerful king of Asante° even tried to persuade a British official in 1820 that reopening the trade would be to their mutual profit. Because the slave trade moved to other parts of Africa, the trans-Atlantic slave trade did not end until 1867.

Asante (uh-SHAHN-tee)

The demand for slaves in the Americas claimed the lives and endangered the safety of untold numbers of Africans, but the trade also satisfied other Africans' desires for the cloth, metals, and other goods that European traders brought in return. To continue their access to those imports, Africans expanded their **"legitimate" trade** (exports other than slaves). They revived old exports or developed new ones as the Atlantic slave trade was shut down. On the Gold Coast, for example, annual exports of gold climbed to nearly 25,000 ounces (750 kilograms) in the 1840s and 1850s, compared to 10,000 ounces (300 kilograms) in the 1790s.

The most successful of the new exports from West Africa was palm oil, a vegetable oil used by British manufacturers for soap, candles, and lubricants. Though still a major source of slaves until the mid-1830s, the trading states of the Niger Delta simultaneously emerged as the premier exporters of palm oil. In inland forests men climbed tall oil palms and cut down large palm-nut clusters, which women pounded to extract the thick oil. Coastal African traders bought the palm oil at inland markets and delivered it to European ships at the coast.

The dramatic increase in palm-oil exports—from a few hundred tons at the beginning of the century to tens of thousands of tons by midcentury—did not require any new technology, but it did alter the social structure of the coastal trading communities. Coastal traders grew rich and used their wealth to buy large numbers of male slaves to paddle the giant dugout canoes that transported palm oil from inland markets along the narrow delta creeks to the trading ports. Niger Delta slavery could be as harsh and brutal as slavery on New World plantations, but it offered some male and female slaves a chance to gain wealth and power. Some female slaves who married big traders exercised great authority over junior members of trading households. Male slaves who supervised canoe fleets were well compensated, and a few even became wealthy enough to take over the leadership of the coastal "canoe houses" (companies). The most famous, known as "Jaja" (ca. 1821–1891), rose from canoe slave to become the head of a major canoe house. In 1869, to escape discrimination by free-born Africans, he founded the new port of Opobo, which he ruled as king. In the 1870s Jaja of Opobo was the greatest palm-oil trader in the Niger Delta.

Another effect of the suppression of the slave trade was the spread of Western cultural influences in West Africa. To serve as a base for their anti-slave-trade naval squadron, the British had taken over the small colony of Sierra Leone° in 1808. Over the next several years,

Sierra Leone (see-ER-uh lee-OWN)

130,000 men, women, and children taken from "captured" vessels were liberated in Sierra Leone. Christian missionaries helped settle these impoverished and dispirited **recaptives** in and around Freetown, the capital. In time the mission churches and schools made many willing converts among such men and women.

Sierra Leone's schools also produced a number of distinguished graduates. For example, Samuel Adjai

King Jaja of Opobo This talented man rose from slavery in the Niger Delta port of Bonny to head one of the town's major palm-oil trading firms, the Anna Pepple House, in 1863. Six years later, Jaja founded and ruled his own trading port of Opobo. (Reproduced from *West Africa: An Introduction to Its History,* by Michael Crowder, by courtesy of the publishers, Addison Wesley Longman)

Crowther (1808–1891), freed as a youth from a slave ship by the British squadron in 1821, became the first Anglican bishop in West Africa in 1864, administering a pioneering diocese along the lower Niger River. James Africanus Horton (1835–1882), the son of slaves liberated in Sierra Leone, became a doctor and the author of many studies of West Africa.

Other Western cultural influences came from people of African birth or descent returning to their ancestral homeland. In 1821, to the south of Sierra Leone, free black Americans began a settlement that grew into the Republic of Liberia, a place of liberty at a time when slavery was legal and flourishing in the United States. After their emancipation in 1865 other African-Americans moved to Liberia. Emma White, a literate black woman from Kentucky, moved from Liberia to Opobo in 1875, where King Jaja employed her to write his commercial correspondence and run a school for his children. Edward Wilmot Blyden (1832–1912), born in the Danish West Indies and proud of his West African parentage, emigrated to Liberia in 1851 and became a professor of Greek and Latin (and later Arabic) at the fledgling Liberia College. Free blacks from Brazil and Cuba chartered ships to return to their West African homelands, bringing Roman Catholicism, architectural motifs, and clothing fashions from the New World. Although the number of Africans exposed to Western culture in 1870 was still small, this influence grew rapidly.

Secondary Empires in Eastern Africa

When British patrols hampered the slave trade in West Africa, slavers moved southward and then around the tip of southern Africa to eastern Africa. There the Atlantic slave trade joined an existing trade in slaves to the Islamic world that also was expanding. Two-thirds of the 1.2 million slaves exported from eastern Africa in the nineteenth century went to markets in North Africa and the Middle East; the other third went to plantations in the Americas and to European-controlled Indian Ocean islands.

Slavery also became more prominent within eastern Africa itself. Between 1800 and 1873 Arab and Swahili° owners of clove plantations along the coast purchased some 700,000 slaves from inland eastern Africa to do the labor-intensive work of harvesting this spice. The plantations were on Zanzibar Island and in neighboring territories belonging to the Sultanate of Oman, an Arabian kingdom on the Persian Gulf that had been expanding its control over the East African coast since 1698. The sultan had even moved his court to Zanzibar in 1840 to take better advantage of the burgeoning trade in cloves. Zanzibar also was an important center of slaves and ivory. Most of the ivory was shipped to India, where much of it was carved into decorative objects for European markets.

Ivory caravans came to the coast from hundreds of miles inland under the direction of African and Arab merchants. Some of these merchants brought large personal empires under their control by using capital they had borrowed from Indian bankers and modern firearms they had bought from Europeans and Americans. Some trading empires were created by inland Nyamwezi° traders, who worked closely with the indigenous Swahili and Arabs in Zanzibar to develop the long-distance caravan routes.

The largest of these personal empires, along the upper Congo River, was created by Tippu Tip (ca. 1830–1905), a trader from Zanzibar, who was Swahili and Nyamwezi on his father's side and Omani Arab on his mother's. Livingstone, Stanley, and other explorers who received Tippu Tip's gracious hospitality in the remote center of the continent praised their host's intelligence and refinement. On an 1876 visit, for example, Stanley recorded in his journal that Tippu Tip was "a remarkable man," a "picture of energy and strength" with "a fine intelligent face: almost courtier-like in his manner."

Tippu Tip also composed a detailed memoir of his adventures in the heart of Africa, written in the Swahili language of the coast. In it he mocked innocent African villagers for believing that his gunshots were thunder. As the memoir and other sources make clear, modern rifles not only felled countless elephants for their ivory tusks but also inflicted widespread devastation and misery on the people of this isolated area.

One can blame Tippu Tip and other Zanzibari traders, along with their master, the sultan of Oman, for the pillage and havoc in the once-peaceful center of Africa. However, the circle of responsibility was broader. Europeans supplied the weapons and were major consumers of ivory and cloves. For this reason histories have referred to the states carved out of eastern Africa by the sultans of Oman, Tippu Tip, and others as "secondary empires," in contrast to the empire that Britain was establishing directly. At the same time, British officials pressured the sultan of Oman into halting the Indian Ocean slave trade from Zanzibar in 1857 and ending the import of slaves into Zanzibar in 1873.

Swahili (swah-HEE-lee)

Nyamwezi (nn-nyahm-WAY-zee)

Egypt's expansion southward during the nineteenth century can also be considered a secondary empire. Muhammad Ali had pioneered the conquest of the upper Nile, in 1821 establishing a major base at Khartoum° that became the capital of Egyptian Sudan. A major reason for his invasion of Sudan was to secure slaves for his army so that more Egyptian peasants could be left free to grow cotton for export. From the 1840s unscrupulous traders of many origins, leading forces armed with European weapons, pushed south to the modern frontiers of Uganda and Zaire in search of cattle, ivory, and slaves. They set one African community against another and reaped profit from the devastation they sowed.

INDIA UNDER BRITISH RULE

The people of South Asia felt the impact of European commercial, cultural, and colonial expansion more immediately and profoundly than did the people of Africa. While Europeans were laying claim to only small parts of Africa between 1750 and 1870, nearly all of India (with three times the population of all of Africa) came under Britain's direct or indirect rule. During the 250 years after the founding of East India Company in 1600, British interests commandeered the colonies and trade of the Dutch, fought off French and Indian challenges, and picked up the pieces of the decaying Mughal° Empire. By 1763 the French were stymied; in 1795 the Dutch East India Company was dissolved; and in 1858 the last Mughal emperor was dethroned, leaving the vast subcontinent in British hands.

Company Men

As Mughal power weakened in the eighteenth century, Europeans were not the first outsiders to make a move. In 1739 Iranian armies defeated the Mughal forces, sacked Delhi, and returned home with vast amounts of booty. Indian states also took advantage of Mughal weakness to assert their independence. By midcentury, the Maratha° Confederation, a coalition of states in central India, controlled more land than the Mughals did (see Map 25.2). Also ruling their own powerful states were the **nawabs°** (a term used for Muslim princes who were deputies of the Mughal emperor, though in name only): the nawab of

Bengal in the northeast; the nawab of Arcot in the southeast, Haidar Ali (1722–1782)—the father of Tipu Sultan and ruler of the southwestern state of Mysore; and many others.

British, Dutch, and French companies were also eager to expand their profitable trade into India in the eighteenth century. Such far-flung European trading companies were speculative and risky ventures in 1750. Their success depended on hard-drinking and ambitious young "company men," who used hard bargaining, and hard fighting when necessary, to persuade Indian rulers to allow them to establish trading posts at strategic points along the coast. To protect their fortified warehouses from attack by other Europeans or by native states, the companies hired and trained Indian troops known as **sepoys°.** In divided India these private armies came to hold the balance of power.

In 1691 Great Britain's East India Company (EIC) had convinced the nawab of the large state of Bengal in northeast India to let the company establish a fortified outpost at the fishing port of Calcutta. A new nawab, pressing claims for additional tribute from the prospering port, overran the fort in 1756 and imprisoned a group of EIC men in a cell so small that many died of suffocation. To avenge their deaths in this "Black Hole of Calcutta," a large EIC force from Madras, led by the young Robert Clive, overthrew the nawab. The weak Mughal emperor was persuaded to acknowledge the East India Company's right to rule Bengal in 1765. Fed by the tax revenues of Bengal as well as by profits from trade, the EIC was on its way. Calcutta grew into a city of 250,000 by 1788.

In southern India, Clive had used EIC forces from Madras to secure victory for the British Indian candidate for nawab of Arcot during the Seven Years War (1756–1763), thereby gaining an advantage over French traders who had supported the loser. The defeat of Tipu Sultan of Mysore at the end of the century (described at the start of the chapter) secured south India for the company and prevented a French resurgence.

Along with Calcutta and Madras, the third major center of British power in India was Bombay, on the western coast. There, after a long series of contests with Maratha Confederation rulers, the East India Company gained a decisive advantage in 1818, annexing large territories to form the core of what was called the "Bombay Presidency." Some states were taken over completely, as Bengal had been, but very many others remained in the hands of local princes who accepted the political control of the company.

Khartoum (khar-TOOM) **Mughal** (MOO-guhl)
Maratha (muh-RAH-tuh) **nawab** (NAH-wab)

---

sepoy (SEE-poy)

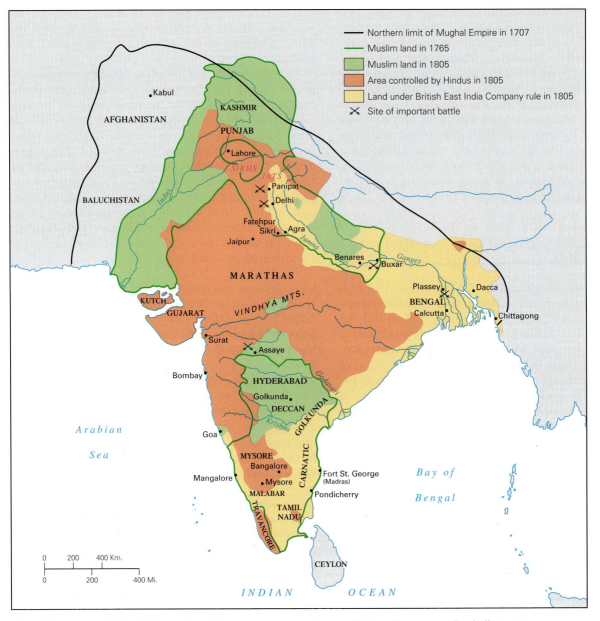

Map 25.2   India, 1707–1805   As Mughal power weakened during the eighteenth century, other Indian states and the East India Company expanded their territories.

Raj and Rebellion, 1818–1857

In 1818 the East India Company controlled an Empire with more people than in all of western Europe and fifty times the population of the colonies the British had lost in North America. One thrust of **British raj** (reign) was to remake India on a British model through administrative and social reform, economic development, and the introduction of new technology. But at the same time the company men—like the Mughals before them—had to temper their interference with Indian social and religious customs lest they provoke rebellion or lose the support of their Indian princely allies. For this reason and because of the complexity of the task of ruling such a vast empire, there were many inconsistencies in Britain's policies toward India.

The main policy was to create a powerful and efficient system of government. British rule before 1850 relied heavily on military power—170 sepoy regiments and 16 European regiments. Another policy very much in the interests of India's new rulers was to disarm approximately 2 million warriors who had served India's many states and turn them to civilian tasks, mostly cultivation. A third policy was to give freer rein to Christian missionaries eager to convert and uplift India's masses. Few converts were made, but the missionaries kept up steady pressure for social reforms.

Another key British policy was to substitute ownership of private property for India's complex and overlapping patterns of landholding. In Bengal this reform worked to the advantage of large landowners, but in Mysore the peasantry gained. Private ownership made it easier for the state to collect the taxes that were needed to pay for administration, the army, and economic reform.

Such policies of "westernization, Anglicization, and modernization," as they have been called, were only one side of British rule. The other side was the bolstering of "traditions"—both real and newly invented. In the name of tradition the Indian princes who ruled nearly half of British India were frequently endowed by their British overlords with greater power and splendor and longer tenure than their predecessors had ever had. Hindu and Muslim holy men were able to expand their "traditional" power over property and people far beyond what had been the case in earlier times. Princes, holy men, and other Indians frequently used claims of tradition to resist British rule as well as to turn it to their advantage. The British rulers themselves invented many "traditions"— including elaborate parades and displays—half borrowed from European royal pomp, half freely improvised from Mughal ceremonies.

The British and Indian elites danced sometimes in close partnership, sometimes in apparent opposition. But the ordinary people of India suffered. Women of every status, members of subordinate Hindu castes, the "untouchables" and "tribals" outside the caste system, and the poor generally experienced less benefit from the British reforms and much new oppression from the taxes and "traditions" that exalted their superiors' status.

The transformation of British India's economy was also doubled-edged. On the one hand, British raj created many new jobs as a result of the growth of internal and external trade and the expansion of agricultural production, such as in opium in Bengal—largely for export to China (see Chapter 26)—coffee in Ceylon (an island off the tip of India), and tea in Assam (a state in northeastern India). On the other hand, competition from cheap cotton goods produced in Britain's industrial mills drove many Indians out of the handicraft textile industry. In the eighteenth century India had been the world's greatest exporter of cotton textiles; in the nineteenth century India increasingly shipped raw cotton fiber to Britain.

Even the beneficial economic changes introduced under Britain rule were disruptive, and there were no safety nets for the needy. Displaced ruling elites, disgruntled religious traditionalists, and the economically dispossessed fomented almost constant local rebellions during the first half of the nineteenth century. British rulers readily handled these isolated uprisings, but they were more concerned about the continuing loyalty of Indian sepoys in the East India Company's army. The EIC employed 200,000 sepoys in 1857, along with 38,000 British officers. Armed with the latest rifles and disciplined in fighting methods, the sepoys had a potential for successful rebellion that other groups lacked.

In fact, discontent was growing among Indian soldiers. In the early decades of EIC rule, most sepoys came from Bengal, one of the first states the company had annexed. The Bengali sepoys resented the active recruitment of other ethnic groups into the army after 1848, such as Sikhs° from Punjab and Gurkhas from Nepal. Many high-caste Hindus objected to a new law in 1856 requiring new recruits to be available for service overseas in the growing Indian Ocean empire, for their religion prohibited ocean travel. The replacement of the standard military musket by the far more accurate Enfield rifle in 1857 also caused problems. Soldiers were ordered to use their teeth to tear open the ammunition cartridges, which were greased with animal fat. Hindus were offended by this order if the fat came from cattle, which they considered sacred. Muslims were offended if the fat came from pigs, which they considered unclean.

Although the cartridge-opening procedure was quickly changed, the initial discontent grew into rebellion by Hindu sepoys in May 1857. British troubles mushroomed when Muslim sepoys, peasants, and discontented elites joined in. The rebels asserted old traditions to challenge British authority: sepoy officers in Delhi proclaimed their loyalty to the Mughal emperor; others rallied behind the Maratha leader Nana Sahib. The rebellion was put down by March 1858, but it shook this piecemeal empire to its core.

Historians have attached different names and meanings to the events of 1857 and 1858. Concentrating on

---

Sikh (seek)

the technical fact that the uprising was an unlawful action by soldiers, nineteenth-century British historians labeled it the **"Sepoy Rebellion"** or the "Mutiny," and these names are still commonly used. Seeing in these events the beginnings of the later movement for independence, some modern Indian historians have termed it the "Revolution of 1857." In reality, it was much more than a simple mutiny, because it involved more than soldiers, but it was not yet a nationalist revolution, for the rebels' sense of a common Indian national identity was weak.

Political Reform and Industrial Impact

Whatever it is called, the rebellion of 1857–1858 was a turning point in the history of modern India. Some say it marks the beginning of modern India. In its wake Indians gained a new centralized government, entered a period of rapid economic growth, and began to develop a new national consciousness.

The changes in government were immediate. In 1858 Britain eliminated the last traces of Mughal and Company rule. In their place, a new secretary of state for India in London oversaw Indian policy, and a new government-general in Delhi acted as the British monarch's viceroy on the spot. A proclamation by Queen Victoria in November 1858 guaranteed all Indians equal protection of the law and the freedom to practice their religions and social customs; it also assured Indian princes that so long as they were loyal to the queen British India would respect their control of territories and "their rights, dignity and honour."[4]

British rule continued to emphasize both tradition and reform after 1857. At the top, the British viceroys lived in enormous palaces amid hundreds of servants and gaudy displays of luxury meant to convince Indians that the British viceroys were legitimate successors to the Mughal emperors. They treated the quasi-independent Indian princes with elaborate ceremonial courtesy and maintained them in splendor. When Queen Victoria was proclaimed "Empress of India" in 1877 and periodically thereafter, the viceroys put on great pageants known as **durbars.** The most elaborate was the durbar at Delhi in 1902–1903 to celebrate the coronation of King Edward VII, at which Viceroy Lord Curzon honored himself with a 101-gun salute and a parade of 34,000 troops in front of 50 princes and 173,000 visitors (see Diversity and Dominance: Ceremonials of Imperial Domination).

Behind the pomp and glitter, a powerful and efficient bureaucracy controlled the Indian masses. Members of the elite **Indian Civil Service** (ICS), mostly graduates of Oxford and Cambridge Universities, held the senior administrative and judicial posts. Numbering only a thousand at the end of the nineteenth century, these men visited the villages in their districts, heard lawsuits and complaints, and passed judgments. Beneath them were a far greater number of Indian officials and employees. Recruitment into the ICS was by open examinations. In theory any British subject could take these exams. But they were given in England, so in practice the system worked to exclude Indians. In 1870 only one Indian was a member of the ICS. Subsequent reforms by Viceroy Lord Lytton led to fifty-seven Indian appointments by 1887, but there the process stalled.

The key reason qualified Indians were denied entry into the upper administration of their country was the racist contempt most British officials felt for the people they ruled. When he became commander-in-chief of the Indian army in 1892, Lord Kitchener declared:

> It is this consciousness of the inherent superiority of the European which had won for us India. However well educated and clever a native may be, and however brave he may have proved himself, I believe that no rank we can bestow on him would cause him to be considered an equal of the British officer.

A second transformation of India after 1857 resulted from involvement with industrial Britain. The government invested millions of pounds sterling in harbors, cities, irrigation canals, and other public works. British interests felled forests to make way for tea plantations, persuaded Indian farmers to grow cotton and jute for export, and created great irrigation systems to alleviate the famines that periodically decimated whole provinces. As a result, India's trade expanded rapidly.

Most of the exports were agricultural commodities for processing elsewhere: cotton fiber, opium, tea, silk, and sugar. In return India imported manufactured goods from Britain, including the flood of machine-made cotton textiles that severely undercut Indian hand-loom weavers. The effects on individual Indians varied enormously. Some women found new jobs, though at very low pay, on plantations or in the growing cities, where prostitution flourished. Others struggled to hold families together or ran away from abusive husbands. Everywhere in India poverty remained the norm.

The Indian government also promoted the introduction of new technologies into India not long after their appearance in Britain. Earlier in the century there were steamboats on the rivers and a massive program of canal building for irrigation. Beginning in the 1840s a

Delhi Durbar, January 1, 1903   The parade of Indian princes on ornately decorated elephants and accompanied by retainers fostered their sense of belonging to the vast empire of India that British rule had created. The durbar was meant to evoke the glories of India's earlier empires, but many of the details and ceremonies were nineteenth-century creations.   (British Empire and Commonwealth Museum, Bristol, UK/The Bridgeman Art Library)

railroad boom (paid for out of government revenues) gave India its first national transportation network, followed shortly by telegraph lines. Indeed, in 1870 India had the greatest rail network in Asia and the fifth largest in the world. Originally designed to serve British commerce, the railroads were owned by British companies, constructed with British rails and equipment, and paid dividends to British investors. Ninety-nine percent of the railroad employees were Indians, but Europeans occupied all the top positions—"like a thin film of oil on top of a glass of water, resting upon but hardly mixing with [those] below," as one official report put it.

Although some Indians opposed the railroads at first because the trains mixed people of different castes, faiths, and sexes, the Indian people took to rail travel with great enthusiasm. Indians rode trains on business, on pilgrimage, and in search of work. In 1870 over 18 million passengers traveled along the network's 4,775 miles (7,685 kilometers) of track, and

more than a half-million messages were sent up and down the 14,000 miles (22,500 kilometers) of telegraph wire. By 1900 India's trains were carrying 188 million passengers a year.

But the freer movement of Indian pilgrims and the flood of poor Indians into the cities also promoted the spread of cholera°, a disease transmitted through water contaminated by human feces. Cholera deaths rose rapidly during the nineteenth century, and eventually the disease spread to Europe. In many Indian minds *kala mari* ("the black death") was a divine punishment for failing to prevent the British takeover. This chastisement also fell heavily on British residents, who died in large numbers. In 1867 officials demonstrated the close connection between cholera and pilgrims who bathed in and drank from sacred pools and rivers. The installation of a new sewerage system (1865) and a filtered water

cholera (KAHL-uhr-uh)

DIVERSITY AND DOMINANCE

CEREMONIALS OF IMPERIAL DOMINATION

This letter to Queen Victoria from Edward Robert Bulwer-Lytton, the Earl of Lytton and the viceroy of India, describes the elaborate durbar that the government of India staged in 1876 in anticipation of her being named "Empress of India." It highlights the effects these ceremonies had on the Indian princes who governed many parts of India as agents ("feudatories") of the British or as independent rulers.

British India's power rested on the threat of military force, but the letter points up how much it also depended on cultivating the allegiance of powerful Indian rulers. For their part, as the letter suggests, such rulers were impressed with such displays of majesty and organization and found much to be gained from granting the British their support.

The day before yesterday (December 23), I arrived, with Lady Lytton and all my staff at Delhi. . . . I was received at the [railroad] station by all the native chiefs and princes, and, . . . after shaking hands . . . , I immediately mounted my elephant, accompanied by Lady Lytton, our two little girls following us on another elephant. The procession through Delhi to the camp . . . lasted upwards of three hours. . . . The streets were lined for many miles with troops; those of the native princes being brigaded with those of your Majesty. The crowd along the way, behind the troops, was dense, and apparently enthusiastic; the windows, walls, and housetops being thronged with natives, who salaamed, and Europeans, who cheered as we passed along. . . .

My reception by the native princes at the station was most cordial. The Maharaja of Jeypore informed Sir John Strachey that India had never seen such a gathering as this, in which not only all the great native princes (many of whom have never met before), but also chiefs and envoys from Khelat, Burmah, Siam, and the remotest parts of the East, are assembled to do homage to your Majesty. . . .

On Tuesday (December 26) from 10 A.M. till past 7 P.M., I was, without a moment's intermission, occupied in receiving visits from native chiefs, and bestowing on those entitled to them the banners, medals, and other honours given by your Majesty. The durbar, which lasted all day and long after dark, was most successful. . . . Your Majesty's portrait, which was placed over the Viceregal throne in the great durbar tent,

was thought by all to be an excellent likeness of your Majesty. The native chiefs examined it with special interest.

On Wednesday, the 27th, I received visits from native chiefs, as before, from 10 A.M. til 1 P.M., and from 1:30 P.M. to 7:30 P.M., was passed in returning visits. I forgot to mention that on Tuesday and Wednesday evenings I gave great State dinners to the Governors of Bombay and Madras. Every subsequent evening of my stay at Delhi was similarly occupied by state banquets and receptions [for officials, foreign dignitaries, and] many distinguished natives. After dinner on Thursday, I held a levee [reception], which lasted till one o'clock at night, and is said to have been attended by 2,500 persons—the largest, I believe, ever held by any Viceroy or Governor-General in India. . . .

The satisfactory and cordial assurances received from [the ruler of] Kashmir are, perhaps, less important, because his loyalty was previously assumed. But your Majesty will, perhaps, allow me to mention, in connection with the name of this prince, one little circumstance which appears to me very illustrative of the effect which the assemblage has had on him and others. In the first interviews which took place months ago between myself and Kashmir, which resulted in my securing his assent to the appointment of a British officer at Gilgit, I noticed that, though perfectly courteous, he was extremely mistrustful of the British Government and myself. He seemed to think that every word I had said to him must have a hidden meaning against which he was bound to be on his guard. During our negotiations he carefully kept all his councillors round him, and he referred to them before answering any question I put to him, and, although he finally agreed to my proposals, he did so with obvious reluctance and suspicion, after taking a night to think them over. On the day following the Imperial assemblage, I had another private interview with Kashmir for the settlement of some further details. His whole manner and language on this last occasion were strikingly different. [He said:] "I am now convinced that you mean nothing that is not for the good of me and mine. Our interests are identical with those of the empire. Give me your orders and they shall be obeyed."

I have already mentioned to your Majesty that one of the sons of Kashmir acted as my page at the assemblage. I can truly affirm that all the native princes, great and small, with whom I was previously acquainted vied with each other in doing honor to the occasion, and I sincerely believe that this great gathering has also enabled me to establish the most cordial and confidential personal relations with a great many others whom I then met for the first time.

. . . If the vast number of persons collected together at Delhi, and all almost entirely under canvas, be fairly taken into consideration—a number alluding the highest executive officers of your Majesty's administration from every part of India, each with his own personal staff; all the members of my own Council, with their wives and families, who were entertained as the Viceroy's personal guests; all the representatives of the Press, native and European; upwards of 15,000 British troops, besides about 450 native princes and nobles, each with a following of from 2 to 500 attendants; the foreign ambassadors with their suites; the foreign consuls; a large number of the rudest and most unmanageable transfrontier chieftains with their horses and camels, &c.; and then an incalculably large concourse of private persons attracted by curiosity from every corner of the country—I say if all this be fairly remembered, no candid person will, I think, deny that to bring together, lodge, and feed so vast a crowd without a single case of sickness, or a single accident due to defective arrangements, without a moment's confusion or an hour's failure in the provision of supplies, and then to have sent them all away satisfied and loud in their expressions of gratitude for the munificent hospitality with which they had been entertained (at an expenditure of public money scrupulously moderate), was an achievement highly creditable to all concerned in carrying it out. Sir Dinkur Rao (Sindiah's great Minister) said to one of my colleagues: "If any man would understand why it is that the English are, and must necessarily remain, the masters of India, he need only go up to the Flagstaff Tower, and look down upon this marvellous camp. Let him notice the method, the order, the cleanliness, the discipline, the perfection of its whole organisation, and he will recognise in it at once the epitome of every title to command and govern which one race can possess over others." This anecdote reminds me of another which may perhaps please your Majesty. [The ruler of] Holkar said to me when I took leave of him: "India has been till now a vast heap of stones, some of them big, some of them small. Now the house is built, and from roof to basement each stone of it is in the right place."

The Khan of Khelat and his wild Sirdars were, I think, the chief objects of curiosity and interest to our Europeans. . . . On the Khan himself and all his Sirdars, the assemblage seems to have made an impression more profound even than I had anticipated. Less than a year ago they were all at war with each other, but they have left Delhi with mutual embraces, and a very salutary conviction that the Power they witnessed there is resolved that they shall henceforth keep the peace and not disturb its frontiers with their squabbles.

The Khan asked to have a banner given to him. It was explained to His Highness that banners were only given to your Majesty's feudatories, and that he, being an independent prince, could not receive one without compromising his independence. He replied: "But I am a feudatory of the Empress, a feudatory quite as loyal and obedient as any other. I don't want to be an independent prince, and I do want to have my banner like all the rest. Pray let me have it."

I anticipate an excellent effect by and by from the impressions which the yet wilder envoys and Sirdars of Chitral and Yassin will carry with them from Delhi, and propagate throughout that important part of our frontier where the very existence of the British Government has hitherto been almost unrealised, except as that of a very weak power, popularly supposed in Kafristan to be exceedingly afraid of Russia. Two Burmese noblemen, from the remotest part of Burmah, said to me: "The King of Burmah fancies he is the greatest prince upon earth. When we go back, we shall tell all his people that he is nobody. Never since the world began has there been in it such a power as we have witnessed here." These Burmese are writing a journal or memoir of their impressions and experiences at Delhi, of which they have promised me a copy. I have no doubt it will be very curious and amusing. Kashmir and some other native princes have expressed a wish to present your Majesty with an imperial crown of great value; but as each insists upon it that the crown shall be exclusively his own gift, I have discouraged an idea which, if carried out, would embarrass your Majesty with the gift of half a dozen different crowns, and probably provoke bitter heart-burnings amongst the donors. The Rajpootana Chiefs talk of erecting a marble statue of the Empress on the spot where the assemblage was held; native noblemen have already intimated and several to me their intention of building bridges, or other public works, and founding charities, to be called after your Majesty in commemoration of the event.

QUESTIONS FOR ANALYSIS

1. What is significant about the fact that Lord Lytton and his family arrived in Delhi by train and then chose to move through the city on elephants?

2. What impression did the viceroy intend to create in the minds of the Indian dignitaries by assembling so many of them together and bestowing banners, medals, and honors on them?

3. What might account for some Indians' remarkable changes of attitude toward the viceroy and the empire? How differently might a member of the Indian middle class or an unemployed weaver have reacted?

Source: Lady Betty Balfour, The History of Lord Lytton's Indian Administration, 1876 to 1880 (London: Longmans, Green, and Co., 1899), 116–125.

supply (1869) in Calcutta dramatically reduced cholera deaths there. Similar measures in Bombay and Madras also led to great reductions, but most Indians lived in small villages where famine and lack of sanitation kept cholera deaths high. In 1900 an extraordinary four out of every thousand residents of British India died of cholera. Sanitary improvements lowered the rate later in the twentieth century.

Rising Indian Nationalism

Ironically, both the successes and the failures of British India stimulated the development of Indian nationalism. Stung by the inability of the rebellion of 1857 to overthrow British rule, some thoughtful Indians began to argue that the only way for Indians to regain control of their destiny was to reduce their country's social and ethnic divisions and promote Pan-Indian nationalism.

Individuals such as Rammohun Roy (1772–1833) had promoted development along these lines a generation earlier. A Western-educated Bengali from a Brahmin family, Roy was a successful administrator for the East India Company and a thoughtful student of comparative religion. His Brahmo Samaj° (Divine Society), founded in 1828, attracted Indians who sought to reconcile the values they found in the West with the ancient religious traditions of India. They supported efforts to reform some Hindu customs, including the restrictions on widows and the practice of child marriage. They advocated reforming the caste system, encouraged a monotheistic form of Hinduism, and urged a return to the founding principles of the Upanishads, ancient sacred writings of Hinduism.

Roy and his supporters had backed earlier British efforts to reform or ban some practices they found repugnant. Widow burning (*sati*°) was outlawed in 1829 and slavery in 1843. Reformers sought to correct other abuses of women: prohibitions against widows remarrying were revoked in 1856, and female infanticide was made a crime in 1870.

Although Brahmo Samaj remained an influential movement after the rebellion of 1857, many Indian intellectuals turned to Western secular values and nationalism as the way to reclaim India for its people. In this process the spread of Western education played an important role. Roy had studied both Indian and Western subjects, mastering ten languages in the process, and helped found the Hindu College in Calcutta in 1816. Other Western-curriculum schools quickly followed, in-

cluding Bethune College in Calcutta, the first secular school for Indian women, in 1849. European and American missionaries played a prominent role in the spread of Western education. In 1870 there were 790,000 Indians in over 24,000 elementary and secondary schools, and India's three universities (established in 1857) awarded 345 degrees. Graduates of these schools articulated a new Pan-Indian nationalism that transcended regional and religious differences.

Rammohun Roy This romanic portrait of the Indian reformer emphasizes his scholarly accomplishments and India's traditional architecture and natural beauty. (Bristol City Museum and Art Gallery, UK/The Bridgemen Art Library)

Bramo Samaj (BRAH-moh suh-MAHJ)   **sati** (suh-TEE)

Many of the new nationalists came from the Indian middle class, which had prospered from the increase of trade and manufacturing. Such educated and ambitious people were angered by the obstacles that British rules and prejudices put in the way of their advancement. Hoping to increase their influence and improve their employment opportunities in the Indian government, they convened the first **Indian National Congress** in 1885. The members sought a larger role for Indians in the Civil Service. They also called for reductions in military expenditures, which consumed 40 percent of the government's budget, so that more could be spent on alleviating the poverty of the Indian masses. The Indian National Congress promoted unity among the country's many religions and social groups, but most early members were upper-caste Western-educated Hindus and Parsis (members of a Zoroastrian religious sect descended from Persians). The Congress effectively voiced the opinions of elite Indians, but until it attracted the support of the masses, it could not hope to challenge British rule.

BRITAIN'S EASTERN EMPIRE

In 1750 Britain's empire was centered on slave-based plantation and settler colonies in the Americas. A century later its main focus was on commercial networks and colonies in the East. In 1750 the French and Dutch were also serious contenders for global dominion. A century later they had been eclipsed by the British colossus that was straddling the world.

Several distinct changes facilitated the expansion and transformation of Britain's overseas empire. A string of military victories pushed aside other rivals for overseas trade and colonies; new policies favored free trade over mercantilism; and changes in shipbuilding techniques increased the speed and volume of maritime commerce. Linked to these changes were new European settlements in southern Africa, Australia, and New Zealand and the growth of a new long-distance trade in indentured labor.

Colonies and Commerce

As the story of Tipu Sultan told at the beginning of this chapter illustrates, France was still a serious rival for dominion in the Indian Ocean at the end of the eighteenth century. However, defeats in the wars of the French Revolution (see Chapter 22) ended Napoleon's dream of restoring French dominance overseas. The wars also dismantled much

of the Netherlands' Indian Ocean empire. When French armies occupied the Netherlands, the Dutch ruler, who had fled to Britain in January 1795, authorized the British to take over Dutch possessions overseas in order to keep them out of French hands. During 1795 and 1796 British forces quickly occupied the Cape Colony at the tip of southern Africa, the strategic Dutch port of Malacca on the strait between the Indian Ocean and the South China Sea, and the island of Ceylon (see Map 25.3).

Then the British occupied Dutch Guiana° and Trinidad in the southern Caribbean. In 1811 they even seized the island of Java, the center of the Netherlands' East Indian empire. British forces had also attacked French possessions, gaining control of the islands of Mauritius° and Réunion in the southwestern Indian Ocean. At the end of the Napoleonic Wars in 1814, Britain returned Java to the Dutch and Réunion to the French but kept the Cape Colony, British Guiana (once part of Dutch Guiana), Trinidad, Ceylon, Malacca, and Mauritius.

The Cape Colony was valuable because of Cape Town's strategic importance as a supply station for ships making the long voyages between Britain and India. With the port city came some twenty thousand descendants of earlier Dutch and French settlers who occupied far-flung farms and ranches in its hinterland. Despite their European origins, these people thought of themselves as permanent residents of Africa and were beginning to refer to themselves as "Afrikaners°" ("Africans" in their dialect of Dutch). British governors prohibited any expansion of the white settler frontier because such expansion invariably led to wars with indigenous Africans. This decision, along with the imposition of laws protecting African rights within Cape Colony (including the emancipation of slaves in 1834), alienated many Afrikaners.

Between 1836 and 1839 parties of Afrikaners embarked on a "Great Trek," leaving British-ruled Cape Colony for the fertile high *veld* (plateau) to the north that two decades of Zulu wars had depopulated. The Great Trek led to the foundation of three new settler colonies in southern Africa by 1850: the Afrikaners' Orange Free State and Transvaal on the high veld and the British colony of Natal on the Indian Ocean coast. Although firearms enabled the settlers to win some important battles against the Zulu and other Africans, they were still a tiny minority surrounded by the populous and powerful independent African kingdoms that had grown up at the beginning of the century. A few thousand British settlers came to Natal and the Cape Colony by midcentury, but

---

Guiana (ghee-AH-nuh)   **Mauritius** (moh-RIHS-uhs)   **Afrikaner** (af-rih-KAHN-uhr)

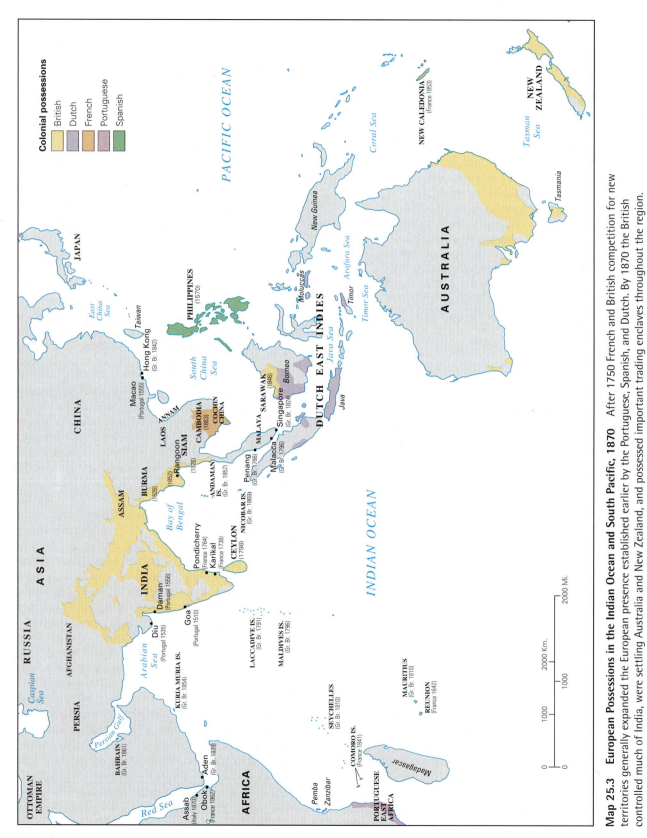

Map 25.3   European Possessions in the Indian Ocean and South Pacific, 1870   After 1750 French and British competition for new territories generally expanded the European presence established earlier by the Portuguese, Spanish, and Dutch. By 1870 the British controlled much of India, were settling Australia and New Zealand, and possessed important trading enclaves throughout the region.

these colonies were important to Britain only as stopovers for shipping between Britain and British India.

Meanwhile, another strategic British outpost was being established in Southeast Asia. One prong of the advance was led by Thomas Stamford Raffles, who had governed Java during the period of British occupation from 1811 to 1814. After Java's return to the Dutch, Raffles helped the British East India Company establish a new free port at Singapore in 1824, on the site of a small Malay fishing village with a superb harbor. By attracting British merchants and Chinese businessmen and laborers, Singapore soon became the center of trade and shipping between the Indian Ocean and China. Along with Malacca and other possessions on the strait, Singapore formed the "Straits Settlements," which British India administered until 1867.

Further British expansion in Malaya (now Malaysia) did not occur until after 1874, but it came more quickly in neighboring Burma. Burma had emerged as a powerful kingdom by 1750, with plans for expansion. In 1785 Burma tried to annex neighboring territories of Siam (now Thailand) to the east, but a coalition of Thai leaders thwarted Burmese advances by 1802. Burma next attacked Assam to the west, but this action led to war with British India, which was concerned for the security of its own frontier with Assam. After a two-year war, India annexed Assam in 1826 and occupied two coastal provinces of northern Burma. As rice and timber trade from these provinces grew important, the occupation became permanent, and in 1852 British India annexed the port of Rangoon and the rest of coastal Burma.

Great Trek Aided by African Servants   The ox-drawn wagons of the Afrikaners struggled over the Drakensberg Mountains to the high plains in an effort to escape British control.   (Hulton Getty/Liaison)

Imperial Policies and Shipping

Through such piecemeal acquisitions, by 1870 Britain had added several dozen colonies to the twenty-six colonies it had in 1792, after the loss of the thirteen in North America (see Chapter 22). Nevertheless, historians usually portray Britain in this period as a reluctant empire builder, its leaders unwilling to acquire new outposts that could prove difficult and expensive to administer. This apparent contradiction is resolved by the recognition that the underlying goal of most British imperial expansion during these decades was trade rather than territory. Most of the new colonies were meant to serve as ports in the growing network of shipping that encircled the globe or as centers of production and distribution for those networks.

This new commercial expansion was closely tied to the needs of Britain's growing industrial economy and reflected a new philosophy of overseas trade. Rather than rebuilding the closed, mercantilist network of trade with its colonies, Britain sought to trade freely with all parts of the world. Free trade was also a wise policy in light of the independence of so many former colonies in the Americas (see Chapter 24).

Whether colonized or not, more and more African, Asian, and Pacific lands were being drawn into the commercial networks created by British expansion and industrialization. As was pointed out earlier, uncolonized parts of West Asia became major exporters to Britain of vegetable oils for industrial and domestic use and forest products for dyes and construction, while areas of eastern Africa free of European control exported ivory that ended up as piano keys and decorations in the elegant homes of the industrial middle class. From the far corners of the world came coffee, cocoa, and tea (along with sugar to sweeten them) for the tables of the new industrial classes in Britain and other parts of Europe, and indigo dyes and cotton fibers for their expanding textile factories.

In return, the factories of the industrialized nations supplied manufactured goods at very attractive prices. By the mid-nineteenth century a major part of their textile production was destined for overseas markets. Sales of cotton cloth to Africa increased 950 percent from the 1820s to the 1860s. British trade to India grew 350 percent between 1841 and 1870, while India's exports increased 400 percent. Trade with other regions also expanded rapidly. In most cases such trade benefited both sides, but there is no question that the industrial nations were the dominant partners.

A second impetus to global commercial expansion was the technological revolution in the construction of oceangoing ships under way in the nineteenth century. The middle decades of the century were the golden age of the sailing ship. Using iron to fasten timbers together permitted shipbuilders to construct much larger vessels. Merchant ships in the eighteenth century rarely exceeded 300 tons, but after 1850 swift American-built **clipper ships** of 2,000 tons were commonplace in the British merchant fleet. Huge canvas sails hung from tall masts made the streamlined clippers faster than earlier vessels. Ships from the East Indies or India had taken six months to reach Europe in the seventeenth century; after 1850 the new ships could complete the voyage in half that time.

This increase in size and speed lowered shipping costs and further stimulated maritime trade. The growth in size and numbers of ships increased the tonnage of British merchant shipping by 400 percent between 1778 and 1860. To extend the life of such ships in tropical lands, clippers intended for Eastern service generally were built of teak and other tropical hardwoods from new British colonies in South and Southeast Asia. Although tropical forests began to be cleared for rice and sugar plantations as well as for timbers, the effects on the environment and people of Southeast Asia came primarily after 1870.

Colonization of Australia and New Zealand

The development of new ships and shipping contributed to a third form of British rule in the once-remote South Pacific. British settlers displaced indigenous populations in the new colonies of Australia and New Zealand, just as they had done in North America. This differs from India, where Britain ruled numerous indigenous populations, and Singapore and Cape Town, which were outposts of a commercial empire.

Portuguese mariners had sighted the continent of Australia in the early seventeenth century, but it was too remote to be of much interest to Europeans. However, after the English adventurer Captain James Cook systematically explored New Zealand and the fertile eastern coast of Australia between 1769 and 1778, expanding

shipping networks brought in growing numbers of visitors and settlers.

At the time of Cook's visits Australia was the home of about 650,000 hunting-and-gathering people, whose Melanesian° ancestors had settled there some forty thousand years earlier. The two islands of New Zealand, lying 1,000 miles (1,600 kilometers) southeast of Australia, were inhabited by about 250,000 Maori°, who practiced hunting, fishing, and simple forms of agriculture, which their Polynesian ancestors had introduced around 1200 C.E. Because of their long isolation from the rest of humanity, the populations of Australia and New Zealand were as vulnerable as the Amerindians had been to unfamiliar diseases introduced by new overseas contacts. In the 1890s only 93,000 aboriginal Australians and 42,000 Maori survived. By then, British settler populations outnumbered and dominated the indigenous peoples.

The first permanent British settlers in Australia were 736 convicts, of whom 188 were women, sent into exile from British prisons in 1788. Over the next few decades, Australian penal colonies grew slowly and had only slight contact with the indigenous population, whom the British called "Aborigines." However, the discovery of gold in 1851 brought a flood of free European settlers (and some Chinese) and hastened the end of the penal colonies. When the gold rush subsided, government subsidies enabled tens of thousands of British settlers to settle "down under." Improved sailing ships made possible a voyage halfway around the world, although it still took more than three months to reach Australia from Britain. By 1860 Australia had a million immigrants, and the settler population doubled during the next fifteen years.

British settlers were drawn more slowly to New Zealand. Some of the first were temporary residents along the coast who slaughtered seals and exported seal pelts to Western countries to be made into men's felt hats. A single ship in 1806 took away sixty thousand sealskins. By the early 1820s overhunting had nearly exterminated the seal population. Special ships also hunted sperm whales extensively near New Zealand for their oil, used for lubrication, soap, and lamps; ambergris°, an ingredient in perfume; and bone, used in women's corsets (see Environment and Technology: Whaling). Military action that overcame Maori resistance, a brief gold rush, and the availability of faster ships and subsidized passages attracted more British immigrants after 1860. The colony especially courted women immigrants to offset

---

Melanesian (mel-uh-NEE-zhuhn)   **Maori** (MOW-ree [*ow* as in *cow*])   **ambergris** (AM-ber-grees)

Whaling

The rapid expansion of whaling aptly illustrates the growing power of technology over nature in this period. Many contemporaries, like many people today, were sickened by the killing of the planet's largest living mammals. American novelist Herman Melville captured the conflicting sentiments in his epic whaling story, *Moby Dick* (1851). One of his characters enthusiastically explains why the grisly and dangerous business existed:

> But, though the world scorns us as whale hunters, yet does it unwittingly pay us the profoundest homage; yea, an all abounding adoration! for almost all the tapers, lamps, and candles that burn around the globe, burn, as before so many shrines, to our glory!

Melville's character overstates the degree to which whale oil dominated illumination and does not mention its many other industrial uses. Neither does he describe the commercial importance of whalebone (baleen). For a time its use in corsets allowed fashionable women to achieve the hourglass shape that fashion dictated. Whalebone's use for umbrella stays, carriage springs, fishing rods, suitcase frames, combs, brushes, and many other items made it the plastic of its day.

New manufacturing technologies went hand in hand with new hunting technologies. The revolution in ship design enabled whalers from Europe and North America to extend the hunt into the southern oceans off New Zealand. By the nineteenth century whaling ships were armed with guns that shot a steel harpoon armed with vicious barbs deep into the whale. In the 1840s explosive charges on harpoon heads ensured the whale's immediate death. Yet, as this engraving of an expedition off New Zealand shows, flinging small harpoons from rowboats in the open sea continued to be part of the dangerous work.

Another century of extensive hunting devastated many whale species before international agreements finally limited the killing of these giant sea creatures.

South Pacific Whaling   One boat was swamped, but the hunters killed the huge whale.   (The Granger Collection, New York)

Asian Laborers in British Guiana The manager of the sugar estate reposes on the near end of the gallery of his house with the proprietor's attorney. At the other end of the gallery European overseers review the plantation's record books. In the yard cups of lifeblood are being drained from bound Chinese and Indian laborers. This allegorical drawing by a Chinese laborer represents the exploitation of Asian laborers by Europeans. (Boston Athenaeum)

the preponderance of single men. By the early 1880s fertile agricultural lands of this most distant frontier of the British Empire had a settler population of 500,000.

Britain encouraged the settlers in Australia and New Zealand to become self-governing, following the 1867 model that had formed the giant Dominion of Canada out of the very diverse and thinly settled colonies of British North America. In 1901 a unified Australia emerged from the federation of six separate colonies. New Zealand became a self-governing dominion in 1907.

Britain's policies toward its settler colonies in Canada and the South Pacific reflected a desire to avoid the conflicts that had led to the American Revolution in the eighteenth century. By gradually turning over governing power to the colonies' inhabitants, Britain accomplished three things. It satisfied the settlers' desire for greater control over their own territories; it muted demands for independence; and it made the colonial governments responsible for most of their own expenses. Indigenous peoples were outvoted by the settlers or even excluded from voting.

North American patterns also shaped the indigenous peoples' fate. An 1897 Australian law segregated the remaining Aborigines onto reservations, where they lacked the rights of Australian citizenship. The requirement that voters had to be able to read and write English kept Maori from voting in early New Zealand elections, but four seats in the lower house of the legislature were reserved for Maori from 1867.

In other ways the new settler colonies were more progressive. Australia developed very powerful trade unions, which improved the welfare of skilled and semi-skilled urban white male workers, promoted democratic values, and exercised considerable political clout. In New Zealand, where sheep raising was the main occupation, populist and progressive sentiments promoted the availability of land for the common person. Australia and New Zealand were also among the first states in the world to grant women the right to vote, beginning in 1894.

New Labor Migrations

Europeans were not the only people to transplant themselves overseas in the mid-nineteenth century. Between 1834 and 1870 many thousands of Indians, Chinese, and Africans responded to labor recruiters, especially to work overseas on sugar plantations. In the half-century after 1870 tens of thousands of Asians and Pacific Islanders made similar voyages.

In part these migrations were linked to the end of slavery. After their emancipation in British colonies in 1834, the freed men and women were no longer willing to put in the long hours they had been forced to work as slaves. When given full freedom of movement in 1839, many left the plantations. To compete successfully with sugar plantations in Cuba, Brazil, and the French Caribbean that were still using slave labor, British colonies had to recruit new laborers.

India's impoverished people seemed one obvious alternative. After planters on Mauritius successfully introduced Indian laborers, the Indian labor trade moved to the British Caribbean in 1838. In 1841 the British government also allowed Caribbean planters to recruit Africans whom British patrols had rescued from slave ships and liberated in Sierra Leone and elsewhere. By 1870 nearly 40,000 Africans had settled in British colonies, along with over a half-million Indians and over 18,000 Chinese. After the French and Dutch abolished slavery in 1848, their colonies also recruited over 150,000 new laborers from Asia and Africa.

Slavery was not abolished in Cuba until 1886, but the rising cost of slaves led the burgeoning sugar plantations to recruit 138,000 new laborers from China between 1847 and 1873. Indentured labor recruits also became the mainstay of new sugar plantations in places that had never known slave labor. After 1850 American planters in Hawaii recruited labor from China and Japan; British planters in Natal recruited from India; and those in Queensland (in northeastern Australia) relied on laborers from neighboring South Pacific islands.

Larger, faster ships made transporting laborers halfway around the world affordable, though voyages from Asia to the Caribbean still took an average of three months. Despite close regulation and supervision of shipboard conditions, the crowded accommodations encouraged the spread of cholera and other contagious diseases that took many migrants' lives.

All of these laborers served under **contracts of indenture,** which bound them to work for a specified period (usually from five to seven years) in return for free passage to their overseas destination. They were paid a small salary and were provided with housing, clothing, and medical care. Indian indentured laborers also received the right to a free passage home if they worked a second five-year contract. British Caribbean colonies required forty women to be recruited for every hundred men as a way to promote family life. So many Indians chose to stay in Mauritius, Trinidad, British Guiana, and Fiji that they constituted a third or more of the to-tal population of these colonies by the early twentieth century.

Although many early recruits from China and the Pacific Islands were kidnapped or otherwise coerced into leaving their homes, in most cases the new indentured migrants had much in common with contemporary emigrants from Europe (described in Chapter 23). Both groups chose to leave their homelands in hopes of improving their economic and social conditions. Both earned modest salaries. Many saved to bring money back when they returned home, or they used their earnings to buy land or to start a business in their new countries, where large numbers chose to remain. One major difference was that people recruited as indentured laborers were generally so much poorer than emigrants from Europe that they had to accept lower-paying jobs in less desirable areas because they could not pay their own way. However, it is also true that many European immigrants into distant places like Australia and New Zealand had their passages subsidized but did not have to sign a contract of indenture. This shows that racial and cultural preferences, not just economics, shaped the flow of labor into European colonies.

A person's decision to accept an indentured labor contract could also be shaped by political circumstances. In India disruption brought by British colonial policies and the suppression of the 1857 rebellion contributed significantly to people's desire to emigrate. Poverty, famine, and warfare had not been strangers in precolonial India. Nor were these causes of emigration absent in China and Japan (see Chapter 26).

The indentured labor trade reflected the unequal commercial and industrial power of the West, but it was not an entirely one-sided creation. The men and women who signed indentured contracts were trying to improve their lives by emigrating, and many succeeded. Whether for good or ill, more and more of the world's peoples saw their lives being influenced by the existence of Western colonies, Western ships, and Western markets.

CONCLUSION

What is the global significance of these complex political and economic changes in southern Asia, Africa, and the South Pacific? One perspective stresses the continuing exploitation of the weak by the strong, of African, Asian, and Pacific peoples by aggressive Europeans. In this view, the emergence of Britain as a dominant power in the Indian Ocean basin and South Pacific continues the European expansion that the

Portuguese and the Spanish pioneered and the Dutch took over. Likewise, Britain's control over the densely populated lands of South and Southeast Asia and over the less populated lands of Australia and New Zealand can be seen as a continuation of the conquest and colonization of the Americas.

From another perspective what was most important about this period was not the political and military strength of the Europeans but their growing domination of the world's commerce, especially through long-distance ocean shipping. In this view, like other Europeans, the British were drawn to Africa and southern Asia by a desire to obtain new materials.

However, Britain's commercial expansion in the nineteenth century was also the product of Easterners' demand for industrial manufactures. The growing exchanges could be mutually beneficial. African and Asian consumers found industrially produced goods far cheaper and sometimes better than the handicrafts they replaced or supplemented. Industrialization created new markets for African and Asian goods, as in the case of the vegetable-oil trade in West Africa or cotton in Egypt and India. There were also negative impacts, as in the case of the weavers of India and the damage to species of seals and whales.

Europeans' military and commercial strength did not reduce Africa, Asia, and the Pacific to mere appendages of Europe. While the balance of power shifted in the Europeans' favor between 1750 and 1870, other cultures were still vibrant and local initiatives often dominant. Islamic reform movements and the rise of the Zulu nation had greater significance for their respective regions of Africa than did Western forces. Despite some ominous concessions to European power, Southeast Asians were still largely in control of their own destinies. Even in India, most people's lives and beliefs showed more continuity with the past than the change due to British rule.

Finally, it must not be imagined that Asians and Africans were powerless in dealing with European expansion. The Indian princes who extracted concessions from the British in return for their cooperation and the Indians who rebelled against the raj both forced the system to accommodate their needs. Moreover, some Asians and Africans were beginning to use European education, technology, and methods to transform their own societies. Leaders in Egypt, India, and other lands, like those in Russia, the Ottoman Empire, China, and Japan—the subject of Chapter 26—were learning to challenge the power of the West on its own terms. In 1870 no one could say how long and how difficult that learning process would be, but Africans and Asians would continue to shape their own futures.

■ Key Terms

Zulu
Sokoto Caliphate
modernization
Muhammad Ali
"legitimate" trade
recaptives
nawab
sepoy
British raj
Sepoy Rebellion
durbar
Indian Civil Service
Indian National Congress
clipper ship
contract of indenture

■ Suggested Reading

Volumes 2 and 3 of *The Oxford History of the British Empire,* ed. William Roger Louis, (1998, 1999), are the most up-to-date global surveys of this period. Less Anglocentric in their interpretations are Immanuel Wallerstein's *The Modern World-System III: The Second Era of Great Expansion of the Capitalist World-Economy, 1730–1840s* (1989) and William Wodruff's *Impact of Western Man: A Study of Europe's Role in the World Economy, 1750–1960* (1982). Atlantic relations are well handled by David Eltis, *Economic Growth and the Ending of the Transatlantic Slave Trade* (1987). For the Indian Ocean basin see Sugata Bose, *The Indian Ocean Rim: An Inter-Regional Arena in the Age of Global Empire* (2003).

Roland Oliver and Anthony Atmore provide a brief introduction to Africa in *Africa Since 1800,* 4th ed. (1994). More advanced works are J. F. Ade Ajayi, ed., *UNESCO General History of Africa,* vol. 6, *Africa in the Nineteenth Century until the 1880s* (1989), and John E. Flint, ed., *The Cambridge History of Africa,* vol. 5, *From c. 1790 to c. 1870* (1976). Although specialized literature has refined some of their interpretations, the following are excellent introductions to their subjects: J. D. Omer-Cooper, *The Zulu Aftermath* (1966); Murray Last, *The Sokoto Caliphate* (1967); A. G. Hopkins, *An Economic History of West Africa* (1973); Robert W. July, *The Origins of Modern African Thought* (1967); and Robert I. Rotberg, ed., *Africa and Its Explorers: Motives, Methods, and Impact* (1970). For eastern and northeastern Africa see Norman R. Bennett, *Arab Versus European: War and Diplomacy in Nineteenth Century East Central Africa* (1985); P. J. Vatikiotis, *The History of Modern Egypt: From Muhammad Ali to Mubarak,* 4th ed. (1991); and, for the negative social impact of Egyptian modernization, Judith Tucker, "Decline of the Family Economy in Mid-Nineteenth-Century Egypt," *Arab Studies Quarterly 1* (1979): 245–271.

Very readable introductions to India in this period are Sugata Bose and Ayeshia Jalal, *Modern South India* (1998); Burton Stein, *A History of India* (1998); and Stanley Wolpert, *A New History of India,* 6th ed. (1999). More advanced treatments in the "New Cambridge History of India" series are P. J. Marshall, *Bengal: The British Bridgehead: Eastern India, 1740–1828* (1988); C. A. Bayly, *Indian Society and the Making of the British Empire* (1988); Sugata Bose, *Peasant Labour and Colonial Capital: Rural Bengal Since 1700* (1993); and Kenneth W. Jones, *Socio-Religious Reform Movements in British India* (1989). Environmental and technological perspectives on India are offered in the appropriate parts of Daniel Headrick, *The Tentacles of Progress: Technology Transfer in the Age of Imperialism, 1850–1940* (1988); Mashav Gadgil and Ramachandra Guha, *This Fissured Land: An Ecological History of India* (1992). For Tipu Sultan see Kate Brittlebank, *Tipu Sultan's Search for Legitimacy: Islam and Kingship in a Hindu Domain* (1997).

A good introduction to the complexities of Southeast Asian history is D. R. SarDesai, *Southeast Asia: Past and Present,* 2nd ed. (1989). More detail can be found in the appropriate chapters of Nicholas Tarling, ed., *The Cambridge History of South East Asia,* 2 vols. (1992). The second and third volumes of *The Oxford History of Australia,* ed. Geoffrey Bolton (1992, 1988), deal with the period covered by this chapter. A very readable multicultural and gendered perspective is provided by *Images of Australia,* ed. Gillian Whitlock and David Carter (1992). *The Oxford Illustrated History of New Zealand,* ed. Keith Sinclair (1990), provides a wide-ranging introduction to that nation.

For summaries of recent scholarship on the indentured labor trade see David Northrup, *Indentured Labor in the Age of Imperialism, 1834–1922* (1995), and Robin Cohen, ed., *The Cambridge Survey of World Migration,* part 3, "Asian Indentured and Colonial Migration" (1995).

An outstanding analysis of British whaling is Gordon Jackson's *The British Whaling Trade* (1978). Edouard A. Stackpole's *Whales & Destiny: The Rivalry Between America, France, and Britain for Control of the Southern Whale Fishery, 1785–1825* (1972) is more anecdotal.

■ Notes

1. Paul E. Lovejoy and Jan S. Hogendorn, *Slow Death for Slavery: The Course of Abolition in Northern Nigeria, 1897–1936* (New York: Cambridge University Press, 1993).
2. Quoted in P. J. Vatikiotis, *The History of Modern Egypt: From Muhammad Ali to Mubarak,* 4th ed. (Baltimore: Johns Hopkins University Press, 1991), 74.
3. David Eltis, "Precolonial Western Africa and the Atlantic Economy," in *Slavery and the Rise of the Atlantic Economy,* ed. Barbara Solow (New York: Cambridge University Press, 1991), table 1.
4. Quoted by Bernard S. Cohn, "Representing Authority in Victorian India," in *The Invention of Tradition,* ed. Eric Hobsbawm and Terence Ranger (Cambridge, England: Cambridge University Press, 1983), 165.

26

Land Empires in the Age of Imperialism, 1800–1870

Muhammad Ali Meets with European Representatives in 1839   This meeting came after the European powers brought the expansive portion of the Egyptian governor's meteoric career to an end.

CHAPTER OUTLINE

The Ottoman Empire

The Russian Empire

The Qing Empire

DIVERSITY AND DOMINANCE: The French Occupation of Egypt

ENVIRONMENT AND TECHNOLOGY: The Web of War

When the emperor of the Qing° (the last empire to rule China) died in 1799, the imperial court received a shock. For decades officials had known that the emperor was indulging his handsome young favorite, Heshen°, allowing him extraordinary privileges and power. Senior bureaucrats hated Heshen, suspecting him of overseeing a widespread network of corruption. They believed he had been scheming to prolong the inconclusive wars against the native Miao° peoples of southwest China in the late 1700s. Glowing reports of successes against the rebels had poured into the capital, and enormous sums of government money had flowed to the battlefields. But there was no adequate accounting for the funds, and the war persisted.

After the emperor's death, Heshen's enemies ordered his arrest. When they searched his mansion, they discovered a magnificent hoard of silk, furs, porcelain, furniture, and gold and silver. His personal cash alone exceeded what remained in the imperial treasury. The new emperor ordered Heshen to commit suicide with a rope of gold silk. The government seized Heshen's fortune, but the financial damage could not be undone. The declining agricultural base could not replenish the state coffers, and much of the income that did flow in was squandered by an increasingly corrupt bureaucracy. In the 1800s the Qing Empire faced increasing challenges from Europe and the United States with an empty treasury, a stagnant economy, and a troubled society.

The Qing Empire's problems were not unique. They were common to all the land-based empires of Eurasia, where old and inefficient ways of governing put states at risk. The international climate was increasingly dominated by industrializing European economies drawing on the wealth of their overseas colonies. During the early 1800s rapid population growth and slow agricultural growth affected much of Eurasia. Earlier military expansion had stretched the resources of imperial treasuries (see Chapter 21), leaving the land-based empires vulnerable to European military pressure. Responses to this pressure varied, with reform and adaptation gaining headway in some lands and tradition being reasserted in others. In the long run, attempts to meet western Europe's economic and political demands produced financial indebtedness to France, Britain, and other Western powers.

This chapter contrasts the experiences of the Qing Empire with the Russian and Ottoman Empires, with a particular look at the Ottomans' semi-independent province of Egypt. While the Qing opted for resistance, the others made varying attempts to adapt and reform. Russia eventually became part of Europe and shared in many aspects of European culture, while the Ottomans and the Qing became subject to ever greater imperialist pressure. These different responses raise the question of the role of culture in shaping western Europe's relations with the rest of the world in the nineteenth century.

As you read this chapter, ask yourself the following questions:

• Why did the Ottoman and Qing Empires find themselves on the defensive in their encounters with Europeans in the 1800s?

• By what strategies did the land-based empires try to adapt to nineteenth-century economic and political conditions?

• How did the Russian Empire maintain its status as both a European power and a great Asian land empire?

THE OTTOMAN EMPIRE

During the eighteenth century the central government of the Ottoman Empire lost much of its power to provincial governors, military commanders, ethnic leaders, and bandit chiefs. In several parts of the empire local officials and large landholders tried to increase their independence and divert imperial funds into their own coffers.

Qing (ching)　**Heshen** (huh-shun)　**Miao** (mee-ow)

A kingdom in Arabia led by the Saud family, and following the puritanical and fundamentalist religious views of an eighteenth-century leader named Muhammad ibn Abd al-Wahhab°, took control of the holy cities of Mecca and Medina and deprived the sultan of the honor of organizing the annual pilgrimage. In Egypt the Mamluk slave-soldiers purchased as boys in Georgia and nearby parts of the Caucasus and educated for war reasserted their influence. Between 1260 and 1517, when they were defeated by the Ottomans, Egypt's sultans had come from the ranks of the Mamluks. Now Ottoman weakness allowed the Mamluk factions to reemerge as local military forces.

For the sultans, hopes of escaping still further decline were few. The inefficient Janissary corps wielded great political power in Istanbul. It used this power to force Sultan Selim III to abandon efforts to train a modern, European-style army at the end of the eighteenth century. This situation unexpectedly changed when France invaded Egypt.

Egypt and the Napoleonic Example, 1798–1840

Napoleon Bonaparte and an invasion force of 36,000 men and four hundred ships invaded Egypt in May 1798 (see Diversity and Dominance: The French Occupation of Egypt). The French quickly defeated the Mamluk forces that for several decades had dominated the country under the loose jurisdiction of the Ottoman sultan in Istanbul. Fifteen months later, after being stopped by Ottoman land and British naval forces in an attempted invasion of Syria, Napoleon secretly left Cairo and returned to France. Three months later he seized power and made himself emperor.

Back in Egypt, his generals tried to administer a country that they only poorly understood. Cut off from France by British ships in the Mediterranean, they had little hope of remaining in power and agreed to withdraw in 1801. For the second time in three years, a collapse of military power produced a power vacuum in Egypt. The winner of the ensuing contest was **Muhammad Ali°**, the commander of a contingent of Albanian soldiers sent by the sultan to restore imperial control. By 1805 he had taken the place of the official Ottoman governor, and by 1811 he had dispossessed the Mamluks of their lands and privileges.

Muhammad ibn Abd al-Wahhab (Moo-HAH-muhd ib-uhn ab-dahl-wa HAHB)
Muhammad Ali (moo-HAM-mad AH-lee)

Muhammad Ali's rise to power coincided with the meteoric career of Emperor Napoleon I. It is not surprising, therefore, that he adopted many French practices in rebuilding the Egyptian state. Militarily, he dutifully sent an army against the Saudi kingdom in Arabia to reclaim Mecca and Medina for the sultan. Losses during the successful war greatly reduced his contingent of Albanians, leaving him free to construct a new army. Instead of relying on picked groups of warriors like the Mamluks, Muhammad Ali instituted the French practice of conscription. For the first time since the days of the pharaohs, Egyptian peasants were compelled to become soldiers.

He also established special schools for training artillery and cavalry officers, army surgeons, military bandmasters, and others. The curricula of these schools featured European skills and sciences, and Muhammad Ali began to send promising young Turks and Circassians (an ethnic group from the Caucasus), the only people permitted to serve as military officers, to France for education. In 1824 he started a gazette devoted to official affairs, the first newspaper in the Islamic world.

To outfit his new army Muhammad Ali built all sorts of factories. These did not prove efficient enough to survive, but they showed a determination to achieve independence and parity with the European powers.

Money for these enterprises came from confiscation of lands belonging to Muslim religious institutions, under the pretext that the French occupation had canceled religious trusts established in earlier centuries, and from forcing farmers to sell their crops to the government at fixed prices. Muhammad Ali resold some of the produce abroad, making great profits as long as the Napoleonic wars kept European prices for wheat at a high level.

In the 1830s Muhammad Ali's son Ibrahim invaded Syria and instituted some of the changes already underway in Egypt. The improved quality of the new Egyptian army had been proven during the Greek war of independence (see below), when Ibrahim had commanded an expeditionary force to help the sultan. In response, the sultan embarked on building his own new army in 1826. The two armies met in 1839 when Ibrahim attacked northward into Anatolia. The Egyptian army was victorious, and Istanbul would surely have fallen if not for European intervention.

In 1841 European pressure, highlighted by British naval bombardment of coastal cities in Egyptian-controlled Syria, forced Muhammad Ali to withdraw to the present-day border between Egypt and Israel. The great powers imposed severe limitations on his army and navy and forced him to dissolve his economic mo-

	Ottoman Empire	Russian Empire	Qing Empire
	C H R O N O L O G Y		
1800	1805–1849 Muhammad Ali governs Egypt 1808–1839 Rule of Mahmud II 1826 Janissary corps dissolved 1829 Greek independence 1839 Abdul Mejid begins Tanzimat reforms	1801–1825 Reign of Alexander I 1812 Napoleon's retreat from Moscow 1825 Decembrist revolt 1825–1855 Reign of Nicholas I	1794–1804 White Lotus Rebellion
1850	1853–1856 Crimean War 1876 First constitution by an Islamic government	1853–1856 Crimean War 1855–1881 Reign of Alexander II 1861 Emancipation of the serfs	1839–1842 Opium War 1850–1864 Taiping Rebellion 1856–1860 Arrow War 1860 Sack of Beijing 1862–1875 Reign of Tongzhi

nopolies and allow Europeans to undertake business ventures in Egypt.

Muhammad Ali remained Egypt's ruler, under the suzerainty of the sultan, until his death in 1849; and his family continued to rule the country until 1952. But his dream of making Egypt a mighty country capable of standing up to Europe faded. What survived was the example he had set for the sultans in Istanbul.

Ottoman Reform and the European Model, 1807–1853

At the end of the eighteenth century Sultan Selim° III (r. 1789–1807), an intelligent and forward-looking ruler who stayed well informed about events in Europe, introduced reforms to create European-style military units, bring provincial governors under the control of the central government, and standardize taxation and land tenure. The rise in government expenditures to implement the reforms was supposed to be offset by taxes on selected items, primarily tobacco and coffee.

These reforms failed for political, more than economic, reasons. The most violent and persistent opposition came from the **Janissaries**°. Originally Christian boys taken from their homes in the Balkans, converted to Islam, and required to serve for life in the Ottoman army, in the eighteenth century the Janissaries became a

significant political force in Istanbul and in provincial capitals like Baghdad. Their interest in preserving special economic privileges made them resist the creation of new military units.

At times, the disapproval of the Janissaries produced military uprisings. An early example occurred in the Balkans, in the Ottoman territory of **Serbia**, where Janissaries acted as provincial governors. Their control in Serbia was intensely resented by the local residents, particularly Orthodox Christians who claimed that the Janissaries abused them. In response to the charges, Selim threatened to reassign the Janissaries to the Ottoman capital at Istanbul. Suspecting that the sultan's threat signaled the beginning of the end of their political power, in 1805 the Janissaries revolted against Selim and massacred Christians in Serbia. Selim was unable to reestablish central Ottoman rule over Serbia. Instead, the Ottoman court had to rely on the ruler of Bosnia, another Balkan province, who joined his troops with the peasants of Serbia to suppress the Janissary uprising. The threat of Russian intervention prevented the Ottomans from disarming the victorious Serbians, so Serbia became effectively independent.

Other opponents of reform included ulama, or Muslim religious scholars, who distrusted the secularization of law and taxation that Selim proposed. In the face of widespread rejection of his reforms, Selim suspended his program in 1806. Nevertheless, a massive military uprising occurred at Istanbul, and the sultan was deposed and imprisoned. Reform forces rallied and recaptured

---

Selim (seh-LEEM)   Janissaries (JAN-nih-say-rees)

파운드폭탄 4발 투하··· 두 아들과 함께 사망 가

심진지 구축··· 이틀째 시가戰

령이 대중 앞에 나타나거나 애국심
을 고취하는 노래만을 내보내던 방
송마저 중단됐다.

라크 전후 대책
의에서는 전후
영국 주도로 하

DIVERSITY AND DOMINANCE

THE FRENCH OCCUPATION OF EGYPT

Napoleon's invasion of Egypt in 1798 strikingly illustrates the techniques of dominance employed by the French imperial power and the means of resistance available to noncombatant Egyptian intellectuals in reasserting their cultural diversity and independence. Abd al-Rahman al-Jabarti (1753–1826), from whose writings the first four passages are drawn, came from a family of ulama, or Muslim religious scholars. His three works concerning the French occupation, which lasted until 1801, provide the best Egyptian account of that period. The selections below start with the first half of Napoleon's first proclamation to the Egyptian people, which was published in Arabic at the time of the invasion and is quoted here from al-Jabarti's text.

In the Name of God the Compassionate the Merciful: There is no god but God. He has not begotten a son, and does not share in His Kingship.

On behalf of the French Republic, which is founded upon the principles of liberty and equality, the Commander-in-Chief of the French armies, the great head-general Bonaparte, hereby declares to all inhabitants of Egyptian lands that the Sanjaqid rulers of Egypt [i.e., the Mamluk commanders] have persisted far too long in their maltreatment and humiliation of the French nation and have unjustly subjected French merchants to all manner of abuse and extortion. The hour of their punishment has now come.

It is a great pity that this group of slave fighters [Mamluks], caught in the mountains of Abkhazia and Georgia, have for such a long time perpetrated so much corruption in the fairest of all lands on the face of the globe. Now, the omnipotent Lord of the Universe has ordained their demise.

O people of Egypt, should they say to you that I have only come hither to defile your religion, this is but an utter lie that you must not believe. Say to my accusers that I have only come to rescue your rights from the hands of tyrants, and that I am a better servant of God—may He be praised and exalted—and that I revere His Prophet Muhammad and the grand Koran more than the group of slave fighters do.

Tell them also that all people stand equally before God and that reason, virtue, and knowledge comprise the only distinguishing qualities among them. Now, what do the group of slave fighters possess of reason, virtue, and knowledge that would distinguish them from the rest of the people and qualify them exclusively to benefit from everything that is desirable in this worldly life?

The most fertile of all agricultural lands, the prettiest concubines, the best horses, and most attractive residences, all are appropriated exclusively by them. If the land of Egypt was ever conferred upon this group of slave fighters exclusively, let them show us the document that God has written for them: of course, the Lord of the Universe acts with compassion and equity toward mankind. With His help—may He be Exalted—from this day on no Egyptian shall be excluded from high positions nor barred from acquiring high ranks, and men of reason, virtue and learning from among them will administer the affairs, and as a result the welfare of the entire Muslim community (*umma*) shall improve.

The following passages provide examples of al-Jabarti's line-by-line commentary on the proclamation and two examples of his more general comments on the French and on French rule.

Explanation of the wretched proclamation composed of incoherent words and vulgar phrases:

By saying, "in the Name of God the Compassionate the Merciful: There is no god but God. He has not begotten a son, and does not share in His Kingship" [the French] implicitly claim in three propositions that they concur with the three religions [Islam, Christianity, and Judaism] whereas in truth they falsify all three and indeed any other [viable] doctrine. They concur with the Muslims in opening [the statement] with the name of God and in rejecting His begetting a son or sharing in His Kingship. They differ from them in not professing the two essential Articles of Faith: refusing to recognize Prophet Muhammad, and rebuffing the essential teachings of Islam in word and deed. They concur with the Christians in most of what they say and do, but diverge over the question of Trinity, in their rejection of the vocation [of Christ], and furthermore in rebuffing their beliefs and rituals, killing the priests, and desecrating places of worship. They concur with the Jews in believing in one God, as the Jews also do not believe in the Trinity but hold on to anthropomorphism. [The French Republicans] do not share in the religious beliefs and practices of the Jews either. Apparently they do not follow any particular religion and do not adhere to a set of specific rituals: each of them fathoms a religion as it suits his own reason. The rest of the [people of France] are Christians but keep it hidden, and there are some real Jews among them as well. However, even those who may follow a religion, when they come to Egypt, they concur with the agents of the Republic in their insistence upon leading the Egyptians astray.

Their saying "On behalf of the French Republic, etc." implies that the proclamation comes from the Republic or their people directly, because unlike other nations they have no overlord or sovereign whom they unanimously appoint, and who has exclusive authority to speak on their behalf. It is now six years since they revolted against their sovereign and murdered him. Subsequently, the people agreed not to have a single ruler but rather to put the affairs of the government, provincial issues, legislation and administration, into the hands of men of discretion and reason among themselves. They chose and appointed men in a hierarchy: a head of the entire army followed in rank by generals and military commanders each in charge of groups of a thousand, two hundred, or ten men. They similarly appointed administrators and advisers by observing their essential equality and non-supremacy of one over the others, in the same way that people are created equally in essence. This constitutes the foundation and touchstone of their system, and this is what "founded upon the principles of liberty and equality" means. The reference to "liberty" implies that unlike the slaves and [the slave fighters ruling over Egypt] they are not anybody's slaves; the meaning of "equality" has already been explained.

[On that day the French] started to operate a new court bureau, which they named the Ad hoc Court (*mahkamat al-qadaya*). On this occasion they drafted a decree that included clauses framed in most unacceptable terms that sounded rather repellant to the ear. Six Copts and six Muslim merchants were appointed to the bureau, and the presiding judge and chief of the bureau was the Copt from Malta who used to work as secretary to Ayyub Bey, the notary (*daftardar*). Ad hoc cases involving commercial, civil, inheritance disputes, and other suits were referred to this bureau. [The French] formulated corrupt principles for this institution that were based on heresy, founded in tyranny, and rooted in all sorts of abominable unprecedented rulings (*bid'a al-sayyi'a*).

[The French] devastated the palace of Yusuf Salah al-Din including the cites where sovereigns and sultans held audiences, and they tore down strong foundations and demolished towering columns. They also destroyed mosques, meditation spots (*zawaya*), and shrines of martyrs (*mashahid*). They defaced the Grand Congregational Mosque, built by the venerable Muhammad b. Qalawan al-Malik al-Nasir: wrecked the pulpit, spoiled the mosque's courtyard, looted its lumber,

undermined its columns, and razed the well-wrought iron enclosure inside of which the sultan used to pray.

*T*he final passage, which is not in any of al-Jabarti's chronicles, is the full text of an announcement distributed to Napoleon's thirty-six thousand troops on board ship as they headed for Egypt.

Soldiers,—You are about to undertake a conquest the effects of which on civilization and commerce are incalculable. The blow you are about to give to England will be the best aimed, and the most sensibly felt, she can receive until the time arrive when you can give her her death-blow.

We must make some fatiguing marches; we must fight several battles; we shall succeed in all we undertake. The destinies are with us. The Mameluke Beys, who favour exclusively English commerce, whose extortions oppress our merchants, and who tyrannise over the unfortunate inhabitants of the Nile, a few days after our arrival will no longer exist.

The people amongst whom we are going to live are Mahometans. The first article of their faith is this: "there is no God but God, and Mahomet is His prophet." Do not contradict them. Behave to them as you have behaved to the Jews—to the Italians. Pay respect to their muftis [jurists], and their Imaums [sic], as you did to the rabbis and the bishops. Extend to the ceremonies prescribed by the Koran and to the mosques the same toleration which you showed to the synagogues, to the religion of Moses and of Jesus Christ.

The Roman legions protected all religions. You will find here customs different from those of Europe. You must accommodate yourselves to them. The people amongst whom we are to mix differ from us in the treatment of women; but in all countries he who violates is a monster. Pillage enriches only a small number of men; it dishonours us; it destroys our resources; it converts into enemies the people whom it is our interest to have for friends.

The first town we shall come to was built by Alexander. At every step we shall meet with grand recollections, worthy of exciting the emulations of Frenchmen.

Bonaparte

QUESTIONS FOR ANALYSIS

1. Why are the reasons for invading Egypt given to the French soldiers different from those announced to the Egyptians?
2. How do Napoleon and al-Jabarti use religious feeling as a political tool?
3. What do texts like these suggest about the role culture plays in confrontations between imperial powers and imperialized peoples?

Source: First selection from *Abd al-Rahman al-Jabarti's History of Egypt*, ed. Thomas Phillipp and Moshe Perlmann (Stuttgart, 1994), translated by Hossein Kamaly. Second selection from Louis Antoine Fauvelet de Bourrienne, *Memoirs of Napoleon Bonaparte* (1843).

the capital, but not before Selim had been executed. Selim's cousin Sultan Mahmud° II (r.1808–1839) cautiously revived the reform movement. The fate of Selim III had taught the Ottoman court that reform needed to be more systematic and imposed more forcefully, but it took the concrete evidence of the effectiveness of radical reform in Muhammad Ali's Egypt to drive this lesson home. Mahmud II was able to use an insurrection in Greece, and the superior performance of Egyptian forces in the unsuccessful effort to suppress it, as a sign of the weakness of the empire and the pressing need for reform.

Greek independence in 1829 was a complex event that had dramatic international significance. A combination of Greek nationalist organizations and interlopers from Albania formed the independence movement. By the early nineteenth century interest in the classical age of Greece and Rome had intensified European desires to encourage and if possible aid the struggle for independence. Europeans considered the war for Greek independence a campaign to recapture the classical roots of their civilization from Muslim despots, and many—including the "mad, bad and dangerous to know" English poet Lord Byron, who lost his life in the war—went to Greece to fight as volunteers. The Ottomans called on Ibrahim Pasha° of Egypt, the son of Muhammad Ali, to help preserve their rule in Greece; but when the combined squadrons of the British, French, and Russian fleets, under orders to observe but not intervene in the war, made an unauthorized attack that sank the Ottoman fleet at the Battle of Navarino, not even Ibrahim's help could prevent defeat (see Map 26.1).

Europeans trumpeted the victory of the Greeks as a triumph of European civilization over the Ottoman Empire, and Mahmud II agreed that the loss of Greece indicated a profound weakness—he considered it backwardness—in Ottoman military and financial organization. With popular outrage over the military setbacks in Greece strong, the sultan made his move in 1826. First he announced the creation of a new artillery unit, which he had secretly been training. When the Janissaries rose in revolt, he ordered the new unit to bombard the Janissary barracks. The Janissary corps was officially dissolved.

Like Muhammad Ali, Mahmud felt he could not implement major changes without reducing the political power of the religious elite. He visualized restructuring the bureaucracy and the educational and legal systems, where ulama power was strongest. Before such strong measures could be undertaken, however, Ibrahim at-

tacked from Syria in 1839. Battlefield defeat, the decision of the rebuilt Ottoman navy to switch sides and support Egypt, and the death of Mahmud, all in the same year, left the empire completely dependent on the European powers for survival.

Mahmud's reforming ideas received their widest expression in the **Tanzimat**° ("reorganization"), a series of reforms announced by his sixteen-year-old son and successor, Abdul Mejid°, in 1839 and strongly endorsed by the European ambassadors. One proclamation called for public trials and equal protection under the law for all, whether Muslim, Christian, or Jew. It also guaranteed some rights of privacy, equalized the eligibility of men for conscription into the army (a practice copied from Egypt), and provided for a new, formalized method of tax collection that legally ended tax farming in the Ottoman Empire. It took many years and strenuous efforts by reforming bureaucrats, known as the "men of the Tanzimat," to give substance to these reforms. At a theoretical level, however, they opened a new chapter in the history of the Islamic world. European observers praised them for their noble principles and rejection of religious influences in government. Ottoman citizens were more divided; the Christians and Jews, about whom the Europeans showed the greatest concern, were generally more enthusiastic than the Muslims. Many historians see the Tanzimat as the dawn of modern thought and enlightened government in the Middle East. Others point out that removing the religious elite from influence in government also removed the one remaining check on authoritarian rule.

With the passage of time, one legal code after another—commercial, criminal, civil procedure—was introduced to take the place of the corresponding areas of religious legal jurisdiction. All the codes were modeled closely on those of Europe. The sharia, or Islamic law, gradually became restricted to matters of family law such as marriage and inheritance. As the sharia was displaced, job opportunities for the ulama shrank, as did the value of a purely religious education.

Like Muhammad Ali, Sultan Mahmud sent military cadets to France and the German states for training. Military uniforms were modeled on those of France. In the 1830s an Ottoman imperial school of military sciences, later to become Istanbul University, was established at Istanbul. Instructors imported from western Europe taught chemistry, engineering, mathematics, and physics in addition to military history. Reforms in military education became the model for more general educational reforms. In 1838 the first medical school was established

---

Mahmud (MAH-mood)
Ibrahim Pasha (ib-rah-HEEM PAH-shah)

Tanzimat (TAHNZ-ee-MAT)   **Abdul Mejid** (ab-dul meh-JEED)

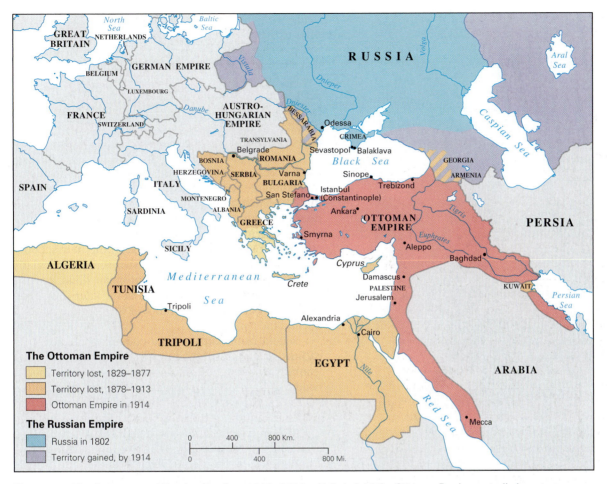

Map 26.1 **The Ottoman and Russian Empires, 1829–1914** At its height the Ottoman Empire controlled most of the perimeter of the Mediterranean Sea. But in the 1800s Ottoman territory shrank as many countries gained their independence. The Black Sea, where the Turkish coast was vulnerable to assault, became a weak spot as Russian naval power grew. Russian challenges to the Ottomans at the eastern end of the Black Sea, and to the Persians east and west of the Caspian aroused fears in Europe that Russia was trying to reach the Indian Ocean.

to train army doctors and surgeons. Later, a national system of preparatory schools was created to feed graduates into the military schools. The subjects that were taught and many of the teachers were foreign, so the issue of whether Turkish would be a language of instruction in the new schools was a serious one. Because it was easier to import and use foreign textbooks than to write new ones in Turkish, French became the preferred language in all advanced professional and scientific training. In numerical terms, however, the great majority of students still learned to read and write in Quran schools down to the twentieth century.

In the capital city of Istanbul, the reforms stimulated the growth of a small but cosmopolitan milieu embracing

European language and culture. The first Turkish newspaper, a government gazette modeled on that of Muhammad Ali, appeared in 1831. Other newspapers followed, many written in French. Travel to Europe—particularly to England and France—became more common among wealthy Turks. Interest in importing European military, industrial, and communications technology remained strong through the 1800s.

The Ottoman rulers quickly learned that limited improvements in military technology had unforeseen cultural and social effects. Accepting the European notion that modern weapons and drill required a change in traditional military dress, beards were deemed unhygienic and, in artillery units, a fire hazard. They were restricted,

Change with Tradition Change in the Ottoman armies was gradual, beginning with the introduction of European guns and artillery. To use the new weapons efficiently and safely, the Janissaries were required to modify their dress and beards. Beards were trimmed, and elaborate headgear was reserved for ritual occasions. Traditional military units attempted to retain distinctive dress whenever possible, and one compromise was the brimless cap adapted from the high hats that some Janissaries had traditionally worn. (Courtesy, Turkish Ministry of Culture and Tourism. Photo: Necmettin Kulahci)

along with the wearing of loose trousers and turbans. Military headgear also became controversial. European military caps, which had leather bills on the front to protect against the glare of the sun, were not acceptable because they interfered with Muslim soldiers' touching their foreheads to the ground during daily prayers. The compromise was the brimless cap now called the *fez*, which was adopted by the military and then by Ottoman civil officials in the early years of Mahmud II's reign.

The changes in military dress—so soon after the suppression of the Janissaries—were recognized as an indication of the empire's new orientation. Government ministries that traditionally drew young men from traditional bureaucratic families and trained them for ministerial service were gradually transformed into formal civil services hiring men educated in the new schools. Among self-consciously progressive men, particularly those in government service, European dress became the fashion in the Ottoman cities of the later 1800s. Traditional dress became a symbol of the religious, the rural, and the parochial.

Secularization of the legal code had special implications for the non-Muslim subjects of the Ottomans. Islamic law had required non-Muslims to pay a special head tax that was sometimes explained as a substitute for military service. Under the Tanzimat, the tax was abolished and non-Muslims became liable for military service—unless they bought their way out by paying a new military exemption tax. Under the new law codes, all male subjects had equal access to the courts, while the sphere of operation of the Islamic law courts shrank. Perhaps the biggest enhancement of the status of non-Muslims, however, was the strong and direct concern for their welfare consistently expressed by the European powers. The Ottoman Empire became a rich field of operation for Christian missionaries and European supporters of Jewish community life in the Muslim world.

The public rights and political participation granted during the Tanzimat applied specifically to men. Private life, including everything connected to marriage and divorce, remained within the sphere of religious law, and at no time was there a question of political participation or reformed education for women. Indeed, the reforms may have decreased the influence of women. The political changes ran parallel to economic changes that also narrowed women's opportunities.

The influx of silver from the Americas that had begun in the 1600s increased the monetarization of some sectors of the Ottoman economy, particularly in the cities. Workers were increasingly paid in cash rather than in goods, and businesses associated with banking, finance, and law developed. Competition drove women from the work force. Early industrial labor and the professions were not open to women, and traditional "woman's work" such as weaving was increasingly mechanized and done by men.

Nevertheless, women retained considerable power in the management and disposal of their own property, gained mostly through fixed shares of inheritance, well into the 1800s. After marriage a woman was often pressured to convert her landholdings to cash in order to transfer her personal wealth to her husband's family, with whom she and her husband would reside; but this was not a requirement, since men were legally obligated to support their families single-handedly. Until the 1820s many women retained their say in the distribution of property through the creation of charitable trusts for their sons. Because these trusts were set up in the religious courts, they could be designed to conform to the wishes of family members, and they gave women of wealthy families an opportunity to exercise significant indirect control over property. Then, in the 1820s and 1830s the secularizing reforms of Mahmud II, which did not always produce happy results, transferred jurisdiction over the charitable trusts from religious courts to the state and ended women's control over this form of property. In addition, reforms in the military, higher education, the professions, and commerce all bypassed women.

Street Scene in Cairo This engraving from Edward William Lane's influential travel book, *Account of the Manners and Customs of the Modern Egyptians Written in Egypt During the Years 1833–1835* conveys the image of narrow lanes and small stores that became stock features of European thinking about Middle Eastern cities. (From Edward William Lane, *The Manners and Customs of the Modern Egyptians*, (London: J. M. D & Co. 1860)

The Crimean War and Its Aftermath, 1853–1877

Since the reign of Peter the Great (r. 1689–1725) the Russian Empire had been attempting to expand southward at the Ottomans' expense (see "Russia and Asia," below). By 1815 Russia had pried the Georgian region of the Caucasus away from the Ottomans, and the threat of Russian intervention had prevented the Ottomans from crushing Serbian independence. Russia seemed poised to exploit Ottoman weakness and acquire the long-sought goal of free access to the Mediterranean Sea. In the eighteenth century Russia had claimed to be the protector of Ottoman subjects of Orthodox Christian faith in Greece and the Balkans. When Muhammad Ali's Egyptian army invaded Syria in 1833, Russia signed a treaty in support of the Ottomans. In return, the sultan recognized an extension of this claim to cover all of the empire's Orthodox subjects. This set the stage for an obscure dispute that resulted in war.

In 1852 the sultan bowed to British and French pressure and named France Protector of the Holy Sepulchre in Jerusalem, a position with certain ecclesiastical privileges. Russia protested, but the sultan held firm. So

Russia invaded Ottoman territories in what is today Romania, and Britain and France went to war as allies of the sultan. The real causes of the war went beyond church quarrels in Jerusalem. Diplomatic maneuvering among European powers over whether the Ottoman Empire should continue to exist and, if not, who should take over its territory lasted until the empire finally disappeared after World War I. The Eastern Question was the simple name given to this complex issue. Though the

Interior of the Ottoman Financial Bureau   This engraving from the eighteenth century depicts the governing style of the Ottoman Empire before the era of westernizing reforms. By the end of the Tanzimat period in 1876, government offices and the costumes of officials looked much more like those in contemporary European capitals.   (From Ignatius Mouradgea d'Ohsson, *Tableau General de l'Empire Ottoman*, large folio edition, Paris, 1787–1820, pl. 178, following p. 340)

powers had agreed to save the empire from Ibrahim's invasion in 1839, Britain subsequently became very suspicious of Russian ambitions. A number of prominent British politicians were strongly anti-Russian. They feared that Russia would threaten the British hold on India either overland through Central Asia or by placing its navy in the Mediterranean Sea.

Between 1853 and 1856 the **Crimean° War** raged in Romania, on the Black Sea, and on the Crimean peninsula. Britain, France, and the Italian kingdom of Sardinia-Piedmont sided with the Ottomans, allowing Austria to mediate the final outcome. Britain and France trapped the Russian fleet in the Black Sea, where its commanders decided to sink the ships to protect the approaches to Sevastopol, their main base in Crimea. An army largely made up of British and French troops landed and laid siege to the city. A lack of railways and official corruption hampered Russian attempts to supply both its land and its sea forces. On the Romanian front, the Ottomans resisted effectively. At Sevastopol, the Russians were outmatched militarily and suffered badly from disease. Tsar Nicholas died as defeat became apparent, leaving his successor, Alexander II (r. 1855–1881), to sue for peace when Sevastopol finally fell three months later.

A formal alliance among Britain, France, and the Ottoman Empire blocked further Russian expansion into eastern Europe and the Middle East. The terms of peace also gave Britain and France a means of checking each other's colonial ambitions in the Middle East; neither, according to the agreement that ended the war, was entitled to take Ottoman territory for its exclusive use.

Crimean (cry-ME-uhn)

The Crimean War brought significant changes to all the combatants. The tsar and his government, already beset by demands for the reform of serfdom, education, and the military (discussed later), were further discredited. In Britain and France, the conflict was accompanied by massive propaganda campaigns. For the first time newspapers were an important force in mobilizing public support for a war. Press accounts of British participation in the war were often so glamorized that the false impression has lingered ever since that Ottoman troops played a negligible role in the conflict. At the time, however, British and French military commanders noted the massive losses among Turkish troops in particular. The French press, dominant in Istanbul, promoted a sense of unity between Turkish and French society that continued to influence many aspects of Turkish urban culture.

The larger significance of the Crimean War was that it marked the transition from traditional to modern warfare (see Environment and Technology: The Web of War). A high casualty count resulted in part from the clash of mechanized and unmechanized means of killing. All the combatant nations had previously prided themselves on the effective use of highly trained cavalry to smash through the front lines of infantry. Cavalry coexisted with firearms until the early 1800s, primarily because early rifles were awkward to load, vulnerable to explosion, and not very accurate. Swift and expert cavalry could storm infantry lines during the intervals between volleys and even penetrate artillery barrages. In the 1830s and 1840s percussion caps that did away with pouring gunpowder into the barrel of a musket were widely adopted in Europe. In Crimean War battles many cavalry units were destroyed by the rapid and relatively accurate fire of rifles that loaded at the breech rather than down the barrel. That was the fate of the British Light Brigade, which was sent to relieve an Ottoman unit surrounded by Russian troops. Ironically, in the charge of the Light Brigade, the heroic but obsolete horsemen were on the side with the most advanced weaponry. In the long run, despite the pathos of Alfred Lord Tennyson's famous poem, the new military technologies pioneered in the Crimean War, not its heroic events, made the conflict a turning point in the history of war.

After the Crimean War, declining state revenues and increasing integration with European commercial networks created hazardous economic conditions in the Ottoman Empire. The men of the Tanzimat dominated government affairs under Abdul Mejid's successors and continued to secularize Ottoman financial and commercial institutions, modeling them closely on European counterparts. The Ottoman imperial bank was founded in 1840, and a few years later currency reform pegged the value of Ottoman gold coins to the British pound. Sweeping changes in the 1850s expedited the creation of banks, insurance companies, and legal firms throughout the empire. These and other reforms facilitating trade contributed to a strong demographic shift in the Ottoman Empire between about 1850 and 1880, as many rural people headed to the cities. Within this period many of the major cities of the empire—Istanbul, Damascus, Beirut, Alexandria, Cairo—expanded. A small but influential urban professional class emerged, as did a considerable class of wage laborers. This shift was magnified by an influx into the northern Ottoman territories of refugees from Poland and Hungary, where rivalry between the European powers and the Russian Empire caused political tension and sporadic warfare, and from Georgia and other parts of the Caucasus, where Russian expansion forced many Muslims to emigrate (discussed later).

The Ottoman reforms stimulated commerce and urbanization, but no reform could repair the chronic insolvency of the imperial government. Declining revenues from agricultural yields and widespread corruption damaged Ottoman finances. Some of the corruption was exposed in the early 1840s. From the conclusion of the Crimean War in 1856 on, the Ottoman government became heavily dependent on foreign loans. In return the Ottoman government lowered tariffs to favor European imports, and European banks opened in Ottoman cities. Currency changes allowed more systematic conversion to European currencies. Europeans were allowed to live in their own enclaves in Istanbul and other commercial centers, subject to their own laws and exempt from Ottoman jurisdiction. This status was known as **extraterritoriality.**

As the cities prospered, they became attractive to laborers, and still more people moved from the countryside. But opportunities for wage workers reached a plateau in the bloated cities. Foreign trade brought in large numbers of imports, but—apart from tobacco and the Turkish opium that American traders took to China to compete against the Indian opium of the British—few exports were sent abroad from Anatolia. Together with the growing national debt, these factors aggravated inflationary trends that left urban populations in a precarious position in the mid-1800s. By contrast, Egyptian cotton exports soared during the American Civil War, when American cotton exports plummeted, but the profits benefited Muhammad Ali's descendants, who had become the hereditary governors of Egypt, rather than the Ottoman government. The Suez Canal, which

The Web of War

The lethal military technologies of the mid-nineteenth century that were used on battlefields in the United States, Russia, India, and China were rapidly transmitted from one conflict to the next. This dissemination was due not only to the rapid development of communications but also to the existence of a new international network of soldiers who moved from one trouble spot to another, bringing expertise in the use of new techniques.

General Charles Gordon (1833–1885), for instance, was commissioned in the British army in 1852, then served in the Crimean War after Britain entered on the side of the Ottomans. In 1860 he was dispatched to China. He served with British forces during the Arrow War and took part in the sack of Beijing. Afterward, he stayed in China and was seconded to the Qing imperial government until the suppression of the Taipings in 1864, earning himself the nickname "Chinese" Gordon. Gordon later served the Ottoman rulers of Egypt as governor of territory along the Nile. He was killed in Egypt in 1885 while leading his Egyptian troops in defense of the city of Khartoum against an uprising by the Sudanese religious leader, the Mahdi.

Journalism played an important part in the developing web of telegraph communications that sped orders to and from the battlefields. Readers in London could learn details of the drama occurring in the Crimea or in China within a week—or in some cases days—after they occurred. Print and, later, photographic journalism created new "stars" from these war experiences. Charles Gordon was one. Florence Nightingale was another.

In the great wars of the 1800s, the vast majority of deaths resulted from infection or excessive bleeding, not from the wounds themselves. Florence Nightingale (1820–1910), while still a young woman, became interested in hospital management and nursing. She went to Prussia and France to study advanced techniques. Before the outbreak of the Crimean War she was credited with bringing about marked improvement in British health care. When the public reacted to news reports of the suffering in the Crimea, the British government sent Nightingale to the region. Within a year of her arrival the death rate in the military hospitals there dropped from 45 percent to under 5 percent. Her techniques for preventing septicemia and dysentery and for promoting healing therapies were quickly adopted by those working for and with her. On her return to London, Nightingale established institutes for nursing that soon were recognized around the world as leaders. She herself was lionized by the British public and received the Order of Merit in 1907, three years before her death.

The importance of Nightingale's innovations in public hygiene is underscored by the life of her contemporary, Mary Seacole (1805–1881). A Jamaican woman who volunteered to nurse British troops in the Crimean War, Seacole was repeatedly excluded from nursing service by British authorities. She eventually went to Crimea and used her own funds to run a hospital there, bankrupting herself in the process. The drama of the Crimean War moved the British public to support Seacole after her sacrifices were publicized. She was awarded medals by the British, French, and Turkish governments and today is recognized with her contemporary Florence Nightingale as an innovative field nurse and a champion of public hygiene in peacetime.

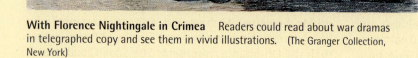

With Florence Nightingale in Crimea   Readers could read about war dramas in telegraphed copy and see them in vivid illustrations.   (The Granger Collection, New York)

was partly financed by cotton profits, opened in 1869, and Cairo was redesigned and beautified. Eventually overexpenditure on such projects plunged Egypt into the same debt crisis that plagued the empire as a whole.

In the 1860s and 1870s reform groups demanded a constitution and entertained the possibility of a law permitting all men to vote. Spokesmen for the Muslim majority expressed dismay at the possibility that the Ottoman Empire would no longer be a Muslim society. Muslims were also suspicious of the motives of Christians, many of whom enjoyed close relations with European powers. Memories of attempts by Russia and France to interfere in Ottoman affairs for the benefit of Christians seemed to some to warrant hostility toward Christians in Ottoman territories.

The decline of Ottoman power and prosperity had a strong impact on a group of well-educated young urban men who aspired to wealth and influence. They believed that the empire's rulers and the Tanzimat officials who worked for them would be forced to—or would be willing to—allow the continued domination of the empire's political, economic, and cultural life by Europeans. Though lacking a sophisticated organization, these **Young Ottomans** (who are sometimes called Young Turks, though that term properly applies to a later movement) promoted a mixture of liberal ideas derived from Europe, national pride in Ottoman independence, and modernist views of Islam. Prominent Young Ottomans helped draft a constitution that was promulgated in 1876 by a new and as yet untried sultan, Abdul Hamid II. This apparent triumph of liberal reform was short-lived. With war against Russia again threatening in the Balkans in 1877, Abdul Hamid suspended the constitution and the parliament that had been elected that year. He ruthlessly opposed further political reforms, but the Tanzimat programs of extending modern schooling, utilizing European military practices and advisers, and making the government bureaucracy more orderly continued during his reign.

THE RUSSIAN EMPIRE

Awareness of western Europe among Russia's elite began with the reign of Peter the Great (r. 1689–1725), but knowledge of the French language, considered by Russians to be the language of European culture, spread only slowly among the aristocracy in the second half of the eighteenth century. In 1812, when Napoleon's march on Moscow ended in a disastrous retreat brought on more by what a later tsar called "Generals January and February" than by Russian military action, the European image of Russia changed. Just as Napoleon's withdrawal from Egypt paved the way for the brief emergence of Muhammad Ali's Egypt as a major power, so his withdrawal from Russia conferred status on another autocrat. Conservative Europeans still saw Russia as an alien, backward, and oppressive land, but they acknowledged its immensity and potential power and included Tsar Alexander I (r. 1801–1825) as a major partner in efforts to restore order and suppress revolutionary tendencies throughout Europe. Like Muhammad Ali, Alexander attempted reforms in the hope of strengthening his regime. Unlike Muhammad Ali, acceptance by the other European monarchs saved a rising Russia from being strangled in its cradle.

In several important respects Russia resembled the Ottoman Empire more than the conservative kingdoms of Europe whose autocratic practices it so staunchly supported. Socially dominated by nobles whose country estates were worked by unfree serfs, Russia had almost no middle class. Industry was still at the threshold of development by the standards of the rapidly industrializing European powers, though it was somewhat more dynamic than Ottoman industry. And the absolute power of the tsar was unchallenged. Like Egypt and the Ottoman Empire, Russia engaged in reforms from the top down under Alexander I, but when his conservative brother Nicholas I (r. 1825–1855) succeeded to the throne, iron discipline and suspicion of modern ideas took priority over reform.

Russia and Europe

In 1700 only 3 percent of the Russian people lived in cities, two-thirds of them in Moscow alone. By the middle of the nineteenth century the town population had grown tenfold, though it still accounted for only 6 percent of the population because the territories of the tsars had grown greatly through wars and colonization (see Chapter 21). Since mining and small-scale industry can be carried out in small communities, urbanization is only a general indicator of modern economic developments. These figures do demonstrate, however, that, like the Ottoman Empire, Russia was an overwhelmingly agricultural land. Moreover, Russian transportation was even worse than that of the Ottomans, since many of the latter's major cities were seaports. Both empires encompassed peoples speaking many different languages.

Well-engineered roads did not begin to appear until 1817, and steam navigation commenced on the Volga in 1843. Tsar Nicholas I built the first railroad in Russia

Raising of the Alexander Monument in St. Petersburg   The death of Alexander I in 1825 brought to power his conservative brother Nicholas I. Yet Alexander remained a heroic figure for his resistance to Napoleon. This monument in Winter Palace Square was erected in 1829.   (Novosti Photo Library)

from St. Petersburg, the capital, to his summer palace in 1837. A few years later his commitment to strict discipline led him to insist that the trunk line from St. Petersburg to Moscow run in a perfectly straight line. American engineers, among them the father of the painter James McNeill Whistler, who learned to paint in St. Petersburg, oversaw the laying of track and built locomotive workshops. This slow start in modern transportation compares better with that of Egypt, where work on the first railroad began in 1851, than with France, which saw railroad building soar during the 1840s. Industrialization projects depended heavily on foreign expertise. British engineers set up the textile mills that gave wool and cotton a prominent place among Russia's industries.

Until the late nineteenth century the Russian government's interest in industry was limited and hesitant. To be successful, an industrial revolution required large numbers of educated and independent-minded artisans and entrepreneurs. Suspicious of Western ideas, especially anything smacking of liberalism, socialism, or revolution, Nicholas feared the spread of literacy and

modern education beyond the minimum needed to train the officer corps and the bureaucracy. Rather than run the risk of allowing the development of a middle class and a working class that might challenge his control, Nicholas I kept the peasants in serfdom and preferred to import most industrial goods and pay for them with exports of grain and timber.

Like Egypt and the Ottoman Empire, Russia aspired to Western-style economic development. But fear of political change caused the country to fall farther behind western Europe, economically and technologically, than it had been a half-century before. When France and Britain entered the Crimean War, they faced a Russian army equipped with obsolete weapons and bogged down by lack of transportation. At a time when European engineers were making major breakthroughs in fast loading of cannon through an opening at the breech end, muzzle-loading artillery remained the Russian standard.

Despite these deficiencies in technology and its institutional supports, in some ways Russia bore a closer resemblance to other European countries than the Ottoman Empire did. From the point of view of the French and the British, the Cyrillic alphabet and the Russian Orthodox form of Christianity seemed foreign, but they were not nearly as foreign as the Arabic alphabet and the Muslim faith of the Turks, Arabs, Persians, and Muslim Indians. Britain and France feared Russia as a rival for power in eastern Europe and the eastern Mediterranean lands, but they increasingly accepted Tsar Nicholas's view of the Ottoman Empire as "the sick man of Europe," capable of surviving only so long as the European powers found it a useful buffer state.

From the Russian point of view, kinship with western Europe was of questionable value. Westernizers, like the men of the Tanzimat in the Ottoman Empire, put their trust in technical advances and governmental reform. Opposing them were intellectuals known as **Slavophiles,** who in some respects resembled the Young Ottomans and considered the Orthodox faith, the solidity of peasant life, and the tsar's absolute rule to be the proper bases of Russian civilization. After Russia's humiliating defeat in the Crimea, the Slavophile tendency gave rise to **Pan-Slavism,** a militant political doctrine advocating unity of all the Slavic peoples, including those living under Austrian and Ottoman rule.

On the diplomatic front, the tsar's inclusion among the great powers of Europe contrasted sharply with the sultan's exclusion. However, this did not prevent the development of a powerful sense of Russophobia in the west. Britain in particular saw Russia as a geostrategic threat and despised the continuing subjection of the serfs, who were granted their freedom by Tsar Alexander II only in 1861, twenty-eight years after the British had abolished slavery. The passions generated by the Crimean War and its outcome affected the relations of Russia, Europe, and the Ottoman Empire for the remainder of the nineteenth century.

Russia and Asia

The Russian drive to the east in the eighteenth century brought the tsar's empire to the Pacific Ocean and the frontiers of China (see Map 21.1) by century's end. In the nineteenth century Russian expansionism continued with a drive to the south. The growing inferiority of the Russian military in comparison with the European powers did not affect these Asian battlefronts, since the peoples they faced were even less industrialized and technologically advanced than Russians. In 1860 Russia established a military outpost on the Pacific coast that would eventually grow into the great naval port of Vladivostok, today Russia's most southerly city. In

Central Asia the steppe lands of the Kazakh nomads came under Russian control early in the century, setting the stage for a confrontation with three Uzbek states farther south. They succumbed to Russian pressure and military action one by one, beginning in 1865, giving rise to the new province of Turkestan, with its capital at Tashkent in present-day Uzbekistan. In the region of the Caucasus Mountains, the third area of southward expansion, Russia first took over Christian Georgia (1786), Muslim Azerbaijan° (1801), and Christian Armenia (1813) before embarking on the conquest of the many small principalities, each with its own language or languages, in the heart of the mountains. Between 1829 and 1864 Dagestan, Chechnya°, Abkhazia°, and other regions that were to gain political prominence only after the breakup of the Soviet Union at the end of the twentieth century became parts of the Russian Empire.

The drive to the south intensified political friction with Russia's new neighbors: Qing China and Japan in the east, Iran on the Central Asian and Caucasus frontiers, and the Ottoman Empire at the eastern end of the Black Sea. In the latter two instances, a flow of Muslim refugees from the territories newly absorbed by Russia increased anti-Russian feelings, but in some cases also brought talented people into Iran and the Ottoman lands. Armenian, Azerbaijani, and Bukharan exiles who had been exposed to Russian administration and education brought new ideas to Iran in the later decades of the century, and a massive migration of Crimean Turks and Circassians from Russia's Caucasian territories affected the demography of the Ottoman Empire, which resettled some of the immigrants as far away as Syria and Jordan and others as buffer populations on the Russian frontiers.

In a broader political perspective, the Russian drive to the south added a new element to the Eastern Question. Many British statesmen and strategists reckoned that a warlike Russia would press on until it had conquered all the lands separating it from British India, a prospect that made them shudder, given India's enormous contribution to Britain's prosperity. The competition that ensued over which power would control southern Central Asia resulted in a standoff in Afghanistan, which became a buffer zone under the control of neither, and direct competition in Iran, where both powers sought to gain an economic and political advantage while preserving the independence of the Qajar dynasty of shahs.

Azerbaijan (ah-zer-by-JAHN)   **Chechnya** (CHECH-nee-yah)
Abkhazia (ab-KAH-zee-yah)

Cultural Trends

Unlike Egypt and the Ottoman Empire, which began to send students to Europe for training only in the nineteenth century, Russia had been in cultural contact with western Europe since the time of Peter the Great (r. 1689–1725). Members of the Russian court knew western languages, and the tsars employed officials and advisers from western countries. Peter had also enlisted the well-educated Ukrainian clerics who headed the Russian Orthodox Church to help spread a western spirit of education. As a result, Alexander I's reforms met a more positive reception than those of Muhammad Ali and Mahmud II.

While Muhammad Ali put his efforts into building a modern army and an economic system to support it, the reforms of Sultan Mahmud II and Alexander promised more on paper than they brought about in practice. Both monarchs hoped to create better organized and more efficient government bureaus, but it took many years to develop a sufficient pool of trained bureaucrats to make the reforms effective. Alexander's Council of State worked better than the new ministerial system he devised. The council coordinated ministry affairs and deliberated over new legislation. As for the ministries, Alexander learned a lesson from Napoleon's military organization. He made each minister theoretically responsible for a strict hierarchy of officers below him, and ordered them to report directly to him as commander-in-chief. But this system remained largely ineffective, as did the provincial advisory councils that were designed to extend the new governing ideas into outlying areas.

Ironically, much of the opposition to these reforms came from well-established families that were not at all unfriendly to western ideas. Their fear was that the new government bureaucrats, who often came from humbler social origins, would act as agents of imperial despotism. This fear was realized during the conservative reign of Nicholas I in the same way that the Tanzimat-inspired bureaucracy of the Ottoman Empire served the despotic purposes of Sultan Abdul al-Hamid II after 1877. In both cases, historians have noted that administrative reforms made by earlier rulers began to take hold under conservative despots, though more because of accumulating momentum and training than because of those rulers' policies.

Individuals favoring more liberal reforms, including military officers who had served in western Europe, intellectuals who read western political tracts, and members of Masonic lodges who exchanged views with Freemasons in the west, formed secret societies of opposition. Some placed their highest priority on freeing the serfs; others advocated a constitution and a republican form of government. When Alexander I died in December 1825, confusion over who was to succeed him encouraged a group of reform-minded army officers to try to take over the government and provoke an uprising. The so-called **Decembrist revolt** failed, and many of the participants were severely punished. These events ensured that the new tsar, Nicholas I, would pay little heed to calls for reform over the next thirty years.

Though the great powers meeting in Paris to settle the Crimean War in 1856 compelled the Ottoman sultan to issue new reform decrees improving the status of non-Muslim subjects, Russia faced a heavier penalty, being forced to return land to the Ottomans in both Europe and Asia. This humiliation contributed to the determination of Nicholas's son and successor, Alexander II, to institute major new reforms to reinvigorate the country. The greatest of his reforms was the emancipation of the serfs in 1861 and the conferral on them of property rights to prevent them from simply becoming hired laborers of big landowners (see Chapter 27). He also authorized new joint stock companies, projected a railroad network to tie the country together, and modernized the legal and administrative arms of government.

Intellectual and cultural trends that began to germinate under Alexander I, and continued to grow under Nicholas, flourished under Alexander II. More and more people became involved in intellectual, artistic, and professional life. Under Alexander I education expanded both at the preparatory and university levels, though Alexander imposed curbs on liberal thought in his later years. Most prominent intellectuals received some amount of instruction at Moscow University, and some attended German universities. Universities also appeared in provincial cities like Kharkov and Kazan. Student clubs, along with Masonic lodges, became places for discussing new ideas.

Nicholas continued his brother's crackdown on liberal education in the universities, but he encouraged professional and scientific training. By the end of his reign Russian scholars and scientists were achieving recognition for their contributions to European thought. Scholarly careers attracted many young men from clerical families, and this helped stimulate reforms in religious education. Perhaps because political activism was prohibited, clubs, salons, and organizations promoting scientific and scholarly activities became more and more numerous. The ideas of Alexander Herzen (1812–1870), a Russian intellectual working abroad who praised traditional peasant assemblies as the heart of Russia, encouraged socialist and Slavophile thinking and gave rise, under Alexander II, to the *narodniki*, a political movement dedicated to making Russia a land of peasant communes. Feodor Dostoyevsky° (1821–1881) and Count Leo Tolstoy (1828–1910), both of whom began to publish their major novels during the reign of Alexander II, aired these and other reforming ideas in the debates of the characters they created.

Just as the Tanzimat reforms of the Ottoman Empire preceded the emergence of the Young Ottomans as a new and assertive political and intellectual force in the second half of the nineteenth century, so the initially ineffective bureaucratic reforms of Alexander I set in motion cultural currents that would make Russia a dynamic center of intellectual, artistic, and political life under his nephew Alexander II. Thus Russia belonged to two different spheres of development. It entered the nineteenth century as a recognized political force in European politics, but in other ways it had a greater resemblance to the Ottoman Empire. Rulers in both empires instituted reforms, overcame opposition, and increased the power of their governments. These activities also stimulated intellectual and political trends that would ultimately work against the absolute rule of tsar and sultan. Yet Russia would eventually develop much closer relations with western Europe and become an arena for every sort of European intellectual, artistic, and political tendency, while the Ottoman Empire would ultimately succumb to European imperialism.

THE QING EMPIRE

In 1800 the Qing Empire faced many of the crises the Ottomans had encountered, but no early reform movement of the kind initiated by Sultan Selim III emerged in China. The reasons are not difficult to understand. The Qing Empire, created by the Manchus, had skillfully countered Russian strategic and diplomatic moves in the 1600s. Instead of a Napoleon threatening them with invasion, the Qing rulers enjoyed the admiration of Jesuit priests who likened them to enlightened philosopher-kings. In 1793, however, a British attempt to establish diplomatic and trade relations—the Macartney mission—turned European opinion against China (see Chapter 21).

For their part, the Qing rulers and bureaucrats faced serious crises of a depressingly familiar sort: rebellions

---

Feodor Dostoyevsky (FE-oh-dor doh-stoh-YEHV-skee)

by displaced indigenous peoples and the poor, and protests against the injustice of the local magistrates. They dealt with these problems in the usual way, by suppressing rebels and dismissing incompetent or untrustworthy officials, and paid little attention to contacts with far-off Europeans. Complaints from European merchants at Canton, who chafed against the restrictions of the "Canton system" by which the Qing limited and controlled foreign trade, were brushed off.

Economic and Social Disorder, 1800–1839

Early Qing successes and territorial expansion sowed the seeds of the domestic and political chaos of the later period. The Qing conquest in the 1600s brought stability to central China after decades of rebellion and agricultural shortages. The new emperors encouraged the recovery of farmland, the opening of previously uncultivated areas, and the restoration and expansion of the road and canal systems. The result was a great expansion of the agricultural base together with a doubling of the population between about 1650 and 1800. Enormous numbers of farmers, merchants, and day laborers migrated in search of less crowded conditions, and a permanent floating population of the unemployed and homeless emerged. By 1800 population strain on the land had caused serious environmental damage in some parts of central and western China.

While farmers tried to cope with agricultural deterioration, other groups vented grievances against the government: Minority peoples in central and southwestern China complained about being driven off their lands during the boom of the 1700s; Mongols resented appropriation of their grazing lands and the displacement of their traditional elites. In some regions, village vigilante organizations took over policing and governing functions from Qing officials who had lost control. Growing numbers of people mistrusted the government, suspecting that all officials were corrupt. The growing presence of foreign merchants and missionaries in Canton and in the Portuguese colony of Macao aggravated discontent in neighboring districts.

In some parts of China the Qing were hated as foreign conquerors and were suspected of sympathy with the Europeans. Indeed, the White Lotus Rebellion (1794–1804)—partly inspired by a messianic ideology that predicted the restoration of the Chinese Ming dynasty and the coming of the Buddha—raged across central China and was not suppressed until 1804. It initiated a series of internal conflicts that continued through the

1800s. Ignited by deepening social instabilities, these movements were sometimes intensified by local ethnic conflicts and by unapproved religions. The ability of some village militias to defend themselves and attack others intensified the conflicts, though the same techniques proved useful to southern coastal populations attempting to fend off British invasion.

The Opium War and Its Aftermath, 1839–1850

Unlike the Ottomans, the Qing believed that the Europeans were remote and only casually interested in trade. They knew little of the enormous fortunes being made in the early 1800s by European and American merchants smuggling opium into China. They did not know that silver gained in this illegal trade was helping finance the industrial transformation of England and the United States. But Qing officials slowly became aware of British colonies in India that grew and exported opium, and of the major naval base at Singapore through which British opium reached East Asia.

For more than a century, British officials had been frustrated by the trade deficit caused by the British demand for tea and the Qing refusal to facilitate the importation of any British product. In the early 1700s a few European merchants and their Chinese partners were importing small quantities of opium. In 1729 the first Qing law banning opium imports was promulgated. By 1800, however, opium smuggling had swelled the annual import level to as many as four thousand chests. British merchants had pioneered this extremely profitable trade; Chinese merchants likewise profited from distributing the drugs. A price war in the early 1820s stemming from competition between British and American importers raised demand so sharply that as many as thirty thousand chests were being imported by the 1830s. Addiction spread to people at all levels of Qing society, including very high-ranking officials. The Qing emperor and his officials debated whether to legalize and tax opium or to enforce the existing ban more strictly. Having decided to root out the use and importation of opium, in 1839 they sent a high official to Canton to deal with the matter.

Britain considered the ban on opium importation an intolerable limitation on trade, a direct threat to Britain's economic health, and a cause for war. British naval and marine forces arrived at the south China coast in late 1839. The power of modern naval forces dawned on the Qing slowly. Indeed, Qing strategists did not learn to distinguish a naval invasion from piracy until the Opium War was nearly ended.

The **Opium War** (1839–1842) broke out when negotiations between the Qing official and British representatives reached a stalemate. The war exposed the fact that the traditional, hereditary soldiers of the Qing Empire—the **Bannermen**—were, like the Janissaries of the Ottoman Empire, hopelessly obsolete. As in the Crimean War, the British excelled at sea, where they deployed superior technology. British ships landed marines who pillaged coastal cities and then sailed to new destinations (see Map 26.2). The Qing had no imperial navy, and until they were able to engage the British in prolonged fighting on land, they were unable to defend themselves against British attacks. Even in the land engagements, Qing resources proved woefully inadequate. The British could quickly transport their forces by sea along the coast; Qing troops moved primarily on foot. Moving Qing reinforcements from central to eastern China took more than three months, and when the defense forces arrived, they were exhausted and basically without weapons.

The Bannermen used the few muskets the Qing had imported during the 1700s. The weapons were matchlocks, which required the soldiers to ignite the load of gunpowder in them by hand. Firing the weapons was dangerous, and the canisters of gunpowder that each musketeer carried on his belt were likely to explode if a fire broke out nearby—a frequent occurrence in encounters with British artillery. Most of the Bannermen, however, had no guns and fought with swords, knives, spears, and clubs. Soldiers under British command—many of them were Indians—carried percussion-cap rifles, which were far quicker, safer, and more accurate than the matchlocks. In addition, the long-range British artillery could be moved from place to place and proved deadly in the cities and villages of eastern China.

Qing commanders thought that British gunboats rode so low in the water that they could not sail up the Chinese rivers. Hence, evacuating the coasts, they believed, would protect the country from the British threat. But the British deployed new gunboats for shallow waters and moved without difficulty up the Yangzi River.

When the invaders approached Nanjing, the former Ming capital, the Qing decided to negotiate. In 1842 the terms of the **Treaty of Nanking** (the British name for Nanjing) dismantled the old Canton system. The number of **treaty ports**—cities opened to foreign residents—increased from one (Canton) to five (Canton, Xiamen, Fuzhou, Ningbo, and Shanghai°), and the island of Hong

Shanghai (shahng-hie)

Map 26.2   Conflicts in the Qing Empire, 1839–1870   In both the Opium War of 1839–1842 and the Arrow War of 1856–1860, the seacoasts saw most of the action. Since the Qing had no imperial navy, the well-armed British ships encountered little resistance as they shelled the southern coasts. In inland conflicts, such as the Taiping Rebellion, the opposing armies were massive and slow moving. Battles on land were often prolonged attempts by one side to starve out the other side before making a major assault.

Kong became a permanent British colony. British residents in China gained extraterritorial rights. The Qing government agreed to set a low tariff of 5 percent on imports and to pay Britain an indemnity of 21 million ounces of silver as a penalty for having started the war. A supplementary treaty the following year guaranteed **most-favored-nation status** to Britain; any privileges that China granted to another country would be automatically extended to Britain as well. This provision effectively

prevented the colonization of China, because giving land to one country would have necessitated giving it to all.

With each round of treaties came a new round of privileges for foreigners. In 1860 a new treaty legalized their right to import opium. Later, French treaties established the rights of foreign missionaries to travel extensively in the Chinese countryside and preach their religion. The number of treaty ports grew, too; by 1900 they numbered more than ninety.

The treaty system and the principle of extraterritoriality resulted in the colonization of small pockets of Qing territory, where foreign merchants lived at ease. Greater territorial losses resulted when outlying regions gained independence or were ceded to neighboring countries. Districts north and south of the Amur River in the northeast fell to Russia by treaty in 1858 and 1860; parts of modern Kazakhstan and Kirgizstan in the northwest met the same fate in 1864. From 1865 onward the British gradually gained control of territories on China's Indian frontier. In the late 1800s France forced the court of Vietnam to end its vassalage to the Qing, while Britain encouraged Tibetan independence.

In Canton, Shanghai, and other coastal cities, Europeans and Americans maintained offices and factories that employed local Chinese as menial laborers. The foreigners built comfortable housing in zones where Chinese were not permitted to live, and they entertained themselves in exclusive restaurants and bars. Around the foreign establishments, gambling and prostitution offered employment to part of the local urban population.

Whether in town or in the countryside, Christian missionaries whose congregations sponsored hospitals, shelters, and soup kitchens or gave stipends to Chinese who attended church enjoyed a good reputation. But just as often the missionaries themselves were regarded as another evil. They seemed to subvert Confucian beliefs by condemning ancestor worship, pressuring poor families to put their children into orphanages, or fulminating against foot-binding. The growing numbers of foreigners, and their growing privileges, became targets of resentment for a deeply dissatisfied, daily more impoverished, and increasingly militarized society.

The Taiping Rebellion, 1850–1864

The inflammatory mixture of social unhappiness and foreign intrusion exploded in the great civil war usually called the **Taiping° Rebellion.** In Guangxi, where the Taiping movement originated, entrenched social problems had been generating disorders for half a century. Agriculture in the region was unstable, and many people made their living from arduous and despised trades such as disposing of human waste, making charcoal, and mining. Ethnic divisions complicated economic distress. The lowliest trades frequently involved a minority group, the Hakkas, and tensions between them

and the majority were rising. Problems may have been intensified by the sharp rises and falls in the trade of opium, which flooded the coastal and riverine portions of China after 1842, then collapsed as domestically grown opium began to dominate the market. Also, the area was close enough to Canton to feel the cultural and economic impact of the growing number of Europeans and Americans.

Hong Xiuquan°, the founder of the Taiping movement, experienced all of these influences. Hong came from a humble Hakka background. After years of study, he competed in the provincial Confucian examinations, hoping for a post in government. He failed the examinations repeatedly, and it appears that he suffered a nervous breakdown in his late thirties. Afterward he spent some time in Canton, where he met both Chinese and American Protestant missionaries, who inspired him with their teachings. Hong had his own interpretation of the Christian message. He saw himself as the younger brother of Jesus, commissioned by God to found a new kingdom on Earth and drive the Manchu conquerors, the Qing, out of China. The result would be universal peace. Hong called his new religious movement the "Heavenly Kingdom of Great Peace."

Hong quickly attracted a community of believers, primarily Hakkas like himself. They believed in the prophecy of dreams and claimed they could walk on air. Hong and his rivals for leadership in the movement went in and out of ecstatic trances. They denounced the Manchus as creatures of Satan. News of the sect reached the government, and Qing troops arrived to arrest the Taiping leaders. But the Taipings soundly repelled the imperial troops. Local loyalty to the Taipings spread quickly; their numbers multiplied; and they began to enlarge their domain.

The Taipings relied at first on Hakka sympathy and the charismatic appeal of their religious doctrine to attract followers. But as their numbers and power grew, they altered their methods of preaching and governing. They replaced the anti-Chinese appeals used to enlist Hakkas with anti-Manchu rhetoric designed to enlist Chinese. They forced captured villages to join their movement. Once people were absorbed, the Taipings strictly monitored their activities. They segregated men and women and organized them into work and military teams. Women were forbidden to bind their feet (the Hakkas had never practiced foot-binding) and participated fully in farming and labor. Brigades of women soldiers took to the field against Qing forces.

Taiping (tie-PING)

Hong Xiuquan (hoong shee-OH-chew-an)

As the movement grew, it began to move toward eastern and northern China (see Map 26.2). Panic preceded the Taipings. Villagers feared being forced into Taiping units, and Confucian elites recoiled in horror from the bizarre ideology of foreign gods, totalitarian rule, and walking, working, warring women. But the huge numbers the Taipings were able to muster overwhelmed attempts at local defense. The tremendous growth in the number of Taiping followers required the movement to establish a permanent base. When the rebel army conquered Nanjing in 1853, the Taiping leaders decided to settle there and make it the capital of the new "Heavenly Kingdom of Great Peace."

Qing forces attempting to defend north China became more successful as problems of organization and growing numbers slowed Taiping momentum. Increasing Qing military success resulted mainly from the flexibility of the imperial military commanders in the face of an unprecedented challenge. In addition, the military commanders received strong backing from a group of civilian provincial governors who had studied the techniques developed by local militia forces for self-defense. Certain provincial governors combined their knowledge of civilian self-defense and local terrain with more efficient organization and the use of modern weaponry. The result was the formation of new military units, in which many of the Bannermen voluntarily served under civilian governors. The Qing court agreed to special taxes to fund the new armies and acknowledged the new combined leadership of the civilian and professional force.

When the Taipings settled into Nanjing, the new Qing armies surrounded the city, hoping to starve out the rebels. The Taipings, however, had provisioned and fortified themselves well. They also had the services of several brilliant young military commanders, who mobilized enormous campaigns in nearby parts of eastern China, scavenging supplies and attempting to break the encirclement of Nanjing. For more than a decade the Taiping leadership remained ensconced at Nanjing, and the "Heavenly Kingdom" endured.

In 1856 Britain and France, freed from their preoccupation with the Crimean War, turned their attention to China. European and American missionaries had visited Nanjing, curious to see what their fellow Christians were up to. Their reports were discouraging. Hong Xiuquan and the other leaders appeared to lead lives of indulgence and abandon, and more than one missionary accused them of homosexual practices. Relieved of the possible accusation of quashing a pious Christian movement, the British and French surveyed the situation. Though the Taipings were not going to topple the Qing,

rebellious Nian ("Bands") in northern China added a new threat in the 1850s. A series of simultaneous large insurrections might indeed destroy the empire. Moreover, since the Qing had not observed all the provisions of the treaties signed after the Opium War, Britain and France were now considering renewing war on the Qing themselves.

In 1856 the British and French launched a series of swift, brutal coastal attacks—a second opium war, called the Arrow War (1856–1860)—which culminated in a British and French invasion of Beijing and the sacking of the Summer Palace in 1860. A new round of treaties punished the Qing for not enacting all the provisions of the Treaty of Nanking. Having secured their principal objective, the British and French forces joined the Qing campaign against the Taipings. Attempts to coordinate the international forces were sometimes riotous and sometimes tragic, but the injection of European weaponry and money helped quell both the Taiping and the Nian rebellions during the 1860s.

The Taiping Rebellion ranks as the world's bloodiest civil war and the greatest armed conflict before the twentieth century. Estimates of deaths range from 20 million to 30 million. The loss of life came primarily from starvation and disease, for most engagements consisted of surrounding fortified cities and waiting until the enemy forces died, surrendered, or were so weakened that they could be easily defeated. Many sieges continued for months, and after starving for a year under the occupation of the rebels, people within some cities had to starve for another year under the occupation of the imperial forces. Reports of people eating grass, leather, hemp, and human flesh were widespread. The dead were rarely buried properly, and epidemic disease was common.

The area of early Taiping fighting was close to the regions of southwest China in which bubonic plague had been lingering for centuries. When the rebellion was suppressed, many Taiping followers sought safety in the highlands of Laos and Vietnam, which soon showed infestation by plague. Within a few years the disease reached Hong Kong. From there it spread to Singapore, San Francisco, Calcutta, and London. In the late 1800s there was intense apprehension over the possibility of a worldwide outbreak, and Chinese immigrants were regarded as likely carriers. This fear became a contributing factor in the passage of discriminatory immigration bans on Chinese in the United States in 1882.

The Taiping Rebellion devastated the agricultural centers of China. Many of the most intensely cultivated regions of central and eastern China were depopulated and laid barren. Some were still uninhabited decades

Nanjing Encircled   For a decade the Taipings held the city of Nanjing as their capital. For years Qing and international troops attempted to break the Taiping hold. By the summer of 1864, Qing forces had built tunnels leading to the foundations of Nanjing's city walls and had planted explosives. The detonation of the explosives signaled the final Qing assault on the rebel capital. As shown here, the common people of the city, along with their starving livestock, were caught in the cross-fire. Many of the Taiping leaders escaped the debacle at Nanjing, but nearly all were hunted down and executed.   (Roger-Viollet/Getty Images)

later, and major portions of the country did not recover until the twentieth century.

Cities, too, were hard hit. Shanghai, a treaty port of modest size before the rebellion, saw its population multiplied many times by the arrival of refugees from war-blasted neighboring provinces. The city then endured months of siege by the Taipings. Major cultural centers in eastern China lost masterpieces of art and architecture; imperial libraries were burned or their collections exposed to the weather; and the printing blocks used to make books were destroyed. While the empire faced the mountainous challenge of dealing with the material and cultural destruction of the war, it also was burdened by a

major ecological disaster in the north. The Yellow River changed course in 1855, destroying the southern part of impoverished Shandong province with flood and initiating decades of drought along the former riverbed in northern Shandong.

Decentralization at the End of the Qing Empire, 1864–1875

The Qing government emerged from the 1850s with no hope of achieving solvency. The corruption of the 1700s, attempts in the very early 1800s to restore waterworks and roads, and de-

We Have Got the Maxim Gun   These two representatives of the Qing Empire visited northern England after the Taiping Rebellion to examine and, if possible, purchase new weapons. They posed for a photograph after watching the famous Maxim gun, one of the first machine guns, shoot a tree in half.   (Peter Newark's Military Pictures)

clining yields from land taxes had bankrupted the treasury. By 1850, before the Taiping Rebellion, Qing government expenditures were ten times revenues. The indemnities demanded by Europeans after the Opium and Arrow Wars foreclosed any hope that the Qing would get out of debt. Vast stretches of formerly productive rice land were devastated, and the population was dispersed. Refugees pleaded for relief, and the imperial, volunteer, foreign, and mercenary troops that had suppressed the Taipings demanded unpaid wages.

Britain and France became active participants in the period of recovery that followed the rebellion. To insure repayment of the debt to Britain, Robert Hart was installed as inspector-general of a newly created Imperial Maritime Customs Service. Britain and the Qing split the revenues he collected. Britons and Americans worked for the Qing government as advisers and ambassadors, attempting to smooth communications between the Qing, Europe, and the United States.

The real work of the recovery, however, was managed by provincial governors who had come to the forefront in the struggle against the Taipings. To prosecute the war, they had won the right to levy their own taxes, raise their own troops, and run their own bureaucracies. These special powers were not entirely canceled when the war ended. Chief among these governors was Zeng Guofan°, who oversaw programs to restore agriculture, communications, education, and publishing, as well as

Zeng Guofan (zung gwoh-FAN)

Cixi's Allies   In the 1860s and 1870s, Cixi was a supporter of reform. In later years she was widely regarded as corrupt and self-centered and as an obstacle to reform. Her greatest allies were the court eunuchs. Introduced to palace life in early China as managers of the imperial harems, eunuchs became powerful political parties at court. The first Qing emperors refused to allow the eunuchs any political influence, but by Cixi's time the eunuchs once again were a political factor.   (Freer Gallery, Smithsonian Institution)

efforts to reform the military and industrialize armaments manufacture.

Like many provincial governors, Zeng preferred to look to the United States rather than to Britain for models and aid. He hired American advisers to run his weapons factories, shipyards, and military academies. He sponsored a daring program in which promising Chinese boys were sent to Hartford, Connecticut, a center of missionary activity, to learn English, science, mathematics, engineering, and history. They returned to China to assume some of the positions previously held by foreign advisers. Though Zeng was never an advocate of participation in public life by women, his Confucian convictions taught him that educated mothers were more than ever a necessity. He not only encouraged but partly over-

saw the advanced classical education of his own daughters. Zeng's death in 1872 deprived the empire of a major force for reform.

The period of recovery marked a fundamental structural change in the Qing Empire. Although the emperors after 1850 were ineffective rulers, a coalition of aristocrats supported the reform and recovery programs. Without their legitimization of the new powers of provincial governors like Zeng Guofan, the empire might have evaporated within a generation. A crucial member of this alliance was Cixi°, who was known as the "Empress Dowager" after the 1880s. Later observers, both Chinese and foreign, reviled her as a monster of corrup-

---

Cixi (tsuh-shee)

tion and arrogance. But in the 1860s and 1870s Cixi supported the provincial governors, some of whom became so powerful that they were managing Qing foreign policy as well as domestic affairs.

No longer a conquest regime dominated by a Manchu military caste and its Chinese civilian appointees, the empire came under the control of a group of reformist aristocrats and military men, independently powerful civilian governors, and a small number of foreign advisers. The Qing lacked strong, central, unified leadership and could not recover their powers of taxation, legislation, and military command once they had been granted to the provincial governors. From the 1860s forward, the Qing Empire disintegrated into a number of large power zones in which provincial governors handed over leadership to their protégés in a pattern that the Qing court eventually could only ritually legitimate.

CONCLUSION

Most of the subjects of the Ottoman, Russian, and Qing rulers did not think of European pressure or competition as determining factors in their lives during the first half of the nineteenth century. They continued to live according to the social and economic institutions they inherited from previous generations. By the 1870s, however, the challenge of Europe had become widely realized. The Crimean War, where European allies achieved a hollow victory for the Ottomans and then pressured the sultan for more reforms, confirmed both Ottoman and Russian military weakness. The Opium War did the same for China. Though all three empires faced similar problems of reform and military rebuilding, Russia enjoyed a comparative advantage in being less appealing to rapacious European merchants and strategists concerned with protecting overseas empires.

The policies adopted by the three imperial governments responded both to traditional concerns and to European demands. The sultans gave first priority to strengthening the central government to prevent territorial losses that began when Serbia, Egypt, and Greece became fully or partially independent. The Qing emperors confronted population growth and agricultural decline that resulted in massive rebellions. The tsars focused on continued territorial expansion. However, each faced different European pressures. In China, the Europeans and Americans wanted trade rights. In the Ottoman Empire, Britain, France, and Russia wanted equality for Christians and freedom from naval and commercial competition in the eastern Mediterranean. In Russia, moral demands for the abolition of serfdom accompanied British determination to stop territorial advances in Asia that might threaten India.

Repeated crises in all three empires would eventually result in the fall of the Qing, Romanov, and Ottoman dynasties in the first two decades of the twentieth century, but in 1870 it was still unclear whether the traditional land empires of Asia would be capable of weathering the storm. One thing that had become clear, however, at least to European eyes, was that Russia was part of Europe, while the other two empires were fundamentally alien. This judgment was based partly on religion, partly on the enthusiasm of westernizing Russian artists and intellectuals for European cultural trends, and partly on the role Russia had played in defeating Napoleon at the beginning of the century, a role that brought the tsars into the highest councils of royal decision making in Europe.

■ Key Terms

Muhammad Ali

Janissaries

Serbia

Tanzimat

Crimean War

extraterritoriality

Young Ottomans

Slavophile

Pan-Slavism

Decembrist revolt

Opium War

Bannermen

Treaty of Nanking

treaty ports

most-favored-nation status

Taiping Rebellion

■ Suggested Reading

For widely available general histories of the Ottoman Empire see Stanford Shaw, *History of the Ottoman Empire and Modern Turkey* (1976–1977), and J. P. D. B. Kinross, *The Ottoman Centuries: The Rise and Fall of the Turkish Empire* (1977).

On the economy and society of the nineteenth-century Ottoman Empire see Huri Islamoglu-Inan, ed., *The Ottoman Empire and the World-Economy* (1987); Resat Kasaba, *The Ottoman Empire and the World Economy: The Nineteenth Century* (1988); Sevket Pamuk, *The Ottoman Empire and European Capitalism, 1820–1913: Trade, Investment, and Production* (1987); Kemal H. Karpat, *Ottoman Population, 1830–1914: Demographic and Social Characteristics* (1985); and Carter V. Findley, *Bureaucratic Reform in the Ottoman Empire: The Sublime Porte, 1789–1922*

(1980). On the reform program and the emergence of national concepts see also Selim Deringil, *The Well-Protected Domains: Ideology and the Legitimation of Power in the Ottoman Empire, 1876–1909* (1998).

Marc Raeff, *Understanding Imperial Russia* (1984), sets nineteenth-century Russian developments in a broad context and challenges many standard ideas. Andreas Kappeler, *The Russian Multi-Ethnic Empire* (2001), and Mark Bassin, *Imperial Visions: Nationalist Imagination and Geographical Expansion in the Russian Far East, 1840–1865* (1999), address Russian expansion and the problems inherent in diversity of population. On economic matters see W. L. Blackwell, *The Beginnings of Russian Industrialization, 1800–1860* (1968). Daniel Field, *The End of Serfdom: Nobility and Bureaucracy in Russia, 1855–1861* (1976), addresses the primary problem besetting Russian society during this period. On the intellectual debates see M. Malia, *Alexander Herzen and the Birth of Russian Socialism* (1961), and Andrzej Walicki, *The Slavophile Controversy* (1975).

On the Qing Empire of the nineteenth century see Pamela Kyle Crossley, *Orphan Warriors: Three Manchu Generations and the End of the Qing World* (1990), and for a more detailed political history see Mary C. Wright, *The Last Stand of Chinese Conservatism: The T'ung-chih Restoration, 1862–1874* (1971). There is a very large literature on both the Opium War and the Taiping Rebellion, including reprinted editions of contemporary observers. For general histories of the Opium War see Peter Ward Fay, *The Opium War, 1840–1842: Barbarians in the Celestial Empire in the Early Part of the Nineteenth Century and the War by Which They Forced Her Gates Ajar* (1975); Christopher Hibbert, *The Dragon Wakes: China and the West, 1793–1911* (1970); and the classic study by Chang Hsin-pao, *Commissioner Lin and the Opium War* (1964). For a recent, more monographic study on Qing political thought in the period of the Opium War see James M. Polachek, *The Inner Opium War* (1992). On the Taiping Rebellion, enduring sources are S. Y. Têng, *The Taiping Rebellion and the Western Powers: A Comprehensive Survey* (1971), and C. A. Curwen, *Taiping Rebel: The Deposition of Li Hsiu-ch'eng* (1976); see also Caleb Carr, *The Devil Soldier: The Story of Frederick Townsend Ward* (1992). The most recent study is Jonathan D. Spence, *God's Chinese Son: The Taiping Heavenly Kingdom of Hong Xiuquan* (1996).

State Power, the Census, and the Question of Identity

Between the American Revolution and the last decades of the nineteenth century, Europe and the Americas were transformed. The ancient power of kings and the authority of religion were eclipsed by muscular new ways of organizing political, economic, and intellectual life. The Western world was vastly different in 1870 than it had been a century earlier. One of the less heralded but enduringly significant changes was the huge expansion of government statistical services.

The rise of the nation-state was associated with the development of modern bureaucratic departments that depended on reliable statistics to measure the nation's achievements and discover its failures. The nation-state, whether democratic or not, mobilized resources on a previously unimaginable scale. Modern states were more powerful and wealthier, and they were also more ambitious and more intrusive. The growth of their power can be seen in the modernization of militaries, the commitment to internal improvements such as railroads, and the growth in state revenues. In recent years historians have begun to examine a less visible but equally important manifestation of growing state power: census taking.

Governments and religious authorities have counted people since early times. Our best estimates of the Amerindian population of the Western Hemisphere in 1500 rest almost entirely on what were little more than missionaries' guesses about the numbers of people they baptized. Spanish and Portuguese kings were eager to count native populations, since "indios" (adult male Amerindians) were subject to special labor obligations and tribute payments. So, from the mid-sixteenth century onward, imperial officials conducted regular censuses of Amerindians, adapting practices already in place in Europe.

The effort to measure and categorize populations was transformed in the last decades of the eighteenth century when the nature of European governments began to change. The Enlightenment belief that the scientific method could be applied to human society proved to be attractive both to political radicals, like the French Revolutionaries, and to reforming monarchs like Maria Theresa of Austria. Enlightenment philosophers had argued that a science of government could remove the inefficiencies and irrationalities that had long subverted the human potential for prosperity and happiness. The French intellectual Condorcet wrote in 1782:

Those sciences, created almost in our own days, the object of which is man himself, the direct goal of which is the happiness of man, will enjoy a progress no less sure than that of the physical sciences. . . . In meditating on the nature of the moral sciences [what we now call the social sciences], one cannot help seeing that, as they are based like the physical sciences on the observation of fact, they must follow the method, acquire a language equally exact and precise, attaining the same degree of certainty.[1]

As confidence in this new "science" grew, the term previously used to describe the collection of numbers about society, *political arithmetic*, was abandoned by governments and practitioners in favor of *statistics*, a term that clearly suggests its close ties to the "state." In the nineteenth century the new objectives set out by Condorcet and others led to both the formal university training of statisticians and the creation of government statistical services.

The ambitions of governments in this new era were great. Nation-states self-consciously sought to transform society, sponsoring economic development, education, and improvements in health and welfare. They depended on statistics to measure the effectiveness of their policies and, as a result, were interested in nearly everything. They counted taverns, urban buildings, births and deaths, and arrests and convictions. They also counted their populations with a thoroughness never before seen. As statistical reporting became more uniform across Europe and the Americas, governments could measure not only their own progress but also that of their neighbors and rivals.

The revolutionary governments of France modernized the census practices of the overthrown monarchy. They spent much more money, hired many more census takers, and devoted much more energy to training the staff that designed censuses and analyzed results. Great Britain set up an official census in 1801, but established a special administrative structure only in the 1830s. In the Western Hemisphere nearly every independent nation provided for "scientific" censuses. In the United States the federal constitution required that a census be taken every ten years. Latin American nations, often torn by civil war in the nineteenth century, took censuses less regularly, but even the poorest nations took censuses when they could. It was as if the census itself confirmed the existence of the government, demonstrating its modernity and seriousness.

Until recently, historians who relied on these documents in their research on economic performance, issues of race and ethnicity, family life, and fertility and mortality asked few questions about the politics of census design. What could be more objective than rows of numbers? But the advocates of statistics who managed census taking were uninhibited in advertising the usefulness of reliable numbers to the governments that employed them. At the 1860 International Statistical Congress held in London one speaker said, "I think the true meaning to be attached to 'statistics' is not every collection of figures, but figures collected with the sole purpose of applying the principles deduced from them to questions of importance to the state."[2] The desire to be useful meant that statistics could not be fully objective.

Subjectivity was an unavoidable problem with censuses. Censuses identified citizens and foreign residents by place of residence, sex, age, and family relationships within households as well as profession and literacy. These determinations were sometimes subjective. Modern scholars have demonstrated that census takers also often undercounted the poor and those living in rural areas.

Because census takers, as agents of nation-states, were determined to be useful, they were necessarily concerned with issues of nationality and, in the Americas, with race because these characteristics commonly determined political rights and citizenship. The assessment and recording of nationality and race would prove to be among the most politically problematic objectives of the new social sciences.

Nationality had not been a central question for traditional monarchies. For the emerging nation-state, nationality was central. A nation's strength was assumed to depend in large measure on the growth of its population, a standard that, once articulated, suggested that the growth of minority populations was dangerous. Who was French? Who was Austrian or Hungarian? European statisticians relied on both *language of use* and *mother tongue* as proxies for *nationality*, the first term being flexible enough to recognize the assimilation of minorities, the second suggesting a more permanent identity based on a person's original language. Both terms forced bilingual populations to simplify their more complex identities. Ethnic minorities, once identified, were sometimes subject to discrimination such as exclusion from military careers or from universities. In parts of Spanish America language was used as a proxy for *race*. Those who spoke Spanish were citizens in the full sense, even if they were indistinguishable from Amerindians in appearance. Those who spoke indigenous languages were "indios" and therefore subject to special taxes and labor obligations and effectively denied the right to vote.

Beyond providing a justification for continuing discrimination, census categories compressed and distorted the complexity and variety of human society to fit the preconceptions of bureaucrats and politicians. Large percentages of the residents of Mexico, Peru, and Bolivia, among other parts of the Americas, were descended from both Europeans and Amerindians and, in the Caribbean region, from Europeans and Africans. Census categories never adequately captured the complexities of these biological and cultural mixtures. We now know that the poor were often identified as "indios" or "blacks" and the better-off were often called something else, "Americanos," "criollos" (creoles), or even whites. Since this process flattened and streamlined the complexities of identity, censuses on their own are not reliable guides to the distribution of ethnicity and race in a population.

In Europe the issue of nationality proved similarly perplexing for census takers and similarly dangerous to those identified as minorities. Linguistic and ethnic minorities had always lived among the politically dominant majorities: Jewish and Polish minorities in areas controlled by German speakers, German speakers among the French, and Serbo-Croatian speakers among Hungarians, for example. The frontiers between these minority populations and their neighbors were always porous. Sexual unions and marriages were common, and two or more generations of a family often lived together in the same household, with the elder members speaking one language and the younger members another. Who was what? In a very real sense, nationality, like race in the Americas, was ultimately fixed by the census process, where the nation-state forced a limited array of politically utilitarian categories onto the rich diversity of ethnicity and culture.

■ Notes

1. Quoted in James C. Scott, *Seeing Like a State. How Certain Schemes to Improve the Human Condition Have Failed* (New Haven: Yale University Press, 1998), 91.
2. This discussion relies heavily on Eliza Johnson (now Ablovatski), "Counting and Categorizing: The Hungarian Gypsy Census of 1893" (M.A. Thesis, Columbia University, 1996), especially Chapter III. She quotes from the *Proceedings of the Sixth International Statistical Congress Held in London*, 1860, 379.

Glossary

The glossary for *The Earth and Its Peoples,* 3/e is for the complete text, Chapters 1 through 34.

Abbasid Caliphate   Descendants of the Prophet Muhammad's uncle, al-Abbas, the Abbasids overthrew the **Umayyad Caliphate** and ruled an Islamic empire from their capital in Baghdad (founded 762) from 750 to 1258.   (*p. 238*)

abolitionists   Men and women who agitated for a complete end to slavery. Abolitionist pressure ended the British transatlantic slave trade in 1808 and slavery in British colonies in 1834. In the United States the activities of abolitionists were one factor leading to the Civil War (1861–1865).   (*p. 650*)

acculturation   The adoption of the language, customs, values, and behaviors of host nations by immigrants.   (*p. 654*)

Acheh Sultanate   Muslim kingdom in northern Sumatra. Main center of Islamic expansion in Southeast Asia in the early seventeenth century, it declined after the Dutch seized **Malacca** from Portugal in 1641.   (*p. 545*)

Aden   Port city in the modern south Arabian country of Yemen. It has been a major trading center in the Indian Ocean since ancient times.   (*p. 384*)

African National Congress   An organization dedicated to obtaining equal voting and civil rights for black inhabitants of South Africa. Founded in 1912 as the South African Native National Congress, it changed its name in 1923. Though it was banned and its leaders were jailed for many years, it eventually helped bring majority rule to South Africa. (*p. 837*)

Afrikaners   South Africans descended from Dutch and French settlers of the seventeenth century. Their Great Trek founded new settler colonies in the nineteenth century. Though a minority among South Africans, they held political power after 1910, imposing a system of racial segregation called apartheid after 1949.   (*p. 758*)

Agricultural Revolution(s) (ancient)   The change from food gathering to food production that occurred between ca. 8000 and 2000 B.C.E. Also known as the Neolithic Revolution.   (*pp. 18, 610*)

agricultural revolution (eighteenth century)   The transformation of farming that resulted in the eighteenth century from the spread of new crops, improvements in cultivation techniques and livestock breeding, and the consolidation of small holdings into large farms from which tenants and sharecroppers were forcibly expelled.   (*p. 610*)

Aguinaldo, Emilio (1869–1964)   Leader of the Filipino independence movement against Spain (1895–1898). He proclaimed the independence of the Philippines in 1899, but his movement was crushed and he was captured by the United States Army in 1901.   (*p. 766*)

Akbar I (1542–1605)   Most illustrious sultan of the Mughal Empire in India (r. 1556–1605). He expanded the empire and pursued a policy of conciliation with Hindus.   (*p. 541*)

Akhenaten   Egyptian pharaoh (r. 1353–1335 B.C.E.). He built a new capital at Amarna, fostered a new style of naturalistic art, and created a religious revolution by imposing worship of the sun-disk. The Amarna letters, largely from his reign, preserve official correspondence with subjects and neighbors.   (*p. 86*)

Alexander (356–323 B.C.E.)   King of Macedonia in northern Greece. Between 334 and 323 B.C.E. he conquered the Persian Empire, reached the Indus Valley, founded many Greek-style cities, and spread Greek culture across the Middle East. Later known as Alexander the Great.   (*p. 143*)

Alexandria   City on the Mediterranean coast of Egypt founded by Alexander. It became the capital of the Hellenistic kingdom of the **Ptolemies.** It contained the famous Library and the Museum—a center for leading scientific and literary figures. Its merchants engaged in trade with areas bordering the Mediterranean and the Indian Ocean.   (*p. 145*)

Allende, Salvador (1908–1973)   Socialist politician elected president of Chile in 1970 and overthrown by the military in 1973. He died during the military attack.   (*p. 890*)

All-India Muslim League   Political organization founded in India in 1906 to defend the interests of India's Muslim minority. Led by Muhammad Ali Jinnah, it attempted to negotiate with the **Indian National Congress.** In 1940, the League began demanding a separate state for Muslims, to be called Pakistan. (See also **Jinnah, Muhammad Ali.**)   (*p. 841*)

amulet   Small charm meant to protect the bearer from evil. Found frequently in archaeological excavations in Mesopotamia and Egypt, amulets reflect the religious practices of the common people.   (*p. 36*)

Amur River   This river valley was a contested frontier between northern China and eastern Russia until the settlement arranged in Treaty of Nerchinsk (1689).   (*p. 562*)

anarchists   Revolutionaries who wanted to abolish all private property and governments, usually by violence, and replace them with free associations of groups.   (*p. 733*)

Anasazi   Important culture of what is now the Southwest United States (1000–1300 C.E.). Centered on Chaco Canyon in New Mexico and Mesa Verde in Colorado, the Anasazi culture built multistory residences and worshipped in subterranean buildings called kivas.   (*p. 317*)

aqueduct   A conduit, either elevated or underground, using gravity to carry water from a source to a location—usually a city—that needed it. The Romans built many aqueducts in a period of substantial urbanization.   (*p. 163*)

Arawak   Amerindian peoples who inhabited the Greater Antilles of the Caribbean at the time of Columbus.   (*p. 423*)

Arkwright, Richard (1732–1792)   English inventor and entrepreneur who became the wealthiest and most successful textile manufacturer of the early **Industrial Revolution.** He invented the water frame, a machine that, with minimal human supervision, could spin many strong cotton threads at once. (*p. 615*)

Armenia One of the earliest Christian kingdoms, situated in eastern Anatolia and the western Caucasus and occupied by speakers of the Armenian language. (*p. 226*)

Asante African kingdom on the **Gold Coast** that expanded rapidly after 1680. Asante participated in the Atlantic economy, trading gold, slaves, and ivory. It resisted British imperial ambitions for a quarter century before being absorbed into Britain's Gold Coast colony in 1902. (*p. 759*)

Ashikaga Shogunate (1336–1573) The second of Japan's military governments headed by a shogun (a military ruler). Sometimes called the Muromachi Shogunate. (*p. 362*)

Ashoka Third ruler of the **Mauryan Empire** in India (r. 270–232 B.C.E.). He converted to Buddhism and broadcast his precepts on inscribed stones and pillars, the earliest surviving Indian writing. (*p. 189*)

Asian Tigers Collective name for South Korea, Taiwan, Hong Kong, and Singapore—nations that became economic powers in the 1970s and 1980s. (*p. 896*)

Atahualpa (1502?–1533) Last ruling Inca emperor of Peru. He was executed by the Spanish. (*p. 440*)

Atlantic Circuit The network of trade routes connecting Europe, Africa, and the Americas that underlay the Atlantic system. (*p. 511*)

Atlantic system The network of trading links after 1500 that moved goods, wealth, people, and cultures around the Atlantic Ocean basin. (*p. 500*)

Augustus (63 B.C.E.–14 C.E.) Honorific name of Octavian, founder of the **Roman Principate,** the military dictatorship that replaced the failing rule of the **Roman Senate.** After defeating all rivals, between 31 B.C.E. and 14 C.E. he laid the groundwork for several centuries of stability and prosperity in the Roman Empire. (*p. 157*)

Auschwitz Nazi extermination camp in Poland, the largest center of mass murder during the **Holocaust.** Close to a million Jews, Gypsies, Communists, and others were killed there. (*p. 827*)

australopithecines The several extinct species of humanlike primates that existed during the Pleistocene era (genus *Australopithecus*). (*p. 6*)

ayllu Andean lineage group or kin-based community. (*p. 321*)

Aztecs Also known as Mexica, the Aztecs created a powerful empire in central Mexico (1325–1521 C.E.). They forced defeated peoples to provide goods and labor as a tax. (*p. 314*)

Babylon The largest and most important city in Mesopotamia. It achieved particular eminence as the capital of the Amorite king **Hammurabi** in the eighteenth century B.C.E. and the Neo-Babylonian king Nebuchadnezzar in the sixth century B.C.E. (*p. 29*)

balance of power The policy in international relations by which, beginning in the eighteenth century, the major European states acted together to prevent any one of them from becoming too powerful. (*p. 468*)

Balfour Declaration Statement issued by Britain's Foreign Secretary Arthur Balfour in 1917 favoring the establishment of a Jewish national homeland in Palestine. (*p. 784*)

Bannermen Hereditary military servants of the **Qing Empire,** in large part descendants of peoples of various origins who had fought for the founders of the empire. (*p. 708*)

Bantu Collective name of a large group of sub-Saharan African languages and of the peoples speaking these languages. (*p. 224*)

Batavia Fort established ca. 1619 as headquarters of Dutch East India Company operations in Indonesia; today the city of Jakarta. (*p. 548*)

Battle of Midway U.S. naval victory over the Japanese fleet in June 1942, in which the Japanese lost four of their best aircraft carriers. It marked a turning point in World War II. (*p. 821*)

Battle of Omdurman British victory over the Mahdi in the Sudan in 1898. General Kitchener led a mixed force of British and Egyptian troops armed with rapid-firing rifles and machine guns. (*p. 753*)

Beijing China's northern capital, first used as an imperial capital in 906 and now the capital of the People's Republic of China. (*p. 352*)

Bengal Region of northeastern India. It was the first part of India to be conquered by the British in the eighteenth century and remained the political and economic center of British India throughout the nineteenth century. The 1905 split of the province into predominantly Hindu West Bengal and predominantly Muslim East Bengal (now Bangladesh) sparked anti-British riots. (*p. 840*)

Berlin Conference (1884–1885) Conference that German chancellor Otto von Bismarck called to set rules for the partition of Africa. It led to the creation of the Congo Free State under King **Leopold II** of Belgium. (See also **Bismarck, Otto von.**) (*p. 755*)

Bhagavad-Gita The most important work of Indian sacred literature, a dialogue between the great warrior Arjuna and the god Krishna on duty and the fate of the spirit. (*p. 190*)

bin Laden, Usama Saudi-born Muslim extremist who funded the al Qaeda organization that was responsible for several terrorist attacks, including those on the World Trade Center and the Pentagon in 2001. (*p. 923*)

bipedalism The ability to walk upright on two legs, characteristic of hominids. (*p. 7*)

Bismarck, Otto von (1815–1898) Chancellor (prime minister) of Prussia from 1862 until 1871, when he became chancellor of Germany. A conservative nationalist, he led Prussia to victory against Austria (1866) and France (1870) and was responsible for the creation of the German Empire in 1871. (*p. 737*)

Black Death An outbreak of **bubonic plague** that spread across Asia, North Africa, and Europe in the mid-fourteenth century, carrying off vast numbers of persons. (*p. 395*)

Bolívar, Simón (1783–1830) The most important military leader in the struggle for independence in South America. Born in Venezuela, he led military forces there and in Colombia, Ecuador, Peru, and Bolivia. (*p. 634*)

Bolsheviks Radical Marxist political party founded by Vladimir Lenin in 1903. Under Lenin's leadership, the Bolsheviks seized power in November 1917 during the Russian Revolution. (See also **Lenin, Vladimir.**) (*p. 784*)

Bonaparte, Napoleon. See **Napoleon I.**

Bornu A powerful West African kingdom at the southern edge of the Sahara in the Central Sudan, which was important in trans-Saharan trade and in the spread of Islam. Also known as Kanem-Bornu, it endured from the ninth century to the end of the nineteenth. (*p. 520*)

Borobodur A massive stone monument on the Indonesian island of Java, erected by the Sailendra kings around 800 C.E. The winding ascent through ten levels, decorated with rich relief carving, is a Buddhist allegory for the progressive stages of enlightenment. (*p. 199*)

bourgeoisie In early modern Europe, the class of well-off town dwellers whose wealth came from manufacturing, finance, commerce, and allied professions. (*p. 457*)

Brant, Joseph (1742–1807) Mohawk leader who supported the British during the American Revolution. (*p. 589*)

Brazza, Savorgnan de (1852–1905) Franco-Italian explorer sent by the French government to claim part of equatorial Africa for France. Founded Brazzaville, capital of the French Congo, in 1880. (*p. 755*)

British raj The rule over much of South Asia between 1765 and 1947 by the East India Company and then by a British government. (*p. 674*)

bronze An alloy of copper with a small amount of tin (or sometimes arsenic), it is harder and more durable than copper alone. The term *Bronze Age* is applied to the era—the dates of which vary in different parts of the world—when bronze was the primary metal for tools and weapons. The demand for bronze helped create long-distance networks of trade. (*p. 40*)

bubonic plague A bacterial disease of fleas that can be transmitted by flea bites to rodents and humans; humans in late stages of the illness can spread the bacteria by coughing. Because of its very high mortality rate and the difficulty of preventing its spread, major outbreaks have created crises in many parts of the world. (See also **Black Death.**) (*pp. 285, 344*)

Buddha (563–483 B.C.E.) An Indian prince named Siddhartha Gautama, who renounced his wealth and social position. After becoming "enlightened" (the meaning of *Buddha*) he enunciated the principles of Buddhism. This doctrine evolved and spread throughout India and to Southeast, East, and Central Asia. (See also **Mahayana Buddhism, Theravada Buddhism.**) (*p. 184*)

business cycles Recurrent swings from economic hard times to recovery and growth, then back to hard times and a repetition of the sequence. (*p. 626*)

Byzantine Empire Historians' name for the eastern portion of the Roman Empire from the fourth century onward, taken from "Byzantion," an early name for Constantinople, the Byzantine capital city. The empire fell to the Ottomans in 1453. (See also **Ottoman Empire.**) (*p. 254*)

caliphate Office established in succession to the Prophet Muhammad, to rule the Islamic empire; also the name of that empire. (See also **Abbasid Caliphate; Sokoto Caliphate; Umayyad Caliphate.**) (*p. 236*)

capitalism The economic system of large financial institutions—banks, stock exchanges, investment companies—that first developed in early modern Europe. *Commercial capitalism,* the trading system of the early modern economy, is often distinguished from *industrial capitalism,* the system based on machine production. (*p. 510*)

caravel A small, highly maneuverable three-masted ship used by the Portuguese and Spanish in the exploration of the Atlantic. (*p. 426*)

Cárdenas, Lázaro (1895–1970) President of Mexico (1934–1940). He brought major changes to Mexican life by distributing millions of acres of land to the peasants, bringing representatives of workers and farmers into the inner circles of politics, and nationalizing the oil industry. (*p. 847*)

Carthage City located in present-day Tunisia, founded by **Phoenicians** ca. 800 B.C.E. It became a major commercial center and naval power in the western Mediterranean until defeated by Rome in the third century B.C.E. (*p. 107*)

Caste War A rebellion of the Maya people against the government of Mexico in 1847. It nearly returned the Yucatán to Maya rule. Some Maya rebels retreated to unoccupied territories where they held out until 1901. (*p. 649*)

Catholic Reformation Religious reform movement within the Latin Christian Church, begun in response to the **Protestant Reformation.** It clarified Catholic theology and reformed clerical training and discipline. (*p. 453*)

Celts Peoples sharing a common language and culture that originated in Central Europe in the first half of the first millennium B.C.E.. After 500 B.C.E. they spread as far as Anatolia in the east, Spain and the British Isles in the west, and later were overtaken by Roman conquest and Germanic invasions. Their descendants survive on the western fringe of Europe (Brittany, Wales, Scotland, Ireland). (*p. 71*)

Champa rice Quick-maturing rice that can allow two harvests in one growing season. Originally introduced into Champa from India, it was later sent to China as a tribute gift by the Champa state. (See also **tributary system.**) (*p. 302*)

Chang'an City in the Wei Valley in eastern China. It became the capital of the Qin and early Han Empires. Its main features were imitated in the cities and towns that sprang up throughout the Han Empire. (*p. 171*)

Charlemagne (742–814) King of the Franks (r. 768–814); emperor (r. 800–814). Through a series of military conquests he established the Carolingian Empire, which encompassed all of Gaul and parts of Germany and Italy. Though illiterate himself, he sponsored a brief intellectual revival. (*p. 254*)

chartered companies Groups of private investors who paid an annual fee to France and England in exchange for a monopoly over trade to the West Indies colonies. (*p. 502*)

Chavín The first major urban civilization in South America (900–250 B.C.E.). Its capital, Chavín de Huántar, was located high in the Andes Mountains of Peru. Chavín became politically and economically dominant in a densely populated region that included two distinct ecological zones, the Peruvian coastal plain and the Andean foothills. (*p. 77*)

Chiang Kai-shek (1886–1975) Chinese military and political leader. Succeeded Sun Yat-sen as head of the **Guomindang** in 1923; headed the Chinese government from 1928 to 1948; fought against the Chinese Communists and Japanese invaders. After 1949 he headed the Chinese Nationalist government in Taiwan. (*pp. 792, 815*)

chiefdom   Form of political organization with rule by a hereditary leader who held power over a collection of villages and towns. Less powerful than kingdoms and empires, chiefdoms were based on gift giving and commercial links.   (*p. 318*)

Chimu   Powerful Peruvian civilization based on conquest. Located in the region earlier dominated by **Moche.** Conquered by **Inca** in 1465.   (*p. 323*)

chinampas   Raised fields constructed along lake shores in Mesoamerica to increase agricultural yields.   (*p. 309*)

city-state   A small independent state consisting of an urban center and the surrounding agricultural territory. A characteristic political form in early Mesopotamia, Archaic and Classical Greece, Phoenicia, and early Italy. (See also **polis.**)   (*p. 32*)

civilization   An ambiguous term often used to denote more complex societies but sometimes used by anthropologists to describe any group of people sharing a set of cultural traits.   (*p. 28*)

Cixi, Empress Dowager (1835–1908)   Empress of China and mother of Emperor Guangxi. She put her son under house arrest, supported antiforeign movements, and resisted reforms of the Chinese government and armed forces.   (*p. 743*)

clipper ship   Large, fast, streamlined sailing vessel, often American built, of the mid-to-late nineteenth century rigged with vast canvas sails hung from tall masts.   (*p. 684*)

Cold War (1945–1991)   The ideological struggle between communism (Soviet Union) and capitalism (United States) for world influence. The Soviet Union and the United States came to the brink of actual war during the **Cuban missile crisis** but never attacked one another. The Cold War came to an end when the Soviet Union dissolved in 1991. (See also **North Atlantic Treaty Organization; Warsaw Pact.**)   (*p. 831*)

colonialism   Policy by which a nation administers a foreign territory and develops its resources for the benefit of the colonial power.   (*p. 754*)

Columbian Exchange   The exchange of plants, animals, diseases, and technologies between the Americas and the rest of the world following Columbus's voyages.   (*p. 474*)

Columbus, Christopher (1451–1506)   Genoese mariner who in the service of Spain led expeditions across the Atlantic, reestablishing contact between the peoples of the Americas and the Old World and opening the way to Spanish conquest and colonization.   (*p. 430*)

Confederation of 1867   Negotiated union of the formerly separate colonial governments of Ontario, Quebec, New Brunswick, and Nova Scotia. This new Dominion of Canada with a central government in Ottawa is seen as the beginning of the Canadian nation.   (*p. 639*)

Confucius   Western name for the Chinese philosopher Kongzi (551–479 B.C.E.). His doctrine of duty and public service had a great influence on subsequent Chinese thought and served as a code of conduct for government officials.   (*p. 64*)

Congress of Vienna (1814–1815)   Meeting of representatives of European monarchs called to reestablish the old order after the defeat of **Napoleon I.**   (*p. 603*)

conquistadors   Early-sixteenth-century Spanish adventurers who conquered Mexico, Central America, and Peru. (See **Cortés, Hernán; Pizarro, Francisco.**)   (*p.436*)

Constantine (285–337 C.E.)   Roman emperor (r. 312–337). After reuniting the Roman Empire, he moved the capital to Constantinople and made Christianity a favored religion.   (*p. 166*)

Constitutional Convention   Meeting in 1787 of the elected representatives of the thirteen original states to write the Constitution of the United States.   (*p. 591*)

contract of indenture   A voluntary agreement binding a person to work for a specified period of years in return for free passage to an overseas destination. Before 1800 most **indentured servants** were Europeans; after 1800 most indentured laborers were Asians.   (*p. 687*)

Cortés, Hernán (1485–1547)   Spanish explorer and conquistador who led the conquest of Aztec Mexico in 1519–1521 for Spain.   (*p. 436*)

Cossacks   Peoples of the Russian Empire who lived outside the farming villages, often as herders, mercenaries, or outlaws. Cossacks led the conquest of Siberia in the sixteenth and seventeenth centuries.   (*p. 569*)

Council of the Indies   The institution responsible for supervising Spain's colonies in the Americas from 1524 to the early eighteenth century, when it lost all but judicial responsibilities.   (*p. 477*)

coureurs des bois **(runners of the woods)**   French fur traders, many of mixed Amerindian heritage, who lived among and often married with Amerindian peoples of North America.   (*p. 493*)

creoles   In colonial Spanish America, term used to describe someone of European descent born in the New World. Elsewhere in the Americas, the term is used to describe all nonnative peoples.   (*p. 483*)

Crimean War (1853–1856)   Conflict between the Russian and Ottoman Empires fought primarily in the Crimean Peninsula. To prevent Russian expansion, Britain and France sent troops to support the Ottomans.   (*p. 700*)

Crusades (1096–1291)   Armed pilgrimages to the Holy Land by Christians determined to recover Jerusalem from Muslim rule. The Crusades brought an end to western Europe's centuries of intellectual and cultural isolation.   (*p. 275*)

Crystal Palace   Building erected in Hyde Park, London, for the Great Exhibition of 1851. Made of iron and glass, like a gigantic greenhouse, it was a symbol of the industrial age.   (*p. 618*)

Cuban missile crisis (1962)   Brink-of-war confrontation between the United States and the Soviet Union over the latter's placement of nuclear-armed missiles in Cuba.   (*p. 869*)

cultural imperialism   Domination of one culture over another by a deliberate policy or by economic or technological superiority.   (*p. 937*)

Cultural Revolution (China) (1966–1969)   Campaign in China ordered by **Mao Zedong** to purge the Communist Party of his opponents and instill revolutionary values in the younger generation.   (*p. 881*)

culture   Socially transmitted patterns of action and expression. *Material culture* refers to physical objects, such as dwellings, clothing, tools, and crafts. Culture also includes arts, beliefs, knowledge, and technology.   (*p. 11*)

cuneiform   A system of writing in which wedge-shaped symbols represented words or syllables. It originated in Mesopotamia and was used initially for Sumerian and Akkadian but later was adapted to represent other languages of western Asia. Because so many symbols had to be learned, literacy was confined to a relatively small group of administrators and **scribes.**   (*p. 37*)

Cyrus (600–530 B.C.E.)   Founder of the Achaemenid Persian Empire. Between 550 and 530 B.C.E. he conquered Media, Lydia, and Babylon. Revered in the traditions of both Iran and the subject peoples, he employed Persians and Medes in his administration and respected the institutions and beliefs of subject peoples.   (*p. 122*)

czar   See **tsar.**

daimyo   Literally, great name(s). Japanese warlords and great landowners, whose armed **samurai** gave them control of the Japanese islands from the eighth to the later nineteenth century. Under the **Tokugawa Shogunate** they were subordinated to the imperial government.   (*p. 551*)

Daoism   Chinese school of thought, originating in the Warring States Period with Laozi (604–531 B.C.E.). Daoism offered an alternative to the Confucian emphasis on hierarchy and duty. Daoists believe that the world is always changing and is devoid of absolute morality or meaning. They accept the world as they find it, avoid futile struggles, and deviate as little as possible from the *Dao,* or "path" of nature. (See also **Confucius.**)   (*p. 64*)

Darius I (ca. 558–486 B.C.E.)   Third ruler of the Persian Empire (r. 521–486 B.C.E.). He crushed the widespread initial resistance to his rule and gave all major government posts to Persians rather than to Medes. He established a system of provinces and tribute, began construction of Persepolis, and expanded Persian control in the east (Pakistan) and west (northern Greece).   (*p. 123*)

Decembrist revolt   Abortive attempt by army officers to take control of the Russian government upon the death of Tsar Alexander I in 1825.   (*p. 706*)

Declaration of the Rights of Man (1789)   Statement of fundamental political rights adopted by the French **National Assembly** at the beginning of the French Revolution.   (*p. 595*)

deforestation   The removal of trees faster than forests can replace themselves.   (*p. 460*)

Delhi Sultanate (1206–1526)   Centralized Indian empire of varying extent, created by Muslim invaders.   (*p. 370*)

democracy   A system of government in which all "citizens" (however defined) have equal political and legal rights, privileges, and protections, as in the Greek city-state of Athens in the fifth and fourth centuries B.C.E.   (*p. 135*)

demographic transition   A change in the rates of population growth. Before the transition, both birthrates and death rates are high, resulting in a slowly growing population; then the death rate drops but the birthrate remains high, causing a population explosion; finally the birthrate drops and the population growth slows down. This transition took place in Europe in the late nineteenth and early twentieth centuries, in North America and East Asia in the mid-twentieth, and, most recently, in Latin America and South Asia.   (*p. 902*)

Deng Xiaoping (1904–1997)   Communist Party leader who forced Chinese economic reforms after the death of **Mao Zedong.**   (*p. 897*)

development   In the nineteenth and twentieth centuries, the economic process that led to industrialization, urbanization, the rise of a large and prosperous middle class, and heavy investment in education.   (*p. 656*)

devshirme   "Selection" in Turkish. The system by which boys from Christian communities were taken by the Ottoman state to serve as **Janissaries.**   (*p. 530*)

dhow   Ship of small to moderate size used in the western Indian Ocean, traditionally with a triangular sail and a sewn timber hull.   (*p. 380*)

Diagne, Blaise (1872–1934)   Senegalese political leader. He was the first African elected to the French National Assembly. During World War I, in exchange for promises to give French citizenship to Senegalese, he helped recruit Africans to serve in the French army. After the war, he led a movement to abolish forced labor in Africa.   (*p. 837*)

Dias, Bartolomeu (1450?–1500)   Portuguese explorer who in 1488 led the first expedition to sail around the southern tip of Africa from the Atlantic and sight the Indian Ocean.   (*p. 428*)

Diaspora   A Greek word meaning "dispersal," used to describe the communities of a given ethnic group living outside their homeland. Jews, for example, spread from Israel to western Asia and Mediterranean lands in antiquity and today can be found throughout the world.   (*p. 101*)

Dirty War   War waged by the Argentine military (1976–1982) against leftist groups. Characterized by the use of illegal imprisonment, torture, and executions by the military.   (*p. 890*)

divination   Techniques for ascertaining the future or the will of the gods by interpreting natural phenomena such as, in early China, the cracks on oracle bones or, in ancient Greece, the flight of birds through sectors of the sky.   (*p. 60*)

division of labor   A manufacturing technique that breaks down a craft into many simple and repetitive tasks that can be performed by unskilled workers. Pioneered in the pottery works of Josiah Wedgwood and in other eighteenth-century factories, it greatly increased the productivity of labor and lowered the cost of manufactured goods. (See also **Wedgwood, Josiah.**)   (*p. 614*)

driver   A privileged male slave whose job was to ensure that a slave gang did its work on a plantation.   (*p. 506*)

Druids   The class of religious experts who conducted rituals and preserved sacred lore among some ancient Celtic peoples. They provided education, mediated disputes between kinship groups, and were suppressed by the Romans as a potential focus of opposition to Roman rule. (See also **Celts.**)   (*p. 73*)

durbar   An elaborate display of political power and wealth in British India in the nineteenth century, ostensibly in imitation of the pageantry of the **Mughal Empire.**   (*p. 676*)

Dutch West India Company (1621–1794)   Trading company chartered by the Dutch government to conduct its merchants' trade in the Americas and Africa.   (*p. 502*)

Edison, Thomas (1847–1931)   American inventor best known for inventing the electric light bulb, acoustic recording on wax cylinders, and motion pictures.   (*p. 726*)

Einstein, Albert (1879–1955)   German physicist who developed the theory of relativity, which states that time, space, and mass are relative to each other and not fixed.   (*p. 800*)

El Alamein   Town in Egypt, site of the victory by Britain's Field Marshal Bernard Montgomery over German forces led by General Erwin Rommel (the "Desert Fox") in 1942–1943.   (*p. 821*)

electricity   A form of energy used in telegraphy from the 1840s on and for lighting, industrial motors, and railroads beginning in the 1880s.   (*p. 726*)

electric telegraph   A device for rapid, long-distance transmission of information over an electric wire. It was introduced in England and North America in the 1830s and 1840s and replaced telegraph systems that utilized visual signals such as semaphores. (See also **submarine telegraph cables.**)   (*p. 620*)

encomienda   A grant of authority over a population of Amerindians in the Spanish colonies. It provided the grant holder with a supply of cheap labor and periodic payments of goods by the Amerindians. It obliged the grant holder to Christianize the Amerindians.   (*p. 482*)

English Civil War (1642-1649)   A conflict over royal versus. Parliamentary rights, caused by King Charles I's arrest of his parliamentary critics and ending with his execution. Its outcome checked the growth of royal absolutism and, with the Glorious Revolution of 1688 and the English Bill of Rights of 1689, ensured that England would be a constitutional monarchy.   (*p. 466*)

Enlightenment   A philosophical movement in eighteenth-century Europe that fostered the belief that one could reform society by discovering rational laws that governed social behavior and were just as scientific as the laws of physics.   (*pp. 456, 582*)

equites   In ancient Italy, prosperous landowners second in wealth and status to the senatorial aristocracy. The Roman emperors allied with this group to counterbalance the influence of the old aristocracy and used the *equites* to staff the imperial civil service.   (*p. 157*)

Estates General   France's traditional national assembly with representatives of the three estates, or classes, in French society: the clergy, nobility, and commoners. The calling of the Estates General in 1789 led to the French Revolution.   (*p. 593*)

Ethiopia   East African highland nation lying east of the Nile River. (See also **Menelik II; Selassie, Haile.**)   (*p. 226*)

ethnic cleansing   Effort to eradicate a people and its culture by means of mass killing and the destruction of historical buildings and cultural materials. Ethnic cleansing was used by both sides in the conflicts that accompanied the disintegration of Yugoslavia in the 1990s.   (*p. 922*)

European Community (EC)   An organization promoting economic unity in Europe formed in 1967 by consolidation of earlier, more limited, agreements. Replaced by the European Union (EU) in 1993.   (*p. 865*)

evolution   The biological theory that, over time, changes occurring in plants and animals, mainly as a result of **natural selection** and genetic mutation, result in new species.   (*p. 5*)

extraterritoriality   The right of foreign residents in a country to live under the laws of their native country and disregard the laws of the host country. In the nineteenth and early twentieth centuries, European and American nationals living in certain areas of Chinese and Ottoman cities were granted this right.   (*p. 701*)

Faisal I (1885–1933)   Arab prince, leader of the Arab Revolt in World War I. The British made him king of Iraq in 1921, and he reigned under British protection until 1933.   (*p.784*)

Fascist Party   Italian political party created by Benito Mussolini during World War I. It emphasized aggressive nationalism and was Mussolini's instrument for the creation of a dictatorship in Italy from 1922 to 1943. (See also **Mussolini, Benito.**)   (*p. 813*)

fief   In medieval Europe, land granted in return for a sworn oath to provide specified military service.   (*p. 263*)

First Temple   A monumental sanctuary built in Jerusalem by King Solomon in the tenth century B.C.E. to be the religious center for the Israelite god Yahweh. The Temple priesthood conducted sacrifices, received a tithe or percentage of agricultural revenues, and became economically and politically powerful. The First Temple was destroyed by the Babylonians in 587 B.C.E., rebuilt on a modest scale in the late sixth century B.C.E., and replaced by King Herod's Second Temple in the late first century B.C.E. (destroyed by the Romans in 70 C.E.)   (*p. 100*)

Five-Year Plans   Plans that Joseph Stalin introduced to industrialize the Soviet Union rapidly, beginning in 1928. They set goals for the output of steel, electricity, machinery, and most other products and were enforced by the police powers of the state. They succeeded in making the Soviet Union a major industrial power before World War II. (See also **Stalin, Joseph.**)   (*p. 806*)

foragers   People who support themselves by hunting wild animals and gathering wild edible plants and insects.   (*p. 12*)

Franklin, Benjamin (1706–1790)   American intellectual, inventor, and politician He helped negotiate French support for the American Revolution.   (*p. 585*)

free-trade imperialism   Economic dominance of a weaker country by a more powerful one, while maintaining the legal independence of the weaker state. In the late nineteenth century, free-trade imperialism characterized the relations between the Latin American republics, on the one hand, and Great Britain and the United States, on the other.   (*p. 768*)

Fujiwara   Aristocratic family that dominated the Japanese imperial court between the ninth and twelfth centuries.   (*p. 301*)

Funan   An early complex society in Southeast Asia between the first and sixth centuries C.E. It was centered in the rich rice-growing region of southern Vietnam, and it controlled the passage of trade across the Malaysian isthmus.   (*p. 198*)

Gama, Vasco da (1460?–1524)   Portuguese explorer. In 1497–1498 he led the first naval expedition from Europe to sail to India, opening an important commercial sea route.   (*p. 428*)

Gandhi, Mohandas K. (Mahatma) (1869–1948)   Leader of the Indian independence movement and advocate of nonviolent resistance. After being educated as a lawyer in England, he returned to India and became leader of the **Indian National Congress** in 1920. He appealed to the poor, led nonviolent demonstrations against British colonial rule, and was jailed many times. Soon after independence he was assassinated for attempting to stop Hindu-Muslim rioting. (*p. 841*)

Garibaldi, Giuseppe (1807–1882) Italian nationalist and revolutionary who conquered Sicily and Naples and added them to a unified Italy in 1860. (*p. 736*)

Genghis Khan (ca. 1167–1227) The title of Temüjin when he ruled the Mongols (1206–1227). It means the "oceanic" or "universal" leader. Genghis Khan was the founder of the Mongol Empire. (*p. 337*)

gens de couleur Free men and women of color in Haiti. They sought greater political rights and later supported the Haitian Revolution. (See also **L'Ouverture, François Dominique Toussaint.**) (*p. 601*)

gentry In China, the class of prosperous families, next in wealth below the rural aristocrats, from which the emperors drew their administrative personnel. Respected for their education and expertise, these officials became a privileged group and made the government more efficient and responsive than in the past. The term *gentry* also denotes the class of landholding families in England below the aristocracy. (*pp. 171, 172, 459*)

Ghana First known kingdom in sub-Saharan West Africa between the sixth and thirteenth centuries C.E. Also the modern West African country once known as the Gold Coast. (*p. 221*)

global culture Cultural practices and institutions that have been adopted internationally, whether elite (the English language, modern science, and higher education) or popular (music, television, the Internet, food, and fashion). (*p. 939*)

globalization The economic, political, and cultural integration and interaction of all parts of the world brought about by increasing trade, travel, and technology. (*p. 920*)

Gold Coast (Africa) Region of the Atlantic coast of West Africa occupied by modern Ghana; named for its gold exports to Europe from the 1470s onward. (*p. 428*)

Golden Horde Mongol khanate founded by Genghis Khan's grandson Batu. It was based in southern Russia and quickly adopted both the Turkic language and Islam. Also known as the Kipchak Horde. (*p. 345*)

Gorbachev, Mikhail (b. 1931) Head of the Soviet Union from 1985 to 1991. His liberalization effort improved relations with the West, but he lost power after his reforms led to the collapse of communist governments in eastern Europe. (*p. 898*)

Gothic cathedrals Large churches originating in twelfth-century France; built in an architectural style featuring pointed arches, tall vaults and spires, flying buttresses, and large stained-glass windows. (*p. 404*)

Grand Canal The 1,100-mile (1,700-kilometer) waterway linking the Yellow and the Yangzi Rivers. It was begun in the **Han** period and completed during the Sui Empire. (*p. 282*)

Great Ice Age Geological era that occurred between ca. 2 million and 11,000 years ago. As a result of climate shifts, large numbers of new species evolved during this period, also called the Pleistocene epoch. (See also **Holocene.**) (*p. 8*)

"great traditions" Historians' term for a literate, well-institutionalized complex of religious and social beliefs and practices adhered to by diverse societies over a broad geographical area. (See also **"small traditions."**) (*p. 222*)

Great Western Schism A division in the Latin (Western) Christian Church between 1378 and 1417, when rival claimants to the papacy existed in Rome and Avignon. (*p. 412*)

Great Zimbabwe City, now in ruins (in the modern African country of Zimbabwe), whose many stone structures were built between about 1250 and 1450, when it was a trading center and the capital of a large state. (*p. 383*)

guild In medieval Europe, an association of men (rarely women), such as merchants, artisans, or professors, who worked in a particular trade and banded together to promote their economic and political interests. Guilds were also important in other societies, such as the Ottoman and Safavid empires. (*p. 401*)

Gujarat Region of western India famous for trade and manufacturing; the inhabitants are called Gujarati. (*p. 379*)

gunpowder A mixture of saltpeter, sulfur, and charcoal, in various proportions. The formula, brought to China in the 400s or 500s, was first used to make fumigators to keep away insect pests and evil spirits. In later centuries it was used to make explosives and grenades and to propel cannonballs, shot, and bullets. (*p. 296*)

Guomindang Nationalist political party founded on democratic principles by **Sun Yat-sen** in 1912. After 1925, the party was headed by **Chiang Kai-shek,** who turned it into an increasingly authoritarian movement. (*p. 791*)

Gupta Empire (320–550 C.E.) A powerful Indian state based, like its Mauryan predecessor, on a capital at Pataliputra in the Ganges Valley. It controlled most of the Indian subcontinent through a combination of military force and its prestige as a center of sophisticated culture. (See also **theater-state.**) (*p. 190*)

Habsburg A powerful European family that provided many Holy Roman Emperors, founded the Austrian (later Austro-Hungarian) Empire, and ruled sixteenth- and seventeenth-century Spain. (*p. 462*)

hadith A tradition relating the words or deeds of the Prophet Muhammad; next to the **Quran,** the most important basis for Islamic law. (*p. 243*)

Hammurabi Amorite ruler of **Babylon** (r. 1792–1750 B.C.E.). He conquered many city-states in southern and northern Mesopotamia and is best known for a code of laws, inscribed on a black stone pillar, illustrating the principles to be used in legal cases. (*p. 34*)

Han A term used to designate (1) the ethnic Chinese people who originated in the Yellow River Valley and spread throughout regions of China suitable for agriculture and (2) the dynasty of emperors who ruled from 206 B.C.E. to 220 C.E. (*p. 166*)

Hanseatic League An economic and defensive alliance of the free towns in northern Germany, founded about 1241 and most powerful in the fourteenth century. (*p. 398*)

Harappa Site of one of the great cities of the Indus Valley civilization of the third millennium B.C.E. It was located on the northwest frontier of the zone of cultivation (in modern

Pakistan), and may have been a center for the acquisition of raw materials, such as metals and precious stones, from Afghanistan and Iran.   (*p. 49*)

Hatshepsut   Queen of Egypt (r. 1473–1458 B.C.E.). She dispatched a naval expedition down the Red Sea to Punt (possibly northeast Sudan or Eretria), the faraway source of myrrh. There is evidence of opposition to a woman as ruler, and after her death her name and image were frequently defaced.   (*p. 86*)

Hausa   An agricultural and trading people of central Sudan in West Africa. Aside from their brief incorporation into the Songhai Empire, the Hausa city-states remained autonomous until the **Sokoto Caliphate** conquered them in the early nineteenth century.   (*p. 520*)

Hebrew Bible   A collection of sacred books containing diverse materials concerning the origins, experiences, beliefs, and practices of the Israelites. Most of the extant text was compiled by members of the priestly class in the fifth century B.C.E. and reflects the concerns and views of this group.   (*p. 97*)

Hellenistic Age   Historians' term for the era, usually dated 323–30 B.C.E., in which Greek culture spread across western Asia and northeastern Africa after the conquests of **Alexander** the Great. The period ended with the fall of the last major Hellenistic kingdom to Rome, but Greek cultural influence persisted until the spread of Islam in the seventh century C.E.   (*p. 144*)

Helsinki Accords (1975)   Political and human rights agreement signed in Helsinki, Finland, by the Soviet Union and western European countries.   (*p. 870*)

Henry the Navigator (1394–1460)   Portuguese prince who promoted the study of navigation and directed voyages of exploration down the western coast of Africa.   (*p. 425*)

Herodotus (ca. 485–425 B.C.E.)   Heir to the technique of *historia*—"investigation"—developed by Greeks in the late Archaic period. He came from a Greek community in Anatolia and traveled extensively, collecting information in western Asia and the Mediterranean lands. He traced the antecedents of and chronicled the **Persian Wars** between the Greek city-states and the Persian Empire, thus originating the Western tradition of historical writing.   (*p. 136*)

Herzl, Theodore (1860–1904)   Austrian journalist and founder of the Zionist movement urging the creation of a Jewish national homeland in Palestine.   (*p. 784*)

Hidalgo y Costilla, Miguel (1753–1811)   Mexican priest who led the first stage of the Mexican independence war in 1810. He was captured and executed in 1811.   (*p. 637*)

Hidden Imam   Last in a series of twelve descendants of Muhammad's son-in-law Ali, whom **Shi'ites** consider divinely appointed leaders of the Muslim community. In occlusion since ca. 873, he is expected to return as a messiah at the end of time.   (*p. 538*)

hieroglyphics   A system of writing in which pictorial symbols represented sounds, syllables, or concepts. It was used for official and monumental inscriptions in ancient Egypt. Because of the long period of study required to master this system, literacy in hieroglyphics was confined to a relatively small group of **scribes** and administrators. Cursive symbol-forms were developed for rapid composition on other media, such as **papyrus.**   (*p. 44*)

Hinduism   A general term for a wide variety of beliefs and ritual practices that have developed in the Indian subcontinent since antiquity. Hinduism has roots in ancient Vedic, Buddhist, and south Indian religious concepts and practices. It spread along the trade routes to Southeast Asia.   (*p. 185*)

Hiroshima   City in Japan, the first to be destroyed by an atomic bomb, on August 6, 1945. The bombing hastened the end of World War II.   (*p. 823*)

history   The study of past events and changes in the development, transmission, and transformation of cultural practices.   (*p. 11*)

Hitler, Adolf (1889–1945)   Born in Austria, Hitler became a radical German nationalist during World War I. He led the National Socialist German Workers' Party—the **Nazis**—in the 1920s and became dictator of Germany in 1933. He led Europe into World War II.   (*p. 813*)

Hittites   A people from central Anatolia who established an empire in Anatolia and Syria in the Late Bronze Age. With wealth from the trade in metals and military power based on chariot forces, the Hittites vied with New Kingdom Egypt for control of Syria-Palestine before falling to unidentified attackers ca. 1200 B.C.E. (See also **Ramesses II.**)   (*p. 84*)

Holocaust   Nazis' program during World War II to kill people they considered undesirable. Some 6 million Jews perished during the Holocaust, along with millions of Poles, Gypsies, Communists, Socialists, and others.   (*p. 827*)

Holocene   The geological era since the end of the **Great Ice Age** about 11,000 years ago.   (*p. 21*)

Holy Roman Empire   Loose federation of mostly German states and principalities, headed by an emperor elected by the princes. It lasted from 962 to 1806.   (*pp. 267, 462*)

hominid   The biological family that includes humans and humanlike primates.   (*p. 7*)

Homo erectus   An extinct human species. It evolved in Africa about 2 million years ago.   (*p. 10*)

Homo habilis   The first human species (now extinct). It evolved in Africa about 2.5 million years ago.   (*p. 8*)

Homo sapiens   The current human species. It evolved in Africa about 200,000 years ago. It includes archaic forms such as Neanderthals (now extinct) and all modern humans.   (*p. 10*)

hoplite   A heavily armored Greek infantryman of the Archaic and Classical periods who fought in the close-packed phalanx formation. Hoplite armies—militias composed of middle- and upper-class citizens supplying their own equipment—were for centuries superior to all other military forces.   (*p. 133*)

horse collar   Harnessing method that increased the efficiency of horses by shifting the point of traction from the animal's neck to the shoulders; its adoption favors the spread of horse-drawn plows and vehicles.   (*p. 274*)

House of Burgesses   Elected assembly in colonial Virginia, created in 1618.   (*p. 489*)

humanists (Renaissance)   European scholars, writers, and teachers associated with the study of the humanities (grammar, rhetoric, poetry, history, languages, and moral philosophy), influential in the fifteenth century and later.   (*p. 407*)

Hundred Years War (1337–1453)   Series of campaigns over control of the throne of France, involving English and French royal families and French noble families. *(p. 413)*

Husain, Saddam (b. 1937) President of Iraq from 1979 until overthrown by an American-led invasion in 2003. Waged war on Iran from 1980 to 1988. His invasion of Kuwait in 1990 was repulsed in the Persian Gulf War in 1991. *(p. 893)*

Ibn Battuta (1304–1369) Moroccan Muslim scholar, the most widely traveled individual of his time. He wrote a detailed account of his visits to Islamic lands from China to Spain and the western Sudan. *(p. 370)*

Il-khan A "secondary" or "peripheral" khan based in Persia. The Il-khans' khanate was founded by Hülegü, a grandson of **Genghis Khan,** and was based at Tabriz in modern Azerbaijan. It controlled much of Iran and Iraq. *(p. 345)*

import-substitution industrialization An economic system aimed at building a country's industry by restricting foreign trade. It was especially popular in Latin American countries such as Mexico, Argentina, and Brazil in the mid-twentieth century. It proved successful for a time but could not keep up with technological advances in Europe and North America. *(p. 851)*

Inca Largest and most powerful Andean empire. Controlled the Pacific coast of South America from Ecuador to Chile from its capital of Cuzco. *(p. 327)*

indentured servant A migrant to British colonies in the Americas who paid for passage by agreeing to work for a set term ranging from four to seven years. *(p. 489)*

Indian Civil Service The elite professional class of officials who administered the government of British India. Originally composed exclusively of well-educated British men, it gradually added qualified Indians. *(p. 676)*

Indian National Congress A movement and political party founded in 1885 to demand greater Indian participation in government. Its membership was middle class, and its demands were modest until World War I. Led after 1920 by Mohandas K. Gandhi, it appealed increasingly to the poor, and it organized mass protests demanding self-government and independence. (See also **Gandhi, Mohandas K.**) *(pp. 681, 840)*

Indian Ocean Maritime System In premodern times, a network of seaports, trade routes, and maritime culture linking countries on the rim of the Indian Ocean from Africa to Indonesia. *(p. 213)*

indulgence The forgiveness of the punishment due for past sins, granted by the Catholic Church authorities as a reward for a pious act. Martin Luther's protest against the sale of indulgences is often seen as touching off the **Protestant Reformation.** *(p. 450)*

Industrial Revolution The transformation of the economy, the environment, and living conditions, occurring first in England in the eighteenth century, that resulted from the use of steam engines, the mechanization of manufacturing in factories, and innovations in transportation and communication. *(p. 609)*

investiture controversy Dispute between the popes and the Holy Roman Emperors over who held ultimate authority over bishops in imperial lands. *(p. 267)*

Irigoyen, Hipólito (1850–1933) Argentine politician, president of Argentina from 1916 to 1922 and 1928 to 1930.

The first president elected by universal male suffrage, he began his presidency as a reformer, but later became conservative. *(p. 850)*

Iron Age Historians' term for the period during which iron was the primary metal for tools and weapons. The advent of iron technology began at different times in different parts of the world. *(p. 82)*

iron curtain Winston Churchill's term for the Cold War division between the Soviet-dominated East and the U.S.-dominated West. *(p. 861)*

Iroquois Confederacy An alliance of five northeastern Amerindian peoples (six after 1722) that made decisions on military and diplomatic issues through a council of representatives. Allied first with the Dutch and later with the English, the Confederacy dominated the area from western New England to the Great Lakes. *(p. 492)*

Islam Religion expounded by the Prophet Muhammad (570–632 C.E.) on the basis of his reception of divine revelations, which were collected after his death into the **Quran.** In the tradition of Judaism and Christianity, and sharing much of their lore, Islam calls on all people to recognize one creator god—Allah—who rewards or punishes believers after death according to how they led their lives. (See also **hadith.**) *(p. 235)*

Israel In antiquity, the land between the eastern shore of the Mediterranean and the Jordan River, occupied by the Israelites from the early second millennium B.C.E. The modern state of Israel was founded in 1948. *(p. 97)*

Jackson, Andrew (1767–1845) First president of the United States to be born in humble circumstances. He was popular among frontier residents, urban workers, and small farmers. He had a successful political career as judge, general, congressman, senator, and president. After being denied the presidency in 1824 in a controversial election, he won in 1828 and was reelected in 1832. *(p. 643)*

Jacobins Radical republicans during the French Revolution. They were led by Maximilien Robespierre from 1793 to 1794. (See also **Robespierre, Maximilien.**) *(p. 596)*

Janissaries Infantry, originally of slave origin, armed with firearms and constituting the elite of the Ottoman army from the fifteenth century until the corps was abolished in 1826. (See also ***devshirme.***) *(pp. 530, 693)*

jati. See ***varna.***

Jesus (ca. 5 B.C.E.–34 C.E.) A Jew from Galilee in northern Israel who sought to reform Jewish beliefs and practices. He was executed as a revolutionary by the Romans. Hailed as the Messiah and son of God by his followers, he became the central figure in Christianity, a belief system that developed in the centuries after his death. *(p. 162)*

Jinnah, Muhammad Ali (1876–1948) Indian Muslim politician who founded the state of Pakistan. A lawyer by training, he joined the **All-India Muslim League** in 1913. As leader of the League from the 1920s on, he negotiated with the British and the **Indian National Congress** for Muslim participation in Indian politics. From 1940 on, he led the movement for the independence of India's Muslims in a separate state of Pakistan, founded in 1947. *(p. 844)*

joint-stock company A business, often backed by a government charter, that sold shares to individuals to raise money for its trading enterprises and to spread the risks (and profits) among many investors. (*p. 459*)

Juárez, Benito (1806–1872) President of Mexico (1858–1872). Born in poverty in Mexico, he was educated as a lawyer and rose to become chief justice of the Mexican supreme court and then president. He led Mexico's resistance to a French invasion in 1863 and the installation of Maximilian as emperor. (*p. 646*)

junk A very large flatbottom sailing ship produced in the **Tang, Ming,** and **Song Empires,** specially designed for long-distance commercial travel. (*p. 295*)

Kamakura shogunate The first of Japan's decentralized military governments. (1185–1333). (*p. 302*)

kamikaze The "divine wind," which the Japanese credited with blowing Mongol invaders away from their shores in 1281. (*p. 361*)

Kangxi (1654–1722) Qing emperor (r. 1662–1722). He oversaw the greatest expansion of the **Qing Empire.** (*p. 559*)

karma In Indian tradition, the residue of deeds performed in past and present lives that adheres to a "spirit" and determines what form it will assume in its next life cycle. The doctrines of karma and reincarnation were used by the elite in ancient India to encourage people to accept their social position and do their duty. (*p. 183*)

keiretsu Alliances of corporations and banks that dominate the Japanese economy. (*p. 896*)

khipu System of knotted colored cords used by preliterate Andean peoples to transmit information. (*p. 321*)

Khomeini, Ayatollah Ruhollah (1900?–1989) Shi'ite philosopher and cleric who led the overthrow of the shah of Iran in 1979 and created an Islamic republic. (*p. 892*)

Khubilai Khan (1215–1294) Last of the Mongol Great Khans (r. 1260–1294) and founder of the **Yuan Empire.** (*p. 352*)

Kievan Russia State established at Kiev in Ukraine ca. 879 by Scandinavian adventurers asserting authority over a mostly Slavic farming population. (*p. 254*)

Korean War (1950–1953) Conflict that began with North Korea's invasion of South Korea and came to involve the United Nations (primarily the United States) allying with South Korea and the People's Republic of China allying with North Korea. (*p. 866*)

Koryo Korean kingdom founded in 918 and destroyed by a Mongol invasion in 1259. (*p. 301*)

Kush An Egyptian name for Nubia, the region alongside the Nile River south of Egypt, where an indigenous kingdom with its own distinctive institutions and cultural traditions arose beginning in the early second millennium B.C.E. It was deeply influenced by Egyptian culture and at times under the control of Egypt, which coveted its rich deposits of gold and luxury products from sub-Saharan Africa carried up the Nile corridor. (*p. 68*)

labor union An organization of workers in a particular industry or trade, created to defend the interests of members through strikes or negotiations with employers. (*p. 732*)

laissez faire The idea that government should refrain from interfering in economic affairs. The classic exposition of laissez-faire principles is Adam Smith's *Wealth of Nations* (1776). (*p. 627*)

lama In Tibetan Buddhism, a teacher. (*p. 352*)

Las Casas, Bartolomé de (1474–1566) First bishop of Chiapas, in southern Mexico. He devoted most of his life to protecting Amerindian peoples from exploitation. His major achievement was the New Laws of 1542, which limited the ability of Spanish settlers to compel Amerindians to labor for them. (See also **encomienda.**) (*p. 480*)

Latin West Historians' name for the territories of Europe that adhered to the Latin rite of Christianity and used the Latin language for intellectual exchange in the period ca. 1000–1500. (*p. 392*)

League of Nations International organization founded in 1919 to promote world peace and cooperation but greatly weakened by the refusal of the United States to join. It proved ineffectual in stopping aggression by Italy, Japan, and Germany in the 1930s, and it was superseded by the **United Nations** in 1945. (*p. 786*)

Legalism In China, a political philosophy that emphasized the unruliness of human nature and justified state coercion and control. The **Qin** ruling class invoked it to validate the authoritarian nature of their regime and its profligate expenditure of subjects' lives and labor. It was superseded in the **Han** era by a more benevolent Confucian doctrine of governmental moderation. (*p. 64*)

"legitimate" trade Exports from Africa in the nineteenth century that did not include the newly outlawed slave trade. (*p. 671*)

Lenin, Vladimir (1870–1924) Leader of the Bolshevik (later Communist) Party. He lived in exile in Switzerland until 1917, then returned to Russia to lead the Bolsheviks to victory during the Russian Revolution and the civil war that followed. (*p. 784*)

Leopold II (1835–1909) King of Belgium (r. 1865–1909). He was active in encouraging the exploration of Central Africa and became the ruler of the Congo Free State (to 1908). (*p. 755*)

liberalism A political ideology that emphasizes the civil rights of citizens, representative government, and the protection of private property. This ideology, derived from the **Enlightenment,** was especially popular among the property-owning middle classes of Europe and North America. (*p. 736*)

Library of Ashurbanipal A large collection of writings drawn from the ancient literary, religious, and scientific traditions of Mesopotamia. It was assembled by the sixth century B.C.E. Assyrian ruler Ashurbanipal. The many tablets unearthed by archaeologists constitute one of the most important sources of present-day knowledge of the long literary tradition of Mesopotamia. (*p. 97*)

Linear B A set of syllabic symbols, derived from the writing system of **Minoan** Crete, used in the Mycenaean palaces of the Late Bronze Age to write an early form of Greek. It was used primarily for palace records, and the surviving Linear B tablets provide substantial information about the economic organization of Mycenaean society and tantalizing clues about political, social, and religious institutions. (*p. 91*)

Li Shimin (599–649) One of the founders of the **Tang Empire** and its second emperor (r. 626–649). He led the expansion of the empire into Central Asia. (*p. 282*)

Little Ice Age A century-long period of cool climate that began in the 1590s. Its ill effects on agriculture in northern Europe were notable. (*p. 460*)

llama A hoofed animal indigenous to the Andes Mountains in South America. It was the only domesticated beast of burden in the Americas before the arrival of Europeans. It provided meat and wool. The use of llamas to transport goods made possible specialized production and trade among people living in different ecological zones and fostered the integration of these zones by **Chavín** and later Andean states. (*p. 77*)

loess A fine, light silt deposited by wind and water. It constitutes the fertile soil of the Yellow River Valley in northern China. Because loess soil is not compacted, it can be worked with a simple digging stick, but it leaves the region vulnerable to devastating earthquakes. (*p. 58*)

Long March (1934–1935) The 6,000-mile (9,600-kilometer) flight of Chinese Communists from southeastern to northwestern China. The Communists, led by **Mao Zedong**, were pursued by the Chinese army under orders from **Chiang Kai-shek**. The four thousand survivors of the march formed the nucleus of a revived Communist movement that defeated the **Guomindang** after World War II. (*p. 816*)

L'Ouverture, François Dominique Toussaint (1743–1803) Leader of the Haitian Revolution. He freed the slaves and gained effective independence for Haiti despite military interventions by the British and French. (*p. 601*)

ma'at Egyptian term for the concept of divinely created and maintained order in the universe. Reflecting the ancient Egyptians' belief in an essentially beneficent world, the divine ruler was the earthly guarantor of this order. (See also **pyramid.**) (*p. 43*)

Macartney mission (1792–1793) The unsuccessful attempt by the British Empire to establish diplomatic relations with the **Qing Empire.** (*p. 564*)

Magellan, Ferdinand (1480?–1521) Portuguese navigator who led the Spanish expedition of 1519–1522 that was the first to sail around the world. (*p. 431*)

Mahabharata A vast epic chronicling the events leading up to a cataclysmic battle between related kinship groups in early India. It includes the Bhagavad-Gita, the most important work of Indian sacred literature. (*p. 190*)

Mahayana Buddhism "Great Vehicle" branch of Buddhism followed in China, Japan, and Central Asia. The focus is on reverence for **Buddha** and for bodhisattvas, enlightened persons who have postponed nirvana to help others attain enlightenment. (*p. 185*)

Malacca Port city in the modern Southeast Asian country of Malaysia, founded about 1400 as a trading center on the Strait of Malacca. Also spelled Melaka. (*p. 385*)

Malay peoples A designation for peoples originating in south China and Southeast Asia who settled the Malay Peninsula, Indonesia, and the Philippines, then spread eastward across the islands of the Pacific Ocean and west to Madagascar. (*p. 196*)

Mali Empire created by indigenous Muslims in western Sudan of West Africa from the thirteenth to fifteenth century. It was famous for its role in the trans-Saharan gold trade. (See also **Mansa Kankan Musa** and **Timbuktu.**) (*p. 372*)

Malthus, Thomas (1766–1834) Eighteenth-century English intellectual who warned that population growth threatened future generations because, in his view, population growth would always outstrip increases in agricultural production. (*p. 902*)

Mamluks Under the Islamic system of military slavery, Turkic military slaves who formed an important part of the armed forces of the **Abbasid Caliphate** of the ninth and tenth centuries. Mamluks eventually founded their own state, ruling Egypt and Syria (1250–1517). (*p. 239*)

Manchu Federation of Northeast Asian peoples who founded the **Qing Empire.** (*p. 551*)

Mandate of Heaven Chinese religious and political ideology developed by the **Zhou,** according to which it was the prerogative of Heaven, the chief deity, to grant power to the ruler of China and to take away that power if the ruler failed to conduct himself justly and in the best interests of his subjects. (*p. 61*)

mandate system Allocation of former German colonies and Ottoman possessions to the victorious powers after World War I, to be administered under League of Nations supervision. (*p. 792*)

manor In medieval Europe, a large, self-sufficient landholding consisting of the lord's residence (manor house), outbuildings, peasant village, and surrounding land. (*p. 262*)

mansabs In India, grants of land given in return for service by rulers of the **Mughal Empire.** (*p. 542*)

Mansa Kankan Musa Ruler of Mali (r. 1312–1337). His pilgrimage through Egypt to **Mecca** in 1324–1325 established the empire's reputation for wealth in the Mediterranean world. (*p. 372*)

manumission A grant of legal freedom to an individual slave. (*p. 509*)

Mao Zedong (1893–1976) Leader of the Chinese Communist Party (1927–1976). He led the Communists on the **Long March** (1934–1935) and rebuilt the Communist Party and Red Army during the Japanese occupation of China (1937–1945). After World War II, he led the Communists to victory over the **Guomindang.** He ordered the **Cultural Revolution** in 1966. (*p. 815*)

maroon A slave who ran away from his or her master. Often a member of a community of runaway slaves in the West Indies and South America. (*p. 509*)

Marshall Plan U. S. program to support the reconstruction of western Europe after World War II. By 1961 more than $20 billion in economic aid had been dispersed. (*p. 863*)

Marx, Karl (1818–1883) German journalist and philosopher, founder of the Marxist branch of **socialism.** He is known for two books: *The Communist Manifesto* (1848) and *Das Kapital* (Vols. I–III, 1867–1894). (*p. 732*)

mass deportation The forcible removal and relocation of large numbers of people or entire populations. The mass deportations practiced by the Assyrian and Persian Empires were meant as a terrifying warning of the consequences of rebellion. They also brought skilled and unskilled labor to the imperial center. (*p. 95*)

mass production The manufacture of many identical products by the division of labor into many small repetitive tasks. This method was introduced into the manufacture of pottery by Josiah Wedgwood and into the spinning of cotton thread by Richard Arkwright. (See also **Arkwright, Richard; Industrial Revolution; Wedgwood, Josiah.**) (*p. 614*)

Mauryan Empire The first state to unify most of the Indian subcontinent. It was founded by Chandragupta Maurya in 324 B.C.E. and survived until 184 B.C.E. From its capital at Pataliputra in the Ganges Valley it grew wealthy from taxes on agriculture, iron mining, and control of trade routes. (See also **Ashoka.**) (*p. 188*)

Maya Mesoamerican civilization concentrated in Mexico's Yucatán Peninsula and in Guatemala and Honduras but never unified into a single empire. Major contributions were in mathematics, astronomy, and development of the calendar. (*p. 310*)

Mecca City in western Arabia; birthplace of the Prophet **Muhammad,** and ritual center of the Islamic religion. (*p. 234*)

mechanization The application of machinery to manufacturing and other activities. Among the first processes to be mechanized were the spinning of cotton thread and the weaving of cloth in late-eighteenth- and early-nineteenth-century England. (*p. 615*)

medieval Literally "middle age," a term that historians of Europe use for the period ca. 500 to ca. 1500, signifying its intermediate point between Greco-Roman antiquity and the Renaissance. (*p. 254*)

Medina City in western Arabia to which the Prophet Muhammad and his followers emigrated in 622 to escape persecution in Mecca. (*p. 235*)

megaliths Structures and complexes of very large stones constructed for ceremonial and religious purposes in **Neolithic** times. (*p. 23*)

Meiji Restoration The political program that followed the destruction of the **Tokugawa Shogunate** in 1868, in which a collection of young leaders set Japan on the path of centralization, industrialization, and imperialism. (See also **Yamagata Aritomo.**) (*p. 744*)

Memphis The capital of Old Kingdom Egypt, near the head of the Nile Delta. Early rulers were interred in the nearby **pyramids.** (*p. 43*)

Menelik II (1844–1911) Emperor of Ethiopia (r. 1889–1911). He enlarged Ethiopia to its present dimensions and defeated an Italian invasion at Adowa (1896). (*p. 759*)

mercantilism European government policies of the sixteenth, seventeenth, and eighteenth centuries designed to promote overseas trade between a country and its colonies and accumulate precious metals by requiring colonies to trade only with their motherland country. The British system was defined by the Navigation Acts, the French system by laws known as the *Exclusif.* (*p. 627*)

Meroë Capital of a flourishing kingdom in southern Nubia from the fourth century B.C.E. to the fourth century C.E. In this period Nubian culture shows more independence from Egypt and the influence of sub-Saharan Africa. (*p. 69*)

mestizo The term used by Spanish authorities to describe someone of mixed Amerindian and European descent. (*p. 487*)

Middle Passage The part of the **Atlantic Circuit** involving the transportation of enslaved Africans across the Atlantic to the Americas. (*p. 511*)

millenarianism Beliefs, based on prophetic revelations, in apocalyptic global transformations associated with the completion of cycles of a thousand years. (*p. 930*)

Ming Empire (1368–1644) Empire based in China that Zhu Yuanzhang established after the overthrow of the **Yuan Empire.** The Ming emperor **Yongle** sponsored the building of the Forbidden City and the voyages of **Zheng He.** The later years of the Ming saw a slowdown in technological development and economic decline. (*pp. 354, 557*)

Minoan Prosperous civilization on the Aegean island of Crete in the second millennium B.C.E. The Minoans engaged in far-flung commerce around the Mediterranean and exerted powerful cultural influences on the early Greeks. (*p. 88*)

mit'a Andean labor system based on shared obligations to help kinsmen and work on behalf of the ruler and religious organizations. (*p. 321*)

Moche Civilization of north coast of Peru (200–700 C.E.). An important Andean civilization that built extensive irrigation networks as well as impressive urban centers dominated by brick temples. (*p. 322*)

Moctezuma II (1466?–1520) Last Aztec emperor, overthrown by the Spanish conquistador Hernán Cortés. (*p. 436*)

modernization The process of reforming political, military, economic, social, and cultural traditions in imitation of the early success of Western societies, often with regard for accommodating local traditions in non-Western societies. (*p. 668*)

Mohenjo-Daro Largest of the cities of the Indus Valley civilization. It was centrally located in the extensive flood-plain of the Indus River in contemporary Pakistan. Little is known about the political institutions of Indus Valley communities, but the large-scale of construction at Mohenjo-Daro, the orderly grid of streets, and the standardization of building materials are evidence of central planning. (*p. 49*)

moksha The Hindu concept of the spirit's "liberation" from the endless cycle of rebirths. There are various avenues—such as physical discipline, meditation, and acts of devotion to the gods—by which the spirit can distance itself from desire for the things of this world and be merged with the divine force that animates the universe. (*p. 184*)

monasticism Living in a religious community apart from secular society and adhering to a rule stipulating chastity, obedience, and poverty. It was a prominent element of medieval Christianity and Buddhism. Monasteries were the primary centers of learning and literacy in medieval Europe. (*p. 268*)

Mongols A people of this name is mentioned as early as the records of the **Tang Empire,** living as nomads in northern Eurasia. After 1206 they established an enormous empire under **Genghis Khan,** linking western and eastern Eurasia. (*p. 337*)

monotheism Belief in the existence of a single divine entity. Some scholars cite the devotion of the Egyptian pharaoh **Akhenaten** to Aten (sun-disk) and his suppression of traditional gods as the earliest instance. The Israelite worship of Yahweh developed into an exclusive belief in one god, and this concept passed into Christianity and Islam. (*p. 101*)

monsoon Seasonal winds in the Indian Ocean caused by the differences in temperature between the rapidly heating and cooling landmasses of Africa and Asia and the slowly changing ocean waters. These strong and predictable winds have long been ridden across the open sea by sailors, and the large amounts of rainfall that they deposit on parts of India, Southeast Asia, and China allow for the cultivation of several crops a year.   (pp. 180, 368)

Morelos, José María (1765–1814)   Mexican priest and former student of Miguel Hidalgo y Costilla, he led the forces fighting for Mexican independence until he was captured and executed in 1814. (See also **Hidalgo y Costilla, Miguel.**)   (p. 638)

most-favored-nation status   A clause in a commercial treaty that awards to any later signatories all the privileges previously granted to the original signatories.   (p. 709)

movable type   Type in which each individual character is cast on a separate piece of metal. It replaced woodblock printing, allowing for the arrangement of individual letters and other characters on a page, rather than requiring the carving of entire pages at a time. It may have been invented in Korea in the thirteenth century. (See also **printing press.**)   (p. 297)

Mughal Empire   Muslim state (1526–1857) exercising dominion over most of India in the sixteenth and seventeenth centuries.   (p. 541)

Muhammad (570–632 C.E.)   Arab prophet; founder of religion of Islam.   (p. 234)

Muhammad Ali (1769–1849)   Leader of Egyptian modernization in the early nineteenth century. He ruled Egypt as an Ottoman governor, but had imperial ambitions. His descendants ruled Egypt until overthrown in 1952.   (p. 668)

mulatto   The term used in Spanish and Portuguese colonies to describe someone of mixed African and European descent.   (p. 488)

mummy   A body preserved by chemical processes or special natural circumstances, often in the belief that the deceased will need it again in the afterlife. In ancient Egypt the bodies of people who could afford mummification underwent a complex process of removing organs, filling body cavities, dehydrating the corpse with natron, and then wrapping the body with linen bandages and enclosing it in a wooden sarcophagus.   (p. 48)

Muscovy   Russian principality that emerged gradually during the era of Mongol domination. The Muscovite dynasty ruled without interruption from 1276 to 1598.   (p. 566)

Muslim   An adherent of the Islamic religion; a person who "submits" (in Arabic, *Islam* means "submission") to the will of God.   (p. 566)

Mussolini, Benito (1883–1945)   Fascist dictator of Italy (1922–1943). He led Italy to conquer Ethiopia (1935), joined Germany in the Axis pact (1936), and allied Italy with Germany in World War II. He was overthrown in 1943 when the Allies invaded Italy.   (p. 821)

Mycenae   Site of a fortified palace complex in southern Greece that controlled a Late Bronze Age kingdom. In Homer's epic poems Mycenae was the base of King Agamemnon, who commanded the Greeks besieging Troy. Contemporary archaeologists call the complex Greek society of the second millennium B.C.E. "Mycenaean."   (p. 90)

Napoleon I (1769–1832)   Overthrew French Directory in 1799 and became emperor of the French in 1804. Failed to defeat Great Britain and abdicated in 1814. Returned to power briefly in 1815 but was defeated and died in exile.   (p. 597)

Nasir al-Din Tusi (1201–1274)   Persian mathematician and cosmologist whose academy near Tabriz provided the model for the movement of the planets that helped to inspire the Copernican model of the solar system.   (p. 347)

National Assembly   French Revolutionary assembly (1789–1791). Called first as the Estates General, the three estates came together and demanded radical change. It passed the **Declaration of the Rights of Man** in 1789.   (p. 594)

nationalism   A political ideology that stresses people's membership in a nation—a community defined by a common culture and history as well as by territory. In the late eighteenth and early nineteenth centuries, nationalism was a force for unity in western Europe. In the late nineteenth century it hastened the disintegration of the Austro-Hungarian and Ottoman Empires. In the twentieth century it provided the ideological foundation for scores of independent countries emerging from **colonialism.**   (p. 733)

nawab   A Muslim prince allied to British India; technically, a semi-autonomous deputy of the Mughal emperor.   (p. 671)

Nazis   German political party joined by Adolf Hitler, emphasizing nationalism, racism, and war. When Hitler became chancellor of Germany in 1933, the Nazis became the only legal party and an instrument of Hitler's absolute rule. The party's formal name was National Socialist German Workers' Party. (See also **Hitler, Adolf.**)   (p. 813)

Nehru, Jawaharlal (1889–1964)   Indian statesman. He succeeded Mohandas K. Gandhi as leader of the **Indian National Congress.** He negotiated the end of British colonial rule in India and became India's first prime minister (1947–1964).   (p. 842)

Neo-Assyrian Empire   An empire extending from western Iran to Syria-Palestine, conquered by the Assyrians of northern Mesopotamia between the tenth and seventh centuries B.C.E. They used force and terror and exploited the wealth and labor of their subjects. They also preserved and continued the cultural and scientific developments of Mesopotamian civilization.   (p. 93)

Neo-Babylonian kingdom   Under the Chaldaeans (nomadic kinship groups that settled in southern Mesopotamia in the early first millennium B.C.E.), **Babylon** again became a major political and cultural center in the seventh and sixth centuries B.C.E. After participating in the destruction of Assyrian power, the monarchs Nabopolassar and Nebuchadnezzar took over the southern portion of the Assyrian domains. By destroying the **First Temple** in Jerusalem and deporting part of the population, they initiated the **Diaspora** of the Jews.   (p. 110)

neo-Confucianism   Term used to describe new approaches to understanding classic Confucian texts that became the basic ruling philosophy of China from the **Song** period to the twentieth century.   (p. 296)

neo-liberalism   The term used in Latin America and other developing regions to describe free-market policies that include reducing tariff protection for local industries; the sale of public-sector industries, like national airlines and public utilities, to private investors or foreign corporations;

and the reduction of social welfare policies and public-sector employment. (*p. 894*)

Neolithic   The period of the Stone Age associated with the ancient **Agricultural Revolution(s).** It follows the **Paleolithic** period.   (*p. 12*)

Nevskii, Alexander (1220–1263)   Prince of Novgorod (r. 1236–1263). He submitted to the invading Mongols in 1240 and received recognition as the leader of the Russian princes under the **Golden Horde.**   (*p. 349*)

New Economic Policy   Policy proclaimed by Vladimir Lenin in 1924 to encourage the revival of the Soviet economy by allowing small private enterprises. Joseph Stalin ended the N.E.P. in 1928 and replaced it with a series of **Five-Year Plans.** (See also **Lenin, Vladimir.**)   (*p. 788*)

New France   French colony in North America, with a capital in Quebec, founded 1608. New France fell to the British in 1763.   (*p. 493*)

New Imperialism   Historians' term for the late-nineteenth- and early-twentieth-century wave of conquests by European powers, the United States, and Japan, which were followed by the development and exploitation of the newly conquered territories for the benefit of the colonial powers.   (*p. 749*)

newly industrialized economies (NIEs)   Rapidly growing, new industrial nations of the late twentieth century, including the **Asian Tigers.**   (*p. 897*)

new monarchies   Historians' term for the monarchies in France, England, and Spain from 1450 to 1600. The centralization of royal power was increasing within more or less fixed territorial limits.   (*p. 413*)

nomadism   A way of life, forced by a scarcity of resources, in which groups of people continually migrate to find pastures and water.   (*p. 337*)

nonaligned nations   Developing countries that announced their neutrality in the **Cold War.**   (*p. 861*)

nongovernmental organizations (NGOs)   Nonprofit international organizations devoted to investigating human rights abuses and providing humanitarian relief. Two NGOs won the Nobel Peace Prize in the 1990s: International Campaign to Ban Landmines (1997) and Doctors Without Borders (1999).   (*p. 934*)

North Atlantic Treaty Organization (NATO)   Organization formed in 1949 as a military alliance of western European and North American states against the Soviet Union and its east European allies. (See also **Warsaw Pact.**)   (*p. 862*)

Olmec   The first Mesoamerican civilization. Between ca. 1200 and 400 B.C.E., the Olmec people of central Mexico created a vibrant civilization that included intensive agriculture, wide-ranging trade, ceremonial centers, and monumental construction. The Olmec had great cultural influence on later Mesoamerican societies, passing on artistic styles, religious imagery, sophisticated astronomical observation for the construction of calendars, and a ritual ball game.   (*p. 75*)

Oman   Arab state based in Musqat, the main port in the southwest region of the Arabian peninsula. Oman succeeded Portugal as a power in the western Indian Ocean in the eighteenth century.   (*p. 547*)

Opium War (1839–1842)   War between Britain and the **Qing Empire** that was, in the British view, occasioned by the Qing government's refusal to permit the importation of opium into its territories. The victorious British imposed the one-sided **Treaty of Nanking** on China.   (*p. 708*)

Organization of Petroleum Exporting Countries (OPEC)   Organization formed in 1960 by oil-producing states to promote their collective interest in generating revenue from oil.   (*p. 884*)

Ottoman Empire   Islamic state founded by Osman in northwestern Anatolia ca. 1300. After the fall of the **Byzantine Empire,** the Ottoman Empire was based at Istanbul (formerly Constantinople) from 1453 to 1922. It encompassed lands in the Middle East, North Africa, the Caucasus, and eastern Europe.   (*pp. 351, 526*)

Páez, José Antonio (1790–1873)   Venezulean soldier who led Simón Bolívar's cavalry force. He became a successful general in the war and built a powerful political base. He was unwilling to accept the constitutional authority of Bolívar's government in distant Bogotá and declared Venezuela's independence from Gran Colombia in 1829.   (*p. 643*)

Paleolithic   The period of the Stone Age associated with the **evolution** of humans. It predates the **Neolithic** period.   (*p. 12*)

Pan-Slavism   Movement among Russian intellectuals in the second half of the nineteenth century to identify culturally and politically with the Slavic peoples of eastern Europe.   (*p. 705*)

Panama Canal   Ship canal cut across the isthmus of Panama by United States Army engineers; it opened in 1915. It greatly shortened the sea voyage between the east and west coasts of North America. The United States turned the canal over to Panama on January 1, 2000.   (*p. 771*)

papacy   The central administration of the Roman Catholic Church, of which the pope is the head.   (*pp. 267, 450*)

papyrus   A reed that grows along the banks of the Nile River in Egypt. From it was produced a coarse, paperlike writing medium used by the Egyptians and many other peoples in the ancient Mediterranean and Middle East.   (*p. 44*)

Parthians   Iranian ruling dynasty between ca. 250 B.C.E. and 226 C.E.   (*p. 211*)

patron/client relationship   In ancient Rome, a fundamental social relationship in which the patron—a wealthy and powerful individual—provided legal and economic protection and assistance to clients, men of lesser status and means, and in return the clients supported the political careers and economic interests of their patron.   (*p. 155*)

Paul (ca. 5–65 C.E.)   A Jew from the Greek city of Tarsus in Anatolia, he initially persecuted the followers of Jesus but, after receiving a revelation on the road to Syrian Damascus, became a Christian. Taking advantage of his Hellenized background and Roman citizenship, he traveled throughout Syria-Palestine, Anatolia, and Greece, preaching the new religion and establishing churches. Finding his greatest success among pagans ("gentiles"), he began the process by which Christianity separated from Judaism.   (*p. 162*)

pax romana   Literally, "Roman peace," it connoted the stability and prosperity that Roman rule brought to the lands of the Roman Empire in the first two centuries C.E. The movement of people and trade goods along Roman roads and safe seas allowed for the spread of cultural practices, technologies, and religious ideas. (*p. 161*)

Pearl Harbor Naval base in Hawaii attacked by Japanese aircraft on December 7, 1941. The sinking of much of the U.S. Pacific Fleet brought the United States into World War II. (*p. 821*)

Peloponnesian War A protracted (431–404 B.C.E.) and costly conflict between the Athenian and Spartan alliance systems that convulsed most of the Greek world. The war was largely a consequence of Athenian imperialism. Possession of a naval empire allowed Athens to fight a war of attrition. Ultimately, Sparta prevailed because of Athenian errors and Persian financial support. (*p. 142*)

perestroika Policy of "openness" that was the centerpiece of Mikhail Gorbachev's efforts to liberalize communism in the Soviet Union. (See also **Gorbachev, Mikhail.**) (*p. 898*)

Pericles (ca. 495–429 B.C.E.) Aristocratic leader who guided the Athenian state through the transformation to full participatory democracy for all male citizens, supervised construction of the Acropolis, and pursued a policy of imperial expansion that led to the **Peloponnesian War.** He formulated a strategy of attrition but died from the plague early in the war. (*p. 138*)

Perón, Eva Duarte (1919–1952) Wife of **Juan Perón** and champion of the poor in Argentina. She was a gifted speaker and popular political leader who campaigned to improve the life of the urban poor by founding schools and hospitals and providing other social benefits. (*p. 852*)

Perón, Juan (1895–1974) President of Argentina (1946–1955, 1973–1974). As a military officer, he championed the rights of labor. Aided by his wife **Eva Duarte Perón,** he was elected president in 1946. He built up Argentinean industry, became very popular among the urban poor, but harmed the economy. (*p. 852*)

Persepolis A complex of palaces, reception halls, and treasury buildings erected by the Persian kings **Darius I** and Xerxes in the Persian homeland. It is believed that the New Year's festival was celebrated here, as well as the coronations, weddings, and funerals of the Persian kings, who were buried in cliff-tombs nearby. (*p. 124*)

Persian Wars Conflicts between Greek city-states and the Persian Empire, ranging from the Ionian Revolt (499–494 B.C.E.) through Darius's punitive expedition that failed at Marathon (490 B.C.E.) and the defeat of Xerxes' massive invasion of Greece by the Spartan-led Hellenic League (480–479 B.C.E.). This first major setback for Persian arms launched the Greeks into their period of greatest cultural productivity. **Herodotus** chronicled these events in the first "history" in the Western tradition. (*p. 138*)

personalist leaders Political leaders who rely on charisma and their ability to mobilize and direct the masses of citizens outside the authority of constitutions and laws. Nineteenth-century examples include José Antonio Páez of Venezuela and Andrew Jackson of the United States. Twentieth-century examples include Getulio Vargas of Brazil and Juan Perón of Argentina. (See also **Jackson, Andrew; Páez, José Antonio; Perón, Juan; Vargas, Getulio.**) (*p. 643*)

Peter the Great (1672–1725) Russian tsar (r. 1689–1725). He enthusiastically introduced Western languages and technologies to the Russian elite, moving the capital from Moscow to the new city of St. Petersburg. (*p. 569*)

pharaoh The central figure in the ancient Egyptian state. Believed to be an earthly manifestation of the gods, he used his absolute power to maintain the safety and prosperity of Egypt. (*p. 43*)

Phoenicians Semitic-speaking Canaanites living on the coast of modern Lebanon and Syria in the first millennium B.C.E. From major cities such as Tyre and Sidon, Phoenician merchants and sailors explored the Mediterranean, engaged in widespread commerce, and founded **Carthage** and other colonies in the western Mediterranean. (*p. 104*)

pilgrimage Journey to a sacred shrine by Christians seeking to show their piety, fulfill vows, or gain absolution for sins. Other religions also have pilgrimage traditions, such as the Muslim pilgrimage to **Mecca** and the pilgrimages made by early Chinese Buddhists to India in search of sacred Buddhist writings. (*p. 276*)

Pilgrims Group of English Protestant dissenters who established Plymouth Colony in Massachusetts in 1620 to seek religious freedom after having lived briefly in the Netherlands. (*p. 490*)

Pizarro, Francisco (1475?–1541) Spanish explorer who led the conquest of the **Inca** Empire of Peru in 1531–1533. (*p. 440*)

Planck, Max (1858–1947) German physicist who developed quantum theory and was awarded the Nobel Prize for physics in 1918. (*p. 800*)

plantocracy In the West Indian colonies, the rich men who owned most of the slaves and most of the land, especially in the eighteenth century. (*p. 505*)

polis The Greek term for a **city-state,** an urban center and the agricultural territory under its control. It was the characteristic form of political organization in southern and central Greece in the Archaic and Classical periods. Of the hundreds of city-states in the Mediterranean and Black Sea regions settled by Greeks, some were oligarchic, others democratic, depending on the powers delegated to the Council and the Assembly. (*p. 132*)

pop culture Entertainment spread by mass communications and enjoying wide appeal. (*p. 938*)

positivism A philosophy developed by the French count of Saint-Simon. Positivists believed that social and economic problems could be solved by the application of the scientific method, leading to continuous progress. Their ideas became popular in France and Latin America in the nineteenth century. (*p. 628*)

Potosí Located in Bolivia, one of the richest silver mining centers and most populous cities in colonial Spanish America. (*p. 480*)

printing press A mechanical device for transferring text or graphics from a woodblock or type to paper using ink. Presses using movable type first appeared in Europe in about 1450. See also **movable type.** (*p. 409*)

Protestant Reformation Religious reform movement within the Latin Christian Church beginning in 1519. It resulted in the "protesters" forming several new Christian denominations, including the Lutheran and Reformed Churches and the Church of England.   (*p. 450*)

proxy wars   During the **Cold War,** local or regional wars in which the superpowers armed, trained, and financed the combatants.   (*p. 888*)

Ptolemies   The Macedonian dynasty, descended from one of Alexander the Great's officers, that ruled Egypt for three centuries (323–30 B.C.E.). From their magnificent capital at Alexandria on the Mediterranean coast, the Ptolemies largely took over the system created by Egyptian pharaohs to extract the wealth of the land, rewarding Greeks and Hellenized non-Greeks serving in the military and administration.   (*p. 145*)

Puritans   English Protestant dissenters who believed that God predestined souls to heaven or hell before birth. They founded Massachusetts Bay Colony in 1629.   (*p. 490*)

pyramid   A large, triangular stone monument, used in Egypt and Nubia as a burial place for the king. The largest pyramids, erected during the Old Kingdom near Memphis with stone tools and compulsory labor, reflect the Egyptian belief that the proper and spectacular burial of the divine ruler would guarantee the continued prosperity of the land. (See also **ma'at.**)   (*p. 43*)

Qin   A people and state in the Wei Valley of eastern China that conquered rival states and created the first Chinese empire (221–206 B.C.E.). The Qin ruler, **Shi Huangdi,** standardized many features of Chinese society and ruthlessly marshaled subjects for military and construction projects, engendering hostility that led to the fall of his dynasty shortly after his death. The Qin framework was largely taken over by the succeeding **Han** Empire.   (*p. 166*)

Qing Empire   Empire established in China by Manchus who overthrew the **Ming Empire** in 1644. At various times the Qing also controlled Manchuria, Mongolia, Turkestan, and Tibet. The last Qing emperor was overthrown in 1911. (*p. 558*)

Quran   Book composed of divine revelations made to the Prophet Muhammad between ca. 610 and his death in 632; the sacred text of the religion of **Islam.**   (*p. 236*)

railroads   Networks of iron (later steel) rails on which steam (later electric or diesel) locomotives pulled long trains at high speeds. The first railroads were built in England in the 1830s. Their success caused a railroad-building boom throughout the world that lasted well into the twentieth century.   (*p. 723*)

Rajputs   Members of a mainly Hindu warrior caste from northwest India. The Mughal emperors drew most of their Hindu officials from this caste, and **Akbar I** married a Rajput princess.   (*p. 542*)

Ramesses II   A long-lived ruler of New Kingdom Egypt (r. 1290–1224 B.C.E.). He reached an accommodation with the **Hittites** of Anatolia after a standoff in battle at Kadesh in Syria. He built on a grand scale throughout Egypt.   (*p. 87*)

Rashid al-Din (d.1318)   Adviser to the **Il-khan** ruler Ghazan, who converted to Islam on Rashid's advice.   (*p. 347*)

recaptives   Africans rescued by Britain's Royal Navy from the illegal slave trade of the nineteenth century and restored to free status.   (*p. 671*)

reconquest of Iberia   Beginning in the eleventh century, military campaigns by various Iberian Christian states to recapture territory taken by Muslims. In 1492 the last Muslim ruler was defeated, and Spain and Portugal emerged as united kingdoms.   (*p. 414*)

Renaissance (European)   A period of intense artistic and intellectual activity, said to be a "rebirth" of Greco-Roman culture. Usually divided into an Italian Renaissance, from roughly the mid-fourteenth to mid-fifteenth century, and a Northern (trans-Alpine) Renaissance, from roughly the early fifteenth to early seventeenth century.   (*pp. 406, 449*)

Revolutions of 1848   Democratic and nationalist revolutions that swept across Europe. The monarchy in France was overthrown. In Germany, Austria, Italy, and Hungary the revolutions failed.   (*p. 604*)

Rhodes, Cecil (1853–1902)   British entrepreneur and politician involved in the expansion of the British Empire from South Africa into Central Africa. The colonies of Southern Rhodesia (now Zimbabwe) and Northern Rhodesia (now Zambia) were named after him.   (*p. 758*)

Robespierre, Maximilien (1758–1794)   Young provincial lawyer who led the most radical phases of the French Revolution. His execution ended the Reign of Terror. See **Jacobins.**   (*p. 596*)

Romanization   The process by which the Latin language and Roman culture became dominant in the western provinces of the Roman Empire. The Roman government did not actively seek to Romanize the subject peoples, but indigenous peoples in the provinces often chose to Romanize because of the political and economic advantages that it brought, as well as the allure of Roman success.   (*p. 161*)

Roman Principate   A term used to characterize Roman government in the first three centuries C.E., based on the ambiguous title *princeps* ("first citizen") adopted by Augustus to conceal his military dictatorship.   (*p. 157*)

Roman Republic   The period from 507 to 31 B.C.E., during which Rome was largely governed by the aristocratic **Roman Senate.**   (*p. 154*)

Roman Senate   A council whose members were the heads of wealthy, landowning families. Originally an advisory body to the early kings, in the era of the **Roman Republic** the Senate effectively governed the Roman state and the growing empire. Under Senate leadership, Rome conquered an empire of unprecedented extent in the lands surrounding the Mediterranean Sea. In the first century B.C.E. quarrels among powerful and ambitious senators and failure to address social and economic problems led to civil wars and the emergence of the rule of the emperors.   (*p. 154*)

Royal African Company   A trading company chartered by the English government in 1672 to conduct its merchants' trade on the Atlantic coast of Africa.   (*p. 400*)

sacrifice   A gift given to a deity, often with the aim of creating a relationship, gaining favor, and obligating the god to provide some benefit to the sacrificer, sometimes in order to sustain the deity and thereby guarantee the continuing vitality of the natural world. The object devoted to the deity could be as simple as a cup of wine poured on the ground, a live animal slain on the altar, or, in the most extreme case, the ritual killing of a human being.   (*p. 135*)

Safavid Empire   Iranian kingdom (1502–1722) established by Ismail Safavi, who declared Iran a Shi'ite state.   (*p. 536*)

Sahel   Belt south of the Sahara; literally "coastland" in Arabic.   (*p. 220*)

samurai   Literally "those who serve," the hereditary military elite of the **Tokugawa Shogunate.**   (*p. 551*)

Sandinistas   Members of a leftist coalition that overthrew the Nicaraguan dictatorship of Anastasia Somoza in 1979 and attempted to install a socialist economy. The United States financed armed opposition by the Contras. The Sandinistas lost national elections in 1990.   (*p. 890*)

Sanger, Margaret (1883–1966)   American nurse and author; pioneer in the movement for family planning; organized conferences and established birth control clinics.   (*p. 799*)

Sasanid Empire   Iranian empire, established ca. 226, with a capital in Ctesiphon, Mesopotamia. The Sasanid emperors established **Zoroastrianism** as the state religion. Islamic Arab armies overthrew the empire ca. 640.   (*p. 230*)

satrap   The governor of a province in the Achaemenid Persian Empire, often a relative of the king. He was responsible for protection of the province and for forwarding tribute to the central administration. Satraps in outlying provinces enjoyed considerable autonomy.   (*p. 123*)

savanna   Tropical or subtropical grassland, either treeless or with occasional clumps of trees. Most extensive in **sub-Saharan Africa** but also present in South America. (*p. 222*)

schism   A formal split within a religious community. See **Great Western Schism.**   (*p. 256*)

scholasticism   A philosophical and theological system, associated with Thomas Aquinas, devised to reconcile Aristotelian philosophy and Roman Catholic theology in the thirteenth century.   (*p. 407*)

Scientific Revolution   The intellectual movement in Europe, initially associated with planetary motion and other aspects of physics, that by the seventeenth century had laid the groundwork for modern science.   (*p. 454*)

"scramble" for Africa   Sudden wave of conquests in Africa by European powers in the 1880s and 1890s. Britain obtained most of eastern Africa, France most of northwestern Africa. Other countries (Germany, Belgium, Portugal, Italy, and Spain) acquired lesser amounts.   (*p. 755*)

scribe   In the governments of many ancient societies, a professional position reserved for men who had undergone the lengthy training required to be able to read and write using **cuneiforms, hieroglyphics,** or other early, cumbersome writing systems.   (*p. 35*)

seasoning   An often difficult period of adjustment to new climates, disease environments, and work routines, such as that experienced by slaves newly arrived in the Americas. (*p. 508*)

Selassie, Haile (1892–1975)   Emperor of Ethiopia (r. 1930–1974) and symbol of African independence. He fought the Italian invasion of his country in 1935 and regained his throne during World War II, when British forces expelled the Italians. He ruled **Ethiopia** as a traditional autocracy until he was overthrown in 1974.   (*p. 838*)

Semitic   Family of related languages long spoken across parts of western Asia and northern Africa. In antiquity these languages included Hebrew, Aramaic, and Phoenician. The most widespread modern member of the Semitic family is Arabic.   (*p. 32*)

"separate spheres"   Nineteenth-century idea in Western societies that men and women, especially of the middle class, should have clearly differentiated roles in society: women as wives, mothers, and homemakers; men as breadwinners and participants in business and politics.   (*p. 730*)

sepoy   A soldier in South Asia, especially in the service of the British.   (*p. 673*)

Sepoy Rebellion   The revolt of Indian soldiers in 1857 against certain practices that violated religious customs; also known as the Sepoy Mutiny.   (*p. 676*)

Serbia   The Ottoman province in the Balkans that rose up against **Janissary** control in the early 1800s. After World War II the central province of Yugoslavia. Serb leaders struggled to maintain dominance as the Yugoslav federation dissolved in the 1990s.   (*p. 693*)

serf   In medieval Europe, an agricultural laborer legally bound to a lord's property and obligated to perform set services for the lord. In Russia some serfs worked as artisans and in factories; serfdom was not abolished there until 1861.   (*pp. 262, 569*)

shaft graves   A term used for the burial sites of elite members of Mycenaean Greek society in the mid-second millennium B.C.E. At the bottom of deep shafts lined with stone slabs, the bodies were laid out along with gold and bronze jewelry, implements, weapons, and masks.   (*p. 90*)

Shah Abbas I   (r. 1587–1629)   The fifth and most renowned ruler of the **Safavid** dynasty in Iran. Abbas moved the royal capital to Isfahan in 1598.   (*p. 538*)

shamanism   The practice of identifying special individuals (shamans) who will interact with spirits for the benefit of the community. Characteristic of the Korean kingdoms of the early medieval period and of early societies of Central Asia.   (*p. 300*)

Shang   The dominant people in the earliest Chinese dynasty for which we have written records (ca. 1750–1027 B.C.E.). Ancestor worship, divination by means of oracle bones, and the use of bronze vessels for ritual purposes were major elements of Shang culture.   (*p. 60*)

Shi Huangdi   Founder of the short-lived **Qin** dynasty and creator of the Chinese Empire (r. 221–210 B.C.E.). He is remembered for his ruthless conquests of rival states, standardization of practices, and forcible organization of labor for military and engineering tasks. His tomb, with its army of life-size terracotta soldiers, has been partially excavated.   (*p. 166*)

Shi'ites   Muslims belonging to the branch of Islam believing that God vests leadership of the community in a descendant of Muhammad's son-in-law Ali. Shi'ism is the state religion of Iran. (See also **Sunnis.**)   (*pp. 230, 537*)

Siberia   The extreme northeastern sector of Asia, including the Kamchatka Peninsula and the present Russian coast of the Arctic Ocean, the Bering Strait, and the Sea of Okhotsk.   (*p. 567*)

Sikhism   Indian religion founded by the guru Nanak (1469–1539) in the Punjab region of northwest India. After the Mughal emperor ordered the beheading of the ninth guru in 1675, Sikh warriors mounted armed resistance to Mughal rule.   (*p. 543*)

Silk Road   Caravan routes connecting China and the Middle East across Central Asia and Iran.   (*p. 209*)

Slavophiles   Russian intellectuals in the early nineteenth century who favored resisting western European influences and taking pride in the traditional peasant values and institutions of the Slavic people.   (*p. 705*)

"small traditions"   Historians' term for a localized, usually nonliterate, set of customs and beliefs adhered to by a single society, often in conjunction with a **"great tradition."** (*p. 222*)

socialism   A political ideology that originated in Europe in the 1830s. Socialists advocated government protection of workers from exploitation by property owners and government ownership of industries. This ideology led to the founding of socialist or labor parties throughout Europe in the second half of the nineteenth century. (See also **Marx, Karl.**)   (*p. 732*)

Socrates   Athenian philosopher (ca. 470–399 B.C.E.) who shifted the emphasis of philosophical investigation from questions of natural science to ethics and human behavior. He attracted young disciples from elite families but made enemies by revealing the ignorance and pretensions of others, culminating in his trial and execution by the Athenian state.   (*p. 140*)

Sokoto Caliphate   A large Muslim state founded in 1809 in what is now northern Nigeria.   (*p. 667*)

Solidarity   Polish trade union created in 1980 to protest working conditions and political repression. It began the nationalist opposition to communist rule that led in 1989 to the fall of communism in eastern Europe.   (*p. 899*)

Song Empire   Empire in central and southern China (960–1126) while the Liao people controlled the north. Empire in southern China (1127–1279; the "Southern Song") while the Jin people controlled the north. Distinguished for its advances in technology, medicine, astronomy, and mathematics.   (*p. 292*)

Songhai   A people, language, kingdom, and empire in western Sudan in West Africa. At its height in the sixteenth century, the Muslim Songhai Empire stretched from the Atlantic to the land of the **Hausa** and was a major player in the trans-Saharan trade.   (*p. 519*)

Srivijaya   A state based on the Indonesian island of Sumatra, between the seventh and eleventh centuries C.E. It amassed wealth and power by a combination of selective adaptation of Indian technologies and concepts, control of the lucrative trade routes between India and China, and skillful showmanship and diplomacy in holding together a disparate realm of inland and coastal territories. (See also **theater-state.**)   (*p. 198*)

Stalin, Joseph (1879–1953)   Bolshevik revolutionary, head of the Soviet Communist Party after 1924, and dictator of the Soviet Union from 1928 to 1953. He led the Soviet Union with an iron fist, using **Five-Year Plans** to increase industrial production and terror to crush all opposition.   (*p. 805*)

Stalingrad   City in Russia, site of a Red Army victory over the German army in 1942–1943. The Battle of Stalingrad was the turning point in the war between Germany and the Soviet Union. Today Volgograd.   (*p. 819*)

Stanley, Henry Morton (1841–1904)   British-American explorer of Africa, famous for his expeditions in search of Dr. David Livingstone. Stanley helped King **Leopold II** establish the Congo Free State.   (*p. 755*)

steam engine   A machine that turns the energy released by burning fuel into motion. Thomas Newcomen built the first crude but workable steam engine in 1712. **James Watt** vastly improved his device in the 1760s and 1770s. Steam power was later applied to moving machinery in factories and to powering ships and locomotives.   (*p. 618*)

steel   A form of iron that is both durable and flexible. It was first mass-produced in the 1860s and quickly became the most widely used metal in construction, machinery, and railroad equipment.   (*p. 724*)

steppes   Treeless plains, especially the high, flat expanses of northern Eurasia, which usually have little rain and are covered with coarse grass. They are good lands for nomads and their herds. Living on the steppes promoted the breeding of horses and the development of military skills that were essential to the rise of the Mongol Empire.   (*p. 222*)

stirrup   Device for securing a horseman's feet, enabling him to wield weapons more effectively. First evidence of the use of stirrups was among the Kushan people of northern Afghanistan in approximately the first century C.E.   (*p. 213*)

stock exchange   A place where shares in a company or business enterprise are bought and sold.   (*p. 459*)

Stone Age   The historical period characterized by the production of tools from stone and other nonmetallic substances. It was followed in some places by the Bronze Age and more generally by the Iron Age.   (*p. 11*)

submarine telegraph cables   Insulated copper cables laid along the bottom of a sea or ocean for telegraphic communication. The first short cable was laid across the English Channel in 1851; the first successful transatlantic cable was laid in 1866. (See also **electric telegraph.**)   (*p. 724*)

sub-Saharan Africa   Portion of the African continent lying south of the Sahara.   (*p. 222*)

Suez Canal   Ship canal dug across the isthmus of Suez in Egypt, designed by Ferdinand de Lesseps. It opened to shipping in 1869 and shortened the sea voyage between Europe and Asia. Its strategic importance led to the British conquest of Egypt in 1882.   (*p. 749*)

Suleiman the Magnificent (1494–1566)   The most illustrious sultan of the **Ottoman Empire** (r. 1520–1566); also known as Suleiman Kanuni, "The Lawgiver." He significantly expanded the empire in the Balkans and eastern Mediterranean.   (*p. 528*)

Sumerians   The people who dominated southern Mesopotamia through the end of the third millennium B.C.E. They were responsible for the creation of many fundamental elements of Mesopotamian culture—such as irrigation technology, **cuneiform,** and religious conceptions—taken over by their **Semitic** successors.   (*p. 31*)

Sunnis   Muslims belonging to branch of Islam believing that the community should select its own leadership. The majority religion in most Islamic countries. (See also **Shi'ites.**)   (*p. 230*)

Sun Yat-sen (1867–1925)   Chinese nationalist revolutionary, founder and leader of the **Guomindang** until his death. He attempted to create a liberal democratic political movement in China but was thwarted by military leaders.   (*p. 791*)

Swahili   Bantu language with Arabic loanwords spoken in coastal regions of East Africa.   (*p. 547*)

Swahili Coast   East African shores of the Indian Ocean between the Horn of Africa and the Zambezi River; from the Arabic *sawahil,* meaning "shores."   (*p. 383*)

Taiping Rebellion (1853–1864)   The most destructive civil war before the twentieth century. A Christian-inspired rural rebellion threatened to topple the **Qing Empire.**   (*p. 710*)

Tamil kingdoms   The kingdoms of southern India, inhabited primarily by speakers of Dravidian languages, which developed in partial isolation, and somewhat differently, from the Aryan north. They produced epics, poetry, and performance arts. Elements of Tamil religious beliefs were merged into the Hindu synthesis.   (*p. 190*)

Tang Empire   Empire unifying China and part of Central Asia, founded 618 and ended 907. The Tang emperors presided over a magnificent court at their capital, Chang'an.   (*p. 282*)

Tanzimat   "Restructuring" reforms by the nineteenth-century Ottoman rulers, intended to move civil law away from the control of religious elites and make the military and the bureaucracy more efficient.   (*p. 696*)

Tecumseh (1768–1813)   Shawnee leader who attempted to organize an Amerindian confederacy to prevent the loss of additional territory to American settlers. He became an ally of the British in War of 1812 and died in battle.   (*p. 648*)

Tenochtitlan   Capital of the Aztec Empire, located on an island in Lake Texcoco. Its population was about 150,000 on the eve of Spanish conquest. Mexico City was constructed on its ruins.   (*p. 314*)

Teotihuacan   A powerful **city-state** in central Mexico (100 B.C.E.–750 C.E.). Its population was about 150,000 at its peak in 600.   (*p. 30*)

terrorism   Political belief that extreme and seemingly random violence will destabilize a government and permit the terrorists to gain political advantage. Though an old technique, terrorism gained prominence in the late twentieth century with the growth of worldwide mass media that, through their news coverage, amplified public fears of terrorist acts.   (*p. 923*)

theater-state   Historians' term for a state that acquires prestige and power by developing attractive cultural forms and staging elaborate public ceremonies (as well as redistributing valuable resources) to attract and bind subjects to the center. Examples include the **Gupta Empire** in India and **Srivijaya** in Southeast Asia.   (*p. 191*)

Thebes   Capital city of Egypt and home of the ruling dynasties during the Middle and New Kingdoms. Amon, patron deity of Thebes, became one of the chief gods of Egypt. Monarchs were buried across the river in the Valley of the Kings.   (*p. 43*)

Theravada Buddhism   "Way of the Elders" branch of Buddhism followed in Sri Lanka and much of Southeast Asia. Therevada remains close to the original principles set forth by the **Buddha;** it downplays the importance of gods and emphasizes austerity and the individual's search for enlightenment.   (*p. 185*)

third-century crisis   Historians' term for the political, military, and economic turmoil that beset the Roman Empire during much of the third century C.E.: frequent changes of ruler, civil wars, barbarian invasions, decline of urban centers, and near-destruction of long-distance commerce and the monetary economy. After 284 C.E. Diocletian restored order by making fundamental changes.   (*p. 163*)

Third World   Term applied to a group of developing countries who professed nonalignment during the **Cold War.**   (*p. 879*)

three-field system   A rotational system for agriculture in which one field grows grain, one grows legumes, and one lies fallow. It gradually replaced two-field system in medieval Europe.   (*p. 395*)

Tiananmen Square   Site in Beijing where Chinese students and workers gathered to demand greater political openness in 1989. The demonstration was crushed by Chinese military with great loss of life.   (*p. 897*)

Tibet   Country centered on the high, mountain-bounded plateau north of India. Tibetan political power occasionally extended farther to the north and west between the seventh and thirteen centuries.   (*p. 289*)

Timbuktu   City on the Niger River in the modern country of Mali. It was founded by the Tuareg as a seasonal camp sometime after 1000. As part of the **Mali** empire, Timbuktu became a major terminus of the trans-Saharan trade and a center of Islamic learning.   (*p. 386*)

Timur (1336–1405)   Member of a prominent family of the Mongols' Jagadai Khanate, Timur through conquest gained control over much of Central Asia and Iran. He consolidated the status of Sunni Islam as orthodox, and his descendants, the Timurids, maintained his empire for nearly a century and founded the **Mughal Empire** in India.   (*p. 346*)

Tiwanaku   Name of capital city and empire centered on the region near Lake Titicaca in modern Bolivia (375–1000 C.E.).   (*p. 323*)

Tokugawa Shogunate (1600–1868)   The last of the three shogunates of Japan.   (*p. 552*)

Toltecs   Powerful postclassic empire in central Mexico (900–1168 C.E.). It influenced much of Mesoamerica. Aztecs claimed ties to this earlier civilization.   (*p. 313*)

trans-Saharan caravan routes   Trading network linking North Africa with **sub-Saharan Africa** across the Sahara.   (*p. 219*)

Treaty of Nanking (1842)   The treaty that concluded the **Opium War.** It awarded Britain a large indemnity from the **Qing Empire,** denied the Qing government tariff control over some of its own borders, opened additional ports of residence to Britons, and ceded the island of Hong Kong to Britain.   (*p. 708*)

Treaty of Versailles (1919)   The treaty imposed on Germany by France, Great Britain, the United States, and other Allied Powers after World War I. It demanded that Germany dismantle its military and give up some lands to Poland. It was resented by many Germans.   (*p. 787*)

treaty ports   Cities opened to foreign residents as a result of the forced treaties between the **Qing Empire** and foreign signatories. In the treaty ports, foreigners enjoyed **extraterritoriality.**   (*p. 708*)

tributary system   A system in which, from the time of the **Han** Empire, countries in East and Southeast Asia not under the direct control of empires based in China nevertheless enrolled as tributary states, acknowledging the superiority of the emperors in China in exchange for trading rights or strategic alliances.   (*p. 285*)

tribute system   A system in which defeated peoples were forced to pay a tax in the form of goods and labor. This forced transfer of food, cloth, and other goods subsidized the development of large cities. An important component of the Aztec and Inca economies.   (*p. 315*)

trireme   Greek and Phoenician warship of the fifth and fourth centuries B.C.E. It was sleek and light, powered by 170 oars arranged in three vertical tiers. Manned by skilled sailors, it was capable of short bursts of speed and complex maneuvers.   (*p. 139*)

tropical rain forest   High-precipitation forest zones of the Americas, Africa, and Asia lying between the Tropic of Cancer and the Tropic of Capricorn.   (*p. 222*)

tropics   Equatorial region between the Tropic of Cancer and the Tropic of Capricorn. It is characterized by generally warm or hot temperatures year-round, though much variation exists due to altitude and other factors. Temperate zones north and south of the tropics generally have a winter season.   (*p. 367*)

Truman Doctrine   Foreign policy initiated by U.S. president Harry Truman in 1947. It offered military aid to help Turkey and Greece resist Soviet military pressure and subversion.   (*p. 866*)

tsar (czar)   From Latin *caesar,* this Russian title for a monarch was first used in reference to a Russian ruler by Ivan III (r. 1462–1505).   (*pp. 350, 567*)

Tulip Period (1718–1730)   Last years of the reign of Ottoman sultan Ahmed III, during which European styles and attitudes became briefly popular in Istanbul.   (*p. 536*)

Tupac Amaru II   Member of Inca aristocracy who led a rebellion against Spanish authorities in Peru in 1780–1781. He was captured and executed with his wife and other members of his family.   (*p. 496*)

tyrant   The term the Greeks used to describe someone who seized and held power in violation of the normal procedures and traditions of the community. Tyrants appeared in many Greek **city-states** in the seventh and sixth centuries B.C.E., often taking advantage of the disaffection of the emerging middle class and, by weakening the old elite, unwittingly contributing to the evolution of **democracy.**   (*p. 134*)

Uighurs   A group of Turkic-speakers who controlled their own centralized empire from 744 to 840 in Mongolia and Central Asia.   (*p. 289*)

ulama   Muslim religious scholars. From the ninth century onward, the primary interpreters of Islamic law and the social core of Muslim urban societies.   (*p. 241*)

Umayyad Caliphate   First hereditary dynasty of Muslim caliphs (661 to 750). From their capital at Damascus, the Umayyads ruled an empire that extended from Spain to India. Overthrown by the **Abbasid Caliphate.**   (*p. 236*)

umma   The community of all Muslims. A major innovation against the background of seventh-century Arabia, where traditionally kinship rather than faith had determined membership in a community.   (*p. 235*)

underdevelopment   The condition experienced by economies that depend on colonial forms of production such as the export of raw materials and plantation crops with low wages and low investment in education.   (*p. 656*)

United Nations   International organization founded in 1945 to promote world peace and cooperation. It replaced the **League of Nations.**   (*p. 862*)

Universal Declaration of Human Rights   A 1946 United Nations covenant binding signatory nations to the observance of specified rights.   (*p. 933*)

universities   Degree-granting institutions of higher learning. Those that appeared in Latin West from about 1200 onward became the model of all modern universities.   (*p. 406*)

Ural Mountains   This north-south range separates Siberia from the rest of Russia. It is commonly considered the boundary between the continents of Europe and Asia.   (*p. 567*)

Urdu   A Persian-influenced literary form of Hindi written in Arabic characters and used as a literary language since the 1300s.   (*p. 386*)

utopian socialism   A philosophy introduced by the Frenchman Charles Fourier in the early nineteenth century. Utopian socialists hoped to create humane alternatives to industrial capitalism by building self-sustaining communities whose inhabitants would work cooperatively. (See also **socialism.**)   (*p. 628*)

Vargas, Getulio (1883–1954)   Dictator of Brazil from 1930 to 1945 and from 1951 to 1954. Defeated in the presidential election of 1930, he overthrew the government and created Estado Novo ("New State"), a dictatorship that emphasized industrialization and helped the urban poor but did little to alleviate the problems of the peasants.   (*p. 851*)

varna/jati   Two categories of social identity of great importance in Indian history. *Varna* are the four major social divisions: the *Brahmin* priest class, the *Kshatriya* warrior/administrator class, the *Vaishya* merchant/farmer class, and the *Shudra* laborer class. Within the system of *varna* are many *jati*, regional groups of people who have a common occupational sphere, and who marry, eat, and generally interact with other members of their group.   (*pp. 182, 183*)

vassal   In medieval Europe, a sworn supporter of a king or lord committed to rendering specified military service to that king or lord.   (*p. 263*)

Vedas   Early Indian sacred "knowledge"—the literal meaning of the term—long preserved and communicated orally by Brahmin priests and eventually written down. These religious texts, including the thousand poetic hymns to various deities contained in the Rig Veda, are our main source of information about the Vedic period (ca. 1500–500 B.C.E.).   (*p. 180*)

Versailles   The huge palace built for French King Louis XIV south of Paris in the town of the same name. The palace symbolized the preeminence of French power and architecture in Europe and the triumph of royal authority over the French nobility.   (*p. 466*)

Victorian Age   The reign of Queen Victoria of Great Britain (r. 1837–1901). The term is also used to describe late-nineteenth-century society, with its rigid moral standards and sharply differentiated roles for men and women and for middle-class and working-class people. (See also **"separate spheres."**) (*p. 730*)

Vietnam War (1954–1975) Conflict pitting North Vietnam and South Vietnamese communist guerrillas against the South Vietnamese government, aided after 1961 by the United States. (*p. 869*)

Villa, Francisco "Pancho" (1878–1923) A popular leader during the Mexican Revolution. An outlaw in his youth, when the revolution started, he formed a cavalry army in the north of Mexico and fought for the rights of the landless in collaboration with **Emiliano Zapata.** He was assassinated in 1923. (*p. 846*)

Wari Andean civilization culturally linked to **Tiwanaku,** perhaps beginning as a colony of Tiwanaku. (*p. 323*)

Warsaw Pact The 1955 treaty binding the Soviet Union and countries of eastern Europe in an alliance against the **North Atlantic Treaty Organization.** (*p. 866*)

Washington, George (1732–1799) Military commander of the American Revolution. He was the first elected president of the United States (1789–1799). (*p. 589*)

water wheel A mechanism that harnesses the energy in flowing water to grind grain or to power machinery. It was used in many parts of the world but was especially common in Europe from 1200 to 1900. (*p. 397*)

Watt, James (1736–1819) Scot who invented the condenser and other improvements that made the **steam engine** a practical source of power for industry and transportation. The watt, an electrical measurement, is named after him. (*p. 619*)

weapons of mass destruction Nuclear, chemical, and biological devices that are capable of injuring and killing large numbers of people. (*p. 923*)

Wedgwood, Josiah (1730–1795) English industrialist whose pottery works were the first to produce fine-quality pottery by industrial methods. (*p. 614*)

Western Front A line of trenches and fortifications in World War I that stretched without a break from Switzerland to the North Sea. Scene of most of the fighting between Germany, on the one hand, and France and Britain, on the other. (*p. 780*)

Wilson, Woodrow (1856–1924) President of the United States (1913–1921) and the leading figure at the Paris Peace Conference of 1919. He was unable to persuade the U.S. Congress to ratify the **Treaty of Versailles** or join the **League of Nations.** (*p. 785*)

witch-hunt The pursuit of people suspected of witchcraft, especially in northern Europe in the late sixteenth and seventeenth centuries. (*p. 453*)

Women's Rights Convention An 1848 gathering of women angered by their exclusion from an international antislavery meeting. They met at Seneca Falls, New York to discuss women's rights. (*p. 655*)

World Bank A specialized agency of the United Nations that makes loans to countries for economic development, trade promotion, and debt consolidation. Its formal name is the International Bank for Reconstruction and Development. (*p. 862*)

World Trade Organization (WTO) An international body established in 1995 to foster and bring order to international trade. (*p. 927*)

Wright, Wilbur (1867-1912), and Orville (1871-1948) American bicycle mechanics; the first to build and fly an airplane, at Kitty Hawk, North Carolina, December 7, 1903. (*p. 800*)

Xiongnu A confederation of nomadic peoples living beyond the northwest frontier of ancient China. Chinese rulers tried a variety of defenses and stratagems to ward off these "barbarians," as they called them, and finally succeeded in dispersing the Xiongnu in the first century C.E. (*p. 173*)

Yamagata Aritomo (1838–1922) One of the leaders of the **Meiji Restoration.** (*p. 746*)

Yi (1392–1910) The Yi dynasty ruled Korea from the fall of the **Koryo** kingdom to the colonization of Korea by Japan. (*p. 359*)

yin/yang In Chinese belief, complementary factors that help to maintain the equilibrium of the world. Yin is associated with masculine, light, and active qualities; yang with feminine, dark, and passive qualities. (*p. 65*)

Yongle Reign period of Zhu Di (1360–1424), the third emperor of the **Ming Empire** (r. 1403–1424). He sponsored the building of the **Forbidden City,** a huge encyclopedia project, the expeditions of **Zheng He,** and the reopening of China's borders to trade and travel. (*p. 355*)

Young Ottomans Movement of young intellectuals to institute liberal reforms and build a feeling of national identity in the Ottoman Empire in the second half of the nineteenth century. (*p. 703*)

Yuan Empire (1271–1368) Empire created in China and Siberia by **Khubilai Khan.** (*p. 342*)

Yuan Shikai (1859–1916) Chinese general and first president of the Chinese Republic (1912–1916). He stood in the way of the democratic movement led by **Sun Yat-sen.** (*p. 791*)

Zapata, Emiliano (1879–1919) Revolutionary and leader of peasants in the Mexican Revolution. He mobilized landless peasants in south-central Mexico in an attempt to seize and divide the lands of the wealthy landowners. Though successful for a time, he was ultimately defeated and assassinated. (*p. 846*)

Zen The Japanese word for a branch of **Mahayana Buddhism** based on highly disciplined meditation. It is known in Sanskrit as *dhyana*, in Chinese as *chan*, and in Korean as *son*. (*p. 296*)

Zheng He (1371–1433) An imperial eunuch and Muslim, entrusted by the Ming emperor **Yongle** with a series of state voyages that took his gigantic ships through the Indian Ocean, from Southeast Asia to Africa. (*pp. 356, 422*)

Zhou The people and dynasty that took over the dominant position in north China from the **Shang** and created the concept of the **Mandate of Heaven** to justify their rule. The Zhou era, particularly the vigorous early period (1027–771 B.C.E.), was remembered in Chinese tradition as a time of prosperity and benevolent rule. In the later Zhou period (771–221 B.C.E.), centralized control broke down, and warfare among many small states became frequent. (*p. 63*)

ziggurat A massive pyramidal stepped tower made of

mudbricks. It is associated with religious complexes in ancient Mesopotamian cities, but its function is unknown.   (*p. 36*)

Zoroastrianism   A religion originating in ancient Iran with the prophet Zoroaster. It centered on a single benevolent deity—Ahuramazda—who engaged in a twelve-thousand-year struggle with demonic forces before prevailing and restoring a pristine world. Emphasizing truth-telling, purity, and reverence for nature, the religion demanded that humans choose sides in the struggle between good and evil. Those whose good conduct indicated their support for Ahuramazda would be rewarded in the afterlife. Others would be punished. The religion of the Achaemenid and Sasanid Persians, Zoroastrianism may have spread within their realms and influenced Judaism, Christianity, and other faiths.   (*p. 128*)

Zulu   A people of modern South Africa whom King Shaka united in 1818.   (*p. 665*)

Index

Abbas I, Shah, 538, 540, 541

Abd al-Qadir, 669

Abdul al-Hamid II, Sultan, 703, 706

Abdul Mejid, Sultan, 696, 701

Abolition (abolitionist movement), 626; in Cuba, 652, 687; in Dutch colonies, 652; in French colonies, 581, 652; Great Britain and, 638, 651, 670, 672; in the United States, 646, 650–651; in Venezuela, 634; in Western Hemisphere, 650–652

Aborigines, Australian, 684, 686

Abu Bakr, Sultan, 367

Acculturation, of immigrants to Western Hemisphere, 654–655

Acheh Sultanate, 545, 548

Adal, 433

Adams, John Quincy, 643

Aden, 384, 434, 435, 528, 547

Administration: *See also* Bureaucracy; Civil service; Government; colonial Latin America, 486; Delhi sultanate (India), 379; Latin American development and, 659; Ottoman, 534; Spanish colonial, 478; in Yuan China, 352

Aegean Sea region, 528

Afghans (Afghanistan), 375, 538, 559, 705; Mughal India and, 541, 542, 544

Afonso I (Kongo), 432, 438–439

Africa: *See also* Africa, tropical; East Africa; North Africa; Southern Africa; Sub-Saharan Africa; West Africa, *and specific countries and peoples;* (1200-1500), 373 *(map);* gold trade of, 371–372, 374, 381, 384, 425, 426, 431, 671; Portuguese exploration of, 414, 426–428, 427 *(map);* navigation around, 428, 429, 430; encounters with Europe (1450-1550), 431–433; European expeditions to (1420-1542), 427 *(map);* Christian missionaries in, 432, 438–439

Africa, in nineteenth century, 666 *(map);* Christian missionaries in, 670, 671; European penetration of, 669–670, 681; legitimate trade in, 670–672; chronology (1795-1889), 665; new states in, 665, 667–668; secondary empires in, 672–673; trade in, 664

Africa, tropical: *See also* Sub-Saharan Africa; *and specific countries;* agriculture in, 370; chronology (1230s-1433), 369; gender division of work in, 388

Africans, 511. *See also specific peoples;* Portuguese exploration of, 426, 427 *(map),* 429, 430; in Madagascar, 421; Atlantic exploration by, 423; Atlantic system and, 515–520; chronology (1500-1730), 501; Gold Coast and Slave Coast, 515–517; laborers, in British colonies, 686, 687

African slaves (slavery), 428; in Brazil, 496, 508, 509, 638, 640–641; in China, 387; in colonial North America, 490; in Europe, 409 *(illus.);* freedom for, 509; in Haiti, 601; in Latin America, 477; in North America, 489; Portuguese and, 428; punishment for, 507 *and illus.;* rebellions by, 486–487, 490, 508, 580 *(illus.),* 581, 587, 651, 670; on sugar plantations, 482, 502–503, 505–509; United States' Constitution and, 591

African slave trade, 384, 514 *(map),* 545, 547, 626; (1551-1850), 503 *(illus.);* Americas and, 460; Portuguese and, 426, 432, 438–439; Atlantic system and, 510, 522, 523; in colonial Latin America, 485, 486, 488; disease and, 476, 508, 515; Dutch and, 502, 503; Europe and, 460; Middle Passage, 511, 513–515; Royal Africa Company and, 496, 500, 511, 513, 515; prisoners of war and, 517, 520; sugar plantations and, 483; trans-Saharan, 667–668; in West Africa and Americas compared, 520–521; end of, 650, 670–671, 672

Afrikaners, 681, 683 *(illus.)*

Afro-Brazilian experience, 640–641, 656

Agincourt, Battle of (1415), 413

Agriculture: *See also* Cotton; Farmers; Landownership (landowners); Peasants (peasantry); Sugar plantations, *and specific crops;* in Japan, 362; in tropics, 370; irrigation for, 370–371, 668, 678; Columbian exchange and, 476–477; Ottoman, 536; Chinese, 565; American crops in Europe and, 609; in British India, 675, 678; in Qing China, 707

Ahmadabad, 386

Ahmad Baba, 520

Ahmed II, Sultan, 536

Ain Jalut, Battle of (Spring of Goliath, 1260), 343

Air pollution, Industrial Revolution and, 623

Akbar, Sultan, 435, 525 *(illus.),* 541, 542–543

Alabama, 616; native peoples in, 648

Alaska, Russians in, 567, 571

Ala-ud-din Khalji, Sultan, 378, 387, 388

Albania (Albanians), 531, 692, 696

Albazin, 562

Alchemists, 358

Aleppo, 533, 535

Alexander I (Russia), 703, 704 *(illus.),* 707; reforms of, 706

Alexander II (Russia), 700, 705, 706, 707

Alexandria, 398

Algebra, 348

Algeria, 528

Algonquin peoples, 493

Al-Hajj Ahmed, 387

Ali (Muhammad's son-in-law), 538

Ali-Quili Jabbadar, 537 *(illus.)*

Al-Jabarti, Abd al-Rahman, 694–695

Al-Kashi, Ghiyas al-Din Jamshid, 349

Al-Umari, 423

Ambergris, 545

Ambon, 548

American Revolution (1776-1779), 587–592, 605; construction of republican institutions in, 591–592; course of, 589–591; French and, 590, 593; frontiers and taxes, 587–588; 590 *(map)*

American system of manufactures, 618

Americas, colonial. *See* Brazil, colonial; Latin America, colonial; North America, colonial

Americas, the (New World; Western Hemisphere), 435–441, 474. *See also* Latin America; North America; South America; African slaves in, 460; smallpox in, 435, 436 *and illus.,* 437, 440; new foods from, 460, 565; chronology (1754-1804), 583; Enlightenment ideas in, 585; food crops from, 609; abolition of slavery in, 650–652; immigration to, 609, 652–654; independence movements in, 633; development and underdevelopment in, 656–659

Amerindians (native peoples), 474, 587; voyages of, 420; in Caribbean, 423–424 *and map,* 435, 505; European diseases and, 435, 436 *and illus.,* 437, 440, 475–476; Christianity and, 478, 480; in colonial Latin America, 481, 482, 483, 486; in colonial North America, 489, 491, 492, 493, 495; horses and, 477, 493; labor of, 481, 482; lands of, 494; Canadian fur trade and, 492 *(illus.);* rebellions by, 496; as slaves, 436; traveling in Europe, 461; nation-states in Americas and, 647–649

Amsterdam, 457, 459 *and illus.*

Amsterdam Exchange, 459, 510

Amur River, 562, 567, 569

Anatolia (modern Turkey): *See also* Turkic (Turkish) peoples; Il-khanate and, 351; Mongols and, 349; Ottoman Empire and, 528, 534

Ancien régime (France), 581, 583, 585

Andean region: *See also* Inca (Inca Empire) *and specific countries;* Amerindian uprising in, 637; volcanic eruption in (1600), 575

Angkor, 371

Anglo-Dutch Wars (1652-1678), 459, 471

Angola: Christianity in, 522; as Portuguese colony, 519; slave trade in, 506, 511, 517–518, 523

Ankara, Battle of (1402), 528

Annam, 363. *See also* Vietnam; as Ming province, 356; Mongol attack on, 342

Anne of Brittany, 413

Anthrax, 395

Antigua, 504 *(illus.)*

Anti-Semitism, 402. *See also* Jews

Apache people, 649

Aqueducts, 504

Aquinas,Thomas, 394, 402, 407

Aquitane, 412

Arabia (Arabian Peninsula), 692; Indian Ocean trade and, 381, 384; pastoralism in, 369

Arabic language, Islam and, 331
Arabic literature, 668
Arabic script, 537
Arabs: *See also* Islam (Islamic civilization); Middle East; Muslim(s); African trade and, 545
Aragon, 425
Arawak people, 435–436, 505; Caribbean exploration by, 423–424 *and map*; Spanish conquest of, 436
Archers. *See* Bows and arrows (archers)
Arches, in Gothic cathedrals, 404 *(illus.)*
Architecture: *See also* Construction materials and techniques; Housing (dwellings); Forbidden City (Beijing), 352, 355–356; Hindu-Muslim, 385–386
Arcot, 673
Argentina, colonial. *See* Latin America, colonial
Argentina, 644, 659; Amerindians in, 647, 649; education of women in, 655; immigrants in, 652, 653; independence of, 637; labor movement in, 654 *(illus.)*, 655; livestock industry in, 656, 660; power of Catholic Church in, 642; racial discrimination in, 656; regional wars and, 646, 647; technology and development in, 656
Aristocracy (nobility): *See also* Elite class; Landowners; Mongol, 344; Mongol, in Yuan China, 353; in late medieval Europe, 410, 412–413; European bourgeoisie and, 459; Enlightenment and, 583; pre-revolutionary France, 592; Qing China, 559, 714; Russian boyars, 569, 570; British, 604
Aristotle, 406; European science and, 454, 455
Arizona, 646
Arkangelsk, 567
Arkwright, Richard, 612, 615, 625, 626
Armed forces: *See also* Cavalry; Infantry; Military, the; Navy; War; Warrior class; Chinese infantry, 422, 572; early modern Europe, 467–468
Armenia (Armenians), 533, 705; as merchants, 457, 535, 539
Armor, body, 413, 436, 438, 440; conquistadors, 436, 440
Aro of Arochukwu, 517
Arrow War (1856-1860), 709 *(map)*, 711
Art and artists: *See also* Painting; *and specific artist*; colonial religious, 478 *(illus.)*; Flemish, 448 *(illus.)*; Renaissance, 409–410; runaway slave, 509 *(illus.)*; Japanese Woodblock print, 556 *(illus.)*
Articles of Confederation (United States), 591, 639
Artillery, 704, 708. *See also* Cannon
Artisans (craftspeople): African, 371 *and illus.*, 383; tanneries (leatherworking), 384, 398; in medieval Europe, 400; plantation slaves, 506; glassmaking, 404, 531 *(illus.)*; Japanese, 552; French Revolution and, 593; cottage industry and, 610; gunmaking and, 618
Asante kingdom, 516–517, 670
Ashikagura Shogunate (Japan), 362–363
Asia. *See also* Central Asia; East Asia; Eurasia; South Asia; Southeast Asia: tropical: chronology (1206-1500), 369

Asians: immigrants to Americas from, 652–653; in British Guiana, 686–687 *and illus.*; Russia and, 705
Askia Muhammad, 387
Assam, 675, 683
Assassins (Islamic sect), 348
Assembly-line production: in Ming China, 557
Assembly of Notables (France), 593
Astrakhan, 567
Astrolabe, 426
Astronomy: in imperial China, 354, 355; Mongols and, 348–349 *and illus.*; European revolution in, 454–455
Atacama Desert, 646
Atahualpa, 440
Ata-Malik Juvaini, 340
Atlantic Circuit, 511
Atlantic Ocean: chronology, 419; exploration of, before 1500, 423–424
Atlantic trading system, 491, 496; capitalism and mercantilism, 510–511; chronology (1530-present), 501; economy of, 510–515, 512 *(map)*; Slave trade (Middle Passage), 511, 513–515, 522, 523
Aurangzeb, Sultan, 543, 544
Australia, 548; as British colony, 684, 686
Austria, 397; conservative retrenchment in, 604; French Revolution and, 595; Holy Alliance and, 603; Napoleonic France and, 597, 601; Crimean War and, 700
Authoritarianism, of Napoleon, 597
Avicenna (Ibn Sina), 406
Avignon, 412
Aya Sofya, in Istanbul, 530 *(illus.)*, 538
Ayuba Suleiman Diallo, 520–521
Azerbaijan, 346, 705
Azores Islands, 423, 426, 482
Aztec Empire, Spanish conquest of, 436–437, 438

Babur, 541
Baghdad, 536; Mongol sack of (1258), 342
Bahamas, 436
Bahmani Empire (India), 378 *(map)*, 380
Balance of power, 673, 688; in seventeenth century Europe, 467, 468–469; Congress of Vienna and, 603
Balboa, Vasco Núñez de, 430–431
Balkans, Ottoman Empire and, 528, 530, 531, 693
Balkh, 343
Baltic states, 395, 398. *See also* Lithuania
Banditry, 534
Banff national park (Canada), 660
Bankers (banking), 471; European (1400s), 401, 404; Dutch, 457, 510; Ottoman, 701
Bannermen, 708, 711
Bantu language, 547
Bantu-speaking peoples, 370
Barbados, 496, 501, 502, 510
Barley, 356
Bastille, storming of (1789), 594 *(illus.)*, 595
Batavia, 548
Batu, khan, 342, 343, 349
Bayazid I, Sultan, 528
Bay Colony, 490. *See also* Massachusetts

Bay of Bengal, 380
Beans, 370
Beer, 388, 460
Beijing, 551, 552, 564; Forbidden City complex in, 352, 355–356; Jesuits in, 558, 559, 563 *(illus.)*; Korea and, 359; as Yuan Empire capital, 338, 348, 354, 359
Beirut, 398
Belgium: Revolution of 1830 in, 605 *(illus.)*; cities in, 623; coal in, 621 *(map)*; industrialization in, 612, 614; railroads in, 620
Belgrade, 528
Belize (British Honduras), 660
Bengal, 387, 543, 673, 675
Benguela, 517
Benin, 432 *and illus.*
Bentham, Jeremy, 627
Berbers, 372
Bering, Vitus, 571
Berlin, 604
Bible, the: Erasmus and, 408; Gutenberg, 409; Hebrew Bible, 453, 455
Bight of Biafra, 517
Bill of Rights (England, 1688), 466
Birthrate, in medieval Europe, 461
Black Death, 391 *(illus.)*, 393, 395, 396 *(map)*. *See also* Bubonic plague
"Black Hole of Calcutta," 673
Blacks: *See also* Africans; Afro-Brazilians; Slaves, African; racial discrimination and, 655–656
Black Sea, 697 *(map)*, 700
Black Sea region, 398, 570, 571
Blake, William, 623
Blyden, Edward Wilmot, 672
Bocaccio, Giovanni, 407–408
Bohemia, 604
Bolívar, Simón, 634, 637, 639, 642; Gran Colombia and, 644
Bolivia, 635, 637, 644, 660; colonial, 480 *and illus.*; independence of, 634; war with Chile, 646–647
Bologna, 406
Bombards, 358. *See also* Explosives
Bombay, 673
Bonaparte, Joseph, 634
Books: *See also* Libraries; Literacy; Literature; Enlightenment, 585
Bordeaux, 461
Borinquen (Puerto Rico), 436, 652
Borneo, 545
Bornu, 387, 522
Bosman, Willem, 516, 517
Bosnia, 531, 693
Boston, 491, 588–589
Boston Massacre, 588
Boulton, Matthew, 609, 619
Bourbon dynasty (France), 466, 467 *(illus.)*, 468, 495
Bourgeoisie: *See also* Middle class; European cities and, 456–457, 459, 461; French Revolution and, 592, 596
Bows and arrows (archers): Mongol, 343, 360; crossbows, 375, 410, 413, 422; flaming arrows, 358 *and illus.*; Ottoman, 530, 531
Boyle, Robert, 455

Brahe, Tycho, 454
Brahmin class (Brahmin priests), 380; Muslim elite and, 379
Brahmo Samj (Divine Society), 680
Brant, Joseph (Thayendanegea), 589
Brazil, 646, 647; abolition of slavery in, 651 *and illus.*; Afro-Brazilian experience, 640–641; chronology (1808-1888), 635; coffee production in, 626, 660; constitutionalism in, 639; end of slave trade in, 652, 670; immigrants in, 652, 653; Minas Gerais mining in, 660; Portuguese monarchy and, 634, 638; racial discrimination in, 656; slave trade in, 650
Brazil, colonial, 428, 477, 479 *(map)*; Amerindians and disease in, 475; chronology, 475; church and state in, 478; Dutch and, 510; market in, 496 (illus.); reform and, 496; slaves in, 508, 509, 511; social structure in, 487; sugar plantations in, 480, 482–483 *and illus.*, 502, 507, 513
British East India Company (EIC), 544, 564, 588, 630, 664, 673, 674 and map, 683. *See also* India, under British rule
British Empire, 504 *and illus.*, 682 *(map). See also* North America, colonial, British; Australia and New Zealand, 684, 686; commerce and, 681, 683; labor migrations to, 686–687; in South Pacific, 682 *(map)*; in West Indies, 501–502, 503, 651–652
British Guiana, 652, 686 *(illus.)*
British North America. *See also* American Revolution; Canada; Amerindians in, 491, 492, 493, 589; chronology, 475; constitutionalism in, 639; disease in, 476; French and Indian War (Seven Years War), 582, 587; Middle Atlantic, 492–493; New England, 490–492; reform in, 497; South, 488–490
British raj. *See* India, British rule in
Bronze, 356
Brueghel, Peter, 448 *(illus.)*
Bruges, 400
Brunei Sultanate, 545
Bubonic plague, 351, 395–396 *and map*, 711; in Asia, 344, 353; as Black Death, in Europe, 391 *(illus.)*, 393, 395, 396 *(map)*; in Crimea, 344, 349
Buddhism, 354; Chan (Zen), 359, 362; in India, Islam and, 387; Tibetan (Lamaism), 352, 558
Buenos Aires, 635, 637, 644; labor movement in, 654 *(illus.)*; port construction in, 658 *and illus.*
Buffalo hunting, 649
Bulwer-Lytton, Edward Robert, 676, 678–679
Bureaucracy (bureaucrats): *See also* Administration; Civil service; in Benin, 432; Delhi sultanate, 380; Benin, 432; Latin American colonial, 478; Enlightenment ideas and, 583; Ottoman, 531; in British India, 676; Ottoman reforms, 703; Russian, 706, 707
Burgoyne, John, 589
Burma (Siam), 385, 683
Business (companies): *See also* Capitalism; Corporations; Merchants; Trade; tax farming, 345, 353; chartered, 502, 510; joint-stock, 459, 510, 544, 546 *(map)*, 706; cycles

of, 626; in Japan, 552; East India trade, 588, 630, 664, 673, 674, 683
Byron, Lord (George Gordon Noel), 696
Byzantine Empire, end of, 351

Cabral, Pedro Alvares, 428, 430
Cairo, 668, 703; street scene in, 699 *(illus.)*
Cajamarca, 440
Calcutta, 673, 680
Calendars, 562; French revolutionary, 596; Mongols and, 348, 355, 357, 360
Calicut, 385, 423, 433, 435
California, 660; gold in, 646
Caliphate of Sokoto, 665
Calvin, John, 451
Calvinism, 451, 452 *(map). See also* Puritans
Cambay, 384, 385, 545
Cambodia, 371
Cambridge University, 406
Canada: as French colony, 493–495; colonial fur trade in, 492 *(illus.)*; American Revolution and, 589, 591; Amerindians in, 648; British trade with, 657; Dominion of, 635, 639, 642 *(map)*, 686; immigrants to, 652, 653–654 *and illus.*; independence of, 639; national park in, 660; technology and development in, 656; women's rights in, 655
Canal du Midi, 459
Canals: irrigation, 370–371; in Europe, 459; in China, 565; in St. Petersburg, 571 *(illus.)*; in Britain, 612, 624; in Europe, 612; in United States, 619; irrigation, 668, 678
Canary Islands, 423, 426, 430
Cannon, 404, 426, 468, 526, 572; in China and Korea, 357, 358, 360; Ethiopian, 668, 669 *(illus.)*; in Hundred Years War, 413; Spanish conquistadors, 438, 440; on warships, 422, 426, 544, 572
Canoes, Polynesian, 420–421 *and illus.*
Canterbury Tales (Chaucer), 397, 401, 407
Canton, 707, 710
Cape Colony (South Africa), 519, 681
Cape Verde Islands, 426, 482
Capitalism, 510, 523, 627
Caramansa, 430, 431
Caravan trade and routes, 672; Silk Road, 349, 526; trans-Saharan trade, 372, 373, 375, 519, 522, 667–668
Caravels (ships), 422 *and illus.*, 426, 429 *and illus.*
Caribbean region (West Indies): *See also* specific island; exploration of, to 1533, 423–424 *and map*; Columbus in, 424 *(map)*, 430, 436; disease in, 435, 476; British colonies in, 501–502, 503, 651–652; sugar plantations in, 487, 495 *(illus.)*, 626; chronology (1500-1795), 501; French colonies in, 501–502, 503, 505, 508, 652; plantations in, 501–503; slave trade in, 511, 513, 514 *(map)*; abolition of slavery in, 651–652; Indian immigrants in, 652, 653
Carib peoples, exploration by, 424 *and map*
Carpet manufacture, 540
Carrío de la Vandera, Alonso, 484, 485
Cartier, Jacques, 493

Cassava, 435, 506 *(illus.)*
Castas (mixed-race), 487 *(illus.)*, 488
Caste War (1847), 649
Castile, 425
Catapults, 343, 358, 360
Cathedrals, Gothic of medieval Europe, 404 *(illus.)*, 406
Catherine of Aragon, 466
Catherine the Great (Russia), 571, 573, 583
Catholic Church, 572. *See also* Jesuits; Papacy (popes); African missions of, 432; Reformation and, 451, 452 *(map)*; Inquisition and, 455; European monarchies and, 466; Latin American colonies and, 477, 478, 480; Enlightenment and, 585–586; French Revolution and, 592, 595, 597; Latin America and, 639, 644
Catholic Reformation, 453
Cattle (cattleherders). *See* Livestock; Pastoralism
Caudillo (personalist leader), 643, 644
Cavalry (horsemen), 422, 519, 701. *See also* Horses; Mongolian, 343, 360; on Chinese warships, 422; European knights, 395, 410, 413, 414; Ottoman Turk, 477, 528, 530, 531, 534; Spanish conquistador, 436
Cayuga peoples, 589
Celibacy, 451
Censorship, 585
Central Africa, Pygmy people of, 369
Central America, Republic of, 644
Central Asia, 526. *See also specific country and people;* chronology (1221-1453), 339; Mongol domination of, 342; Qing China (Manchu) power in, 558; Russia and, 705; Safavid Iran and, 538; tea trade in, 564; Turkic peoples of, 354, 375, 569
Central Europe, mining in, 397
Ceramics, in Ming China, 357 *(illus.)*. See also Porcelain
Ceuta, 414
Ceylon (Sri Lanka), 380, 675, 681; water-control systems in, 370–371
Chaldiran, Battle of (1514), 528
Champa, 342, 363. *See also* Vietnam
Champagne region, 400
Champa rice, 362, 363
Champlain, Samuel de, 493
Chan (Zen) Buddhism, 359, 362
Chappe, Claude, 610
Charles I (England), 466
Charles II (England), 497
Charles III (Spain), 583
Charleston, South Carolina, 489–490
Charles V (Holy Roman emperor), 462, 463 *(illus.)*, 469
Charles VII (France), 414
Charles X (France), 604
Chartered companies, 502, 510
Chartism (Great Britain), 604, 628
Chaucer, Geoffrey, 397, 401, 407
Cherokee peoples, 648
Child labor, in Industrial Revolution, 609, 625 *and illus.*, 628
Children: *See also* Education; Family; Schools; education of, 461; as plantation workers,

Children (*cont.*)
505; Ottoman devshirme, 530; French revolution and, 593

Chile, 639, 659; colonial, 486; Amerindians in, 647, 649; Catholic Church in, 642; immigrants in, 652; independence of, 637; mining in, 656, 660; regional war in, 646–647; women's rights in, 655

China, Great Britain and, 629, 707, 713; Arrow War (1856-1860) and, 711; opium trade, 708, 743; Opium War (1839-1842) and, 708–709; Taiping Rebellion (1850-1864), 709 *(map)*, 710–712 *and illus.*; Treaty of Nanking (1842), 708

China, imperial, 429. *See also* Ming Empire; Qing Empire; Yuan Empire; chronology (1206-1449), 339; Mongol domination in (1271-1368), 337, 351–354; Tanggut Empire, 338, 352; Il-khanate and, 347; Jin Empire, 352; Southern Song Empire, 343, 352; Zheng He's explorations and, 355 *(map)*, 356, 422–423; Japan and, 363; Song Empire, 358, 405, 616–617; African slaves in, 387; Indian Ocean trade and, 380; piracy and, 385; navy of, and Portuguese compared, 429; Christian missionaries in, 456, 458; Indian Ocean exploration by, 421–423; porcelain production by, 554; Portuguese port in, 434; printing in, 408; Dutch trade with, 553; Korea and, 552, 558; British naval attacks on, 629; climate change in, 575; treaty ports in, 434, 707, 708–709, 711

Chinese Exclusion Act (United States, 1882), 653

Chinese immigration: to Americas, 652, 653 *and illus.*; as plantation laborers, 686, 687; United States' ban on, 711

Choctaw peoples, 474, 648

Cholera, 624, 677, 680

Christian Church: *See also* Catholic Church; Papacy; condemnation of usury by, 404; European monarchies and, 410, 412

Christianity (Christians): *See also* Bible, the; Christian church; Crusades; Orthodox Christianity; Priests (clergy); *and specific Christian sects*; in Ethiopia, 372, 386 *and illus.*, 433, 668; Crusades and, 345, 350–351, 398; Russian Orthodox, 349, 350, 699; persecution of Jews by, 400, 402–403; theology and, 407; militancy of, 425; Portuguese promotion of, 426; Protestant Reformation and, 450–454; in colonial Americas, 477, 478; Caribbean slaves and, 508; in Angola, 522; in Japan, 553–555; in Ottoman Empire, 703

Christian missionaries, 426, 545, 675, 698. *See* Jesuits (Society of Jesus); Missionaries, Christian. *See also* Jesuits (Society of Jesus); in Africa, 432, 438–439, 670, 671; in Americas, 432, 436; in China, 456, 458, 558–559, 707, 709, 710, 711; in India, 675; in Indian Ocean states, 544; Japan and, 553–554, 573; in Latin America, 480; in North America, 493; Orthodox in Siberia, 567

Churches (buildings): Ethiopian, 386 *and illus.*; Gothic cathedrals, 404 *(illus.)*, 406; Saint Peter's Basilica, 450

Church of England (Anglicanism), 452 *(map)*, 466, 490

Circassians, 705

Cities and towns (urban areas): *See also* City-states; Urbanization; *and specific cities and towns*; Mongol seige of, 343–344; Gujarati, 384–385; late medieval European revival of, 398–401, 404; Malacca, 434; European bourgeoisie and, 456–457, 459; colonial Latin America, 484–485; Ottoman and Iranian compared, 538–539; Ming China, 557; European industrialization and, 622–624; Ottoman Empire, 701; Chinese treaty ports, 707, 708–709, 711

City-states, Hausa (Africa), 375, 520, 522, 667

City-states, northern Italy, 425. *See also* Florence; Genoa; Venice

Civil Code of 1804 (France), 597

Civil service: *See also* Administration; Bureaucracy; in British India, 676; Ottoman, 698

Civil wars: in Japan, 361, 363, 551; in England (1642), 466; Amerindian, 474; in Argentina, 644; Mexican (1858-1861), 646; Amerindians and, 649; United States (1861-1865), 646, 650–651; Taiping Rebellion (China), 709 *(map)*, 710–712 *and illus.*

Cixi (China), 714–715 *and illus.*

Class. *See* Social classes (social stratification)

Clergy. *See* Priests (Clergy); Religion

Climate and weather (climate change): *See also* Monsoons; Korean science of, 360; tropical, 367–369; population growth and, 443–444; Little Ice Age (1590s), 460, 557, 575

Clipper ships, 684

Clive, Robert, 673

Clocks: in Europe, 405 *and illus.*; in Korea, 359

Clothing, 377. *See also* Cotton textiles; Textiles (textile industry); Mongol aristocracy, 344; colonial Americas, 485; Safavid Iran, 539; Russian elite, 550 *(illus.)*; Ottoman military, 698 *and illus.*

Clove plantations, 672

Coal, and industrialization, 460; in Britain, 617, 618 *(illus.)*, 624; in Europe, 612, 614, 621 *(map)*; steam engines and, 619

Cochin, 435

Coeur, Jacques, 414

Coffee, 533, 650, 675; in Brazil, 626, 660

Coinage: copper, 353; dies for, 535 *(illus.)*; gold, 426, 701; Ottoman inflation of, 535

Coke-iron production, 617–618, 624

Colbert, Jean Baptiste, 459, 460, 471

Coleridge, Samuel Taylor, 352

Colleges and Universities: in Europe, 406–407; in Egypt, 668; in India, 680; in Liberia, 672; in Russia, 706

Colombia, 635, 642; independence of, 643, 644

Colonies (colonization): *See also* British Empire; French colonies; Expansion (expansionism); Latin America, colonial; North America, colonial; Black sea area, 398; European, in Indian Ocean states, 546 *(map)*; Enlightenment and, 585

Columbian exchange, 474–477; animal and plant transfer in, 476–477; chronology, 475; disease in, 474, 475–476

Columbus, Christopher, 415, 417 *(illus.)*, 430, 436

Comanche peoples, 649

Commerce. *See* Trade

Commercial and Political Atlas, The (Playfair), 613

Committee of Public Safety (France), 596

Common Sense (Paine), 589

Communication(s): *See also* Language(s); Writing; Enlightenment, 584; overland China, 559; telegraph, 620–621, 656, 702

Companies, 488. *See also* Business (companies); Joint-stock companies

Company men (British India), 673

Compass, 382, 426

Comte, Auguste, 628

Concordat of 1801 (France), 597

Condorcanqui, José Gabriel, 496

Confederate States of America (Confederacy), 646, 650

Confederation of 1867 (Canada), 639

Confucianism: in East Asia (other than China), 352, 359, 363; in China, 354, 556, 562, 572, 710

Congo River, 432

Congress of Vienna (1814-1815), 604

Conquistadors, 436–438, 440

Constantinople: *See also* Istanbul; Ottoman capture of, 351, 398; Russia and, 349, 350

Constitutional Convention (United States), 591

Constitutions, 643; in Americas, 639, 642; French, 595, 604; Haitian, 581; in Latin America, 639, 642; Ottoman Empire, 703; Russia, 742; state, 591; United States, 591, 644, 651

Construction materials and techniques, 385–386. *See also* Architecture; Engineering; Housing; stone, in Great Zimbabwe, 383 *and illus.*; for Gothic cathedrals, 404; Mughal India, 525 *(illus.)*

Conté, Nicolas-Jacques, 584

Continental Congress, 585, 589, 590, 591

Cook, James, 684

Cooke, William, 621

Copernicus, Nicolas, 348, 454, 582

Copper, 397, 404; in Africa, 371, 372, 383, 387; coinage, 353; in industrialization, 353, 535

Córdoba (Argentina), 484

Corn Laws (Britain,1815), 604, 628

Cornwallis, Charles, 590

Corporations, for tax farming, 345, 353

Cort, Henry, 617

Cortés, Hernán, 436–437, 438, 475

Cossacks, 526, 569

Cotton (cotton industry), 477. *See also* Cotton textiles; Textiles (textile industry); in imperial China, 353, 356; in Africa (Hausa), 375; in Korea, 359, 360; Ottoman, 536; Arawak, 435, 436; child labor in, 625 *and illus.*; mechanization of, 615–616; in United States, 615–616, 624, 626, 660; women in, 625–626; Egyptian, 673, 701, 703

Cotton gin, 615
Cotton textiles, 684; in Britain, 612; Indian, 384, 385, 388 and illus., 511, 515, 542, 615, 628–629, 675; Industrialization and, 612, 615, 628–629
Council of the Indies, 477
Council of Trent (1563), 453
Counter Enlightenment, 585–586
Coureurs de bois, 493
Crafts and craftspeople. See Artisans (craftspeople) and specific crafts
Cranach, Lucas, 450 (illus.)
Creek people, 648
Creoles, 634; in colonial Latin America, 483, 485, 486, 487 and illus.
Crete, 398, 528, 532
Crimea, plague in, 344, 349
Crimean peoples, 567
Crimean War (1853-1856), 699–701, 702, 704
Crompton, Samuel, 615
Cromwell, Oliver, 466
Crossbows, 375, 410, 413, 422
Crowther, Samuel Adjai, 671–672
Crusades, 345, 350–351, 398
Cruzado (gold coin), 426
Crystal Palace, 618
Cuba, 653; slave trade in, 650, 651; abolition of slavery in, 652, 687; racial discrimination in, 656; sugar production in, 659–660; end of slave trade in, 670
Cueta, 425
Cult of domesticity, 626
Cultural change, 385–389
Culture: See also Art and artists; Literature; Society (societal conditions); and specific cultures; exchange of, 337; of the Americas and immigration, 654–655; folk traditions, 453, 586–587; Russian Empire, 706–707
Currency: coinage, 353, 426, 701; copper bars as, 371; Ottoman, 535, 701; paper money, 345, 349, 353, 535, 588
Curzon, Lord, 676
Custer, George Armstrong, 649
Cuzco, 440
Cyprus, 528

Da Gama, Christopher, 433
Da Gama, Vasco, 428, 429, 433
Dagestan, 705
Dagur peoples, 562
Daimyo (Japanese warlord), 551
Dalai Lama, 558
Damascus, 347, 533
Dams, 397
Dante Alighieri, 407
Darby, Abraham, 617
Darby, Abraham, III, 618
Dardanelles strait, 528
Darwin, Erasmus, 609, 615
Davar, Cowasjee Nanabhoy, 630
Da Vinci, Leonardo, 410
Debt. See Foreign debt (International loans)
Decameron (Boccaccio), 407
Deccan Plateau, 369, 380
Decembrist revolt (Russia), 706

Declaration of Independence (1776, United States), 589, 595, 634, 650
Declaration of the Rights of Man (France, 1789), 595, 634
Deforestation, 505, 684; in Africa, 383–384; in Europe, 398, 460; in China, 357, 565, 617; in Cuba, 659; in the Americas, 660
De Las Casas, Bartolomé, 480
Delft, 614
Delhi, 544
Delhi Durbar, 677 (illus.)
Delhi Sultanate (India), 346, 378–380, 378 (map); Gujarat and, 385; Hinduism and, 375, 379, 380, 385, 387, 388; leadership in, 376, 378, 379; learning and literacy in, 386, 387; slavery in, 387–388; water-control systems in, 370; women in, 378, 387–388
De Mendoza, Antonio, 477
Democracy (democratic reforms): in United States and Britain, 604
De mulieribus claris (Boccacio), 407–408
Denmark, 604
Depression (economic): French Revolution and, 594, 595, 596; Ming China, 535
De Ulloa, Antonio, 484–485
Developing countries (non-industrial world), 609, 629–630. See also specific countries and regions
Devshirme, 530
De Witt Clinton (locomotive), 620 (illus.)
Dhows (ships), 380, 382 (illus.), 421, 433
Dias, Bartolomeu, 428, 430
Dictatorship: See also Napoleon Bonaparte, and specific dictators; personalist leaders, in Americas, 642–644
Diderot, Denis, 582
Diet. See Food (diet; nutrition)
Diplomacy: McCartney mission to China, 564; Russian, 571
Directory (France), 597, 602
Disease: See also Bubonic plague; Medicine (physicians); plague (Black Death), 393, 395, 396 (map); Amerindians and, 435, 436 and illus., 437, 440, 475–476; smallpox, 344, 436 and illus., 440, 624; yellow fever, 476, 602; in Columbian exchange, 474, 475–476; slaves and, 476, 508, 515; cholera in British India, 624, 677, 680; industrialization and, 623–624; influenza, 344, 476; native peoples and, 684
Disraeli, Benjamin, 626
Diu, 434, 435
Divine Comedy (Dante), 407
Division of labor, 614, 616–617. See also Labor; gender differences and, 388; working class, 624–625, 630
Dnieper River, 526
Doctors. See Medicine (physicians)
Dominicans, 554, 558, 563; scholasticism of, 406, 407; in Spanish America, 478, 480 (illus.)
Dominion of Canada, 635, 639, 642 (map), 686. See also Canada
Doré, Gustave, 622 (illus.)
Dostoyevsky, Feodor, 707
Douglass, Frederick, 650

Draft animals, 396. See also Horses; Oxen; and specific animals
"Drivers" of slave gangs, 506
Drought, in Sahara Desert, 368
Duke, Antara, 522
Dupleix, Joseph François, 544
Durbars (pageants) in India, 676, 677(illus.), 678–679
Dushan, Stephen, 351
Dutch. See Netherlands (the Dutch, Holland)
Dutch colonies, 682 (map); abolition of slavery in, 652; in South America, 509, 681
Dutch Guiana, 681
Dutch studies (Japan), 555
Dutch World Map (1641), 458 (illus.)

Earthquake, Lisbon (1755), 453
East Asia: See also specific country; reintegration of, under Mongols, 352; centralization and militarism in, 359–363; Indian Ocean trade and, 421
Easter Island, 420
Eastern Africa: See also specific countries; pastoralists in, 366 (illus.); farming in, 370; Indian Ocean trade and, 381, 383; Swahili Coast, 373 (map) 381, 385, 433, 522, 545; ivory trade in, 545, 547, 672, 683; secondary empires in, 672–673
Eastern Europe, 460, 528. See also specific countries; Mongols and, 349, 350; landownership in, 609; immigrants to Americas from, 652, 653
East India Company English/British (EIC), 544, 564, 630, 683; American Revolution and, 588; British India and, 664, 673, 674 and map; East India Company, Dutch (VOC), 459 (illus.), 510, 516, 519, 544, 673; in China, 558; porcelain trade and, 544 and illus.; spice trade and, 547–548; West India Company, Dutch, 492, 502, 510, 511, 513. See also East India Company, Dutch (VOC)
East Indies, 418, 420; Muslim traders in, 545
Ecological crisis, 383–384. See also Environment, the (environmental stress)
Economic crisis: See also Inflation; French Revolution and, 594, 595, 596; Spanish decline and, 469; Ming China depression, 535
Economics (economic theories): See also Inflation; Taxation; Trade (trading); business cycles, 626; capitalism, 510, 523, 627; laissez faire, 627, 628
Economy: British industrial growth and, 611; European industrialization and, 612; Ilkhanate, 345; Russia, under Mongols, 350; government role in, 471; Japanese, 556; British India, 675
Ecuador, 483–484, 635; independence of, 644
Edict of Nantes (1685), 466
Education (educational institutions): See also Colleges and Universities; Schools; in British India, 680; of military, in Egypt, 692; Ottoman devshirme, 530–531; Ottoman reforms, 696–697; in Russia, 706; of women, 461–462, 680, 714

Edward II (England), 413

Edward III (England), 413, 414

Edward VII (Great Britain), 676

Egypt: Mamluk rule in, 350, 527, 528, 530, 536, 537, 538, 692; industrialization in, 609, 629; modernization in, 668; Muhammad Ali and, 673, 690 (illus.), 703; Napoleon's invasion of, 664, 668, 694–695; Ottoman empire and, 691, 692–693; cotton industry in, 673, 701, 703

Elba, 601

Electricity, 585; telegraph and, 620–621

Elephants, 542 (illus.), 677 (illus.)

Elite class: See also Aristocracy (nobility); Landowners; Warrior class; Muslim in India, 379; in colonial Latin America, 486; Caribbean plantation, 505, 509; Ottoman ulama, 531, 538, 693, 696

Elizabeth I (England), 465

Elmina, 431, 502, 511

Emancipation Proclamation (1863, United States), 651

Empires. See Colonies (colonization); European Expansion; Expansion and specific empires and emperors

Enclosure movement (England), 609

Encomienda labor, 482, 483

Encyclopédie (Diderot), 582, 610

Engineering: See also Construction materials and techniques; in Persia (Il-khanate), 348 (illus.)

England: See also Great Britain; British Empire; India, British rule in, and individual monarchs; watermills in, 397; wool trade in, 400, 414; Magna Carta in, 412 and illus.; Hundred Years War (1337-1453) and, 413; government in, 414; science in, 455; Dutch rivalry with, 459, 471; merchant fleet of, 459; religion and state in, 466; royal dynasties in, 467 (illus.); as sea power, 468; French and Indian War (1756-1763) and, 495; slave trade and, 496; trading companies and, 502; Atlantic trade and, 510–511; monopoly charters and, 511; sugar consumption in, 511, 513; trade with Iran, 526; Mughal India and, 542; McCartney mission to China, 564; pencil making in, 584; education of women in, 585; population growth in, 609; graph-making in, 613

English East India Company. See East India Company, British (EIC)

Enlightenment, the, 456, 582–586, 634, 650; Catholic response to, 585–586; reforms of, 583–584, 587, 606

Environment, the (environmental stress), 624, 661. See also Climate and weather; deforestation and, 357, 383–384, 398, 617, 659, 660, 684; tropical, 367–369; medieval industry and, 398; mining in Latin America, 481; colonial sugar plantation, 505; soil erosion and, 660; in Qing China, 707

Epidemics, 494. See also Disease

Erasmus, 408, 409

Ericsson, Leif, 423

Erie Canal, 619

Estates General (France), 414, 466, 593, 601

Ethiopia, 384, 519; Christianity in, 372, 386 and illus., 433, 668; Church of Saint George in, 386 (illus.); Portuguese alliance with, 433; modernization in, 668

Ethnicity and race in colonial Americas, 484–485, 487 (illus.), 488

Eunuchs: as harem slaves, 387; in Chinese imperial court, 522, 534, 539, 714 (illus.)

Eurasia, empires in: See also Mongolian Empire; Russia; Mongol domains in (1300), 343 (map)

Europe. See Eastern Europe; European Expansion (1400-1550); Latin West (Europe 1200-1500); Western Europe

European Expansion (1400-1550), 424–431, 427 (map), 431–441; Americas and, 435–441; Eastern Africa, 433; Indian Ocean states, 433–435; motives for, 425; patterns of dominance, 438–439, 440; Portuguese voyages, 425–428, 429 and illus.; Spanish voyages, 427 (map), 428, 430–431; Western Africa and, 431–432

European immigration, 687; to Americas, 609, 652, 653; labor movement and, 654 (illus.), 655

European trading companies, 558. See also specific companies

Europe (1500-1750), 448–472; in 1740, 470 (map); culture and ideas in, 449–456; English and French monarchies, 466–467; Enlightenment ideas in, 456; Holy Roman Empire in, 463 (map); mapmaking in, 458 and illus.; Ottoman trade and, 536; political craft in, 464–465; political innovations in, 462–471; price revolution in, 535; religious policies in, 463, 466; religious reformation, 450–454, 452 (map); Renaissance, 449; scientific revolution in, 454-455; state development in, 462–463

Europe and Europeans (1750-1900): See also specific individuals; disease and, 476; in Africa, 519; African trade and, 523; Atlantic economy and, 510; China trade and, 564, 573; chronology (1755-1848), 583; as indentured servants, 502, 503; India and, 544; Indian Ocean trade and, 535; Japan and, 553–555; middle class in, 585; conservative Holy Alliance in, 603; Napoleon and, 600 (map); nationalism in, 604; population growth in, 609–610; industrialization in, 621 (map); trading companies of, 673; balance of power and, 688; colonies in Indian Ocean and South Pacific, 682 (map); Greek independence and, 696; in Ottoman Empire, 701; Ottoman reform and, 703; Qing China and, 708–710; slave trade and, 496, 522

Evenk peoples, 562

Exchange, Columbian, 474–477. See also Merchants; Trade (trading)

Exclusif (France), 511

Expansion (expansionism): See also Colonies (colonization); European Expansion; Maritime expansion; Mongol (1215-1283), 338, 342–344, 398; Chinese and Russian compared, 572–573; Delhi sultanate, 379; Ethiopian (15th century), 384; European,

late medieval, 415; Ottoman Empire, 425, 528–530, 529 (map); Qing China, 559 (map), 562; Russian, 565–567, 699, 700, 701, 705; United States, 644, 645 (map), 657, 659 (illus.)

Experiments and Observations on Electricity (Franklin), 585

Exploration (expeditions): See also European Expansion; Zheng He, 355 (map), 356, 422–423; Portuguese in Africa, 414; Europeans in Africa, 670

Explosives, 358, 360. See also Weapons and military technology

Exports. See Trade (trading)

Extraterritoriality, 701, 710

Factory Act of 1833 (Great Britain), 628

Fallen Timbers, Battle of (1794), 648

Family (family life): See also Children; Marriage; Women; in Europe, 461; Istanbul, 540 (illus.); nomadic, in Central Asia, 338; slave, on plantations, 507; industrialization and, 625

Famine: in Europe (1315-1317), 395; in Ireland (1847-1848), 626

Farey, John, 611

Farmers (farming): See also Agriculture; Peasants (peasantry); nomadic conflict with, 338; Yuan China, 353; Korean, 360; late medieval Europe, 395; European, 609; in China, 707

Fatima, 341

Fatwas, 532–533

Ferdinand (Spain), 414–415, 430

Ferdinand VII (Spain), 634, 635, 639

Festivals: durbars in India, 676, 677(illus.), 678–679; Zulu, 667

Fez (hat), 698 and illus.

Fiji, 420

Finance: See also Bankers (banking); Foreign debt; Inflation; European governments and, 471

Financial markets (stock exchanges), 459, 510

Finney, Ben, 420–421

Finns (Finland), 350

Firearms (guns), 358, 540. See also Cannon; Gunpowder; Weapons and military technology; in late medieval Europe, 410, 413; Amerindians and, 489, 649; in colonial North America, 493; guns, 522, 530; interchangeable parts for, 618; Ottoman, 531; in Japan, 553; muskets, 430–431, 432, 440, 516, 519, 534, 675, 701, 708; African trade in, 672; rifles, 675, 701, 708

First Estate (France), 594

Firuz Shah, 379, 387

Fiscal crises, 582. See also Inflation; French Revolution and, 593

Fishing (fishermen), 369

Fishwife, The (van Ostade), 457 (illus.)

Flanders, 398, 400, 410, 448 (illus.); Black death in, 391 (illus.)

Floods (flooding), in China, 353, 565

Florence, 400, 407, 410; banking in, 401, 404

Florida, colonial, 436

Folk cultures: and popular protest, 586–587; witchcraft and, 453

Food crops: from Africa to New World, 505; American in China, 565; Amerindian in Africa, 506 *(illus.)*

Food (diet): *See also* Famine; and immigration to Americas, 654; preparation of, by women, 388

Forbidden City (Beijing), 352, 355–356

Foreign debt (international loans): British war, 582, 587, 613 *(illus.)*; European wars, 469, 471; American Revolution, 591; French wars, 593, 669; Egyptian, 668, 703; Ottoman, 701; Chinese to Britain, 713

Forests: *See also* Deforestation; tropical, 368 *and map*; of medieval Europe, 398; Russian, 460, 567, 624

Fortifications: Great Zimbabwe, 383 *and illus.*; Japanese against Mongols, 361; Kremlin, 350 *(illus.)*; Portuguese, in Musqat, 547 *and illus.*

"Forty-Seven Ronin" incident (Japan), 556 *and illus.*

Fourier, Charles, 628

Fourth Crusade (1202-1204), 398, 528

Fractions, mathematics and, 349

France, 409. *See also* French colonies; French Revolution; peasants in, 394 *(illus.)*, 395–396; watermills in, 397; stone quarries in, 397–398; medieval trade in, 400; printshop in, 408 *(illus.)*; medieval monarchy in, 412; Hundred Years War (1337-1453) and, 413; canals in, 459; aristocracy in, 459; deforestation in, 460; peasant revolts in, 461; religion and state in, 466; royal dynasties in, 467 *(illus.)*; Spain and, 468; tax reforms in, 471; Atlantic trade and, 513; pencil production in, 584 *and illus.*; Seven Years War (1756-1763), 582, 587, 673; American Revolution and, 590, 593; conservative retrenchment in, 603; revolutions of 1848 and, 604; graph-making in, 613; industrialization in, 612, 614; railroads in, 620, 621 *(map)*; steamships in, 619; invasion of Mexico by, 633, 646; slavery and, 651; Louisiana Purchase and, 644; India and, 664; Algeria and, 669–670; Seven Years War (1756-1763), 673; colonies of, 682 *(map)*; Indian Ocean dominion and, 681; invasion of Egypt by, 692, 694–695; Crimean War and, 699, 700, 701; government in, 414; monopoly charters and, 511; Qing China and, 711, 713; Russia and, 704, 705; trading companies and, 502; Vietnam and, 710

Franciscans, 554, 558, 563; scholasticism of, 406, 407

Francis I (France), 462

Francis Xavier, 553

Franklin, Benjamin, 585, 610

Franz Josef (Austria), 604

Frederick (Holy Roman Emperor), 350

Frederick the Great (Prussia), 583

Frederick William IV (Denmark), 604

Free-market capitalism, 627

Freemasons, 706

Free trade, 628, 629, 683

French and Indian War (1756-1763), 494 *(map)*, 495, 582, 587, 673

French Assembly, 581

French colonies: in Indian Ocean, 546 *(map)*; in North America, 475, 476, 488, 493–495; in West Indies, 501–502, 503, 505, 508, 652

French Revolution (1783-1789), 592–601, 605; Napoleon's Europe, 600 *(map)*; protest beginning, 593–595; reaction to, and dictatorship, 597, 601; Reign of Terror, 595–597, 598–599; society and fiscal crisis, 592–593

Fresco painting, 410

Fugger family, 404

Fugitive slave clause, 591

Fulani people, 370, 387, 667

Fur trade: in colonial North America, 489, 490, 492 *(illus.)*, 493, 494, 587; Russian, 550 *(illus.)*, 567, 571

Fynn, Henry Francis, 667

Gage, Thomas, 588

Galdan (Mongolia), 558, 562, 567

Galilei, Maria Celeste, 462

Galileo Galilei, 454–455 *and illus.*

Gallipoli, 528

Gambia, 520

Ganges River, 369

Garnet, Henry Highland, 650

Gates, Horatio, 589

Gender differences: *See also* Men; Women; in late medieval Europe, 394; in Muslim India, 388 *and illus.*; working class, 624–625, 630

Genghis Khan (Temüjin), 337, 338, 343, 345

Genoa, 423, 425, 528; Portuguese competition with, 435; sea routes of, 399 *(map)*; trading colonies of, 398

Gens de couleur, 601

Gentry, 353, 459; British, 626

George III (England), 589

Georgia (Asia), 705

Georgia (United States), 616, 660

Germany (Germans), 395, 451; expansion by, 350; nationalism of, 462; in North America colonies, 493; industrialization of, 614; railroads in, 621 *(map)*; roads in, 624; Ruhr district, 614, 621 *(map)*, 623; customs union in, 627

Ghana (Gold Coast), 371, 428, 431, 511, 515; Berber attack on, 372; end of slave trade in, 670, 671

Ghazan, kahn, 345

Ghent, 400

Gilbert, Humphrey, 488

Giotto, 409

Giraffes, 423

Girondists, 596

Glassmakers, 404, 531 *(illus.)*

Glorious Revolution of 1688 (England), 466, 497

Goa, 530, 547; Portuguese in, 433–434

Go-Daigo (Japan), 361

Gods and goddesses: Inca sungod, 437; Mongol "Heaven," 338

Gold Coast (Ghana), 371, 428, 431, 511, 515; Berber attack on, 372; end of slave trade in, 670, 671

Gold coinage, 426, 701

Golden Horde (Kipchak Khanate), 346 *(map)*, 566; rivalry with Il-Khans, 345–346; Russia and, 342, 343 *(map)*, 349–350, 351

"Golden Speech of Queen Elizabeth, The," 465

Gold (gold trade), 349, 571; African, 374, 381, 384, 425, 426, 522, 545; in Brazil, 483, 496; in Caribbean, 435–436; coinage, 426, 701; from colonial Americas, 440, 469, 478, 480, 510, 535; in California, 646; in Australia, 684; West African, 371–372, 431, 671

Gomes, Fernão, 428

Gordon, Charles, 702

Gothic cathedrals, 404 *(illus.)*, 406

Government: *See also* Administration; Bureaucracy; Monarchy; Il-khanate, 345; Delhi India and Mali compared, 376–377; European, 414; economic management by, 471; colonial North America, 489; popular protest of, 587; Latin American colonial, 478; United States revolutionary, 591–592; British industrialization and, 611; laissez faire economics and, 627; Constitutionalism in Americas, 639, 642; in British India, 676; Ottoman, 531; Ottoman reforms, 701

Gozzoli, Benozzo, 409 *(illus.)*

Granada, 414, 425

Gran Colombia, 635, 636 *(map)*, 643, 644, 646

Grand Canal (China), 565

Grand National Consolidated Trade Union, 628

Graphite, for pencils, 584

Graphs, origin of, 613

Great Britain, 468. *See also* British Empire; England; India, British rule in; sea power of, 582; American Revolution and, 588–591; Napoleon and, 597, 600; Amerindians and, 648; Argentine investment by, 658; business cycles in, 626; Canada and, 657; child labor in, 625; chronology (1763-1877), 665; democratic reforms in, 604; enclosure movement in, 609; end of slave trade and, 638, 651, 670, 672; imperial policies and shipping, 683–684; invasion of Ethiopia by, 668; Latin American investment by, 659; Sierra Leone and, 671; trading empire of, 688; War of 1812 and, 646; Crimean War and, 699–700, 701; health care in, 702; Russia and, 704, 705

Great Britain, China and, 707, 713; Arrow War (1856-1860) and, 711; opium trade, 708, 743; Opium War (1839-1842) and, 708–709; Taiping Rebellion (1850-1864), 709 *(map)*, 710–712 *and illus.*; Treaty of Nanking (1842), 708

Great Britain, Industrial Revolution in (1760-1851), 611–612 *and map*, 630; child labor in, 625; cotton industry in, 612, 615; iron industry in, 617–618; laissez faire, 627, 628; population growth and, 609, 622, 623; pottery industry, 614–615 *and illus.*; protests and reforms; railroads in, 612 *(map)*, 620; rural environments, 624; social changes, 626–627; steamships in, 619, 629; working conditions, 624

Greater Antilles, 424, 436. *See also* Caribbean region

Great Famine of 1315-1317 (Europe), 395
Great Lakes region, colonial, 493
Great Northern War (1700-1721), 469, 570
Great Trek, 681, 683 *(illus.)*
Great Western Schism (1378-1415), 412
Great Western (steamship), 619 *(illus.)*, 620
Great Zimbabwe, 383 *and illus.*
Greco-Roman traditions, 407, 409, 454
Greece, 528; independence of, 604, 696
Greenland, 423
Gregory X, Pope, 402
Gregory XIII, Pope, 455
Grimké, Sarah, 655
Guadeloupe, 501, 502
Guangxi, 710
Guatemala, 476, 660
Guianas, 509
Guilds, 401, 406; in late medieval Europe, 396
Gujarat, 388; Delhi sultanate and, 379, 380;
    mosque architecture in, 386; as trade and
    manufacturing hub, 384–385; Portuguese
    in, 434, 435
Gunpowder, 360, 516, 708; in China, 357, 358;
    invention of, 358; in medieval Europe, 410;
    in Japan, 553, 572; Ottoman use of, 528
Guns. *See* Firearms
Gutenberg, Johann, 409
Güyük, Great khan, 341

Habsburg dynasty, 462, 467 *(illus.)*, 495
Hafez, 538
Haidar Ali, 673
Haiti (St. Domingue), 503, 505, 508, 634;
    revolution in, 601–603 *and illus.*, 602 *(map)*,
    605; slave rebellion in, 580 *(illus.)*, 581, 587,
    651, 670; unknown maroon of, 509 *(illus.)*
Hakkas, 710
Halil, Patrona, 536
Halil rebellion, 536
Hall, John, 610
Han'gul, 359
Hannibal (slave ship), 496, 514
Hanoi, 342, 363
Hanoverian dynasty, 467 *(illus.)*
Hanseatic League, 398, 410
Harsha Vardhana, 542
Hart, Robert, 713
Hausa city-states, 375, 520, 522, 667
Hawaiian Islands, 420, 687
Heaven (god), 338
Heavenly Kingdom of Great Peace (Chinese
    religious movement), 710, 711
Hebrew Bible, 453, 455. *See also* Bible, the
Helena (Ethiopia), 433
Henry IV (France), 466
Henry of Navarre, 466
Henry the Navigator, 425–426
Henry VIII (England), 466, 468
Heresy, 466
Herodotus, 338
Herzen, Alexander, 706
Heshen, 691
Heyerdahl, Thor, 420
Hidalgo y Costilla, Miguel, 637–638 *and illus.*
Hidden Imam, 538
Hideyoshi, 552

Himalaya Mountains, 368
Hindus (Hinduism), 680. *See also* India (Indian civilization); Delhi sultanate and, 375,
    379, 380, 385, 387, 388; Muslim relations, in
    Mughal India, 541, 542–543; women and,
    388; holy men, 675
Hispaniola, 435–436, 436, 509
Hogarth, William, 586 *(illus.)*
Hokulea (ship), 420–421
Holy Alliance, 603
Holy Land, 533
Holy Roman Empire, 467; (1519-1556), 463
    (map); in 1453, 411 *(map)*
Homosexuality, in Islam, 540
Hong Kong, 708–709, 711
Hongwu, 354
Hong Xiuquan, 710, 711
Hormuz, 434, 530, 541
Horses, 381, 395, 559. *See also* Cavalry;
    Amerindians and, 477, 493; Conquistador,
    436, 440; iron stirrups for, 375; military use
    of, 413; conquistadors, 436, 440; Amerindi-
    ans and, 649
Horton, James Africanus, 672
Hospitallers, 528
House of Burgesses (Virginia), 489
House of Commons (Britain), 604
House of Representatives (United States), 591
Housing (dwellings): *See also* Construction
    materials and techniques; Parisian poor,
    592 *(illus.)*; colonial Americas, 491 *(illus.)*;
    London tenements, 622 *(illus.)*; Paris apart-
    ment, 623 *(illus.)*
Huang Dao Po, 353
Huang (Yellow) River, 353, 712
Hülegü, Il-khan, 343, 345, 347
Human rights, 595, 597
Hume, David, 585
Hundred Years War (1337-1453), 413
Hungary, 350, 604, 701; copper mining in, 397,
    404
Hunting: in tropics, 369; by Amerindians, 649
Huron peoples, 493
Husayn, 538
Hyderabad, 544
Hydraulic works (waterpower), 370, 397 *and
    illus.*, 615. *See also* Water control systems
Hygiene, 702. *See also* Sanitation

Iberian expansion. *See* Portuguese explo-
    ration; Spanish exploration
Iberian peninsula: *See also* Portugal; Spain;
    expansion and, 424, 440–441; unification of,
    414–415
Ibn Abd al-Wahhab, Muhammad, 536, 692
Ibn Battuta, Muhammad ibn Abdullah, 367,
    381 *(map)*, 383, 384; in Delhi, 376, 379, 388;
    in Mali, 374, 376–377, 389
Ibn Khaldun, 347
Ibn Tughluq, Muhammad, Sultan, 376, 379
Ibrahim, 692, 696
Ice Age, Little (1590s), 460, 557, 575
Iceland, 423
Ideas (ideology): *See also* Intellectuals; Politi-
    cal thought (ideology); popular protest, 587
Ife kingdom, 371 *(illus.)*

Ignatius of Loyola, 453
Il-khanate (Iran), 342 *(illus.)*, 343 *(map)*, 345–
    348, 351; rivalry with Golden Horde, 345–
    346; science and technology in, 348, 349
Illinois, native peoples in, 648
Iltutmish, Sultan, 375, 378
Immigration: to colonial North America, 489,
    497; acculturation and, 654–655; to Ameri-
    cas, 652–655; to Australia and New Zealand,
    684; Russian Empire, 705
Imperialism: *See* Colonies (colonization); Ex-
    pansion (expansionism) *and specific empires*
Imperial Maritime Customs Service, 713
Import duties, 627, 628
Imports. *See* Trade (trading)
Inca (Inca Empire), 475, 486; Spanish con-
    quest of, 437, 440
Indentured labor (indentured servants), 489,
    502, 503, 687
Independence: *See also* Latin American
    independence; Nationalism; American
    Revolution and, 589; revolutionary era, 581;
    Greek, 604, 696; Haitian, 602; of Nether-
    lands, 470
India (Indian civilization), 369, 528. *See also*
    Hindus (Hinduism); Mughal Empire (In-
    dia); agriculture in, 370; water-control
    systems in, 370; Bahmani Empire, 378
    (map), 380; cotton textiles from, 384, 385,
    388, 615, 628–629; gold trade in, 372; Ma-
    japahut Empire, 378 *(map)*, 385; Indian
    Ocean trade and, 381; literacy in, 386;
    Chinese voyages to, 422–423; Portuguese
    and, 428, 433–434 *and illus.*, 435; cotton
    textiles from, 511, 515, 518; industrializa-
    tion in, 609; railroads in, 630; British trade
    with, 684; steam tractor in, 629 *(illus.)*;
    African ivory trade and, 672
India, Delhi Sultanate, 346, 378–380, 378
    (map); Gujarat and, 385; Hinduism and,
    375, 379, 380, 385, 387, 388; leadership in,
    376, 378, 379; learning and literacy in, 386,
    387; slavery in, 387–388; water-control
    systems in, 370; women in, 378, 387–388
India, Mughal Empire, 529 *(map)*, 537, 541–
    544; building techniques in, 525 *(illus.)*;
    chronology, 527; decay and regional chal-
    lenges to, 544; Hindu-Muslim coexistence
    in, 541, 542–543; Iran and, 346, 526, 673;
    political foundations of, 541–542; Por-
    tuguese threat to, 435
India British rule in, 664, 673–681, 683, 705,
    708; (1707-1805), 674 *(map)*; chronology
    (1756-1885), 665; company men in, 673;
    cotton textiles and, 629–630; disease in,
    677–678; durbar ceremonials in, 676, 677–
    679; Hinduism and, 675, 680; impact of
    industry in, 676–677; nationalism in, 676,
    680–681; political reform in, 676; railroads
    in, 663 *(illus.)*; raj and rebellion in, 674–676
Indiana, native peoples in, 648
Indian Civil Service (ICS), 676
Indian immigrants: in British colonies, 686,
    687; in Caribbean, 652, 653
Indian Ocean region (Indian Ocean states),
    433–435; chronology (1405-1539), 419;

exploration of, before 1450, 419, 420 *(map)*, 421–423; Portuguese exploration of, 418; chronology (1511-1742), 527; Portuguese threat in, 528, 530; European possessions in, 682 *(map)*

Indian Ocean trade (maritime system), 367, 380–385, 421, 441, 544, 672; expansion of (1200-1500), 378 *(map)*; Arabia and, 381, 384; monsoons and, 380, 384; East Africa and, 381, 383; ship-building technology and, 380–381, 382 *(illus.)*; Ming China and, 422–423; Europe and, 433–435; Portuguese and, 429, 431, 433–435, 547 *(illus.)*; European colonization and, 546 *(map)*; Muslims in East Africa, 545, 547

Indian Removal Act (United States,1830), 648

Indigo plantations, 384, 490

Indonesia (Indonesians), 421, 530

Indulgence selling, 450

Indus River, 369, 543

Industrial countries, 609; overseas trade of, 683–684

Industrialization (industry), 660–661. *See also* Industrial Revolution; Iron industry and tools; Porcelain; Textile industry; Steel industry; late medieval Europe, 397–398; tobacco in colonial Mexico, 473 *(illus.)*; in Americas, 650; in British India, 676–677; of Egypt, 668; in Europe, 621 *(map)*; laissez faire economics and, 627; nonindustrial world and, 629–630; railways and, 620; in Russia, 704

Industrial Revolution (1760-1851), 608–630; agriculture and, 610; in Britain and Europe, 611–612, 614; causes of, 609–614; changes in society and, 626–627; child labor in, 609, 625 *and illus.*, 628; chronology, 611; cities and towns in, 622–624; division of labor in, 616–617; impact of, 622–627; iron industry, 616–618; mass production in, 614–615, 618; mechanization of cotton industry in, 615–616; new economic and political ideas, 627–628; population growth and, 609–610; railroads and, 612 *(map)*, 620, 621 *and map*, 623, 624, 656; rural areas and, 624; steam engine and, 608 *(illus.)*, 615, 618–620; technological revolution in, 614–621; telegraph and, 620–621, 656; trade and inventiveness in, 610–611; working conditions in, 624–626

Inequality. *See* Gender differences; Social classes (social stratification); Women

Infantry, Chinese, 422, 572. *See also* Armed forces; Military, the

Inflation: in Europe, 535; in Ming China, 535, 557; in Ottoman Empire, 534, 535; in Safavid Iran, 541

Influenza, 344, 476

Inheritance: European monarchies and, 413; women and, 699

Inner Asia. *See also* Central Asia; Tibet *and specific country*: Mongol control of, 354

Inquisition, 455, 466

Institutes of the Christian Religion (Calvin), 451

Intellectuals (intellectual life): *See also* Culture; Philosophy; Political thought; Science;

Enlightenment, 582–586; revolutionary era and, 581; Russian Slavophiles, 705, 706–707

Interchangeable parts, for manufacturing, 618

Iran, 705. *See also* Safavid Empire (Iran); Islam in, 331, 332 *(illus.)*; Mongol Il-khanate in, 342 *(illus.)*, 343 *(map)*, 345–348, 351; Mughal India and, 346, 526, 673

Iraq, 528, 538

Ireland (Irish), 412, 460; British annexation of, 468; colonization of, 488; emigration from, 626, 639; famine in (1847-1848), 626

Iron industry and tools, 571. *See also* Steel production; English, and deforestation, 460; late medieval Europe, 397, 398; in Ming China, 356; stirrups, 375; in tropics, 371; Turkic, 338; Conquistador weaponry, 438; Industrial Revolution and, 612, 616–618, 624; British coke and, 617–618

Iroquois Confederacy, 491, 492, 493, 589

Irrigation: in tropics, 370–371; in British India, 678; in Egypt, 668

Isabella (France), 413

Isabella (Spain), 414–415, 430; Columbus and, 415, 430

Isfahan, 538–539

Islamic empires. *See also* Delhi sultanate (India); Khans and khanates; Mali; Mongolian Empire; Mughal Empire (India); Safavid Empire (Iran)

Islam (Islamic civilization), 344. *See also* Muslims; Christian rivalry with, 351; conversion to, 331, 332 *(illus.)*, 372, 387, 531, 543; culture and science of, 346–349; trade and travel in (850-1500), 381 *(map)*; Gujarat and, 384, 385; in Iran, 331, 332 *(illus.)*; Mongolian Empire and (1260-1500), 342, 344–349; mosques, 385–386, 530 *(illus.)*, 538; Shi'ite, 345, 348, 384; Shi'ite in Iran, 529 *(map)*, 536, 537, 538; slaves in, 522; Sunni, 345, 529 *(map)*, 536, 537; African trade and, 518–522; Indian Ocean trade and, 421, 544–545, 547; in Russia, 567; ulama, 531, 538, 693, 696; in West Africa, 665, 667; Egypt and, 668

Ismail, Shah, 537, 538

Ismail (Egypt), 668

Istanbul, 528, 536, 540. *See also* Constantinople; and Isfahan compared, 538–539; mosque in, 530 *(illus.)*; Ottoman modernization and, 696, 697

Italy (Italian peninsula), 409, 604; city-states of, 398, 410, 425; roads in, 624; immigrants to Americas from, 654–655

Iturbide, Augustín de, 638, 642

Ivan III (Russia), 350

Ivan IV (the Terrible; Russia), 526, 566

Ivory trade, 432 *(illus.)*, 545, 547, 672, 683

Izmir (Smyrna), 535–536

Jackson, Andrew, 604, 643, 648

Jacobins, 596

Jacquerie revolt (1358), 395–396

Jagadai khanate, 342, 343 *(map)*, 346

Jaja of Opobo, 671 *(illus.)*, 672

Jakarta, 548

Jamaica, 651; slave rebellion in, 508; sugar plantations in, 503, 504–505, 507 *(illus.)*, 508 *(illus.)*

James I (England), 466, 501

James II (England), 466, 492, 497

Jamestown, 488–489

Janissaries, 530–531, 534, 536; Ottoman modernization and, 692, 693, 696

Japan (Japanese), 360–363, 572, 705; chronology (1274-1338), 339; Mongol invasions of, 336 *(illus.)*, 342; Ashikaga Shogunate, 362–363; steel production in, 356, 357, 361; trade, 363; Kamakura Shogunate, 361; chronology (1543-1792), 553; civil war in, 551; elite decline and social crisis in, 555–556; Europeans and, 553–555, 558; invasion of Korea by, 552; reunification of, 551–556; Tokugawa shogunate, 552–556, 572, 573; immigration to Brazil, 653

Java, 385, 548, 681, 683

Jefferson, Thomas, 595

Jenkinson, Anthony, 526

Jerusalem, 350, 533, 699

Jesuits (Society of Jesus), 455, 544; Reformation and, 453; in North America, 493; in China, 456, 458, 558–559, 562–563 *and illus.*, 572, 707; in Japan, 553–554

Jewelry, 372, 384

Jews, 384; Christian persecution of, 400, 402–403; mapmaking by, 374 *(illus.)*, 425–426; merchants, 385; as moneylenders, 404; as scholars, 406; in Spain, 400; expelled from Spain, 415, 469; in Germany, 457; in Ottoman Empire, 531; immigrants in Americas, 653; in Ottoman Empire, 698

Jihad (holy war), 667

Jim Crow laws (United States), 651

Jin Empire (China), 352

Jingdezhen, 357, 554, 557

Joan of Arc, 413

João III (Portugal), 438

Job Solomon, 520–521

John (England), 412

Johnson, Samuel, 582

Johnson, Sir William, 589

Johnson, William, home of, 491 *(illus.)*

John VI (Portugal), 634, 638

Joint-stock companies, 459, 490, 510, 544, 546 *(map)*, 706

Joseph Bonaparte, 634

Journalism, Crimean War and, 702

Juan, Jorge, 484–485

Juárez, Benito, 633, 646, 647*(illus.)*

Jubbadar, Ali-Quli, 537 *(illus.)*

Junks (ships), 380–381, 422 *and illus.*

Junta Central (Spain), 634, 635

Juvaini, 347

Kaffa, black death in, 344, 395, 396 *(map)*

Kamakaze, 361

Kamakura Shogunate (Japan), 361 *and map*

Kanem-Bornu, 375

Kangxi (China), 559, 562 *and illus.*, 563, 572

Karakorum, 342

Kashmir, 678

Kazakhstan (Kazakhs), 705, 710

Kazan, 567
Kenya, 545
Kepler, Johannes, 454
Keraits, 337
Khans and khanates: *See* Golden Horde khanate; Il-khanate (Iran); Jagadai khanate; White Horde; Yuan Empire (China) and *specific khan*
Khubilai, Great Khan, 342, 343, 348, 351, 352, 354, 398; invasion of Japan by, 361 *and map*
Khwarezm, 338
Kilwa, 383, 547
Kingship. *See* Monarchy (kingship)
Kinship, in colonial Latin America, 486
Kiowa peoples, 649
Kipchak khanate. *See* Golden Horde khanate
Kirgizstan, 710
Kitchener, Lord, 676
Knights, 395, 410, 413, 414
Knights of the Hospital of St. John, 528
Kola nut, 522
Kongo, 432, 438–439
Kon Tiki (ship), 420
Korea (Koreans), 361 *(map)*; chronology (1258-1392), 339; technology of, 357, 359–360; China and, 552, 558; Japan and, 363, 552, 553
Koryo, 359. *See also* Korea
Kosovo, Battle of (1389), 351, 528
Kremer, Gerhard (Mercator), 458 *and illus.*
Kremlin (Moscow), 350 *(illus.)*
Kyoto, 362, 363, 551

Labor: *See also* Slaves (slavery); Working class; Amerindian, 436; Andean mit'a, 482, 496; *encomienda*, 482, 483; indentured, 489, 502, 503, 687; of children, in Industrial Revolution, 609, 625 *and illus.*, 628; division of, 388, 614, 616–617, 624–625, 630; migrations, to British colonies, 686–687
Labor movement, in Americas, 654 *(illus.)*, 655
Lahore, 375
Laissez faire economics, 627, 628
Lake Tana, 670
Lake Victoria, 670
Lalibela (Ethiopia), 386 *and illus.*
Lamaism (Tibetan Buddhism), 352, 558
Land grants, 542, 543, 544
Landowners (landownership): tax farming and, 345; Chinese gentry, 353, 459; Amerindians and, 494; in late medieval Europe, 394; plague in Europe and, 396; European nobility and, 459; in colonial Latin America, 486; Ottoman, 531, 534; Russian serfs and, 569; Europe, 609; British gentry, 626; in British India, 675
Lane, Edward William, 699 *(illus.)*
Language: *See also* Writing *and specific language;* religious conversion and, 331; Latin, 392, 406, 408; European vernacular, 407; Persian, 386; Polynesian, 420; Russian, 349; Swahili, 381, 672; and immigrants to Americas, 653–654; French, 697, 703
Laos, 711
Lateen sails, 382, 426, 429 *and illus.*, 430

Latin America, colonial, 469, 477–488, 479 *(map)*, 505, 509. *See also* Brazil; *and specific colony;* Amerindians in, 481, 482, 483, 486; in Caribbean, 435–436; chronology, 475; culture of, 477, 480; economy in, 480, 482–483; gold and silver from, 510; imperial reforms and, 495–496; Inca Empire and, 437, 440; Mexico, 436–437, 438; race and ethnicity in, 484–485, 487 *(illus.)*, 488; and Russia compared, 572; silver refinery in, 481; society in, 483, 486–488; state and church in, 477–478, 480
Latin America (Latin Americans): *See also* South America *and specific countries and regions;* by 1830, 636 *(map)*; constitutional experiments in, 639, 642; development in, 659; immigration to, 652; personalist leaders in, 642–644; positivism in, 628; racial discrimination in, 655–656; underdevelopment in, 656–657
Latin American independence, 633–661, 636 *(map)*; Brazil, 638, 640–641; chronology (1810-1888), 635; Mexico, 637–638 *and illus.;* roots of revolution, 634; Spanish South America, 634–635, 637
Latin language, 392, 406, 408
Latin West (Europe 1200-1500), 392; in 1453, 411 *(map)*; Black Death in, 391, 393, 395, 396 *(map)*; cathedrals in, 404, 406; chronology, 393; culture in, 393; humanism and printers in, 407–409; Hundred Years War (1337-1453) and, 413; Iberian unification in, 414–415; mines and mills in, 396–397; monarchy and aristocracy in, 410, 412–413; Mongolian Empire and, 344, 350–351, 398; new monarchies in, 413–414; peasant revolts in, 393–394, 395–396; persecution of Jews in, 400, 402–403; politics and society in, 393; Renaissance artists, 409–410; rural life, 393–395; technology and environment in, 393; universities in, 406–407; urban revival in, 398–401
Laws (legal codes): *See also* Constitutions; Vietnamese, 363; Enlightenment ideas and, 583; British factories (1833), 628; Jim Crow (United States), 651; Napoleonic France, 597; Ottoman reforms, 693, 696, 698
Leatherworking (tanneries), 375, 384, 398
Lebanon, 345
Legislative Assembly (France), 595
Leo X, Pope, 450
Lepanto, Battle of (1571), 531
Lesotho, 667
Liberia, 672
Libraries: in Timbuktu, 386–387; Vatican, 408; Franklin and, 585; Jesuit at Beijing, 563 *(illus.)*
Limbourg brothers, 394 *(illus.)*
Lincoln, Abraham, 644, 646; abolition of slavery and, 650–651
Linnaeus, Carolus, 582
Lisbon, 414; earthquake in (1755), 453
List, Frederich, 627
Literacy: of European women, 462; Muslim, 386
Literature: of late medieval Europe, 407–408; Ming China, 357; Mughal India, 543; Arabic, 668

Lithuania, 351; in 1453, 411 *(map)*; Poland and, 567, 569
Little Bighorn, Battle of (1876), 649
Little Ice Age (1590s), 460, 557, 575
Liverpool and Manchester Railway, 622
Livestock, 476 *(illus.)*, 477. *See also* Pastoralism; in East Africa, 366 *(illus.)*; in Argentina, 656, 660
Livingstone, David, 670, 672
Li Zicheng, 551, 558
Loans, 414. *See also* Foreign debt
Locke, John, 467, 582–583, 605
London, 586 *(illus.)*, 623; growth of, 622; tenements in, 622 *(illus.)*
Longbows, 413
"Lost-wax" method, 371
Louisiana, 494, 495, 616
Louisiana Purchase, 644, 645 *(map)*
Louis IX (France), 412
Louis Philippe (France), 604, 652
Louis XIII (France), 466
Louis XIV (France), 466–467, 468
Louis XV (France), 593
Louis XVI (France), 593, 594, 595
Louis XVIII (France), 604
Lovett, William, 628
Lowell, Francis Cabot, 625
Lunar Society, 609, 615
Luanda, 502, 517
Lunda kingdoms, 506, 517
Luo Guanzhong, 357
Luther, Martin, 450–451 *and illus.*, 455, 462
Lutheranism, 451, 452 *(map)*, 462

Macao, 434, 547, 558, 707
Macartney, George (Macartney mission), 564, 565 *(illus.)*, 707
Machiavelli, Niccoló, 464–465
Madagascar, 421
Madeira, 423, 426, 482
Madison, James, 639, 643
Madras, 544, 673
Madrasas (Islamic schools), 406, 534, 538
Madurai (India), temple in, 379 *(illus.)*
Magellan, Ferdinand, 418, 420, 431
Magna Carta, 412 *(illus.)*
Mahmud II, Sultan, 696, 706
Ma Huan, 384
Mai Ali (Bornu), 522
Maize (corn), 435, 476, 506, 565; in Europe, 460, 609
Majapahit Empire (India), 378 *(map)*, 385
Malabar Coast, 380, 385, 434; Portuguese threats to, 433, 434
Malacca, 530, 683; as trading center, 385; Islam in, 387, 545; Portuguese and, 434, 548
Malacca, Strait of, 381, 384
Malaria, 371, 476, 562; slaves and, 508, 515
Malaya (Malaysia), 420, 421, 683
Malay Peninsula, 385, 420, 548
Malcomb, John, 588 *(illus.)*
Mali, 373 *(map)*, 387, 423; disintegration of, 374–375; kingship in, 372, 376–377; women in, 388–389
Malindi, 423, 433, 545, 547
Malinke people, 372, 375
Malthus, Thomas, 627

Mamluks, 343, 345

Mamluk sultanate (Egypt), 350, 537, 538, 694; Ottoman Empire and, 527, 528, 530, 536, 692

Manchester, 622, 623, 624

Manchu China (Manchus), 551, 710. *See also* Qing Empire (China); Japanese invasion of Korea and, 552

Manchuria, 552, 562

Mangonès, Albert, 509 *(illus.)*

Manioc, 476

Mansabhars, 542, 543

Mansa Kankan Musa, 373 *(illus.)*, 423; kingship of, 372

Mansa Muhammad, 423

Mansa Suleiman, 374, 376–377

Manuel (Portugal), 433

Manufactured goods (manufacturing), 469. *See also* Industrial Revolution; Textiles; *and specific manufactures;* trade in, 383; Gujarati, 384; late medieval Europe, 398, 399 *(map)*, 400; Indian Ocean trade and, 380; African slave trade and, 511; carpets in Iran, 540; Japanese, 552; Ming (China) porcelain, 557; pencils, 584 *and illus.*; Industrial Revolution and, 609; mass production of, 614–615 *and illus.*, 618; division of labor in, 614, 616–617; in Latin America, 659; interchangeable parts in, 618; overseas markets for, 683

Manumission (freedom), 487, 509

Manuzio, Aldo, 409

Maori peoples, 684, 686

Mapmaking: Japanese, 555 *(illus.)*; Jewish, 374 *(illus.)*, 425–426; Portuguese, of West Africa, 428 *(illus.)*; Dutch, 458 *and illus.*

Mapuches (Araucanians), 649

Maragheh, observatory at, 348

Maratha Confederation, 673, 675

Marathas, 543, 544

Marie Antoinette (France), 595

Maritime expansion: before 1450, 418–424; Atlantic Ocean, 419, 423–424; Indian Ocean, 418, 421–423, 421 *(map)*; Pacific Ocean, 418, 419–421, 419–421 *and map*

Maroons, 509

Marquesas Islands, 420

Marriage: Mongol, 338; Muslim-Hindu in India, 379; spread of Islam and, 387; Indian, 388; European monarchies and, 413; in late medieval Europe, 461; Henry VIII and, 466; Hindu-Muslim, 543

Martin, P.-D., 468 *(illus.)*

Martin de Porres, Saint, 478 *(illus.)*

Martinique, 501, 502

Mary of Burgundy, 413

Masamune, Date, 554

Masonic lodges, 706

Massachusetts, 588, 591, 625; colonial, 490–491

Mass production, 614–615, 618

Mataram, 548

Mathematics (mathematicians), 454, 455; Persian Il-khanate, 348, 349

Mauritius, 681, 687

Maximilian of Habsburg, 633, 646

Maximillian II (Bohemia), 550 *(illus.)*

Maxim (machine) gun, 713 *(illus.)*

Maya people, 475, 649

Measles, 476

Mecca, 541; pilgrimage to, 372, 522

Mechanization, 360; of cotton industry, 615

Medici, Cosimo de', 410

Medici, Lorenzo de', 410

Medici family, 404, 409 *(illus.)*, 450

Medicine (physicians): in imperial China, 352, 354; Jesuit, in China, 562, 563; Portuguese in Africa, 439; women and, 655, 702 *and illus.*

Medina, 541

Mediterranean region, 425; Ottoman Empire and, 528

Meenakshi, temple of, 379 *(illus.)*

Mehmed I, Sultan, 528

Mehmed II, Sultan, 528

Mehmet I, Sultan, 351

Meissen, 614

Melanesia (Melanesians), 420, 684

Melville, Herman, 685

Mercantilism, 510–511, 627

Mercator (Gerhard Kremer), 458 *and illus.*

Merchants (merchant class): *See also* Trade (trading); Mongolian Empire and, 344; in Yuan China, 352, 353; Arabian, 384; Indian Ocean trade and, 381, 385; Jews as, 385; late medieval Europe, 398; Portuguese, in Africa, 432; taxes on, 414; Muslim traders, 385, 387, 421, 425, 434, 544; European, 457; North American, 491; African slave trade and, 517; Japanese, 552, 553, 555–556; East African, 672; in Chinese treaty ports, 710

Mestizos (mixed race), 484, 488

Metals (metallurgy): *See also* Bronze; Copper; Gold; Iron industry and tools; Steel; in Japan, 356; British, 611

Metternich, Klemens von, 603, 604

Mexican-American War (1846-1848), 646

Mexico, 475, 659; Spanish conquest of, 436–437; Aztecs in, 436–437, 438; colonial, 473 *(illus.)*, 495; Amerindians in, 647, 649; anti-Chinese prejudice in, 653; chronology (1810-1867), 635; civil war in, 646; constitutionalism in, 639, 642; independence of, 634, 636 *(map)*, 637–638; labor movement in, 655; mining in, 656, 660; nationalism in, 633; power of Catholic Church in, 642; railroads in, 632 *(illus.)*; war with United States (1846-1848), 633

Miao peoples, 691

Michelangelo, 410

Michigan, native peoples in, 648

Middle Atlantic colonies, 492–493

Middle class (bourgeoisie): Enlightenment and, 585; European cities and, 456–457, 459, 461; French Revolution and, 592, 596; Revolutions of 1848 and, 604; British industrialization and, 626, 627; Indian nationalism and, 681

Middle East, 564. *See also* Arabs; Islam (Islamic civilization); *and specific countries, cultures, empires and regions;* Chinese trade with, 356; chronology (1221-1453), 339; Timur's conquests in, 346

Middle Passage, 511, 513–515

Military, the: *See also* Infantry; Navy; War (warfare): Weapons and military technol-ogy; slaves as, 387, 530, 540–541; in Egypt, 692; Latin America, 642; Amerindians and, 649; Ottoman Janissaries, 530–531, 534, 536, 692, 693, 696–697; sepoy in British India, 673, 675–676; Qing China, 711

Military slaves, 387, 530, 540–541

"Milton" (Blake), 623

Mindanao, 545

Ming Empire (China), 354–357, 355 *(map)*, 551, 556–558; achievements of, 357; Mongol foundation of, 354–356; technology and population of, 356–357; Vietnam and, 363; Indian Ocean exploration by, 421–423; collapse of, 558

Mining (minerals): *See also* Coal, and industrialization; in late medieval Europe, 397; in tropics, 371–372; in colonial Americas, 495; English graphite, 584; in Great Britain, 611, 612, 628; Industrial Revolution and, 656; new technology in, 657 *(illus.)*; environmental impact of, 660

Missionaries, Christian, 426, 545, 675, 698. *See also* Jesuits (Society of Jesus); in Africa, 432, 438–439, 670, 671; in Americas, 432, 436; in China, 456, 458, 558–559, 707, 709, 710, 711; in India, 675; in Indian Ocean states, 544; Japan and, 553–554, 573; in Latin America, 480; in North America, 493; Orthodox in Siberia, 567

Mississippi, 616; native peoples in, 648

Mississippi River, 619

Missouri, native peoples in, 648

Mit'a (labor system), 482, 496

Mitsui companies, 552

Moby Dick (Melville), 685

Mocha, 536

Moctezuma II, 436–437 *and illus.*, 438

Modernization: *See also* Industrialization; Westernization; in Egypt and Ethiopia, 668

Mogadishu, 367

Mohawk people, 491, 589

Moluccas (Spice Islands), 385, 430, 431

Mombasa, 545, 547

Monarchy (kingship). *See also specific monarchs and emperors;* in Mali, 372, 376–377; in late medieval Europe, 410, 412–413; Congress of Vienna and, 603; European nationalism and, 462, 467 *(illus.)*, 604, 606; in France (Bourbons), 466–467 *and illus.*, 468, 495, 604; in Great Britain, 466, 467 *and illus.*; Enlightenment and, 583–584; popular protest and, 586, 587; in Russia, 567; in Spain, 467 *(illus.)*; in Brazil, 634, 638

Mongolia, Galdan in, 558, 562, 567

Mongolian Empire (Mongols), 337–364. *See also* Golden Horde; Il-khanate (Iran): Yuan Empire (China); *and specific khans;* chronology (1206-1449), 339; conquests of (1215-1283), 338, 342–344; culture and science in, 346–349; Europeans and, 344, 350–351, 398; invasion of Japan by, 336 *(illus.)*, 360–361; Islam and (1260-1500), 344–349; Korea and, 359; nomadic way of life and, 337–338; passports in, 344 *(illus.)*; plague and disease in, 344; rise of (1200-1260), 337–344; rulers of (1206-1260), 342

Mongolian Empire (Mongols) (cont.)
(illus.); trade in, 344; Vietnam and, 363; women and politics in, 340–341; Yuan Empire (China), 351–354, 363; China and, 707

Monopolies, 511, 657; colonial trade, 483, 491, 494, 495, 496, 502; royal, 432, 510; trading, 434, 435, 548

Monsoons, 368 and map, 421; Indian Ocean trade and, 380, 384

Montana, 660

Montgolfier brothers, 610

Montserrat, 501

Moral guides, 408

Morality, Victorian, 627

Morelos, José María, 638

Morocco, 414, 519, 522; Portuguese in, 425

Moro Wars, 545

Morse, Samuel, 621

Moscow, 349, 566, 567; Kremlin in, 350 (illus.); Napoleon's invasion of, 601

Mosques: Aya Sofya in Istanbul, 530 (illus.), 538; in India, 385–386

Most-favored nation status, 709

Mountain, the (France), 596

Mount Huanyaputina, 575

Movable type, for printing, 359, 360 (illus.)

Mozambique, 547

Mughal Empire (India), 526, 529 (map), 537, 673; Timurids and, 346; building techniques in, 525 (illus.); chronology, 527; decay of, and regional challenges to, 544; Hindu-Muslim coexistence in, 541, 542–543; political foundations of, 541–542; Portuguese and, 435

Muhammad Ali, 664, 690 (illus.), 692–693, 696; industrialization and, 629; invasion of Sudan by, 673; modernization of, 668, 692; reforms of, 703, 706

Muir, John, 660

Mule (spinning device), 615

Muscovy, 550 (illus.), 566. See also Moscow

Muscovy Company, 526

Music, and immigrants in Americas, 654–655

Muskets, 432, 534; and European trade, in Africa, 430–431, 440, 516, 519; and rifles compared, 675, 708

Muslim Empires, (1520-1656), 529 (map). See also Ottoman Empire; Mughal Empire (India); Safavid Empire

Muslims, 425, 531, 544. See also Islam (Islamic civilizations); as traders in India, 385, 387; hospitality to travelers by, 367; driven from Iberian peninsula, 414–415; Indian Ocean trade and, 421, 434; expelled from Spain, 469; in Africa, 433, 667

Muslim Turks, 462. See also Ottoman Empire

Musqat, Portuguese fort in, 547 and illus.

Mysore, 664, 675

Nadir Shah, 541, 544

Nagasaki, 554, 555

Nalanda, 387

Nanak, 543

Nana Sahib, 675

Nanjing (Nanking), 355, 711, 712 (illus.)

Nanking, Treaty of (1842), 708

Napoleon Bonaparte, 624, 634, 669; Civil Code of, 597; defeat of, 603, 606; Europe of, 600 (map); Haitian revolution and, 602; invasion of Egypt by, 664, 692, 694–695; invasion of Russia by, 597, 601, 703; as personalist leader, 643

Napoleonic Code, 597

Napoleon III, 604, 633

Narodniki (Russian movement), 707

Nasir al-Din Tusi, 347–348

Natal, 681

National Assembly (France), 594, 595

National Colored Convention, 650

National Convention (France), 595–597, 602

Nationalism, 581. See also Independence; Belgian, 605 (illus.); in British India, 676, 680–681; in Europe, 604, 606; German, 462; Mexican, 633

National parks, 660

Native Americans. See Amerindians

Natural disasters: flooding, in China, 353, 565; Lisbon earthquake (1755), 453

Natural law, 627

Nature. See Environment, the

Navajo peoples, 477, 648 (illus.)

Navarino, Battle of (1829), 696

Navigation Acts (Great Britain), 497, 511

Navigation (navigational instruments), 425; compass, 382, 426; Polynesian, 421; Portuguese, 426; Viking, 423

Navy (warships), 526; Korean, 360, 552; Mongol warship, 336 (illus.); European in Mughal India, 542; of Safavid Iran, 541; Portuguese in Africa, 433; Portuguese in Indian Ocean, 433–434, 435; English, 468, 469 (illus.), 471; Ottoman, 531; Spanish Armada, 469 (illus.); Russian, 570; in Northern Eurasia, 572; British, 582, 597, 629, 670, 692, 708

Nawabs, 673

Nemesis (steamship), 629

Nepal, 387

Nerchinsk, Treaty of (1689), 562, 567

Netherlands (the Dutch; Holland), 536, 548, 582. See also East India Company, Dutch, (VOC); Atlantic economy and, 510; bourgeoisie in, 457; colonies of, 681, 682 (map); India trade and, 673; mapmaking by, 458 and illus.; Mughal India and, 542; in North America, 492, 493; slave trade and, 502, 503; Spain and, 469–470; weaving in, 401 (illus.); West India Company, (Dutch) 492, 502, 510, 511, 513; Japan and, 553, 554, 555

Nevada, 660

Nevskii, Alexander, 349

New England, 511, 588; colonial, 476, 497; cotton mills in, 616, 625–626

Newfoundland, 423, 488, 493

New France (colonial Canada), 493–495

New Guinea, 420

New Jersey, voting rights in, 591

New Lanark, 628

New Spain, 478. See also Latin America, colonial

Newspapers, Crimean War and, 697, 702

Newton, Isaac, 455, 582

New York City, 492, 622

New Zealand, 420, 548, 685; as British colony, 684, 686

Nguni peoples, 665

Nian rebellions, 711

Nicaragua, 660

Nicholas I (Russia), 700, 703, 704, 706

Nicholas IV, Pope, 345

Niger Delta, 370, 432, 671

Nigeria, 371 (illus.)

Niger River, 369, 371, 670

Nightingale, Florence, 702 and illus.

Nile River, search for source of, 670

Niña (ship), 430

Nizam al-Mulk, 544

Nomadic peoples, 337–338, 540, 541. See also Mamluks; Mongolian Empire; Berbers, 372; Kazakh, 705, 710

Nonindustrial world (developing countries), 609. See also specific countries and regions; industrialization and, 629–630

North Africa, 519. See also specific peoples and countries; Portuguese and, 414, 425; Portuguese in, 425

North America. See also Canada; United States; constitutionalism in, 639

North America, colonial, 494 (map). See also American Revolution; Canada; British colonies, 488–493; chronology, 475; disease in, 476; Middle Atlantic, 492–493; New England, 490–492; New France (Canada), 493–495; reform in, 497; Russian Alaska, 567, 571; Seven Years War (French and Indian War), 494 (map), 495, 582, 587; South, 488–490

North China Plain, 351

North River (steamboat), 619

Novgorod, 566

Nubia, 372

Nyamwezi traders, 672

Nzinga (Angola), 518 (illus.)

Oath of the Tennis Court (France), 594

Observatories: Il-Khanate, 348; in imperial China, 354, 355, 356

O'Connor, Fergus, 628

Ogé, Vincent, 601

Oglethorpe, James, 521

Ögödei, Great Khan, 338, 340, 342, 343, 351

Ohio, native peoples in, 648

Ohio River, 619

Ohio River Valley, 493

Okinawa, 558

Oman, 547 and illus.; sultanate of, 672

Omar Khayyam, 348

Oneida peoples, 589

Onin War (1477), 363

Onondaga peoples, 589

Opium trade, 675, 701, 708

Opium War (1839-1842), 708–710, 709 (map)

Oral tradition, in Africa, 383

Orange Free State, 681

Order of Christ, 426

Order of Knights Templars, 426

Order of Teutonic Knights, 350–351, 395

Orozco, José Clemente, 647 *(illus.)*

Orthodox Christianity, Russian, 569, 699; Mongol rule of Russia and, 349, 350; missionaries to Siberia, 567, 572; Ottoman Turks and, 570

Osaka, 552

Osmanli language, 531

Ottawa peoples, 587

Ottoman Empire (Ottoman Turks), 526–536, 691–693, 696–701; in 1453, 411 *(map)*; Timur and, 346; capture of Constantinople by, 351; Holy Roman Empire and, 462; Portuguese rivalry with, 433, 435; chronology (1500-1730), 527; central institutions, 530–531; expansion of, 425, 519, 528–530, 529 *(map)*; crisis in (1585-1650), 534; economic change and weakness in (1650-1750), 534–536; Islamic law (Shari'a) and, 531–533; Istanbul, 536, 538–539; Islam and, 541; Russia and, 567, 570, 571, 705, 707; Egypt and, 629; Greek independence and, 604, 698; (1829-1914), 697 *(map)*; chronology (1805-1876), 693; European reform model for, 693, 696–699; Tanzimat reforms, 696–699, 700 *(illus.)*, 701; Crimean War and aftermath, 699–701, 703

Owen, Robert, 628

Oxen, 395

Oxford University, 406

Oyo kingdom, 516

Pacific Ocean: chronology, 419; exploration of, before 1450, 419–421 *and map*; exploration of, before 1500, 419–421 *and map*; Magellan's exploration of, 418; Spanish exploration of, 430–431; whaling in, 685 *(illus.)*; European possessions in, 682 *(map)*

Páez, José Antonio, 643

Paine, Thomas, 589

Paintings: *See also* Art and artists; Iranian miniatures, 347; Japanese, 362 *and illus.*; of French peasants, 394 *(illus.)*; Renaissance, 409–410 *and illus.*; of Luther, 450 *(illus.)*; of Versailles, 468 *(illus.)*; colonial Spanish, 487 *(illus.)*; Mughal India, 525 *(illus.)*, 542 *(illus.)*, 543; Safavid Iran, 537 *(illus.)*; Revolution of 1830, 605 *(illus.)*

Palembang, 385

Palestine, 345

Palmares, 487

Palm oil trade, 671

Panipat, Battle of (1526), 541

Pan-Slavism, 705

Papacy (popes), 563. *See also* Catholic Church; *and individual popes;* Crusades and, 350; annual collection by, 401; European monarchies and, 410, 412; Henry VIII and, 466; reformation and, 450; treaty negotiation by, 430

Paper currency, 345, 349, 588; in China, 353, 535

Papermaking: in Europe, 400; in India, 386; Chinese wallpaper, 653

Paraguay, 637, 644, 647, 651

Paris: watermills in, 397 *(illus.)*; population of, 456; University of, 406; breweries in, 460;

inflation in, 535; women's salons in, 585; French Revolution and, 595, 596; housing in, 592 *(illus.)*, 623 *(illus.)*; Parlement of, 593; Reign of Terror and, 599; revolutions of 1848 and, 604

Paris, Treaty of (1783), 590–591

Parliament (England), 398, 414, 466, 509, 564; American Revolution and, 588; Chartism and, 628; enclosure movement and, 609

Parsis, 681

Passports, 344 *(illus.)*, 435

Pastoralism, 387. *See also* Livestock; Eastern African, 366 *(illus.)*; in tropics, 369–370

Patriarch of Alexandria, 433

Patriarch of Serbia, 351

Paul, 450

Pawnee peoples, 649

Peace of Augsburg (1555), 462

Peasants (peasantry), 605. *See also* Farmers; Rural societies; in rural France, 394 *(illus.)*; revolts by, 393–394, 395–396, 461, 573; European, 460; French Revolution and, 593, 595; Russian serfs, 569, 570, 573, 704, 705, 706

Pedro I (Brazil), 638, 642

Pedro II (Brazil), 638, 651

Pencil manufacture, 584 *and illus.*

Penn, William, 492

Pennsylvania, 585, 619; colonial, 492–493

Percussion cap rifles, 701, 708

Persian language, 386, 537, 538

Personalist leaders, 642–644

Peru, 420, 635, 637; colonial, 478, 480, 495, 496; Chinese immigration to, 652, 653; war with Chile, 646–647

Peter's pence, 401

Peter the Great (Russia), 569–570 *and illus.*, 706; Westernization of Russia and, 569, 570, 573, 703

Petrarch, Francisco, 407

Petroski, Henry, 584

Philadelphia, 492, 493

Philip II (Spain), 463, 466, 469

Philippine Islands, 482, 546 *(map)*, 558; Magellan in, 418, 431; Spanish conquest of, 545

Philip "the Fair" (France), 412

Philip V (Spain), 495

Phillips, Thomas, 496

Physicians. *See* Medicine (physicians)

Pilgrims (pilgrimages), 490; Islamic, 372, 522, 541, 545; Safavid Iran, 538; in India, 677

Pin-makers workshop, 616–617 *and illus.*

Pinta (ship), 430

Pirates (piracy), 483; China and, 558, 572; Korea and, 359, 360; in Southeast Asia, 385

Pi (symbol), 349

Piccolomini, Aeneas Silvius, 392

Pizarro, Francisco, 440, 486

Plague. *See* Bubonic plague

Plantations, 687. *See also* Sugar plantations; in British Guiana, 686 *(illus.)*; clove, 672; economy of, 490

Planter elite (plantocracy), 505, 509

Plato, 406

Playfair, William, 613 *and illus.*

Plymouth colony, 490

Poets and poetry: Safavid Iran, 538

Poland, 350, 351, 571, 701; Roman Catholicism of, 573

Poland-Lithuania, 567, 569

Political thought (ideology): Industrial Revolution and, 628; Locke and, 467; Machiavelli and, 464–465

Politics (political institutions): *See also* Administration; Democracy; Government; Monarchy; Political thought; *and specific institutions;* Mongol women and, 340–341; Delhi sultanate and, 380; Southeast Asian rivalry, 385; European innovation in, 462–471; North American colonial, 491; Japanese, 552; revolutionary era, 581; Enlightenment and, 582

Pollution: in Europe, from medieval industry, 398; Industrial Revolution and, 623

Polo, Marco, 344, 382, 384, 398; route of, 343 *(map)*

Polygamy, Islam and, 387

Polynesians, Pacific exploration of, 419–421 *and illus.*

Pombal reforms, 496

Ponce de León, Juan, 436

Pondicherry, 544

Pontiac (Ottawa chief), 587

Poor Richard's Almanac (Franklin), 585

Pope, Alexander, 456

Popular authoritarianism, 597

Popular protest, 586–587

Population movement. *See* Immigration

Population (population growth): in China, 353, 356; in late medieval Europe, 395; Amerindian, 440; climate and, to 1500, 443–444; in colonial Americas, 482, 490, 491, 494, 495; Columbian exchange and, 476; European cities, 456; in Ming China, 557; in Qing China, 564–565, 707; in industrialized Europe, 609–610, 623; in Russian Empire, 703

Porcelain, 344; Ming Chinese, 357 *and illus.*, 557; Japanese, 552, 553, 554 *and illus.*; mass production of, 614–615 *and illus.*

Portugal (Portuguese), 430; expulsion of Jews from, 415; African slave trade and, 426, 432, 438–439; African trade with, 431–433, 519; Atlantic trade and, 513, 517; Brazil and, 475; in China, 558; Dutch in Brazil and, 502; Hormuz and, 541; Indian Ocean trade and, 429, 431, 433–435, 434 *(illus.)*, 528, 530, 547; monopoly trade of, 483; Napoleon and, 597, 634; Brazilian independence and, 638; rivalry with Ottomans, 433, 435

Portuguese colonies, 582, 633, 682 *(map)*. *See also* Brazil, colonial; coastal China, 707; in Indian Ocean, 546 *(map)*

Portuguese exploration, 418, 424, 425–428, 427 *(map)*, 429 a*nd illus.*, 429 *and illus.*; of Africa: 414, 426-428, 427 *(map)*; in Atlantic, before 1500, 423; in the Atlantic Ocean, 423; Henry the Navigator and, 425–426; map of West Africa and, 428 *(illus.)*; Vasco da Gama, 428, 429 *and illus.*

Positivism, 628

Potatoes, 460, 476, 506; in Europe, 609; Irish famine and, 626

Potosí, 482; silver refinery, 480, 481 and illus.
Pottery. See also Porcelain: mass production of, 614–615 and illus.
Poverty (the poor): See also Peasants (peasantry); in late medieval Europe, 394–395; American crops and, 460; in early modern Europe, 460–461; French Revolution and, 593; housing for, 623, 624; disease and, 624; factory work and, 627; laissez faire theory and, 627
Price controls, 378
Priestley, Joseph, 609
Priests (clergy): See also Missionaries; Papacy; Religions; Religious orders; Indian Brahmins, 379, 380; European monarchies and, 414; in Spanish American colonies, 478 and illus., 480; French Revolution and, 594, 595, 597
Prince, The (Machiavelli), 464–465
Printing: woodblock, 359; in Korea, 359, 360 and illus.; movable type for, 359, 360 (illus.), 552; in medieval Europe, 408–409 and illus.; Dutch, 457; press for, 450
Proclamation of 1763, 587
Property rights: Russian serfs, 706; women and, 699
Prophet (Tenskwatawa), 648
Prostitutes (prostitution), 461, 593, 627, 678
Protestant Reformation, 450–454, 452 (map)
Protests, industrialization and, 628
Prussia, 395, 398, 570, 595; armed forces of, 467, 468; Napoleonic France and, 597, 601; democratization in, 604; Holy Alliance and, 603
Ptolemy, 348
Puerto Madero, 658 and illus.
Puerto Rico, 436, 652
Punjab, 543
Puritans, 466, 490
Pygmy people, of Central Africa, 369
Pythagoras, 454

Qajar dynasty (Iran), 705
Qazvin, 526
Qianlong (China), 559, 563, 564, 565 (illus.)
Qing Empire (China), 559 (map), 691, 705, 707–715; climate and diversity in, 566 (map); rise of, 558; trading companies in, 558; missionaries in, 558–559, 562–563; Emperor Kangxi, 559, 562 and illus.; European trade and, 563; Yangzhou Massacre, 560–561; population and social stress, 564–565; tea and diplomacy, 564; and Russia compared, 572–573; chronology (1794-1875), 693; conflicts in (1839-1870), 709 (map); economic and social disorder in, 707–708; Opium War (1839-1842) and aftermath, 708–710; Arrow War (1856-1860), 709 (map), 711; decentralization at end of, 712–715
Quaque, Philip, 522
Quebec, 587; colonial, 493, 495
Quetzalcoatl, 436, 438
Quito (Ecuador), 483–484
Quran, 386. See also Islam (Islamic civilizations); Muslims
Quran schools, 697. See also Madrasas

Race, and ethnicity in colonial Americas, 484–485, 487(illus.), 488
Raffles, Thomas Stamford, 683
Railroads, 623, 656; in Britain, 612 (map); canal systems and, 624; in Europe, 621 (map); in India, 630, 663 (illus.), 677; in Mexico, 632 (illus.); in Russia, 703–704; telegraph and, 621; in United States, 620 and illus., 657, 659 (illus.)
Rainfall, tropical. See Monsoons
Rajputs, 542, 543
Rangoon, 683
Rashid al-Din, 347
Raziya, Sultan, 378
Rebellions (revolts): See also Revolutionary era; Slave rebellions; and specific rebellions; in China, 551, 565, 707; of European peasants, 393–394, 395–396, 461; Indian sepoys, 675–676; in Ottoman Empire, 534, 536; Taiping, 709 (map), 710–712
Red Sea area, 528; trade in, 384
Red Shoes (Shulush Homa), 474
Reforms: Protestant, of Christianity, 450–454, 452 (map); colonial Americas, 495–496; Enlightenment, 583–584, 587; democratic, in Europe, 604; industrialization and, 628; in Mexico, 633; in Americas, 650; Islamic, in West Africa, 665, 667; in British India, 676; Ottoman Empire, 693, 696–699; Russian, 706
Regionalism, in Americas, 644, 646
Reign of Terror (France), 595–597, 598–599
Religion(s): See also Buddhism; Catholic Church; Christianity; Churches (buildings); Confucianism; Hinduism; Islam; Priests (clergy); Sacrifice; Salvation; Temples; Mongol, 338; Mongol synthesis in China, 352; Aztec, 436, 437; and statecraft, early modern Europe, 463, 466, 469; on Caribbean plantations, 508; in Russia, 567; Enlightenment and, 583; revolutionary era, 581; Heavenly Kingdom of Great Peace, 710, 711
Religious conversion, 331–332
Religious orders, 406, 543. See also Dominicans; Franciscans; Jesuits
Religious reformation, 450–454, 452 (map), 456
Renaissance, 406; artists of, 409–410
Republican Party (United States), 650
Réunion, 681
Revolutionary era (1750-1850), 580–606. See also Rebellions (revolts); American Revolution (1776-1779), 587–592, 590 (map), 605; colonial wars and fiscal crises, 582; eighteenth century crisis, 582–587; Enlightenment and old order, 582–586; folk cultures and popular protest, 586–587; in France, 592–599, 605; Haitian Revolution (1789-1804), 601–603 and illus., 602 (map); Napoleonic France, 597, 600 (map), 601, 602; national reform (1821-1850), 604–605; Conservative retrenchment in (1815-1820), 603, 606
Revolution of 1830, 605 (illus.)
Revolution of 1857 (India), 675–676
Revolutions of 1848, 604–605
Ricardo, David, 627

Ricci, Matteo, 456, 458, 558–559, 563
Rice and rice cultivation, 356; in Africa, 370; Champa, 362, 363; in North America, 490; in India, 543; in Japan, 552
Rickets (bone disease), 624
Rifles: breech-loading, 701; Enfield, 675; percussion-cap, 708
Rights: See also Voting rights; French Revolution and, 595, 634; Napoleonic France, 597
Roads, industrialization and, 624
Robespierre, Maximilien, 596–597, 598–599
Rocket (locomotive), 620
Romance of the Three Kingdoms, 357
Romania, 699, 700
Romanov, Mikhail, 569
Rome, 412, 604. See also Popes (papacy); Renaissance art of, 410; reformation and, 450
Roosevelt, Theodore, 660
Rosas, Juan Manuel de, 644
Rousseau, Jean-Jacques, 583, 585, 605
Roy, Rammohun, 680 and illus.
Royal African Company (RAC), slave trade and, 496, 500, 511, 513, 515
Royal monopolies, 432, 510
Royal Society (London), 455, 614
Ruhr district, 614, 621 (map), 623
Rural societies (rural areas): See also Farmers; Peasants; in late medieval Europe, 394–395; industrialization and, 624
Russian Orthodox Church, 567, 699; missionaries to Siberia, 567, 572; Mongol rule of Russia and, 349, 350; Ottoman Turks and, 570
Russia (Russian Empire), 565–573, 703–707. See also Muscovy; chronology (1221-1505), 339; Golden Horde in, 342, 343 (illus.), 349–350; ambassadors to Holland, 550 (illus.); and China compared, 572–573; chronology (1547-1799), 553; consolidation of, 571; war with Sweden, 469, 570; Qing China and, 562; expansion of, 565–567, 568 (map); forest resources in, 460, 567, 624; Peter the Great and, 569–570 and illus., 573, 703, 706; society and politics to 1725, 567, 569; Napoleon's invasion of, 597, 601, 703; Holy Alliance and, 603; railroads in, 620; Ottoman Empire and, 526, 691, 697 (map), 699, 701, 707; chronology (1801-1861), 693; Crimean War and, 700; cultural trends, 706–707; Europe and, 703–705

Sacrifice, Aztec, 436, 437
Sa'di, 538
Safavid Empire (Iran), 526, 535, 536–541, 567; chronology, 527; economic crisis and collapse of, 540–541; Ottomans and, 531, 532; Shi'ite Islam in, 529 (map), 536, 537, 538; society and religion in, 537–538
Sagres, 425
Sahara Desert, lack of rainfall in, 368
Sahara region: pastoralism in, 369–370; salt-making in, 375 (illus.)
Sailing (seafaring): See also Exploration (expeditions); Navigation; Ships and shipping; Polynesian canoes, 420–421 and illus.
St. Domingue (Haiti), 503, 505. 508. 634; revolution in, 601–603 and illus., 602 (map),

605; slave rebellion in, 580 *(illus.)*. 581, 587, 651, 670; unknown maroon of, 509 *(illus.)*

St. George of the Mine (Elmina), 431, 502, 511

St. Lawrence River, 493

St. Petersburg, 570, 571 *(illus.)*, 704 *and illus.*

Saint Peter's Basilica, 450

Saint-Simon, duke of, 467, 628

Salt, 383; in Central Sahara, 375 *(illus.)*

Salvation: Buddhism and, 354; Calvinist, 451

Samarkand, 347, 348; tomb of Timur in, 347 *(illus.)*

Samurai warriors, 551, 552, 555, 556

Sanitation, 702; disease and, 680

San Martín, José de, 637

Santa Anna, Antonio López de, 633

Santa María (ship), 430

Santo Domingo, 602

São Tomé, 428, 432, 482

Sarai, 349

Sardinia, 700

Sati (widow burning), 388, 680

Saud family, 692

Savannah (steamship), 620

Scandanavians, 451, 460. *See also* Denmark; Finns; Sweden; Vikings

Schism, 412

Scholasticism, 407

Schools, 534. *See also* Education; Colleges and Universities; in Timbuktu, 386–387; Muslim, 406; women and, 461–462; in Egypt, 668, 692; immigrants and, 653, 654; in India, 680; Islamic, 667, 697; Ottoman military, 696

Science: *See also* Astronomy; Engineering; Mathematics; Technology; European revolution in, 454–455; Jesuit, in China, 563 *(illus.)*

Scotland, 468

Seacole, Mary, 702

"Seasoning" of slaves, 508

Second Treatise on Civil Government (Locke), 467

Seine River, 397 *(illus.)*

Self-determination, 581, 604, 686. *See also* Independence; Nationalism

Selim I, Sultan, 528, 538

Selim II, Sultan, 532

Selim III, Sultan, 692, 693, 696

Senate (United States), 591

Seneca Falls, New York, 655

Seneca peoples, 589

Sepoy rebellion (India), 675–676

Sepoys, 673

Serbia, 351, 699; Ottoman Empire and, 693

Serfs (serfdom), 394, 396, 460. *See also* Peasants (peasantry); Russian, 569, 570, 573, 704, 705, 706

Sesshu Toyo, 362 *and illus.*

Sevastopol, 700

Seven Years War (1756-1763), 494 *(map)*, 495, 582, 587, 673

Seville, 400

Sèvres, 614

Sexuality: homosexuality in Islam, 540; prostitution, 461, 593, 627, 678

Shaka (Zulu), 665, 667

Shamanism, Mongol, 338, 345

Shandong, 712

Shanghai, 710, 712

Shari'a (Islamic law), 531–533, 539, 545, 696; in Mughal India, 543

Shifting cultivation, 370

Shi'ite Islam, 345; Assassin sect, 348; in Iran, 529 *(map)*, 536, 537, 538; rivalry with Sunnis, 384

Ships and shipping: *See also* Navigation; Navy (warships); Pirates; Sailing (seafaring), 683, 684; Indian dhows, 380, 382 *(illus.)*; Chinese junks, 380–381, 422 *and illus.*; lateen sails for, 382, 426, 429 a*nd illus.*; 430; Polynesian canoes, 420–421 *and illus.*; Portuguese caravels, 422 *and illus.*, 426, 429 *and illus.*; Dutch merchant, 457, 459 *(illus.)*; English merchant, 459; colonial Americas, 483; slave trade, 496, 510, 513 *(illus.)*, 514–515; steamships, 619–620 *and illus.*, 620, 629, 656; port construction and, 658 *and illus.*

Shoa kingdom, 668

Shulush Homa (Red Shoes), 474

Siam (Burma), 385, 683

Siberia, 562, 567, 569, 573

Sibir (khanate), 567

Siege weapons: *See also* Fortifications; Weapons and military technology; catapults, 343, 358, 360

Sierra Leone, 426, 428 *(illus.)*, 671, 687; Portuguese in, 426, 428 *(map)*

Sikhism (Sikhs), 543, 675

Silk Road, 349, 526

Silk trade, 541; Mongols and, 344

Silver, 349, 397, 557, 564; as medium of exchange, 354; in colonial Americas, 440, 480–481 *and illus.*, 482, 495; from Americas, 469, 510, 534, 535, 541, 698

Singapore, 683, 711

Sinhalese kingdom (Ceylon), 371

Sioux people, 649

Sirius (steamship), 619 *(illus.)*, 620

Sistine Chapel, 410

Slave Coast (Africa), 515–517, 523

Slave rebellions, 486–487, 490, 508; St. Domingue, 580 *(illus.)*, 581, 587, 651, 670

Slavery, abolition of, 581, 626, 687; in Cuba, 652, 687; in Dutch colonies, 652; in France, 602; in French colonies, 581, 652; Great Britain and, 638, 651, 670, 672; in the United States, 646, 650–651; in Venezuela, 634; in Western Hemisphere, 650–652

Slave soldiery, 387, 530, 540–541. *See also* Janissaries

Slaves (slavery): Amerindians as, 436, 482, 489; freedom for, 487, 509; Islam and, 522; in Islamic India, 387–388, 542; rebellions of, 486–487; and serfdom compared, 569; on sugar plantations, 528

Slaves (slavery), African, 428; in Brazil, 496, 508, 509, 638, 640–641; in China, 387; in colonial North America, 490; in Europe, 409 *(illus.)*; freedom for, 509; in Haiti, 601; in Latin America, 477; in North America, 489; punishment for, 507 *and illus.*; rebellions, 486–487, 490, 508, 580 *(illus.)*, 581, 587, 651, 670; on sugar plantations, 482, 487, 502–503, 504–509, 507 *(illus.)*, 650; US Constitution and, 591

Slave trade, African, 384, 514 *(map)*, 523, 626; Portuguese and, 426, 432, 438–439; Americas and, 460; Europe and, 460; malaria and, 476; sugar plantations and, 483; in colonial Latin America, 485, 486, 488; (1551-1850), 503 *(illus.)*; Dutch and, 502, 503; Atlantic system and, 510; Middle Passage, 511, 513–515; prisoners of war and, 517, 520; in West Africa and Americas compared, 520–521; in Eastern Africa, 545, 547; Islam and, 522; Great Britain and, 638, 651, 672; Sokoto Caliphate and, 667–668; trans-Saharan, 667–668; in Zanzibar, 672; end of, 650, 670–671, 672

Slavophiles, 705, 707

Smallpox, 344, 496, 515, 563, 624; Amerindians and, 436 *(illus.)*, 437, 440, 475

Smith, Adam, 616–617, 627

Smyrna, 535–536

Social classes (social stratification): *See also* specific class; colonial Latin America, 477, 483, 486–488; in colonial North America, 490; Europe (1500-1750), 456–457, 459–461; in Yuan China, 352; Islam and, 387; in late medieval Europe, 394; marriage and, 461; in medieval Europe, 400; pre-revolutionary France, 592; British industrialization and, 611; Parisian housing and, 623 *(illus.)*; industrial revolution and, 626–627; in slave plantations, 508–509

Social Contract, The (Rousseau), 583

Socialism, utopian, 628

Society (social conditions), 385–389; black death and, 395–396 *and map*; Mongol influence on Chinese, 337

Sodom, 453

Sokoto Caliphate, 665, 667–668

Solano López, Francisco, 647

Solomon, 384

Somali, 384, 387; pastoralism, 369

Song Empire (China): clocks in, 405; explosives in, 358; iron industry in, 616–617; Southern Song, 342, 352

Songhai Empire, 387, 519, 522

Sons of Liberty, 588

Sophia (Russia), 570

South America. *See also* Latin America, *and specific countries*; European expeditions to (1420-1542), 427 *(map)*; Iberian claims to, 428, 430; Spanish conquest of, 437, 440; chronology (1808-1888), 635

South Asia, empires and maritime trade in, 378 *(map)*. *See also* Indian Ocean trade, *and specific countries*

South Carolina, 489–490, 492, 615, 660

South China Sea, 380

Southeast Asia, 420, 558, 683. *See also* specific country; island, or region; Chinese travellers in, 355 *(map)*, 356; empires and maritime trade in, 378 *(map)*; farming in, 370; Indian Ocean trade and, 380; Mongols and, 339; trade in, 385; water control systems in, 371

Southern Africa, 665

Southern Song Empire (China), 342, 352. *See also* Song Empire

Southwest Asia (1500-1750). *See* Ottoman Empire; Safavid Empire

Spain, 468, 582; windmills in, 397; Jews in, 400; unification of, 414–415; conquest of Granada by, 425; royal dynasties in, 467 (illus.); economic decline in, 469; Netherlands and, 469–470; popular protest in, 586–587; Asian trade of, 558; Napoleon and, 597, 634; end of slave trade and, 652

Spanish American War (1898-1899), 646

Spanish Armada, 469 (illus.)

Spanish colonies, 582, 633, 682 (map). See also Latin America, colonial; Caribbean, 435–436; Philippines, 431, 545, 546 (map); popular protest in, 586–587

Spanish expeditions (exploration), 418, 424, 427 (map), 428, 430–431

Spanish Inquisition, 466

Spice trade, 385, 535, 547–548; Portuguese and, 434, 435

Spinning: by Indian women, 388 and illus.; mechanization of (jenny), 615

Sri Lanka (Ceylon), 380, 675, 681; water-control systems in, 370–371

Stained glass, 404

Stamp Act of 1765, 588

Standard Oil Company, 657

Stanley, Henry Morton, 670, 672

Starry Messenger, The (Galileo), 454, 455

Steam engine, 608 (illus.), 615, 618–620; for ships, 619–620 and illus.

Steamships, 619–620 and illus., 629, 656

Steam tractor, 629 (illus.)

Steel production, 657; in Japan, 356, 357, 361

Steel swords, Spanish conquistadors, 436, 440

Stephenson, George, 620

Stirrups, 375

Stock exchanges, 459, 510

Stono Rebellion (1739), 490

Strasbourg, 403; cathedral of, 404 (illus.); clock in, 405

Strikes: of millworkers, 626; in Ming China, 535

Strogonov family, 567, 569

Stuart dynasty, 467 (illus.)

Students, 406

Sub-Saharan Africa, 518, 519. See also Africa, tropical; Great Zimbabwe in, 383 and illus.; intensive cultivation in, 370; Islam in, 522; European trade and, 515, 523; climate changes in, 575; new states in, 665

Sudan, 520, 522, 547, 673. See also Western Sudan

Suez Canal, 701

Sufism, 380, 387, 538, 543

Sugar consumption, 511, 513

Sugar plantations, 432, 476, 483 (illus.), 501–509, 528, 626, 649, 651; in Africa, 428, 432, 482; colonial Americas, 480; in colonial Brazil, 480, 482–483 and illus., 502, 507, 513; in Cuba, 659; slave labor for, 482, 487, 502–503, 505–509, 650; technology and environment for, 504–505; in West Indies, 501–503; windmills on, 495 (illus.), 504

Sugar trade, 610

Suleiman the Magnificent, 528

Sulu Empire (Philippines), 545

Sumanguru (Mali), 372

Sumatra, 356, 385, 528, 548

Summa Theologica (Aquinas), 402, 407

Sundiata, 372

Sun gods, Inca, 437

Sunni Islam, 345, 529 (map), 536, 537

Supernatural, European witchcraft and, 453

Surinam (Dutch Guiana), 509

Swahili Coast, 373 (map), 381, 385, 433, 522, 545

Swahili language, 547, 672

Swazi kingdom, 665, 667

Sweden, 460, 467, 567, 569, 624; war with Russia (1700-1721), 469, 570

Sweet potatoes, 357, 435, 477, 565

Swords, 436, 440

Sybil; or, The Two Nations (Disraeli), 626

Syria, 345, 533, 692, 696; Mamluks in, 527, 528, 530, 537, 538

Tabriz, 352

Tacky (slave), 508

Tahiti, 420

Tahmasp, Shah, 537

Taiping Rebellion, 709 (map), 710–712 and illus.

Taiwan, 558, 559

Takrur (Mali), 372

Tamerlane. See Timur, Il-khan

Tanggut Empire (China), 338, 352

Tanneries (leatherworking), 375, 384, 398

Tanzimat reforms, 696–699, 700 (illus.), 701, 703

Tariffs, 627

Tashkent, 705

Tasman, Abel, 548

Taxation (taxes): in Yuan China, 352; Delhi sultanate, 375, 378; by French monarchy, 412, 414; on trade, by Portuguese, 435; French nobility and, 459; in England, 466; peasant revolts against, 461; reform of, in France, 471; in Indian Ocean empires, 548; Enlightenment and, 583; Safavid Iran, 541; American Revolution and, 588; French Revolution and, 592, 593, 595; in African Caliphate, 667; in British India, 675; Mongol rule in Russia, 350; Ottoman Empire, 693, 696–699, 698; Spanish decline and, 469

Tax farming, 345, 353, 471, 534–535

Tea trade, 564, 610, 675, 708; American Revolution and, 588

Technology: See also Construction materials and techniques; Engineering; Manufactured goods; Metals (metallurgy); Science(s); Ships and shipping; Weapons and military technology; Yuan China, 353–354; Ming China, 356–357; in Japan, 362; Columbian exchange and, 474; Renaissance Europe, 451; colonial sugar plantation, 504; Jesuit, in China, 563 (illus.); Enlightenment, 584 and illus.; and modernization in Egypt, 668; for whaling, 685; European, in Ottoman Empire, 697

Technology, Industrial Revolution and, 609, 610, 614–621. See also Railroads; chronology (1759-1851), 611; division of labor, 616–617; iron industry, 616–618; mass production and, 614–615, 618; mechanization in cotton

industry, 615–616; steam engine and, 608 (illus.), 615, 618–620 and illus.; telegraph, 620–621, 656, 702

Tecumseh, 648

Telegraph, 620–621, 656, 702

Temples, 385–386; Indian, 379 (illus.)

Temüjin, 337. See also Ghenghis Khan

Tenements, 622 (illus.), 623

Tennyson, Alfred Lord, 701

Tenochtitlan, Spanish conquest of, 436, 437

Terror: in Delhi sultanate, 379; Mongol, 351

Teutonic Knights, 350–351, 395

Téwodros II (Ethiopia), 668, 669 (illus.)

Texas, 616, 646, 649

Textiles (textile industry), 384, 460, 523. See also Cotton (cotton industry); Cotton textiles; Spinning; Weaving; African, 375; in late medieval Europe, 399 (map), 400; in thirteenth century Ypres, 401 (illus.); Netherlands, 457; African trade and, 515; in Russia, 704; women in, 588, 625–626; British, 683

Thailand (Siam), 683

Theology, 406–407

Third Estate, 593–594

Thirty Years War (1618-1648), 467

Thomas Aquinas, 394, 402, 407

Three-field system, 395

Tibet, 387, 710; Buddhism in (Lamaism), 352, 558

Timber and Stone Act of 1878 (US), 660

Timbuktu, 519 (illus.); library in, 386–387

Timor, 547, 548

Timur, Il-khan, 346–347, 351, 528; capture of Delhi by, 380; tomb of, 347 (illus.)

Timurids, 346–347, 348, 541

Tin mines, 612

Tippu Tip, 672

Tipu Sultan, 664, 673

Tobacco, 501, 502, 536, 537; in colonial Americas, 435, 473 (illus.), 477, 489

Tokugawa Ieyasu, 552

Tokugawa shogunate (Japan), 552–556, 572, 573; economics in, 552–553; elite decline and crisis in, 555–556; European missionaries and closing of, 553–555; porcelain industry in, 552, 553, 554 and illus.

Tokyo (Edo), 552, 554, 556

Toledo, 414

Tolstoy, Leo, 707

Tomatoes, 477

Tomb, of Timur in Samarkand, 347 (illus.)

Tordesillas, Treaty of (1494), 427 (map), 430, 431, 546 (map)

Töregene Khatun, 340, 341

Torture, in Delhi sultanate, 376

Toussaint L'Ouverture, François Dominique, 581, 601–602

Trade (trading), 423, 431, 441. See also Free trade; Indian Ocean trade; Merchants (merchant class); and specific commodities; in Mongol Russia, 349; Chinese, 352, 356; Japanese, 363; spread of Islam and, 372, 387; late medieval cities and, 398–401, 399 (map), 425; African, 428; Dutch, 457; Anglo-Dutch rivalry in, 471; colonial, 488; North

American colonies and, 491; English with Iran, 526; Ottoman, 536; Mughal India, 542; English with China, 564; Industrial Revolution and, 609; laissez faire and, 627; British Empire and, 664; in nineteenth century Africa, 666 *(map)*; East African, 672; legitimate, with Africa, 670–672; in British India, 678; industrialized nations and, 683–684; Opium war (1839-1842) and, 708

Trade routes, 441. *See also* Atlantic trading system; Caravan trade and routes; Trans-Saharan trade routes

Trading companies: *See also specific companies;* European, in China, 558

Trading monopolies, 434, 435, 548; colonial, 483, 491, 494, 495, 496, 502

Traditions, 675

Trafalgar, Battle of (1805), 597, 600

Transportation: *See also* Railroads; Industrial Revolution and, 612; in Russia, 703–704

Trans-Saharan trade routes, 375; sub-Saharan Africa and, 372, 373 *(map)*, 522; slave trade and, 519, 667–668

Transvaal, 681

Travel (travelers): African, 367. *See also* Ibn Battuta, Muhammad ibn Abdullah; to and from China, 384; colonial Americas, 484–485; Marco Polo, 343 *(map)*, 344, 382, 384, 398; in Mongolian Empire, 344; Zheng He, 355 *(map)*, 356, 422–423

Treaty of Paris (1783), 590–591

Treaty ports, in China, 434, 707, 708–709, 711

Trent, Council of (1545), 453

Trevithick, Richard, 620

Tribute system, Chinese, 363, 552

Trigonometry, 348

Trinidad, 681

Trinidad (ship), 418, 420

Tropics, the, 367–372; environment of, 367–369; human ecosystems in, 369–370; irrigation and water systems in, 370–371

Tsar, 350, 567

Tuareg, 370, 375

Tudor dynasty, 467 *(illus.)*

Tulip Period (Ottoman Empire), 536

Tunisia, 528

Tupac Amaru II, 496, 637

Turkestan, 705

Turkic (Turkish) peoples, 342, 526, 537, 541. *See also* Ottoman Empire (Ottoman Turks); in Central Asia, 354; of Central Asia, 569; Delhi sultanate, 379; in India, 375; iron-working by, 338; Keraits, 337; Kipchak, 349; threat to Europe by, 392; Uzbeks, 540

Tuscarora peoples, 589

Tyler, Wat, 396

Typhus, 344, 476

Ukraine, 349, 569

Ulama (Islamic elite), 531, 538, 693, 696

Ulugh Beg, 348–349

Underdevelopment, 656–657

United Provinces of the Río de la Plata, 637

United States: abolition of slavery in, 650–651; Amerindians in, 647, 648–649 *and illus.;*

ban on Chinese immigration to, 711; chronology (1789-1890s), 635; civil war (1861-1865) in, 646; constitutional experiment in, 639; end of slave trade and, 670; expansion in, 644, 645 *(map)*, 657, 659 *(map)*; immigration to, 652, 653; labor movement in, 655; Latin American investment by, 659; mining in, 657 *(illus.)*; national parks in, 660; personalist leaders in, 642–644; Qing China and, 713, 714; racial discrimination in, 656; slavery debate in, 644; technology and development in, 656; territorial growth of (1783-1853), 645 *(map)*; voting rights in, 604; war with Mexico, 633, 646; war with Spain (1898-1899), 646

United States, Industrial Revolution in, 624–625; mechanization of cotton industry, 615–616, 624, 626, 660; steamships in, 619; telegraph in, 621; railroads in, 620 *and illus.,* 657, 659 *(illus.)*; rural areas in, 624

Universities, 406–407, 706. *See also* Colleges and Universities

Upanishads, 680

Ural Mountains, 567

Urbanization: *See also* Cities and towns (urban areas); environment and, 660; and immigration in Americas, 652; Ottoman Empire, 701

Urdu language, 386, 543

Uruguay, 637, 638, 644, 647, 660; education of women in, 655

Usuman dan Fodio, 667

Usury (interest), 404

Utopian socialism, 628

Uzbeks (Uzbekistan), 540, 705

Valiente, Juan, 486

Valois dynasty, 466, 467 *(illus.)*

Vancouver, Canada, Chinese in, 653 *(illus.)*

Van Eyck, Jan, 410

Variolation, 563

Vassals, monarchy and, 410, 412–413

Vatican, 554. *See also* Papacy (popes)

Venezuela, 635, 639; independence of, 634, 643, 644

Venice, 400, 409; Muslim alliances of, 425; Ottoman Empire and, 528, 532; Portuguese competition with, 435; sea routes of, 399 *(map)*; trading colonies of, 398

Vernacular languages, 407

Versailles, 593, 594

Versailles palace, 466–467, 468 *(illus.)*

Vespucci, Amerigo, 430

Victoria (Great Britain), 676

Victorian morality, 627

Victoria (ship), 418

Vienna, 528; defeat of Ottomans in, 462

Vienna, Congress of (1814-1815), 604

Vietnam, 710, 711; Annam, 356, 363; Mongol attack on, 342

Vijayanagar Empire (India), 378 *(map)*, 380

Vikings, Atlantic exploration by, 423, 443

Vinland, 423

Virginia, 591

Virginia Company, 488–489

Vivaldo brothers, 423

Vladivostok, 705

Volta, Alessandro, 620

Voltaire, 456, 563, 583, 585

Voting rights (franchise), 591–592, 604; for blacks, 655–656; for women, 655, 686

Wages, 395–396; colonial Americas, 482; controls, 378; European peasants and, 460

Wales, 412, 609

Wallpaper, Chinese, 563

Walsh, Robert, 640–641

Wappers, Gustav, 605 *(illus.)*

Warfare: Mongol invasion of Japan, 360–361; Renaissance Europe, 451; Anglo-Dutch (1652-1678), 459, 471; in colonial North America, 493, 494; and diplomacy in early modern Europe, 451 *(illus.)*, 467–469; French-Algerian, 669; prisoners of, as slaves, 517; regional, in Americas, 646

War of 1812, 604, 646, 648

War of the Austrian Succession (1740-1748), 582, 593

War of the Spanish Succession (1701-1714), 468, 582

Warrior class: Japanese, 361–362, 363, 551–552; Ottoman Janisseries, 530–531, 534, 536, 692, 693, 696; Russian Cossacks, 526, 569

Wars of religion (1562-1598), 453

Washington, George, 589, 590, 591, 639

Water-control systems: *See also* Canals; Irrigation; Watermills; dams in medieval Europe, 397; Irrigation, 370–371, 668, 678

Water frame, 615

Waterloo, 603

Water Margin, 357

Watermills, 397 *and illus.,* 504

Waterways. *See* Canals; Flooding *and specific rivers*

Water wheel, 615

Watt, James, 609, 612, 619; steam engine of, 608 *(illus.)*

Wealth of Nations, The (Smith), 616, 627

Weapons and military technology, 518. *See also* Bows and arrows; Cannon; Firearms; body armor, 413, 436, 438, 440; steel swords, 436, 440; cannon, 426, 438, 440, 468, 526, 540, 544, 572; catapults, 343, 358, 360; conquistadors, 436, 438, 440; Delhi sultanate, 375; gunpowder, 357, 358, 360, 410, 516, 528, 553, 572, 708; Japanese, 361, 553; Korean, 360; early modern Europe, 467–468; Ming China, 357, 358; Mongol, 343, 360; Portuguese, 433–434; in Northern Eurasia, 572; Ottoman Empire, 528, 531, 697–698; Qing China, 708, 711; Russian, 704; transition to modern warfare, 701; Maxim (machine) gun, 713 *(illus.)*; Zulu, 667 *(illus.)*

Weather. *See* Climate and weather

Weaving: *See also* Cotton textiles; Textiles (textile industry), 388 *and illus.,* 401 *(illus.),* 615; industrial revolution and, 626

Wedgwood, Josiah, 609, 614–615, 626

Weld, Theodore, 650

West Africa, 510, 670. *See also specific countries or peoples;* Portuguese map of, 428 *(illus.)*; European traders and, 431–432; slave trade and, 496, 520; Songhai Empire in, 519–520; trade and, 515, 516 *(map)*; Islam in, 387, 667; new states in, 665; western culture in, 671–672

Western Europe: *See also* European Expansion (1400-1550); Latin West (Europe 1200-1500); China trade and, 563; Russia and, 350, 703–705, 706; sugar consumption in, 513; telegraph in, 621

Western Hemisphere. *See* Americas, the (Western Hemisphere)

Westernization (Western culture): *See also* Modernization; of Russia, 569, 570, 573, 703–705; in West Africa, 671

Western Sudan, 374 *(map)*, 385

West Indies. *See* Caribbean region (West Indies)

Whaling, 684–685 *and illus.*

Wheat, 356, 370, 460

Wheatstone, Charles, 621

Whistler, James McNeill, 704

White, Emma, 672

White Horde (khanate), 349

White Lotus Rebellion (1794-1804), 707

Whitney, Eli, 610, 615

Whydah, 496, 516

Widow burning (sati), 388, 680

William and Mary (England), 497

Williams, Eric, 503

Windmills, 397, 400; sugar plantation, 495 *(illus.)*, 504

Winds: *See also* Monsoons; Indian Ocean routes and, 367, 368 *(map)*

Witch-hunts, 453–454 *and illus.*

Wollstonecraft, Mary, 598, 599

Women: *See also* Children; Family; Marriage; Delhi sultanate (India), 378, 387–388; Mongol, 338; Mongol politics and, 340–341; Muslim, 377; Muslim, in Mali, 388–389; spinning by, 388 *(illus.)*; spread of Islam and, 387; in late medieval Europe, 394 *and illus.*; in medieval Guilds, 401; textile production by, 401 *(illus.)*; in medieval European literature, 407–408; as witches, 453–454 *and illus.*; Dutch, 457 *(illus.)*; and family in Europe, 461–462; in colonial Latin America, 485, 496 *(illus.)*; agricultural work of, 506; slave, 507; Islam and, 522; Ottoman and Iranian compared, 539; as Acheh rulers: 545; role in American Revolution, 588, 591; French Revolution and, 595, 596, 597; Haitian revolution and, 602; as factory workers, 625–626; as prostitutes, 593, 627, 678; cult of domesticity and, 626; industrialization and, 630; as abolitionists, 650; voting rights for, 655, 686; abuses of, in India, 680; in British India, 678; education of, 680, 714; in colonial Australia, 684; inheritance and, 699; in Ottoman Empire, 698–699; as prostitutes, 461, 593, 627, 678; Taiping Rebellion and, 710, 711

Women's Rights Convention, 655

Woodblock printing, 359

Wool industry, 615; English, 400, 414; in late medieval Europe, 400

Working class: *See also* Labor; French Revolution and, 594, 596, 597; Revolutions of 1848 and, 604, 605; housing for, 622 *(illus.)*; Industrial Revolution and, 624–626, 627; reforms for, 628

World economy, 657

Writing: Korean, 359, 360, 552; Russian language, 349; Urdu, in India, 386

Wu Sangui, 551

"Xanadu" (Coleridge), 352

Yakutsk, 562

Yams, 370

Yangzhou Massacre, 560–561

Yanjing. *See* Beijing

Yaws (skin disease), 508

Yellow fever, 476, 602

Yellow River, 712; flooding of, 353

Yellowstone national park, 660

Yemen, 536, 547; Indian Ocean trade and, 384

Yi dynasty (Korea), 359–360, 552

Yohannes IV (Ethiopia), 668

Yongle (China), 355–356

Yoruba kingdoms, 371 *(illus.)*

Yosef, 384

Young Ottomans, 703

Ypres, 400; weavers in, 401 *(illus.)*

Yuan Empire (China), 342, 351–354; Beijing as capital of, 338, 348, 352, 354, 355–356, 359; cannon in, 358; cultural and scientific exchange in, 353–354; fall of, 354, 363; Korea and, 359; Vietnam and, 363

Yucatán region, 649

Yunnan, 353

Zambezi River, 372, 670

Zamorin, 385

Zanzibar, 672

Zeila, 384

Zen Buddhism, 359, 362

Zeng Guofan, 713–714

Zheng He, 355 *(map)*, 356, 422–423 *and illus.*

Zhu Yuanzhang, 354

Zimbabwe, 383 *and illus.*, 665

Zollverein, 627

Zulu kingdom, 665, 667 *and illus.*, 681